Blacks in the United States

Chandler Publications in Anthropology *and* Sociology
LEONARD BROOM, *General Editor*

Sociology
CHARLES M. BONJEAN, *Editor*

BLACKS
IN THE
UNITED STATES

Edited by

NORVAL D. GLENN
CHARLES M. BONJEAN

The University of Texas at Austin

Expanded from the *Social Science Quarterly,* December, 1968

Chandler Publishing Company

124 Spear Street, San Francisco, California 94105

Distributed by Science Research Associates, Inc., A Subsidiary of IBM
259 East Erie Street, Chicago, Illinois 60611

Contents

Preface

President Lyndon B. Johnson's Executive Order 11365 of July 29, 1967, established the National Advisory Commission on Civil Disorders and instructed it to, "As best you can, find the truth and express it in your report." In the pursuit of this objective, the Commission relied heavily upon the testimony, methods, and previous research of social scientists.

However much too early it is to assess in full the social consequences of the Order, the Commission, and its Report, one effect has been obvious—social scientists have approached the study of Blacks in the United States with increased vigor and new perspectives. As journal editors we recognized this fact in the summer of 1967 when we began to receive increasing numbers of manuscripts dealing with this topic. By fall, we began to plan a topical issue on "Black America" and informed the editors of the *Social Science Quarterly* and other colleagues to be alert to current studies that might significantly enhance the issue.

By the spring of 1968 we had accepted enough manuscripts to fill an issue of regular length, but relevant submissions, many of good quality, were still coming. We then decided to prepare a double-length issue and we sought additional funds for its support. Chandler Publishing Company generously offered an advance on royalties in exchange for the use of the issue contents in an anthology. Because of the rapidly changing nature of intergroup relations in the United States, both editors and publisher agreed that work on the anthology and topical issue of the *Quarterly* should proceed simultaneously so that the time usually lost between the completion of a manuscript and its publication could be held to a minimum. Thus, one of our purposes is to present the reader with quality examples of *current* social science research on Blacks in the United States. Indeed, most of the selections included in this volume were *written* in 1967 and 1968. Several of the *Quarterly* articles were written as late as October 1968 and the most recent contribution to this anthology was not completed until January 1969.

In addition to the contents of the December 1968 *Quarterly* and several original contributions, we decided to include thirteen articles from other publications because they met one or more of the four following criteria: (a) they were major contributions to our understanding of Blacks in the United States, (b) they covered important topics not found among the *Quarterly* selections, (c) they were written in a manner which we thought would be clear and stimulating to advanced undergraduate students, and (d) they were (in five instances) excellent articles about blacks *by* blacks.

While we expect this collection of articles to be most useful for our colleagues and students in sociology, the list of contributors includes scholars in the disciplines of political science, history, economics, marketing, psychology and communications, as well as all shades of sociology from humanist to positivist. This variety reflects our belief that the understanding of blacks and their relationships with whites is a task which will not be accomplished without cross-disciplinary awareness and cooperation.

This collection of articles is the product of the efforts of hundreds of individuals and we cannot hope to acknowledge them all here. In addition to the authors, we owe a special debt of gratitude to Ann C. Hardy, Jean Plummer Baker, Leta Partney, Robert Ankeny, Patricia Morrison, Michael D. Grimes, Bobby Gierisch, and Ann Miles, our *Quarterly* staff members, and graduate assistants. Associate and advisory editors who provided helpful suggestions to authors for revision included Dan D. Nimmo, Harold Osborne, C. Norman Alexander, Ira Sharkansky, Harry Scoble, Gaylord Jentz, Jim Pearson, James Chase, Eleanor Main, James Anderson, J. Allen Williams, Jr., Fred Whitam, Louis A. Zurcher, Grady D. Bruce, and B. Joe Colwell. Also assisting us in the review of manuscripts were Leonard Broom, David Gottlieb, James Geschwender, S. Dale McLemore, Carl Akins, Hiram Friedsam, Leonard Gordon, Clifton McCleskey, Kenneth Land, and Roderick Bell. Finally, we are most grateful to the members and officers of the Southwestern Social Science Association whose interest and efforts have made the *Social Science Quarterly* possible.

We acknowledge the shortcomings of this anthology (and take full responsibility for them), but we hope the reader will agree that the new findings and fresh interpretations warranted earliest possible publication at the sacrifice of some academic and editorial niceties. It is our sincere hope that continued progress in the social sciences and our society will soon make *this* volume obsolete or, at best, a satisfactory record of the nature of research in this area in the late 1960s.

Austin, Texas   Norval D. Glenn
January 2, 1969   Charles M. Bonjean

Contributors

CARL AKINS is assistant professor of political science at the University of Houston.

LEWIS BOWMAN is professor of political science at Emory University.

LEONARD BROOM is Ashbel Smith professor of sociology at the University of Texas.

GRADY D. BRUCE is associate professor of marketing at the University of Texas.

THOMAS R. BURTIS is a graduate student in psychology and sociology at Texas Technological College.

JAY CAMPBELL, JR., is assistant professor of human development at Pennsylvania State University.

WALTER J. CARTWRIGHT is associate professor and chairman of the department of sociology and anthropology at Texas Technological College.

M. MARGARET CONWAY is associate professor of government and politics at the University of Maryland.

KEITH K. COX is associate professor of marketing at the University of Houston.

ROBERT L. CRAIN is associate professor of social relations at Johns Hopkins University.

STEPHEN W. BURKS is a graduate student in the department of political science at Michigan State University.

M. RICHARD CRAMER is associate professor of sociology at the University of North Carolina at Chapel Hill.

THOMAS R. CRIPPS is associate professor of history at Morgan State College.

WILLIAM S. DONALDSON is research associate at the University of Virginia.

LEWIS DONOHEW is associate professor of communications at the University of Kentucky.

BRYAN T. DOWNES is assistant professor of political science at Michigan State University.

G. FRANKLIN EDWARDS is professor and chairman of the department of sociology at Howard University.

JOHN LEE EIGHMY is chairman of the division of social sciences at Oklahoma Baptist University.

JOE R. FEAGIN is assistant professor of sociology at the University of California, Riverside.

JAMES A. GESCHWENDER is associate professor of sociology at the University of Western Ontario.

ELI GINZSBERG is Hepburn professor of economics at Columbia University.

NORVAL D. GLENN is associate professor of sociology at the University of Texas.

DAVID GOTTLIEB is professor of human development at Pennsylvania State University.

JEFFREY K. HADDEN is associate professor of sociology at Case Western Reserve University.

CHARLES DESMOND HART is assistant professor of history at the University of Toronto.

JAMES B. HIGGINBOTHAM is president of Higginbotham and Associates, Houston, Texas.

JOSEPH HIMES is professor of sociology at North Carolina College at Durham.

HERBERT HIRSCH is assistant professor of government at the University of Texas.

HARRY HOLLOWAY is professor of political science at the University of Oklahoma.

DENNIS IPPOLITO is assistant professor of political science at Emory University.

VINCENT JEFFRIES is assistant professor of sociology at San Fernando Valley State College.

CLIFTON R. JONES is lecturer in sociology at Howard University.

MARTIN LUTHER KING, JR., was president of the Southern Christian Leadership Conference.

JOYCE LADNER is curriculum specialist at Southern Illinois University.

RAYMOND W. MACK is professor of sociology at Northwestern University.

GERALD A. McWORTER is assistant professor of sociology at Atlanta University.

GARY T. MARX is assistant professor of sociology at Harvard University.

AUGUST MEIER is professor of history and senior research fellow, Center for Urban Regionalism, Kent State University.

RICHARD T. MORRIS is professor and chairman of the department of sociology at the University of California, Los Angeles.

CHARLES C. MOSKOS, JR., is associate professor of sociology at Northwestern University.

AMY W. ORUM is a candidate for the doctorate of philosophy in history at Emory University.

ANTHONY M. ORUM is assistant professor and director of undergraduate studies in the department of sociology at Emory University.

JEWEL PRESTAGE is professor and chairman of the department of political science at Southern University.

DANIEL O. PRICE is professor of sociology at the University of Texas.

ELLIOTT RUDWICK is professor of sociology and senior research fellow, Center for Urban Regionalism, Kent State University.

DAVID A. SCHULZ is assistant professor of sociology at Pennsylvania State University.

DAVID O. SEARS is associate professor of psychology at the University of California, Los Angeles.

MONTROSE SOMMERS is associate professor of marketing at the University of Toronto.

JAMES E. STAFFORD is associate professor of marketing at the University of Houston.

BRUCE C. STRAITS is assistant professor of sociology at the University of California, Santa Barbara.

FREDERICK D. STURDIVANT is professor of marketing at the University of Texas.

T. M. TOMLINSON is a research psychologist with the Office of Economic Opportunity.

JACK R. VAN DER SLIK is assistant professor of political science at Southern Illinois University.

FRANK WESTIE is professor of sociology at Indiana University.

WALTER T. WILHELM is a student in the graduate school of business at the University of Southern California.

ERNEST WORKS is assistant professor of sociology at California State College at Fullerton.

Blacks in the United States

INTRODUCTION

We have heard our students remark that in their other courses, the questions may vary but the answers stay the same; while in their social-science courses, the questions stay the same but the answers change. Most of the forty-five selections in this volume will support at least the latter half of this assertion. The answers in regard to questions concerning the social and demographic characteristics of the 22 million blacks in the United States, the manner in which whites react to them, the nature of black response to white reactions and the nature of public policy *have* changed and, in themselves, are the stimuli for further changes. Thus, the answers have changed because the phenomena about which the questions are directed have changed. In some cases the changes have been so rapid that predictions made only a few years ago (see contribution 2 below) have had to be revised (see contribution 3). For this reason, one of the goals of this volume is to present the student with the most recent data possible. In fact, only two of the forty-five contributions to this anthology were written before 1965 and the majority were published in 1968.

There is another equally important reason why the answers keep changing. As social scientists' concepts, theories, and research designs and techniques have been improved and refined, it has not only been possible to describe with greater precision, but also to offer some new explanations *for* the changes which have been and are taking place. Thus, our second purpose is to acquaint the student with those theories and methods which are furthering our knowledge and understanding of blacks and their relationships with whites. In regard to theory, the contributions range from a discussion and test of the widely accepted Myrdal theory (contribution 15) to attempts at introducing new concepts or new ways of looking at social phenomena (contribution 25). Equally varied are the research designs, types of data gathered, and methods of analysis. The reader will be exposed to a wide range of social-science methods from the rich descriptions based on participant observation (see, for example, contributions 11 and 32) to the precise generalizations based on census data (for example those in contributions 2, 3 and 4), from chi-square to Q-sort (see contribution 6), and from the analysis of historical documents (contributions 22 and 44) to the execution of a field experiment (contribution 19). Indeed, the importance of methodology and how it may contribute to changing interpretations is itself documented in contribution 14.

Our third goal is not an academic one. For those seeking to understand the problems existing in the United States today between blacks and whites and for those who want to do something about them, we offer the following forty-five selections as a point of departure.

In addition to this brief introduction, we have divided this book into four sections, each with an introduction and a bibliography. Section I concerns social and demographic characteristics of blacks in the United States—their occupations, income, consumption patterns, family structure, and attitudes. This is followed by a group of contributions dealing with white reactions to blacks and some of the social and psychological correlates of these reactions. The third section includes articles dealing with both institutionalized and noninstitutionalized black responses to white reactions. The final section involves public policy and blacks in the United States and it includes the views of prominent black and white social scientists on the *Report of the National Advisory Commission on Civil Disorders*. Only a month after the establishment of the Commission, the late Dr. Martin Luther King discussed "The Role of the Behavioral Scientist in the Civil Rights Movement" at the annual meeting of the American Psychological Association. He suggested that there were many areas of research related to the civil-rights movement that should be pursued by social scientists, but that three in particular had an especially urgent quality: the problem of Negro leadership, political action, and psychological and ideological changes among Negroes. Indeed, since mid-1967 there have been significant research efforts on all three of these fronts and some of the published findings are included in this volume. Negro leadership is discussed in several contributions, but especially in contributions 13 and 32. Political action is the central topic of contributions 9, 28, and 35 to 42. Recent findings in regard to psychological and ideological changes are presented in a wide spectrum of articles, including especially contributions 5, 6, and 30.

These articles and the others in this anthology fail to provide the final answers posed by Dr. King, but they do represent an impressive beginning, especially considering the fact that all of those cited in the previous paragraph (as well as the vast majority in this anthology) were published *since* the speech which follows.

The Role of the Behavioral Scientist in the Civil Rights Movement*

MARTIN LUTHER KING, JR.

IT IS ALWAYS A VERY RICH AND REWARDING EXPERIENCE WHEN I CAN TAKE a brisk break from the day-to-day demands of our struggle for freedom and human dignity and discuss the issues involved in that struggle with concerned friends of good will all over the nation. It is particularly a great privilege to discuss these issues with members of the academic community, who are constantly writing about and dealing with the problems that we face and who have the tremendous responsibility of moulding the minds of young men and women all over our country.

THE CIVIL RIGHTS MOVEMENT NEEDS THE HELP OF SOCIAL SCIENTISTS

In the preface to their book, *Applied Sociology* (1965), S. M. Miller and Alvin Gouldner state: "It is the historic mission of the social sciences to enable mankind to take possession of society."[1] It follows that for Negroes who substantially are excluded from society this science is needed even more desperately than for any other group in the population.

For social scientists, the opportunity to serve in a live-giving purpose is a humanist challenge of rare distinction. Negroes too are eager for a rendezvous with truth and discovery. We are aware that social scientists, unlike some of their colleagues in the physical sciences, have been spared the grim feelings of guilt that attended the invention of nuclear weapons of destruction. Social scientists, in the main, are fortunate to be able to extirpate evil, not to invent it.

If the Negro needs social sciences for direction and for self-understanding, the white society is in even more urgent need. White America needs to understand that it is poisoned to its soul by racism and the understanding needs to be carefully documented and consequently more difficult to reject. The present crisis arises because although it is historically imperative that our society take the next step to equality, we find ourselves psychologically and socially imprisoned. All too many white Americans are horrified not with conditions of Negro life but with the product of these conditions—the Negro himself.

White America is seeking to keep the walls of segregation substantially

* Reprinted by permission from the *Journal of Social Issues*, 24 (April, 1968), pp. 1–12. Invited Distinguished Address given at the 75th Annual Convention of the American Psychological Association, September 1, 1967, Washington, D.C. Dr. King was President of the Southern Christian Leadership Conference, Atlanta, Georgia. Copyright 1967 by Martin Luther King, Jr. Reprinted by permission of the Southern Christian Leadership Conference.

[1] S. M. Miller and Alvin Gouldner, *Applied Sociology* (New York: The Free Press, 1965).

intact while the evolution of society and the Negro's desperation is causing them to crumble. The white majority, unprepared and unwilling to
accept radical structural change, is resisting and producing chaos while
complaining that if there were no chaos orderly change would come.

Negroes want the social scientist to address the white community and
"tell it like it is." White America has an appalling lack of knowledge
concerning the reality of Negro life. One reason some advances were made
in the South during the past decade was the discovery by northern whites
of the brutal facts of southern segregated life. It was the Negro who
educated the nation by dramatizing the evils through nonviolent protest.
The social scientist played little or no role in disclosing truth. The Negro
action movement with raw courage did it virtually alone. When the majority of the country could not live with the extremes of brutality they
witnessed, political remedies were enacted and customs were altered.

These partial advances were, however, limited principally to the South
and progress did not automatically spread throughout the nation. There
was also litle depth to the changes. White America stopped murder, but
that is not the same thing as ordaining brotherhood; nor is the ending of
lynch rule the same thing as inaugurating justice.

After some years of Negro-white unity and partial success, white America shifted gears and went into reverse. Negroes, alive with hope and
enthusiasm, ran into sharply stiffened white resistance at all levels and
bitter tensions broke out in sporadic episodes of violence. New lines of
hostility were drawn and the era of good feeling disappeared.

The decade of 1955 to 1965, with its constructive elements, misled us.
Everyone, activists and social scientists, underestimated the amount of
violence and rage Negroes were suppressing and the amount of bigotry
the white majority was disguising.

Science should have been employed more fully to warn us that the
Negro, after 350 years of handicaps, mired in an intricate network of
contemporary barriers, could not be ushered into equality by tentative
and superficial changes.

Mass nonviolent protests, a social invention of Negroes, were effective
in Montgomery, Birmingham and Selma in forcing national legislation
which served to change Negro life sufficiently to curb explosions. But
when changes were confined to the South alone, the North, in the absence of change, began to seethe.

The freedom movement did not adapt its tactics to the different and
unique northern urban conditions. It failed to see that nonviolent marches
in the South were forms of rebellion. When Negroes took over the streets
and shops, southern society shook to its roots. Negroes could contain their
rage when they found the means to force relatively radical changes in
their environment.

In the North, on the other hand, street demonstrations were not even
a mild expression of militancy. The turmoil of cities absorbs demonstrations as merely transitory drama which is ordinary in city life. Without
a more effective tactic for upsetting the status quo, the power structure

could maintain its intransigence and hostility. Into the vacuum of inaction, violence and riots flowed and a new period opened.

Urban Riots. Urban riots must now be recognized as durable social phenomena. They may be deplored, but they are here and should be understood. Urban riots are a special form of violence. They are not insurrections. The rioters are not seeking to seize territory or to attain control of institutions. They are mainly intended to shock the white community. They are a distorted form of social protest. It enables the most enraged and deprived Negro to take hold of consumer goods with the ease the white man does by using his purse. Often the Negro does not even want what he takes; he wants the experience of taking. But most of all, alienated from society and knowing that this society cherishes property above people, he is shocking it by abusing property rights. There are thus elements of emotional catharsis in the violent act. This may explain why most cities in which riots have occurred have not had a repetition, even though the causative conditions remain. It is also noteworthy that the amount of physical harm done to white people other than police is infinitesimal and in Detroit white and Negroes looted in unity.

A profound judgment of today's riots was expressed by Victor Hugo a century ago. He said, "If a soul is left in darkness, sins will be committed. The guilty one is not he who commits the sin, but he who causes the darkness."

The policy makers of the white society have caused the darkness; they create discrimination; they structured slums; and they perpetuate unemployment, ignorance and poverty. It is incontestable and deplorable that Negroes have committed crimes; but they are derivative crimes. They are born of the greater crimes of the white society. When we ask Negroes to abide by the law, let us also demand that the white man abide by law in the ghettos. Day-in and day-out he violates welfare laws to deprive the poor of their meager allotments; he flagrantly violates building codes and regulations; his police make a mockery of law; and he violates laws on equal employment and education and the provisions for civil services. The slums are the handiwork of a vicious system of the white society; Negroes live in them but do not make them any more than a prisoner makes a prison. Let us say boldly that if the total violations of law by the white man in the slums over the years were calculated and compared with the law-breaking of a few days of riots, the hardened criminal would be the white man. These are often difficult things to say but I have come to see more and more that it is necessary to utter the truth in order to deal with the great problems that we face in our society.

Vietnam War. There is another cause of riots that is too important to mention casually—the war in Vietnam. Here again, we are dealing with a controversial issue. But I am convinced that the war in Vietnam has played havoc with our domestic destinies. The bombs that fall in Vietnam explode at home. It does not take much to see what great damage this war has done to the image of our nation. It has left our country politically and morally isolated in the world, where our only friends happen to be puppet nations like Taiwan, Thailand and South Korea. The major allies in the world that have been with us in war and peace are not with us in this war. As a result we find ourselves socially and politically isolated.

The war in Vietnam has torn up the Geneva Accord. It has seriously impaired the United Nations. It has exacerbated the hatreds between continents, and worse still, between races. It has frustrated our development at home by telling our underprivileged citizens that we place insatiable military demands above their most critical needs. It has greatly contributed to the forces of reaction in America, and strengthened the military-industrial complex, against which even President Eisenhower solemnly warned us. It has practically destroyed Vietnam, and left thousands of American and Vietnamese youth maimed and mutilated. And it has exposed the whole world to the risk of nuclear warfare.

As I looked at what this war was doing to our nation, and to the domestic situation and to the Civil Rights movement, I found it necessary to speak vigorously out against it. My speaking out against the war has not gone without criticisms. There are those who tell me that I should stick with civil rights, and stay in my place. I can only respond that I have fought too hard and too long to end segregated public accommodations to segregate my own moral concerns. It is my deep conviction that justice is indivisible, that injustice anywhere is a threat to justice everywhere. For those who tell me I am hurting the Civil Rights movement, and ask, "Don't you think that in order to be respected, and in order to regain support, you must stop talking against the war," I can only say that I am not a consensus leader. I do not seek to determine what is right and wrong by taking a Gallup Poll to determine majority opinion. And it is again my deep conviction that ultimately a genuine leader is not a searcher for consensus, but a molder of consensus. On some positions cowardice asks the question, "Is it safe?" Expediency asks the question, "Is it politic?" Vanity asks the question, "Is it popular?" But conscience must ask the question, "Is it right?" And there comes a time when one must take a stand that is neither safe, nor politic, nor popular. But one must take it because it is right. And that is where I find myself today.

Moreover, I am convinced, even if war continues, that a genuine massive act of concern will do more to quell riots than the most massive deployment of troops.

Unemployment. The unemployment of Negro youth ranges up to 40 percent in some slums. The riots are almost entirely youth events—the are range of participants is from 13 to 25. What hypocricy it is to talk of saving the new generation—to make it the generation of hope—while consigning it to unemployment and provoking it to violent alternatives.

When our nation was bankrupt in the 30's we created an agency to provide jobs to all at their existing level of skill. In our overwhelming affluence today what excuse is there for not setting up a national agency for full employment immediately?

The other program which would give reality to hope and opportunity would be the demolition of the slums to be replaced by decent housing built by residents of the ghettos.

These programs are not only eminently sound and vitally needed, but they have the support of an overwhelming majority of the nation—white and Negro. The Harris Poll on August 21, 1967, disclosed that an astounding 69 percent of the country support a works program to provide employment to all and an equally astonishing 65 percent approve a program to tear down the slums.

There is a program and there is heavy majority support for it. Yet, the administration and Congress tinker with trivial proposals to limit costs in an extravagant gamble with disaster.

The President has lamented that he cannot persuade Congress. He can, if the will is there, go to the people, mobilize the people's support and thereby substantially increase his power to persuade Congress. Our most urgent task is to find the tactics that will move the government no matter how determined it is to resist.

Civil Disobedience. I believe we will have to find the militant middle between riots on the one hand and weak and timid supplication for justice on the other hand. That middle ground, I believe, is civil disobedience. It can be aggressive but nonviolent; it can dislocate but not destroy. The specific planning will take some study and analysis to avoid mistakes of the past when it was employed on too small a scale and sustained too briefly.

Civil disobedience can restore Negro-white unity. There have been some very important sane white voices even during the most desperate moments of the riots. One reason is that the urban crisis intersects the Negro crisis in the city. Many white decision makers may care little about saving Negroes, but they must care about saving their cities. The vast majority of production is created in cities; most white Americans live in them. The suburbs to which they flee cannot exist detached from cities. Hence powerful white elements have goals that merge with ours.

The Role for the Social Scientist

Now there are many roles for social scientists in meeting these problems. Kenneth Clark has said that Negroes are moved by a suicide instinct in riots and Negroes know there is a tragic truth in this observation. Social scientists should also disclose the suicide instinct that governs the administration and Congress in their total failure to respond constructively.

What other areas are there for social scientists to assist the civil rights movement? There are many, but I would like to suggest three because they have an urgent quality.

Social science may be able to search out some answers to the problem of Negro leadership. E. Franklin Frazier, in his profound work, *Black Bourgeoisie*, laid painfully bare the tendency of the upwardly mobile Negro to separate from his community, divorce himself from responsibility to it, while failing to gain acceptance into the white community.[2] There has been significant improvements from the days Frazier researched, but anyone knowledgeable about Negro life knows its middle class is not yet bearing its weight. Every riot has carried strong overtone of hostility of lower class Negroes toward the affluent Negro and vice versa. No contemporary study of scientific depth has totally studied this problem. Social science should be able to suggest mechanisms to create a wholesome black unity and a sense of peoplehood while the process of integration proceeds.

As one example of this gap in research, there are no studies, to my knowledge, to explain adequately the absence of Negro trade union leadership. Eighty-five percent of Negroes are working people. Some 2,000,000 are in trade unions but in 50 years we have produced only one national leader—A. Philip Randolph.

Discrimination explains a great deal, but not everything. The picture is so dark even a few rays of light may signal a useful direction.

Political Action. The second area for scientific examination is political action. In the past two decades, Negroes have expended more effort in quest of the franchise than they have in all other campaigns combined. Demonstrations, sit-ins and marches, though more spectacular, are dwarfed by the enormous number of man-hours expended to register millions, particularly in the South. Negro organizations from extreme militant to conservative persuasion, Negro leaders who would not even talk to each other, all have been agreed on the key importance of voting. Stokely Carmichael said black power means the vote and Roy Wilkins, while saying black power means black death, also energetically sought the power of the ballot.

A recent major work by social scientists Matthews and Prothro concludes that "The concrete benefits to be derived from the franchise—under conditions that prevail in the South—have often been exaggerated," . . . that voting is not the key that will unlock the door to racial equality because "the concrete measurable payoffs from Negro voting in the South will not be revolutionary."[3]

James A. Wilson supports this view, arguing, "Because of the structure of American politics as well as the nature of the Negro community, Negro politics will accomplish only limited objectives."[4]

If their conclusion can be supported, then the major effort Negroes have invested in the past twenty years has been in the wrong direction and the major pillar of their hope is a pillar of sand. My own instinct is that these views are essentially erroneous, but they must be seriously examined.

The need for a penetrating massive scientific study of this subject cannot be overstated. Lipset in 1957 asserted that a limitation in focus in political sociology has resulted in a failure of much contemporary re-

[2] E. Franklin Frazier, *Black Bourgeoisie* (New York: Macmillan, 1962).
[3] Donald R. Matthews and James W. Prothro, *Negroes and the New Southern Politics* (New York: Harcourt, 1966).
[4] James A. Wilson, "The Negro in Politics," *Daedalus*, (Fall, 1965).

search to consider a number of significant theoretical questions.[5] The time is short for social science to illuminate this critically important area. If the main thrust of Negro effort has been, and remains, substantially irrelevant, we may be facing an agonizing crisis of tactical theory.

The third area for study concerns psychological and ideological changes in Negroes. It is fashionable now to be pessimistic. Undeniably, the freedom movement has encountered setbacks. Yet I still believe there are significant aspects of progress.

Negroes today are experiencing an inner transformation that is liberating them from ideological dependence on the white majority. What has penetrated substantially all strata of Negro life is the revolutionary idea that the philosophy and morals of the dominant white society are not holy or sacred but in all too many respects are degenerate and profane.

Negroes have been oppressed for centuries not merely by bonds of economic and political servitude. The worst aspect of their oppression was their inability to question and defy the fundamental precepts of the larger society. Negroes have been loath in the past to hurl any fundamental challenges because they were coerced and conditioned into thinking within the context of the dominant white ideology. This is changing and new radical trends are appearing in Negro thought. I use radical in its broad sense to refer to reaching into roots.

Ten years of struggle have sensitized and opened the Negro's eyes to reaching. For the first time in their history, Negroes have become aware of the deeper causes for the crudity and cruelty that governed white society's responses to their needs. They discovered that their plight was not a consequence of superficial prejudice but was systemic.

The slashing blows of backlash and frontlash have hurt the Negro, but they have also awakened him and revealed the nature of the oppressor. To lose illusions is to gain truth. Negroes have grown wiser and more mature and they are hearing more clearly those who are raising fundamental questions about our society whether the critics be Negroes or white. When this process of awareness and independence crystallizes, every rebuke, every evasion, become hammer blows on the wedge that splits the Negro from the larger society.

Social science is needed to explain where this development is going to take us. Are we moving away, not from integration, but from the society which made it a problem in the first place? How deep and at what rate of speed is this process occurring? These are some vital questions to be answered if we are to have a clear sense of our direction.

We know we haven't found the answers to all forms of social change. We know, however, that we did find some answers. We have achieved and we are confident. We also know we are confronted now with far greater complexities and we have not yet discovered all the theory we need.

[5] Seymour Martin Lipset, "Political Sociology" in Robert K. Merton, Leonard Broom and Leonard S. Cottrell, Jr. (eds.), *Sociology Today* (New York: Basic Books, 1959), pp. 81–114.

And may I say together, we must solve the problems right here in America. As I have said time and time again, Negroes still have faith in America. Black people still have faith in a dream that we will all live together as brothers in this country of plenty one day.

But I was distressed when I read in the *New York Times* of August 31, 1967 that a sociologist from Michigan State University, the outgoing president of the American Sociological Society, stated in San Francisco that Negroes should be given a chance to find an all Negro community in South America: "that the valleys of the Andes Mountains would be an ideal place for American Negroes to build a second Israel." He further declared that "The United States Government should negotiate for a remote but fertile land in Equador, Peru, or Bolivia for this relocation." I feel that it is rather absurd and appalling that a leading social scientist today would suggest to black people, that after all these years of suffering an exploitation as well as investment in the American dream, that we should turn around and run at this point in history. I say that we will not run– Professor Loomis even compared the relocation task of the Negro to the relocation task of the Jews in Israel. The Jews were made exiles. They did not choose to abandon Europe, they were driven out. Furthermore, Israel has a deep tradition, and Biblical roots for Jews. The Wailing Wall is a good example of these roots. They also had significant financial aid from the United States for the relocation and rebuilding effort. What tradition does the Andes, especially the valley of the Andes mountains, have for Negroes?

And I assert at this time that once again we must reaffirm our belief in building a democratic society, in which blacks and whites can live together as brothers, where we will all come to see that integration is not a problem, but an opportunity to participate in the beauty of diversity.

The problem is deep. It is gigantic in extent, and chaotic in detail. And I do not believe that it will be solved until there is a kind of cosmic discontent enlarging in the bosoms of people of good will all over this nation.

There are certain technical words in every academic discipline which soon become stereotypes and even clichés. Every academic discipline has its technical nomenclature. You who are in the field of psychology have given us a great word. It is the word maladjusted. This word is probably used more than any other word in psychology. It is a good word; certainly it is good that in dealing with what the word implies you are declaring that destructive maladjustment should be destroyed. You are saying that all must seek the well-adjusted life in order to avoid neurotic and schizophrenic personalities.

But on the other hand, I am sure that we will recognize that there are some things in our society, some things in our world, to which we should never be adjusted. There are some things concerning which we must always be maladjusted if we are to be people of good will. We must never adjust ourselves to racial discrimination and racial segregation. We must never adjust ourselves to religious bigotry. We must never adjust ourselves to economic conditions that take necessities from the many to give luxuries to the few. We must never adjust ourselves to the madness of militarism, and the self-defeating effects of physical violence.

In a day when Sputniks, Explorers and Geminies are dashing through outer space, when guided ballistic missiles are carving highways of death through the stratosphere, no nation can finally win a war. It is no longer a choice between violence and nonviolence, it is either nonviolence or nonexistence. As President Kennedy declared, "Mankind must put an end to war, or war will put an end to mankind." And so the alternative to disarmament, the alternatives to a suspension in the development and use of nuclear weapons, the alternative to strengthening the United Nations and eventually disarming the whole world, may well be a civilization plunged into the abyss of annihilation. Our earthly habitat will be transformed into an inferno that even Dante could not envision.

Creative Maladjustment. Thus, it may well be that our world is in dire need of a new organization. The International Association for the Advancement of Creative Maladjustment. Men and women should be as maladjusted as the prophet Amos, who in the midst of the injustices of his day, could cry out in words that echo across the centuries, "Let justice roll down like waters and righteousness like a mighty stream"; or as maladjusted as Abraham Lincoln, who in the midst of his vacillations finally came to see that this nation could not survive half slave and half free; or as maladjusted as Thomas Jefferson, who in the midst of an age amazingly adjusted to slavery, could scratch across the pages of history, words lifted to cosmic proportions, "We hold these truths to be self evident, that all men are created equal. That they are endowed by their creator with certain inalienable rights. And that among these are life, liberty, and the pursuit of happiness." And through such creative maladjustment, we may be able to emerge from the bleak and desolate midnight of man's inhumanity to man, into the bright and glittering daybreak of freedom and justice.

I have not lost hope. I must confess that these have been very difficult days for me personally. And these have been difficult days for every civil rights leader, for every lover of justice and peace. They have been days of frustration—days when we could not quite see where we were going, and when we often felt that our works were in vain, days when we were tempted to end up in the valley of despair. But in spite of this, I still have faith in the future, and my politics will continue to be a politic of hope. Our goal is freedom. And I somehow still believe that in spite of the so-called white backlash, we are going to get there, because however untrue it is to its destiny, the goal of America is freedom.

Abused and scorned though we may be, our destiny as a people is tied up with the destiny of America. Before the Pilgrim fathers landed at Plymouth, we were here. Before Jefferson scratched across the pages of history the great words that I just quoted, we were here. Before the beautiful words of the "Star Spangled Banner" were written, we were here.

For more than two centuries, our forebears labored here without wages. They made Cotton King. They built the home of their masters in the midst of the most humiliating and oppressive conditions.

And yet out of a bottomless vitality, they continued to grow and develop. If the inexpressable cruelties of slavery could not stop us, the opposition that we now face will surely fail. We shall win our freedom because both the sacred heritage of our nation, and the eternal will of the almighty God, are embodied in our echoing demands.

And so I can still sing, although many have stopped singing it, "We shall overcome." We shall overcome because the arch of the moral universe is long, but it bends toward justice. We shall overcome because Carlyle is right, "No lie can live forever." We shall overcome because William Cullen Bryant is right, "Truth crushed to earth will rise again." We shall overcome because James Russell Lowell is right, "Truth forever on the scaffold, wrong forever on the throne, yet that scaffold sways a future." And so with this faith, we will be able to hew out of the mountain of despair a stone of hope. We will be able to transform the jangling discords of our nation into a beautiful symphony of brotherhood. This will be a great day. This will not be the day of the white man, it will not be the day of the black man, it will be the day of man as man.

A Selected Bibliography of
General Works on Blacks in the United States
and on Racial and Ethnic Minorities

Berry, Brewton, *Race and Ethnic Relations*, third edition (Boston: Houghton Mifflin, 1965).

Broom, Leonard, and Norval D. Glenn, *Transformation of the Negro American* (New York: Harper, 1965).

Carter, Robert L., Dorothy Kenyon, Peter Marcuse, and Loren Miller, *Equality* (New York: Pantheon, 1965).

Clark, Kenneth B., *Dark Ghetto* (New York: Harper, 1965).

Cox, Oliver C., *Caste, Class and Race* (Garden City: Doubleday, 1948).

Davie, Maurice, *Negroes in American Society* (New York: McGraw-Hill, 1949).

Drake, St. Clair, and Horace R. Cayton, *Black Metropolis*, revised edition (New York: Harper, 1962).

Franklin, John Hope, *From Slavery to Freedom: A History of American Negroes*, revised edition (New York: Knopf, 1956).

Franklin, John Hope, and Isidore Star (editors), *The Negro in Twentieth Century America* (New York: Random House, 1967).

Frazier, E. Franklin, *The Negro in the United States* (New York: Macmillan, 1949).

Ginzberg, Eli, and Alfred S. Eichner, *The Troublesome Presence: American Democracy and the Negro* (New York: Free Press, 1964).

Handlin, Oscar, *Race and Nationality in American Life* (Boston: Little, Brown, 1950).

Isaacs, Harold R., *The New World of Negro Americans* (New York: John Day, 1963).

Logan, Rayford W., *The Negro in the United States: A Brief History* (Princeton: Van Nostrand, 1957).

Marden, Charles F., and Gladys Meyer, *Minorities in American Society*, third edition (New York: American Book, 1968).

Miller, Elizabeth W. (compiler), *The Negro in America: A Bibliography* (Cambridge: Harvard University Press, 1966).

Myrdal, Gunnar, *An American Dilemma* (New York: Harper, 1944).

Parsons, Talcott, and Kenneth B. Clark (editors), *The Negro American* (Boston: Houghton Mifflin, 1966).

Pettigrew, Thomas F., *A Profile of the Negro American* (Princeton: Van Nostrand, 1964).

Rose, Peter I., *They and We: Racial and Ethnic Relations in the United States* (New York: Random House, 1964).

Shibutani, Tamotsu, and Kian M. Kwan, *Ethnic Stratification* (New York: Macmillan, 1965).

Simpson, George E., and J. Milton Yinger, *Racial and Cultural Minorities:*

An Analysis of Prejudice and Discrimination, third edition (New York: Harper, 1965).

van den Berghe, Pierre L., *Race and Racism* (New York: Wiley, 1967).

Vander Zanden, James W., *American Minority Relations,* second edition (New York: Ronald, 1966).

Part I

SOCIAL AND DEMOGRAPHIC CHARACTERISTICS OF BLACKS IN THE UNITED STATES

The contributions in this section deal with a variety of characteristics of black Americans that are affected by their subordinate status. These range from occupations to rates of intracity movement, from consumption patterns to kinship ties, from political attitudes to leadership. In more than half the articles, characteristics of blacks are placed in perspective by comparisons with characteristics of whites.

Contributions 2, 3, and 4 deal with trends in the economic, occupational, and other stratification characteristics of black Americans. This topic is clearly important to anyone concerned with the welfare of the largest racial minority in the United States. To the social scientists, it is also important because it is relevant to understanding recent changes in the posture of black *vis-à-vis* whites. "The Occupations and Income of Black Americans," by Leonard Broom and Norval D. Glenn, was written primarily to help explain the increase in demonstrations and other protest activity during the early 1960's. It emphasizes that whereas black gains during the 1950's were substantial in an absolute sense, they were small

relative to the rise in black expectations and aspirations, and they involved
no appreciable closing of the gap between Negroes and whites.

"Changes in the Social and Economic Conditions of Black Americans
during the 1960's," by Norval D. Glenn, brings the story of blacks' occupations and income more nearly up-to-date and includes data on amount
and quality of education, life expectancy, infant mortality, and family
disorganization. It shows that whereas some aspects of black-white
inequality have recently diminished at an accelerated rate, other aspects
have increased or ceased to decline.

In contributions 2 and 3, occupational data are handled in the conventional manner. That is, in most black-white comparisons, persons in the
labor force of all ages are lumped together. For some purposes, such
treatment is adequate, but additional valuable information is yielded by
a more sophisticated treatment known as cohort analysis. A cohort consists of persons born during a given period of time, such as 1920 through
1929 or 1930 through 1934. By tracing cohorts from one census year to the
next, one can detect occupational shifts that occur as people progress
through their careers, and the career patterns of different cohorts can be
compared. "Occupational Changes in the Negro Population," by Daniel
O. Price, is an excellent illustration of the potential of cohort analysis for
the study of occupational change.

In "Winners and Losers in the Race for the Good Life: A Comparison
of Blacks and Whites," David Gottlieb and Jay Campbell present evidence
relating to a longstanding controversy among students of social stratification concerning differences by social level in values and aspirations.
Some scholars have claimed that in the United States basic values and
aspirations are essentially the same regardless of social level, whereas
others have described a "lower-class subculture," which they claim de-emphasizes the goals and aspirations that would be attained through
upward mobility and represents a collective adaptation to failure. Significantly, Gottlieb and Campbell report black-white difference in the
relationship between aspirations and the failure of young lower-class
men to progress toward a higher social level. In general, the white "losers"
soon lowered their aspirations to a level more consistent with their realistic prospects, whereas the blacks tended to retain high aspirations. The
difference, the authors suggest, may result from the fact that the blacks
could blame their failure on racial injustice, whereas the whites were
more likely to attribute their failure to their own shortcomings.

The Gottlieb and Campbell findings has several implications the authors do not pursue. For instance, it suggests that during a period of
diminishing discrimination and widespread verbal support of egalitarian
values, the effects of minority status on such characteristics of the individual as his self image and his optimism are complex and not entirely
detrimental. If, however, blacks tend to attribute their failures entirely
to racial injustice, this tendency may lead them to expect eventual attainment of their high aspirations without their overcoming any personal
limitations (which, to be sure, are in large measure the result of racial
injustice). Therefore, it may lead in the long run to extreme frustration

and intense hostility toward whites. Such a consequence may already be prevalent in some ghettos and may help explain some of the recent ghetto violence.

Contributions 6 to 10 also report black-white comparisons, and some of them also reveal that variables are related in different ways in the black and white populations. For instance, in "Blacks, Whites, and Products: Relative Deprivation and Reference Group Behavior," Montrose Sommers and Grady D. Bruce show that attitudes toward products bear a different relationship to social level among blacks than among whites, at least in one community. However, to show this is not the purpose of their article.

The consumer practices and preferences of blacks and whites have often been compared to detect black-white subcultural differences. In their article, Sommers and Bruce demonstrate that studies of product preferences and ownership can also illuminate other issues relating to racial and ethnic relations. The concepts of relative deprivation and reference group have been used by several authors to explain why black protest has increased in recent years while the objective conditions of blacks, considered as a whole, have improved.[1] It is believed that Negroes have changed the standards by which they judge their conditions and thus have experienced psychological losses, or an increase in feelings of deprivation, while they have experienced objective gains. However, there have been few attempts to measure relative deprivation and to test empirically the explanations that utilize the concept of relative deprivation. The major contribution of Sommers and Bruce is that they have devised a measure of one kind of relative deprivation, and they report evidence on the standards of reference of different classes of blacks and whites. However, as they are careful to point out, one should not generalize from their findings to blacks and whites in the country as a whole. The study was conducted in a community in which there has been little black protest. Blacks in many other communities may well experience a greater amount of relative deprivation than those in Austin, Texas.

A study that reports similar data but that has a different purpose is "Some Consumption Pattern Differences between Urban Whites and Negroes," by James E. Stafford, Keith K. Cox, and James B. Higginbotham. Social scientists are interested in differences between the consumption patterns of blacks and whites with similar incomes because these differences may reflect differences in values, needs, and adjustment problems. Businessmen are interested in black-white consumption differences because many of their decisions can be aided by knowledge of the "Negro market." The research reported by Stafford, Cox, and Higginbotham was performed to serve businessmen rather than social scientists, but the latter can make good use of its findings. The study corroborates a con-

[1] For instance, see Thomas F. Pettigrew, *A Profile of the Negro American* (Princeton: Van Nostrand, 1964); Ruth Searles and J. Allen Williams, Jr., "Negro College Students' Participation in Sit-Ins," *Social Forces*, 40 (March, 1962), pp. 215–220; and contributions 25 and 26 in this volume.

clusion arrived at by several other studies, namely, that blacks and whites with similar incomes spend their money somewhat differently. The usual interpretation of this finding is that it reflects black-white differences in culture and in status needs. Although none of the research has demonstrated conclusively that some of the consumption differences do not result from differences on the average in age, family size, stage of family cycle, and the like, such differences as those in the amount and kind of liquor purchased do very likely reflect differences in values and needs.

In recent years a prevalent belief among liberal whites has been that there is no black subculture in the United States and that black-white differences in attitudes and behavior are totally "social-class" and regional differences, explained by differences in education, occupation, income, region of residence, and region of origin. In view of the many unique experiences of blacks in this country during their centuries of slavery and subordination, and in view of their continued segregation and involuntary social isolation, the theoretical perspectives of sociology and social psychology would lead one to expect subcultural differences between blacks and whites, although not a completely separate and autonomous black culture. Surprisingly, however, many social scientists have subscribed to the popular "liberal" belief in no racial differences except "social-class" and regional differences.[2] Since the mid-1960's, a convincing array of empirical evidence has been published that rather conclusively refutes this point of view. "A note on Negro-White Differences in Attitude toward the Supreme Court," by Herbert Hirsch and Lewis Donohew, is but one of the many reports of black-white differences in attitudes and behavior that cannot be explained by socioeconomic variables or by region of residence or origin. The difference Hirsch and Donohew report is to be expected in view of the several highly publicized recent Supreme Court decisions favorable to civil rights, but the reasons for many of the differences found by other studies are less obvious and more complicated.[3]

However, it is still important to keep in mind that differences in socioeconomic standing and region of residence and origin *do* account for a substantial proportion (and possibly for most) of all the attitudinal and behavioral differences between blacks and whites in the United States.

In "Political Orientations among Negroes and Whites," Dennis Ippolito, William S. Donaldson, and Lewis Bowman report a finding similar to that of Hirsch and Bowman, namely, that blacks at each socioeconomic level, considered as an aggregate, were more favorable to government support of a program of vocational rehabilitation than were their white counterparts.

At least in this respect, middle-class blacks in one city were more liberal than middle-class whites, and "social-class" differences were small-

[2] This view apparently was never held by most black social scientists and race leaders, and it is now vehemently denounced by the more militant and less "integrationist" black protest leaders.

[3] It should be stressed that there is no reason to believe that any of these differences result from innate, genetic differences between blacks and whites.

er among blacks than among whites. There apparently is a similarity of some political attitudes among blacks, if not true political solidarity, that cuts across social strata.

Many social scientists would attribute the liberalism of middle-class blacks on this issue to their low degree of status consistency, that is, to the fact that their ranks on the different dimensions of social stratification are dissimilar. Even though they are well-educated and in high-status occupations, they are denied the prestige, the social acceptance, and the privilege of moving into "better" neighborhoods generally accorded middle-class whites. According to Gerhard Lenski and other theorists, such a condition is conducive to discontent with the *status quo* and thus to political liberalism.

Ironically, the remaining discrimination against middle-class blacks probably benefits lower-class blacks in several ways. Without this discrimination, there probably would not be sufficient liberalism in the black middle class, nor sufficient ideological solidarity among blacks, for a successful protest movement. If prosperous, talented, well-educated blacks were generally accepted by whites as social equals, most of the potential leaders of political and social action on behalf of lower-class blacks would be co-opted by the majority population. Under such conditions, there would be no black protest movement and probably no "war on poverty." There traditionally has been little political action on behalf of the most poverty-stricken whites in the United States. (The welfare legislation of Franklin D. Roosevelt's "New Deal" and Harry Truman's "Fair Deal" benefited some working-class people and farmers but had relatively little effect on those who needed help the most.) Poor whites capable of leading movements for such action have usually been "bought off" by opportunities for upward mobility.[4] Therefore, it was not until a substantial black middle class emerged and the civil-rights movement had considerable momentum that there was a capable leadership experienced in social action and ideologically committed to bring pressure on the federal government to take steps to abolish poverty.[5]

The Mexican-Americans of the southwestern United States are an example of a minority whose most economically successful and well-educated members have generally been co-opted by the majority population while discrimination at the lower levels has continued. The Mexican-American who has been upwardly mobile to an upper-middle social stratum in spite of his many handicaps has usually become, for all intents and purposes, an "Anglo" (the word used in the southwest for a white not of Mexican or Spanish descent). The result has been a relative lack

---

[4] This "buying off" process may not be deliberate and consciously motivated but rather may be simply an unintended consequence of the relatively "open" class structure among whites in the United States.

[5] The leadership of the United States labor movement during its earlier stages may be an exception to this generalization, but the time was not then ripe for the kind of federal programs initiated under the recent ambitious, if largely unsuccessful, federal "war on poverty." When the time became ripe, the labor movement was busy furthering the interests of the more prosperous manual workers rather than the interests of the very poor.

of leadership for lower-class Mexican-Americans and, until recently, very little protest activity or political action on their behalf.

The last article reporting a Negro-white comparison deals not with attitudes but with changes of residence. A number of analyses of survey data gathered by the Bureau of the Census have shown that intracity residential moves are more frequent for blacks than for whites. In "Residential Movement among Negroes and Whites in Chicago," Bruce C. Straits demonstrates that the difference in Chicago is not explained by differences either in age, stage of family life cycle, amount of education, occupation, or intercity migration, and he thinks it improbable that all these together account for the difference in intracity moves. He tentatively concludes that a higher prevalence of a number of "push" factors accounts for the greater tendency of blacks to change place of residence.

Straits is concerned only with explaining this black-white difference; he does not discuss its probable consequences. However, the consequences are likely to be important. The frequent moves of blacks no doubt are adverse to neighborhood solidarity and stable social ties and probably contribute to the characteristically high rates of family instability in the ghetto. Of course, the family instability may also contribute to the frequency of moves. Instability of place of residence very likely aggravates the detrimental consequences of family instability on the adjustment and socialization of children.

There is a moderately large literature on black family characteristics, including several treatments of the prevalence and characteristics of female-headed households. However, relatively little attention has been given to black families in which the husband and father is present. In "Variations in the Father Role in Complete Families of the Negro Lower Class," David A. Schulz reports some observations of such families and presents a typology of the fathers based on their sexual ties. This typology, in turn, is related to the father's mode of legitimating his authority in the household. Although Schulz does not deal explicitly with the effects of the different kinds of families on the children, his observations suggest that the situation of children in many complete lower-class black families is little if any better than that of children in father-absent families.

Although the relative instability of conjugal relationships in black ghettos is well documented, to attribute a generally high degree of "family instability" to ghetto residents is somewhat misleading, because ties within the extended family appear to be stronger, and in a sense more stable, in black ghettos than in the white urban middle class. In fact, the frequent interaction and mutual aid among relatives seem to compensate to some degree for the insecurity and instability that often characterize marital relations. Joe R. Feagin reports data on this aspect of social organization in Boston's largest ghetto in "The Kinship Ties of Negro Urbanites."

Although continued social discrimination against all classes of blacks has prompted and sustained at least some small degree of social solidarity and political and ideological uniformity among black Americans, observers of the black protest movement agree that important schisms, jealousies, and ideological conflicts continue in the black community and in the protest movement. Since a major source of prestige in the black community is leadership of protest activity, some of the divisiveness grows simply out of a struggle among organizations and individuals for prestige rather than out of basic disagreement on goals and means to reach those goals. Whereas all careful students of the protest movement recognize the prevalence of this competition, they do not agree on its consequences for the effectiveness of the movement. In "Subcommunity Gladiatorial Competition: Civil Rights Leadership as a Competitive Process," Gerald A. McWorter and Robert L. Crain report evidence that the consequences vary according to whether the competition is among individuals or organizations, and they conclude that each kind of competition affects the attainment of different kinds of goals in different ways. McWorter and Crain also examine the community conditions conducive to different kinds and degrees of competition.

The last contribution in this section—"Race and Intelligence: Changing Opinions in Social Science," by Walter J. Cartwright and Thomas R. Burtis—deals not so much with the characteristics of black Americans as with the beliefs of social scientists about black Americans. Almost any American layman with some familiarity with the social and behavioral sciences knows that most scholars in these disciplines do not believe there is convincing evidence of racial differences in innate intelligence. However, the layman is less likely to know that just a few decades ago the social and behavioral sciences generally supported the popular belief in black inferiority. Critics of social science have charged that ideological influences brought about the switch. However, Cartwright and Burtis, after a detailed documentation of the change, conclude that it resulted from scientific discovery.

A related story is the corresponding change in the beliefs of white laymen in the United States about race and intelligence, which has been almost as swift and dramatic, if not quite as nearly complete, as the change in social scientists' beliefs. According to data collected by the National Opinion Research Center, only 21 percent of the whites in the South and 50 percent in the North said in 1942 they believed Negroes were as intelligent as whites. By 1964, these percentages had risen to 57 and 84, and most of the change occurred before 1956.[6]

[6] Herbert Hyman and Paul Sheatsley, "Attitudes toward Desegregation," *Scientific American*, 211 (July, 1964), pp. 2–9.

The Occupations and Income of Black Americans*

LEONARD BROOM
THE UNIVERSITY OF TEXAS AT AUSTIN

NORVAL D. GLENN
THE UNIVERSITY OF TEXAS AT AUSTIN

DURING RECENT DECADES THERE HAVE BEEN IMPROVEMENTS OF THE GREATest consequences in the occupational and economic standing of Negro Americans. Viewed in absolute terms, these gains are impressive. For instance, in 1940 only 8.5 percent of employed Negro workers had whitecollar or skilled manual occupations, whereas by 1960 almost 20 percent were employed in such work. The percentage employed as laborers and domestic service workers fell from 54 percent in 1940 to 33 percent in 1960. Unemployment in the nonwhite labor force fell during this period from 16.8 percent to 8.7 percent. The median wage and salary income of gainfully employed nonwhite males rose from $460 in 1939 to $3,023 in 1962. In actual buying power, in constant (1962) dollars, the increase was threefold—from $995 in 1939 to $3,023 in 1962.

However, these substantial occupational and income gains have not been sufficient to forestall Negro restivenesss. Advancement may bring not satiation of ambition but desire for even greater advancement. Success is companion to a discovery of the possible and an increase in aspiration. But this is not the full story. Men evaluate their achievements not only in absolute but in relative terms, not only in dollars earned but also in relation to the earnings of coworkers and competitors. Many Negroes lack precise knowledge of the gap between Negro and white economic status, but they are nevertheless aware that the gap has not narrowed greatly. The satisfaction derived from increased prosperity has been diluted by the observation that whites are also more prosperous and that Negroes are nearly the same distance behind. Furthermore, the rate of Negro advancement, which was very rapid during World War II, declined during the postwar period and therefore fell far short of the hopes, kindled by wartime experience, that Negroes were at last catching up.

Improved occupational and educational status has made keener the Negro's perception of his relative disadvantage. For the first time, many Negroes have a vantage point from which to estimate with some accuracy their relative condition. A semiliterate agricultural laborer can easily tell that his economic status is far below that of most whites, but he is unlikely to be able to make a meaningful comparison. In contrast, an in-

*Reprinted by permission from Leonard Broom and Norval D. Glenn, *Transformation of the Negro American* (New York: Harper & Row, 1967), pp. 105–134.

dustrial worker knows where he stands in the labor hierarchy and can guess how far he would have to go to be on a par with white workers. A Negro college professor in a predominantly Negro college knows reasonably well what his degree is worth compared with the same degree (perhaps from the same institution) held by a white professor teaching in a neighboring university. Negroes now are not only more able but also more inclined to gauge their standing relative to whites because more of them have contacts with whites on an equal footing. Where Negro social isolation has decreased and egalitarian social contacts have increased, one effect undoubtedly has been a rise in aspirations and a heightened sense of deprivation. Because high income and high occupational status are rare among Negroes, the middle-status Negro (by white standards) ranks above most other Negroes and therefore enjoys high prestige in the Negro community.[1] As long as he evaluates his economic status in relation to other Negroes, he may be fairly well satisfied, but when he begins to judge his status in relation to whites, he ranks himself lower and is less satisfied. To use the hackneyed metaphor, he is no longer a big frog in a little pond but a little frog in a big pond.

THE TURNING POINT: WORLD WAR II

Neither the occupational nor the economic gap between Negroes and whites was markedly closed between emancipation and the entry of the United States into World War II. In 1890, when the Census Bureau first gathered data on Negro occupations, almost 90 percent of Negro workers were in agriculture and domestic and personal service; about 60 percent of the native white workers were so employed. Early in the twentieth century, large numbers of Negroes moved from agriculture and domestic service into industrial occupations. However, there was an even greater movement of white workers, so that by 1940 only 20 percent of white workers remained in agriculture and domestic and personal service, compared with about 55 percent of Negro workers. In addition, many more white than Negro workers moved into skilled and white-collar occupations, resulting in a somewhat wider occupational gap between Negroes and whites in 1940 than in 1890. Accurate data on Negro and white incomes are not available for years prior to 1939, but there is little reason to believe that in 1939 Negro income compared more favorably with white income than it did late in the nineteenth century.

With the entry of the United States into World War II, Negro workers for the first time took a giant step toward equality with whites. The drafting of hundreds of thousands of civilian workers into the Armed Services created an acute labor shortage, and the dearth of qualified white males led to the recruitment of white women and Negroes of both sexes into types of work that previously had been largely closed to them. President Roosevelt's Executive Order 8802 in June 1941 forbade discrimination on the basis of race, creed, or national origin by employers who held govern-

---

[1] Norval D. Glenn, "Negro Prestige Criteria: A Case Study in the Bases of Prestige," *American Journal of Sociology*, 68 (May, 1963), pp. 645–657.

ment war contracts. The Fair Employment Practices Committee was set up to implement the order, and in several cases the committee was able to prevent discrimination and to open new jobs to Negroes. With the return of veterans to the civilian labor force at the end of the war, with the end of the Fair Employment Practices Committee in 1946, and with the decline of industries that mainly served the war effort, Negroes suffered losses in occupational status. However, not all wartime gains were lost, and conditions remained more favorable for Negro advancement than they had been before the war. Negro servicemen and workers in war industries gained valuable training and experience that enabled them to compete more effectively, and their employment in large numbers in unionized industries during the war left them in a stronger position in the labor movement. (Negroes first joined labor unions in large numbers after the founding of the CIO in 1935.)

However, the continuation of Negro gains after the war was not so much due to the residual effects of the war as to the nearly continuous prosperity and sustained growth of the whole economy. During and since the war, hundreds of thousands of new jobs have been created at intermediate and upper levels, and many Negroes have been able to move up without displacing whites.[2] Between 1940 and 1960, the total number of employed white-collar workers increased by nearly 12 million, or 81 percent, while the total employed labor force increased by only 37 percent. Hundreds of thousands of white workers have moved into new higher-level jobs, leaving vacancies at intermediate levels that could be filled by Negroes. For instance, of white males 25 through 34 years old in 1950 who were employed as clerical and kindred workers, 61,000—or 9 percent —had moved out of these occupations or died by 1960 and had not been replaced by other white males of the same cohort (a "cohort" is made up of all persons born during a given period of time). Some of these whites were replaced by younger whites, but many were replaced by Negroes. Because Negro gains could occur without loss to whites, white resistance to Negro advancement was less than it otherwise would have been. Expansion of jobs at the upper levels is not a new trend; it goes back to the start of industrialization, but until recently the upward movement of workers generated by this change did not greatly benefit Negroes. As long as large numbers of European immigrants were entering the country, they, rather than Negroes, replaced most of the native-born whites who moved up. World War I slowed European immigration and the Immigration Act of 1924 reduced it to a mere trickle, so that by the 1940s there was no longer a large pool of immigrants at the lowest occupational levels to replace the upward-moving native workers. The opportunity for the first great occupational advancement of Negro Americans was at hand.

THE OCCUPATION GAP

Some aspects of the occupational advancement of employed Negroes in in relation to employed whites from 1940 to 1960 are shown in Table 4.

[2] Norval D. Glenn, "Some Changes in the Relative Status of American Nonwhites, 1940 to 1960," *Phylon*, 24 (Summer, 1963), pp. 111–113.

TABLE 4

Ratio of Actual to Expected Proportion of Employed Workers Who Were Negro, in Each Occupational Group, United States, 1940, 1950, 1960[*]

Occupational group	Male			Female		
	1940	1950	1960	1940	1950	1960
Professional, technical, and kindred workers	.33	.29	.30	.33	.45	.55
Farmers and farm managers	1.44	1.28	.77	2.20	2.24	1.06
Managers, proprietors, and officials, except farm	.13	.19	.17	.19	.30	.28
Clerical and kindred workers	.19	.47	.70	.04	.14	.25
Sales workers	.13	.17	.19	.07	.16	.19
Craftsmen, foremen, and kindred workers	.30	.42	.50	.16	.41	.54
Operatives and kindred workers	.69	1.05	1.23	.34	.76	.82
Private household workers	7.00	5.71	5.32	3.38	4.87	4.60
Service workers, except private household	1.92	2.27	2.32	.92	1.55	1.58
Farm laborers and foremen	2.44	2.14	2.55	4.49	2.61	2.47
Laborers, except farm and mine	2.44	2.92	2.96	.96	1.88	1.85

Source: Computed from data from the 1940, 1950, and 1960 census of U.S. population.

[*]The "expected" proportion of Negroes in each group is the proportion of Negroes in the total employed labor force.

The "expected" proportion of Negroes in each occupational group is the proportion of Negroes in the total employed labor force. For instance, 8.4 percent of all employed males in 1960 were Negro, and one might "expect" 8.4 percent of employed males in each occupational group to be Negro. If the actual proportion of Negroes in an occupational group was more than this parity, the ratio is greater than 1.00; if the actual proportion was less than expected, the ratio is less than 1.00.

The greatest gains for both Negro males and females from 1940 to 1960 were in intermediate-level occupations, such as clerical workers, craftsmen, foremen, and operatives. There was negligible increase in the representation of Negro males in the highest-level occupations during the two decades. The ratio of the actual to expected proportion of employed Negro males who were managers, officials, and proprietors increased only slightly, from .13 in 1940 to .17 in 1960. The ratio for professional and technical workers declined, from .33 in 1940 to .30 in 1960.

This decline is accounted for by a large decrease in Negro clergymen, from 17,102 in 1940 to 13,955 in 1960. The number of male clergymen per 10,000 population declined from 13.3 in 1940 to 7.4 in 1960 for Negroes but increased from 9.8 to 11.4 for whites. This decline in Negro clergymen reflects the passing from the scene of the older traditional minister, perhaps a declining interest in religion among Negro Americans, and increased opportunities for young Negroes in more lucrative lines of work. Since most Negro clergymen in 1940 were poorly educated, poorly paid, and professional workers only in the extended sense, a decline in their numbers may be regarded as a gain for Negroes.

If clergymen are excluded from the professional and technical category, there was a slight increase in the ratio from .24 for 1940 to .27 for 1960. In contrast to males, the ratio for Negro females increased appreciably in each of the highest-level occupational categories, from .33 in 1940 to .55 in 1960 as professional and technical workers, and from .19 to .28 as managers, officials, and proprietors.

In spite of Negro gains in the 1940s and 1950s, both males and females in 1960 were far from proportionally represented in all of the white-collar occupational groups and as craftsmen and foremen. Furthermore, the recent rate of Negro increase in these occupations is not great enough to lead to occupational equality in the near future. For instance, assuming that the representation of Negro males as professional, technical, and kindred workers (excluding clergymen) were to continue to increase at the 1940–1960 rate, it would not be for *530 years* after 1960 (until the year 2490) that proportional representation would be attained. By the same calculations, proportional representation of Negro males would not be attained as managers, officials, and proprietors within 415 years and as sales workers not for 270 years. Since these projections extend several generations beyond the lifetime of Negroes now living, it is small wonder that Negroes imbued with the ideal of equality are less than satisfied with the recent pace of occupational gains. To be sure, neither Negroes nor whites are aware of the arithmetic of trends nor their harsh implications, but some Negroes may sense the rate of change. (The reader must be cautioned that these figures are projections, not predictions. Alterations in the rates of change probably will occur and we point to some of the conditions that may cause such changes. Nevertheless, the projections do dramatize the gap that remains.)

Small as the ratios were in the higher-level occupational groups in 1960, they do not fully reveal the extent of inequality. Within each occupational group, Negroes were relatively concentrated in the lower-paying and lower-prestige occupations. For instance, the occupational group of professional, technical, and kindred workers includes such diverse occupations as physicians, engineers, school teachers, social workers, and medical and dental technicians. In 1960, only 11.4 percent of the employed Negro male professional, technical, and kindred workers were architects, dentists, engineers, lawyers, judges, physicians, and surgeons. In contrast, 31.4 percent of the employed white male professionals had these higher-paying occupations. In addition, the rate of increase of Negroes in the higher-level professional and technical occupations has generally been less (see Table 5). For instance, from 1940 to 1960 there was no increase in the representation of Negro males as physicians and surgeons or as college presidents, professor, and instructors, and the increase in Negro representation as dentists was very small. The big gains were in relatively low-paying semiprofessional occupations, such as welfare and recreation workers and medical and dental technicians.

Not only are Negroes concentrated in the lower-paying occupations; they generally earn less than whites in the same occupations. The 1959 median earnings of white and nonwhite males in selected occupations are shown in Table 6. The gap between whites and nonwhites was generally less in governmental occupations such as postal workers, firemen, and policemen. For the seven occupations of this type in the table, the average ratio of nonwhite to white median earnings was .92, whereas for the other occupations the average was only .72. Present-day discrimination in government employment, where it exists, more often takes the form of exclusion than of lower pay. Even at the state and local levels, wages and salaries are fairly well standardized, and Negroes and whites with similar jobs and similar seniority are usually paid about the same. Highly trained Negro workers, such as engineers and electronics technicians, who are employed mainly by private industry also are paid almost as much as their white counterparts. In contrast, an appreciable earnings gap existed in 1959 between Negroes and whites in most manual occupations and in those occupations in which Negroes serve other Negroes as entrepreneurs or as employees of Negro institutions. Some, but not all, of the Negro-white disparity in earnings within occupations is due to greater unemployment of Negroes in most occupations.

The Negro-white occupational gap obviously is still very wide, and it is closing so slowly that it will not disappear within the next century unless the rate of Negro gains sharply accelerates. Some acceleration, especially at the highest levels, is likely and may already have occurred since 1960. The increased race consciousness of Negroes is making the opening of higher-level government jobs to Negroes a political necessity and is making the hiring of Negroes by private firms requisite to the attraction and holding of a large Negro clientele. There will be some discrimination in favor of Negroes, but unless it becomes more widespread than seems probable, near equality in occupational status must await near equality in occupational qualifications. As we point out above, near equality in qualifications is at least several decades away.

THE INCOME GAP

Until recently, the moderate closing of the occupational gap between employed Negroes and whites was accompanied by a similar narrowing of the income gap. The income gap closed appreciably during World

TABLE 5

Ratio of Actual to Expected Proportion of Negro Males in Selected
Occupations, United States, 1940, 1950, and 1960

	1940	1950	1960
Accountants and auditors	n.a.[a]	.04	.07
Architects	.05	.07	.10
Artists and art teachers	.08	.14	.20
Authors, editors, and reporters	.09	.09	.11
Bookkeepers	n.a.	.06	.12
Chemists	.06	.12	.24
Clergymen	1.48	1.31	.85
College presidents, professors, and instructors (not elsewhere classified)	.30	.30	.30
Dentists	.24	.24	.30
Designers and craftsmen	.01	.05	.13
Engineers			
—aeronautical	n.a.	.02	.07
—civil	.01	.05	.10
—electrical	.01	.03	.08
—mechanical	.01	.03	.05
Insurance agents and brokers	n.a.	.23	.18
Lawyers and judges	.07	.09	.12
Mail carriers	.54	.87	1.24
Medical and dental technicians	n.a.	.44	.95
Musicians and music teachers	.82	.86	.83
Natural scientists (not elsewhere classified)	n.a.	.16	.18
Pharmacists	.12	.16	.20
Physicians and surgeons	.25	.24	.24
Real estate agents and brokers	.13	.20	.20
Salaried managers, officials, and proprietors (not elsewhere classified)			
—in manufacturing	n.a.	.03	.05
—in retail and wholesale trade	n.a.	.13	.11
in finance, insurance, and real estate	n.a.	.10	.12
Salesmen and sales clerks			
—in manufacturing	n.a.	.05	.06
—in wholesale trade	n.a.	.05	.06
—in retail trade	n.a.	.20	.25
Self-employed managers, officials, and proprietors (not elsewhere classified)			
—in construction	n.a.	.20	.21
—in manufacturing	n.a.	.06	.10
—in wholesale trade	n.a.	.17	.24
—in eating and drinking places	n.a.	.46	.45
—in other retail trade	n.a.	.46	.45
Social scientists	n.a.	.15	.19
Social, welfare, and recreation workers	n.a.	.73	1.17
Teachers(not elsewhere classified)	.63	.76	.77

Source: Computed from data from the 1940, 1950, and 1960 censuses of U.S. population.

[a] Not available.

TABLE 6

Ratio of Nonwhite to White Median Earnings of Males in
Selected Occupations, United States, 1959

Occupation	Ratio of nonwhite to white	Occupation	Ratio of nonwhite to white
Electrical and electronics technicians	.98	Secondary school teachers	.76
Firemen, fire protection	.96	Foremen (not elsewhere classified)	.74
Mail carriers	.96	Compositors and typesetters	.73
Postal clerks	.95	Automobile mechanics and	
Policemen and detectives	.95	repairmen	.71
Aeronautical engineers	.94	Dentists	.70
Electrical engineers	.91	Linemen and servicemen, telegraph,	
Inspectors, public administration	.90	telephone, and power	.69
Bookkeepers	.90	Laborers, except farm and mine	.69
Designers and draftsmen	.88	Musicians and music teachers	.67
Airplane mechanics and repairmen	.88	Painters, construction and	
Mechanical engineers	.88	maintenance	.64
Bus drivers	.87	Clergymen	.64
Electricians	.86	Barbers	.64
Civil engineers	.86	Insurance agents, brokers,	
Accountants and auditors	.84	and underwriters	.63
Officials and administrators,		Salesmen and sales clerks	
public administration	.83	(not elsewhere classified)	.63
Office machine operators	.83	Brickmasons, stonemasons,	
Elementary school teachers	.82	and tile setters	.61
Medical and dental technicians	.80	Truck and tractor drivers	.59
Radio and television		Cement and concrete finishers	.59
mechanics and repairmen	.79	Plumbers and pipe fitters	.58
Chemists	.78	Plasterers	.56
College professors and instructors	.77	Carpenters	.55
Mine operatives and laborers		Farm laborers, wage workers	.52
(not elsewhere classified)	.77	Physicians and surgeons	.39
Shipping and receiving clerks	.77	Farmers and farm managers	.33

Source: Computed from data from U.S. *Census of Population: 1960*, Final Report
PC(2)-7B, Table 1 (US. Bureau of the Census, Washington, D.C.).

War II but very slowly and erratically during the postwar period. White
and nonwhite median family incomes in constant (1962) dollars are
shown for each year from 1947 to 1962 in Figure 2. Incomes for both
races went up steeply during the period, but the ratio of the nonwhite to
the white median hardly changed; it was exactly the same in 1962 as it
was in 1948. The absolute gap between the white and nonwhite medians
increased. The data in Table 7 on the median income of individuals show
greater improvement in the relative standing of nonwhites. However,
these data are only for persons *with* income, and since a greater percentage of Negro than of white adult males had no income, the comparison of
family incomes is more meaningful. Nevertheless, it is important that the
ratio of Negro to white median income of males with income did not increase from 1949 to 1959.

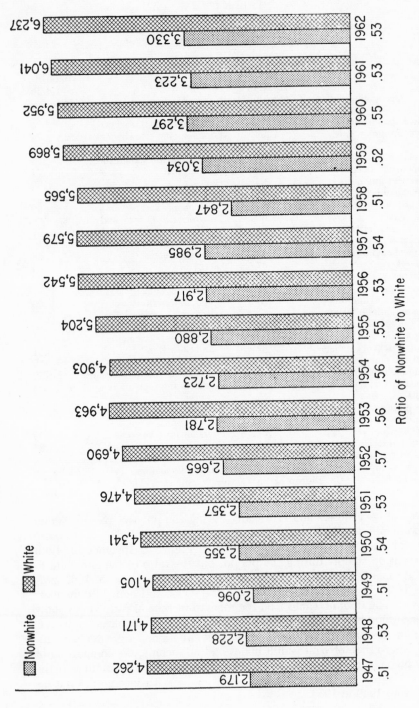

Figure 2. Median Family Income in Constant (1962) Dollars, by Color, United States, 1947–1962 (Source: Computed from data reported annually by the U.S. Bureau of the Census in *Current Population Reports*, Series P–60.)

TABLE 7

Median Income of Persons with Income, by Race and Sex,
United States, 1949 and 1959

	Negro	White	Ratio of Negro to White
Both sexes			
1949	961	2,058	.47
1959	1,519	3,026	.50
Male			
1949	1,356	2,582	.53
1959	2,254	4,338	.52
Female			
1949	703	1,139	.62
1959	905	1,509	.60

Source: *U.S. Census of Population: 1960*, Final Report PC(1)-ID, p. 578 (U.S. Bureau of the Census, Washington, D.C.)

The slower rate of income gains as compared to occupational gains of Negroes is largely accounted for by (1) an increase in the difference between white and nonwhite unemployment rates and (2) an increase in the income gap between lower-level and other occupations. The ratio of nonwhite to white percentage of workers unemployed increased from 11.8 in 1940, to 1.73 in 1950, to 1.85 in 1960. The absolute differences between the percentages for the same three years were 2.6, 3.3, and 4.0. Mechanization of industrial processes that eliminated many jobs in occupations in which Negroes are concentrated largely accounts for this widening of the unemployment gap.

Demand for unskilled and semiskilled labor has declined more rapidly than Negroes have acquired the education and training requisite to upgrading into expanding lines of work, and unless Negro education and skills improve more rapidly than is likely, the difference between Negro and white unemployment rates is likely to grow with further mechanization and automation. If so, the effects may offset many past as well as future occupational gains. The occupational advances of Negro workers after 1940 were largely into intermediate-level jobs that are subject to elimination by automation. The largest movement of Negro workers was into the occupational group of operatives and kindred workers, a category which is already hard hit by technological unemployment. In 1960, 6.4 percent of the males and 9.9 percent of the females in this occupational group were unemployed—higher unemployment than among any other class of workers except laborers. (Only part, however, was technological unemployment; much of it was caused by reduced production in some industries.) Many kinds of skilled workers also are being displaced by mechanization, although Negro craftsmen generally are more secure than Negro operatives. Unemployment in 1960 was relatively low among clerical and kindred workers, the other occupational group into which

Negroes moved in large numbers. However, clerical jobs appear to be next in line to feel the impact of automation. Most of the occupational gains of Negroes during the past quarter of a century, in fact, are vulnerable to automation and other technological changes.

The reduced demand for unskilled labor has prevented incomes of unskilled workers from rising as fast as incomes of other workers. Wage and salary income of unskilled workers was little higher in 1959 than in 1949. Wages and salaries in general rose steeply during the decade, so the gap between unskilled and other workers widened. Since Negroes are overrepresented in unskilled work, this change tended to widen the income gap between Negroes and whites even though Negro representation increased at the higher occupational levels during the same period.

For similar reasons, the closing of the educational gap during the 1950s was not accompanied by a corresponding closing of the economic gap. The ratio of nonwhite to white median years of school completed by persons 25 years old and older increased from .71 in 1950 to .75 in 1960. Because the income gap is to a large extent a reflection of the educational gap, one might have expected similar marked improvement in the relative economic status of Negroes during the 1950s. Yet such improvement did not occur, because the economic gap between all poorly educated workers and others widened and Negroes remained highly represented among the poorly educated. In 1949, the median income of males who had completed one to four years of elementary school was 45 percent of the median income of those who had completed high school and was 31 percent of the median income of those who had completed four or more years of college. By 1959, these percentages had declined to 34 and 24.

Negro Americans are on a treadmill. They must keep gaining on whites in education and occupation simply to stay the same distance behind in income. Undoubtedly, this condition adversely affects Negro morale. Many Negroes find it increasingly difficult to get and keep jobs, and many who manage to remain employed most of the time do not share in the general increase in real income in the United States. While their own economic condition becomes worse or improves only slowly, their appetite for a more affluent style of life is whetted by direct observation of increased consumption by other Americans (both whites and the growing number of middle-class Negroes) and by increased exposure to the mass media of communication. Their feelings of deprivation increase even if their absolute economic condition improves.

The increased sense of deprivation of poorly educated Negroes is not unique but is shared by many poorly educated and unskilled whites. However, the consequences of Negro discontent are different. Negroes tend to define their troubles in racial terms, especially since the recent increased publicity given to the struggle for equal rights. The plight of the large percentage of Negroes who are poorly educated and unskilled has appreciable effects upon other Negroes. Self-employed Negro businessmen and professionals are dependent upon other Negroes and can hope to improve their economic condition only as the economic condi-

tion of the entire Negro population improves. Middle-class Negroes employed in the integrated economy have less reason to be concerned about
the plight of poor Negroes, but whether they care or not, their fates are
linked in important ways. Middle-class Negroes often must live in neighborhoods with lower-class Negroes, send their children to schools in
which most of the pupils come from lower-class families, and in general
have more frequent and closer contacts with lower-class people than do
middle-class whites. An increasing number of middle-class Negroes owe
their jobs to the political influence and buying power either of the entire
Negro population or of the local Negro community. In addition, these
people know that whites are likely to judge them on the basis of stereotypes that reflect the characteristics of the lower class. Therefore, a condition that adversely affects any segment of the Negro population has
some adverse effects on all. Negroes are apparently becoming more sensitive to this fact, and the plight of unskilled workers causes some unrest
among all classes.

As we suggest above, improvement in the relative occupational status
of Negro Americans since the beginning of World War II seems, to a
large extent, to be an outgrowth of a high level of nationwide prosperity,
a high rate of economic growth and changes in the occupation structure
generating many upper- and intermediate-level jobs. The evidence for
this reasoning is convincing if not conclusive. For example, Negroes generally made their greatest occupational gains in lines of work in which the
number of jobs increased most rapidly.[3] Their relative economic status
improved during years of rapid economic growth and generally declined
or was static during years of little or no economic growth. These facts
might lead one to conclude that future Negro gains are largely contingent upon continued economic growth and changes in the economic structure. Such changes probably are necessary for Negro gains, but they are
hardly sufficient, and there is reason to believe that they will be less beneficial to Negroes than they have been. Rapid economic growth in the past
has helped Negroes mainly by reducing unemployment. The economic
status of Negroes has generally risen during years of full employment in
the total labor force and fallen during years of high unemployment. Now,
however, a rapid rate of economic growth does not reduce unemployment
as much as it once did; high rates of economic growth and high rates of
unemployment recently have occurred together. For instance, the rate of
economic growth in the United States from 1958 to 1959 was about 8.5
percent, well above the average for the previous decade, but unemployment in 1959 was 5.5 percent, also well above the average for the previous decade. (The rate of economic growth is defined roughly as the
annual percentage increase in the value, in constant dollars, of all goods
and services purchased for final use.)

In the future, unemployment may actually increase during years of
rapid economic growth, and if so, rapid expansion of the economy may no

[3] Glenn, "Some Changes in the Relative Status of American Nonwhites, 1940 to
1960," p. 112.

longer tend to improve the relative status of Negroes. Furthermore, the opening of new jobs at the higher and intermediate occupational levels may no longer be greatly beneficial to the Negro population as a whole if there is an accompanying large decrease in jobs at the lower levels. The number of Negroes displaced from lower-level jobs may be larger than the number who are qualified to take advantage of openings at intermediate and higher levels. In short, economic and occupational trends of the future may benefit Negroes appreciably only if their occupational qualifications improve very rapidly. And the improvement of Negro occupational qualifications depends largely, although not completely, upon improvement in the quantity and quality of Negro education. The obstacles to rapid improvement in Negro education are formidable; and perhaps the obstacles to rapid improvement of the occupational qualifications of adult Negroes who have completed their formal education are even greater. Therefore, the relative economic status of Negroes may drop below its present level within the next few years. Only unforeseen developments could bring about a rapid increase in the near future.

INTERRELATIONS AMONG EDUCATION, OCCUPATION, AND INCOME

The gap between Negroes and whites in the amount of formal education accounts for much, but not all, of the occupation and income gaps. Negroes and whites with the same amount of schooling differ greatly in their incomes and occupations (see Tables 8 and 9). The differences are due in part to persisting discrimination and to the handicaps under which self-employed Negroes work. But . . . Negroes and whites with the same number of years of school are frequently not equally qualified. All these factors combine to create a particularly stubborn obstacle to Negro achievement and a heavy burden to Negro morale. The inequality between Negroes and whites with the same amount of formal education is perhaps even more burdensome to morale than the economic inequality that can be attributed to differences in the amount of schooling.

TABLE 8

Ratio of Nonwhite to White Median Income of Males 25 Years Old and Older, by Educational Level, United States, 1949 and 1959

School years completed	1949	1959
none	.68	.66
1–4	.54	.80
5–7	.70	.73
8	.72	.73
1–3 high school	.67	.65
4 high school	.68	.68
1–3 college	.64	.66
4 or more college	.59	.62

Sources: Computed from data from *U.S. Census of Population: 1950*, Special Report PE No. 5B, Table 12, and *U.S. Census of Population: 1960*, Final Report, PC(1)-1D, p. 590 (Washington, D.C., U.S. Bureau of the Census).

TABLE 9

Index of Occupational Dissimilarity[a] between Nonwhite and White Males
25–44 Years Old, by Educational Level, United States, 1950 and 1960

Years of school completed	25–34 years old, 1950	35–44 years old, 1960	25–34 years old, 1960
Less than 5	21.9	19.45	18.4
5–7	26.1	26.65	26.1
8	28.95	26.9	26.95
1–3 high school	29.05	30.65	28.0
4 high school	32.05	30.5	30.65
1–3 college	30.05	29.65	26.15
4 or more college	11.45	8.85	6.3

Source: Computed from data from the 1950 and 1960 censuses of U.S. population.
[a] The index of occupational dissimilarity is the percentage of nonwhite workers who would have to move from one occupational category to another in order for the nonwhite and white occupational distributions to be equal. Nine broad occupational categories were used to compute the index values shown here.

The gaps in both occupation and income are generally greater at upper educational levels. For instance, in 1949 and in 1959, nonwhite males with from five to eight years of school fared better relative to their white counterparts than did nonwhite males at any higher educational level. In 1959, the biggest gap between nonwhite and white incomes was at the highest educational level. This difference perhaps in part reflects a greater difference in average qualifications at higher levels. The relatively small gap at the *lower* levels reflects the fact that the quality of formal education has little relevance to qualifications for many of unskilled and semiskilled jobs.

The greater income and occupational disparity at the higher educational levels is an additional reason why the increased average educational status of Negroes probably has led to increased discontent and feelings of deprivation. Not only is the well-educated Negro better able to perceive the status gap between himself and his white educational counterpart—he also perceives a wider gap. And the wider gap probably contributes to the restiveness and urge to protest that seem to be engendered by increased education.

If the status differences between Negroes and whites with the same amount of education were diminishing rapidly, Negro discontent might be less. However, changes from 1950 to 1960 were small. Ratios of nonwhite to white median income of males in 1949 and in 1959 are shown for each of eight educational levels in Table 8. The ratio increased from 1949 to 1959 at five levels, decreased at two levels, and stayed the same at one. However, only one change—the increase in the relative status of nonwhites with one to four years of school—was large enough to be important, and this increase came about not because the median income of nonwhites increased steeply but because the median income of white males at this educational level *declined* in constant dollars during the decade.

Nonwhite income at the one-through-four-year educational level was very low in 1949, and it probably was kept from dropping by relief payments and the extention of minimum-wage legislation.

There was little change during the 1950s in the relative economic standing of nonwhite males with high school education, and the increase was small among the college educated. However, the incomes of well-educated nonwhites did rise in relation to the incomes of whites with less education—one aspect of the general widening of the economic gap between the well educated and the poorly educated. For instance, in 1949 the median nonwhite male with four or more years of college had an income only 3 percent higher than the income of the median white male with an eighth-grade education. By 1959 this difference had risen to 20 percent. Even so, in 1959 the median income of nonwhite males with four or more years of college did not yet equal the median income of white males with one to three years of high school.

The data on Table 9 give a rough indication of the occupational status of nonwhite males compared to white males in 1950 and 1960. The index of dissimilarity reported is simply the percentage of nonwhites who would have to move from one occupational category to another in order for the distribution of nonwhites and whites among nine broad occupational categories to be the same. Therefore, the higher the index, the wider is the occupational gap. The occupational categories from which the data have been computed are the same as those used in the U.S. census, except that clerical and sales workers are combined into a single category and professional and technical workers are combined with managers, officials, and proprietors. The combination of groups similar in prestige and incomes results in nine categories that form a hierarchy, in prestige and desirability, of the occupations they include. Crude though it is, the index of occupational dissimilarity correlates highly with more complex and refined indexes of occupational differences. Its major weakness is that it does not reflect the considerable vertical differences between nonwhites and whites *within* the occupational groups. This weakness could not easily be overcome because the Bureau of the Census did not tabulate complete data on detailed occupations by educational level. Consequently, the index understates the extent of nonwhite disadvantage, but it is still a convenient way of summarizing such statistics.

The occupational difference between nonwhite and white males who were 25 through 34 years old in 1950 (a category that included approximately the same people who were 35 through 44 years old in 1960) changed very little during the decade. The biggest decline in the index was among those with four years or more of college, and the decline is not clearcut evidence of an increase in opportunity for Negroes. The change could stem from differences in the career patterns of nonwhites and whites with a college education. Since more whites began their careers in the top category, white upward movement was more often within the category and did not affect the distribution of white workers among the nine categories.

The difference between the index values for workers who were 25 through 34 years old in 1950 and those of the same age in 1960 is greater. The index declined some at each level of schooling except the five-to-seven-year level, and it declined appreciably at the college levels. A much larger percentage of college-educated young nonwhite males was in professional and technical occupations in 1960, and the nonwhite increase was greater than the white increase. Again, however, there is no clearcut evidence of increased opportunity. The higher relative status of the younger nonwhites could be the consequence of improvement in their qualifications and in the quality of Negro education.

Much of the discrimination-caused difference in status between whites and nonwhites with the same amount of education is likely to disappear within a decade or two. This trend is especially evident at the higher educational levels. Many corporations are recruiting Negroes for fairly high positions because it has become good public relations to do so. Likewise, many colleges and universities are adding Negro faculty and staff members either because of the shortage of qualified white personnel or to show a lack of discrimination. Appointment of Negroes to high posts in the federal government and to many state agencies in the North and West has become good politics. Such lowering of the color bar is as yet hardly more than "tokenism" and will not in itself go far toward solving the economic problems of Negroes. However, conspicuous employment of Negroes has become prevalent enough within the past two or three years so that the demand for competent and personable Negro college graduates probably exceeds the supply. The appearance of well-qualified Negroes in conspicuous positions of responsibility has diverse effects. White coworkers who never before associated with Negroes in an egalitarian setting—perhaps who never before associated with Negroes—have an opportunity to observe the Negro as a man and react to him as a person. Whites whose image of the Negro is bound by stereotypes find that the stereotypes do not stand up under daily observations in the work setting. Negroes whose lives were lived out in a world of Negroes find broader horizons and gain greater familiarity with middle-class white standards and styles.

At the lower educational levels, the extension and more stringent enforcement of antidiscrimination legislation may lessen discrimination, and the widespread use of boycotts and demonstrations may be even more effective in bringing down the color bar. However, lessened job discrimination depends upon continued favorable economic conditions whereby interests of large segments of the white population will not be threatened by Negro gains. If upper- and intermediate-level jobs do not increase fast enough to provide job opportunities for almost all qualified workers of both races, white resistance to Negro advancement probably will stiffen and discrimination may increase. The sober fact is that, in spite of recent gains in Negro power, any large segment of the white population still has an advantage over Negroes. White customers, with their greater buying power, could, if they wished, influence the employment practices of business firms more than Negroes. Any sizeable number of white voters, properly distributed, could offset the political influence of Negroes. In short, any large segment of the white population that so desired could use the same means to increase discrimination that Negroes are now using to lessen it.

Nevertheless, it seems unlikely that white resistance will now reverse the trend away from discrimination. Only a business depression or other major disruption of the economy could make Negro advancement a serious threat to a large number of white workers, except perhaps in a few localities in which the Negro population is relatively large. Furthermore, social and cultural change, once underway, gathers momentum that enables it to continue in the face of increased opposing influences. For instance, the more widespread acceptance of egalitarian values during recent years would make it hard to justify increased discrimination. Whites who would gain from greater discrimination no doubt could justify it to themselves, but egalitarian values would deter many other whites from supporting it. Even if there is no real threat, some white workers may *feel* threatened and oppose the trend toward equal opportunity, but their resistance is not likely to halt the trend.

It might be possible to eliminate the more important kinds of discrimination within the next few years, but the quality of Negro education cannot be improved so rapidly, and Negro-white status differences will persist for a long time. A shortage of skills and educational qualifications may soon become a much greater obstacle to Negro advancement than a dearth of available jobs. Indeed, such may already be the case.

THE ROLE OF ORGANIZED LABOR

Organized labor has played both beneficial and detrimental roles in Negro economic and occupational status. During the past few decades the detrimental effects have decreased and the beneficial ones have increased, but union discrimination remains a major obstacle to Negro advancement.

Countervailing influences have blunted and diverted the ability of organized labor either to hinder or to help. On the negative side, many white union members are recruited from some of the more prejudiced parts of the white population. Although the evidence is not clearcut and consistent, it seems that manual workers are somewhat more anti-Negro on the average than white-collar workers.[4] Members of ethnic minorities and migrants from the rural South, numerous among union members, are also prone to strong anti-Negro sentiments. In general, manual workers are more directly in competition with large numbers of Negroes and may feel threatened by Negro advancement. These union members, motivated by their own perceived interests, tend to exclude Negroes from unions or

[4] But the presumed greater prejudice of "working-class" people may be more apparent than real. Manual workers express prejudice less subtly and their realizations are less sophisticated. They do not so clearly understand the purpose of paper-and-pencil tests and interviewers' questions that are designed to measure prejudice and are more likely to make "prejudiced" responses than are white-collar workers with basically similar attitudes.

to discriminate against them if they are admitted. Since craft unions are more fraternal than industrial unions, membership in them more clearly implies social equality; the incentive of prejudiced members to exclude Negroes has therefore been especially strong.

On the positive side, intellectuals in the labor movement have espoused the ideal of racial equality, but their liberalism affects the formal policies of international unions more than the practices of locals. No doubt the international policy has been filtering down to the local level, although the extent of such influence is not fully documented. Egalitarian values are more apparent in industrial than craft unions, but decreased discrimination in them may be motivated by self-interest and necessity as well as ethical conviction. The egalitarian ideology may be as much a reflection of practice as a molder of it. Industrial unions, whose members are largely semiskilled and unskilled, often organized industries in which a large number of Negroes were already employed, and in order to attain their objectives, they had to be inclusive in their membership. Before Negroes were admitted to many unions, management used Negroes as strikebreakers, and it was in the interest of some industrial unions to lower racial bars. Craft unions, in contrast, organized workers by specific occupations rather than by industry, and few Negroes were employed in the typical craft occupations. Since craft-union membership was skilled, unskilled Negroes could not be used as strikebreakers against them; craft unions thus had no self-interest in lowering racial bars. It is not surprising, therefore, that the Congress of Industrial Organizations (CIO) espoused a policy of nondiscrimination when it was formed in 1935, whereas most craft unions in the American Federation of Labor (AFL) continued to discriminate.

Although Negro and white manual workers compete for jobs, they have many interests in common, and their cooperation in the labor movement can be mutually advantageous. Both benefit from industrial expansion that creates more jobs and from improvements in wages, fringe benefits, and working conditions. Both are threatened by automation, retarded economic growth, and antilabor legislation. While these common interests and concerns have not led to a high degree of solidarity between Negro and white workers, organized labor and Negroes have occasionally formed effective political coalitions. A few such liberal alliances have been formed in parts of the South; prospects of further ones are provoking segregationists, especially the White Citizens Councils, to expend considerable effort to foster anti-Negro feelings among union members in order to prevent such alliance.[5] Since most Southern workers probably have stronger race consciousness than class conciousness, a general Southern coalition of Negroes and unions is unlikely in the near future.

Government action against discrimination has tended to make organized labor deal more favorably with Negroes. About half of the states have legislation specifically prohibiting discrimination in unions, even

[5] Ray Marshall, "The Negro and Organized Labor," *Journal of Negro Education*, 32 (Fall, 1963), pp. 384–385.

though effective enforcement is rare. Some federal labor legislation also prohibits discrimination, but some does not. For instance, the Railway Labor Act and the Wagner-Connery Act require unions that are granted exclusive bargaining rights to represent all workers fairly but do not require them to admit Negroes to membership; their effects upon discriminatory union practices have thus been small.[6] The National Labor Relations Board has used its regulatory powers only to a limited extent to prevent discrimination. It has threatened to revoke the certification of discriminating unions, but it has not done so.[7]

The most effective governmental action against union discrimination has been taken by Presidential committees set up to police employment practices of firms with government contracts. These include President Roosevelt's wartime Fair Employment Practices Committee, President Eisenhower's Committee on Government Contracts, and President Kennedy's Committee on Equal Employment Opportunity (CEEO). The first two of these, which applied their sanctions to employers only, had only an indirect effect upon union practices. The CEEO, however, was directed to "cause any labor union . . . [which] is or may be engaged in work under government contracts to cooperate with and to comply in the implementation of the purposes of the order [which forbade discrimination in work done under government contracts]." As a result of the committee's activity, a few unions have integrated their locals in the South and a few additional jobs have opened to Negroes. The personal effects of President Kennedy and Johnson have been at least as effective as the activities of the committee. President Kennedy persuaded unions that include 90 percent of the AFL-CIO's membership to sign pledges to comply with his executive order prohibiting discrimination in work done under government contracts. The short-run effect of these pledges upon practice is not clear, but the long-run consequences may be important.

Government pressure, unfavorable publicity, and other influences have fostered considerable change in union racial policies, if not in practice. In 1930, at least twenty-two unions officially barred Negroes from membership, but the number fell to thirteen in 1943, to nine in 1949, and to two in 1963. Discrimination on the unofficial level did not decline correspondingly, however, and continues in numerous unions—for example, by refusal to admit Negroes to apprenticeship programs, by agreements not to sponsor Negroes for membership, and by rigging examinations to refuse Negroes journeymen status. Auxiliary Negro locals, controlled by white locals, were once numerous, but most were integrated with white locals or given "separate but equal" status before the Landrum-Griffin Act of 1959 made it possible for Negro employees to bring legal action to abolish auxiliary locals. However, "separate but equal" Negro locals are still common in the South. In some trades, the existence of separate locals denies Negroes equal job opportunities, but in others Negroes have

[6] *Ibid.*, p. 385.
[7] *Ibid.*, p. 386.

protected territories and therefore have little to gain from integration. Some Negroes feel they have greater freedom of action, especially in pursuing nonunion interests, by having their own locals.[8] However, younger Negroes tend to oppose segregation on principle, and greater agitation for integration of locals is to be expected.

Most remaining discrimination is in craft unions, where it is probably rooted primarily in the desire of present members to reduce competition by keeping membership low. In this situation, race prejudice as such is not a basic motivation for action, but it is manipulated to achieve economic objectives. Many craft unions limit membership and the number of persons in their apprenticeship programs to create a shortage of qualified workers and thus maintain high wages and job security. Consequently, it has been difficult for many whites as well as for Negroes to enter certain trades. Some craft unions allegedly practice nepotism; one must have close ties to a union member to become a member or an apprentice. In those crafts, Negroes may be discriminated against not because of race but because they have no relatives or close friends in the union.

Whatever the basis, the exclusion of Negroes from craft unions and segregation into separate locals with limited access to jobs are major obstacles to Negro advancement. Most Negro Americans are now denied entry into business, professional, technical, and many clerical and sales jobs because they are poorly educated. The only well-paying and rapidly expanding lines of work that do not require a high level of formal education are the skilled trades, and Negro entry into these occupations is impeded by union policy, tradition, and the present makeup of membership.

Negroes are now well represented in semiskilled work and in the industrial unions, but the importance of this kind of work is declining. Mechanization has eliminated some semiskilled jobs of many types and will soon eliminate others, thus undermining the influence of unions that organize semiskilled workers. The total experienced civilian labor force increased by 15 percent from 1950 to 1960, but semiskilled workers increased by only 9 percent. Some types of skilled workers were also hard hit by mechanization, but skilled workers as a whole increased almost as much as the total labor force—by about 13 percent. Technological changes have increased the demand for such skilled workers as electricians, aircraft mechanics, television repairmen, and the like. In fact, there is an acute shortage of workers in some skills. Median earnings of skilled workers in 1959 were well above the median for the entire labor force and well above the medians for clerical and sales workers. In short, skilled work is almost the only kind of work for which a college education is not required that has a relatively bright future. To an increasing extent, the skilled trades offer the greatest hope for above-average income and style of life to the man with no college training.

Breaching the barrier to the skilled trade is the one possible major

[8] *Ibid.*, pp. 379–380.

breakthrough in Negro occupations that is not dependent on drastically improved quantity and quality of education. Of course, some formal education is required for skilled work, but thousands of Negro youths have the basic education and aptitudes for successful apprenticeship. Many have acquired marketable skills through vocational training in high school, although too often such training is in obsolescent lines of work. Therefore, Negroes are in a position to make appreciable gains whenever restrictive union practices are discontinued. But past experience suggests that union discrimination will be discontinued only under strong government pressures. More legislation and executive orders that prohibit discrimination by unions are probably forthcoming, but their effective enforcement will be difficult and may be politically inexpedient. White craftsmen outnumber all Negro workers and, like Negroes, are highly concentrated in populous states with many electoral votes. These whites can be expected to use political influence to oppose government removal of racial barriers in unions, to protect themselves from competition from Negroes. Or, they may meet the Negro "threat" through tokenism, that is, by admittting enough Negroes to lessen charges of discrimination but not enough to reduce appreciably the jobs available to whites. Therefore, the immediate prospects for large Negro gains in skilled work do not seem bright.

Changes in the Social and Economic Conditions of Black Americans during the 1960's[*]

NORVAL D. GLENN

UNIVERSITY OF TEXAS AT AUSTIN

DURING THE 1940's, BLACKS IN THE UNITED STATES EXPERIENCED AN UN-precedented improvement in their social and economic conditions; for the first time, the gap between black and white Americans in income and oc-cupational status closed substantially and rapidly. The near cessation of European immigration two decades earlier had placed blacks in line to benefit from any considerable economic expansion or favorable balance of upward over downward mobility, and the massive commitment of man-power to the war effort created an acute labor shortage that made the low-ering of racial bars to many desirable lines of work a virtual necessity. Although many of the wartime gains were lost when white service men returned to the civilian labor force, blacks had gained a foothold in many industries and occupations, and the end of the decade found the black population as a whole in a much better position than it was in ten years earlier.

The 1950's was a decade of continued but less dramatic gains. The dif-ference between the median number of years of school completed by whites and by nonwhites continued to decline, and the occupational gap narrowed, but only at a rate at which it would have taken centuries for blacks to have attained proportional representation in many of the more desirable occupations.[1] The ratio of nonwhite to white median family in-come was virtually the same at the end of the decade as at the beginning,[2] although most classes of blacks participated in the appreciable gains in real income that characterized the labor force as a whole. The failure of the white-nonwhite income gap to become smaller, in spite of the modest closing of the occupational gap, was due to a general increase in income differences between highly educated workers and unskilled, poorly edu-cated ones; among the latter, blacks remained disproportionately numer-ous. Also, the black-white difference in unemployment rates became great-er during both the 1940's and the 1950's.

Full documentation of the gains of blacks during the 1960's must await publication of detailed data from the 1970 Census of Population, probably in 1972 and 1973. However, data from sample surveys conducted by the Bureau of the Census and other data gathered by the federal government allow an examination of many changes during the first half of the decade and a few changes through the first half of 1968.

[*] First published in this volume.
[1] See Leonard Broom and Norval D. Glenn, "When Will America's Negroes Catch Up?" *New Society* (March 25, 1965), pp. 6–7.
[2] See Figure 2 in contribution 2, preceding this.

Several reasons suggest that there has been an acceleration in the improvement in the objective conditions of blacks during the 1960's. This has been the decade of the "black revolution," which has brought about a multiplication of the attention devoted to the "Negro problem" by politicians, public officials, educators, social scientists, clergymen, business leaders, journalists, and the white public in general. The most important civil-rights legislation since Reconstruction was passed in 1964 and 1965; the United States Supreme Court and the lower federal courts have continued to rule in favor of equal rights for blacks; and efforts to enforce earlier rulings have been intensified. And, indeed, evidence is presented below that in many respects the improvement in the conditions of blacks has been greater during the 1960's than during the 1950's.

Unfortunately, however, the tone of this paper cannot be entirely optimistic, because the trends of the 1960's have not all been favorable to black Americans, and some of the gains have been quite small. In fact, social commentators in general are now noticeably less sanguine about the progress of blacks in American society than they were a decade ago. For instance, Pat Watters, Director of Information for the Southern Regional Council, recently wrote in a report on school desegregation in the South: "This time there seems almost no hope, virtually no reason to find optimistic words, to say things may improve. The mistakes of the past are repeated . . ."[3] In a similar vein, the National Advisory Commission on Civil Disorders, in its report issued early in 1968, concluded: "Our nation is moving toward two societies, one black, one white—separate and unequal."[4] Pessimism concerning the social integration of blacks into the mainstream of society in the United States certainly seems warranted, but some kinds of objective gains by blacks may be accelerated at the same time that violence, conflict, and black expressions of hostility and resentment increase. Nevertheless, it is clear that the objective gains have not kept up with the increase in black aspirations and expectations. It is also clear that the faith placed in civil-rights legislation, litigation, and "direct-action" techniques as means to the solution of the most basic problems of blacks has not been warranted, although it is difficult to suggest available means that are likely to be substantially more effective. Some obstacles to black progress seem so refractory and stubborn that they are not likely to be overcome in the near future.

In this paper I shall strive for a balanced treatment and shall attempt not to give undue emphasis either to the causes for optimism or to the causes for despair. Although I do not think there is much hope for greater interracial harmony in the near future, I do think there is hope for fairly rapid improvements in the economic standing and living conditions of blacks. In fact, a temporary increase in conflict, violence, and social separation of the races may be an inevitable concomitant of an acceleration in some kinds of black progress.

Blacks' occupational advancement during this decade has already ex-

[3] *Lawlessness and Disorder* (Atlanta: Southern Regional Council, 1968).
[4] *Report of the National Advisory Commission on Civil Disorders* (New York: Bantam Books, 1968), p. 1.

ceeded the gains of the 1950's and may also exceed the gains of the 1940's. Unfortunately, the only data available for recent dates are for all non-whites rather than specifically for blacks. Although about 92 percent of all nonwhites are blacks, well under that percentage of the nonwhites in professional and other high-status occupations are blacks. Nevertheless, the data for nonwhites in Table 1 roughly indicate the rate of progress of black Americans from 1940 to 1968.

The white-nonwhite occupational gap is summarized by the index of dissimilarity at the bottom of the table. The index is the percentage of nonwhites (or of whites) who would have to change occupational categories to make the white and nonwhite distributions identical.[5] The index

TABLE 1

Ratio of Actual to Expected* Proportion of Employed Nonwhite Workers in Each Occupation Group, 1940, 1950, 1960 and 1968

Occupational Group	1940§	1950§	1960§	1968§
Professional, Technical and Kindred Workers	.36	.40	.49	.59
Farmers and Farm Managers	1.31	1.22	.78	.52
Managers, Officials, and Proprietors, Except Farm	.17	.22	.23	.28
Clerical and Kindred Workers	†	.29	.46	.67
Sales Workers	†	.18	.23	.30
Craftsmen, Foremen, and Kindred Workers	.27	.38	.49	.60
Operatives and Kindred Workers	.57	.94	1.08	1.27
Private Household Workers	4.66	5.92	5.46	4.22
Service Workers, except Private Household	1.53	2.00	2.02	1.81
Farm Laborers and Foremen	2.57	2.28	2.46	2.08
Laborers, except Farm and Mine	2.06	2.56	2.59	2.00
Index of Dissimilarity‡	47.8	40.9	38.5	31.9

* The "expected" proportion is the proportion of all employed workers in the occupational group.

† In the 1940 census reports, clerical and sales workers are not separated. The ratio for clerical, sales, and kindred workers for 1940 is .12.

‡ This index is the percentage of nonwhites (or of whites) who would have to change occupational categories to make the white and nonwhite distributions identical.

§ The ratios and indexes for 1940, 1950, and 1960 are computed from decennial census data gathered in April of those years. The 1968 figures are computed from data from a sample survey conducted in June. See United States Department of Labor, Bureau of Labor Statistics, *Employment and Earnings and Monthly Report on the Labor Force* (July, 1968).

[5] Although this index is widely used to summarize the disparity between two occupational distributions, it has several limitations. For instance, nonwhite underrepresentation in the low-status category of "farmers and farm managers" in 1960 and 1968 contributes to the index as well as does nonwhite representation in the high-status occupations; underrepresentation in intermediate-status occupations has the same effect on the index as underrepresentation in upper-status occupations.

declined by 7.6 points from 1940 to 1950, by 2.4 points from 1950 to 1960, and by 6.6 points from 1960 to 1968. If the index declines at the 1960–1968 rate until 1970, the total decrease for the decade will be 8.3—an unprecedented ten-year rise in the relative occupational standing of nonwhites in the United States.

Acceleration in occupational gains is also evident from the projected dates of proportional nonwhite representation in the high-status occupational categories on the basis of the 1950–1960 and 1960–1968 rates of change (Table 2). All the dates projected from the 1960–1968 rates of change are earlier, some substantially so. Nevertheless, proportional representation of nonwhites as managers, officials, and proprietors is still more than a century away unless the rate of nonwhite gain increases, and proportional representation as sales workers is eighty years away at the 1960–1968 rate of change. These projections are not predictions, of course, but they indicate how great recent gains have been in relation to the distance yet to be traveled before equality is attained.

The data in Table 1 reveal that representation of blacks in United States business is still meager. The ratio of real to "expected" or proportional representation of nonwhites is only .28 for managers, officials, and proprietors. and .30 for sales workers. In fact, the picture is even bleaker than it seems from superficial examination of these data. A substantial proportion of the nonwhites in these categories are undoubtedly Orientals rather than blacks, and unless the situation has changed dramatically since 1960 (which is unlikely), the nonwhites are highly concentrated in low-paying managerial positions, ownership of marginal small business, and low-paying retail sales jobs.[6] The representation of blacks as executives, as prosperous entrepreneurs, and in sales jobs in which high commissions are possible almost certainly is still miniscule.

The meaning of the moderately high representation of nonwhites as professional, technical, and kindred workers will not be clear until the 1970 census data are reported, but in 1960 blacks in this category were highly

TABLE 2

Dates of Proportional Nonwhite Representation in High-Status Occupational Categories Projected from 1950–1960 and 1960–1968 Rates of Change

Occupational Group	1950–1960 Rate*	1960–1968 Rate**
Professional, Technical, and Kindred Workers	2017	2001
Managers, Officials, and Proprietors, except Farm	2730	2083
Clerical and Kindred Workers	1992	1981
Sales Workers	2114	2048
Craftsmen, Foremen, and Kindred Workers	2005	1995

* The base date for the projections is 1960.
** The base date for the projections is 1968.

6 See Table 5 in contribution 2, preceding this.

concentrated in the lower-paying occupations, and it is likely that the greatest black gains have come in these same occupations. For instance, the various programs of the Office of Economic Opportunity have made many minor professional positions available to blacks, but there have been no similar reasons for increased black representation in medicine, dentistry, architecture, engineering, and pharmacy—fields in which Negro representation in 1960 ranged from small to negligible.

On the brighter side, nonwhites have become moderately well represented as clerical workers and craftsmen and foremen—categories in which there has not been so much difference in the distributions of blacks and whites among the higher-status and lower-status detailed occupations. Four years ago, Leonard Broom and I wrote that the immediate prospects for large Negro gains in the skilled trades were not good,[7] but it now seems that we were somewhat too pessimistic. The "major breakthrough" that we considered unlikely has not yet occurred, but nonwhite representation in skilled work has increased somewhat more than we had anticipated. The reasons for the important, although moderate, increase apparently have been greater pressures from the federal government to end discrimination by labor unions and employers and a continued shortage of many kinds of skilled workers that has prevented the increased recruitment of blacks from being a serious threat to white craftsmen.

The greatest increase in nonwhite representation since 1960 has been in clerical work. Significantly, clerical jobs are not generally very highly rewarded, with either money or prestige, even though they are "middle-class" jobs and blacks were almost entirely excluded from them prior to World War II. It is likely that black entry into these jobs is to a large extent a movement into a labor vacuum created by the upward mobility of whites into higher-status work and a very rapid increase in the number of clerical jobs. White female clerical workers have fewer opportunities than the males to move into more desirable work, and not surprisingly, the increase in black representation in clerical work has been greater for males than for females.[8]

The continued steep decline in nonwhite representation as farmers and farm managers must be considered a gain for blacks, in view of the very low earnings of black farmers in 1959,[9] although undoubtedly many of the black ex-farmers are now unemployed rather than in more desirable work. The decline in nonwhite representation in other low-status occupational categories has not been so great. For instance, the ratios for nonfarm laborers and private household workers were little higher in 1940 than in 1968. At the latter date, nonwhites still did more than four times their proportional share of private household work and twice their share of unskilled labor.

The data in Tables 1 and 2 pertain only to employed workers. To mention unemployment is to turn to one of the bleakest aspects of the total picture. The rate of unemployment of nonwhites has fluctuated consider-

[7] See contribution 2, preceding this.
[8] See Table 4 in contribution 2, preceding this.
[9] See Table 6 in contribution 2, preceding this.

ably during the decade and is now well below the average rate before escalation of the Vietnam war, but the ratio of the nonwhite rate to the white rate has remained almost constant, at about two to one. Seasonally adjusted quarterly averages of unemployment rates show that the ratio of the nonwhite rate to the white rate was at or above 2.0 from the third quarter of 1954 through the second quarter of 1968 (the latest quarter for which data are available as this is written), except that the ratio dipped slightly below 2.0 during the third quarter of 1960 and the second quarter of 1965.[10] Most of the fluctuations in the ratio were so small that sampling variability may account for them.

No doubt there is still some tendency for blacks to be the "last hired and first fired," but much of the difference in the unemployment rates of blacks and whites would remain even if there were no discrimination in hiring and firing. Blacks are concentrated in the kinds of work most susceptible to technological unemployment and to layoffs occasioned by temporary cutbacks in production. Furthermore, a larger percentage of the blacks than of the whites in the labor force are recent entrants, who are more prone to unemployment than older and more experienced workers. The failure of the incomes of small-scale farm operators to rise proportionally with the incomes of most other workers has pushed hundreds of thousands of farmers off the land in recent years, and a larger percentage of black farmers than of white have been displaced. The number of jobs in the urban labor force that these people are qualified to do has not increased rapidly enough to absorb all the displaced farmers, and thus many are unemployed.

The story of the relative economic position of black families in the United States cannot be brought up-to-date much beyond the data shown in Figure 2 of contribution 2 in this volume. However, in 1966 there was, for the first time since World War II, a rather steep increase in the ratio of nonwhite to white median family income. The 1966 ratio was .60, compared with the .55 in 1955. Whether or not this rise signals the beginning of a continuing upward trend remains to be seen. The income data come from sample surveys and thus are subject to sampling variability; and even if the increase was as great as the data indicate, it could have been a temporary gain resulting from the involvement of the United States in the Vietnam conflict. During the Korean conflict of the early 1950's, the relative economic standing of nonwhites increased temporarily, but it declined to its previous level by the late 1950's. Massive military involvement reduces unemployment (although it does not necessarily reduce the ratio of nonwhite to white unemployment), and in spite of the recent automation of many industrial processes, it still increases the demand for unskilled and semiskilled labor. Therefore, a peace settlement in Vietnam before 1970 might leave black Americans in about the same relative economic position at the end of the decade as at the beginning.[11]

[10] United States Department of Labor, Bureau of Labor Statistics, *Employment and Earnings and Monthly Report on the Labor Force* (July, 1968).

[11] I do not want to create the impression that the war in Vietnam has been in the balance favorable to the interests and welfare of black Americans, because it probably

Nevertheless, improvements in the absolute economic conditions of blacks have been substantial. For instance, in 1960, 48 percent of all nonwhite families were below the "poverty line" defined by the Social Security Administration,[12] whereas in 1966 the percentage was only 35. When income is expressed in terms of the value of the dollar in 1965, only 17 percent of all nonwhite families had incomes of $7,000 or more in 1960, but the percentage had risen to 28 in 1966. This increase was reflected in rising life styles. For instance, in 1960, 44 percent of all nonwhite families lived in housing classified as "dilapidated" or that lacked basic plumbing facilities, whereas by 1966 the percentage had declined to 29.[13]

The improvement in amount of education is perhaps the most impressive gain made by black Americans so far during this decade. The median number of years of school completed by nonwhites 25 years old and older was 5.8 in 1940, 6.9 in 1950, 8.2 in 1960, and 9.4 in 1967. Although the white median also rose steadily, the ratio of the nonwhite to the white median rose from .67 in 1940 to .71 in 1950, to .75 in 1960, to .78 in 1967. If the 1960–1967 rate of change continues, the ratio will be .80 in 1970 (and 1.00 in 2010), and the gain of the 1960's will be slightly greater than that of either of the two preceding decades.

The improvement in the relative standing of nonwhites is more striking if one focuses on persons aged 25 through 29—the youngest age level in which a large majority of the persons have completed their formal education. In 1960, the median years of school completed by persons in this age level was 12.3 for whites and 10.8 for nonwhites, a difference of 1.5. By March of 1967, the median was 12.6 for whites and 12.1 both for all nonwhites and for blacks, a difference of only a half year. However, in spite of the narrow gap between the medians, there were important differences in the educational distributions of Negro and white young adults. Whereas 15.7 percent of the whites had completed four or more years of college, only 5.4 percent of the Negroes had done so.[14] And 17.5 percent of the Negroes had completed no more than eight years of school, compared with 9.1 percent of the whites. The traditional tendency remains for more

---

has not been. United States involvement in the war has diverted financial resources and attention from the "war on poverty" and other federal programs that could have been more beneficial to Negro Americans if these programs had been more adequately financed, planned, and administered. Furthermore, blacks have borne a disproportionate share of the costs of the war in life and health. Although Negroes were only 9 percent of the men in the armed forces in June of 1967, they had suffered 15 percent of the deaths in Vietnam. See United States Department of Commerce, Bureau of the Census, *Current Population Reports*, Series P-23, No. 24, *Social and Economic Conditions of Negroes in the United States* (October, 1967), p. 83.

[12] The poverty line varies according to the number, age, and sex of persons in the family and according to place of residence (urban or rural). It also varies from year to year as the cost of living changes.

[13] The data in this paragraph are from various issues of the *Current Population Reports*, published by the Bureau of the Census. Data in subsequent paragraphs are from the same sources unless other sources are indicated.

[14] I shift here to data for Negroes rather than data for all nonwhites because the *Current Population Reports* have just recently started publishing separate education data for Negroes.

Negro females than males to enroll in and complete college. In the 25-through-29 age level in 1967, 16 percent of the Negro females but only 12.9 percent of the males had completed one or more years of college, and 6.3 percent of the females but only 4.2 percent of the males had completed four or more years.

Perhaps of more consequence than the remaining gap between blacks and whites in amount of education is the considerable gap in quality. On the average, the increment of knowledge and skills resulting from a year in school is appreciably less for Negroes than for whites. Some evidence relating to this conclusion is given in Table 3. It is important that the gap in achievement test scores is greater at the higher grades. From these data alone, one cannot tell whether the Negro-white gap in scholastic achievement becomes greater as a cohort of pupils progresses through the grades or whether there is going to be a smaller gap among the younger children throughout their school careers. However, data from earlier studies make it clear that the gap in achievement scores is greater at the higher grades primarily because it increases as children grow older.

There are no data that allow an accurate tracing of recent trends in the quality gap between Negro and white education, but there is little reason to believe the gap has diminished much during the 1960's. Batchelder claims that it widened during the 1950's,[15] and the trends he believes were responsible have generally continued since 1960. For instance, *de facto* school segregation, based on residential segregation, has increased in some northern cities. School desegregation in the south is still rarely more than tokenism (in the fall of 1967, 86 percent of southern Negro pupils were enrolled in segregated schools), and the desegregation that has occurred may have *lowered* the average quality of Negro education. Transferring a few of the very best pupils from the Negro classrooms has hardly improved the intellectual atmosphere for the great majority left behind.

TABLE 3

Mean Achievement Levels on National Standardized Tests of Reading and Other School Subjects, Fall, 1965, by Race

| | | Mean Test-Level Grade | |
Grade in School	Negro	White	Difference
Sixth	4.4	6.8	−2.4
Ninth	7.0	9.9	−2.9
Twelfth	9.2	12.7	−3.5

Source: United States Department of Commerce, Bureau of the Census, *Current Population Reports*, Series P-23, No. 24, *Social and Economic Conditions of Negroes in the United States* (October, 1967), p. 49. Computed from the 1965 survey on "Equality of Educational Opportunity," directed by James S. Coleman for the United States Department of Health, Education, and Welfare.

[15] Alan B. Batchelder, "Decline in the Relative Income of Negro Men," *Quarterly Journal of Economics*, 78 (November, 1964), pp. 525–548.

Trends in the relative quality of Negro education at the college level are probably no more favorable than those in the public schools. About half of all Negro college students are still enrolled in predominantly Negro institutions, and according to Jaffe, Adams, and Meyers, 63 percent of these, or about a third of all Negro college students, are in the academically poorer Negro colleges.[16] At the college level, as at lower levels, desegregation may have done more harm than good. Predominantly white colleges and universities have tended to draw the best Negro students, to the detriment of the intellectual atmosphere on the black campuses. Furthermore, predominantly white colleges and universities, eager to demonstrate their liberalism and in some cases yielding to the demands of their own black students, have enticed many of the more competent black professors to leave the Negro colleges. The token desegregation of predominantly white faculties has not had a truly devastating effect on Negro colleges only because many dedicated and competent black professors have chosen to remain at the Negro institutions.[17] Such high-quality colleges and universities as Howard, Fisk, and Atlanta (and several others) have been quite successful in retaining their black professors who have had opportunities to join predominantly white faculties, but it seems likely that the faculties of most of the weaker institutions have suffered. If so, the effects on the quality of Negro education are compounded by the fact that the weaker colleges supply most of the teachers to the Negro schools in the southern and border states and more than a few teachers to ghetto schools in the north and west.

A crucial difference in the "life chances" of American blacks and whites has been in life expectancy. This difference declined moderately during the 1930's and 1940's and slightly during the 1950's.[18] During the first half of the 1960's, however, the difference remained almost constant, even though nonwhites experienced slight absolute gains in life expectancy (see Table 4).

Infant mortality is very sensitive to changes in the percentage of families living in poverty, and therefore the infant mortality rate for nonwhites has declined dramatically since 1940 (see Table 5). However, the white rate has declined even more rapidly, so that in 1965 the ratio of the nonwhite rate to the white rate was greater than it was in 1940. In 1965, the nonwhite rate was one and a half times the white rate for infants less than a month old and almost three times the white rate for infants from a month to a year old. Significantly, the nonwhite rates in 1960 were

[16] A. J. Jaffe, Walter Adams, and Sandra G. Meyers, "A Report on Negro Colleges," *College Board Review* (Winter, 1967–1968).

Many Negro students enrolled in predominantly white colleges and universities are also attending institutions of relatively poor quality.

[17] It is acknowledged the decision of a black professor to remain at a Negro college may be motivated primarily not by altruism or by commitment to black students but rather by such considerations as preference for the social situation at the Negro college and desire to avoid the pressure to publish and the competitiveness of the "major league" institutions.

[18] See Leonard Broom and Norval D. Glenn, *Transformation of the Negro American* (New York: Harper and Row, 1965), p. 167.

TABLE 4

Additional Years of Life Expected at Selected Ages, by Color, 1960 and 1965

| | 1960 | | | 1965 | | |
Age	Nonwhite	White	Ratio of Nonwhite to White	Nonwhite	White	Ratio of Nonwhite to White
Birth	63.6	70.6	.90	64.1	71.0	.90
25	43.1	48.3	.89	43.3	48.6	.89
35	34.3	38.8	.88	34.6	39.2	.88
45	26.2	29.7	.88	26.6	30.0	.89
55	19.3	21.5	.90	19.6	21.8	.90

Sources: United States Department of Commerce, Bureau of the Census, *Current Population Reports*, Series P-23, No. 24, *Social and Economic Conditions of Negroes in the United States* (October, 1967), p. 63; and Leonard Broom and Norval D. Glenn, *Transformation of the Negro American* (New York: Harper and Row, 1965), p. 167 of 1967 printing.

TABLE 5

Infant Deaths per 1,000 Live Births, 1940, 1950, 1960, and 1965, by Color

| | Age Less than 1 Month | | | Age 1 Month to 1 Year | | |
Date	Nonwhite	White	Ratio of Nonwhite to White	Nonwhite	White	Ratio of Nonwhite to White
1940	39.7	27.2	1.46	34.1	16.0	2.13
1950	27.5	19.4	1.42	17.0	7.4	2.30
1960	26.9	17.2	1.56	16.4	5.7	2.88
1965	25.4	16.1	1.58	14.9	5.4	2.76

Source: United States Department of Commerce, Bureau of the Census, *Current Population Reports*, Series P-23, No. 24, *Social and Economic Conditions of Negroes in the United States* (October, 1967), p. 64.

about the same as the whites rates in 1940—an indication of a twenty-year lag in the reduction of nonwhite infant deaths. However, unless the decline in nonwhite infant mortality is much greater during the second half of the 1960's than during the first half, the nonwhite rates in 1970 will be well above the white rates in 1950.

Much attention has been devoted recently to characteristics of Negro families, and some observers believe that family disorganization in the black ghettos has reached crisis proportions.[19] Although many of the discussions of Negro lower-class families are guilty of moralism and middle-

[19] See especially Daniel P. Moynihan, *The Negro Family: The Case for National Action* (Washington, D.C.: United States Department of Labor, 1965), commonly known as "The Moynihan Report." For a good treatment of the controversy precipitated by this document, see Lee Rainwater and William Yancey, *The Moynihan Report and the Politics of Controversy* (Boston: MIT Press, 1967).

class ethnocentrism,[20] high rates of divorce, separation, and illegitimacy and a large percentage of the children in fatherless homes undoubtedly do handicap the black population in its struggle for an equitable share of the "good things" of American society. Therefore, from one value perceptive, any decline in these phenomena is a gain for blacks and any increase is a loss.

Most indicators of Negro family disorganization show little or no improvement during the 1960's but neither do they show marked deterioration. For instance, the percentage of unmarried nonwhite children under 18 years old who were living with both parents declined from 75 in 1960 to 71 in 1966. The corresponding percentages for whites were 92 and 91. In both 1960 and 1966, 16 percent of the nonwhite women who had ever married were either divorced or separated from their husbands because of marital discord, compared with 5 percent of the white women in 1960 and 6 percent in 1966. The percentage of nonwhite families with female heads increased rather steeply from 17.6 in 1950 to 22.4 in 1960 but rose only to 23.7 in 1966. The white percentage remained near nine during the entire period.

Negro illegitimacy is a controversial and sensitive subject, and objective discussion of it has been hampered by a lack of accurate data as well as by its sensitivity. Estimates of illegitimacy are based on data from only 34 states, in which there is undoubtedly some underreporting of illegitimate births. Many social scientists believe that underreporting is greater for whites than for nonwhites and that published estimates exaggerate the white-nonwhite difference.

For whatever they are worth, the estimates show an increase in the percentage of illegitimate births, from 21.6 in 1960 to 26.3 in 1965 for nonwhites and from 2.3 to 4.0 for whites.[21] However, there is an interesting white-nonwhite difference in the trends in recorded illegitimacy by age of the mothers. Among whites, recorded illegitimacy increased from 1960 to 1965 among unmarried females at all ages from 15 through 44, whereas among nonwhites, it increased only among women aged 30 and older and decreased moderately at the younger ages. It seems that the cohort of nonwhite females now in the upper ranges of the reproductive years has had an unusually high rate of illegitimacy ever since it entered the reproductive age span.[22] As this cohort matures out of the reproductive ages, there is likely to be at least a moderate decline in nonwhite illegitimacy. However, a large proportion of several more generations of Negro children are likely to suffer any adverse consequences that come from spending some of the formative years in a fatherless home.[23]

[20] Although it has had many critics, the Moynihan Report is not flagrantly moralistic or ethnocentric.

[21] There was a slower increase in recorded illegitimacy before 1960. The nonwhite percentage was 16.8 in 1940, 18.0 in 1950, and 20.2 in 1955. The white percentage was 2.0 in 1940, 1.8 in 1950, and 1.9 in 1955.

[22] For discussion of how the experiences of this cohort of nonwhites may have contributed to its unusually high illegitimacy, see Jessie Bernard, *Marriage and Family among Negroes* (Englewood Cliffs: Prentice-Hall, 1966).

[23] Although only about a fourth of all Negro children and adolescents are in father-

In summary, the 1960's have seen a moderate acceleration in the reduction of some dimensions of black-white inequality but a slowing down or cessation of progress on other dimensions. In general, the conditions of black Americans have improved substantially in an absolute sense, but in several respects they have not improved relative to the conditions of whites. The gains have been great enough to convince blacks that further change is possible and worth striving for, but the lack of appreciable reduction of some kinds of inequality has contributed to restiveness, impatience, and bitterness. These different feelings, which may co-exist in the same individuals but which have differing relative strength among the several classes and age levels, may each conduce to the selection and emphasis of particular techniques of protest. However, they all seem to be strong motives for protest activity, and the combination and interaction of these feelings will assure the continuation, and perhaps intensification, of vigorous black protests during the rest of the decade and into the 1970's.

---

less homes at any one time, probably a substantial majority are in such a home at some time before they reach adulthood.

Occupational Changes among Whites and Nonwhites, with Projections for 1970[1]

DANIEL O. PRICE
THE UNIVERSITY OF TEXAS AT AUSTIN

THE IMPORTANCE OF OCCUPATIONS IN THE STUDY OF SOCIAL STRUCTURE, economic development, and social mobility is too well known to need elaboration here. However, very little work has been done in studying the occupational characteristics of cohorts, that is, taking a population group as they enter the labor force and looking at the occupational character-istics of this group as they age.[2]

The present article examines the occupational characteristics of cohorts of white and nonwhite males and females from the period of 1920 to 1960. Only broad occupational categories can be made comparable over this period of time, utilizing census data. These cohorts show surprising sta-bility in trends for most occupational groups, and from these trends it is possible to extrapolate the projected occupational distribution for 1970.

OCCUPATIONAL DISTRIBUTION OF FOUR COHORTS

Figure 1 shows the occupational distribution of nonwhite males who were 14 to 24 years of age in 1920. This is the approximate age range at which this group entered the labor force and this figure shows the per-centage distribution by occupation throughout most of their labor force life, to age 55–64. In the occupational group of professionals and manag-ers, at the top of the chart, it can be seen that age 14–24 a negligible pro-portion of this cohort was employed in this category, but that the propor-tion increased gradually throughout the life of the cohort until by 1960, when this group was 55–64 years old, about 5 per cent of the cohort was employed in this occupational category. Looking at farm laborers and foremen (category 8) we see that at age 14–24 this category included the largest proportion of this cohort. The proportion employed as farm laborers and foremen dropped sharply by age 25–34 but remained fairly stable, decreasing slightly as the cohort grew older. In other words, if the Negro male did not move out of the farm laborer category by age 25–34 he was unlikely to move out of it at older ages. Category 7, farmers and farm managers, increased slightly during the first 10 years of labor force experience, but showed no appreciable increase after age 25–34, and declined at older ages.

[1] Revision of a paper given at the Southern Sociological Society meetings, Atlanta, Georgia, April 2, 1968. Most of the material in this article is taken from "Changing Characteristics of the Negro Population: Trends in Migration, Occupation, Education and Marital Status," a manuscript accepted in 1965 by the Bureau of the Census for publication as a Census monograph, but still unpublished. Appreciation is expressed to Harriet Betty Presser and Audie Blevins for assistance in compilation of data.

[2] See Otis Dudley Duncan, "Occupation Trends and Patterns of Net Mobility in the United States," *Demography*, 3 (1966), pp. 1–18.

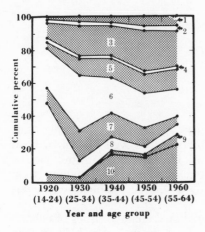

FIGURE 1. Occupational Distribution by Age of Nonwhite Male Cohort 14–24 Years in 1920

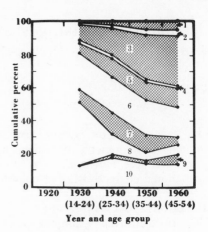

FIGURE 2. Occupational Distribution by Age of Nonwhite Male Cohort 14–24 Years in 1930

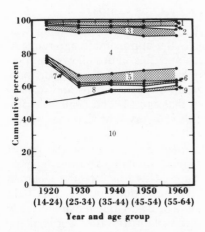

FIGURE 3. Occupational Distribution by Age of Nonwhite Female Cohort 14–24 Years in 1920

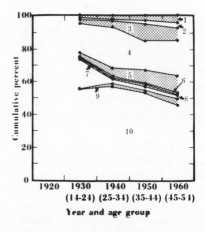

FIGURE 4. Occupational Distribution by Age of Nonwhite Female Cohort 14–24 Years in 1930

Identification of occupational groups for Charts 1, 2, 3, and 4.

1. Professional and managerial
2. Clerical and sales
3. Craftsmen and operatives
4. Private household workers
5. Other service workers

6. Laborers except farm laborers
7. Farmers and farm managers
8. Farm laborers
9. Occupation not reported
10. Not in the experienced civilian labor force

Category 6, laborers other than farm laborers, increased during the first 10 years of labor force experience. Apparently, some of the farm laborers moved into this category by age 25–34, but the number employed here decreased slightly as the cohort increased in age.

Category 3, craftsmen and operatives, showed a fairly steady increase in proportion employed in this category throughout the life of the cohort. The largest increase in this category was between 1940 and 1950, reflecting the impact of World War II; there were declines between 1950 and 1960.

The proportion not in the labor force was very small for nonwhite males in this cohort under the age of 34 but showed a general increase as age increased beyond 34. Category 9, "occupation not reported," also showed an increase with increasing age. Part of this increase derived from the facts that prior to 1940 this category was not reported by the U.S. Census and that two things happened to increase the size of this category in the 1960 Census. More people did not report their occupations in 1960, and the editing procedures used in 1960 classified in "occupation not reported" many persons that in previous censuses would have been classified as not in the labor force.

Figure 2 shows the occupational distribution of the next cohort of Negro males, those who were 14–24 years old in 1930. One of the important differences between this cohort and the previous one is the large increase in proportion not in the labor force at ages under 34. The proportion not in the labor force started fairly high for this cohort but did not show the same sort of continuing increase showed by the previous cohort. This high beginning point may have been a consequence of the Depression. In this cohort the same large proportion was employed in agriculture, but the decline in the proportion of farm laborers, category 8, continued throughout the first 20 years of the cohort's working life rather than during only the first 10 years, as for the previous cohort. The proportion employed as laborers, category 6, was more stable in this cohort, and the proportion employed as craftsmen and operatives showed a steadier increase in this cohort than in the older one.

Figure 3 shows the occupational distribution of the nonwhite female cohort that was 14–24 years in 1920. Compared to males, of course, there was a large proportion in category 10, "not in the experienced labor force." Private household workers, category 4, showed an increase in proportion in this category during the first 10 years of labor force experience, and apparently much of this increase came from the decrease in farm laborers, category 8. With increasing age, the proportion employed as private household workers decreased somewhat, with some increase in other service workers, category 5. It is not surprising to find that this cohort had very few employed in clerical and sales occupations, category 2.

Shifting to the next younger cohort of nonwhite females, the cohort 14–24 years in 1930, Figure 4 shows again the large proportion employed as farm laborers during the first 10 years of labor force experience. At younger ages this group had a much larger proportion employed in the top three occupational categories than did the previous cohort.

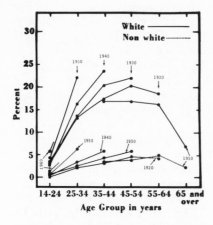

FIGURE 5. Percentage by Age of White and Nonwhite Male Cohorts in Professional and Managerial Occupations, with Cohorts Identified by Year in which Members Were 14–24 Years of Age

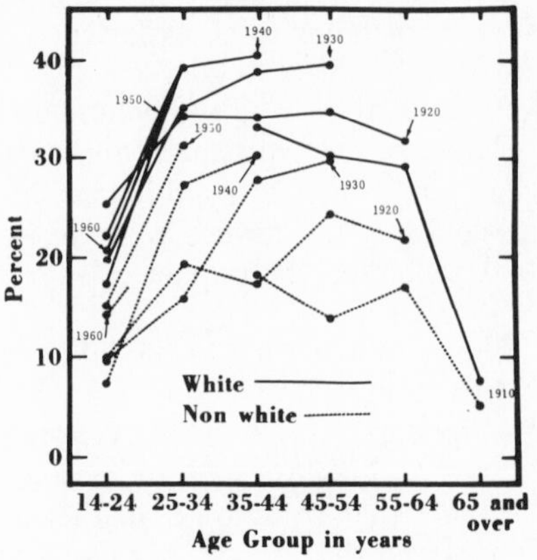

FIGURE 6. Percentage by Age of White and Nonwhite Male Cohorts in Craftsmen and Operative Occupations, with Cohorts Identified by Year in which Members Were 14–24 Years of Age

SPECIFIC OCCUPATIONAL GROUPS

MALES. Figures are not presented for the occupational distribution of other cohorts. It is possible, however, by using the same data from which these figures of cohort occupational distribution were prepared, to prepare figures for individual occupations showing the trends in individual occupations by cohorts. For example, Figure 5 shows the percentage of the white and nonwhite male cohorts employed in professional and managerial occupations. Again the cohorts are identified by year in which the members were 14–24 years of age. The upper lines are for white males and the lower for nonwhite males. The line for the cohort for 1910 shows the percentage of members of this cohort of white males who were 14–24 years in 1910 employed in professional and managerial occupations by age. They were first picked up at age 35–44 in 1920, at which time about 16 per cent were employed in professional and managerial occupations; the percentage declined slowly to age 55–64, then dropped sharply at ages 65 and over. Each younger cohort of white males seems to be following a similar pattern but at a higher level than the previous cohort. Nonwhite males in the lower part of this figure show much lower proportions employed in professional and managerial occupations but the proportion increases for each successive cohort.

Figure 6 shows the percentage of white and nonwhite males by cohorts in craftsmen and operative occupations. It is interesting to note the similarity of patterns of employment of whites and nonwhites in similar cohorts. For both white and nonwhite each succeeding cohort has higher proportions employed as craftsmen and operative workers, but the increase from one cohort to the next is considerably greater for nonwhites than for whites. Both whites and nonwhites show sharp increases in proportion in this occupational group during the first 10 years of labor force experience, with some increase or leveling during the middle years and a decline at older ages. The dips in the lines for nonwhites are the result of the Depression and reflect the sensitivity of nonwhite employment to economic conditions.

Figure 7 shows the percentage of males employed in clerical and sales occupations by cohorts. The higher proportion of whites relative to non-whites in this category is immediately obvious. The white cohorts also show a sharp increase in proportion employed in this category during the first 10 years of labor force experience, then a fairly regular decline at older ages. Nonwhites, on the other hand, seem to show small but regular increases in this occupational category during their work histories. It can also be seen that the proportion of whites in this category has been decreasing somewhat in more recent cohorts, but among nonwhites each cohort shows a considerably higher proportion than the preceding one. It is clear that increasing proportions of nonwhite males in this occupational category at all ages can be expected.

Figure 8 shows the pattern of employment of white and nonwhite males in the category of farmers and farm managers (not farm laborers). In the white and nonwhite comparison here, each nonwhite cohort started with a higher proportion employed as farmers and farm managers than the proportion so employed in the corresponding white cohort. However, during the work history these percentages cross over. The final point in each cohort shows the nonwhite percentage employed as farmers and farm managers lower than the white percentage. The crossover point occurs 10 years earlier for each successive cohort, and the starting point of the cohort 14–24 years in 1960 shows nonwhites employed as farmers and farm managers starting with a smaller percentage than whites so employed. The patterns in this figure are so consistent and the trends so clear that it is not difficult to make projections for the future distribution by age of white and nonwhite males employed as farmers and farm managers.

Figure 9, the last one for males, shows the proportions employed as farm laborers and foremen. Here again is seen the sharp decline in proportion employed as farm laborers and foremen during the first 10 years in the labor force, with the decline being much greater for nonwhites than for whites. This sharp decline is one aspect of the rural-to-urban migration. Both whites and nonwhites show declines in the proportion employed as farm laborers for each successive cohort with the decline being greater for the nonwhites than for whites, indicative of the rapid movement of nonwhites out of agriculture. The beginning points for the 1960 cohorts are quite similar for whites and nonwhites.

FEMALES. Figure 10 shows female employment in professional and managerial occupations. We see here that the difference in percentage of white and nonwhite females employed in professional and managerial occupations is not nearly as large as the differences in percentage of white and nonwhite males so employed. The cohorts of nonwhite females clear-

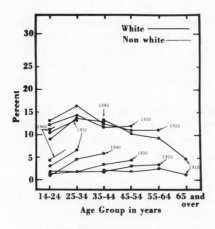

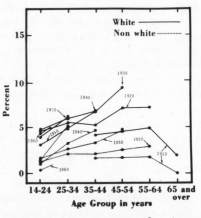

FIGURE 7. Percentage by Age of White and Nonwhite Male Cohorts in Clerical and Sales Occupations, with Cohorts Identified by Year in which Members Were 14–24 Years of Age

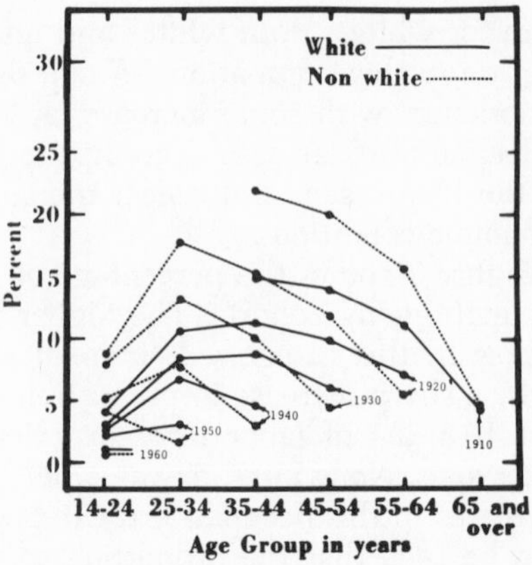

FIGURE 8. Percentage by Age of White and Nonwhite Male Cohorts in Farm and Farm Manager Occupations, with Cohorts Identified by Year in which Members Were 14–24 Years of Age

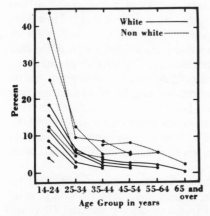

FIGURE 9. Percentage by Age of White and Nonwhite Male Cohorts in Farm Laborer and Foreman Occupations, with Cohorts Identified by Year in which Members Were 14–24 Years of Age

FIGURE 10. Percentage by Age of White and Nonwhite Female Cohorts in Professional and Managerial Occupations, with Cohorts Identified by Year in which Members Were 14–24 Years of Age

ly show increasing proportions employed in professional and managerial occupations, although this pattern is not clear at ages 14–24. White females do not show a clear pattern of consistent increases from cohort to cohort although the cohort of 1940 (that is, those white females that came of labor force age in 1940) is the main group out of line, showing smaller-than-expected percentages employed in professional and managerial occupations—possibly a consequence of the war.

Figure 11 shows the percentage of white and nonwhite females employed in clerical and sales occupations and is important for two reasons. In the first place it shows the consistent large increase in proportion of Negro females employed in this occupation, with younger cohorts starting at higher levels and increasing the proportions in this occupational category rapidly. The pattern for nonwhites has also been one of consistent increases in this occupational category with increasing age. Among white females there is a decrease and then an increase in proportion in this occupational group with increasing age. An examination of the total labor force participation of white females by cohorts shows declines in labor force participation during the childbearing years, with most of these declines coming from the clerical and sales occupations. A fairly clear consequence of this development is that white females tend to have increasing proportions in this occupational category on the whole but reduced proportions during the childbearing years. The rate of increase of white females (probably married) over age 35 in this occupational group seems to be fairly high and may act to maintain or even increase the differential white-nonwhite female employment in this occupational category.

Figure 12 shows the proportion of females employed in private household occupations, and the white and nonwhite differences are immediately obvious. Equally obvious is the decreasing proportion of nonwhite females in this occupational category for the three most recent cohorts. The proportion of the cohort of 1930 employed in this occupational category at age 14–24 was nearly three times the corresponding proportion for the cohort of 1960.

Figure 13 shows the percentage of females employed in other service occupations and is most striking because of the rapid increase in the proportion of nonwhite females employed in other service occupations. White females also show an increase in this occupational category but at a lower rate than nonwhite females.

Figure 14 shows employment of females as farm laborers and foremen. It is clear that this occupation has never been an important one for white females and that it is rapidly becoming an occupation of little relative importance for nonwhite females, even though the cohort of 1920 started with over 25 per cent employed in this occupational group at ages 14–24. This cohort ended up with less than 2 per cent so employed at age 55–64 in 1960.

SUMMARY AND IMPLICATIONS

The patterns of employment by occupations shown in Figures 5 through 14 are so stable that it is possible to take these figures and figures for other occupations (not shown) and extrapolate the trends. This has been done and Table 1 shows the projected occupational distribution by age, race, and sex for 1970. It should be kept in mind that these figures shown

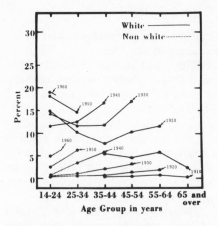

FIGURE 11. Percentage by Age of White and Nonwhite Female Cohorts in Clerical and Sales Occupations, with Cohorts Identified by Year in which Members Were 14–24 Years of Age

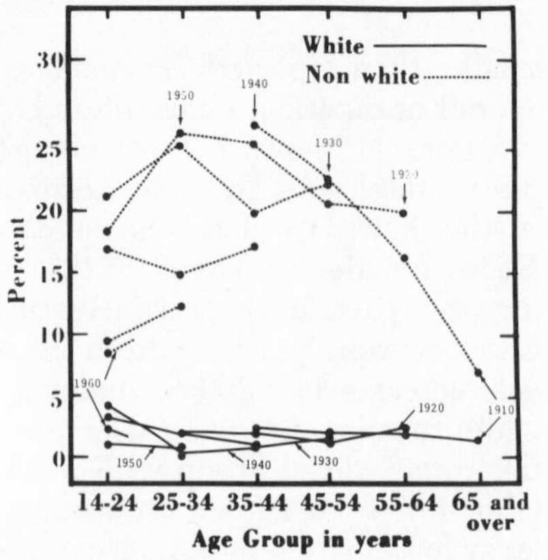

FIGURE 12. Percentage by Age of White and Nonwhite Female Cohorts in Private Household Occupations, with Cohorts Identified by Year in which Members Were 14–24 Years of Age

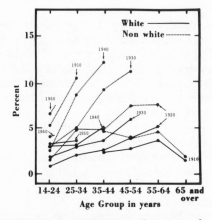

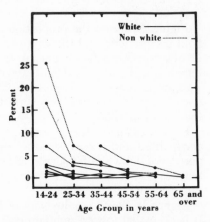

FIGURE 13. Percentage by Age of White and Nonwhite Female Cohorts in Other Service Occupations, with Cohorts Identified by Year in which Members Were 14–24 Years of Age

FIGURE 14. Percentage by Age of White and Nonwhite Female Cohorts in Farm Laborer and Foremen Occupations, with Cohorts Identified by Year in which Members Were 14–24 Years of Age

in Table 1 are based on past trends. To the extent that they do not agree with the Census data for 1970 they give an indication of changes in trends. It will be important to examine these changes and look for the factors involved.

If the gains in occupational distribution of nonwhites are not greater by 1970 than those projected in Figure 1 on the basis of past trends, it

TABLE 1
Projected Occupational Distribution of Age Groups in 1970 by
Race and Sex

Sex and Occupa-tional Category	Color and Age							
	Per Cent White				Per Cent Nonwhite			
	25–34	35–44	45–54	55–64	25–34	35–44	45–54	55–64
Males								
All occupations	100.0	100.0	100.0	100.0	100.0	100.0	100.0	100.0
Professional and managerial	23.0	25.0	25.0	20.0	7.0	8.5	7.5	5.0
Clerical and sales	15.0	13.0	12.5	12.0	8.0	8.0	6.0	5.0
Craftsmen and operatives	37.0	42.5	41.0	38.5	33.5	35.0	32.0	28.5
Private house-hold workers	–	–	–	0.1	0.3	0.4	0.5	0.7
Other service workers	3.7	3.5	4.5	5.3	9.7	10.6	10.5	13.3
Laborers, except farm	4.0	3.5	4.0	5.0	13.0	15.0	15.5	16.5
Farmers and farm managers	1.5	2.5	3.0	3.5	0.8	1.5	2.0	2.5
Farm laborers	1.5	0.8	0.8	0.8	4.0	5.0	5.0	5.0
Not in the expe-rienced labor force (including occupation not reported)	(14.3)	(9.2)	(9.2)	(14.7)	(23.7)	(16.0)	(21.0)	(23.5)
Females								
All occupations	100.0	100.0	100.0	100.0	100.0	100.0	100.0	100.0
Professional and managerial	6.0	8.0	9.0	11.0	5.0	6.5	6.0	6.0
Clerical and sales	16.0	19.0	19.0	19.0	10.0	10.0	8.0	4.5
Craftsmen and operatives	6.0	7.0	8.0	8.0	7.0	8.0	8.0	7.0
Private house-hold workers	2.0	1.0	1.5	2.0	12.0	14.0	16.0	20.0
Other service workers	4.5	5.0	6.0	7.0	11.0	13.0	13.0	12.5
Laborers, except farm	–	0.1	0.1	0.2	0.3	0.4	0.5	0.6
Farmers and farm managers	0.2	0.2	0.2	0.2	0.2	0.2	0.2	0.2
Farm laborers	–	–	–	–	0.1	0.1	0.1	0.1
Not in the expe-rienced labor force (including occupation not reported)	(65.3)	(59.7)	(56.2)	(52.6)	(54.4)	(47.8)	(48.2)	(49.1)

Note: The proportion not in the experienced civilian labor force is not a pro-jection but is included to clarify the 100 per cent base.

cannot necessarily be assumed that civil rights legislation and other efforts have been fruitless. It is possible that these efforts were necessary to maintain past trends. Hopefully, however, the occupational distribution of nonwhites will be better than that projected. By comparing the projected and actual distributions the changes in trends can be observed and the specific areas where greater efforts are needed can be indicated.

The changes examined in this article reflect two basic trends in the nonwhite population. One is the increasing urbanization of the nonwhite population and the consequent decreasing involvement in farm occupations. The other basic trend is the general upward occupational movement of nonwhites, especially nonwhite females. The upward movement of nonwhite males, which gave some evidence of slowing during the 1950–1960 decade, is reflected primarily in the decreasing proportions in agricultural occupations and the increasing proportions in craftsmen and operative occupations. Shifts out of agricultural occupations and private household work into clerical and sales and service occupations other than private household are seen among nonwhite females. There are also shifts of nonwhites into those occupations requiring higher levels of education, but these shifts occur more slowly.

Winners and Losers in the Race for the Good Life: A Comparison of Blacks and Whites

DAVID GOTTLIEB
THE PENNSYLVANIA STATE UNIVERSITY

JAY CAMPBELL, JR.
THE PENNSYLVANIA STATE UNIVERSITY

I N THIS STUDY, TWO RATHER SIMPLE QUESTIONS ARE TO BE INVESTIGATED: (1) What do poor youth want? and (2) What is the impact of race on the social factors that appear to facilitate or block attainment of their expressed goals?

The exclusion of the poor from middle-class society is a "forced" alienation. True, one can surmise that the poor might not like the "good life of the middle class' if they had it; but one must have it to be able to reject it. Efforts to attribute unique value systems to the lower classes, it is here contended, have confused how the poor feel they *must* live with how they would prefer to live.[1] Observed life styles at any given time may be as much a result of contemporary social and economic conditions as they are a preference to live in a certain way.[2] The difference between the abilities and the desires of the individual has been frequently overlooked.[3]

Questionnaire data which originated in Job Corps Centers and in urban high schools lend some credence to the proposition that poor adolescents do not seek to stand on the sidelines.[4] They do not see the middle-class culture as either crass or overly commercial, nor are they inclined to reject a regulated 9–to–5 employment pattern. Their exclusion is more a product of an inability to come up with the resources, material, social and psychological requirements for middle-class goal attainment than is it a rejection of middle-class goals and values. Unlike their middle-class counterparts, poor adolescents do not have access to adults who have the power and desire to assist in the socialization process. They have few who can help explain or prove the real payoff of formal education. Racial prejudice compounds the burden on black youth. Too frequently they learn from their elders that formal education by no means insures tangible rewards.

[1] The attribution of unique value systems to the lower classes is elaborated in many standard stratification texts. See, for example, Joseph A. Kahl, *The American Class Structure* (New York: Holt, Rinehart and Winston, Inc., 1957).

[2] This point of view is supported by Gabriel Kolko, "Economic Mobility and Social Stratification," *American Journal of Sociology*, 63 (July, 1957), pp. 30–38; and Eli Ginzburg, Sol W. Ginsburg, Sidney Axelrod, and John L. Herma, *Occupational Choice: An Approach to a General Theory* (New York: Columbia University Press, 1951).

[3] A significant exception is Ely Chinoy, *The Automobile Worker and the American Dream* (New York: Doubleday and Company, Inc., 1955).

[4] This information was not originally collected in order to conduct a comparative analysis. Both sets of data were obtained independently as part of two separate investigations. In both cases paper and pencil questionnaires were the primary source of information. In instances where comparisons are made, similar questions were asked of respondents in both samples. Despite certain methodological shortcomings, the data do help pinpoint where variations exist between Winners and Losers.

♦ First published in *Social Science Quarterly* 49, No. 3 (December, 1968).

WINNERS AND LOSERS

Comparisons were made between a group of low-income male students (white and black) who were in high school in three different Eastern cities (N=737), and a select group of Job Corps trainees composed of urban males aged 16–18 (white and black) who were neither in school nor employed when they were admitted (N=3,602).[5] For the sake of brevity this article will refer to the high school students as "Winners," because they were apparently succeeding in their education. The Job Corps trainees will be called "Losers". In general, the Job Corps population (100,000 males) presented the following profile: the average age was about 17.5 years; the subjects had completed an average of nine years of formal education, although their reading scores tested at the 6.7 grade level; 27 per cent had a record of minor delinquency and 10 per cent had relatively serious delinquency records; for 10 years prior to entrance into the Job Corps, over 75 per cent had not had contact with a doctor or a dentist; over 90 per cent were unemployed at the time of admission and the 10 per cent that had worked had been paid less than $1.00 per hour.

The majority of both Winners and Losers expressed a desire for jobs with good pay and steady work, wanted an opportunity to use their own ideas, and believed that if one works hard be can get ahead. (See Table 1.)

Table 2 indicates that, although they were not "making it," most Losers liked to watch TV and listen to the radio, liked new model cars, liked to go to church events, liked athletic events, would vote for president if they were old enough, were interested in recent elections, wanted to marry and have children, and believed that "religion is truth." In short these items indicate a preference for activities often associated with middle-

TABLE 1

Winners and Losers: Race and
Desired Job Characteristics

| | Per Cent Selecting Each (Multiple Choice Item) | | | |
| | Winners | | Losers | |
Characteristics	White	Black	White	Black
The pay is good	86	91	89	88
Sure of steady employment	93	89	89	85
If you work hard you can get ahead	93	89	92	89
Opportunity to use own ideas	66	70	70	74
N =	(443)	(260)	(2,097)	(1,411)

[5] This latter was not a random sample, as the Job Corps includes rural and urban youth aged 16–21.

class culture and not too unrelated to what have been described as the dominant value orientations in American society.[6]

With regard to self-concept, Table 3 shows that roughly half of the Losers felt that they were in a rut with no way out, that most people are unhappy and cannot do anything about it, and that it was hard to do what they really wanted.

TABLE 2

Losers: Race and
Personal Preferences and Beliefs

Items	Per Cent Selecting Each (Multiple Choice Item) Losers	
	White	Black
Like to watch TV and listen to radio	79	80
Like new model cars	81	84
Interested in recent elections	69	72
Would vote for president if old enough	88	90
Would like to have children when I marry	87	88
Like to go to church events	77	81
Like athletic events	75	86
Religion is truth	87	86
Like to read newspapers	74	80
N =	(2,063)	(1,392)

TABLE 3
Losers:[a] Race and Self-Concept—Alienation

Items	Per Cent Selecting Each (Multiple Choice Item) Losers	
	White	Black
Most people are unhappy and can't do anything about it.	49	44
Sometimes I feel I am in a rut with no way out.	52	43
Hard to do what I really want	46	57
N =	(2,063)	(1,392)

[a] Data on Winners unavailable.

[6] Robin J. Williams, *American Society* (New York: Alfred A. Knopf, Inc., 1951), Ch. 11.

In contrast (see Table 4), about 90 per cent of the Winners selected, "I feel that I am a person of worth, at least on an equal plane with others," and "I enjoy being with people." Table 4 also indicates that over two-thirds of the Winners claimed they were interested in their school work (although they did not particularly enjoy it) but felt they must do it to be able to get things they would want later.

Other important differences between Winners and Losers are apparent in selected characteristics of their families. Winners and whites were more likely than Losers and blacks to be living with both of their parents, and to be most likely to have working fathers.

In the case of fathers' education, the variation between Losers and Winners is greater than that found between blacks and whites (see Table 5).

TABLE 4

Winners:[a] Race and Self-Concept—Alienation

Items	Per Cent Selecting Each (Multiple Choice Item) Losers	
	White	Black
I feel that I am a person of worth, at least on an equal plane with others.	84	96
I enjoy being with people.	87	91
I am interested in my school work.	71	88
I don't enjoy school work, but I feel that I must do it in order to be able to get things I will want later	66	54
N =	(436)	(251)

[a] Data on Losers unavailable.

TABLE 5

Winners and Losers: Race and
Selected Family Characteristics

Selected Family Characteristics	Winners				Losers			
	White		Black		White		Black	
	%	N	%	N	%	N	%	N
Living with both parents	73	426	58	252	64	2,014	48	1,461
Fathers working	88	443	92	251	72	2,003	51	1,362
Fathers who completed high school	41	458	46	269	24	2,001	25	1,462

TABLE 6

Winners: Race and Parental Ability
and Desire to Assist

| | Per Cent Selecting Each Winners | | | |
| | Father | | Mother | |
Desire to Assist	White	Black	White	Black
Able and willing	74	65	79	82
Able but not willing	7	10	3	2
Willing but not able	13	18	15	12
Neither willing nor able	6	7	3	4
Total	100	100	100	100
N =	(302)	(111)	(327)	(119)

TABLE 7

Losers: Race and Parental Involvement

| | Per Cent Selecting Each Losers | |
Parental Involvement	White	Black
Interest and involvement	31	36
Interest but little involvement	46	43
No interest, no involvement	19	18
Active interference	4	3
Total	100	100
N =	(1,989)	(1,164)

Tables 6 and 7 deal with the perceptions of respondents with regard to parental attitudes and involvement in matters of career choice.

Well over two-thirds of the Winners' parents were selected by their sons as willing and able to provide assistance, whereas the Losers claimed that only slightly more than a third of their parents were interested and involved.

Table 8 shows that less than a fifth of the Losers perceived a high degree of consensus between their school experience and their personal goals.

BLACKS AND WHITES

Certain racial differences stand out with reference to family background. There was only a 16 per cent difference between the white Winners and Losers on the percentage of fathers working—88 per cent for the winners versus 72 per cent for the Losers—whereas a striking 41 per cent difference was discovered between the black Winners and Losers (see Table 5). Table 6 shows that among the winners, there was only a 5 per cent difference between the ability and desire of mothers and fathers to assist among the whites. In contrast there was a 27 per cent difference among the blacks.[7]

Racial differences in career aspirations are found in Table 9. Over three-fourths of the black Winners and less than two-thirds of the white Winners selected an occupation which could be considered within the indoor–white-collar job setting (i.e., professional, managerial, sales, and clerical). The greatest differences are found in the "professional" group, with blacks showing the stronger preference, and in the "skilled trade or craft" group, with whites indicating the greater interest.

TABLE 8

Losers: Race and School—Goal Consensus

	Per Cent Selecting Each Losers	
Perception	White	Black
High consensus	14	19
Moderate consensus	35	40
Low consensus	51	41
Total	100	100
N =	(2,016)	(1,409)

TABLE 9

Winners:[a] Race and Career Plans

	Per Cent Selecting Each Winners	
Career Category	White	Black
Professional-technical	49	59
Farm-ranch owner	1	1
Manager-official	6	7
Clerical	5	12
Sales	3	1
Skilled trade-craft	27	12
Machine operator	5	4
Service	3	3
Laborer	1	1
Total	100	100
N =	(436)	(228)

[a] Data on Losers unavailable.

[7] Variations in the father role among Negro families are explored in another article in this issue. See David Schulz's "Variations in the Father Role in Complete Families of the Negro Lower Class."

The racial differences of occupational preference among Winners are not inconsistent with their Job Corps experience. Upon entrance into the Job Corps, blacks expressed a greater desire for training in white-collar areas, such as data processing, clerical, sales, and general office-centered work, while Caucasians showed a greater initial interest in training related to machinery and construction.

Table 10 presents perceived barriers to the good life. Among both Winners and Losers, about a quarter of the blacks see race as a barrier to the good life versus well under 10 per cent of the whites. Other racial differences are noted in regard to race-relevant items such as family background.

Discussion and Speculation

Even among the poor, those youth who are less impoverished in terms of family resources seem to fare better. If the family is intact, the father educated and working, and if both parents are willing and able to help, the chances appear much better that the youth will at least stay in school. Racial prejudice has compounded the burden on Negroes in that the black father, though he may be as well educated as the white father, is much more likely to be unemployed. The poor black youth is faced with the example of a father who has attempted education as a means to success but has failed to reap the benefit of increased employment. The disillusionment of the black father may explain in part the greater willingness of the mother, compared with the father, to vouch for the "socially appropriate" avenues of entrance into the good life.

If both parents reinforce by their own experiences, attitudes, and involvement with their children that ability, hard work, and education are the keys to entrance into the good life, then their offspring tend to achieve, or at least to question their own abilities and inclinations, with a consequent lowering of their levels of aspiration. This stern, but not es-

TABLE 10

Winners and Losers: Race and
Barriers to the Good Life

| Barriers | Per Cent Selecting Each (Multiple Choice Item) | | | |
| | Winners | | Losers | |
	White	Black	White	Black
Lack of ability	36	41	50	52
Lack of education	81	88	69	76
Lack of breaks	49	59	43	55
Lack of clear goals	31	36	65	67
Family background	5	16	11	24
Race	9	21	6	28
Unrealistic goals	27	38	41	54
N =	(437)	(255)	(2,019)	(1,416)

sentially unfair, message transmitted from the parents to their sons is supported by the proponents of the "they-want-in-but-can't-make-it" or "they-want-in-but-get-it-knocked-out-of-them" school of thought.[8] Data in the present study suggest that this holds true for whites but is more complicated for blacks. In the latter case, "not making it" can be attributed to an unjust system which penalizes a person because of his race as well as to personal inadequacies. The relatively lower level of aspiration of the white Losers versus the black Losers suggests the whites have accepted their lack of ability and have consequently adjusted their goals to a lower level of occupational aspiration. Though defeated, they adjust—through acceptance of their own inadequacy. The black Loser, on the other hand, probably sees his defeat more as the product of an unjust system than of any particular lack of ability on his part. Consequently he retains his level of aspirations, though he is likely confused and embittered.

Poor youths evidence that they do, in fact, want to be "middle class" but it is far from easy for them to make the grade. The question is not one of a lower-class value system or subculture containing elements opposed to, or in conflict with, legitimate means and ends. It is not, as is frequently the case among middle-class adolescents, an opposition to that life style which is called "middle class." Rather the poor adolescent finds himself alienated because he is without the resources and referents which have become increasingly more important for goal attainment in American society. Little variation was found in this study between Winners and Losers with regard to aspirations and goals; the greater difference here was between blacks and whites in both groups. At the same time there were fairly sharp differences between Winners and Losers in matters of the availability of referents and resources. Both were poor and both were deprived, the Losers much more so than the Winners. Finding himself without these resources and referents within the structure of his own family, the poor adolescent becomes more dependent on others outside the home, but even here he finds himself deprived. Few among his relatives or peers can be of assistance. His alternatives are limited, for the most part, to the resources of the school; yet here again there is little that will compensate for his general deprivation. The slum school, aside from its many other shortcomings, is like many other schools (both high school and college) in that it fails to provide the student with a setting which enables him to see and feel the real "payoff." He cannot see a meaningful or legitimate relation between the demands of the formal educational process and the better life he seeks. At the same time, unlike his more affluent counterpart, he does not have the referents who possess the power and desire to keep him within the system. There are few poor parents with the ability to buy him off with promises of material rewards and leisure-time activities. He is limited in his contacts with adults who can explain,

---

[8] Robert K. Merton, "Social Structure and Anomie," in Robert K. Merton, ed., *Social Theory and Social Structure* (Chicago: Free Press, 1957), pp. 131–160; Albert K. Cohen, *Delinquent Boys* (Chicago: Free Press, 1954); and Albert K. Cohen and James F. Short, "Juvenile Delinquency," in R. K. Merton and R. A. Nisbet, eds., *Contemporary Social Problems* (New York: Harcourt, Brace and World, 1961), p. 106.

clarify, and illustrate the benefits of education. Little is offered him in the way of guidance and counseling, much less the more frequently needed intensive therapy. The poor adolescent's deprivation is not limited solely to occupational, social, and intellectual resources. He even lacks those who can provide him with medical and dental care.

It is interesting to note that for many years poor youths have migrated from one community to the next with little attention or assistance from others, yet with the sudden "hippie" movement not only has massive media coverage emerged, but also countless spontaneous service centers to aid the rebellious middle-class adolescent. Seemingly, despite expressions to the contrary, Americans do maintain the status quo: the rich must stay rich, no matter their preference, while the poor must stay poor.

There appear to be few referents who can help convince the poor youngster that there is a meaningful relationship between what he is being asked to do in school and what his own goals are. For the black youth, the message may be more clear: daddy tried it—he finished school —and he's still out of a job. Through everyday experiences the poor come to learn that inadequate skills and lack of socially appropriate means together minimize their chances for success. If the ability is there and skills are developed, there should be a payoff. Apathy may be the end result for the inadequate and lethargic; from the talented and energetic we should expect rebellion.

SUMMARY AND CONCLUSIONS

Observations, impressions, and questionnaire data originating in action programs and urban high schools were analyzed and compared in order to delineate what poor youth want and to find out how race affects their aspirations, resources, and achievement. In general the proposition that poor youngsters aspire to middle-class participation (whether they were making it or not) was supported. Those winning the race for the good life were most likely to come from intact, interested families in which the father was working and had completed high school.

The wheel of fortune, though stern, seemed more generous to the white youngsters. Those whose familial resources were relatively superior (in education, employment, and interest) were more likely to continue in high school. The losing whites (those in the Job Corps) apparently accepted their lots and adjusted their levels of aspiration to the skilled trades and manual endeavors. The relationship between paternal education and employment was vague and inconsistent for the black youth. Although the fathers of the blacks were almost as well educated as the fathers of the whites, they were much more likely to be unemployed. Education had not spelled increased employment for black fathers. The most striking difference between black youths who were in high school and those who had dropped out of school and had entered the Job Corps was the employment of their fathers. Ninety-two per cent of the fathers of the black high school students were working whereas only 51 per cent of the black Job Corps members' fathers were employed. In contrast to the white Job Corps trainees, the blacks retained a relatively higher level of occupational aspiration, shooting for the white-collar, professional, and managerial positions.

This study concludes that poor youth in general aspire to middle-class affluence. Those who are making it through high school have substantially greater familial referents and resources. Racial prejudice has compounded the burden on the black youth. In addition to overcoming deprivation, he must fight an unfair and unjust system. The white Loser has apparently introjected his failure and lowered his sights, while the black Loser retains his aspirations and very likely projects his failure onto the injustice of the system.

Blacks, Whites, and Products: Relative Deprivation and Reference Group Behavior[1]

MONTROSE S. SOMMERS
UNIVERSITY OF TORONTO

GRADY D. BRUCE
THE UNIVERSITY OF TEXAS AT AUSTIN

A MAJOR PROBLEM IN EMPIRICAL RESEARCH RELATING TO REFERENCE GROUP theory and relative deprivation is determining the referent used by a person or social category in evaluating life circumstances and in setting aspirations and standards.[2] A second problem concerns measuring the degree of relative deprivation experienced when comparisons are made.[3] This paper reports the application of Q-sort methodology to these problems in the study of black and white housewives.

CONCEPTUAL FRAMEWORK

The study is conceptualized and designed in the context of product symbolism.[4] That is, products are said to symbolize action or activity patterns. A product is *both* a recognizable object and an object which has activity potential. Those products which individuals use and prefer, then, symbolize their activities (real or idealized) and present an aspect of the culture or subculture to which they belong.

A product or cluster of products can symbolize a social role or an aspect of it; for example, kitchen furniture may symbolize the wife or mother role. Such furniture may be important in the behavior of some women and, therefore, have high symbolic value. For others, this same furniture may symbolize prescribed, but distasteful, behavior and have low symbolic value. Thus, for a given set of products, interpersonal variations in symbolic value may reflect differences in social roles and self-conceptions viewed as ways of behaving. Variations are discernible, of course, only for roles and role-related products included in such a set.

1 This study was financed by a grant from the Research Committee of the Graduate School of Business, The University of Texas at Austin. The authors wish to thank Norval D. Glenn for reading an earlier version of the manuscript and for making a number of helpful suggestions on its revision.

2 See the discussions in W. G. Runciman, "Problems of Research on Relative Deprivation," in Herbert H. Hyman and Eleanor Singer, eds., *Readings in Reference Group Theory and Research* (New York: The Free Press, 1968), pp. 69–76; and Robert K. Merton and Alice S. Rossi, "Contributions to the Theory of Reference Group Behavior," in Robert K. Merton, ed., *Social Theory and Social Structure* (New York: The Free Press, 1957), pp. 225–280.

3 Runciman, "Problems of Research," p. 70.

4 An expanded discussion of product symbolism may be found in Montrose S. Sommers, "The Use of Product Symbolism to Differentiate Social Strata," *Houston Business Review*, 11 (Fall, 1964), pp. 16–26.

♦ First published in *Social Science Quarterly* 49, No. 3 (December, 1968).

RESEARCH DESIGN

APPROACH. This concept of product symbolism, when it becomes the perspective for studying relative deprivation and reference group behavior, can be made operational in a number of ways. In research designed to study black and white housewives, relative deprivation must be operationally defined and the potential influence of social levels within the black and white communities must be "controlled."

A person or social category may be relatively deprived: (1) in comparison with an Ideal, however established, or (2) in comparison with some other reference individual or group.[5] Relative deprivation may be measured: (1) by the disparity between a self-conception and an Ideal, and/or (2) by the disparity between the self-conceptions of different social categories (potential reference points). Products are used to obtain such measurements in this design. Subjects are asked to rank products in a given set on two bases: the first to describe themselves on a current basis (the Self) and the second to describe or symbolize themselves on a future basis (the Ideal). Comparisons then made among the various Selves and Ideals serve to identify reference points and to measure relative deprivation.

The need for a "control" for social level is suggested by Pettigrew's discussion of class differences in the aspirations of blacks. Lower-class blacks are so deprived, he found, that they "give up the fight" and therefore show an unusually low need for achievement compared to similarly situated whites.[6] But upper-class blacks exhibit very high levels of need for achievement compared to upper-class whites, lower-class whites, and lower-class blacks.[7] Measurements should be made, then, within the black and white segments of a community on at least two societal levels. This requirement introduces "sticky" problems concerning the delineation of levels and the extent of their comparability. One can use socioeconomic indicators (income, occupation, and education) to measure strata objectively and can control on this basis; or one can subjectively establish "lower" and "middle" strata in terms of the structures of the black and white communities.

While objective comparability results from the first approach, its validity is questionable: blacks, as a group, are not part of the white community—they are separate and unequal. While objective comparability does not result with the second approach, the structure of the particular community can be considered. In Austin, Texas (the study community), no predominantly black census tract existed which could be defined objectively as equivalent to a predominantly white tract. Four census tracts, therefore, were selected—two predominantly white and two predominantly black—on the basis of their general conformity, in subjective terms, to certain levels of the Warner dwelling area classification. Warner's dwelling

---

[5] Runciman, "Problems of Research," pp. 70–72.

[6] Thomas F. Pettigrew, *A Profile of the Negro American* (Princeton, N.J.: C. Van Nostrand Company, Inc., 1964), pp. 30–31.

[7] *Ibid.*, pp. 31–34.

area classification of "below average" here represents a "lower" stratum and a combination of Warner's "average" and "above average" levels here represents a "middle" stratum.[8] The actual designation as "lower" and "middle" strata was made by white and black interviewers and the investigators, based on their knowledge of the city. Thirty-eight subjects were selected in each tract, using area sampling with quota controls. The socioeconomic characteristics of the subjects are shown in Table 1. For both strata, blacks differ from whites in family size, occupation of the male household head, and family income. Control is not achieved, then, in a purely objective sense; rather, the validity of the subjective designations must be relied upon. In addition, the process by which strata were established and the possibility that blacks in Austin, Texas, are atypical suggest that one should be cautious in generalizing from the findings.

SUBJECT:. Subjects were housewives in the "fullnest I" stage of the life cycle, as defined by Katona.[9] This stage includes married couples with dependent children and with the housewife in the 30–45 age category. These women are appropriate subjects for two reasons. First, they are in households which have recently spent considerable money in establishing a life style. It may be assumed that they, as representatives of the household, have been involved with products—in obtaining, using, or developing aspirations for them. Second, housewives are generally good culture bearers. They are the prime socializing agents in the family—perhaps more in the case of black families than of white.[10]

The quota for each tract was 38 completed house calls. Housewives living in single, detached dwelling units were interviewed in their homes;

TABLE 1

Socioeconomic Characteristics of Subjects

Characteristics	"Lower" Stratum		"Middle" Stratum	
	Black	White	Black	White
Age (mean) in years	34.7	35.0	36.6	35.2
Number of children (mean)	3.1	2.6	3.3	2.8
Husband's occupation	Laborers and other unskilled workers	Craftsman, foreman, and kindred workers	Operative and kindred workers	Sales worker, official, and proprietor
Annual family income	$3,000–$4,000	$5,000–$6,000	$5,000–$6,000	$7,000–$8,000

[8] W. Lloyd Warner, Marchia Meeker, and Kenneth Eells, *Social Class in America* (New York: Harper and Brothers, 1960), p. 153.

[9] George Katona, *The Powerful Consumer* (New York: McGraw-Hill Book Company, 1960), pp. 155–156.

[10] See the discussion abstracted from E. Franklin Frazier, *The Negro Family in the United States* (Chicago: The University of Chicago Press, 1939) in Leonard Broom and Philip Selznick, *Sociology* (New York: Harper & Row, 1963), pp. 509–512.

male Negro interviewers worked in black tracts and male white interviewers, in white tracts.

INTERVIEW PROCESS. Interviewers used the following process to obtain Self and Ideal descriptions. Subjects were presented a deck of 38 cards with the name of a common household product printed on each card (see Table 2). The housewife was instructed to examine the deck and then to divide it into two stacks, one listing products that she used or owned and the other listing products she did not use or own. From the stack naming used or owned products, she was instructed to select that single item which best described her and to place it on position 1 of a sorting board. The board contained 38 positions and the housewife was instructed to continue placing cards on the board (in order of decreasing descriptive power of products) until the stack naming used or owned products was exhausted. A similar procedure was followed for products not used or owned. The housewife placed the product which least described her in position 38 and continued until the second stack was exhausted. Upon completion, there resulted for each subject an array of ranked products scaled from "best describes" (position 1) to "least describes" (position 38), with the Self used as a frame of reference. Each subject also sorted products with the Ideal as a frame of reference. The distribution of product sorts (by race, strata and frame of reference) thus obtained is shown in Table 3.

MEASUREMENT. After products are sorted by a subject, they appear on the sorting board in the pattern of a forced quasi-normal distribution. This distribution provides, first, a rank ordering of products amenable to non-parametric analysis. Second, it allows areas under the curve, consisting of categories of ranking, to be defined and scored for parametric analysis.[11]

TABLE 2

Items Included in the Product Test

Suits	Cake mix	Electric iron
Frozen orange juice	Permanent waves	Gloves
Blouses	Flour	Stove
Shoes	Magazines	Newspaper
Deodorant	Toothpaste	Vacuum cleaner
Television set	Refrigerator	Eye shadow
Bread	Shortening	Electric toaster
Hair spray	Hair shampoo	Potatoes
Nail polish	Washing machine	Hi-fi set
Slacks	Skirts	Lipstick
Catsup	Hand soap	Records
Hosiery	Lingerie	Hats
Dresses		Books

[11] The technique is termed Q-sorting and the product array is called a Q-sort. The approach used here is a slightly modified version (in that it has items ranked separately) of that suggested in William Stephenson, *The Study of Behavior* (Chicago: University of Chicago Press, 1953).

TABLE 3

Distribution and Number of
Product Sorts Obtained

| Subjects | Frame of Reference | Stratum | | Total |
		Low	Middle	
Negro	Self	38	38	76
Negro	Ideal	38	38	76
White	Self	38	38	76
White	Ideal	38	38	76
Total		152	152	304

TABLE 4

Frequency Distribution and Scores for
38 Ranked Products

	"Best Describes"					"Least Describes"			
Frequency	2	3	5	6	6	6	5	3	2
Rank	1,2	3–5	6–10	11–16	17–22	23–28	29–33	34–36	37,38
Score	9	8	7	6	5	4	3	2	1

The forced distribution and scores for the categories are shown in Table 4.

The individual measurements generated from the four groups of subjects—the 304 product sorts—were converted into eight product profiles.[12] Each profile is based on 38 product sorts, as indicated by the classifications shown in Table 3. The profiles, presented as Table 5, allow for comparisons between blacks (B) and whites (W) representing "lower" (L) and "middle" (M) strata, and between blacks and whites at the two levels and for the frames of reference Self (S) and Ideal (I). The various correlations between product profiles are reported in Table 6;[13] differences between selected pairs of correlations and the associated levels of significance are shown in Table 7.

FINDINGS

As indicated earlier, relative deprivation may be measured by the disparity between the Self and the Ideal for a category of subjects. The findings, as reported in Table 6, suggest that both of the black strata experi-

[12] The profile for each stratum can be determined by using either the individual subject rankings or the category scores assigned to sets of ranks. In this case the sums of the ranks assigned to each item by subjects within a stratum were calculated. The lowest R_i for an item designates the item ranked first in the stratum array; the highest R_j is ranked in the last position.

[13] The product arrays are correlated using the method suggested in Arnold Hilden, "Manual for Q-sort and Random Sets of Personal Concepts" (St. Louis: Washington University, 1954), mimeographed.

TABLE 5

Product Profiles for Blacks and Whites by Frame of Reference by Stratum

Rank	Q-Score	WMS	WLS	BMS	BLS	WMI	WLI	BMI	BLI
1	9	washing machine	stove	stove	stove	toothpaste	dresses	dresses	dresses
2	9	stove	refrigerator	refrigerator	refrigerator	dresses	lingerie	washing machine	refrigerator
3	8	toothpaste	washing machine	electric iron	dresses	newspaper	hosiery	stove	shoes
4	8	hand soap	electric iron	washing machine	deodorant	hi-fi set	skirts	deodorant	stove
5	8	deodorant	dresses	dresses	washing machine	deodorant	shoes	skirts	suits
6	7	electric iron	bread	deodorant	toothpaste	lipstick	deodorant	refrigerator	blouses
7	7	refrigerator	blouses	shoes	lingerie	shoes	blouses	electric iron	washing machine
8	7	newspaper	potatoes	television set	shoes	lingerie	hair shampoo	toothpaste	deodorant
9	7	vacuum cleaner	toothpaste	toothpaste	newspaper	books	toothpaste	blouses	lingerie
10	7	television set	shoes	hand soap	television set	stove	lipstick	television set	newspaper
11	6	lipstick	flour	lingerie	electric iron	skirts	hair spray	lingerie	television set
12	6	hair shampoo	shortening	vacuum cleaner	hand soap	hand soap	suits	shoes	skirts

No.	Freq.								
13	6	blouses	television set	suits	books	records	television set	hosiery	magazines
14	6	shoes	hand soap	electric toaster	blouses	suits	magazines	suits	hosiery
15	6	dresses	hair shampoo	bread	hosiery	refrigerator	newspaper	vacuum cleaner	books
16	6	lingerie	skirts	hosiery	magazines	hair spray	books	hand soap	toothpaste
17	5	bread	deodorant	newspaper	suits	television set	records	gloves	electric iron
18	5	books	newspaper	shortening	electric toaster	hosiery	hats	electric toaster	gloves
19	5	flour	hosiery	blouses	skirts	hair shampoo	hi-fi set	records	hand soap
20	5	magazines	catsup	skirts	bread	blouses	hand soap	hi-fi set	electric toaster
21	5	skirts	electric toaster	flour	shortening	gloves	nail polish	books	hats
22	5	potatoes	lingerie	books	lipstick	magazines	refrigerator	hair shampoo	vacuum cleaner
23	4	cake mix	hair spray	potatoes	flour	washing machine	slacks	hats	hi-fi set
24	4	records	cake mix	frozen orange juice	hats	flour	stove	lipstick	bread
25	4	hair spray	lipstick	lipstick	lipstick	shortening	bread	bread	records
26	4	shortening	books	magazines	hair shampoo	slacks	permanent waves	magazines	lipstick

Rank Order	Q-Score	WMS	WLS	BMS	BLS	WMI	WLI	BMI	BLI
27	4	electric toaster	magazines	hats	vacuum cleaner	potatoes	vacuum cleaner	newspaper	flour
28	4	slacks	slacks	gloves	potatoes	cake mix	gloves	flour	hair shampoo
29	3	suits	vacuum cleaner	records	hi-fi set	nail polish	washing machine	shortening	frozen orange juice
30	3	hi-fi set	frozen orange juice	cake mix	records	vacuum cleaner	potatoes	potatoes	slacks
31	3	frozen orange juice	suits	hair shampoo	frozen orange juice	hats	cake mix	slacks	potatoes
32	3	hosiery	records	catsup	slacks	bread	electric iron	nail polish	cake mix
33	3	catsup	permanent waves	slacks	cake mix	permanent waves	flour	frozen orange juice	nail polish
34	2	gloves	hi-fi set	hi-fi set	nail polish	electric toaster	shortening	hair spray	shortening
35	2	hats	hats	nail polish	catsup	electric iron	electric toaster	cake mix	hair spray
36	2	permanent waves	nail polish	hair spray	hair spray	eye shadow	frozen orange juice	catsup	catsup
37	1	nail polish	gloves	permanent waves	eye shadow	catsup	catsup	permanent waves	eye shadow
38	1	eye shadow	eye shadow	eye shadow	permanent waves	frozen orange juice	eye shadow	eye shadow	permanent waves

TABLE 6

Correlation Matrix of Black and White
Self and Ideal Product Arrays by Strata

	BLS	BMS	WLS	WMS	BLI	BMI	WLI	WMI
BLS	1.00							
BMS	.92	1.00						
WLS	.75	.77	1.00					
WMS	.80	.77	.76	1.00				
BLI	.88	.81	.55	.61	1.00			
BMI	.83	.83	.62	.71	.87	1.00		
WLI	.45	.26	.20	.30	.60	.54	1.00	
WMI	.57	.36	.31	.48	.61	.54	.76	1.00

ence deprivation at nearly the same low level: r(BLS:BLI) = .88 and
r(BMS:BMI) = .83. These high correlations also indicate a very low
"need for achievement" for both of the black strata insofar as this need is
expressed and measured by the products in the test. Among white housewives the findings on relative deprivation are quite different. Each white
stratum experiences deprivation to a much greater extent than the black
strata: r(WLS:WLI) = .20 and r(WMS:WMI) = .48. It should be further noted that the level experienced by "lower" stratum whites in the
community examined is quite pronounced.

Insofar as relative deprivation is measured by differences in the Self-
concept of each strata, it appears that "lower" stratum blacks experience
less relative deprivation in comparison with their "middle" stratum counterparts than do "lower" stratum whites compared with "middle" stratum
whites: r(BLS:BMS) = .92, as opposed to r(WLS:WMS) = .76. It also
appears that Negro subjects in this sample may experience close to the
same level of relative deprivation in comparison with whites, regardless
of strata considerations: r(BLS:WLS)=.75, r(BMS:WLS)=.77, and
r(BMS:WMS) = .77.

The reference group behavior of these subjects is also indicated by the
data in Table 6. It is clear that the "lower" stratum black subject uses her
perception of the "middle" stratum black Self and Ideal as the model for
her Ideal: r(BLI:BMS) = .81 and r(BMI:BLI) = .87. As regards the
"middle" stratum black subjects, the black points of reference are apparent: r(BMI:BLS) = .83 and r(BMI:BLI) = .87. But this black stratum
also takes the "middle" stratum white Self (and clearly not the "middle"
stratum white Ideal), as well as the "lower" stratum white Self, as moderate points of reference. This is reflected in the following correlations:
r(BMI:WMS) = .71; r(BMI:WMI) = .54; and r(BMI:WLS) = .62.
Also, the "middle" stratum white seems to be a more important reference
point for the "middle" stratum black than for the "lower" stratum black:
r(BLI:WMI) = .61; r(BLI:WMS) = .61; r(BLI:WLI) =.60; and

TABLE 7

Selected Comparative Relationships among and between r's for Blacks and
Whites, by Strata

Relationship			Difference	Significance
r(BMS:BLS)	=	.92	.05	p=.84
r(BMI:BLI)	=	.87		
r(BMI:BLI)	=	.87	.06	p=.80
r(BLI:BMS)	=	.81		
r(BMI:WMS)	=	.71	.23	p=.17
r(BMI:WMI)	=	.54		
r(BMI:WMS)	=	.71	.09	p=.35
r(BMI:WLS)	=	.62		
r(BMI:WMS)	=	.71	.10	p=.34
r(BLI:WMS)	=	.61		
r(BLS:BLI)	=	.88	.05	p=.84
r(BMS:BMI)	=	.83		
r(WMS:WLS)	=	.76	.16	p=.26
r(BMS:BLS)	=	.92		
r(WMI:WLI)	=	.76	.11	p=.32
r(BMI:BLI)	=	.87		
r(WMS:WMI)	=	.48	.28	p=.12
r(WLS:WLI)	=	.20		
r(WMS:WMI)	=	.48	.45	p=.03
r(BMS:BMI)	=	.83		
r(WLS:WLI)	=	.20	.68	p=.002
r(BLS:BLI)	=	.88		
r(BLS:WLS)	=	.75	.02	p=.94
r(BMS:WMS)	=	.77		
r(BLI:WLI)	=	.60	.06	p=.80
r(BMI:WMI)	=	.54		

r(BLI:WLS) = .55. This finding is consistent with Pettigrew's observation that as status increases, the black community moves toward the white community rather than away from it. [14]

When the reference behavior of white housewives is examined, it is clear that the "lower" stratum white subject does not emphasize the "middle" stratum white Self as a model for her Ideal: r(WLI:WMS) = .30. Unlike the behavior of "lower" stratum Negroes, in which r(BLI:BMS) = .81, the "lower" stratum white housewife appears to look beyond the

[14] Pettigrew, *A Profile*, pp. 178–201.

"middle" stratum white Self in the formation of her Ideal. Indeed, both "lower" and "middle" stratum white subjects show moderate agreement on another reference point for their Ideal: $r(WMI:WLI) = .76$.

It is also of interest to note that not only are the "lower" stratum white subjects extremely relatively deprived in their Self, $r(WLS:WLI) = .20$, but also the "middle" stratum whites and both strata of blacks agree with the undesirability of that Self: any WLS correlation shown in Table 6 is comparatively very low.

Besides indicating levels of relative deprivation and aiding in the discovery of reference points, the data also say something about the role behavior and role preferences of subjects. For example, a comparison of the four most prominent items in the product profiles in Table 5 indicates that the wife and mother roles are considered most important in the behavior of "lower" stratum whites and "middle" stratum blacks. This is reflected in the positioning of the following items: stove, refrigerator, washing machine, and electric iron. The "lower" stratum black Self, on the other hand, differs in evaluating the importance of these roles; as symbols of femininity (dresses and deodorants) have very high Q-scores.

If the ten most descriptive items in the four Self profiles are compared, it appears that, while homemaking is important for "middle" stratum whites, it is even more important for blacks in both strata. It would also appear that media exposure (reflected in the ranking of newspapers and television sets) is more important in the behavior formation of "lower" stratum Negroes and "middle" stratum whites than in that of other subjects.

If selected Self profiles are compared with corresponding Ideal profiles, further observations regarding behavior may be made. For example, the "lower" stratum black Ideal emphasizes the feminine role and de-emphasizes somewhat the wife and mother roles in comparison with the "lower" stratum black Self. Five of the ten most descriptive items for the Ideal are clothing, but only three are clothing for the Self profile.

The Ideal for "lower" stratum whites is vastly different from the Self. Six of the ten most descriptive items for the Ideal are clothing, and the other four are personal-care items. The essential emphasis is on the female role and femininity in visual terms. All other roles are de-emphasized in this Ideal to a much greater extent than for other subjects. In relative terms, this profile shows a radical shift in role preference.

SUMMARY AND IMPLICATIONS

As regards this application of Q-sort methodology per se, it seems important to re-emphasize the number of analyses that are possible. Through the product profiles and the correlations among them, one can

1. measure relative deprivation in two ways: in terms of what one wants (an Ideal) and in terms of what others have

2. examine the correlations among Selves and Ideals to identify reference groups

3. infer the importance of different roles and identify differences in role preferences.

From a broader perspective, empirical field research in processes of self-conception and related aspects of symbolic interaction theory is limited essentially, it seems, because of problems in operationalizing and measuring self-conceptions.[15] In this regard, the application of Q-sort to the development of product arrays offers interesting possibilities beyond those suggested in this study. Subjects might be asked to describe categories of subjects other than themselves, thereby measuring a "generalized other" which may be used in additional comparisons as it was here for the Self and Ideal.

In the study of minority groups, characterizations are possible, of course, for subjects other than blacks. These characterizations might be developed using controls other than social level or, more specifically, using controls dictated by the structures of such groups. Also, it is possible to expand or change roles involved in the characterizations by adding and/or deleting products. Through changes in the set of products used in the Q-sort, other dimensions of the Self and Ideal could be investigated (*e.g.*, religious roles and related symbols) and conclusions could be drawn regarding the prominence of such roles.

Finally, it is of no little importance that in this study products are treated as something more than objects of economic exchange. They are that, of course, but they are also symbols in man's symbolic environment and, as such, are useful in behavioral research. In such research, their economic aspects are not lost, since ownership is, in part, the effect of an economic process. Rather, ownership, aspirations for ownership, and deprivations are seen to be observable and tangible effects of both an economic and social process; and a large part of the case for using products in behavioral research would appear to lie in their existence as tangible objects in the "real world."

[15] Leo G. Reeder, George A. Donohue, and Arturo Biblarz, "Conceptions of Self and Others," *American Journal of Sociology*, 66 (Sept., 1960), pp. 153–159.

Some Consumption Pattern Differences between Urban Whites and Negroes

JAMES E. STAFFORD
UNIVERSITY OF HOUSTON

KEITH K. COX
UNIVERSITY OF HOUSTON

JAMES B. HIGGINBOTHAM
HIGGINBOTHAM AND ASSOCIATES

DURING THE PAST 20 YEARS, THE "NEGRO MARKET" HAS BEEN VIRTUALLY ignored in the United States, except by a few farsighted companies. Most mass-market–oriented firms assumed that the advertising message, as well as the product itself, reached the Negro, even though both were directed almost exclusively at the white audience. As a result, few companies have realized their potential with Negro consumers, and many opportunities have been overlooked. In recent years, however, increased political, social, and economic pressure has forced more companies either to consider for the first time, or to re-evaluate, the nature of the Negro market.

A very basic question being asked is, "Does a Negro market really exist?" The answer appears, on the surface, to be a simple and straight-forward "yes." If the problem is carefully delineated, however, it is found that there are several sides to the question, and they must be uncovered, evaluated, and integrated before a definitive answer can be stated. Several studies, for example, have noted that the Negro market is a distinct geographic, social, and psychological reality based not only on certain physical characteristics, but also on common experiences of exclusion and deprivation.[1] Similarly, from an economics standpoint, there is little doubt that Negroes constitute a segment of the population separate from the majority of whites. The Negro's relatively low economic status is clearly demonstrated by the fact that 35 per cent of Negro families had incomes below $3,000 in 1965, compared with only 14 per cent of white families. At the other end of the spectrum, 42 per cent of the white families had family incomes greater than $8,000, while only 16 per cent of the Negroes had comparable family incomes.[2] When these facts, plus other enlightening economic comparisons, are coupled with the severe educational and hous-

[1] See T. F. Pettigrew, *A Profile of the American Negro* (Princeton, N.J.: D. Van Nostrand Company, 1964); Talcott Parsons and K. B. Clark, eds., *The American Negro* (Boston, Mass.: Houghton-Mifflin Company, 1966); Henry Bullock, "Consumer Motivations in Black and White," *Harvard Business Review* (May-June, July-Aug., 1961), pp. 89–104, 110–124; L. E. Black, "The Negro Market," *Sales Management*, 91 (Oct. 4, 1963), pp. 42–47; Raymond Bauer *et al.*, "The Marketing Dilemma of Negroes," *Journal of Marketing*, 29 (July, 1965), pp. 1–6; and Leonard Broom and Norval D. Glenn, *Transformation of the Negro American* (New York: Harper & Row, 1965).

[2] U.S., Bureau of the Census, *Current Population Reports*, Series P-60, No. 53, "Income in 1966 of Families and Persons in the U.S.," (Washington, D.C.: U.S. Government Printing Office, 1967), p. 19.

♦ First published in *Social Science Quarterly* 49, No. 3 (December, 1968).

ing deprivations suffered by Negroes, it should be no great revelation to learn that, on an aggregate basis, Negroes have distinct consumption patterns, relative to whites.[3] Some of these same economists, however, have argued that even when income discrepancies are controlled statistically, comparable Negroes and whites still allocate their incomes differently. The alleged difference in spending behavior of Negroes and whites is attributed to the economic and social discrimination which has been part of the Negro heritage. Not being able to live, relax, or dine where they please, American Negroes are said to have developed aggregate consumption patterns different from those of their white counterparts.[4]

It is apparent from the foregoing discussion that Negroes, as a group of individuals having certain characteristics and behavior patterns in common with—yet distant from—whites, could be viewed as a "market." To marketers, however, such a segment exists only to the extent that Negroes *behave differently* from whites *as consumers.* A group of individuals with certain characteristics in common does not, in itself, constitute a realistic market segment. Only when people have common characteristics as consumers may they be thought of as a market segment.

Marketers, therefore, are basically concerned with determining if consumption-pattern differences exist between Negroes and whites and, if they do, whether they are attributable to income differentials, racial differences, or other factors often overlooked.[5] It may be that race, for example, is secondary to income as an influence on purchase behavior; in fact, it is conceivable that 100 per cent of the consumption-pattern differences between Negroes and whites could be accounted for by income and other sociodemographic differentials. Klein and Mooney reach somewhat the same conclusion when they state that "this explanation of racial differentials is not solely adequate" to explain consumption differences. They go on to say that the "effects of [socio]demographic variables have been found to be statistically significant. . . . but not clear in direction."[6]

In the study reported here, the authors hoped to shed light on the prob-

---

[3] Horst Mendershausen, "Differences in Family Savings between Cities of Different Size and Location, Whites and Negroes," *Review of Economic Statistics*, 22 (Aug., 1940), pp. 122–137; Dorothy Brady and Rose Friedman, "Savings and Income Distribution," *Studies in Income and Wealth*, 10 (New York: National Bureau of Economic Research, 1947), pp. 247–265; J. Duesenberry, *Income, Saving and the Theory of Consumer Behavior* (Cambridge, Mass.: Harvard University Press, 1949); Marcus Alexis, "Some Negro-White Differences in Consumption," *American Journal of Economics and Sociology* (Jan., 1962), pp. 11–28.

[4] Alexis, *ibid.*, p. 11.

[5] At least one writer argues very strongly that most studies to date have de-emphasized the consideration that many factors other than race influence the determination of consumption patterns. In fact, he concludes that because of the number of uncontrolled variables, "the concept of race as a factor in the statistical analyses of group economic behavior . . . has no more validity than lefthandedness, eye pigmentation, or height." B. E. Sawyer, "An Examination of Race as a Factor in Negro-White Consumption Patterns," *The Review of Economics and Statistics*, 44 (May, 1962), p. 220.

[6] L. R. Klein and H. W. Mooney, "Negro-White Savings Differentials and the Consumption Function Problem," *Econometrics* (July, 1953), p. 455.

lem of Negro-white consumption-pattern differences over and above that shed by earlier studies. These studies approached the comparisons on a macro-economic level, that is, their basic concern was to make aggregate comparisons of how Negroes and whites allocated their incomes. More specifically, the purposes of the present study were (1) to determine if there existed between Negroes and whites consumption-pattern differences which were not accounted for by income differentials, and (2) to specify, where possible, the nature or possible origin(s) of those differences.

Methodology

SAMPLE. The consumption-pattern data for both Negro and white housewives was taken from a large-scale commercial survey conducted in the Houston Standard Metropolitan Statistical area in 1967. A probability sample of 1,546 housewives was obtained through personal interviews in the respondents' homes. This sample survey was cited by Advertising Research Foundation as conforming to the standards set forth in ARF's *Criteria for Marketing and Advertising Research*. With no substitutes allowed in the sample survey, a completion rate of 80 per cent was achieved by the researchers, who made up to eight call-backs to housewives who were not at home. The accuracy of the field interviewing was verified by ARF, which conducted a 100 per cent verification of the field interviewing, using FACT (Field Audit and Completion Test).[7] Because of the procedures used in this survey, the usual problems of sampling errors (and nonsampling errors due to interviewing) were considered to be minimal.

LIMITATIONS. Due to the nature of the original proprietary survey, several limitations were imposed on this study. First, since the search objectives of the company conducting the project were much broader in scope than a simple study of Negro-white consumption patterns, they made no attempt to be all-inclusive in the product categories chosen. As a result, the present study was restricted to a survey of only a small list of household product purchases. Second, even though the Negro sample selected was unusually large (see Table 1), it was still not large enough to permit a completely satisfactory breakdown of income classes, particularly at the middle ($3,000–$6,000) and upper ($8,000 plus) levels. Similarly, multiple cross-classifications by income and other sociodemographic characteristics were impossible, due to inadequate cell sizes. Isolation of the impact of these other sociodemographic characteristics on consumption patterns was limited to inferences drawn from Table 2. Great care, however, was taken by the authors not to become over-enchanted with implying cause and effect relationships relative to these characteristics. Finally, any generalizations from this study must be tempered with the realization that the data were collected from one large urban metropolitan area located in a Southern state.

---

[7] Pilot Study of FACT, Arrowhead Study No. 4 (New York: Advertising Research Foundation, Inc., 1968).

TABLE 1

Sample Breakdown by Income Classifications

Income	Whites		Negroes	
	N	Per Cent	N	Per Cent
Under $3,000	151	11.3	86	40.8
$3,000–5,999	236	17.7	77	36.5
$6,000–7,999	298	22.3	26	12.3
$8,000 and Over	650	48.7	22	10.4
	1,335[a]	100.0	211[a]	100.0

[a] These are the base numbers used hereafter in each of the tables except where stated differently.

RESULTS

While of general interest to marketers, aggregate income-allocation differences do not provide any information about actual product- or brand-choice comparisons, which are so vital to marketing strategy decisions. It may be, for example, that even though Negroes spend more money on food, their product and brand choices are very similar to those of whites in comparable circumstances. In this study (see Table 3), specific usage comparisons were made between Negroes and whites for ownership of a selected number of household products (by holding income constant). An evaluation of brand preferences will be left to a future study.

CONSUMPTION DIFFERENCES. 1. *Food products.* Table 3 clearly demonstrates that, at every income level, Negroes consumed more butter than did whites. In fact, Negroes at the lowest income level (under $3,000) spent more on butter than did whites at the highest level of income ($8,000 and over). Obviously, factors other than income must account for these variations, but none of the sociodemographic characteristics shown in Table 2 seem to provide any substantial clues.[8]

Nondietary soft drink consumption varied drastically across income classes between the two groups. Negro usage was double that of whites at the lowest income level, but then tended to decline with increasing wealth. Among whites, consumption followed somewhat a reverse trend, with usage rising as income increased. Consumption differences at the low-income level can be attributed primarily to dissimilarities in occupations between the groups. The data in Table 2 indicate that the 77 per

8 Among other possible explanations, two stand out as likely sources of influence. The first is "status." Bauer, in a recent study, stated that Negroes are extremely interested in quality and are "even more concerned with the symbolic value of goods than are whites." (Bauer, "Marketing Dilemma," p. 2.) The possibility exists, therefore, that a certain amount of status usually is associated with highly conspicuous goods—clothing and automobiles. A more likely explanation is that Negroes are compensating for their narrower spectrum of choice relative to potential uses of their income. In other words, since the Negro has less selectivity in the purchase of a home, of a vacation, etc., he spends more per item on the things that are available to him.

cent of the low-income whites were retired, as compared to only 30 per cent of the Negroes. As a result, the low-income Negro families were considerably larger and had more children than the average low-income white families. Why Negro consumption of nondietary soft drinks was so erratic in the high-income brackets is difficult to answer.

Dietary soft drinks were more popular with Negroes until the highest-income bracket was reached. At this point, usage among whites was almost double that among Negroes. Again, the larger size of Negro families probably is sufficient to explain larger consumption patterns in the low-income groups. At the highest income level, it may be that Negroes are less diet-conscious than are whites and, as a result, have turned their attentions to other "drinks."

2. *Liquor.* Negroes, in every income bracket but the highest, purchased more liquor than did whites. For both groups, however, liquor consumption rose steadily with increases in income. Scotch whiskey was preferred to a substantial degree by Negroes in almost every income group, when compared with whites. This observation supports the findings of several other studies, which indicate that Negroes drink at least 25 per cent of the Scotch consumed in the United States, although they represent only 12 per cent of the population.[9] Scotch, among all consumers, has always been thought of as a "quality," high-class product. Therefore, it appears likely that, among Negroes, drinking Scotch has become associated with high status. Bauer also found that "those Negroes who see themselves as moving upward self-perceived mobility from their fathers' position in society are most likely to . . . regard Scotch as a 'status' drink, and are most likely to report being regular Scotch drinkers."[10]

3. *Personal hygiene products.* In 11 of 12 possible income groupings, Negroes purchased more deodorant, toothpaste, and mouthwash than comparable groups of whites. Negroes, on the other hand, did not purchase as much shampoo, although the differences were slight in most cases. More household disinfectants were used by Negroes, except in one income group.

The bulk of the differences, particularly at the lower income levels, can be attributed to larger Negro families with more children. Higher rates for usage of household disinfectants by Negroes probably result from the difficulty of keeping their average substandard housing facilities clean.

4. *Major home appliances and home ownership.* A very striking point was that, except for the lowest income bracket, almost as many Negroes owned their own home as did whites. The difference at the lowest income level can be explained by the occupational discrepancies mentioned earlier.

Substantial differences in ownership of various major appliances were noted between the two groups at all income levels. Ownership differences for washing machines, clothes dryers, and dishwashers were particularly apparent. Part of the reason for these differences is income; for example,

9 "The Negro Market, Accent on Quality," *Media-scope* (April, 1964), p. 77.
10 Bauer, "Marketing Dilemma," p. 3.

TABLE 2

Total Sample Breakdown by Income and by Various
Sociodemographic Characteristics (in per cent)

Sociodemographic Characteristics	Annual Family Income							
	Less than $3,000		$3,000–5,999		$6,000–7,999		$8,000 or more	
	Whites	Negroes	Whites	Negroes	Whites	Negroes	Whites	Negroes
Occupation								
Prof/semi-prof/tech	—	—	4	4	8	8	19	9
Prof/mgr/official	—	—	6	1	9	11	22	14
Clerical/sales/kindred	3	5	16	6	15	11	16	18
Craftsmen/foremen/kindred	6	3	24	25	34	8	26	23
Operatives/service	10	48	24	49	26	31	12	14
Farm/laborers	3	14	8	8	2	19	1	9
Retired	77	30	18	6	5	8	3	9
Others/not reported	1	—	—	1	1	4	1	4
Total	100	100	100	100	100	100	100	100
Education								
Less than high school	48	53	28	26	15	19	7	9
Some high school	22	23	26	30	23	23	15	9
High school grad.	18	17	26	31	34	31	27	14
Some college	9	3	15	9	18	8	25	32
College graduate	2	1	2	—	7	8	17	23
Graduate or prof. training	1	—	1	—	3	8	9	9
Not reported	—	3	2	4	—	3	—	4
Total	100	100	100	100	100	100	100	100
Sex—head of household								
Male	40	48	77	83	94	88	96	91
Female	60	52	23	17	6	12	4	9
Total	100	100	100	100	100	100	100	100

Age of household head								
Less than 24 years	3	9	14	6	9	4	2	9
25–34 years	1	10	16	27	31	31	21	32
35–44 years	7	26	16	32	27	31	33	27
45–54 years	10	19	19	22	18	22	26	23
55–64 years	18	20	18	13	11	8	15	9
65 years or older	60	14	16	—	4	—	3	—
Not reported	1	2	1	—	—	4	—	—
Total	100	100	100	100	100	100	100	100
Total living in household								
1	44	17	11	4	2	—	1	—
2	43	32	33	20	21	15	22	14
3	7	13	25	22	23	20	21	36
4	3	13	11	18	26	23	27	14
5–7	3	19	18	23	26	38	27	32
8 or more	—	6	2	13	2	4	2	4
Total	100	100	100	100	100	100	100	100
Total no. employed in household								
None	75	17	14	3	4	4	2	5
1	21	50	64	47	70	46	58	18
2	4	29	19	44	24	50	33	68
3	—	2	2	5	2	—	6	9
4 or more	—	—	1	1	—	—	1	—
Not reported	—	2	—	—	—	—	—	—
Total	100	100	100	100	100	100	100	100
Stage in life cycle								
Younger children only	3	12	18	14	25	11	12	23
Younger and older children	1	16	15	26	21	27	17	27
Older children only	9	23	16	35	29	35	36	18
None–head less than 45	3	15	10	10	7	8	7	9
None–head over 45	31	14	27	9	16	19	24	18
None–single head over 45	52	19	14	4	2	—	3	5
Not reported	1	1	—	2	—	—	1	—
Total	100	100	100	100	100	100	100	100

TABLE 3

Percentage of Negroes and Whites Who Had Recently
Purchased or Who Owned Various Household Products

| Products | Annual Family Income | | | | | | | |
| | Less than $3,000 | | $3,000–5,999 | | $6,000–7,999 | | $8,000 or more | |
	Whites	Negroes	Whites	Negroes	Whites	Negroes	Whites	Negroes
Food Products[a]								
Butter	6.6	23.3	8.0	31.2	7.7	26.9	14.1	45.4
Margarine	58.3	61.6	63.6	72.7	69.8	57.7	69.5	81.8
Frozen vegetables[b]	30.5	31.4	28.0	50.6	39.6	34.6	47.1	54.6
Canned vegetables[c]	20.5	35.6	35.6	44.5	37.9	40.4	40.6	43.2
Dietary soft drinks	7.3	17.4	11.9	23.4	20.8	23.1	25.5	13.6
Nondietary soft drinks	26.5	60.5	55.5	71.4	62.4	23.1	67.1	45.4
Liquor								
All respondents[d]	15.2	26.7	29.7	39.0	39.3	46.2	56.5	54.6
Scotch[e]	3.3	9.3	4.2	22.1	7.7	34.6	19.7	27.3
Bourbon[e]	7.3	15.1	20.3	23.4	29.2	7.7	40.9	40.9

Personal Hygiene Products[f]

Shampoo	42.4	41.9	59.3	52.0	74.5	65.4	72.6	50.0
Deodorant	39.7	65.1	56.8	79.2	74.5	92.3	76.6	81.8
Toothpaste	48.3	76.7	75.0	89.6	86.9	88.5	89.1	86.4
Mouthwash	43.7	61.6	58.5	75.3	56.7	88.5	63.5	86.4
Disinfectants	52.3	69.8	56.4	80.5	70.1	61.5	68.6	86.4
Home Appliances[g]								
Auto. washing machine	47.4	19.8	57.6	29.9	78.6	50.0	85.5	72.7
Auto. clothes dryer	12.6	5.8	16.5	7.8	34.2	15.4	54.9	27.3
Auto. dishwasher	2.0	—	5.5	—	14.1	3.8	33.8	—
B&W television	87.4	91.8	89.5	98.7	83.7[h]	97.9[h]	—	—
Color television	3.3	0.6	5.7	1.9	24.3[h]	6.2[h]	—	—
Home Ownership								
Own home	68.3	39.5	49.4	57.1	70.8	73.0	81.5	77.3

[a] Purchased within the past seven days.
[b] Includes all types of frozen vegetables.
[c] Includes canned corn, peas, green beans, and tomatoes.
[d] Percentage to total respondents purchasing some alcoholic beverages within past 12 months.
[e] Percentage of Scotch and Bourbon purchases among total respondents.
[f] Purchased within past 30 days.
[g] Percentage "having" in the home.
[h] Last two income classes were combined because of small number of respondents.

ownership of washing machines among Negroes increased across each income level until it was fairly close to the white ownership level. Another reason which helps explain the differentials is that many of the dwellings occupied by Negroes, regardless of income, are not equipped with the plumbing and electrical connections necessary for installation of those appliances. The additional installation cost makes it impractical or impossible to purchase washers and dryers. A further comment on automatic dishwashers is in order, since ownership variances are so prominant, even at the highest income level. The reason for these variances is that the majority of dishwasher sales are made to home builders who install them in new homes. Since even higher-income Negroes have had limited opportunity to purchase new homes, it should not be surprising that dishwasher ownership is so low.

Color television ownership was much higher among whites at every income level, although the reverse was true for black-and-white television. No simple explanation is available for this phenomenon, unless Negroes: (1) do not care much about color TV, or (2) cannot afford or are not willing to replace a working black-and-white TV for a new color set.

Consumption similarities. A major finding of this study was that, for many household products, consumption-pattern differences were small both in number and magnitude. In fact, many similarities existed. For example, purchases of margarine, frozen and canned vegetables, and bourbon were nearly identical for both groups. Even among those products for which group differences existed, there were similarities in overall consumption patterns (for example, high total usage of personal hygiene products in both groups) as well as expanding usage as income rose.

Discussion

Most of the earlier economic studies were concerned with comparing and analyzing aggregate consumption-pattern differences between Negroes and whites. They concluded that, essentially, the consumption differences were a reflection of the greater need of Negroes to save, rather than a result of cultural differences. This type of aggregate analysis, however, tends to conceal any internal variations in consumption which might exist within each group.

Although extensive consumption-pattern differences were found for a variety of household products, most of the discrepancies could be explained by income and/or other sociodemographic differentials between the two groups. Consider, for example, major home appliances, for which ownership appears to be primarily a function of income and a lack of proper utility connections. Even though a large portion of the consumption differences could be attributed to economic and sociodemographic considerations, usage patterns for several products—particularly Scotch, butter, soft drinks, and frozen foods—could not be so explained.

One reason behind the varying consumption patterns in the Negro market versus the white market is the Negro's narrower spectrum of choice:

> The Negro has less selectivity in the purchase of a home, of a vacation, of travel, dining, entertainment, etc. This results in a greater expenditure

per unit in the things that are available to him. Whites have more places to put their discretionary income while Negroes, even in the same income level as whites, use their dollars differently because of their narrower selectivity.[11]

Another reason for consumption differences is that minority groups today are apt to engage in compensatory consumption. Most Negro families have little opportunity to base their self-respect on occupational, educational, or other accomplishments. This poverty of opportunity tends to reinforce for these families the significance of consumption as at least one sphere in which they can make progress toward the American dream of success. Appliances, automobiles, and a home of their own can become compensations for blocked social mobility.[12] Bullock agrees and notes that "the main criterion for determining social class in many urban Negro communities of the South is overt consumption rather than wealth, family background, or church affiliation."[13] Similarly, Negroes who are insecure in their status or who believe their status is not widely accepted may participate in conspicuous consumption. "For instance," according to Broom and Glenn, "those who have recently improved their economic standing may buy conspicuously expensive items to communicate the fact that they have 'arrived.' "[14]

Because material goods have such an important symbolic role in American society, their acquisition symbolizes to the Negro his achievement of full status. Yet, this often creates a dilemma for the Negro consumer: whether to strive against odds for middle-class values, as reflected in material goods, or to give in and live for the moment.[15]

Summary and Implications

A probability sample of 1,335 whites and 211 Negroes was interviewed in Houston, Texas, to determine if, and to what extent, consumption patterns varied for a selected list of household products. The results for both groups were broken down and analyzed across four income categories. Sample variations for other sociodemographic characteristics were noted and utilized in explaining the resulting product-usage differences.

For the five product categories evaluated—food, soft drinks, liquor, personal hygiene products, and major home appliances—variations in consumption were found between Negroes and whites. A substantial portion of these differences, however, were explainable more in terms of income or sociodemographic variations than by purely "racial" influences. The evidence, in fact, disclosed as many similarities as differences in consumption patterns. There were, however, certain products for which unexplained differences in consumption patterns still existed between Negroes and

11 "Is There Really a Negro Market?," *Marketing Insights*, Jan. 29, 1968, p. 14.
12 David Caplovitz, *The Poor Pay More* (New York: The Free Press, 1963), pp. 12–13, 181.
13 H. A. Bullock, *Pathways to the Houston Negro Market* (Ann Arbor, Mich.: Edwards Brothers Publishing Co., 1957), p. 190.
14 Broom and Glenn, *Transformation*, pp. 28–29.
15 Bauer, "Marketing Dilemma," p. 3.

whites even after an attempt was made to separate out the influence of income and other sociodemographic factors. Two such examples were butter and Scotch. No economically "rational" explanation exists why Negroes at every income level consume more of these products than do whites. The two most likely reasons put forth by this and other studies are compensatory consumption and status or conspicuous consumption. Unfortunately, too few products were studied to ascertain accurately which types of people or products would most likely be subject to these influences.

In conclusion, it can be said from a businessman's point of view that a Negro market does exist, not so much identifiable by color as by patterns of consumption. Marketers who assume that product buying in Negro households is roughly a match for that in white families of similar economic circumstances are far from correct. A combination of societal constraints; cultural traditions; and differences in values, preferences, and psychological needs have led Negroes not only to spend a larger proportion of their incomes on food, drink, clothing, and home entertainment than do whites, but also to vary their expenditures across different products and, probably, brands compared with whites.[16] However, as the Negro continues to climb the economic and social ladder, some of these patterns of consumption will undoubtedly change, as the more prosperous persons raise their sights from compensatory spending to financing nice homes, education, medical care, and travel. In other words, it is likely that a smaller percentage of the Negro's income will be channeled into traditionally popular product categories—food, clothing, liquor, and entertainment—while there will be an increase in forms of consumption which heretofore have been either unattainable or unwanted. This means that opportunities will continue to expand very rapidly for companies willing to cultivate the Negro as a market. If this is to be, then marketing must keep up with the changes occurring inside and outside this market.

[16] Marketers should keep in mind, however, that the indications in this study are that the Negro market is not completely homogeneous. Even as Negroes at the top income levels find the lines separating them from the rest of America becoming less of a barrier, those at the bottom income level still find themselves essentially isolated from their total environment. As a result, there has been increasing economic and cultural stratification within the Negro community which, among other things, has led to internal consumption-pattern variations.

A Note on Negro-White Differences in Attitudes toward the Supreme Court

HERBERT HIRSCH
THE UNIVERSITY OF TEXAS AT AUSTIN

LEWIS DONOHEW
UNIVERSITY OF KENTUCKY

RESEARCH ON RACE AS A VARIABLE IN ATTITUDES TOWARD GOVERNMENTAL institutions has been very sketchy. The present article will examine this variable as it applies to an institution expected to emphasize its saliency —the United States Supreme Court.

Since 1954, the Court has been in the forefront of the civil rights "revolution" and in general has been sympathetic to the Negro. Consequently, one would expect Negroes to display a positive attitude toward the Court, but expectations regarding white attitudes are not as clear. Previous research using race as a variable has produced conflicting evidence. On the one hand, research by Brink and Harris did not reveal much difference between Negroes and whites. They noted that Negroes were overwhelmingly positive in their evaluation of the Court, but that most whites were also positive, except in the South.[1] This finding is somewhat surprising when compared to research which has indicated very real differences in other categories between Negroes and whites. For example, Broom and Glenn in their analysis of Negro and white responses to questions from ten national public opinion surveys concluded that "there are important Negro-white differences in attitudes that cannot be explained by Negro-white differences in educational level or regional distribution."[2] In the absence of race as a variable, Kessel found that demographic factors other than geographic area had no significant relationship to public attitudes toward the Court.[3] There is also evidence to suggest that Negroes and whites differ in patterns of political socialization[4] and it is known that the two racial groups differ on a large number of other variables.[5]

[1] William Brink and Louis Harris, *The Negro Revolution in America* (New York: Simon and Schuster, 1964), pp. 131, 143.

[2] Leonard Broom and Norval D. Glenn, "Negro-White Differences in Reported Attitudes and Behavior," *Sociology and Social Research*, 50 (Jan., 1966), p. 199.

[3] John H. Kessel, "Public Perceptions of the Supreme Court," *Midwest Journal of Political Science*, 10 (May, 1966), pp. 185–186. For additional studies of public perceptions of the Supreme Court see: Kenneth M. Dolbeare, "The Public Views the Supreme Court," in Herbert Jacob, ed., *Justice and Politics in the Supreme Court* (Boston: Little, Brown & Company, 1967); Kenneth M. Dolbeare and Phillip E. Hammond, "The Political Party Basis of Attitudes Toward the Supreme Court," *Public Opinion Quarterly*, 32 (Spring, 1968), pp. 16–30; and Walter F. Murphy and Joseph Tannenhaus, "Public Opinion and Supreme Court: The Goldwater Campaign," *Public Opinion Quarterly*, 32 (Spring, 1968), pp. 31–50.

[4] Kenneth P. Langton and M. Kent Jennings, "Political Socialization and the High School Civics Curriculum in the United States," *American Political Science Review* (Sept., 1968), pp. 852–867. Also see Dwaine Marvick, "The Political Socialization of the American Negro," *The Annals*, 361 (Sept., 1965), pp. 112–127.

[5] See, for example, Marcus Alexis, "Some Negro-White Differences in Consumption,"

♦ First published in *Social Science Quarterly* 49, No. 3 (December, 1968).

Thus, it seemed reasonable to expect that the importance of race as a variable would extend into attitudes toward a governmental institution whose activities have often been identified with race relations. In this study, Negro-white attitudes toward the Supreme Court have been re-examined, using data from a source other than that used by Brink and Harris.

METHOD

The data used here are from the University of Michigan's Survey Research Center post-election study of the 1964 Presidential election.[6] The sample included 1,399 whites and 159 Negroes.

In one part of the study, respondents were asked, "Have you had time to pay attention to what the Supreme Court of the United States has been doing in the past few years?" If the answer was "no," interviewers passed on to another line of questioning. If "yes," respondents were then asked, "Is there anything in particular that it has done that you have liked or disliked?" Interviewers probed for answers, seeking up to three positive and three negative responses. The present analysis is based on these responses.

When we set out to analyze the results, it was discovered that less than 2 per cent of the sample gave a second and third response, either positive or negative. To simplify computations, these were eliminated. For the present purposes an answer was sought to the question: which persons tend to answer positively in the first response to the above question, and which tend to answer negatively? This was done in two ways. First, by computing the ratios of positive to negative responses among Negroes and among whites and then comparing the two, holding certain variables constant (education, income, etc.). The amount of variance accounted for by race in each instance is reported through a $\emptyset^2$ coefficient. This is roughly comparable to reporting between-groups variance in an analysis of variance procedure.[7] Second, comparing the proportions of positive and negative responses within each group (Negroes

---

American Journal of Economics and Sociology, 21 (Jan., 1962), pp. 11–28; Ira L. Reiss, "Premarital Sexual Permissiveness among Negroes and Whites," American Sociological Review, 29 (Oct., 1964), pp. 688–698; Hadley Cantril, ed., Public Opinion, 1936–1946 (Princeton, N.J.: Princeton University Press, 1951); Herbert Hyman and Paul B. Sheatsley, "Attitudes toward Desegregation," Scientific American, 211 (July, 1964), pp. 16–23; Frank R. Westie and David H. Howard, "Social Status Differentials and the Race Attitudes of Negroes," American Sociological Review, 19 (Oct., 1954), pp. 584–591; and Donald R. Matthews and James W. Prothro, Negroes and the New Southern Politics (New York: Harcourt, Brace & World, 1966).

[6] Data were made available to the Department of Political Science, University of Kentucky through the Inter-University Consortium.

[7] Probability levels are not reported because, strictly speaking, the sample from which the data are taken is not a random sample but an area probability sample. Further problems arose since the large degree of nonresponse probably entered an additional source of bias. The $\emptyset^2$ coefficient is reported to indicate the amount of variance accounted for in the data. Thus, when attitudes of whites and Negroes are compared, a high coefficient indicates that race accounts for the variance. When the coefficient is computed down the column it indicates the amount of variation accounted for by the control variable.

and whites) at each level on the control variable (e.g., at low-, medium-, and high-income levels among Negroes) and again computing the amount of variation accounted for through a $\emptyset^2$ coefficient. This is roughly comparable to reporting within-group variance in analysis of variance.

Demographic Variables

The overall evaluation of the Court may be seen in Table 1, which indicates that there is a large difference between white and Negro attitudes toward the Court. Whites responded negatively to the Court and Negroes responded positively. In an effort to explain the difference, a number of demographic variables have been controlled.[8] Table 2 shows differences between white and Negro attitudes when education is controlled, and indicates that education level does not explain these differences. At all levels Negroes had a positive attitude toward the Court and whites had a negative attitude toward it.

Closer examination of Table 2 reveals that white attitudes become more positive as education increases. It can be observed in Table 2 that the ratio of positive to negative responses is only .24 for white respondents who have completed grade school but that this increases consistently upward to a ratio of .54 for whites who have attended college. The $\emptyset^2$ coefficient equals .01, indicating that differences among whites according to education level account for a small amount of the variation.

For Negroes, those who have attended college also have a slightly more positive attitude than those who have attended only grade school, and again the variation accounted for is small ($\emptyset^2 = .01$). Consequently, the considerable difference between Negro and white attitudes at all levels indicates that differences in education do not explain differences in attitudes toward the Court.

The analysis next turned to geographic area in which the respondent grew up, but there were not enough Negro respondents in five of the

TABLE 1

White and Negro Attitudes toward the Supreme Court

Attitude	Race	
	White	Negro
Positive	172	46
Negative	414	18
Total	586	64
Ratio of positive to negative responses	.42	2.55
	$\emptyset^2 = .06$	

[8] Unfortunately, because of the size of the sample, finer distinctions in the control variables could not be made. It is probable, therefore, that the Negro respondents were lower, on the average, in both education and income than the white respondents. The fact remains, however, that they continued to be more positive toward the Court.

TABLE 2

Attitudes toward the Supreme Court: Ratio of Positive to Negative
Responses by Race and Education Level

Education Level	Race		
	White	Negro	ϕ^2
Grade school	.24	2.67	.16
Junior high school and some high school	.27	2.50	.13
High school graduate	.39	2.00	.03
Some college and college graduate	.54	3.00	.04

TABLE 3

Attitudes toward the Supreme Court: Ratio of Positive to Negative Responses
by Race and Geographic Area in Which Respondent Grew Up

Geographic Area	Race		
	White	Negro	ϕ^2
Middle Atlantic	.68	1.67	.01
East North Central	.56	*	*
West North Central	.46	*	*
Solid South	.14	2.29	.31
Border States	.18	*	*
Mountain States	.56	*	*
Pacific States	.71	*	*

* Too few Negro respondents to permit analysis.

TABLE 4

Attitudes toward the Supreme Court: Ratio of Positive
to Negative Responses by Race and Income

Income	Race		
	White	Negro	ϕ^2
$0–$3,999	.42	2.13	.08
$4,000–$7,499	.38	2.83	.16
$7,500–$9,999	.43	*	*
$10,000+	.49	*	*

* Too few Negro respondents to permit analysis.

seven geographic areas to permit analysis. Data for the areas in which attitudes among the races could be compared are presented in Table 3,
which reports a considerable difference in the solid South between white
and Negro attitudes toward the Court. In the Middle Atlantic area the

differences appear to be much smaller, although Negroes here also tended to be more positive toward the Court than did whites. Interestingly, white respondents in the Middle Atlantic and Pacific regions were the most positively disposed toward the Court. Negro respondents in the Middle Atlantic area, however, were somewhat less positive in their evaluation of the Court than their counterparts in the solid South. White respondents in the South were, of course, the least positive and the most negative.

Differences of opinions within each of the racial groups are indicated by looking down the columns from geographic area to geographic area. Among white respondents, $\emptyset^2 = .07$. This finding undoubtedly results from the more positive orientations expressed by white respondents in the Middle Atlantic and Pacific regions. For Negroes, $\emptyset^2 = .03$, indicating that geographic area accounts for little of the variance.

The last demographic variable to be examined was income. Again the analysis was faced with the problem of too few Negro respondents in two of the four income brackets. The data are presented in Table 4, which indicates that white respondents at all income levels perceived the Court negatively while Negroes (at least in the two lower income brackets) perceived it positively. Holding race constant and looking at differences

TABLE 5

Attitudes toward the Supreme Court: Ratio of Positive to Negative
Responses by Race and Political Party Identification

| | Race | | |
Party	White	Negro	$\emptyset^2$
Strong Democrat	.48	2.15	.09
Not very strong Democrat	.39	2.25	.06
Independent, closer to Democrat	.85	*	*
Independent	.64	*	*
Independent, closer to Republican	.33	*	*
Not very strong Republican	.32	*	*
Strong Republican	.25	*	*

* Too few Negro respondents to permit analysis.

TABLE 6

Attitudes toward the Supreme Court: Ratio of Positive to Negative
Responses by Race and Political Efficacy

| | Race | | |
Efficacy	White	Negro	$\emptyset^2$
Low	.27	1.80	.08
Medium	.33	2.83	.12
High	.60	2.67	.03

between income groups, one finds no systematic differences ($\emptyset^2=.002$ for whites; $\emptyset^2=.002$ for Negroes). Thus, only when the racial variable was considered in this analysis was a substantial amount of variance accounted for by the data.

POLITICAL VARIABLES

In general, the above analysis indicated that demographic variables did not differentiate positive from negative attitudes as successfully as did the racial variable. Next, the study turned to the political dimension in which two variables were examined: political party identification and political efficacy. Here again, there were substantial differences in the way whites and Negroes responded to the Supreme Court. Tables 5 and 6 support the conclusion that Negroes perceive the Court more positively than whites regardless of their political party identification or their level of political efficacy. Among whites, there were differences in attitudes toward the Court according to party identification. White "independents" and "independents closer to Democrats" were the most positive, while white Republicans were the most negative. Yet, party identification accounted for little variance ($\emptyset^2=.02$).

Among white respondents, those having a high sense of political efficacy registered more positive attitudes than those with low or medium efficacy scores. The variance accounted for remains small ($\emptyset^2=.02$). Among Negroes, systematic differences in attitudes do not result when the respondents are compared according to party identification or political efficacy.

CONCLUSION

The above analysis has demonstrated that there are consistent differences between white and Negro attitudes toward the United States Supreme Court. Negroes evaluated the Court more positively and less negatively than whites. These differences remained, moreover, when geographic area, education, income, political party identification, and sense of political efficacy were controlled. The analysis further demonstrates that the racial variable accounts for a greater amount of the variance in the data than any of the control variables.

Political Orientations among Negroes and Whites[1]

DENNIS S. IPPOLITO
EMORY UNIVERSITY

WILLIAM S. DONALDSON
UNIVERSITY OF VIRGINIA

LEWIS BOWMAN
EMORY UNIVERSITY

IT IS POSSIBLE THAT THE SUCCESS OF SOCIAL MOVEMENTS AND PUBLIC POL-
icies designed to improve the social and economic conditions of lower-
class Negroes will be highly dependent upon the political orientations of
the growing Negro middle class.[2] The effect which upward mobility has
had upon other groups in the United States has been to weaken their
political links with their class of origin through emulation and political
reorientation, and, traditionally, this reorientation has been toward conservatism.[3] Thus, one of the situational variables affecting the strength of
social and political action on behalf of the poor could be the political
orientations of middle-class Negroes.[4] Since one of the determinants of
collective behavior is attitudinal consistency, the political effectiveness of
the Negro community would appear to be strongly related to the maintenance of a consistent political orientation.[5]

As Lopreato has stated, "The likelihood of retaining political links with
the class of origin (avoiding resocialization) increases with the degree of

[1] The data reported here are derived from research conducted for the Governor's
Study Commission on Vocational Rehabilitation in Virginia and financed by a statewide comprehensive planning grant from the Rehabilitation Services Administration,
United States Department of Health, Education, and Welfare to the Virginia Department of Vocational Rehabiliation and, as associate sponsor, to the Virginia Commission
for the Visually Handicapped.

[2] As Tomlinson has pointed out, one of the prerequisites for effective political action
is: "The unification of the street militant and the Negro middle class in the common
cause of Negro development." T. M. Tomlinson, "The Development of a Riot Ideology
among Urban Negroes," American Behavioral Scientist, 11 (March–April, 1968), p. 30.

[3] For a brief summary of the major findings in this area, see Joseph Lopreato, "Upward Social Mobility and Political Orientation," American Sociological Review, 32
(Aug., 1967), p. 587. For a somewhat different interpretation of why this reorientation
occurs, see Harry C. Bredemeier, "The Politics of the Poverty Cold War," Urban Affairs
Quarterly, 3 (June, 1968), pp. 3–35, esp. p. 17.

[4] As Matthews and Prothro stated, "Perhaps when the Negro middle class becomes
fairly large, it tends to become more isolated from other Negroes, more preoccupied
with the middle-class round of life, less identified with the black masses." Donald R.
Matthews and James W. Prothro, Negroes and the New Southern Politics (New York:
Harcourt, Brace, and World, 1966), pp. 121–122.

[5] There are, of course, other determinants. See, for example, James A. Geschwender,
"Status Inconsistency, Social Isolation, and Individual Unrest," Social Forces, 46
(June, 1968), pp. 477–483. Geschwender also deals with some of the factors related
to the disproportional representation of status-inconsistents among the leadership and
the rank and file of social movements, and some of these are relevant to the question
of political reorientation noted here.

♦ First published in Social Science Quarterly 49, No. 3 (December, 1968).

status discrepancies, namely, rejection."[6] Since discrimination against and social rejection of middle-class Negroes is quite evident, the hypothesized effect would be to maintain the identification between middle-class and lower-class Negroes with respect to political orientations.

A number of studies have shown the attitudinal consistency of Negroes, irrespective of class, toward policies of high political saliency.[7] The question remains, however, of whether inter-racial differences in support of governmental involvement are a function of immediate programs highly identified with the Negro community or whether they are a manifestation of essentially differing attitudes toward the role of government. If Negroes and whites exhibit differential attitudes toward governmental implementation and involvement in a program of low political saliency, it is probable that the political orientations of the two groups are dissimilar, particularly if both groups show strong support for the program.[8] Further, if Negro attitudes are consistent, regardless of social class, it is equally probable that the political reorientation of middle-class Negroes has not occurred.

The present study investigates these questions in the policy area of vocational rehabilitation.[9] We shall report the inter-racial differences in advocacy of public or private implementation and federal involvement in programs to aid the handicapped, and, finally, the correlates of the subgroups advocating various types of implementation and involvement.

THE DATA

The data are based on personal interviews conducted in Petersburg, Virginia, and Norfolk, Virginia, in August and October of 1967. The samples were drawn by area probability techniques to represent a cross-section of the adult population in each locale. The response rates were 91 per cent in Petersburg and 84 per cent in Norfolk. Negro interviewers interviewed all Negro respondents, and white interviewers interviewed all white respondents.

Petersburg is a city of close to 40,000 population situated on the border of the southside and central regions of Virginia. Almost one-half of its population is Negro. Norfolk, a city of over 300,000, is part of Tidewater Virginia's standard metropolitan statistical area, which also includes Newport News, Portsmouth ,and Chesapeake. Slightly over one-fourth of Norfolk's population is Negro.

[6] Lopreato, "Upward Social Mobility," p. 592.

[7] See, among others, William Brink and Louis Harris, *Black and White: A Study of U.S. Racial Attitudes Today* (New York: Simon and Schuster, 1967).

[8] The operational meaning of political orientation varies widely. Lopreato's study, for example, used party preference as the relevant political orientation. This study used attitudes toward governmental versus private implementation and federal involvement, since these represent the basis of the liberal versus conservative approaches to social welfare issues.

[9] It should be noted that the potential relevance of this program is particularly great for Negroes. As its traditional focus on physical restoration shifts to the more complex mental and emotional handicaps, including cultural and educational, benefits to Negroes should increase disproportionately. The program is also part of the CAMPS program which is a comprehensive federal-state planning system designed to maximize job opportunities among other objectives.

PROGRAM SUPPORT

RELEVANCE OF PROGRAM. Among Negroes and whites in these two communities, there is a high level of support for the rehabilitation program. Table 1 indicates that a substantial majority of respondents viewed this policy area as highly relevant to their community and supported the premise that handicapped persons should be trained in order to be able to work. Support of this magnitude is generally considered to be consensual.

COMMUNITY VERSUS PERSONAL BENEFITS. General perceptions of the program, moreover, were similar among Negroes and whites. Table 2 shows nearly three-fourths of the Negro and white respondents in both communities characterized the program as an educational rather than a welfare program. And there was substantial agreement that the personal benefits of the program, as opposed to the more general community benefits, were the more pressing concern.

The Negro-white differences in terms of program relevance and program benefits, then, were not significant. Indeed, both races were in substantial agreement on the relevance and humanitarian nature of the program. Striking differences between Negroes and whites, however, did occur when the question of public versus private implementation was raised.

GOVERNMENT OR PRIVATE INVOLVEMENT?

ATTITUDES TOWARD IMPLEMENTATION. Table 3 indicates Negro support of governmental implementation was much higher than that evidenced by whites. In both communities, nearly three-fourths of the Negro respondents favored governmental implementation, while only about one-half of the whites favored governmental implementation. Relative support for mixed as opposed to private involvement also was higher among Negroes than whites.

TABLE 1
Negro and White Attitudes toward Relevance of Rehabilitation
Policy for Local Community[a]

| | Petersburg | | Norfolk | |
	Per Cent Negro	Per Cent White	Per Cent Negro	Per Cent White
Important problem in community	90	81	78	72
Not important problem in community	7	15	14	20
NA, DK	3	3	8	7
	100	99	100	99
N =	(134)	(145)	(78)	(259)

[a] In response to the question: "Would you say that helping handicapped people so that they are able to work is an important problem in your community?"

TABLE 2

Negro and White Perceptions of Personal and Community Benefits
of the Rehabilitation Program[a]

| | Petersburg | | Norfolk | |
	Per Cent Negro	Per Cent White	Per Cent Negro	Per Cent White
Personal-benefit orientation	78	68	71	60
Community-benefit orientation	4	6	3	6
Other (including IA)	1	11	8	15
NA, DK	17	15	18	19
	100	100	100	100
N =	(134)	(144)	(76)	(254)

[a] These responses are derived from open-ended explanations of why the respondent felt that helping the handicapped was or was not an important problem
in his community. Personal-benefit orientations included responses such as "they
deserve help," "they need special attention," etc. Community-benefit orientations
included responses such as "takes burden off taxpayers," "helps employers who
need laborers," etc.

TABLE 3

Negro and White Attitudes toward Governmental versus Private
Implementation of Policy[a]

| | Petersburg | | Norfolk | |
	Per Cent Negro	Per Cent White	Per Cent Negro	Per Cent White
Government implementation better	73	46	72	53
Government and private implementation better	14	22	14	20
Private implementation better	10	25	11	22
NA, DK	3	7	3	6
	100	100	100	101
N =	(134)	(144)	(76)	(254)

[a] In response to the question: "Do you think it is better for government or for
private groups to help train the handicapped?"

ORIENTATION AND EFFECT. Among respondents of both races who supported governmental involvement, the most frequently expressed reason
was that government was better able to do the job. Over four-fifths of the
Negroes and nearly three-fourths of the whites who supported governmental involvement articulated their explanation in a pragmatic manner.
Table 4 shows this approach also was evident in the Negroes' response to

the question about the use of federal funds. In both communities, opposition among whites to the use of federal funds in the rehabilitation program was substantially greater than among Negroes. For a majority of Negroes, however, the positive orientation toward the use of federal funds was based on the premise that the source of funds was irrelevant. And particularly striking in the context of Virginia politics, opposition among whites to the use of federal funds was more frequently rationalized in terms of state obligation than in terms of opposition to federal involvement (see Table 5).

TABLE 4

Negro and White Attitudes toward the Use of Federal Funds in
Rehabilitation Programs

| | Petersburg | | Norfolk | |
	Per Cent Negro	Per Cent White	Per Cent Negro	Per Cent White
Opposed	14	46	8	25
Unopposed	63	35	70	61
NA, DK	23	20	22	13
	100	101	100	99
N =	(134)	(144)	(76)	(254)

TABLE 5

Reasons for Attitudes toward Use of Federal Funds in
Rehabilitation Programs

| | Petersburg | | Norfolk | |
	Per Cent Negro	Per Cent White	Per Cent Negro	Per Cent White
Opposed				
States have obligation	13	33	7	19
Federal government should not be involved	1	13	1	6
Unopposed				
Good to have federal government involved	13	5	12	7
Source of funds irrelevant	50	30	57	53
Other	0	0	1	1
NA, DK	23	20	22	13
	100	101	100	99
N =	(134)	(144)	(76)	(254)

Attitudes among Negroes and whites toward governmental implementation and federal involvement in the rehabilitation program, then, differ. Among Negroes there is greater support for governmental implementation and relatively little support for private implementation. Further, opposition to the use of federal funds and hence toward federal involvement is more widespread among whites than among Negroes. This occurs, moreover, within a context of rather limited information about the program in question. Within both communities, 50 per cent or fewer of the respondents in both races had ever heard of the state vocational rehabilitation program. In addition, information about the operation of the program was even more limited. In many cases the differing attitudes of Negroes and whites are probably relatively "pure" responses to the questions of governmental implementation and federal involvement. Further, the differences noted reflect differing political orientations between the groups.

THE CORRELATES OF ADVOCACY

The question remains: Are racial or class differences being measured? In other words, do the inter-racial differences remain when variables such as income and education are introduced?[10] Relatedly, does knowledge of the program affect attitudes?

GOVERNMENT OR PRIVATE IMPLEMENTATION. Among Negroes and whites, income does not appear to affect attitudes toward governmental versus private implementation. Table 6 shows that at each income level, greater numbers of Negroes than whites favor governmental implementation and oppose private implementation. Education, however, does have some effect on inter-racial differences. Negroes in both the high and medium educational levels are more strongly in favor of governmental implementation than whites in either of these categories or than Negroes with low educational levels. Moreover, Negroes and whites in the low-education category display relatively similar attitudes toward governmental or private implementation. Knowledge of the program has no substantial effect upon inter-racial differences. An orientation toward governmental implementation characterizes both Negroes who have heard about the program and Negroes who have not heard about the program. And, in both cases, the inter-racial differences are relatively similar.

ATTITUDES TOWARD USE OF FEDERAL FUNDS. Similar relationships emerge when attitudes toward federal involvement are examined (see Table 7). With the exception of Negroes and whites in the low-education category, Negroes at all income levels, at the medium and high educational levels, and in both categories of knowledge about the program are less opposed than whites to federal involvement.

10 The data in Tables 6 and 7 are not broken down by community. This was done, in part, to secure large enough N's in some cells, particularly the high-income and education cells for Negroes. In addition, the introduction of income and education tends to reduce the intercommunity differences among whites, although substantial differences remain. Among Negroes, however, the effects of community are minimal, particularly when income and education are introduced. In effect, the inter-racial differences are substantial despite community, and community affects mainly the degree of inter-racial differences.

TABLE 6

The Relationship of Family Income Level, Educational Level, and
Knowledge of Program to Attitudes Favoring Governmental
or Private Involvement

Orientation	High Per Cent Negro	High Per Cent White	Medium Per Cent Negro	Medium Per Cent White	Low Per Cent Negro	Low Per Cent White
			Income Level[a]			
Government	70	51	72	56	78	57
Government and private	22	20	11	16	11	16
Private	9	21	14	21	6	21
NA, DK	0	8	3	6	5	5
	101	100	100	99	100	99
N =	(23)	(149)	(88)	(171)	(89)	(56)
			Educational Level[b]			
Government	76	32	82	56	63	64
Government and private	10	27	12	19	14	13
Private	10	36	6	20	20	15
NA, DK	3	4	0	6	4	9
	99	99	100	101	101	101
N =	(29)	(96)	(68)	(197)	(110)	(102)

Orientation	Has Heard of Program Per Cent Negro	Has Heard of Program Per Cent White	Has Not Heard of Program Per Cent Negro	Has Not Heard of Program Per Cent White
		Knowledge of Program		
Government	74	49	69	53
Government and private	13	23	15	20
Private	13	22	14	21
NA, DK	1	6	3	5
	101	100	101	99
N =	(80)	(184)	(116)	(213)

[a] Income level is for total family income. High income is defined as $7500 or more annually; medium income is defined as $3000–$7499 annually; low income is defined as less than $3000 annually.

[b] High educational level includes those with at least some college education; medium educational level includes those who attended high school and/or trade school; low educational level includes those who attended only elementary and/or junior high school.

TABLE 7

The Relationship of Family Income Level, Educational Level, and
Knowledge of Program to Attitudes toward Use of Federal Funds

Use of Federal Funds	High		Medium		Low	
	Negro Per Cent	White Per Cent	Negro Per Cent	White Per Cent	Negro Per Cent	White Per Cent
	Income Level[a]					
Unopposed	70	47	71	55	62	55
Opposed	13	37	12	29	10	15
NA, DK	17	16	17	16	28	30
	100	100	100	100	100	100
N =	(23)	(149)	(88)	(171)	(89)	(56)
	Educational Level[a]					
Unopposed	75	40	74	55	53	57
Opposed	17	48	8	31	22	27
NA, DK	6	12	16	15	25	17
	98	100	98	101	100	101
N =	(29)	(96)	(68)	(197)	(110)	(102)

Knowledge of Program

	Has Heard of Program		Has Not Heard of Program	
	Per Cent Negro	Per Cent White	Per Cent Negro	Per Cent White
Unopposed	72	55	60	51
Opposed	10	35	17	29
NA, DK	18	11	24	19
	100	101	101	99
N =	(80)	(184)	(116)	(213)

[a] For definitions of income and educational levels, see Table 6.

This indicates that inter-racial differences, apart from social class, characterize Negro and white attitudes toward governmental implementation
and federal involvement. Indeed, inter-racial differences increase at the
higher income and educational levels. It could be that the better educated
Negroes are more aware of the implications of governmental implementation and federal involvement. While the differences were minor, Negroes
who had heard of the program were more oriented toward governmental
implementation and federal involvement than Negroes who had not heard
of the program. Thus, knowledge of the program or a level of education
sufficient to deal with the abstract questions of implementation and involvement seem to reinforce inter-racial differences.

SUMMARY

In this study the political orientations of Negroes and whites have been examined by comparing the attitudes of both groups toward government-al versus private implementation and federal involvement in a policy area of low political saliency. While a majority of the respondents in both races had never heard of the state program, differing political orientations emerged. These were not, however, related to differential attitudes toward the program. Most Negroes and whites accepted the relevance of the rehabilitation program for their communities and supported its objectives. Moreover, Negroes and whites tended to emphasize the "personal" as opposed to the "community" benefits of the program.

Where Negro and white attitudes differed was with respect to public or private implementation and toward federal involvement in the program. In both communities almost three-fourths of the Negroes favored governmental implementation, while nearly a majority of the whites favored private or "mixed" implementation. Also, Negroes favored mixed implementation over strictly private implementation.

While the differences by community varied, Negroes were more favorably disposed than whites toward federal involvement in the program. In both communities, nearly three times as many whites as Negroes expressed some opposition to the use of federal funds.

It is apparent, then, that inter-racial differences in political orientation are not simply a function of class differences. Negroes at all income levels gave greater support to governmental implementation and federal involvement than did whites. And with the exception of respondents in both races at the lowest educational level, the same relationship occurs when education is controlled.

Of particular importance is the finding that Negroes in the middle- and upper-income and education categories are substantially closer to Negroes in the low-income and education levels than they are to whites with comparable incomes and education. Indeed, higher status Negroes are closer to whites with low education than they are to higher status whites.

The data, then, indicate that Negroes have similar political orientations, irrespective of class, and that these orientations differ from those of whites. Further, these differing orientations are not a function of the particular policy area.

There is no evidence of inconsistency in the political orientations of Negroes, at least insofar as the political orientations examined here are concerned. And the continued maintenance of this consistent political orientation should increase the political effectiveness of the Negro community.[11]

[11] In general, the Negroes in the middle and upper education and income categories can be classified as upwardly mobile on the basis of the parent's occupation. Thus, the findings here support Lopreato's thesis that discrimination minimizes political reorientation among upwardly mobile groups.

Residential Movement among Negroes and Whites in Chicago[1]

BRUCE C. STRAITS

UNIVERSITY OF CALIFORNIA, SANTA BARBARA

CENSUS SURVEYS TAKEN IN RECENT YEARS INDICATE THAT NONWHITES change residences more frequently within metropolitan areas than do whites.[2] The annual rate of local (intra-county) residential mobility for whites living in standard metropolitan statistical areas have been remarkably stable since shortly after World War II: about one out of every eight persons has moved to a different residence each year since 1949.[3] In contrast, the nonwhite mobility rate rose slightly during the same period, and presently nearly one out of every five nonwhite urban dwellers moves locally during a given year.

The present study of longitudinal intra-city movement in Chicago is intended to offer some insight into the differential mobility patterns of white and nonwhite urban dwellers. First, data are presented to show that controlling for factors (inter-city mobility, family life-cycle position, educational attainment, occupation, and financial standing) prominent in previous studies of residential mobility does not eliminate the observed racial differentials in rate of mobility. On the basis of these findings and data on net distance of movement, the thesis is advanced that the higher incidence of residential mobility among Negroes is a consequence of factors that, for the most part, affect only Negroes, including occupational and residential discrimination, the Negro housing market, and family and employment instability.

DATA AND METHOD

The "Problems of Living in the Metropolis" survey[4] contains, among numerous other items, a complete inventory of residence changes within the Chicago area (with data of move and street address) for 839 white

---

[1] For criticizing an earlier version of this article, I am indebted to Robert M. Terry, Thomas P. Wilson, and Paul L. Wuebben. I wish especially to thank Harvey L. Molotch for his helpful suggestions.

[2] U.S., Bureau of the Census, *Current Population Reports*, Series P-20, Nos. 36, 49, 57, 61, 73, 82, 85, 104, 113, 118 ,127, 134, 141, 150, 156, and 171; and Seventeenth Census (1960), IV, No. 5A, Tables 2 and 2a.

[3] Statistics for earlier periods have not been considered because of the difficulties involved in comparing data based on different time intervals (most of the earlier surveys and censuses were based on a five-year or longer periods). For an excellent discussion of this problem, see Henry S. Shryock, *Population Mobility within the United States* (Chicago: Community and Family Study Center, 1964), Ch. 3.

[4] The author wishes to thank Donald J. Bogue, director of the Community and Family Study Center, for permission to use these data. The research reported here was performed under a grant from the Ford Foundation for research in urban sociology.

and 721 nonwhite[5] household heads.[6] Special care was taken in the coding of these responses in order to assure accuracy and temporal continuity, not only within the mobility histories but also with respect to other factual information contained in the questionnaire.[7] Each residential history was summarized as a single rate by means of a computer search routine:[8]

Average Annual Rate of Mobility	Per Cent of Whites	Per Cent of Nonwhites
.00–.09	16.9	5.3
.10–.19	34.1	21.5
.20–.29	18.5	15.7
.30–.49	13.8	23.4
.50 or higher	16.6	34.1
Total	100.0	100.0

[5] Although nonwhites (as defined by the 1960 Census) other than Negroes were included in the sample, 96 per cent of the nonwhite total was Negro. Therefore, "nonwhite" and "Negro" will be used interchangeably in this paper.

[6] Negroes and inhabitants of slum neighborhoods were disproportionately sampled by a stratified cluster sample method (conducted by the National Opinion Research Center). Respondents were obtained by selecting three (cluster) dwelling units in randomly selected blocks having particular preselected characteristics (strata). To assure that the findings would represent the 1960 Chicago population (interviewing was conducted between May, 1959 and September, 1961), the respondents were weighted by the incidence of their particular strata in the total population. Although the weighted totals are used throughout this paper to compute percentages, the unweighted totals are shown in the tables. The weighted totals for white and nonwhites are 8, 148 and 2,625, respectively. The unweighted totals are 839 and 721, respectively. Because of the exploratory nature of this study and problems associated with cluster-stratified sampling, statistical tests of significance have not been employed.

[7] Whenever a date of move was unknown or in conflict with other dates of move, items such as year of marriage, date of moving to Chicago (if a migrant), the work history (which includes the year in which each job began), and a question relating to the length of stay in the present neighborhood were studied in order to determine if a reasonable estimate could be made of the year of movement. For instance, if a nonmigrant mentioned that he moved because he got married, the coder would refer to the marital history section of the questionnaire to ascertain if the date of marriage was available.

[8] Unfortunately, the thorough coding of the residential histories disclosed frequent gaps in the middle of the mobility histories, found to be caused by the structure of the questionnaire. The respondents were asked several questions about their first two residences in Chicago and then a final question which was intended to pick up information on any other residences in Chicago. Many respondents mentioned their most recent residences and their first two residences in Chicago, but neglected to account for the intervening years. Missing information was assigned a special coding category in order that the mobility rates might be adjusted for the discontinuities in the residential histories. Then by means of a computer search routine, each residential history was summarzed as a single rate:

$$\text{Annual rate of mobility (within Chicago)} = \frac{T}{Y - G}$$

where T is the total number of known residences in Chicago (including last place lived as a dependent or before age 13 if a nonmigrant)
  Y is the total number of years lived in Chicago (from age 18 if living as a dependent at that age)
  G is the number of years of missing information.

In comparison with the white respondents, the Negroes had higher average rates of mobility; slightly over one-half of the whites moved on the average less frequently than once every five years (that is, an annual rate of less than .20), while nearly three-fourths of the Negroes moved at least every five years.

Negro-White Differentials in Rate of Movement: A Preliminary Accounting

The literature on residential mobility suggests several factors which may account for the observed higher rates of Negro mobility:

1. A much higher proportion of the nonwhites are migrants (76 per cent compared to 50 per cent of the whites), and migrants, at least initially, exhibit higher rates of intra-city movement than do nonmigrants.

2. The two groups may differ in ability to recall past mobility history; lifetime residents of Chicago may forget more residences than do recent migrants.

3. The higher rates of Negro mobility may be attributed to differences in age composition or life-cycle stage between the two groups.

4. Given the large disparities in educational attainment, income, and occupations between Negro and white urban populations, the higher mobility rates of Negroes may be a consequence of these differentials in socioeconomic status.

Although the above accounting scheme is purposely limited to variables contained in the present study, it does include most of the important correlates of mobility as reported in other studies.[9] Other possible explanations for the higher rates of Negro mobility will be discussed after the above possibilities are explored.

Migration status. In this study a respondent was classified as a nonmigrant if he was born in Chicago or moved to the city before age 16 or if he was born in Chicago, moved away for less than five years after age 16, and then returned to Chicago. All other individuals were considered migrants. The findings of earlier studies,[10] which showed that migrants (inter-city movers) had higher rates of intra-city movement than nonmigrants, are clearly borne out in this study:

[9] References to these studies are listed in footnotes 10, 12, 20, and 25.

[10] See Sidney Goldstein, *Patterns of Mobility, 1910-1950* (Philadelphia: University of Pennsylvania, 1958); and Peter A. Morrison, "Duration of Residence and Prospective Migration: The Evaluation of a Stochastic Model," *Demography*, 4 (1967), pp. 553–561.

Annual Rate of Mobility	Per Cent of White Nonmigrants	Per Cent of Nonwhite Nonmigrants	Per Cent of White Migrants	Per Cent of Nonwhite Migrants
.00–.09	23.5	10.5	10.3	3.7
.10–.19	39.6	23.6	28.5	20.8
.20–.29	19.4	18.2	17.6	14.8
.30–.49	11.8	22.7	15.8	23.6
.50 or higher	5.8	24.9	27.7	37.1
Total	100.0	100.0	100.0	100.0

Mobility rates for both racial groups are higher for migrants than for nonmigrants, but the nonwhite mobility rate exceeds the white rate even when migration status is held constant.

DURATION OF PRESENT RESIDENCE. Another technique for estimating the rate of movement of a given population is to ask people how long they have lived at their present residences. Although the usefulness of this method is rather limited for studying individual behavior, since past mobility is not taken into account, the problem of memory errors is not as critical as it is in the annual rate of mobility measure. In this case, respondents may report their length of residence incorrectly by a few years, while in the former measure, people may not only err in giving dates of their previous residences, but they may also forget to mention some.

In terms of duration of present residence, the Negroes reported a slightly shorter average length of residence than did the white respondents. About 52 per cent of the whites had lived at their present residences more than five years, while only 42 per cent of the nonwhites reported having lived at their present residences that long. The duration of present residence statistics thus gives support to the hypothesis that the higher rates of mobility for Negroes are real, that is, they are not caused by white and nonwhite differences in recall of residential histories.[11]

FAMILY LIFE CYCLE. Since changes in work status and family composition often necessitate a residential move, many investigators have attempted to explain residential mobility in terms of the typical family life cycle.[12] Two variables, age of the head of the household and a family type classification (based on marital status and the number of dependent children living in the household at the time of the interview), are used in this study to describe the family life cycle.[13]

The possibility that the higher mobility rates of Negroes can be attributed to age differentials is quickly dispelled by the data in Table 1. Mobil-

[11] It was also evident from a cross-tabulation of annual rate of mobility of whites and nonwhites by duration of present residence that the Negro rates remained higher even when duration of present residence was held constant.

[12] See Edgar W. Butler, Georges Sabagh, and Maurice D. Van Arsdol, Jr., "Demographic and Social Psychological Factors in Residential Mobility," *Sociology and Social Research*, 48 (Jan., 1964); Gerald R. Leslie and Arthur H. Richardson, "Life-Cycle, Career Pattern, and the Decision to Move," *American Sociological Review*, 26 (Dec., 1961), p. 890; Peter H. Rossi, *Why Families Move* (Glencoe, Ill: The Free Press, 1955); and Shryock, *Population Mobility*, p. 408.

[13] J. B. Lansing and L. Kish, "Family Life Cycle as an Independent Variable," *American Sociological Review*, 22 (Oct., 1957), pp. 512–519.

TABLE 1

Average Annual Rate of Intra-city Mobility of White and Nonwhite Household Heads, by Age: Chicago Sample

Average Annual Rate of Intra-city Mobility	Total Per Cent	Age of Household Head				
		5–24 Per Cent	25–34 Per Cent	35–44 Per Cent	45–64 Per Cent	65+ Per Cent
White						
.00–.09	16.9	5.1	1.0	5.6	21.3	43.8
.10–.19	34.1	10.4	17.2	39.0	38.3	45.8
.20–.29	18.5	25.9	22.4	14.7	12.4	1.9
.30–.49	13.8	–	29.1	21.8	18.7	4.8
.50+	16.6	58.6	30.2	19.0	9.3	3.7
(Number of respondents)	(825)	(42)	(178)	(163)	(296)	(146)
Nonwhite						
.00–.09	5.3	–	1.7	2.9	9.3	13.0
.10–.19	21.5	3.5	4.3	20.3	36.8	37.8
.20–.29	15.7	2.8	8.6	22.6	18.8	16.8
.30–.49	23.4	7.7	31.0	29.3	16.0	18.5
.50+	34.1	85.9	54.4	25.0	19.2	13.9
(Number of respondents)	(709)	(43)	(188)	(191)	(231)	(56)

ity rates for both racial groups start at a relatively high level and then decline with age, and the nonwhite mobility rate exceeds the white rate within each age group.[14] When both migration status and age composition are held constant, the rate of residential mobility is still higher for nonwhites than it is for whites.

It is evident from Table 2, which cross-classifies rate of mobility by migration status and family type, that families with dependent children have the highest rates of intra-city movement. Moreover, families with three or more dependent children are more mobile than families with only one or two children. These data agree with Rossi's findings that families with children are most likely to express desires and plans about moving.[15]

Are the observed rates of residential mobility for nonwhites merely a reflection of differences in the proportion of whites and nonwhites in the various stages of the family life cycle, especially since families with three or more children are more prevalent among nonwhites (26 per cent) than among whites (13 per cent)? A comparison of the mobility rates of white migrants and nonmigrants in each family type with corresponding rates for nonwhites clearly indicates that the difference between white and nonwhite mobility rates does not disappear when migration status and family type are held constant (see Table 2).[16]

SOCIOECONOMIC STATUS. Table 3 cross-classifies rate of movement by race, migration status, and educational attainment, revealing that a positive association between rate of mobility and level of educational attainment is strongly apparent for both white nonmigrants and migrants, slightly evident for nonwhite migrants, and not present for nonwhite nonmigrants.[17] Thus, holding the level of educational attainment constant does not eliminate the mobility differentials by race.

It is possible that the positive relationship between mobility and education among whites reflects the real rise in educational attainment in the United States during the last few decades; older persons, on the average, have lower mobility rates and lower educational attainment. Since nonwhites have also made substantial gains in educational attainment in re-

[14] One must be cautious in interpreting the decline in mobility rates between successive age categories as representing true mobility patterns, since these data do not represent the same individuals at different periods of time, but rather groups of people ("cohorts") of similar age who were interviewed at approximately the same point in time. Thus, in 20 years the survivors of the 15–24 age cohort may display different patterns of mobility than their elders now in the 34–44 age category, and vise versa.

[15] Rossi, *Why Families Move*, p. 6.

[16] The cautious reader may wish to challenge the preceding interpretation of Table 2 since the family type classification is based on a single period of time (date of interview) whereas the mobility rate is based on a span of time (lifetime residence in Chicago). For instance, the family type classification fails to distinguish between childless families and households whose children have grown up and left the home. Nevertheless, the white-nonwhite mobility differentials are also evident when duration of present residence is cross-classified by color and family type.

[17] The absence of a strong association between education and intra-city mobility for nonwhites seems to preclude the possibility that the positive association for whites is attributed to differential recall of residential histories by level of educational attainment.

cent years,[18] however, one must look elsewhere for an explanation of this phenomenon. The observed relationship between mobility and education may simply reflect certain characteristics of the occupations (for example, financial remuneration and rate of job turnover) held by people with different levels of educational preparation. The lower association between mobility and education for nonwhites might be attributed to racial discrimination in employment; that is, Negroes receive a relatively lower "return" for a given educational investment.[19]

As Table 4 shows, controlling for occupation also fails to eliminate race differentials in rate of movement. Most of the differences in mobility rates between occupational groups are quite small, perhaps because of the grossness of the occupational categories. Nevertheless, a similar pattern is evident for whites and nonwhites: frequent movers were most numerous among laborers and operatives and least represented among household and service workers.[20]

Although Census figures show higher rates of intra-county mobility among nonwhites, the whites have a higher inter-county mobility. Henry S. Shryock, Jr., offers the following explanation of this phenomenon:

> The greater extent of short-distance mobility among nonwhites may reflect the facts that a larger proportion of them than of whites live in rented homes and that renters are more mobile than owners. On the other side, greater financial resources, on the average, and greater ability to secure a job in another area may be major factors in the larger proportion of inter-county movers among whites.[21]

Economic factors do appear to be an important reason for the higher short-distance mobility of Negroes. Although the mobility histories in the present study did not include information on home ownership, this factor alone would not be sufficient to explain the higher mobility rates of nonwhites, since only a small minority of white (32.9 per cent) and nonwhite (12.1 per cent) households in Chicago in 1950 were owner-occupied dwelling units.[22] Furthermore, many of the homeowners who were inter-

[18] John K. Folger and Charles B. Nam, "Educational Trends from Census Data," *Demography*, 1 (1964), pp. 247–257.

[19] Racial discrimination is not consistent across all occupations, but is most apparent in managerial, sales, craft, and operative occupations. See Donald J. Brogue, *The Population of the United States* (Glencoe, Ill.: The Free Press, 1959), pp. 511–514; and Paul M. Siegel, "On the Cost of Being a Negro," *Sociological Inquiry*, 35 (Winter, 1965), pp. 41–57.

[20] With the exception of household and service workers, the pattern of rates in Table 4 agrees with national estimates of intra-county mobility from the Census *Current Population Reports* (see the excellent review in Bogue, *Population of the United States*, pp. 384–386) and with the migration expectancy rates (intra- and inter-county mobility) computed by George L. Wilber ("Migration Expectancy in the United States," *Journal of the American Statistical Association*, 58 [June, 1963], pp. 444–453) from the 1958 *Current Population Report* on mobility in the United States.

[21] Shryock, *Population Mobility*, pp. 335–336.

[22] Otis Dudley Duncan and Beverly Duncan, *The Negro Population of Chicago* (Chicago: The University of Chicago Press, 1957), Table 23, p. 80.

TABLE 2

Average Annual Rate of Intra-city Mobility of White and Nonwhite Household Heads, by Migration Status and by Family Type: Chicago Sample

| Average Annual Rate of Intra-city Mobility | Total Per Cent | Family Type | | | | | | | | |
| | | Male head | | | Female head | | | Single person | |
		No dep. children Per Cent	1-2 children Per Cent	3+ children Per Cent	No dep. children Per Cent	1-2 children Per Cent	3+ children Per Cent	Male Per Cent	Female Per Cent
White Nonmigrant									
.00–.09	23.5	31.6	9.9	10.9	46.7	21.4	8.3	25.4	47.6
.10–.19	39.6	39.3	46.3	40.1	26.2	15.1	16.7	53.2	42.7
.20–.29	19.4	14.0	24.3	28.5	15.6	18.2	–	14.3	2.9
.30–.49	11.8	10.1	14.8	12.4	8.0	24.5	16.7	4.0	6.8
.50+	5.8	5.0	4.7	8.1	3.4	20.8	58.3	3.2	–
Total	100.0	100.0	100.0	100.0	100.0	100.0	100.0	100.0	100.0
N =	(359)	(90)	(109)	(49)	(52)	(16)	(5)	(24)	(14)
Nonwhite Nonmigrant									
.00–.09	10.5	31.2	8.9	7.0	9.0	6.5	1.9	18.7	–
.10–.19	23.6	14.6	32.5	32.0	32.1	25.8	4.6	18.7	41.7
.20–.29	18.2	27.1	12.2	9.0	35.9	15.1	19.4	6.2	–

									Total
.30–.49	16.7	6.2	19.4	36.6	15.4	26.0	20.3	21.9	22.7
.50+	41.7	50.0	54.6	16.1	7.7	26.0	26.0	5.2	24.9
Total	100.0	100.0	100.0	100.0	100.0	100.0	100.0	100.0	100.0
N=	(4)	(7)	(24)	(19)	(19)	(31)	(44)	(26)	(174)

White Migrant

									Total
.00–.09	16.8	7.5	3.1	1.9	13.0	0.7	4.1	16.3	10.3
.10–.19	10.3	19.5	21.9	31.2	49.9	24.1	21.6	32.7	28.5
.20–.29	27.7	1.3	3.1	18.8	12.1	23.0	22.1	15.9	17.6
.30–.49	20.3	17.3	14.1	4.5	4.5	14.0	23.9	15.2	15.8
.50+	24.8	54.4	57.8	43.5	20.4	38.2	28.3	19.9	27.7
Total	100.0	100.0	100.0	100.0	100.0	100.0	100.0	100.0	100.0
N =	(23)	(34)	(9)	(15)	(51)	(47)	(107)	(180)	(466)

Nonwhite Migrant

									Total
.00–.09	4.2	–	–	4.3	9.2	1.3	5.9	2.2	3.7
.10–.19	–	22.0	13.0	10.1	32.2	12.8	20.8	25.0	20.8
.20–.29	10.4	34.1	9.9	18.0	21.0	12.2	12.2	14.2	14.8
.30–.49	20.8	17.1	39.1	19.4	18.6	26.3	20.1	24.0	23.6
.50+	64.6	26.8	37.9	48.2	19.0	47.4	40.9	34.6	37.1
Total	100.0	100.0	100.0	100.0	100.0	100.0	100.0	100.0	100.0
N=	(13)	(12)	(37)	(35)	(84)	(88)	(94)	(172)	(535)

TABLE 3

Average Annual Rate of Intra-city Mobility of White and Nonwhite Household Heads, by Migration Status and by Educational Attainment:
Chicago Sample

Average Annual Rate of Intra-city Mobility	Total Per Cent	Last Grade Completed							
		Less than 4 Per Cent	5–7 Per Cent	8 Per Cent	9–11 Per Cent	12 Per Cent	13–15 Per Cent	16 Per Cent	More than 16 Per Cent
				White Nonmigrant					
.00–.09	23.5	56.4	41.7	33.4	27.4	16.9	8.0	4.5	20.5
.10–.19	39.6	43.6	37.1	49.8	41.2	38.2	42.6	26.4	16.7
.20–.29	19.4	–	–	9.9	12.8	26.1	33.0	40.6	37.9
.30–.49	11.8	–	7.6	5.8	11.4	12.3	11.3	24.4	25.0
.50+	5.8	–	13.6	1.1	7.1	6.5	5.0	4.0	–
N =	(359)	(8)	(35)	(50)	(97)	(91)	(40)	(25)	(13)
				Nonwhite Nonmigrant					
.00–.09	10.5	25.0	–	7.9	4.5	20.4	10.6	–	42.9
.10–.19	23.6	75.0	35.1	36.8	19.4	15.9	17.2	78.3	57.1
.20–.29	18.2	–	35.1	7.9	10.9	22.3	27.2	–	–

.30–49	22.7	—	21.6	18.4	30.3	15.3	25.2	17.4	—
.50+	24.9	—	8.1	28.9	34.8	26.1	19.9	4.3	—
N=	(174)	(4)	(15)	(12)	(46)	(47)	(38)	(9)	(3)

White Migrant

.00–09	10.3	18.7	7.1	13.1	9.5	8.2	11.9	11.0	2.1
.10–19	28.5	33.9	40.3	29.0	22.6	31.8	20.6	20.0	21.4
.20–29	17.6	7.8	16.8	14.2	22.8	21.8	21.8	3.7	27.6
.30–49	15.8	10.7	16.5	23.5	16.3	8.1	22.0	21.0	8.3
.50+	27.7	28.9	19.3	20.1	28.8	30.1	23.7	44.3	40.7
N =	(466)	(58)	(75)	(74)	(79)	(74)	(48)	(32)	(26)

Nonwhite Migrant

.00–09	3.7	1.8	3.8	6.2	4.5	2.1	5.4	—	—
.10–19	20.8	25.2	28.4	28.4	11.7	9.6	18.9	27.8	38.5
.20–29	14.8	18.0	9.9	14.9	15.0	18.8	18.0	9.3	—
.30–49	23.6	19.5	22.3	20.7	28.0	28.8	19.8	9.3	61.5
.50+	37.1	35.4	35.4	29.8	40.8	40.8	37.8	53.7	—
N =	(535)	(92)	(113)	(80)	(118)	(79)	(34)	(15)	(4)

TABLE 4

Average Annual Rate of Intra-city Mobility of White and Nonwhite Household Heads, by Occupation in Labor Force: Chicago Sample

Average Annual Rate of Intra-city Mobility	Total Per Cent	Occupation in Labor Force						
		Professionals, proprietors, and managers Per Cent	Clerical and sales Per Cent	Craftsmen Per Cent	Operatives Per Cent	Household and service Per Cent	Laborers Per Cent	Not in labor force Per Cent
White								
.00–09	16.9	13.4	15.4	14.7	8.1	22.7	5.3	36.0
.10–19	34.1	27.2	34.0	35.1	32.7	41.7	21.0	45.2
.20–29	18.5	25.6	22.8	26.4	14.7	3.4	12.5	6.5
.30–49	13.8	13.2	16.8	15.8	15.4	16.6	27.1	2.4
.50+	16.6	20.5	11.0	8.0	29.0	15.6	34.2	9.9
Total	100.0	100.0	100.0	100.0	100.0	100.0	100.0	100.0
N =	(825)	(166)	(136)	(133)	(150)	(54)	(47)	(139)
Nonwhite								
.00–09	5.3	7.7	8.3	7.2	3.1	6.2	0.4	5.9
.10–19	21.5	28.2	16.3	24.2	20.2	21.7	16.9	24.7
.20–29	15.7	9.6	14.7	14.4	12.4	23.0	14.7	16.9
.30–49	23.4	39.7	21.9	16.0	24.7	23.7	22.1	21.5
.50+	34.1	14.7	38.8	38.1	39.6	25.4	45.9	30.9
Total	100.0	100.0	100.0	100.0	100.0	100.0	100.0	100.0
N =	(709)	(57)	(99)	(56)	(178)	(107)	(65)	(147)

viewed during this study very likely resided in rented dwelling units during their earlier years of residence in Chicago.[23]

Although this study does not have available information on home ownership, it does have an income-welfare index which shows the difference between a family's income and its needs.[24] Presumably, families with a more favorable income-welfare ratio (higher surplus) would contain a higher proportion of home owners, or at least would have less trouble renting and retaining an apartment adequate for their needs in a neighborhood of their choice. In general, mobility is weakly associated with the income-welfare ratio in an inverse fashion (see Table 5). Controlling for the income-welfare ratio, however, does not eliminate the higher mobility rates among nonwhites.[25]

SUMMARY. An accounting scheme composed of factors prominent in previous studies of metropolitan residential mobility fails to explain the observed racial differentials in rate of movement. The higher rates of Negro mobility persist when inter-city mobility, family life-cycle position,

[23] Indirect evidence from a multiple regression analysis performed with 1960 Chicago Census tract statistics also tends to refute the possibility that the slightly higher proportion of homeowners among whites is sufficient to account for the observed differentials. The limitations of the ecological correlation model for drawing inferences about individual behavior is minimized as the proportion of individuals having a certain characteristic approaches either 0 or 100 per cent in each ecological unit. That is, if all Census tracts were either 100 per cent white or 100 per cent nonwhite and contained the same number of inhabitants, then an ecological correlation between per cent nonwhite and a second characteristic may be used to draw inferences about the corresponding individual correlation. Neither of these two conditions, of course, are met in the Chicago Census tract statistics. These data, however, suggest that home ownership is not sufficient to account for the mobility differentials: the zero-order correlation between the per cent of local movers (resided in a different house in the same county in 1955) and the per cent nonwhite was +0.42, and this was not substantially changed (+0.41) when the per cent of owner-occupied housing was held constant.

[24] The income-welfare ratio was calculated by dividing family income by an estimate of family need based on annual rent and personal needs for all relations in the dwelling unit. Each household was assigned to one of eight categories:

Ratio	Category	Per Cent of Whites	Per Cent of Nonwhites
less than 0.5	Destitute	4.5	18.4
0.5–0.9	Poor	6.0	22.3
1.0–1.2	Minimum Adequate	8.2	15.4
1.3–1.4	Adequate	10.2	8.1
1.5–1.9	Minimum Comfortable	23.1	14.7
2.0–2.4	Comfortable	15.9	9.4
2.5–2.9	Affluent	15.5	7.2
3.0 or higher	Wealthy	16.6	4.5
Total		100.0	100.0

[25] Interpretation of this table is hampered by the multi-dimensionality of the income-welfare ratio, since a shift in this index may reflect either a change in family size or a change in family income. Thus, it is not clear whether the high mobility of the destitute and poor is related to economic factors or to an above-average family size. The *Current Population Reports* on mobility for 1962–1963, 1963–1964, 1964–1965 and 1965–1966 provide a partial answer to this question: the rate of intra-county mobiltiy is inversely related to income, and this relationship is slightly enhanced when age is controlled.

TABLE 5

Average Annual Rate of Intra-city Mobility of White and Nonwhite Household Heads, by Income-Welfare Ratio

Average Annual Rate of Intra-city Mobility	Total Per Cent	Destitute Per Cent	Poor Per Cent	Minimum Adequate Per Cent	Adequate Per Cent	Minimum Comfort. Per Cent	Comfortable Per Cent	Affluent Per Cent	Wealthy Per Cent
				White					
.00–.09	16.9	21.4	22.3	18.1	16.1	11.3	17.7	18.7	19.2
.10–.19	34.1	27.9	32.1	44.9	32.0	36.9	26.3	35.9	34.6
.20–.29	18.5	5.2	4.5	13.4	21.7	18.3	26.0	19.6	20.0
.30–.49	13.8	4.7	13.8	10.0	12.8	16.9	20.0	14.5	7.8
.50+	16.6	40.9	27.4	13.7	17.5	16.6	10.0	11.2	18.3
Total	100.0	100.0	100.0	100.0	100.0	100.0	100.0	100.0	100.0
N =	(825)	(60)	(67)	(80)	(76)	(189)	(121)	(113)	(119)
				Nonwhite					
.00–.09	5.3	4.4	4.2	4.9	8.6	5.1	1.7	13.2	5.2
.10–.19	21.5	18.1	22.0	23.1	11.5	21.8	22.4	27.5	32.8
.20–.29	15.7	16.8	14.2	13.9	19.6	6.8	30.0	16.4	17.2
.30–.49	23.4	21.7	17.9	25.2	23.0	26.9	24.5	23.8	37.1
.50+	34.1	38.9	41.7	32.9	37.3	39.4	21.5	19.0	7.8
Total	100.0	100.0	100.0	100.0	100.0	100.0	100.0	100.0	100.0
N =	(709)	(137)	(128)	(102)	(65)	(112)	(80)	(56)	(29)

and socioeconomic status indicators are controlled. Of course, there is a very slight possibility that the differences between the two races might vanish if it had been technically possible to control all of these factors simultaneously. A more likely explanation for the higher rates of Negro mobility, which emphasizes the "push" dimension of the "push-pull" migration model, is offered below.

DISCUSSION

The observed Negro-white differentials in frequency of residential movement may be caused either by push or pull factors or by a combination of the two. If the family is pushed, residential movement is precipitated by factors related to the previous place of residence: overcrowding, an increase in rent, eviction, a change in neighborhood character, etc. Since nonwhites are more likely than whites to be renters, to be residents of areas undergoing urban renewal, and to be financially impoverished, the observed mobility differences may be attributed to a higher incidence of push factors among nonwhites.

The distribution of pulls, factors pertaining to residential possibilities, may also vary between the two racial groups. According to the literature, aspirations for social status in the forms of home ownership and a better neighborhood are the prominent pull factors among whites.[26] Even though Negroes may share some of the values and norms of the white community regarding social mobility, these aspirations are likely to be tempered by the reality of residential segregation. Indeed, in the present study, Negroes moved less frequently to a higher-status neighborhood than did whites.[27] Thus, it is doubtful that pull factors would contribute very much to an explanation of the higher rates of Negro mobility.

From a structural standpoint, the Negro mobility patterns may be viewed as a partial consequence of residential segregation and the Negro housing market. Generally, Negroes have received lower-quality housing than whites for a given rent rate (or sale price) and have faced a stronger seller's market.[28] Perhaps, because of the characteristics of this market, Negroes often settle temporarily in inadequate or substandard housing

[26] Inquiries into the relationship between vertical and horizontal residential mobility include Wendell Bell, "Familism and Suburbanization: One Test of the Social Choice Hypothesis," *Rural Sociology*, 21 (Sept.-Dec., 1956), pp. 276–283; Butler, Sabagh, and Van Arsdol, Jr., "Demographic Factors"; Leslie and Richardson, "Life-Cycle"; H. Laurence Ross, "Reasons for Moves to and from a Central City Area," *Social Forces*, 40 (March, 1962), pp. 261–263; Rossi, *Why Families Move*; Harold L. Wattell, "Levittown: A Suburban Community," in William M. Dobriner, ed., *The Suburban Community* (New York: G. P. Putnam's Sons, 1958), pp. 287–313; and Vincent H. Whitney and Charles M. Grigg, "Patterns of Mobility among a Group of Families of College Students, *American Sociological Review*, 23 (Dec., 1958), pp. 643–652.

[27] Bruce C. Straits and Paul L. Wuebben, "Occupational Advancement and Vertical Residential Mobility among Negroes and Whites in Chicago," paper read at the 1968 meetings of the American Sociological Association, Boston, August, 1968.

[28] See Duncan and Duncan, *Negro Population of Chicago*, pp. 80–82; and Karl E. Taeuber and Alma F. Taeuber, *Negroes in Cities* (Chicago: Aldine Publishing Co., 1965).

and move as often as they find a better situation.[29] In addition, Negroes may be forced to move more often than whites for involuntary reasons such as shifts in land usage precipitated by urban renewal or freeway construction.

Recent changes in the quality and quantity of housing units available to nonwhites, caused by whites fleeing to the suburbs, is also an important factor.[30] In Chicago, the city's white population decreased by 13 per cent (from 3,111,525 to 2,712,748) between 1950 and 1960, while the Negro population during the same decade increased by 65 per cent (from 492,265 to 812,637).[31] It is possible that the "population pressure" built up in the ghettos by the influx of recent Negro migrants leads to the displacement of whites by Negroes along the periphery of the Negro residential areas. As people opt for the resulting vacancies, there is a chain of moves within the Negro community.

One of the most prominent features of Negro ghetto life, according to ethnographic accounts, is the transient character of personal, family, and employment relationships.[32] This fluidity and change which characterizes the life style of many urban Negroes may be an important push determinant of Negro residential mobility. Although the "static" measures of family composition and employment status contained in the present study are inadequate to test a hypothesis linking Negro residential mobility to family and employment instability, some suggestive data are available on mobility by type of neighborhood. These findings, which show slightly greater spatial mobility (net distance of movement) among Negro than among white slum residents, are described below.

The residences reported by the respondents in this study were located by Census tract, and the net distance in miles between the first adulthood place of residence in Chicago (last place lived as a dependent or before age 18 for Chicago-born respondents) and the present residence was computed from the geometric coordinates of the Census tracts.[33] Census tract statistics for 1950 were employed to classify the present neighborhood of each respondent as either a slum, a blighted area, a middle-class section, or an upper-class housing area.[34]

[29] One index of inadequate housing, the per cent of housing units with 1.01 or more persons per room (the average obtained by dividing the number of persons by the number of rooms in the unit), was strongly correlated with the per cent of nonwhites ($+0.75$) and the per cent of local moves ($+0.40$) in 1960 Chicago Census tracts.

[30] Easing of the tight housing market that had prevailed during World War II facilitated this expansion of the urban Negro housing market.

[31] Evelyn M. Kitagawa and Karl E. Taeuber, eds., *Local Community Fact Book, Chicago Metropolitan Area,* 1960 (Chicago: Chicago Community Inventory, University of Chicago, 1963), Table I-3, p. 9.

[32] See, for example, Elliot Liebow, *Tally's Corner* (Boston: Little, Brown and Company, 1967); E. Franklin Frazier, *The Negro Family in the United States* (Chicago: University of Chicago Press, 1939); and U.S., Department of Labor, Office of Policy Planning and Research, *The Negro Family: The Case for National Action* (The Moynihan Report), March, 1965.

[33] *Guide for Coding Street Address to Community Area and Census Tract* (Chicago: Chicago Community Inventory, University of Chicago, May, 1961).

[34] The following criteria were used:

Table 6, which cross-tabulates net distance of movement by race, migration status, and type of area, reveals that over half of the slum residents are now living within two miles of their first places of residence within Chicago, whereas about one-third of the respondents living in middle-class neighborhoods and slightly less than one-tenth of those living in upper-class neighborhoods now live this close to their first residences. These data strongly suggest that the majority of slum dwellers either were raised in such a neighborhood or moved into a slum area when they migrated to Chicago. This statement may be challenged on the ground that an area within a two-mile radius of the center of a slum census tract may contain upper- and middle-class neighborhoods, or did so in the past.[35] Such a challenge proves irrelevant, however. Indeed, the relationship between net distance of movement and type of neighborhood is even stronger if one examines the proportion of respondents who are now living within *one* mile of their first place of residence (see table 6). A similar relationship is observed when distance of movement is measured in terms of miles from the center of Chicago or in terms of the proportion of respondents who have not moved out of their first Census tract of residence.[36]

Slum: All Census tracts in 1950 where 20 per cent or more of the dwelling units
      were substandard (either dilapidated structures or structures without a
      private bath and hot and cold running water)
Blighted: All Census tracts where 10–19 per cent of the dwellings were substandard
Middle: Less than 10 per cent substandard, median income under $4,500.
Upper: Median income over $4,500.
The terms "neighborhood" and "Census tract" of residence will be used interchangeably throughout the rest of this article.

[35] Inspection of a map showing the distribution of Chicago Census tracts classified by type of area revealed that most of the residential areas lying within a two-mile radius from any slum location contain either slum or blighted neighborhoods. Similarly, the majority of tracts contiguous to upper-class tracts are also upper-class neighborhoods, and the remainder are almost entirely middle-class. While there is some intermingling of slum and blighted tracts, and of middle-class and upper-class tracts, the separation between the slum and blighted tracts on the one hand, and the middle- and upper-class tract on the other, is very pronounced. Thus, most of the 69 per cent of white nonmigrant slum residents and 46 per cent of nonwhite nonmigrant slum residents who reported living presently within two miles of their first Chicago addresses were raised in areas which are now slums. Whether these areas were slums at the time of the respondents' adolescences is not easy to determine, but available evidence indicates that these areas have been deteriorated for many years. For instance, 70 per cent of the Chicago Community Areas classified as slums in 1950 (which meant that they had a higher proportion of substandard dwelling units than the average for the city of Chicago—19.6 per cent) contained a higher proportion of dwelling units in need of major repair in 1930 than the city average for that period (source: Louis Wirth and Eleanor H. Bernert, eds., *Local Community Fact Book of Chicago* [Chicago: The University of Chicago Press, 1949]).

[36] A further problem in interpreting these data on neighborhood type is that the four types of residential areas have had different rates of growth or decline in the last few decades. That is, the probability that a nonmigrant (or a migrant, though to a lesser extent) will still be living near his first place of residence may be seriously understated for upper-class neighborhoods because of the large population expansion in these areas in recent decades. Adjustment of the figures in Table 6 to control for popu-

TABLE 6

Net Distance between First and Present Residence of White and Nonwhite Household Heads, by Migration Status and by Type of Area: Chicago Sample

Net Distance between First and Present Residence	Total Per Cent	Type of Area			
		Slum Per Cent	Blighted Per Cent	Middle Per Cent	Upper Per Cent
White Nonmigrant					
Less than 1 mile	21.0	51.7	31.7	14.4	6.6
1–1.9 miles	12.5	16.9	22.2	11.9	4.6
2–2.9 miles	11.5	6.1	6.0	14.1	11.2
3–3.9 miles	14.1	8.1	25.2	14.7	11.4
4–4.9 miles	7.7	4.0	8.5	8.7	7.7
5–5.9 miles	5.6	4.6	—	4.3	14.0
6–6.9 miles	5.5	0.3	0.7	8.5	3.2
7–7.9 miles	8.1	3.9	3.2	8.4	14.5
8–8.9 miles	3.1	—	—	4.8	2.4
9–9.9 miles	3.0	0.3	—	2.5	9.3
10 miles or more	7.8	4.1	2.2	7.8	15.1
Total	100.0	100.0	100.0	100.0	100.0
N =	(354)	(96)	(52)	(154)	(52)
Nonwhite Nonmigrant					
Less than 1 mile	19.0	25.7	12.5	18.1	—
1–1.9 miles	17.6	20.8	29.2	15.9	1.5
2–2.9 miles	19.4	25.7	50.0	9.3	6.1
3–3.9 miles	10.0	1.1	—	9.7	54.5
4–4.9 miles	5.3	5.9	—	6.2	3.0
5–5.9 miles	2.6	1.1	—	4.0	6.1
6–6.9 miles	7.4	7.8	—	3.5	24.2
7–7.9 miles	8.2	4.5	—	16.8	—
8–8.9 miles	5.6	1.1	8.3	11.9	—

9-9.9 miles	3.0	–	–	–	0.3
10 miles or more	1.5	4.4	–	6.3	4.6
Total	100.0	100.0	100.0	100.0	100.0
N =	(21)	(60)	(16)	(71)	(168)

White Migrant

Less than 1 mile	9.2	22.7	33.2	36.0	26.6
1–1.9 miles	3.6	12.0	16.5	19.6	13.9
2–2.9 miles	8.8	15.5	10.7	8.6	11.9
3–3.9 miles	21.0	5.5	12.2	6.4	9.0
4–4.9 miles	3.2	13.2	11.3	8.5	10.3
5–5.9 miles	6.2	4.4	7.1	5.7	5.5
6–6.9 miles	10.2	3.7	0.3	4.0	4.0
7–7.9 miles	3.2	7.6	0.3	2.2	4.2
8–8.9 miles	3.0	6.2	–	0.3	3.0
9–9.9 miles	3.4	3.8	1.9	2.0	2.9
10 miles or more	28.3	5.4	6.5	6.6	8.9
Total	100.0	100.0	100.0	100.0	100.0
N =	(40)	(128)	(74)	(220)	(462)

Nonwhite Migrant

Less than 1 mile	2.6	18.5	7.2	34.9	26.8
1–1.9 miles	5.3	18.2	21.0	16.1	17.0
2–2.9 miles	2.6	10.9	13.8	16.0	14.0
3–3.9 miles	15.8	5.7	18.0	10.4	9.7
4–4.9 miles	10.5	13.8	7.2	6.5	8.9
5–5.9 miles	55.3	10.6	18.6	2.1	7.2
6–6.9 miles	2.6	10.8	3.6	4.7	6.4
7–7.9 miles	–	6.7	1.8	3.1	4.0
8–8.9 miles	2.6	0.7	1.2	2.1	1.6
9–9.9 miles	2.6	0.7	5.4	1.1	1.3
10 miles or more	–	3.4	2.4	2.9	3.0
Total	100.0	100.0	100.0	100.0	100.0
N =	(24)	(133)	(55)	(319)	(531)

Pull factors, such as a desire to own a home or to live in a better neighborhood, may explain a substantial portion of the larger net distances of movement displayed by residents of middle- and upper-class neighborhoods. For slum inhabitants, on the other hand, push factors most likely account for much of their residential movement. If this is true, the ratio of Negro to white net distance of movement should be high for inhabitants of slum and blighted areas (because of the greater prevalence of pushes among Negroes) and low for residents of upper-class neighborhoods (because of the scarcity and spatial location of better housing opportunities for Negroes). Findings based on data presented in Table 6 confirm these expectations:[37]

MEDIAN DISTANCE IN MILES BETWEEN FIRST AND PRESENT
CHICAGO RESIDENCE, BY TYPE OF AREA

	Slum	Blighted	Middle	Upper
White nonmigrants	1.0	1.8	3.7	5.6
Nonwhite nonmigrants	2.1	2.2	3.7	3.8
White migrants	1.7	2.0	3.0	5.7
Nonwhite migrants	1.9	3.4	3.4	5.2

The Negro-white differentials in net distance of movement take on added significance when one realizes that the Negro residential area in Chicago is much smaller and has a higher population density than the area containing white neighborhoods. Consequently, a short-distance move within a Negro ghetto involves greater change in community environment and social milieu, including disruption of social ties, etc., than a move of the same distance within an upper-class white neighborhood. While these findings should be regarded as exploratory, they clearly support the hypothesis that the observed mobility differences between the two races may be attributed to a higher incidence of push factors among Negroes.

---

lation change did not, however, eliminate the observed differences in distance from first Chicago residence by type of area.

[37] The median was calculated rather than the mean, the former measure being less affected by extreme values; these extremes are more prevalent among whites, since the maximum possible distance of movement is greater within the white than within the Negro residential areas.

Variations in the Father Role in Complete Families of the Negro Lower Class

DAVID A. SCHULZ

THE PENNSYLVANIA STATE UNIVERSITY

IN SPITE OF THE FACT THAT THERE ARE NUMEROUS STUDIES OF THE NEGRO IN America, very few have been concerned primarily with the family.[1] Those that have taken the family as a central concern[2] have not been based upon intensive studies such as, for example, Oscar Lewis' studies of poor families in Mexico.[3] Indeed, it is common to think of lower-class Negro families in terms of a simple "fatherless-complete" typology.[4] Consequently Hylan Lewis had to say recently, "In focusing on family homes . . . the present father tends to be forgotten. Forgotten also is the fact that we know very little about him."[5]

Negro family structure has been studied more intensively in the Caribbean. Here the work has been motivated to a large extent by a concern to determine if patterns of nonresidential mating do or no not indicate a breakdown or "disorganization" of the family—a concern originating in the markedly high rates of illegitimacy.[6]

[1] Studies such as Allison Davis and John Dollard, *Children of Bondage* (Washington, D.C.: American Council of Education, 1940); Abram Kardiner and Lionel Ovesey, *The Mark of Oppression* (New York: Meridian Books, 1962); and Hertha Reise, *Heal the Hurt Child* (Chicago: University of Chicago Press, 1962) concentrate on the children. Those such as Kenneth Clark, *Dark Ghetto* (New York: Harper and Row, 1965); Hylan Lewis, *Blackways of Kent* (Chapel Hill: University of North Carolina Press, 1961); and Sinclair Drake and Horace Cayton, *Black Metropolis* (New York: Harcourt, Brace and World, 1945) consider the family as a small portion of a much broader concern for community studies, although Lewis does develop a family typology based on genealogical data.

[2] For example E. Franklin Frazier's *The Negro Family in the United States* (Chicago: University of Chicago Press, 1960) is based largely upon census data and other gross indices of family life combined with the author's own intuitive interpretation of their meaning. It is not based on an examination of how particular families function. The one intensive participant observation study of the Negro lower class by Elliot Liebow (*Tally's Corner* [Boston: Little and Brown, 1967]) only touches upon the family as its main concern is with "corner men."

[3] *The Children of Sanchez* (New York: Random House, 1961) and *Five Families* (New York: Science Editions, Inc., 1962).

[4] This tendency is heightened by the accessibility of Census data. A good idea of the extent to which this dichotomy is considered central to the study of the lower-class Negro family is provided in Thomas Pettigrew, *Profile of the Negro American* (Princeton, N.J.: D. Van Nostrand, Inc., 1964) on page 15 and following. The issue of the relevance of this simple typology was brought forward in the controversy over the Department of Labor's, *The Negro Family: The Case for National Action*, now attributed to Daniel Patrick Moynihan.

[5] Lee Rainwater and William Yancy, *The Moynihan Report and the Politics of Controversy* (Boston: MIT Press, 1967), p. 322.

[6] For a summary of this work see Raymond T. Smith, "Cultural and Social Structure in the Caribbean: Some Recent Work on Family and Kinship Studies" in *Comparative*

Several types of mating patterns are described. Hyman Rodman, for example, found that the natives of Coconut Village distinguished between three types of "marital" relations: "friending," "living," and "married."[7] Friending was a nonresidential pattern similar to one called "visiting" by Roberts and Braithwaite.[8]

The concern of the present study, however, is to describe and analyze some of the variations in the husband-father role in the category that is ordinarily thought of as "married."[9]

THE SAMPLE

The field work focused upon 10 lower-class Negro families living in a large public housing project in a midwestern city. Five of the families were complete, five were fatherless.[10] The age of the parents ranged from 33 to 55. All except two families had teenage children living in the households. The size of the families varied from six to 18 persons and the households from five to 18 persons. The latter included some kin at times but no other boarders. Although about 88 persons lived in these households during most of the study, only three of the households remained relatively stable in size. Data were collected on all household members and most family members.

METHODOLOGY

The majority of the data on these households were collected by means of participant observation[11] and open-ended interviewing. While the researcher did not live with the families, he did spend about 250 ten-hour days on site interacting with the family members in various ways—sometimes obviously studying them and asking direct questions, at other times just enjoying their company at home, in a bar, or on the street. Extensive biographies were taken of all parents and many teenaged members of the

---

Studies in Society and History (The Hague, The Netherlands: Mouton & Co., Oct., 1963).

[7] "Marital Relationships in a Trinidad Village," *Journal of Marriage and Family Living*, 23 (May, 1961), pp. 166–170.

[8] "A Cross-Mating Table for a West Indian Population," *Population Studies*, 14: 3 (1961).

[9] John F. Cuber and Peggy B. Harroff develop a fivefold typology of marriage for the upper middle class that parallels in several respects this attempt, particularly in their discussion of the "conflict habituated" type of marriage which seems similar to this study's "indiscreet free-man." See "The More Total View: Relationships Among Men and Women of the Upper Middle Class," in Hyman Rodman, ed., *Marriage, Family and Society: A Reader* (New York: Random House, 1961).

[10] In the project 54 per cent of the families were headed by females. See Jerome Stromberg, *A Preliminary Report on Housing and Community Experiences: Occasional Paper # 1* (St. Louis: The Social Science Institute of Washington University, 1966). Lefcowitz estimates that only about 23 per cent of the entire lower-class Negro family population was headed by females in 1960. See "Poverty and Negro-White Family Structure," paper presented to the White House Conference, "To Fulfill These Rights," 1965.

[11] In point of fact neither detached observation nor totally immersed participation was ever achieved; the working balance always tended toward one or the other pole.

households, and the assessment of the role played by the father in each household was based upon information obtained from most, if not all, family members plus observations of family interaction. All periods of the waking day were covered in most families, and in one the researcher was invited to spend the night.

Whenever possible a tape recorder was used to record conversations and interviews. Notes were made of all encounters. To supplement the information obtained from family members and to provide additional perspectives on the families, data were obtained from the files of the Housing Authority, the schools, and the police.

A TYPOLOGY OF MARGINALITY

As an exploratory study attempting to document the variety to be found in lower-class Negro family life, the first objective was to describe each family. This objective alone could easily result in ten case studies. Indeed, each family has enough distinctive characteristics to be considered by some researchers as a separate culture.[12] To dichotomize the 10 families simply into "complete" and "fatherless," however, is to grossly oversimplify. A useful compromise can be achieved if one looks at the husband-father role in terms of several significant variables: (1) the "strength" of the conjugal bond, (2) the support given by the father to his family and (3) the relationship of the father to the children. At this stage of the research, none of these variables was rigorously defined or measured, but an immense amount of qualitative data[13] have enabled the researcher to make and support judgments about the relative placement of these families along the dimension of adult male marginality. The 10 families suggest six types. This articles describes the three types of "complete" families.[14]

THE INDISCREET FREE-MAN

The most marginal type of father observed is the indiscreet free-man.[15] What is apparent in his relationship to his family is a split in allegiance between his legitimate family and one or more "illegitimate" families. This outside interest is continually paraded before his wife and family either in a constant, chiding reference to the "other woman" or by the delib-

[12] Jules Henry, "An Anthropological Approach to Cultural, Idiosyncratic and Universal Factors in Behavior," *American Anthropologist.*

[13] The researcher's personal notes on observations and interviews exceed 2,500 typewritten pages and the data on the larger study exceed 20,000 pages.

[14] The researcher is greatly indebted to Lee Rainwater's "notes" entitled "Three Patterns of Separateness and Connectedness in Lower-Class Families: A Typology" although the typology presented in this study is a modification of his. The sixfold typology derived from these families is as follows: monogamous, discreet free-man, indiscreet free-man, quasi-father, supportive biological father, and supportive companion. A seventh and most marginal type, the pimp, was described by the family members but not observed. The last four types are discussed in David A. Schulz and Lee Rainwater, "The Role of the Boyfriend in Lower-Class Negro Life," paper presented to the Midwest Sociological Society, Des Moines, Iowa, 1967.

[15] This type resembles the type of father described as Jesus Sanchez by Lewis in *Children of Sanchez.*

erate engineering of an encounter with her. His interests outside the family are reflected in his spending on behalf of the other woman and, if he has had children by her, a regular amount of money may be set aside each month in their behalf—regardless of whether or not the court has intervened—or, more commonly, he will buy shoes, clothing, and gifts for them from time to time. Such a father's interests have repercussions upon his legitimate children, creating an intensified kind of sibling rivalry with his "outside" children who, in some instances, are known personally by his legitimate children. Life within such families is thus one of constant conflict and bickering. That the family stays intact at all is probably related to (1) the advancing age of the wife which, combined with her many children, makes her less and less attractive to other men and more and more destined to head a household should her husband leave, (2) her continuing hope that he will reform his ways, and (3) his positive, if sporadic contributions in support and affection to his family.

Two families fit this type: the Pattersons and the Boikens. Illustration from the Patterson case will suffice. They had been married 22 years; he was 45, she was 42. They had 18 children including eight "outsiders."[16] All but two were his by other women. Their present household included eight children in age from 9 to 19. Mr. Patterson's earnings as a machine operator for a local automobile manufacturer accounted for $5,593 of the family's $6,072 annual income; his wife's earnings accounted for the balance. He was in complete charge of the money and allowances, expecting his wife to live within her allowance, adequate or not.

About four years ago he left his family to live with another woman by whom he sired two children. Prior to that, in 1955, his wife had had him put in the workhouse for six months for nonsupport while he was living with another woman. His spending, even when he was at home, extended to his several "outside" children, a fact that was fully and painfully known by his wife and legitimate children. When he was at home he generally was shunned by his family and usually ate alone.

He once commented on his marriage:

> I would say that if I had to do it all over again, I don't think I would select this route that I have gone. It hasn't been too pleasant at all times. I mean there's a ruling to everything. You can't run what's in the house and what's on the outside of the house both at the same time . . . so I don't know whether I came in the house too much or whether I stayed on the outside too long. It's a problem somewhere. . . . I don't think it would get serious enough where it would cause another separation. . . . [You] make the best out of what you have. . . . I can walk, shun them, a lot easier than the other person could shun me.

His wife's account of their marriage reflected his indiscretion more vividly:

> Well before we came to the city my husband and I were separated three times on the sake of fighting. He used to fight me all the time. He was in

---

[16] As the term is used in the project it means "outside a particular relationship" which ordinarily terminated in marriage—not simply "outside of wedlock."

the city about nine months before I came. When I came up he was living
with another woman at my uncle's house. . . . I have never walked out in
front of him, but this lady he used to live with, he have had her right out
in front of my door. . . . I asked him not to do it again because he seemed
like he was boasting about it. And the next time he did it . . . I got a gun
and started down the steps and he ran down there by the car. But by the
time I got down under the building he had done pulled off.

His relationships with his children were also strained, particularly those
with his older boys, who generally took the side of their mother against
him. Their oldest boy once lived with the family, but he moved out about
midway in this study in order to avoid a fight with his father, who at the
last encounter had "hit him up side of the head with a shoe." After that
Pattersons' wife claimed that when he walked in the door, "the actual sight
of him made me nervous . . . because I had a fear of his ways."

The older girls, on the other hand, tried to cover up the family feuding
as much as possible, stressing the fact that their father "will still give" to
them. His 18-year-old daughter, B., noted "every family has its ups and
downs . . . some parents be arguing and fighting all the time . . . but they
don't hardly quarrel. . . . One of them will walk away from it. I guess
because they have us and don't want to be setting a bad example in front
of us." The implied denial could not, even for B., cover up Patterson's obvious and flagrant infidelity, which lay at the base of the family conflict.
Mr. Patterson's indiscretion as a free-man made his home all but intoler-
able for him, and a source of embarrassment and hurt for his wife and
children as well.

THE DISCREET FREE-MAN

In contrast to the indiscreet free-man, the discreet free-man's "cutting
out" is clearly a secondary concern, which he does not use to antagonize
his wife and children. As a result his indiscretions are understood and
both partners are likely to admit "we get along well enough." His relationship to his children is not particularly impaired as a result of his
interests outside the home and they often look upon him as an ideal father.
Typically, just as he is able to cover up or minimize his activities with
other women, so also he is able to carry on deviant activities such as
gambling or pimping without these appreciably interfering with his home
life. The relationship can be considered as a separate type, therefore,
because it does not result simply from the fact that the "old man" has not
been caught yet. His indiscretions are known to his wife and family, but
he manages in such a way as not to antagonize them, and thus maintains a relatively comfortable relationship with his legitimate family,
which persists over time.

Two families fit this type: the Washingtons and the Bardwells. The
Washingtons can provide the illustration. The researcher knew them for
over three and one-half years and only toward the end of the study discovered why he knew comparatively little about them. Mr. Washington,
51, and seven of his boys had long police records connected mainly with

gambling and narcotics. The father had once been "sent up" for possession of lottery equipment. Nevertheless, the home was neat, well kept, and his children well mannered. An impression of warmth and intimacy was characteristic of their interactions. He and his wife, who was 47, had been married 26 years and for 19 of these years Mr. Washington had been the major wage earner. During the time of the study he supplemented his wife's earnings as a domestic through efforts at odd jobs and through gambling. Neither source of income was reported in the family's annual income of $4,370. The Washingtons had 12 children including two "outsiders" born before they married.

Mr. Washington said that he had managed to stay married 26 years because "we don't raise a lot of cain. If a little something happens we don't jump down each other's throat." He expressed his conception of marital fidelity in a way that implied he "cuts out" but does not play the field and does not brag about his antics in front of his wife:

> I am this type of fellow. I talk to anyone before my wife or behind my wife. But just to go out and say I've got a bunch of women and that type of thing, that's all baloney. . . . I see some women that look good to me, sure, and if you push it you can get caught in the right corner and you might step out. You're human and you're a good one if you don't. If you just go out and strive directly for that then you're going to find somebody that wants to do these things. The average woman that does it ain't doing it because she likes to but because she wants to do something just like you . . . something different . . . it's not a big deal.

His wife presented a complementary picture of tolerating his discreet outside activities:

> I think I've been a nice lady. I ain't bragging on myself, but it takes a steady head I guess. I never was a wild person and like to get in the streets. I stayed home and took care of my children . . . I didn't leave my children to nobody.

One impressive indicator of the control the parents were able to exercise over themselves and their children was their willingness not to exchange gifts at Christmas time. Mr. Washington said, "It's pretty rough when you know everybody else is receiving them and giving them and you're not . . . but if you understand life . . . you just have to grit your teeth and say, 'Well we doing the best we can, and thank the Lord.'"

Finally, instead of denouncing his delinquent children, as many parents did, Mr. Washington said of his oldest boy, who had the longest record, "He's just another one of my kids regardless of the troubles he's been in. Maybe he made a mistake and maybe he didn't. Maybe he just got the wrong break. That happens too. Sometimes to the best of people."

The family, despite what went on outside, was a central concern for all its members, and Mr. Washington's discretion in handling what went on outside was a major factor in its continuing relative stability.

The Monogamous Father

The last type of father is called the monogamous type because he is proud of the fact that he is able to say, "Where you see me, you will see my wife." This type, although rare in fact, is reflected in the data in numerous references to its desirability. In such a family the father does not "cut out" and if he has had any "outside" children they are the result of youthful indiscretions and not of his violation of monogamous marriage. His home and family are his major concerns and receive his constant attention. Typically, such fathers have good relationships with their children and high status in the family regardless of their ability to earn a living.

Only one family fitted this type in the data: the Fraziers. They had been married 20 years, were the least urbanized of the families studied (lived in the city only seven years) and were the only family in which the father was younger than the mother. He was 37, she 40. He, nevertheless, was an advocate of the patriachal type of family and his wishes in this regard were respected.[17] Because of illiteracy and a fear of the streets the family spent most of its time inside the small row apartment it had rented in the heart of the city—the last of five residencies in which they lived during the last two years of the study. Mr. Frazier received disability checks and his wife received ADC, giving the family an annual income of $4,896 for a family of 11.

For both of the Fraziers "cutting out" was unheard of. They believed that for the parents to do so would result in their complete inability to control their children. Mr. Frazier said:

> I have been to lots of houses and I've seen some pretty rough deals with kids. I'll tell you what that come from. That comes from mother and daddy. If you do any and everything over your child you can't expect no better can you? . . . I don't let my children see me do no wrong thing. . . . I'm not playing [cutting out]. I ain't got nane that can tell you that today. They ain't never seen daddy come in here drunk, cussing, clowning, or nothing. They'll tell you that right now. Daddy is going to come in here as he leaves.

Being thus strong believers in teaching children by example rather than precept, both Fraziers labored to keep themselves respectable "in front of the children" for they knew that the accusation "Mamma, you and Daddy do it" had no acceptable reply—"It ain't nothing for us to say." Thus despite his educational handicaps and his poor earning power, Mr. Frazier was very well thought of in his family and his children were well behaved. The Frazier family was a warm, intimate shelter from the harsh realities

---

[17] In his article "The Impact of Urban Civilization upon Negro Family Life," *American Sociological Review*, 2 (1939), E. Franklin Frazier described a type of family organization originating in rural southern communities of Negro, white, and Indian ancestry that was relatively isolated from the main currents of Negro life and that maintained a strictly patriarchal tradition. The Fraziers seem to have been influenced by this tradition.

of the street and if they had the earning legitimate capacity to become upwardly mobile, such a family would have followed the style of living more characteristic of the working-class nuclear family. Ironically, however, given their economic status, their conception of appropriate family living was a handicap in teaching the children how to cope with the world in which they found themselves. Thus they obtained a degree of intimacy at the expense of acquiring effective survival techniques.

MARGINALITY AND THE MODE OF LEGITIMATING AUTHORITY

An interesting aspect of the internal dynamics of these families was the fact that each type of father made his claim to hold authority in the household on somewhat different grounds.

(1) The monogamous father tended to legitimate his authority on the basis of two more or less equal aspects of his relationship to the external world: his ability as an adequate provider (or the fact that his inability to provide was "understood"), and his ability to say, "There ain't nane that can speak slack of me"—that is, he was an adequate model for respectable behavior. He was not an adaptive strategist because he had been able to "make it" by legitimate means and because his principles prohibited him from being one.

(2) The "discreetly free" fathers, on the other hand, tended to legitimate their authority within the household on the basis of being warm, loving "pals" to their children and expressive companions to more instrumentally oriented wives. They tended also to be able to muster respect for their ability to cope with the environment by means of manipulative strategies such as gambling, "working game" on friends, and discreet affairs with other women, which provided them with victories their sons would have liked to emulate. They were, or at one time had been, adequate providers and their current disability was understood by their families. They expressed concern for "skeletons" in the family closet, indicating they would have liked to draw upon past respectable behavior to provide an example for their children, but could not.

(3) The "indiscreet" fathers had least control over their children because they had little to justify their authority. If they were able to provide for their family, this ability was marred by their split in allegiance. If they were unable, their disability was not accepted and they had to prefabricate an instrumental role in order to protect themselves in this vulnerable area—thus Mr. Boiken, though unemployed, thought of himself as earning $150 a week, the amount earned by the construction crew with which he once worked. They generally had little justification for authority on the basis of their expressive ability, and none as a model for traditional respectable behavior.

CONCLUSION

In an exploratory study based primarily upon such a small number of families the conclusions drawn can only be suggestive. However, the father in lower-class Negro families does not appear to be simply subordinate to his wife, as the term "matriarchal" would indicate and the term "matrifocal" might imply. His status, these data suggest, depends not only upon his capacity to earn a living and his further willingness to share that living with his family, but also upon the degree of his adher-ence to the norms of monogamous marriage, his ability to cope with the harsh realities of the ghetto, and his capacity to be a pal to his children. The family that seems best able to survive as a family unit in a situation where there is little hope of upward mobility or of sufficient income from legitimate sources is the family that is best able to cope with its environment as it presents itself. In such a family the father is typically the discreet free-man.

The cohesiveness of such families in spite of their extreme openness to the life of the street was a source of constant amazement to the researcher, and the extent of the father's influence, particularly as a model for effective coping behavior, was greater than expected.

The Kinship Ties of Negro Urbanites

JOE R. FEAGIN

UNIVERSITY OF CALIFORNIA, RIVERSIDE

IN THE PAST DECADE NUMEROUS EMPIRICAL STUDIES HAVE DISCOVERED IM-portant, if in some cases limited, kinship ties among urban dwellers.[1] Although kinship ties have been found to be of importance to both low-status and high-status urbanites, Gans and Berger, among others, have reported that residents of working-class communities are especially likely to be involved in kinship networks.[2]

In regard to the kinship ties of urban Negro families, whether working class or middle class, the data are much less extensive. Two studies of Detroit and Philadelphia Negroes have reported some data indicating that most Negro urbanites have relatives living in their vicinity and that a majority interact with these relatives regularly.[3] It is the purpose of this paper to report research which corroborates and amplifies these earlier findings and to explore dimensions of Negro kinship ties not yet investigated.

THE SAMPLE

This paper utilizes data collected in connection with an evaluation study of a low-income housing demonstration program in Boston's "Roxbury" Negro ghetto, a rent-supplementation program carried out by the Boston Housing Authority with the financial aid of the U.S. Department of Housing and Urban Development.[4] The evaluation study included three rough-

---

[1] See, for example, Scott Greer and Ella Kube, "Urbanism and Social Structure: A Los Angeles Study," in *Community Structure and Analysis*, edited by M. B. Sussman (New York: Thomas Y. Crowell, 1959), p. 103; Wendell Bell and Marion D. Boat, "Urban Neighborhoods and Informal Social Relations," *American Journal of Sociology*, 62 (Jan., 1957), p. 394.

[2] Herbert J. Gans, *The Urban Villagers* (New York: The Free Press, 1962); Bennett M. Berger, *Working-Class Suburb* (Berkeley: University of California Press, 1960). See also Michael Young and Peter Willmott, *Family and Kinship in East London* (Baltimore: Penguin Books, 1957); Floyd Dotson, "Patterns of Voluntary Associations among Working-Class Families," *American Sociological Review*, 16 (Oct., 1957), pp. 687–693; and J. M. Mogey, *Family and Neighborhood* (London: Oxford University Press, 1956).

[3] Leonard Blumberg and Robert R. Bell, "Urban Migration and Kinship Ties," *Social Problems*, 6 (Spring, 1959), pp. 328–333; Kathryn P. Meadow, "Negro-White Differences among Newcomers to a Transitional Urban Area," *Journal of Intergroup Relations*, 3 (1962), pp. 320–330. See also Clyde V. Kiser, *Sea Island to City: A Study of St. Helena Islanders in Harlem and Other Urban Centers* (New York: Columbia University Press, 1952).

[4] In this paper the terms "Roxbury ghetto" and "Roxbury area ghetto" will be used as shorthand for the more accurate "Roxbury-South End-Dorchester ghetto area and its immediate fringe." This is an area with a core of heavily Negro Census tracts surrounded by a fringe of disproportionately Negro tracts; the overwhelming majority of Boston's Negroes reside in this area. Two of the sample respondents moved out of the ghetto area to another part of inner Boston a few months before being interviewed; they were retained in the sample because they maintained ties with the ghetto.

♦ First published in *Social Science Quarterly* 49, No. 3 (December, 1968).

ly matched subsamples of large, low-income Negro families from three
housing markets in the Roxbury ghetto: (1) rent-supplementation families
in fha-financed, nonprofit units; (2) families who had moved into public
housing units; and (3) families in private housing units.[5] Also included
was a group of otherwise similar middle-income, blue-collar families who
had moved into the same fha-financed, nonprofit projects as the supplementation families. For the purposes of this analysis these four subsamples
have been combined into one predominantly blue-collar sample of 120
families; interviews were conducted with wives, most being interviewed
several months after moving within the ghetto area. Comparisons with
Roxbury U.S. Census data indicate that this sample is representative of
the larger, poorer, and younger families in the area.[6] The sample does not
include representatives from the single or best-paid segments of the ghetto
population.

The Data

Closely paralleling Meadow's Detroit findings, 84.2 per cent of the Roxbury area sample had relatives in the Boston area (Table 1). Somewhat
less than two-thirds had from one to three relatives in the area, while
22.5 per cent had four or more. Sixteen per cent reported no relatives in
the area, a percentage similar to the ones reported for Meadow's Detroit
sample and Blumberg's and Bell's Philadelphia sample.[7] The mean number of relatives per respondent was 2.6. This figure seems relatively high,
especially in light of the fact that half of the respondents had migrated to
Boston since 1950, three-quarters since 1940.

To what extent do these Negro urbanites interact with their relatives in
the Boston area? Table 2 presents data relevant to this question. Coding
for contact with each relative listed ran from zero ("never see") to six ("at
least three times a week"); scores for each relative listed were summed to
get an overall intensity score for each respondent. Such a score has the advantage of incorporating data on each relative listed, not just on relatives
in general. The mean contact score per respondent was 11.2. Such a score
typically meant personal contact several times a week with one relative
and weekly to monthly contact with one or two others. Looking at the

[5] Under this supplementation program a number of large low-income Negro families
displaced by urban renewal were enabled by means of a rent subsidy to move into nonprofit housing financed under fha Section 221(d)3, a provision which provides mort-
gage insurance for financing such housing. I am indebted to the Boston Housing
Authority for permission to publish these data from the evaluation study.

[6] Ninety-seven per cent of the respondents were between the ages of 20 and 54; 84
per cent of the families earned less than $6,000 in 1964 (compared with 72 per cent of
Boston nonwhites in 1959); the mean number of children per family was 4.5. Because
of the relatively large proportion (47 per cent) of female-headed households, data on
spouse's occupation were available for only 71 of the 120 families; of these husbands,
only 10 per cent held white-collar jobs. Because of this, and the fact that most respondents subjectively labeled themselves "lower class" or "working class," the sample will
hereafter be referred to as a blue-collar sample.

[7] Meadow, "Negro-White Differences," p. 328; Blumberg and Bell, "Urban Migration," p. 330.

TABLE 1

Distribution of Respondents by Number of Relatives:
Roxbury Area Sample (N=120)

Number of Relatives in Boston	Percentage of Respondents
0	15.8
1	20.8
2–3	40.8
4–5	8.3
6 or more	14.2
Total	99.9

TABLE 2

Percentage of Boston Negro Respondents at Several Levels of Interaction
with Kin: Roxbury Area Sample (N=120)

Intensity Score	Percentage of Respondents
0	18.3
5 or less	17.5
6–15	38.3
16 or more	25.8
Total	99.9

percentage distribution in Table 2, one can see that a quarter of the respondents were extensively involved in kinship interaction, having scores greater than 15. The largest proportion of the respondents fell into the 6–15 intensity of interaction bracket. About one-fifth were completely isolated from relatives. These figures are similar to other findings on Negro samples and, for that matter, to some findings on white samples.[8]

Cohen and Hodges have reported data indicating more kin contacts for a lower-status, blue-collar group than for a higher-status, blue-collar group.[9] The Roxbury data, however, do not corroborate this finding. Split-

[8] Because of the attempt to devise a measure indicating the magnitude of total interaction intensity, it is difficult to compare these data in detail with the findings of Blumberg and Bell, "Urban Migration," and Meadow, "Negro-White Differences." One rough way to compare the scores of the Roxbury sample is to use the intensity score equivalent to one weekly contact or more with one relative (a score of 5 or 6). Since a 5 or 6 score could be gained by seeing two (or more) relatives less often than weekly, it would perhaps be best simply to compare those with a score of 6 or greater; the number with a score of 6, which means less than weekly contact, is probably offset by the number of those with a 5 score, who should be counted as seeing kin weekly. In any event, 64 per cent of this Roxbury sample had a score of 6 or greater. Meadow, "Negro-White Differences," states that a similar proportion of her respondents reported at least weekly contact with relatives. These figures compare favorably with the findings of Bell and Boat, "Urban Neighborhoods," pp. 394–395, on the general urban samples.

[9] Albert K. Cohen and Harold M. Hodges, Jr., "Characteristics of the Lower–Blue-Collar Class," *Social Problems*, 10 (Spring, 1963), pp. 309–311.

ting the Roxbury area sample into two groups of somewhat differing status, (1) those 29 nonsubsidized and generally higher-status respondents in FHA-financed, nonprofit housing and (2) the rest of the sample, revealed that the higher-status respondents were somewhat more involved with their kin than the lower-status respondents, although the difference between the two subsamples was not statistically significant.

Assessing the extent of mutual aid between relatives is another means of measuring the quality and meaning of kinship interaction. Important types of aid investigated in previous research have included help during illness, financial aid, and business advice. The Roxbury area respondents were asked how many times they had given financial aid to and received personal or business advice from a relative (see Table 3). Twenty-two per cent reported having given aid to a relative in financial trouble; 24 per cent reported having received personal or business advice. Data collected by Sharp and Axelrod on a predominantly white Detroit sample are not too dissimilar: 30 per cent of their Detroit female respondents had given financial aid to a relative; 12 per cent had received business advice from relatives.[10] It should be noted that the questions, as phrased, were unidirectional; presumably the proportions of these Negro respondents receiving financial aid or giving advice would be similar. One additional piece of information available for the Boston sample also indicated that relatives were important to many Negroes in times of minor family crises, such as moving from one area to another. Forty-eight per cent of the Roxbury area respondents reported that they had received aid from their kin in moving into their present homes or apartments.

Research by Meadow and Sussman, among others, suggests that the closer the relatives live to one another, the more intensive the interaction; or perhaps, the more intensive the interaction, the greater the propinquity

TABLE 3

Relatives and Mutual Aid: Roxbury Area Sample (N=120)

Number of Times	Question A[a] Percentage of Respondents	Question B[b] Percentage of Respondents
0	78.3	75.8
1	5.0	7.5
2 or more	16.7	16.7
Total	100.0	100.0

[a] Question A: "How many times in the last year have you given money to a relative who was in financial trouble?"

[b] Question B: "How many times in the last year have you gotten personal or business advice from a relative?"

[10] Harry Sharp and Morris Axelrod, "Mutual Aid Among Relatives in an Urban Population," in *Principles of Sociology*, edited by R. Freedman, Amos H. Hawley, Werner S. Landecker, Gerhard E. Lenski and Horace M. Miner (New York: Holt, Rhinehart and Winston, 1952), pp. 436–437.

of residence.[11] This relationship between proximity and interaction held true for the Roxbury sample. The data in Table 4 indicate that average intensity of contact was greatest for those relatives living within one block of the respondents. Mean intensity declined somewhat beyond that point. The proximity phenomenon could also be seen when the total number of relatives reported was distributed across the spatial categories. Computing the distance each relative lived from the relevant respondent revealed that a majority of all the relatives listed by the sample lived within a one-mile radius of the respondents; 83 per cent lived within a two-mile radius. Correlatively, plotting the addresses of the relatives on a map revealed that 97 per cent lived within the Negro ghetto and its immediate fringe. These Negro respondents and their kin were clearly encapsulated.

That working-class slum or ghetto dwellers are enmeshed in "peer group" sociability is the suggestion of Gans' study of Boston's West End.[12] By "peer group" Gans means a group based primarily on ties of kinship and composed of relatives of roughly the same generation and life cycle. Friends also are members, but often participate less frequently. In order to investigate the applicability of one aspect of Gans' sociability model to residents of a Negro ghetto, tabulations of the number and frequency of interaction with "peer" and "nonpeer" relatives were made for the Roxbury respondents. Altogether the 120 respondents listed 184 relatives as being seen "once a week or more often." Sixty-two per cent of these relatives were peer relatives in Gans' sense of the term. The same was true for relatives seen "once a month or more often." Additional tabulations revealed that a majority of these Negro wives were involved in kinship groups which were predominantly composed of peers. These data tend to substantiate Gans' contention that peer-dominated kin groups reflect working-class values, not just the values of one ethnic group.

TABLE 4

Proximity and Number of Kin: Roxbury Area Sample (N=120)

Distance of Kin from Respondent	Number of Kin	Cumulative Percentage	Mean Intensity of Contact Per Relative[a]
Within 500 feet	16	5.4	6.0
500 feet–2,000 feet	37	18.0	4.9
2,000 feet–1 mile	102	52.7	4.4
1 mile–2 miles	90	83.3	4.2
Boston SMSA (beyond 2 miles)	49	100.0	3.9

[a] Maximum score = 6.0.

11 Meadow, "Negro-White Differences," p. 328; Marvin B. Sussman and Sherwood B. Slater, "A Reappraisal of Urban Kin Networks: Empirical Evidence," a paper given at the 58th Annual Meeting of the American Sociological Association, Los Angeles, California, Aug. 28, 1963. See also Albert K. Cohen and Harold M. Hodges, "Characteristics of the Lower–Blue-Collar Class."

12 Gans, *Urban Villagers*, esp. p. 74.

SUMMARY AND CONCLUSION

This paper has presented data on the extensity, intensity, encapsulation, and types of kinship ties for a sample of Negro urbanites, a sample most representative of the larger and poorer families in Boston's Negro ghetto area. The overwhelming majority of these Negro respondents had relatives in the Boston area, almost all of whom lived within the ghetto and its fringe. They averaged 2.6 relatives each and a frequency of interaction score of 11.2. Almost half depended on relatives for aid in moving to their present address; nearly a quarter had given financial aid to or received advice from relatives in the past year. Given the relatively recent migration of these respondents to the Boston area, this extent of kinship interaction seems significant. Relatives were of some importance to most of these Negro urbanites in terms of both mutual visitation and reciprocal aid.

Depending on which research studies one uses for comparison, these ties may seem relatively weak or relatively strong. They do not seem as strong or as extensive as those of Gans' Italian families. However, rough comparisons with certain other studies, such as that of Bell and Boat, suggest more similarities than differences between the kin contacts of these Negro urbanites and others so far studied. Yet it is generally not possible to determine the number of relatives interacted with from the data in most of these other studies; comparisons of the size and ecology of kinship networks are also not yet possible. Moreover, very little comparable, systematic data are available on rural families, white or Negro; such data would be necessary to test the argument that kinship ties have declined in significance with urbanization. Further research should be directed toward making these important comparisons.

Much social science research has focused on the pathology of ghetto areas, their negative aspects, rather than on ordinary types of social organization which also exist in such areas. These data on Roxbury Negro families point to the existence and importance of one type of informal social network in urban ghettos. In addition to this type, other informal networks, such as friendship and neighboring networks, probably function in Negro ghetto areas. At least one recent study has pointed to the role of such networks in integrating migrants into the urban social fabric.[13] One might hypothesize that such informal networks also function as essential communication and aid networks in ghetto areas, passing information on such things as jobs, housing, welfare, and the like. These networks may provide an organized context in which many, if not most, ghetto dwellers are able to cope with an essentially inhospitable societal environment.

[13] Charles Tilly and C. Harold Brown, "On Uprooting, Kinship, and the Auspices of Migration," *International Journal of Comparative Sociology* (forthcoming).

Subcommunity Gladiatorial Competition:
Civil Rights Leadership as a Competitive Process*

GERALD A. McWORTER
ATLANTA UNIVERSITY

ROBERT L. CRAIN
JOHNS HOPKINS UNIVERSITY

As IS OFTEN THE CASE, THE FOLKLORE OF AMERICAN POLITICS CONTAINS two conflicting statements about the value of competition for political leadership. On the one hand, competition for political office is assumed to be the measure of a thriving democracy. On the other hand, we tend to think of intensely competitive politics as the breeding ground for the spectacular demagogue. In particular, the American Negro civil rights movement is seen as an example of a situation in which high levels of competition have promoted "irresponsible" leadership.[1] In this paper we will examine the civil rights movement in 14 cities, and present an analysis of the factors which cause variations in the degree and character of leadership competition and the way in which this competition has affected these movements.

THE PROBLEM

Much of the literature on the social bases of competition for leadership centers around the word "pluralism." One position is that stated by Kornhauser:

A plurality of independent and limited-function groups supports liberal democracy by providing social bases of free and open competition for leadership, widespread participation in the selection of leaders, restraint in the application of pressures on leaders, and self-government in widespread areas of social life. Therefore, where social pluralism is strong, liberty and democracy tend to be strong; conversely, forces which weaken social pluralism also weaken liberty and democracy.[2]

Here, the competition referred to is clearly functional to a democracy. While the mass society theorists claim that severe social conflict is prevented by these same forces which produce moderate competition, Gusfield has described ways in which pluralism can encourage such conflict.[3]

---

* Reprinted by permission of the University of North Carolina Press from *Social Forces*, 46 (September, 1967), pp. 8-21.

[1] As an example of this diagnosis, see Daniel Bell, "Plea for a 'New Phase in Negro Leadership'," *The New York Times Magazine*, May 31, 1964.

[2] William Kornhauser, *The Politics of Mass Society* (New York: The Free Press of Glencoe, 1959), pp. 230–231.

[3] Joseph Gusfield, *Symbolic Crusade: Status Politics and the American Temperance Movement* (Urbana: The University of Illinois Press, 1963). See especially "A

This is clarified by James S. Coleman, who distinguishes between participation in voluntary organizations which tend to integrate a community by weaving community-wide patterns of communication and influence, and attachments to ethnic and other subcommunity organizations which encourage a division of the community.[4] William A. Gamson's study of 16 middle-sized and small New England cities presented evidence to support this distinction, showing that rancorous conflict was more likely to occur in communities which had isolated subcommunities within their boundaries.[5] By either argument, we might expect the pluralistic community, with a more elaborate network of voluntary organizations, and a larger supply of potential leaders, to provide the greatest degree of leadership competition, although whether such competition sustains or weakens democratic values is left an open question.

However, one apparent difficulty with the pluralism argument is that it would lead us to expect a fairly low level of leadership competition. There is no reason to expect a more elaborate structure of voluntary associations within the generally low socioeconomic status Negro community than in a white community of similar status.[6] And there is little basis for severe ideological cleavage on civil rights as major civil rights leaders command the overwhelming endorsement of the Negro community.[7]

There is another approach to the question which provides a somewhat different set of hypotheses; Ralf Dahrendorf has noted that one can contrast an "integration" theory of society—stressing equilibrium and continuity—with a coercion theory which emphasizes strains and change.[8] He accepts these as compatible viewpoints reflecting the "two faces" of society, but focuses on the coercion theory and writes:

I shall try to show how, on the assumption of the coercive nature of social structure, relations of authority became productive of clashes of role interest which under certain conditions lead to the formulation of organized antagonistic

---

Dramatistic Theory of Status Politics," chap. 7, pp. 166–188. See also "Mass Society and Extremist Politics," *American Sociological Review*, 27 (February, 1962), pp. 19–30.

[4] James S. Coleman, *Community Conflict* (Glencoe, Illinois: The Free Press, 1957).

[5] William A. Gamson, "Rancorous Conflict in Community Politics," *American Sociological Review*, 31 (February, 1966), pp. 71–81.

[6] See Anthony M. Orum, "A Reappraisal of the Social and Political Participation of Negroes," *American Journal of Sociology*, 72 (July, 1966), pp. 32–46.

[7] For national data see William Brink and Louis Harris, *The Negro Revolution in America* (New York: Simon & Schuster, 1964), and for a local example (Durham, North Carolina) see M. Elaine Burgess, *Negro Leadership in a Southern City* (Chapel Hill: The University of North Carolina Press, 1962).

[8] Ralf Dahrendorf, *Class and Class Conflict in Industrial Society* (Stanford: Stanford University Press, 1959). See Part II, "Toward a Sociological Theory of Conflict in Industrial Society," pp. 157–318. He writes that the integration theory of society "conceives of social structure in terms of a functionally integrated system held in equilibrium by certain patterned and recurrent processes; the other one, the *coercion theory* of society, views social structure as a form of organization held together by force and constraint and reacting continuously beyond itself in the sense of producing within itself the forces that maintain it in an unending process of change" (p. 159).

groups within limited social organizations as well as within total societies.[9]

This suggests that in analyzing groups such as those of the civil rights movement, we should keep in mind the possibility that a seemingly stable status hierarchy within the Negro community can itself create competition and conflict. Dahrendorf's remarks lead us back to a traditional viewpoint which says that conflict in politics is to be expected as long as there are bases of power available to competitors.

Much of the existing discussion of the consequences of competition is irrelevant to our concern because it assumes a competition between stable two-party systems. Local studies of competition in nonpartisan or one-party political systems would be more relevant, but there is little material. V. O. Key and others have pointed out the way in which "every man for himself" politics in southern states rewards ideological extremists,[10] and several writers have noted that in Louisiana, where stable party factions have persisted for several decades, racism did not play a major role in electoral contests.[11] James Q. Wilson has noted that the structured politics of Chicago has produced Congressman William Dawson, while the unstructured (and probably more competitive politics of New York City has recruited Adam Clayton Powell.[12] Following this line of reasoning, Wilson has hypothesized that the growth of amateur political clubs in both major political parties has caused ideology to become more important in electoral campaigns and has tended to restrict the freedom of elected officials by binding them to more detailed party platforms.[13] Whether introducing ideology and platform loyalty are good or bad depends not only on one's point of view, but also on the particular community studied. Hunter, for example, suggests that the limiting of competition by the influentials of Atlanta has tended to discourage innovation and prevent the masses from winning new programs.[14]

There does seem to be one consistent finding: political party competition results in increased political participation. Milbrath found a high correlation between party competition and general turnout for senatorial and gubernatorial elections,[15] and Agger *et al.*, in a comparative study of four

[9] *Ibid.*, p. 165.

[10] V. O. Key, *Southern Politics in State and Nation* (New York: Alfred A. Knopf, 1949); Hugh D. Price, *The Negro and Southern Politics* (New York: New York University Press, 1957).

[11] For a comprehensive analysis of the data see Robert Crain, Morton Inger, and Gerald A. McWorter, *School Desegregation in New Orleans: A Comparative Study of the Failure of Social Control* (Chicago: National Opinion Research Center, 1966), pp. 15–106.

[12] James Q. Wilson, *Negro Politics: The Search for Leadership* (New York: The Free Press of Glencoe, 1960); and "Two Negro Politicians: An Interpretation," *Midwest Journal of Political Science*, 4 (November, 1960), pp. 346–369.

[13] James Q. Wilson, *The Amateur Democrat* (Chicago: University of Chicago Press, 1962).

[14] Floyd Hunter, *Community Power Structure: A Study of Decision-Makers* (Chapel Hill: The University of North Carolina Press, 1954).

[15] Lester W. Milbrath, "Political Participation in the States," in Herbert Jacob and Kenneth Vines (eds.), *Comparative State Politics* (Boston: Little, Brown & Co., 1965).

cities, demonstrate how elite competition stimulates mass participation in politics.[16] This is especially true if the basis of the competition is ideological. Lane,[17] and Matthews and Prothro[18] have presented similar findings about contested primary elections and rates of voter turnout.

Similar themes have emerged from studies of leadership in the Negro subcommunity. Hunter found the Negro subcommunity of Atlanta had managed to sustain a monolithic leadership structure despite considerable competition for leadership.[19] Studies of Providence, Rhode Island[20] and "Pacific City"[21] suggest the same pattern. More recently, Ladd has found similar monolithic patterns in Greenville, South Carolina, and Winston-Salem, North Carolina.[22] However, Ladd notes that Winston-Salem does have considerable competition for leadership, and suggests that this is the pattern for the Negro communities of the "new South."

One study found that during periods of intense racial controversy new leaders appeared;[23] another study noted that during a similar controversial period, the opposing factions within the Negro subcommunity merged during the crisis.[24]

Both Glick[25] and Walker [26] hypothesize that competition within the civil rights movement has unanticipated consequences which benefit the Negro subcommunity. Walker concludes that "disputes among the leadership tend to increase, not decrease, the effectiveness of the Negro community's battle against the institution of segregation."[27]

In general, our analysis follows the essential questions being raised in this literature. After clarifying the concept of leadership competition in the civil rights movement, we will investigate: (1) What are the social

[16] Robert E. Agger, Daniel Goldrich, and Bert Swanson, *The Rulers and the Ruled: Political Power and Importance in American Communities* (New York: John Wiley & Sons, 1964).

[17] Robert E. Lane, *Political Life: Why People Get Involved in Politics* (Glencoe, Illinois: The Free Press, 1959).

[18] Donald R. Matthews and James W. Prothro, "Political Factors and Negro Voter Registration in the South," *American Political Science Review*, 57 (June, 1963), pp. 355–367.

[19] Hunter, *op. cit.*

[20] Harold Pfantz, "The Power Structure of the Negro Sub-Community: A Case Study and Comparative View," *Phylon*, 23 (Summer, 1962), pp. 156–166.

[21] Ernest Barth and Baha Abu-Laban, "Power Structure and the Negro Sub-Community," *American Sociological Review*, 24 (February, 1959), pp. 69–76.

[22] Everett C. Ladd, *Negro Political Leadership in the South* (Ithaca: Cornell University Press, 1966).

[23] Lewis Killian and Charles Smith, "Negro Protest Leaders in a Southern Community," *Social Forces*, 38 (March, 1960), pp. 253–257. Also see Tillman Cothran and William Phillips, "Negro Leadership in a Crisis Situation," *Phylon*, 22 (1961), pp. 107–118.

[24] Jacquelyn Johnson Clarke, "Standard Operating Procedures in Tragic Situations," *Phylon*, 22 (Winter, 1961), pp. 318–328.

[25] Clarence E. Glick, "Collective Behavior in Race Relations," *American Sociological Review*, 13 (June, 1948), pp. 287–294.

[26] Jack Walker, "The Functions of Disunity: Negro Leadership in a Southern City," *Journal of Negro Education*, 32 (1963), pp. 227–236.

[27] *Ibid.*, p. 228.

bases which generate and sustain competition? and (2) What are the social consequences of competition?

THE DATA

The research reported here is part of a larger study conducted by the National Opinion Research Center on decision-making with regard to school integration.[28] Fifteen cities were studied by teams of graduate student interviewers who spent from ten to 15 man-days in each city during the winter of 1964–1965. Techniques employed included (a) formal questionnaire interviews with decision-makers, (b) unstructured interviews (up to eight hours in length) with decision-makers and informants, and (c) collecting documentary materials. An average of 20 respondents were interviewed in each city, including an average of four civil rights leaders. In general, there was no difficulty in obtaining interviews with the leading civil rights leaders. The civil rights leaders interviewed included those with important formal positions (e.g., the NAACP president) and those identified as important actors in the school segregation issue. The sample is thus biased (partly, but not completely) toward those persons concerned with education.

The 15 cities included eight in the North, drawn from a sampling frame including all cities between 250,000 and 1,000,000 which were at least ten percent Negro in population. The cities were selected randomly, with substitutions then made for cities which had not faced demands for school integration. The seven southern cities were selected to maximize the range of behavior on school integration, and include three cities which are the largest in their state, three smaller cities from the same states for comparison, and a fourth small city; the smallest city contained 158,623 people. One small southern city is deleted from this analysis because of insufficient direct interviews.

VARIATIONS IN LEVELS OF COMPETITION

As the word is used here, competition for leadership includes competition for formal offices in the government and in voluntary organizations such as the NAACP; but also (and more importantly) competition for status, influence, and power, for the loyalty of masses of civil rights activists, and for control over the policy and the program of the civil rights movement. A civil rights leader may be one who has the reputation for leadership, has the loyalty of a following, holds a formal office, or who is able to use other sources of prestige and status to influence the white subcommittee regarding civil rights. A civil rights leader, by our definition, may be either white or Negro. While it follows that competition can occur in several different ways, the most important distinction is between organized and individual competition. By organized competition we refer to competition between competing organizations or groups, each committed

[28] For the case studies and an analysis of the data, see Robert Crain, with Morton Inger, Gerald A. McWorter, and James J. Vanecko, *School Desegregation in the North: Eight Comparative Case Studies of Community Structure and Policy Making* (Chicago: National Opinion Research Center, 1966), and Crain, Inger, and McWorter, *op. cit.*

more or less permanently to a program or ideological stance. By individual competition, we refer to the competition between individuals for leadership in such as way that a majority of the civil rights leaders are not permanently committed to one side of a conflict. While in principle it would be useful to distinguish competition for leadership from conflict over ideology, in practice the two go hand in hand.

The variables were constructed primarily from the interviews with civil rights leaders. Our judgment of the leader and types of competition is based largely upon three factors—the response to sociometric questions about other leaders; the attitudes expressed by leaders about different civil rights organizations; and a detailed history of the relationships between the groups during the course of the school desegregation issue, which in the North was usually the most important civil rights issue. While the result is a largely impressionistic judgment, we are more confident about its reliability than we might otherwise be because of the great variance among the cities. The differences among cities is quite large, as will be shown when some of the cases are described.

In all 14 cities there is some degree of competition and conflict among civil rights leaders. However, in five of the cities the level of competition is so low that for present purposes we describe them as having minimal competition. These five cities are Baltimore and Miami, where most civil rights activity is handled by the NAACP and competition within the NAACP is light; Columbus, Georgia, where a "ruling elite" of five men work as a close-knit unit; and Pittsburgh and Buffalo, where various groups work in reasonable harmony, again with only a small number of highly active leaders. In all five of these cities, there are no civil rights leaders who were willing to criticize other leaders, and no case when a civil rights group opposed or criticized publicly a program advanced by another.

TABLE 1

Level and Intensity of Civil Rights Leadership Competition
in 14 Cities, by Region

Level of Competition	Region of Cities	
	North	South
Individual competition:		
Intense	San Francisco	Montgomery
Moderate	Oakland	New Orleans
	Boston	
Minimal competition	Baltimore	Miami
	Pittsburgh	Columbus
	Buffalo	
Organized competition	St. Louis	Jacksonville
	Newark	Atlanta

Four cities—St. Louis, Newark, Atlanta, and Jacksonville—fit our model of having intense organized competition. In all four cases, the conflict can be briefly described as between the establishment and the outsiders. The conflict tends to polarize the entire movement; even the leaders who try to think of themselves as nonaligned can only be understood by their relationships to one of the opposing factions. In each case, most leaders interviewed were critical, not merely of other leaders, but other particular civil rights groups as well.

The remaining five cities have individual competition for leadership. In two, San Francisco and Montgomery, the competition can be described as intense and persisting over long periods of time without clear factional alignments. In the other three—Oakland, Boston, and New Orleans—competition and conflict tend to come and go, and are often pushed into the background. Because, as we shall see, the cities without competition are in some ways intermediate between those which have organized competition and those which have individual competition, it is useful to present them graphically in the center of the typology. The civil rights leaders in these cities often qualified their criticism of other leaders in terms of how much support was offered or available for their own program. Since each actor appeared to be a free agent, everyone was considered a possible ally, as well as a potential enemy.

The five cities with individual competition have in common a volatile style of civil rights activity. In all five, since the temporary withdrawal of one or another leader can alter the picture considerably, it is difficult to predict the level and style of civil rights activity. This is especially true of Montgomery, whose leaders have been consistently drafted into the national civil rights movement. As new leaders appear, the pattern of competition changes, and civil rights programs change with them.

The Social Bases of Organized Competition

Let us first consider the roots of organized competition; later we will consider the causes of individual competition. In all four cities in this category, it is possible to locate sources of structural competition in the different bases of power available to competing factions. In the two northern cities the conflict is between the political "establishment" and militant neighborhood-based groups. In St. Louis, the demands for school integration were first made by the West End Community Council with the support of CORE. At first, the NAACP lent its support to the campaign, but later they began to withdraw. After some important victories, an open split between the militant grassroots groups and the NAACP brought about the collapse of the school integration drive. The militants generally accused the NAACP of being conservative and tied to the Democratic party organization in the Negro wards, though one of the militants used his civil rights activity to win control of one ward.[29]

[29] A key actor in St. Louis described this pattern: "Traditionally there have been certain Negroes who are recognized as leaders and they start off as militant, but somewhere along the line they become part of the establishment. They first become

In Newark the pattern was nearly identical. The most militant leader in the NAACP was also a leader of the community organization in a middle-income integrated neighborhood. Under the stress of the school integration campaign, he left the NAACP and the community group continued to battle the school system without the NAACP branch's support. Again, the militants accused the NAACP of being too close to the ruling faction of the Democratic party.

The only other city in the sample with a strong patronage-based Negro political machine is Jacksonville, and here again the result has been organized competition for leadership. However, the cast is a bit different, since the NAACP is militant and anti-machine, and the machine leadership does not have a civil rights organization. In part, this is the effect of Jacksonville being a southern city; the NAACP is not legitimate enough to be accepted by white politicians, and Negro political leaders without autonomous bases of power cannot afford to be active in it. In addition, there is less distinction in the South between generalized community leadership and civil rights leadership, so that the Negro political leader does not need to be a representative of a civil rights group in order to claim status as a civil rights leader.[30]

The fourth city with organized competition is Atlanta. The competition here is between the generations, older and less militant leaders being attacked by young upwardly-mobile militants.[31]

A general but simple proposition fitting all four cities is that organized competition will occur if and only if one faction has access to status independent of an appeal to mass support, and the other faction can successfully appeal to the masses for its power. In the first three cities the political machine can supply patronage and other material incentives maintaining Negro political leaders without requiring that they make a mass appeal on ideological grounds. The competing group is a neighborhood-

---

militant, and this is caused by being anti-establishment, and then they become part of the establishment—they shift from one position to another. Of course, you can't remain a revolutionary as part of the establishment."

[30] A clear example of this in Jacksonville occurred during a recent three-day school boycott run by a militant NAACP-oriented leadership. On the second day of the boycott, a major establishment Negro politician appeared on television to appeal to the Negro community to return to normal and send the children back to school. However, his appeal was not legitimated by his political role, but by his "leadership in many areas, such as civil rights, etc." Further, while appearing on television a NAACP sign was visible in front of him. He warded off charges of fraudulent representation made by NAACP, local and national officials, by declaring that his life membership allowed him such prerogative.

[31] The data were collected prior to significant changes in the political involvement of Negroes in the South, particularly Atlanta. Our findings are essentially similar to those presented by Walker (see Walker, *op. cit.*). After reapportionment in Georgia, the summer primary and general elections added up to two Negro state senators, and five Negro state representatives including Attorney Ben Brown and Julian Bond, both former leaders of the Atlanta Student Movement during 1960–1961 sit-ins. What seems to have subsequently developed is the abdication of leadership by the two key figures (one died, one moved to New York), which in effect has turned over the power to the younger more militant cadre of leaders.

based mass organization in St. Louis and Newark, and a traditional civil rights group in Jacksonville. Since their claim to leadership is based upon the loyalty of a visible group of followers, all three cities have engaged in considerable direct action. Neighborhood-based groups are more successful competitors to the NAACP than city-wide groups such as CORE, probably because they have a more committed following. Thus in all four cities the contest is between militant direct-action groups and moderates.

In Atlanta the same proposition seems to hold. One faction draws its power from its association with the elites of Atlanta's Negro business and academic communities. Of all the cities, Atlanta has the greatest amount of resources for such an elite; the second largest Negro-owned life insurance company and the second largest Negro-owned bank are in Atlanta,[32] in addition to seven Negro colleges and universities. These same resources (especially the colleges) have produced the following for the mass-oriented activists.[33]

To put it another way, the machine city makes it possible for the white leadership to offer resources to particular Negro leaders in exchange for conservative behavior on civil rights. It was probably once true that most cities were able to maintain a conservative group of leaders in this way by offering money or various symbols of honor and prestige. Indeed, the threat of physical violence in some cases might have made such an offering unnecessary. But in the eleven nonmachine cities in our sample, we found little evidence of this today. One reason is that the civil rights revolution has placed these Negro leaders under attack, and the white community has usually been unwilling or unable to counter by inflating their payments to them.

The white leadership also has a negative sanction; it can withhold recognition from civil rights leaders by simply refusing to deal with them. While we have no example of a city which was able to suppress an issue in this fashion, it seems probable that this tactic has increased the turnover of leadership as unrecognized leaders drop into the background. Actually, this is not an "effective" device; as we shall see, an increase in competition tends to increase militancy, so that the whites may find the new leadership more difficult to deal with.

At first it would seem that almost any city could provide a basis for power independent of a mass following, and hence have organized competition, but this is apparently not the case. In Boston there is only one Negro elected official and very few in appointed posts. In the other north-

---

[32] Andrew F. Brimmer, "The Negro in the National Economy," in John P. Davis (ed.), *The American Negro Reference Book* (Englewood Cliffs, New Jersey: Prentice-Hall, 1966), see especially the section titled "Negroes as Enterpreneurs," pp. 291–321.

[33] The largest Negro-owned bank and insurance firm are both in Durham along with a large Ph.D.-granting Negro university. At times, Durham seems to have a pattern of civil rights competition resembling Atlanta's. For a detailed analysis of Durham see Burgess, *op. cit.*; E. Franklin Frazier, "Durham: Capital of the Black Middle Class," in Alain Locke (ed.), *The New Negro* (New York: A. and C. Boni, 1925); and on the early development of Atlanta see August Meier and David Lewis, "History of Negro Upper Class in Atlanta, Georgia, 1890–1958," *Journal of Negro Education* (Spring, 1959), pp. 128–139.

ern cities the absence of a machine vote requires that ambitious political leaders take militant positions, or at least give public support to the militant leaders. Of the northern cities, none has the elaborate Negro economy of Atlanta; furthermore, the Negro economic leaders are sometimes either politically active or are newspaper publishers and therefore still dependent upon a mass following. Similarly, in the South, Jacksonville is represented as a home office of one of the large Negro-owned insurance firms but is otherwise not an important Negro economic center, and the other cities have even less Negro-owned business.[34] Outside of Atlanta, there are so few Negroes holding political positions that they can hardly constitute a fraction. One might expect competition on general ideological grounds between militants and conservatives, but there has been a constantly accelerating rise of militancy in the Negro community since World War II. Conservative ideologies no longer offer a competitive alternative to this increased militancy. Unless the "Uncle Tom" is propped up with a considerable number of favors from white sources, it seems he is fast becoming a mere anachronism.[35]

The general hypothesis predicts that one other type of city will not have organized competition; this is the city where there is no basis for a grass-roots movement. A city with a low-status population, without (for example) the resources of a Negro college, might fall into this class. But even here this is unlikely because of a strong general endorsement of civil rights activity by the Negro masses. If any city in our sample can be described this way it is Columbus, Georgia, where the "ruling elite" has up to now been able to handle civil rights activity with little competition from direct-action groups. Columbus has the lowest status Negro population of the cities in our sample; with a higher status population, there might be a conflict between the generations here as in Atlanta (but it is also possible that the elite might become more militant).

It would also be possible for a city to be led by a group of elites who have enough prestige to be "above criticism." This may have been the case in Montgomery during the early days of the Montgomery Improvement Association, when the MIA leadership combined their prestige as nationally recognized civil rights leaders with their local prestige as ministers of the church.[36] And of course this would have been more often the case before the current thrust of civil rights activities. But in most cities, the holders of traditional status can be attacked (with or without justification) as being conservative. Even when the traditional prestige hierarchy retains its importance, an increase in civil rights activity may encourage competition among elites for the leadership of the movement.

---

[34] Brimmer, *op. cit.*

[35] For a more detailed analysis of this pattern of increasing militancy see Louis Lomax, *The Negro Revolt* (New York: Harper & Row, 1962); August Meier, "New Currents in the Civil Rights Movement," *New Politics* (Summer, 1963), pp. 7–31; and August Meier and Francis L. Broderick (eds.), *Negro Protest Thought in the Twentieth Century* (Indianapolis: The Bobbs-Merrill Co., 1965).

[36] For a general interpretive discussion see Martin Luther King's *Stride Toward Freedom* (New York: Ballantine Books, 1960).

The Bases for Individual Competition

If by individual competition we refer to competition between individuals without permanent factional coalitions or stable ideological differences, we can choose between two seemingly contradictory hypotheses. First, competition will be most present in the "mass society" since there will be few loyalties or agreements binding people into "follower" roles; anyone who wants to be a leader is free to do so. This is a special case of Coleman's hypothesis that a person without an elaborate network of social attachments is free to take controversial positions.[37] However, the more commonly accepted opposing hypothesis is that the pluralistic society, with its complex network of associations, is the training ground for potential leaders. The arguments are not really contradictory, and taken together suggest that we should find greatest competition in (a) the community with many leadership roles and many people in high-status positions, but with little in the way of interdependent relations and a weak internal prestige structure, and less competition in either, (b) the community with a large number of roles for training potential leaders, but with a stable prestige hierarchy and interdependence, or (c) the community with few leadership roles, which will not have competition even if it has an inadequate prestige hierarchy.[38]

We would expect a city of type (a) to have a fast growing middle-class Negro community which is partially assimilated. In such a situation, many persons with leadership skills will be holding "white" jobs, some of the civil rights leaders will be white, and there will not be a traditional prestige structure. All three of the northern cities with individual competition seem to fit this description. In Boston, San Francisco, and Oakland, a large number of civil rights leaders are either white, hold "white" jobs, or live in predominantly white areas. Thus they are autonomous vis-à-vis the Negro economic structure, and have ambiguous status in the Negro prestige hierarchy. Table 2a suggests the lack of autonomy of the Negro community in these cities compared to the less competitive Pittsburgh and Baltimore. In all three individual competition cities, Negroes are less segregated, and the lack of autonomy of the Negro community is reflected in the unimportance of the Negro press. The table also suggests that if it were not for the political organization of St. Louis and Newark, these two cities would have little competition—St. Louis because it has a Negro elite which would maintain considerable power, Newark because it has almost no basis for a grass-roots movement. In general, Table 2a indicates that in the non-machine cities of the North, the higher the status of the Negro community, the greater the individual competition. This pattern does not hold in the four southern cities which do not have organized competition.

In the South, Negro subcommunities are somewhat more self-sufficient, have more visible prestige structures, and have lower status populations.

[37] Coleman, op. cit., p. 26.

[38] A possible fourth type, the community which maintains a stable elite but has no leadership roles, is almost an internal contradiction, and seems to be rare; but as we noted earlier Columbus, Georgia, comes close to this type.

TABLE 2a

Selected Social Factors Influencing Competition (North)

	Socioeconomic Status			Level of Segregation:	
Level of Competition	Percent White Collar	Percent High School Graduates	Size: Percent Population Negro	Index of Residential Segregation°	Importance of Negro Newspapers†
Individual competition:					
Intense:					
San Francisco	27	40	9.0	69.3	Low
Moderate:					
Boston	17	37	9.8	83.9	Low
Oakland	18	32	26.4	73.1	Low
Minimal competition:					
Baltimore	15	19	35.0	89.6	High
Pittsburgh	14	25	16.7	84.6	High
Buffalo	11	22	13.8	86.5	Low
Organized competition:					
St. Louis	15	24	28.8	90.6	Medium
Newark	11	22	34.4	71.6	Medium

° Data compiled from Karl E. Taeuber and Alma F. Taeuber, *Negroes in Cities* (Chicago: Aldine Publishing Co. 1965)

† Data compiled from *Negro Newspapers in the United States* (Jefferson City, Missouri: Lincoln University, Dept. of Journalism, 1964). The Baltimore *Afro-American* and the Pittsburgh *Courier* are well-known: the St. Louis *Argus* and the Newark *Afro-American* are weeklies with circulations of 9,000 and 7,000 respectively.

There is little variation in the degree of autonomy of these highly segregated subcommunities. Hence, we would expect them to have less individual competition. Two cities, New Orleans and Montgomery, do have a limited amount of individual competition, but this may be the result of unique historical factors in each case. A pioneering thrust of civil rights activity in 1955 established the MIA as the model for a mass-based organization in the South. However, several key leaders moved to regional and national levels of leadership, notably Dr. Martin Luther King and Rev. Ralph Abernathy (successive presidents of the MIA). At the time of our interviews, several leaders in the MIA were struggling to organize activity, and thus were competing for power. But our proposition holds that if a direct-action program was organized successfully, the level of competition would decline considerably. Similarly, this appears to be the case for New Orleans which has always had a relatively weak civil rights movement.[39] The cities without competition do have in common a lower supply of "troops" for mass demonstrations; neither has a Negro college whose student body could be used for demonstrations.

[39] Detailed analysis can be found in Crain, Inger, McWorter, *School Desegregation in New Orleans . . . op. cit.*, and Daniel Thompson, *The Negro Leadership Class* (Englewood Cliffs, New Jersey: Prentice-Hall, 1963).

Social Sources of Competition: A Summary

There seems to be some evidence in these data to support several propositions about the causes of competition.

1. A necessary condition for competition is an adequate supply of social resources.

2. A necessary condition for competition to be organized or factional is that there be distinctly different ways to mobilize resources. In our case, this means a choice between appealing for mass support and obtaining resources in other ways; in another context it would include appealing to different sectors of the population for support.

3. Individual competition is facilitated by a weak or ambiguous prestige structure. Social control over potential leaders and loyalty to factions can exist only to the extent that the Negro subcommunity is in fact a subcommunity with binding integrative attachment mechanisms.

Social Consequences of Leadership Competition

In a competitive environment, prospective leaders must make appeals for support. It is commonly assumed that this produces a more militant movement, and our data support this assumption. Without competition, leadership remains in traditional hands, which suggests that the leadership in noncompetitive cities will be older and have higher status. Our data indicate that this is also the case, at least partially. Table 3 gives the age, educational attainment, and income of the civil rights leaders inter-

TABLE 2b

Factors Influencing Competition (South) *

Level of Competition	Socioeconomic Status		Size: Percent Population Negro	Number of Negro Colleges†
	Percent White Collar	Percent High School		
Individual competition:				
Intense:				
Montgomery	14.3	17.8	38.1	1
Moderate:				
New Orleans	11.6	14.5	30.8	2
Minimal competition:				
Miami	8.5	18.1	14.7	0
Columbus	11.9	12.7	29.0	0
Organized competition:				
Atlanta	12.7	21.1	38.2	6
Jacksonville	10.7	18.2	23.2	1

* Importance of Negro Newspapers and the Index of Residential Segregation are not relevant to the study of southern Negro leadership: see text.

† Data compiled from Earl J. McGrath, *The Predominantly Negro Colleges and Universities in Transition* (New York: Columbia University, Teachers College, 1965).

viewed in each class of city; the data suggest that the noncompetitive cities have older leaders who have high incomes, but without especially high educational attainment. However, the South presents a reverse pattern with the noncompetitive cities having younger leaders who are better educated with lower incomes. In both of the noncompetitive southern cities, the leadership was occupied by upwardly-mobile professionals. The Negro professional holds an indisputable status in the Negro subcommunity functionally similar to that of a member of a traditional elite.[40]

Militancy is measured by a four-item scale from a longer agree-disagree questionnaire.[41] The meaning of this militancy scale is perhaps best captured by one of these items which asks the respondent to agree or disagree that "Too many times Negroes have compromised when they could have made more progress if they had held out a little longer." But another component of militancy is the willingness to disagree that "The average white man really wants the Negro to have his rights." Apparently the militant feels there is little to be gained from appealing to the better nature of whites, and therefore the only hope is to make discrimination so unpleasant or costly that whites will give in out of self-interest. In Table 4,

TABLE 3

Social Characteristics of Civil Rights Leaders, by Type of
Leadership Competition and Region

	Competition	Median Age		Percent With Professional Education		Percent Income Over $10,000	
North	Individual	33	(8)	67	(9)	50	(8)
	Minimal	41	(12)	42	(12)	67	(9)
	Organized	34	(6)	58	(12)	20	(5)
South	Individual	53	(7)	43	(7)	50	(4)
	Minimal	46	(7)	50	(8)	0	(6)
		49	(9)	44	(9)	67	(9)

[40] One can interpret leadership competition of the minority community as mechanisms of mobility. The northern pattern differs from the South in part because protest leadership is a functional alternative to establish routes of leadership mobility, whereas in the South it is ofttimes the same as the total minority leadership. This is particularly true in cities without established political leadership; thus, the one Negro attorney in Columbus being elected to the Georgia House of Representatives following reapportionment was predicated on both his station in the Negro community and moderate acceptability to whites.

[41] The two items not cited above are (a) "Unless you dramatize an issue through mass protests and demonstrations it seems that there is scarcely any progress made," and (b) "It is sometimes better to have white resistance to Negro requests, because then you have a basis for bringing the overall problem to the public's attention." Yules Q was used as a measure of association and produced the following matrix:

	2	3	4
1	.45	.73	.89
2	—	.62	.69
3	—	—	.54

we see that the cities with competition, both organized and individual, have more militant leaders. It is understandable that the southern leaders would generally be more militant than those in the North.

Thus far, we have observed that leadership in competitive cities differs in means-orientations. Let us now consider two other factors, differences in goal orientation, and differences in the actual amount of civil rights activity. Here we will draw upon the 15 case studies without attempting to present the data in each case. The reader is referred to the parent monograph for a more complete story.

One might suppose that under conditions of intense competition, the goals of the local civil rights movement might become more attuned to the national civil rights climate as competing leaders draw upon the idioms of the national movement for legitimation. This is partly true in cities where competition is individualized. In these cities the leadership goals have been set in an effort to bid for the support of the entire Negro community, hence the goals have been stated in the most diffuse way. In all three cities, the goals have stressed the elimination of *de facto* segregation and have been highly symbolic.[42] In the two cities with organized competition, the goals have been determined (it seems) by the need of the anti-establishment leaders to build a specific base in one sector of the community from which to wage war on the establishment. The result is that the stated

TABLE 4

Militancy of Civil Rights Leaders, by Competition Level
of City and Region[*]

Level of Competition	Region of Cities					
	North		South		Total[†]	
Individual competition	2.14	(7)	2.74	(9)	.78	(16)
Minimal competition	1.30	(10)	2.00	(7)	.07	(17)
Organized competition	2.00	(9)	2.50	(10)	.72	(19)
Mean	1.77	(26)	2.42	(26)	.77	(52)

[*] Each civil rights leader interviewed was given a militancy score, the average number of militant responses to four statements. The possible range of scores is from very militant (score=4) to not militant at all (score=0).

[†] The total column is derived after reducing the southern militancy scores by .65 so that the North-South differences will not influence the result. In the total column the level of militancy in the two competitive cases are each significantly higher than the militancy in the minimal competition case (at the .05 level, one-tailed test).

[42] In this discussion of civil rights goals we have employed two axes of differentiation, status (symbolic) to welfare, and diffuse to specific. Wilson clearly states that the first basis of distinction is between tangible *things* (welfare) and intangible *principles* (status or symbolic). See Wilson, *Negro Politics: The Search for Leadership*, esp., pp. 185–199. The second dimension concerns the level of specificity of the goals, the extent to which the goals reflect a limited set of concrete propositions as compared to an ever expanding set of general claims.

goals have been set to meet the particular needs of only one part of the subcommunity. In both cases, the base was a racially changing neighborhood which developed a mixture of city-wide and local goals (and a mixture of symbolic and welfare goals) designed to encourage whites to stay in the area and to meet the most salient needs of the incoming Negroes. The two southern cities with organized competition have also shown a tendency toward a mixture of "symbolic" and "welfare" goals; this is particularly true in Jacksonville. The three cities without internal competition developed a set of goals which are in some ways more traditional. Although they were generally city-wide in orientation, they tended to be more specific; in Baltimore and Pittsburgh, focus was upon techniques for eliminating overcrowding by an integration plan; in Buffalo, the movement stressed integration of particular schools.

In the South, there is a narrower range of alternative goals available since the elimination of *de jure* segregation has been the main target. In the one city where there is competition between civil rights groups and a Negro political "establishment," the movement has adopted a heavy welfare orientation which led to a three-day boycott aimed at forcing the upgrading of Negro schools. As in the North, the movements with individual competition for leadership (New Orleans and Montgomery) have stated their goals in abstract terms, and have not paid much attention to specific goals or goals designed to benefit any particular sector or neighborhood of the Negro community. Thus, the data suggest that individualized competition leads to diffuse goals stressing symbolic issues, that cities with organized competition become welfare-oriented, while the cities with low competition tend to stress general and symbolic goals phrasing them in specific terms.

This is only a general tendency, and the data are confounded by three factors. First, the high-status city can be expected to develop more symbolic and diffuse goals since it tends to have an audience for mass-media exhortations, and (we assume) weaker neighborhood orientations. But, as we have discussed above, the high-status cities have individualized competition. Thus our correlation of individualized competition and diffuse goal orientation may be spurious. Secondly, the movements with low competition for leadership are better able to negotiate (since the school board knows who it has to negotiate with), a factor which probably affects the kinds of demands developed and made. And third, the willingness of the school system to meet the particular demands affects the goals of the movement. Since these extraneous factors are important, it is probably wisest to conclude that competition is not necessarily the most important factor in determining the goal orientation of the movement.

Competition also places great pressure on leaders to achieve results. However, in the case of northern school desegregation, the movement has relatively little impact on the degree to which the school board will acquiesce to the demands made.[43] Therefore there is some tendency for the

[43] The major analysis of the parent study revealed that characteristics of the school board and its members so explained acquiescence that adding the effect of civil rights activity did not appreciably add to the predictability. Moreover, the explanatory re-

movement to become means-oriented and evaluate its leaders by their ability to put together a good demonstration or boycott. Again, it is easy to exaggerate the importance of competition in determining level of activity. Much depends upon the amount of resources—especially manpower—available to the movement; and much depends upon whether the school system chooses to be resistant and invite demonstrations. However, with these two qualifications, we can suggest such a pattern. Within the northern sample, both cities with organized competition tend to have aggressive demonstrations, although they tend not to be able to sustain civil rights activity over a long period of time. There is almost an element of desperation in the style of militant groups in these cities. In St. Louis, for example, a blockade of school buses was agreed upon late the preceding evening, and final plans were not developed until a few hours before the blockade. However, it is difficult to sustain civil rights activity without complete support of the Negro community, and in both cities the presence of an organized opposition group eventually crippled the movement.[44] In the three cities with individualized competition, demonstrations have been sporadic, but have continued over a long period of time. In the noncompetitive cities, as expected, the decision to demonstrate is a purely tactical one; the demonstration is regarded as the ultimate weapon and is infrequently used.

The same general pattern seems to hold in the South, even though activity in connection with court-ordered desegregation is quite different from activity generated within a northern context. In the cities with organized competition (Atlanta and Jacksonville), there has been direct action in connection with the schools; there has not been such action in the other four cities. Accordingly, in these four cities, it is difficult to establish a relationship between competition and activity, although the civil rights action does seem more predictable when there is little competition.

The most important effect of competition in the civil rights movement has been to make negotiation with white leadership much more complex. In all northern cities, the movements with individualized competition have been more unpredictable. The San Francisco school superintendent has had to deal with nine civil rights groups. In another city the civil rights movement virtually forced the board to break off negotiations so that a boycott could be held. In the third city, the demands were so vague as to be perceived as merely antagonistic slogans.[45] In the two cities with organ-

---

lationship is opposite this, i.e., the initial reaction or acquiescence of the school board is a cause of civil rights activity rather than being caused by it.

[44] Related to a movement's resource needs for sustaining activity, there is probably an inverse relationship between the number of "troops" needed and the intensity/quality of commitment. But an opposition group affects both factors by drawing off some troops and immobilizing others, and providing alternative gratification which depletes the urgency of the initial controversy.

[45] Killian poses one explanation for cases when ". . . the Negro leader-agent takes the white agent's arguments as the rationalizations of a prejudiced person rather than the tactics of a bargaining agent. When he reiterates his demands, almost as slogans, rather than countering the tactics, he appears either unintelligent or unreasonable. This leads the white agent, in turn, into the psychodynamic fallacy, and he breaks off the

ized competition, the main difficulty with negotiations is that the school board could not know how large an element of the Negro community was "represented" by a group of civil-rights leaders vis-à-vis their opponents or competitors.[46] In contrast, the three cities with minimal competition have had much more orderly processes of negotiation—although in one case, the school board was so disorganized that the civil rights leaders didn't quite know with whom *they* should be talking.

SOCIAL CONSEQUENCES OF COMPETITION: A SUMMARY

Table 5 summarizes the data presented above. From this summary table we can clarify Walker's contention that competitive movements are more successful in achieving their goals.[47] It is probably true that organized competition is beneficial to a civil rights movement in that it stimulates the most intense (though sometimes short-lived) activity. On the other hand, individual competition, which produces a constant circulation of

TABLE 5

Style of Civil Rights Activity, by City Competition Level and Region

| Region | Level of Competition | Style of Civil Rights Activity | | |
		Goals	Action	Militancy
North	Individual	Symbolic, Diffuse, City-wide	Demonstration (sporadic)	Medium
	Minimal	Symbolic, Specific City-wide	Bargain-table negotiation (extensive)	Low
	Organized	Welfare and Symbolic, Local and City-wide	Demonstration (intense, but short-lived)	Medium
South	Individual	Symbolic, City-wide	Court action (limited)	High
	Minimal	Symbolic, City-wide	Court action (extensive)	Medium
	Organized	Welfare and Symbolic, Diffuse, City-wide	Court action and demonstration (short-lived)	High

negotiations on the ground that the Negro is simply an agitator who makes impossible demands for the sake of 'stirring up trouble.' " See Lewis Killian, "Community Structure and the Role of the Negro Leader-Agent," *Sociological Inquiry*, 35 (Winter, 1965), pp. 69–79.

[46] School boards have normally faced the representation question with regard to teachers' unions and parent groups. But civil rights leaders face different problems because the above two are more easily defined constituencies, with longer traditions of negotiating with school boards, and are working within the context of a clearer uncontroversial set of legal guidelines.

[47] Walker, *op. cit.*

leaders, probably equips the movement best for sustained activity over a period of years. However, the city without competition is probably best able to carry out a tightly planned campaign to achieve specific goals, although in the process its small leadership may become stolid and lose the initiative to raise new issues or the courage to use ultimate sanctions.

Race and Intelligence: Changing Opinions in Social Science

WALTER J. CARTWRIGHT
TEXAS TECHNOLOGICAL COLLEGE

THOMAS R. BURTIS
TEXAS TECHNOLOGICAL COLLEGE

SINCE THE 1920's, SOCIAL SCIENCE OPINION IN THE UNITED STATES HAS undergone a complete reversal from general acceptance to an almost unanimous rejection of the theory of innate racial inferiority of Negroes. Although this theory of inherent Negro inferiority has been applied to various apparent physical, psychological, and cultural differences between the races, most of the argument has come to be centered on intelligence, a characteristic which is "relatively easy" to measure and which has important sociological and genetic implications. Most social scientists today seem to believe that most, if not all, of the differences between Negro and white intelligence test-score averages must be caused by cultural and environmental influences and by limitations of mental measurement devices.

An examination of changing social science opinion concerning racial differences may explain both the reinforcement of racist ideas at one period and their elimination at another. This would, in addition, support Tumin's observation that there is a lag of about 20 years between basic findings in race-relations research and the beginning of their implementation by government and society.[1] Current public attitudes on race reflect, in part, earlier opinions in the social sciences.

Since 1897, there have been hundreds of small research studies and two mass comparisons (resulting from military testing during World Wars I and II) all of which have shown that Negro Americans, on the average, score lower on intelligence tests than do white Americans.[2] There is general agreement that the difference in averages in uncontrolled studies has been 15 to 20 Intelligence Quotient (IQ) points.[3] Most studies of supposedly "comparable" groups still have shown average differences of about 5 to 10 IQ points although a number of studies have shown that the upper limit of Negro mental ability corresponds with that of whites.[4] Usually

---

[1] Melvin M. Tumin, "Some Social Consequences of Research on Racial Relations," *American Sociologist*, 3 (May, 1968), pp. 117–124.

[2] Robert D. North, "The Intelligence of American Negroes," *Research Reports of Anti-Defamation League*, 3 (1956), pp. 2–8.

[3] Wesley Critz George, *The Biology of the Race Problem* (New York: National Putnam Letters Committee, 1962), p. 19; Otto Klineberg, "Negro-White Differences in Intelligence Test Performance: A New Look at an Old Problem," *American Psychologist*, 18 (April, 1963), pp. 198–203.

[4] Leona E. Tyler, *The Psychology of Human Differences*, 3d ed. (New York: Appleton-Century-Crofts, 1965), p. 322; Ralph M. Dreger and Kent S. Miller, "Comparative Psychological Studies of Negroes and Whites in the United States," *Psychological Bulletin*, 57 (1960), pp. 361–402.

♦ First published in *Social Science Quarterly* 49, No. 3 (December, 1968).

less than 25 per cent of the Negroes score above the white median, with differences in averages increasing consistently from the youngest to the oldest age groups.[5]

All writers agreed substantially on these facts, but there has been considerable disagreement on interpretation between hereditarians and environmentalists. The former have maintained that group as well as individual differences in intelligence or culture are largely determined by heredity and that environmental factors have little limiting influence on mental or cultural development. The latter have admitted that there are individual differences in inherited mental potential, and that these differences tend to be reflected in family histories; but they have argued that mental and cultural development is determined largely by environmental conditions and that there has been no evidence to suggest any innate racial differences (as distinguished from individual and family differences) in mental ability or cultural potential.

This article is intended to provide a better understanding of the opposing scientific approaches to the study of racial differences, the historical background leading to an emphasis on race and intelligence, the changes which have occurred in the experts' opinions, possible reasons for these changes, and the degree of disagreement which persists.

HISTORICAL BACKGROUND

Although racial doctrines did not reach their peak until the nineteenth century arguments over slavery, ideas of ethnic or racial superiority have their roots in ancient times and even Aristotle has been quoted on this topic.[6]

Gossett credits the age of exploration and the resulting contacts between Europeans and other races with stimulating European thought concerning race differences.[7] In a study of early Spanish contacts with the American Indians, Hanke explains the enslavement of the Indians as an application of the Aristotelian doctrine of natural slavery for an inferior race.[8] Many Spanish explorers thought the Indians were a subhuman species. Largely through the efforts of Bishop Bartolomé de Las Casas, the "Apostle of the Indians," a royal decree was obtained in 1530 and a papal proclamation in 1537 prohibiting enslavement of the Indians. The papal proclamation held that the Indians are "truly men" and not "dumb brutes."[9]

Among early English colonists in America, popular ideas of superiority of the white race, and particularly of Anglo-Saxons, soon developed from contact with the Indians and Negro slaves.[10] These ideas found little ac-

[5] Tyler, *Psychology of Human Differences*, p. 306.

[6] Thomas F. Gossett, *Race: The History of an Idea in America* (Dallas, Tex.: Southern Methodist University Press, 1963), p. 6.

[7] *Ibid.*, p. 16.

[8] Lewis Hanke, *Aristotle and the American Indians: A Study in Race Prejudice in the Modern World* (Chicago: Henry Regnery, 1959), pp. ix, 12–13.

[9] Gossett, *Race*, pp. 12–13.

[10] *Ibid.*, pp. 17–29.

ceptance, however, among leading theologians and philosophers of Europe. The essential unity of mankind was emphasized both by the religious doctrine of divine creation and by the belief of the enlightenment that the mind at birth is a *tabula rasa,* an empty receptacle to be filled by education and environment. In the eighteenth century, egalitarian ideas of the enlightenment were supported by Johann Friedrich Blumenbach and George Louis Leclerc Buffon, the founders of anthropology, and by most of the scientific and religious thinkers in America.[11]

In the late eighteenth century, however, a number of thinkers applied to the Negro race the doctrine of polygenesis, which the early Spanish explorers had applied to the Indians. Thomas Jefferson of America, Voltaire of France, Lord Kames of Scotland, and Charles White of England were among those who argued that Negroes were not merely an inferior race, but a distinct subhuman species.[12]

Although the separate-species argument was still a novelty in the eighteenth century and was originated by individuals who generally opposed slavery, it was repeated often in the nineteenth century as justification for slavery. Further, during the nineteenth century, the idea of Negro inferiority, whether as an inferior race or a subhuman species, gained not only in popular opinion but also among scientific thinkers and scholars.[13] Sir William Lawrence (1783–1867) of the Royal College of Surgeons of London, and Samuel George Morton (1799–1851) of Philadelphia were typical of early nineteenth-century anthropological thinkers who accepted Negro inferiority as undeniable, based on general observation. Both sought to explain Negro inferiority through an analysis of physical differences emphasizing the Negro's ape-like physical characteristics.[14]

The shift in scientific thinking from the eighteenth to the nineteenth centuries may be explained as a result of the acceptance of popular assumptions in the culture based on the undeniable evidence of the senses. In addition, there was an absence of any data which would lead to doubt or critical examination of the popular assumptions. Whereas earlier thinkers had considered mankind in the abstract—in philosophical and theological terms—nineteenth-century thinkers in anthropology began to look at the races and accept the "facts." The facts were that Europe's worldwide colonial expansion placed dark-skinned peoples in inferior positions throughout the world, and the American slavery system helped to create the "racial" inferiority which was required for its justification.

Unlike the long-standing Greek, Roman, and Mediterranean institution of slavery, the American system was based on race. The complete severance of any ties with the previous African tribal culture, the isolation of the field hands from any cultural influences of the master's household, the large-scale prevention of marriage and family ties, and the lack of opportunity for experience with responsibility or planning all combined to make the slaves obviously inferior to their masters. Since the slaves

11 *Ibid.,* pp. 35–41.
12 *Ibid.,* pp. 42–48.
13 *Ibid.,* pp. 51–53.
14 *Ibid.,* pp. 56–59.

were all Negroes, it was equally obvious that their inferiority was racial.[15]

Those who sought to stop the slave trade or to free the slaves did so primarily on humanitarian or religious grounds rather than because of any idea of racial equality. The obvious fact of Negro inferiority was convincing not only to white Americans but also to the slaves themselves. Even after Emancipation early Negro leaders were forced to accept the fact that freedom could not produce equality. Both Silberman and Gossett give excellent descriptions of the conditions which produced the American Negro's inferiority and of the widely accepted interpretations of this inferiority in Biblical, philosophical, and legal spheres.[16]

Thus anthropologists of the nineteenth century searched for evidence of physical differences, not to establish the obvious Negro inferiority, but to explain it. In the later nineteenth century, this search was further stimulated by Darwin's theory. Various physical measures of racial difference —such as skin color, felting of hair, shape of skull, facial angle, cranial capacity, brain weight, and body proportions—were advanced successively to explain Negro inferiority. None of these measureable physical characteristics, however, proved to be a consistent indication of racial difference or of intellectual capacity.[17]

Gossett detailed many of these uncontrolled nineteenth-century studies and their refutation of each other. Morton, for example, the leading authority on cranial capacity, established with the skulls of only five English felons that the English "race" had the largest cranial capacity of all races, and with 85 Negro skulls, indistinguishable as to sex, he concluded that Negroes had nearly the smallest capacity.[18] Montagu reports that modern studies show that the Negro has an average cranial capacity of 1,350 cc., or 50 cc. less than the white average.[19]

Most of the nineteenth-century social scientists assumed that the study of human societies was the study of innate racial differences. These racial theories were basic to Herbert Spencer's Social Darwinism, which represented the most sophisticated theoretical system for explaining white superiority. His influence was world-wide, especially among the leaders in the developing disciplines of sociology (William Graham Sumner and Charles H. Cooley), psychology (G. Stanley Hall), eugenics (Francis Galton), and education (James Mark Baldwin).[20] Even the late nineteenth-century challenges to Social Darwinism by Lester F. Ward and others were based on social and economic differences, not on any differences over racial theories. Ward, for example, saw rape of a white woman by a Negro as not mere lust but the "voice of nature" commanding the Negro

---

[15] Charles E. Silberman, *Crisis in Black and White* (New York: Random House, 1964), pp. 77–93.

[16] *Ibid.*, pp. 77–93; Gossett, *Race*, pp. 17–53.

[17] Gossett, *Race*, pp. 82–83.

[18] *Ibid.*, pp. 73–74.

[19] Ashley Montagu, *Man's Most Dangerous Myth: The Fallacy of Race*, 4th ed. (Cleveland, Ohio: World, 1964), p. 100.

[20] Gossett, *Race*, pp. 144–160.

to "raise his race to a little higher level" and the white reaction of lynch-law as evidence of the "biological law of race preservation."[21]

In tracing the status of the Negro from 1865 to 1915, Gossett shows that "scientific fact" and the prevailing opinion of scientists in general, and social scientists in particular, supported the racists.[22] Those who opposed racial injustice ignored by the "obvious facts" of the Negro's inferior intelligence and character traits, and they offered only appeals to humanitarianism as their rationale. Nobody offered any hard facts which might raise doubts about the established racial doctrine. Negro inferiority had been neither explained nor refuted by the attempts to measure physical differences. Innate character deficiencies were easy to see but hard to measure objectively. The Negro's inferiority had been most readily apparent in his intellectual capacities, but these qualities were not measurable directly until the development of mental tests.

It was thought that mental tests would provide the objective measure of racial inferiority which had long been known to exist. In one of the first such experiments in this country, Bache found race differences in reaction time which favored Indians and Negroes over whites. He interpreted these results as showing that whites were superior because they were more deliberate and reflective.[23] Early reviews of the literature of psychology showed that all studies emphasized the racial inferiority of the Negro.[24]

Finally, the statistical analyses of World War I Army "Alpha" and "Beta" test scores by race and state provided what was thought to be the incontrovertible proof of inherent Negro inferiority. R. M. Yerkes reported that the tests were "definitely known to measure native intellectual ability."[25] They showed that for each state, the Negro average was substantially lower than the white average.

Later analyses of these same test results, however, raised the first challenge to scientific racist theories and ushered in a period of active investigation and changing scientific opinion.[26] Public opinion turned more highly racist, however, during the 1920's and continued to rely on the intelligence test as the "scientific proof" of Negro inferiority.[27]

A PERIOD OF CHANGE

The change of scientific opinion during the 1920's and 1930's is reflected in a series of quotations by North from a number of leading authorities of

[21] Lester F. Ward, *Pure Sociology*, 2nd ed., New York: Macmillan Co., 1921), p. 359.

[22] Gossett, *Race*, pp. 253–286.

[23] R. M. Bache, "Reaction Time with Reference to Race," *Psychological Review*, 2 (1895), pp. 474–486, as reported in Gossett, *Race*, p. 364.

[24] North, "Intelligence of American Negroes."

[25] R. M. Yerkes, ed., *Psychological Examining in the United States Army, Memoirs of the National Academy of Science*, 15 (1921), p. 794.

[26] North, "Intelligence of American Negroes"; Tyler, *Psychology of Human Differences*.

[27] Gossett, *Race*, p. 373.

that period. Typical are the following quotations from Thomas R. Garth, a psychologist described as "one of the most eminent scientists in the field."[28] Garth said,

a) In 1925, that studies he had seen "seem to indicate the mental superiority of the white race."[29]

b) In 1931, after a review of the literature on racial differences in mental ability, that "there are no sure evidences of real racial differences in mental traits," although he had begun his review with "a silent conviction that he would find clear-cut racial differences in mental processes."[30]

c) In 1934, "that one race has a temporary advantage over another."[31]

d) In 1937, that intelligence-test differences "found when we measure races can be more readily attributed to differences in opportunity than to any native racial determinants."[32]

North credited the change of viewpoint by Garth and other leading social scientists to (1) the inability of scientists to relate intelligence to biological features such as anthropoid nose structure (a Negroid feature), anthropoid hairiness (a white feature), electrical brain potential, brain size or weight, or relative proportion of white and Negro ancestry in a given subject, and (2) the increasing evidence of the large role of cultural and environmental influences.[33]

No biological explanation could be found for the striking differences between World War I Army Alpha Test scores of Northern and Southern Negroes and of Northern and Southern whites, nor for the fact that *Negro* averages in three Northern states were higher than *white* averages in three Southern states. Nor did statistical evidence support an explanation by the theory of "selective migration"—that the more intelligent Negroes and whites move north. The only explanation supported by statistics was that the intelligence test scores of Southern Negro children improved after they moved to the North, and that they showed greater improvement for children who moved to the North at a younger age and for those who had been there longer.[34]

This change of opinion on race was part of the increased emphasis on scientific method throughout the sciences, but particularly in the social

[28] North, "Intelligence of American Negroes."

[29] *Ibid.*

[30] Thomas R. Garth, *Race Psychology: A Study of Racial Mental Differences* (New York: 1931), p. 211, as quoted in Gossett, *Race*, p. 425.

[31] North, "Intelligence of American Negroes."

[32] Thomas R. Garth, "The Hypothesis of Racial Difference," *Journal of Social Philosophy*, 2 (1937), pp. 224–231.

[33] North, "Intelligence of American Negroes."

[34] Otto Klineberg, *Negro Intelligence and Selective Migration* (New York: Columbia University Press, 1935), p. 59; Everett S. Lee, "Negro Intelligence and Selective Migration: A Philadelphia Test of the Klineberg Hypothesis," *American Sociological Review*, 16 (April, 1951), pp. 227–233.

sciences. It represented a change from social thought to social science, with more attention to the use of controls and the collection and analysis of data. Gossett noted in this connection the gradual change of emphasis from biological to social factors to explain cultural differences.[35]

Despite Spencer's own reliance on racial theories to explain superior and inferior societies, he was a major contributor to this change of direction and method of social inquiry. Rumney noted that Spencer called for the use of scientific methods derived from biology for sociological study, that is, the collection and analysis of data on differences between social groups, classes, and races and their social structures.[36] The role of Spencer's teachings in the growing emphasis on environment and education was recognized and protested by Osborn in the 1916 Preface to Madison Grant's controversial racist tome, *The Passing of the Great Race.*[37]

Another contribution to the trend toward change in the social sciences was the advent of the new cultural anthropology. This new approach resulted from the work of Sir Edward Burnett Tylor (1832–1917), a self-made anthropologist who developed his own methods of study, and Franz Boaz (1858–1942), who received his doctorate in physics before turning to anthropology. Boaz developed a method of studying each culture from its own rationale, rather than from the preconceptions of an outside culture.[38]

Boaz, a German-born and German-educated Jew who was professor of anthropology at Columbia University from 1889 to 1936, has been both credited and blamed for starting the change in scientific opinion on race. Gossett credited Boaz with being the first to demand scientific evidence for the prevailing theory of innate Negro inferiority and to produce scientific evidence of environmental influences rather than mere humanitarian arguments against racial discrimination.[39] George, a biologist commissioned by the Governor of Alabama to prepare a study on the biology of race, blamed Boaz for producing a first generation of misguided social scientists (Ruth Benedict, Kenneth B. Clark, Otto Klineberg, Margaret Mead, and others) and maintained that these scientists, in turn, misled the majority in all American social science fields.[40]

MODERN OPINION

MAJORITY VIEW. In 1956, a joint statement[41] by 18 leading American social scientists headed by Klineberg reviewed a number of authoritative statements of scientific opinion holding that there has been no scientifically demonstrated relationship between race and innate intellectual capacity

[35] Gossett, *Race*, p. 416.

[36] Jay Rumney, *Herbert Spencer's Sociology* (New York: Atherton Press, 1966), pp. 58–59.

[37] Henry Fairfield Osborn in Madison Grant, *The Passing of the Great Race: The Racial Basis of European History* (New York: Scribner's, 1916), p. vii.

[38] Gossett, *Race*, pp. 417–422.

[39] *Ibid.*, p. 418.

[40] George, *Biology of the Race Problem*, pp. 78–87.

[41] Otto Klineberg, *et al.*, "Intelligence of the American Negro: Statement by Social Scientists," *American Journal of Orthopsychiatry*, 27 (1957), pp. 420–422.

or other inborn psychological characteristics. They noted that the American Anthropological Association and the Society for the Psychological Study of Social Issues, the latter being a division of the American Psychological Association, made such statements in 1938 and 1939.

The American social scientists introduced their 1956 statement with three quotations from earlier statements which reflect current scientific thinking on this issue:

a) From a Statement on Race which a group of distinguished social scientists issued in Paris in 1950: "Whenever it has been possible to make allowances for differences in environmental opportunities, [intelligence] tests have shown essential similarity in mental characters among all human groups. In short, given similar degrees of cultural opportunity to realize their potentialities, the average achievement of the members of each ethnic group is about the same."

b) From a statement which "an equally distinguished assembly" of geneticists and physical anthropologists issued in Paris in 1952: "The scientific material available to us at present does not justify the conclusion that inherited genetic differences are a major factor in producing the differences between the cultures and cultural achievements of different peoples or groups. It does indicate, on the contrary, that a major factor in explaining such differences is the cultural experience which each group has undergone."

c) From a 1953 statement submitted by more than 30 American social scientists to the U.S. Supreme Court: "The available scientific evidence indicates that much, perhaps all, of the observable differences among various racial and national groups may be adequately explained in terms of environmental differences . . . It seems clear, therefore, that fears based on the assumption of innate differences in intelligence are not well founded."

The social scientists noted that only a few specialists disagreed with these three earlier statements, usually on two main grounds: (1) Negro-white differences in intelligence test performance are found even when opportunities for the two groups are "equated," and (2) these test performance differences also are found when "noncultural questions" are used.

Neither of these premises will stand up under an examination of its evidential foundations. The joint statement questioned the possibility of measuring "equated" social and educational opportunities and denied the possibility at that time of culture-free testing. In 1950, Goodenough agreed with many other investigators who had found her earlier "culture-free" Draw-a-Man Test to be far from culture-free. She said that "the search for a culture-free test, whether of intelligence, artistic ability, personal-social characteristics, or any other measurable trait is illusory," and that the 1926 Goodenough study reporting racial differences on the Draw-a-Man Test "is certainly no exception. . . . The writer hereby apologizes for it!"[42]

The Klineberg group indicated that they knew of no new research which would contradict any of these earlier statements.[43] Later claims to the contrary advanced by George[44] were reviewed in a report[45] for the American Association for the Advancement of Science by its Committee on Science in the Promotion of Human Welfare, which concluded "that the available evidence on the measurable differences among racial groups cannot properly support a challenge to the principle of human equality, which is assured by the Constitutiion of the United States. The use of purported 'scientific evidence' to justify noncompliance with the Constitution debases both science and the human conscience."[46]

The 18 American social scientists in the 1956 statement interpreted the difference between average intellectual achievements of Negro and white children in America "in terms of the *whole* pattern of educational opportunities associated with the social environment, and which may affect both the physical and mental development of the child."[47]

The data which provide the basis for these modern opinions on race and intelligence are quite voluminous and too complex for summary within the scope of this article. There have been a number of reviews of the scientific literature which include excellent summaries, as well as detailed analyses, of these data. The most widely accepted and one of the most recent and thorough of these reviews is Leona E. Tyler's *The Psychology of Human Differences*, third edition, (1965). Her text is rigorously neutral, as is a more limited review by Dreger and Miller (1960) covering mostly psychological studies during the period 1943–1958.[48] Pettigrew (1964), Klineberg (1963), North (1956), Bloom (1964), and Kessler (1965) have provided careful and accurate reviews, though frankly from the environmental viewpoint.[49]

The opinions of the various reviewers of recent years could best be summarized by these comments from Tyler's 1965 revision (which agrees substantially on this point with her 1956 edition). Concerning individual differences in intelligence, she wrote:

[42] Florence L. Goodenough and Dale B. Harris, "Studies in the Psychology of Children's Drawings," *Psychological Bulletin*, 27 (Sept., 1950), pp. 369–433.

[43] Klineberg, *et al.*, "Intelligence of the American Negro."

[44] George, *Biology of the Race Problem*, pp. 73–74.

[45] American Association for the Advancement of Science, "Science and the Race Problem," *Science*, 142 (Nov. 1, 1963), pp. 558–561.

[46] *Ibid.*, p. 560.

[47] Klineberg, *et al.*, "Intelligence of the American Negro."

[48] Tyler, *Psychology of Human Differences*; Dreger and Miller, "Comparative Psychological Studies."

[49] Thomas F. Pettigrew, *Profile of the Negro American* (Princeton, N.J.: D. Van Nostrand, 1964); Klineberg, "Intelligence of the American Negro"; North, "Intelligence of American Negroes"; Benjamin Bloom, *Stability and Change in Human Characteristics* (New York: John Wiley, 1964); Jane W. Kessler, "Environmental Components of Measured Intelligence," *School Review*, 73 (1965), pp. 339–358.

Until we have equal opportunity for all, we can never know with certainty
that inequalities would persist in spite of it. . . . The philosophy that differences are basic and ineradicable lends itself very conveniently to those
who need a rationalization for the existence of privileged classes.[50]

Hereditarians and environmentalists no longer divide themselves into two
hostile camps. Increasing knowledge about what is inherited, how learning
processes change various mental characteristics, and what kinds of environmental situations have favorable influences on mental growth has changed
the whole pattern of the controversy.[51]

Tyler explained that mental development at every stage depends not
only upon opportunities available at that stage but also upon the *interaction* between individual capacity and prior learning.[52] The biological
mechanism at any stage is something more than the inherited mechanism.
She concluded that, insofar as racial differences are concerned, when apparent differences in socioeconomic conditions and educational opportunity have been eliminated, most social scientists attribute the remaining
differences in average measured intelligence to one or both of the following reasons: (1) Tests designed for white subjects may not adequately measure Negro intelligence, and (2) "some developmental influence
other than educational and socio-economic handicaps," perhaps inferior
caste status, may consistently depress the mental growth of Negro children.[53] Tyler, among other reviewers, cites evidence of a number of effects
of inferior caste status which have been clearly shown to retard mental
growth. A detailed discussion of these effects is, however, beyond the
scope of this paper.

THE HOLDOUTS. A small group of scientists, including Wesley Critz
George (who has been since 1949 professor emeritus of anatomy at the
University of North Carolina and who published the 1962 study[54] on biology and race commissioned by the Governor of Alabama) and Henry
E. Garrett (President of the American Psychological Association in 1946
and since 1956, professor emeritus of psychology at Columbia University)
have conducted a crusade for the past two decades to promote the
older theory of innate Negro inferiority, particularly in intelligence.[55]
They and several others have written under the apparent auspices of the
International Association for the Advancement of Ethnology and Eugenics, an organization dedicated to "encouraging the free flow of information between scholars . . . in the United States and in other countries of
the Western World and in restoring freedom of inquiry to those areas
(particularly the study of race and race relations) where extraneous political and philosophical predispositions have frequently terminated discussions to the general detriment of the social and biological sciences."[56]

[50] Tyler, *Psychology of Human Differences*, p. 4.
[51] *Ibid.*, pp. 14–15.
[52] *Ibid.*, pp. 65–66.
[53] *Ibid.*, p. 315.
[54] George, *Biology of the Race Problem.*
[55] Tyler, *Psychology of Human Differences*, p. 300.
[56] Clairette P. Armstrong, "Psychodiagnosis, Prognosis, School Desegregation and

Other writers for the organization are retired New York psychologist Clairette P. Armstrong, retired British psychologist Sir Cyril Burt, former South African psychologist A. James Gregor, and Ernest van den Haag, adjunct professor of social philosophy at New York University.

Finally, the most thorough of the holdouts is Audrey M. Shuey, since 1944 chairman of the psychology department at Randolph-Macon Woman's College in Lynchburg, Virginia. In 1958, she published *The Testing of Negro Intelligence*,[57] the most thorough, but also the most severely criticized, of the earlier reviews. It had been claimed that her work covered *"all"* of the comparative studies of Negro-white performance on mental tests over the preceding 40 years, but Pettigrew noted that she had missed a number of important studies published from 1936 to 1956 which directly contradicted her conclusions that there are "some native differences between Negroes and whites as determined by intelligence tests."[58] Dreger and Miller described Shuey's work as "an attempt to prove a nonegalitarian hypothesis" and as doing the "same rationalizing from an hereditarian standpoint that Klineberg (1944) did in his earlier 'review' from an environmental standpoint."[59]

In 1966, Shuey published a larger (578 pages) and more complete second edition of *The Testing of Negro Intelligence* in which she reviewed 380 original investigations and 62 reviews pertaining to Negro intelligence, as well as 122 publications dealing with the various tests used. She introduced the 1966 edition with the statement that it is "not the purpose of this book to prove that Negroes are socially, morally, or intellectually inferior to whites" and ended it with the conclusion that all of the evidence taken together "inevitably point to the presence of native differences between Negroes and whites as determined by intelligence tests."[60] She noted Dreger and Miller's citation of 13 research reports as having been omitted from her first edition. She admitted that eight were omitted, but pointed out that one was included directly, and that the other four were included in their earlier or later form. Though she took note of other criticisms by Pettigrew, she failed to mention his list of 12 omissions which contradicted her conclusions.[61]

THE NEW HEREDITARIANS. Although the majority of modern social scientists clearly believe that there is no evidence of inherent Negro intellectual inferiority, a minority of "new hereditarians" have made themselves heard in recent years. Generally, the new hereditarians acknowledge the major contribution of environmental factors in measured intelligence differences among individuals and races. They differ from majority opinion,

Delinquency," IAAEE *Reprint No. 13* from *The Mankind Quarterly*, 5 (1964), back cover.

[57] Audrey M. Shuey, *The Testing of Negro Intelligence* (Lynchburg, Va.: J. P. Bell Co., 1958).

[58] Pettigrew, *Profile*, p. 102, fn. 3.

[59] Dreger and Miller, "Comparative Psychological Studies," p. 364.

[60] Audrey M. Shuey, *The Testing of Negro Intelligence*, 2d ed. (New York: Social Science Press, 1966), pp. 1, 521.

[61] *Ibid.*, p. 2; Pettigrew, *Profile*, p. 102, fn. 3.

however, in that they place more emphasis on hereditary factors in individual, family, or social-class differences, and they believe hereditary factors also have a major influence on racial and ethnic differences in intelligence. Most of them agree that a need exists for further social change to correct environmental handicaps among Negroes. They seem to favor such environmental improvements, however, in a context of racial segregation or separation, at least by implication.

Some of the new hereditarians, such as Ingle, professor of physiology at the University of Chicago, and Shockley, Nobel Prize-winning physicist at Stanford University, use sociological data or behavioral logic, rather than biological or genetic data, to support their arguments for inherent racial differences and for the need of urgent genetic research aimed at possible eugenic solution, or genetic prevention, of race problems.[62] They have been joined by some social scientists, including Arthur R. Jensen, an educational psychologist in the Institute of Human Learning at the University of California at Berkeley.

In response to Shockley's urgent call to the National Academy of Sciences for expanded racial research to "evaluate the relative effects of heredity and environment on human intelligence and performance," the National Academy in 1967 issued an official statement of its position on racial studies. The Academy recognized that the formulation of "heredity *vs* environment" is a "loaded question that might be destructively exploited by racists if the Academy even ratified it as the right question."[63]

The Academy statement noted that "there is no scientific basis for a statement that there are or that there are not substantial hereditary differences in intelligence between Negro and white populations. In the absence of some now-unforseen way of equalizing all aspects of the environment, answers to this question can hardly be more than reasonable guesses. Such guesses can be easily biased, consciously or unconsciously, by political and social views. . . . There is surely a substantial and perhaps overriding environmental and social component. Therefore, society need not wait for future heredity-environmental research in order to attempt environmental improvements, nor will it do so." On the other hand, the Academy statement made it clear that environmental improvements must be made before meaningful heredity-environment research in race differences is possible. The statement continued that, although the Academy stood for freedom of inquiry, recognized value in genetic research of all kinds, and supported research in human genetics, it did not see any social urgency in the proposed research aimed at establishing inherent Negro inferiority, and it would not sponsor any crash program in that direction.

[62] Dwight J. Ingle, "Racial Differences and the Future," *Science*, 146 (Oct. 16, 1964), pp. 375–379; William Shockley, "Proposed Research to Reduce Racial Aspects of the Environment-Heredity Uncertainty," *Science*, 160 (April 26, 1968), p. 443. The article refers to an earlier speech.

[63] National Academy of Sciences, "Racial Studies: Academy States Position on Call for New Research," *Science*, 158 (Nov. 17, 1967), pp. 892–893.

The Academy statement was prepared with the help of four prominent geneticists.[64]

Jensen, in his invited address to the 1967 Annual Meeting of the American Educational Research Association, reported racial and ethnic differences in *patterns* of learning abilities. He called for study of the causes of individual and group differences, both genetic and environmental, in order to provide appropriately different educational opportuinties for different needs. He pointed to the distinct patterns of learning abilities as evidence that all individuals and groups cannot profit from identical educational experience. He maintained that for many minority-group children, the normal educational experiences becomes psychologically damaging. Their exposure to repeated inappropriate and unrewarding experiences early in their schooling acts like Pavlov's experimental neurosis to condition them against the whole educational process.[65]

Jensen based his belief in inherent ethnic and racial intelligence differences, in part, on studies showing significantly different patterns of learning abilities among different ethnic and racial groups, with Negroes and Jews, for example, having higher verbal than reasoning, numerical, or spatial test averages, and Chinese-Americans and Puerto Ricans averaging consistently lower on the verbal than on the other tests. In part, his belief was based on findings that show racial, ethnic, and class differences in correlation patterns between IQ and basic learning test scores. There is a high correlation for middle-class Anglo-American children, but not for Negro, Latin-American, or lower socioeconomic-status (SES) Anglo-Americans. The latter racial, ethnic, and lower SES groups showed high means in basic learning test scores, even when mean IQ's were low. Jensen interpreted both of these differences in patterns of intellectual abilities as showing hereditary differences (including those between classes within the Anglo-American group).[66] It appears, however, that these differences might be due to language problems and environmental handicaps rather than to hereditary effects. His interpretation is consistent with his proposal that racial research should begin with "the simplest possible hypothesis": that intelligence-test differences between races or groups are caused by inherited factors to the same extent as are differences between individuals. However, in view of the different genetic principles involved in individual heredity, on the one hand, and population genetics, on the other, Jensen's hypothesis is by no means the "simplest" one.[67]

---

[64] *Ibid.*

[65] Arthur R. Jensen, "Social Class, Race, and Genetics: Implications for Education," *American Educational Research Journal*, 5 (1968), pp. 1–42.

[66] *Ibid.*

[67] *Ibid.*; for discussions of these genetic principles, see Theodosius Dobzhansky, "Genetics of Race Equality," *Eugenics Quarterly*, 10 (Dec., 1964), pp. 151–160; Ernst Caspari, "Genetic Endowment and Environment in the Determination of Human Behavior: Biological Viewpoint," *American Educational Research Journal*, 5 (Jan., 1968), pp. 43–55; Bruce K. Eckland, "Genetics and Sociology: A Reconsideration," *American Sociological Review*, 32 (April, 1967), pp. 173–194; and Jerry Hirsch, "Be-

THE SYNTHESIZERS. Scholars from several disciplines have attempted to resolve the continuing controversy over "nature versus nurture" by finding a synthesis of the best from both viewpoints. They add to the position of Tyler (above) by pointing out that a knowledge of genetics is necessary for fully appreciating the importance of culture in human development, especially in a highly complex polygenic trait like human intellectual capacity. Sociologist Bruce K. Eckland of the University of North Carolina, noted in a 1967 paper[68] that sociologists have been particularly resistant to any synthesis between genetics and social science, with the last major sociological reference to interdependence of heredity and environment having been Sorokin's 1927 essay on social mobility.[69]

Eckland's discussion argues that sociologists should re-examine their positions and integrate their views on genetic and social processes, especially in sociological investigations of such problems as those involving intelligence, race, and social-class differences in fertility. He stressed that rather than set heredity and environment against each other, scientists should accept evidence from both.

Ernst Caspari, professor of biology at the University of Rochester, elaborated the same arguments for synthesis from the biological point of view. He emphasized the large number of genes, particularly in higher organisms, whose expression is different in different environments. In the higher human traits especially, "most behavioral characters are either strongly influenced by environmental factors or may be completely dependent on it. . . . Furthermore, the environment to which we refer in man is his previous learning environment, determined by his socioeconomic background."[70] He stated that the question of how much variance is due to heredity and how much to environment is not a useful question, because the answer would depend upon how much variation existed in environmental conditions and thus would be valid only for a temporary and local cultural situation. He stressed that the important question is how heredity and environment interact in the development of intelligence. He also stressed the need to create educational methods and environments to permit the full development of unique individuals.

Geneticist Dobzhansky of the Rockefeller Institute, in a 1964 essay on the genetics of race equality, pointed out that the environmental plasticity of physic traits in man greatly exceeds that of his physical traits or of the temperamental traits deliberately bred into different strains of domesticated animals. "Mankind's singular and singularly powerful adaptive instrument is culture. Culture is not inherited through the genes, it is acquired by learning from other human beings. The ability to learn, and thus to acquire a culture and to become a member of a society is, how-

---

havior-Genetic, or 'Experimental,' Analysis: The Challenge of Science versus the Lure of Technology," *American Psychologist*, 22 (Feb., 1967), pp. 118–130.

[68] Eckland, "Genetics and Sociology."

[69] Pitirim A. Sorokin, *Social and Cultural Mobility* (New York: The Free Press of Glencoe, 1964).

[70] Caspari, "Genetic Endowment."

ever, given by the genetic endowment that is mankind's distinctive biological attribute."[71]

Most of these synthesizers distinguish clearly between the hereditary influence in *individual* differences and innate *racial* differences in intelligence or personality. Eckland, for example, pointed out that random individual variations do not become stable population characteristics, even over time and with an isolated population, if they are maladaptive.[72] It appears that intelligence would have as much positive survival value among primitive peoples facing tribal enemies and jungle dangers in equatorial Africa as among equally primitive tribes roaming the forests of prehistoric Europe.[73] Eckland noted, however, that intelligence variations may be genetically determined in part among individuals and families, as well as between social classes, by assortative mating, a factor not present between races.[74]

CONCLUSIONS

Coincident with the world-wide expansion of European colonialism and the rapid growth of the unique American slavery system, social thinkers of the eighteenth and early nineteenth centuries began to base their thinking on observed "facts." The universally inferior position of dark-skinned peoples led these thinkers to accept without critical examination the prevailing assumptions of their culture that darker races were inherently inferior. Early social science investigations seeking to explain this apparent inferiority served to reinforce the popular assumptions.

Eventually, however, the repeated failure to find a consistent explanation of Negro inferiority in any significant physical differences led to a weakening of the assumption of inherent Negro inferiority. The continuing development and application of social science techniques forced in time a re-examination of World War I Army test scores and similar data. This re-examination of the data also brought a challenge to the previously accepted face evaluation as supporting the theory of inherent Negro inferiority.

During the 1920's and 1930's, the studies generated by this reconsideration resulted in a complete shift of social science opinion to an almost unanimous rejection of the idea that there is convincing evidence of innate racial differences in intelligence. Although some differences of opinion have persisted, the social sciences generally assume social, rather than genetic, causes for social and cultural differences between races and ethnic groups and support further social changes to alleviate environmental handicaps of racial and ethnic minorities.

A significant cohort of synthesizers from various scientific disciplines is working toward relating social science and genetic knowledge about heredity and socially significant traits, such as intelligence. These scholars agree with the majority of social scientists that race as a variable offers

[71] Dobzhansky, "Genetics of Race Equality."
[72] Eckland, "Genetics and Sociology," pp. 173–194.
[73] Pettigrew, *Profile*, pp. 66–67.
[74] Eckland, "Genetics and Sociology."

no valuable explanations yet search for findings on heredity-environment interaction elsewhere. Rejecting the false antithesis of heredity *vs* environment, questions may be proposed for research in test situations which raise (or lower) "intelligence as measured." This marks the close of the controversy we have noted above and indicates a shift to a new area of inquiry.

Increasingly social scientists may be asked to measure the effectiveness of current social policies, largely as a basis for planning future policy. This provides an opportunity for wider research in the effects of *any* program felt to produce a result in effective intelligence. Some research might be in experimental situations with rigid controls. Much more, probably, could make use of social experiments available in the larger society. Current national policies, public school desegregation, preschool programs, and youth programs are not established for the purposes of social science test; they may, however, be used for this purpose by qualified researchers. A complete test will require as wide an experimental group as possible, making use of the extremes of any "normal distribution" of intelligence as well as the mean. Race has been shown to be irrelevant to these extremes but not yet have conclusive results been disclosed that would be relevant to the heredity-environment interaction. With the distracting red flag of race out of the way, one may now deal with more important problems with which the idea of race has been accidentally entwined.

A Selected Bibliography on Social and Demographic Characteristics of Blacks in the United States

Alexis, Marcus, "Some Negro-White Differences in Consumption," *American Journal of Economics and Sociology*, 21 (Jan., 1962), pp. 11–28.

Babchuck, Nicholas, and Ralph V. Thompson, "The Voluntary Associations of Negroes," *American Sociological Review*, 27 (Oct., 1962), pp. 647–655.

Back, Kurt W., and Ida Harper Simpson, "The Dilemma of the Negro Professional," *Journal of Social Issues*, 20 (April, 1964), pp. 60–70.

Bahr, Howard M., and Jack P. Gibbs, "Racial Differentiation in American Metropolitan Areas," *Social Forces*, 45 (June, 1967), pp. 521–532.

Batchelder, Alan B., "Decline in the Relative Income of Negro Men," *Quarterly Journal of Economics*, 78 (Nov., 1964), pp. 525–548.

Batchelder, Alan B., "Poverty: The Special Case of the Negro," *American Economic Review*, 55 (May, 1965), pp. 530–540.

Bates, William M., "Narcotics, Negroes and the South," *Social Forces*, 45 (Sept., 1966), pp. 61–67.

Bauer, Raymond, *et al.*, "The Marketing Dilemma of Negroes," *Journal of Marketing*, 29 (July, 1965), pp. 1–6.

Bell, R. R., "Lower Class Negro Mothers' Aspirations for their Children," *Social Forces*, 43 (May, 1965), pp. 493–500.

Bernard, Jessie, *Marriage and Family among Negroes* (Englewood Cliffs: Prentice-Hall, 1966).

Berry, Brewton, *Almost White: A Study of Certain Racial Hybrids in the Eastern United States* (New York: Macmillan, 1963).

Billingsley, Andrew, *Black Families in White America* (Englewood Cliffs: Prentice-Hall, 1968).

Black, L. E., "The Negro Market," *Sales Management*, 91 (Oct. 4, 1963), pp. 42–47.

Blum, Alan F., "Lower-Class Negro Television Spectators: The Concept of Pseudo-Jovial Scepticism," in Arthur B. Shostak and William Gomberg (editors), *Blue-Collar Worlds* (Englewood Cliffs: Prentice-Hall, 1964).

Bock, E. Wilbur, "The Decline of the Negro Clergy: Changes in Formal Religious Leadership in the United States in the Twentieth Century," *Phylon*, 29 (Spring, 1968), pp. 48–64.

Brazziel, William F., "Correlates of Southern Negro Personality," *Journal of Social Issues*, 20 (1964), pp. 46–54.

Broderick, C. B., "Social Heterosexual Development among Urban Negroes and Whites," *Journal of Marriage and the Family*, 27 (May, 1965), pp. 200–203.

Broom, Leonard, and Norval D. Glenn, "Negro-White Differences in Reported Attitudes and Behavior," *Sociology and Social Research*, 50 (Jan., 1966), pp. 199.

Broom, Leonard, and Norval D. Glenn, *Transformation of the Negro American* (New York: Harper, 1965).

Broom, Leonard, and Norval D. Glenn, "When Will America's Negroes Catch Up?" *New Society* (March 25, 1965), pp. 6–7.

Bullock, Henry Allen, "Consumer Motivations in Black and White—Part I," *Harvard Business Review*, 33 (May–June, 1961), pp. 89–104 —— "Part II," *ibid.* (July–August, 1961), pp. 110–124.

Burgess, M. Elaine, *Negro Leadership in a Southern City* (Chapel Hill: University of North Carolina Press, 1962).

Burma, John H., "Interethnic Marriage in Los Angeles, 1948–1959," *Social Forces*, 42 (Dec., 1963), pp. 156–165.

Caplovitz, David, *The Poor Pay More* (New York: Free Press, 1963).

Carter, Wilmoth A., *The New Negro of the South* (New York: Exposition Press, 1967).

Chalmers, W. Ellison, and Nathaniel W. Dorsey, "Research on Negro Job Status," *Journal of Intergroup Relations*, 3 (Fall, 1962), pp. 344–359.

Clark, Kenneth B. "Alternative School Systems," *Harvard Educational Review*, 38 (Winter, 1968), pp. 100–113.

Clark, Kenneth B., *Dark Ghetto* (New York: Harper, 1965).

Clark, Kenneth B., and Mamie P. Clark, "Racial Identification and Preference in Negro Children," in Theodore M. Newcomb and E. L. Hartley (editors), *Readings in Social Psychology* (New York: Holt, 1947).

Clift, Virgil A., Archibald W. Anderson, and H. Gordon Hullfish, *Negro Education in America: Its Adequacy, Problems and Needs* (New York: Harper, 1962).

Cohen, Albert K., and Harold M. Hodges, "Characteristics of the Lower-Blue-Collar Class," *Social Problems*, 10 (Spring, 1963), pp. 303–334.

Cohen, David K., "Policy for the Public Schools: Compensation and Integration," *Harvard Educational Review*, 38 (Winter, 1968), pp. 114–137.

Coleman, James S., "The Concept of Equality of Educational Opportunity," *Harvard Educational Review*, 38 (Winter, 1968), pp. 7–22.

Coleman, James S., *et al.*, *Equality of Educational Opportunity* (Washington, D.C.: Government Printing Office, 1966).

Conant, James B., *Slums and Suburbs* (New York: McGraw-Hill, 1961).

Conot, Robert, *Rivers of Blood, Years of Darkness* (New York: Bantam, 1967).

Coon, Carleton S., *The Origin of Races* (New York: Knopf, 1962).

Coon, Carleton S., with Edward E. Hunt, Jr., *The Living Races of Man* (New York: Knopf, 1965).

Cramer, M. Richard, *et al.*, *Social Factors in Educational Achievement and Aspirations among Negro Adolescents* (Chapel Hill: Institute for Research in Social Science of the University of North Carolina, 1966).

Cruse, Harold, *The Crisis of the Negro Intellectual* (New York: Morrow, 1967).

David, Stephen M., "Leadership of the Poor in Poverty Programs," in *Urban Riots: Violence and Social Change* (New York: Academy of Political Science, 1968).

Davie, Maurice, *Negroes in American Society* (New York: McGraw-Hill, 1949).

Davis, Allison, and John Dollard, *Children of Bondage* (Washington, D.C.: American Council of Education, 1940).

Davis, Allison, Burleigh B. Gardner, and Mary R. Gardner, *Deep South* (Chicago: University of Chicago Press, 1941).

Dentler, Robert A., Bernard Mackler, and Mary Ellen Warshauser (editors), *The Urban R's: Race Relations as the Problem in Urban Education* (New York: Praeger, 1967).

Deutsch, Martin, and Bert Brown, "Social Influences in Negro-White Intelligence Difference," *Journal of Social Issues*, 20 (1964), pp. 4–24.

Dobzhansky, Theodosius, "Genetics of Race Equality," *Eugenics Quarterly*, 10 (Dec., 1964), pp. 151–160.

Doddy, Hurley H., "The Status of the Negro Public College: A Statistical Summary," *Journal of Negro Education*, 31 (Summer, 1962), pp. 370–385.

Dollard, John, *Caste and Class in a Southern Town*," third edition (Garden City: Doubleday, 1957).

Drake, St. Clair, "The Social and Economic Status of the Negro in the United States," *Daedalus*, 94 (Fall, 1965), pp. 771–814.

Drake, St. Clair, and Horace R. Cayton, *Black Metropolis*, revised edition (New York: Harper, 1962).

Dreger, Ralph M., and Kent S. Miller, "Comparative Psychological Studies of Negroes and Whites in the United States," *Psychological Bulletin*, 57 (1960), pp. 361–402.

Duncan, Otis D., and Beverly Duncan, *The Negro Population of Chicago: A Study of Residential Succession* (Chicago: University of Chicago Press, 1957).

Eckland, Bruce K., "Genetics and Sociology: A Reconsideration," *American Sociological Review*, 32 (April, 1967), pp. 173–194.

Edwards, G. Franklin, *The Negro Professional Class* (New York: Free Press, 1959).

Edwards, G. Franklin, "The Occupational Mobility of Negro Professional Workers," in E. W. Burgess and D. J. Bogue (editors), *Contributions to Urban Sociology* (Chicago: University of Chicago Press, 1964).

Elkins, Stanley M., *Slavery: A Problem in American Institutional and Intellectual Life* (Chicago: University of Chicago Press, 1959).

Epps, Edgar G., Irwin Katz, and Leland J. Axelson, "Relation of Mother's Employment to Intellectual Performance of Negro College Students," *Social Problems*, 11 (1964), pp. 414–419.

Fauset, Arthur H., *Black Gods of the Metropolis* (Philadelphia: University of Pennsylvania Press, 1944).

Fein, Rashi, "An Economic and Social Profile of the Negro American," *Daedalus*, 94 (Fall, 1965), pp. 1055–1084.

Fichter, Joseph H., "American Religion and the Negro," *Daedalus*, 94 (Fall, 1965), pp. 1085–1106.

Finestone, Harold, "Cats, Kicks, and Color," *Social Problems*, 5 (July, 1957), pp. 3–13.

Franklin, John Hope, *From Slavery to Freedom: A History of American Negroes*, revised edition (New York: Knopf, 1956).

Franklin, John Hope, "History of Racial Segregation in the United States," *Annals of the American Academy of Political and Social Science* (March, 1956), pp. 1–9.

Frazier, E. Franklin, *Black Bourgeoisie* (New York: Free Press, 1957).

Frazier, E. Franklin, "The Impact of Urban Civilization upon Negro Family Life," *American Sociological Review*, 2 (Oct., 1937), pp. 609–618.

Frazier, E. Franklin, *The Negro Church in America* (New York: Schocken, 1963).

Frazier, E. Franklin, *The Negro Family in Chicago* (Chicago: University of Chicago Press, 1932).

Frazier, E. Franklin, *The Negro Family in the United States* (Chicago: University of Chicago Press, 1960).

Frazier, E. Franklin, *The Negro in the United States*, rev. ed. (New York: Macmillan, 1957).

Frazier, E. Franklin, *Negro Youth at the Crossroads* (New York: Harper, 1940).

Freeman, Howard E., J. Michael Ross, David Armor, and Thomas F. Pettigrew, "Color Gradation and Attitudes among Middle-Income Negroes," *American Sociological Review*, 31 (June, 1966), pp. 365–374.

Gerson, Walter M., "Mass Media Socialization Behavior: Negro-White Differences," *Social Forces*, 45 (Sept., 1966), pp. 40–50.

Gibbs, Jack P., "Occupational Differentiation of Negroes and Whites in the United States," *Social Forces*, 44 (Dec., 1965), pp. 159–165.

Ginzberg, Eli (editor), *The Negro Challenge to the Business Community* (New York: McGraw-Hill, 1964).

Ginzberg, Eli, *et al.*, *The Middle-Class Negro in the White Man's World* (New York: Columbia University Press, 1967).

Gist, Noel P., and William S. Bennett, Jr., "Aspirations of Negro and White Students," *Social Forces*, 42 (Oct., 1963), pp. 40–48.

Gittell, Marilyn, "Community Control of Education," in *Urban Riots: Violence and Social Change* (New York: Academy of Political Science, 1968).

Glazer, Nathan, and Davis McEntire (editors), *Studies in Housing and Minority Groups* (Berkeley: University of California Press, 1960).

Glenn, Norval D., "Negro Population Concentration and Negro Status," *Journal of Negro Education*, 36 (Fall, 1967), pp. 353–361.

Glenn, Norval D., "Negro Prestige Criteria: A Case Study in the Bases of Prestige," *American Journal of Sociology*, 68 (May, 1963), pp. 645–657.

Glenn, Norval D., "Negro Religion and Negro Status in the United States," in Louis Schneider (editor), *Religion, Culture and Society* (New York: Wiley, 1964).

Glenn, Norval D., "The Relative Size of the Negro Population and Negro Occupational Status," *Social Forces*, 43 (Oct., 1964), pp. 42–49.

Glenn, Norval D., "Some Changes in the Relative Status of American Nonwhites, 1940 to 1960," *Phylon*, 24 (Summer, 1963), pp. 109–122.

Goldwin, Robert A. (editor), *100 Years of Emancipation* (Chicago: Rand McNally, 1963).

Greer, Scott, *Last Man In: Racial Access to Union Power* (New York: Free Press, 1959).

Grier, Eunice S., and George Grier, *Privately Developed Interracial Housing: An Analysis of Experience* (Berkeley: University of California Press, 1960).

Gurin, Patricia, and Edgar Epps, "Some Characteristics of Students from Poverty Backgrounds Attending Predominantly Negro Colleges in the Deep South," *Social Forces*, 45 (Sept., 1966), pp. 27–40.

Handlin, Oscar, *The Newcomers: Negroes and Puerto Ricans in a Changing Metropolis* (Cambridge: Harvard University Press, 1959).

Hare, Nathan, "Recent Trends in the Occupational Mobility of Negroes, 1930–1960: An Intracohort Analysis," *Social Forces*, 44 (Dec., 1965), pp. 166–173.

Heilbrun, James, and Stanislaw H. Wellisz, "An Economic Program for the Ghetto," *Urban Riots: Violence and Social Change* (New York: Academy of Political Science, 1968).

Henderson, Vivian W., *The Economic Status of Negroes: In the Nation and in the South* (Atlanta: Southern Regional Council, 1963).

Henry, Jules, "White People's Time, Colored People's Time," *Trans-action*, 3 (March–April, 1965), pp. 31–34.

Herskovits, Melville J., *The Anthropometry of the American Negro* (New York: Columbia University Press, 1930).

Herskovits, Melville J., *The Myth of the Negro Past* (New York: Harper, 1941).

Hiestand, Dale L., *Economic Growth and Employment Opportunities for Minorities* (New York: Columbia University Press, 1964).

Holloway, Harry, "'The Negro and the Vote: The Case of Texas," *Journal of Politics*, 23 (August, 1961), pp. 526–556.

Hope, John, II, and E. Shelton, "The Negro in the Federal Government," *Journal of Negro Education*, 32 (Fall, 1963), pp. 367–374.

Horton, John, "Time and Cool People," *Trans-action*, 5 (April, 1967), pp. 5–12.

Ingle, Dwight J., "Racial Differences and the Future," *Science*, 146 (Oct., 1964), pp. 375–379.

Jensen, Arthur R., "Social Class, Race, and Genetics: Implications for Education," *American Educational Research Journal*, 5 (1969), pp. 1–42.

Johnson, Charles S., *Growing Up in the Black Belt* (New York: Harper, 1941).

Kessler, Jane W., "Environmental Components of Measured Intelligence," *School Review*, 73 (1965), pp. 339–358.

Keech, William R., *The Impact of Negro Voting: The Role of the Vote in the Quest for Equality* (Chicago: Rand McNally, 1968).

Key, V. O., Jr., *Southern Politics in State and Nation* (New York: Knopf, 1949).

Killian, Lewis M., and Charles M. Grigg, "Urbanism, Race and Anomia," *American Journal of Sociology*, 67 (May, 1962), pp. 661–665.

Kinzer, Robert H., and Edward Sagarin, *The Negro in American Business: The Conflict between Separation and Integration* (New York: Greenberg, 1950).

Klein, L. R., and W. H. Mooney, "Negro-White Savings Differentials and the Consumption Function Problem," *Econometrics*, 21 (July, 1953), pp. 435–456.

Kleiner, R. J., and H. Taylor, *Social Status and Aspirations in Philadelphia's Negro Population* (Philadelphia: Commission on Human Relations, 1962).

Klineberg, Otto, *et al.*, "Intelligence of the American Negro: Statement by Social Scientists," *American Journal of Orthopsychiatry*, 27 (1957), pp. 420–422.

Klineberg, Otto, "Negro-White Differences in Intelligence Test Performance: A New Look at an Old Problem," *American Psychologist*, 18 (April, 1963), pp. 198–203.

Klineberg, Otto, *Negro Intelligence and Selective Migration* (New York: Columbia University Press, 1935).

Krueger, A. D., "The Economics of Discrimination," *Journal of Political Economy*, 71 (Oct., 1963), pp. 481–486.

Krueger, E. T., "Negro Religious Expression," *American Journal of Sociology*, 38 (July, 1932), pp. 22–31.

Kuvlesky, William P., and George W. Ohlendorf, "A Rural-Urban Comparison of the Occupational Status Orientations of Negro Boys," *Rural Sociology*, 33 (June, 1968), pp. 144–152.

Ladd, Everett C., *Negro Political Leadership in the South* (Ithaca: Cornell University Press, 1966).

Ladd, W. M., "The Effect of Integration on Property Values," *American Economic Review*, 52 (September, 1962), pp. 801–808.

Laurenti, Luigi, *Property Values and Race: Studies in Seven Cities* (Berkeley: University of California Press, 1960).

Lee, Everett S., "Negro Intelligence and Selective Migration: A Philadelphia Test of the Klineberg Hypothesis," *American Sociological Review*, 16 (April, 1951), pp. 227–233.

Lee, Frank F., *Negro and White in Connecticut Town* (New Haven: College and University Press, 1961).

Lefton, Mark, "Race, Expectations and Anomia," *Social Forces*, 46 (March, 1968), pp. 347–352.

Leggett, John C., "Working-Class Consciousness, Race, and Political Choice," *American Journal of Sociology*, 69 (Sept., 1963), pp. 171–176.

Lenski, Gerhard, *The Religious Factor* (Garden City: Doubleday, 1961).

Leventman, Seymour, "Race and Mental Illness in Mass Society," *Social Problems*, 16 (Summer, 1968), pp. 73–78.

Lewis, Hylan, *Blackways of Kent* (Chapel Hill: University of North Carolina Press, 1955).

Lewis, Hylan, "Juvenile Delinquency among Negroes: A Critical Summary," *Journal of Negro Education*, 28 (Summer, 1959), pp. 371–387.

Lieberson, Stanley, and Glenn V. Fuguitt, "Negro-White Occupational Differences in the Absence of Discrimination," *American Journal of Sociology*, 73 (Sept., 1967), pp. 188–200.

Liebow, Elliot, *Tally's Corner* (Boston: Little, Brown, 1966).

Logan, Rayford W., *The Negro in the United States: A Brief History* (Princeton: Van Nostrand, 1957).

Lott, Bernice E., and Albert J. Lott, *Negro and White Youth: A Psychological Study in a Border State Community* (New York: Holt, 1963).

McDill, Mary Sexton, Arthur L. Stinchcombe, and Dollie Walker, "Segregation and Educational Disadvantage: Estimates of the Influence of Different Segregating Factors," *Sociology of Education*, 41 (Summer, 1968), pp. 239–246.

McEntire, Davis, *Residence and Race* (Berkeley: University of California Press, 1960).

McGrath, Earl J., *The Predominantly Negro Colleges and Universities in Transition* (New York: Bureau of Publications, Teachers College, Columbia University, 1965).

Mack, Raymond W., *Our Children's Burden: School Desegregation in Ten American Communities* (New York: Random House, 1968).

Marden, Charles F., and Gladys Meyer, *Minorities in American Society*, third edition (New York: American Book, 1968).

Marvick, Dwaine, "The Political Socialization of the American Negro," *Annals of the American Academy of Political and Social Science*, 381 (Sept., 1965), pp. 112–127.

Matthews, Donald R., and James W. Prothro, *Negroes and the New Southern Politics* (New York: Harcourt, 1966).

Matthews, Donald R., and James W. Prothro, "Political Factors and Negro Voter Registration in the South," *American Political Science Review*, 57 (June, 1963), pp. 355–367.

Matthews, Donald R., and James W. Prothro, "Social and Economic Factors and Negro Voter Registration in the South," *American Political Science Review*, 57 (March, 1963), pp. 24–44.

Matthews, Donald R., and James W. Prothro, "Southern Images of Political Parties: An Analysis of White and Negro Attitudes," *Journal of Politics*, 26 (Feb., 1964), pp. 82–111.

Mays, Benjamin E., and Joseph W. Nicholson, *The Negroes' Church* (New York: Institute of Social and Religious Research, 1933).

Meadow, Kathryn P., "Negro-White Differences among Newcomers to a Transitional Urban Area," *Journal of Intergroup Relations*, 3 (1962), pp. 320–330.

Meier, August, and Elliott Rudwick (editors), *The Making of Black America* (New York: Atheneum, 1968).

Middleton, Russell, and John Moland, "Humor in Negro and White Subcultures: A Story of Jokes among University Students," *American Sociological Review*, 24 (Feb., 1959), pp. 61–69.

Middleton, Russell, and Snell Putney, "Dominance in Decisions in the Family: Race and Class Differences," *American Journal of Sociology*, 65 (May, 1960), pp. 605–609.

Miller, C., C. Wertz, and S. Counts, "Racial Differences on the MMPI," *Journal of Clinical Psychology*, 17 (April, 1961), pp. 159–161.

Miller, Herman P., *Rich Man, Poor Man* (New York: Crowell, 1964).

Moynihan, Daniel Patrick, "Employment, Income and the Ordeal of the Negro Family," *Daedalus*, 94 (Fall, 1965), pp. 745–770.

Moynihan, Daniel Patrick, *The Negro Family: The Case for National Action* (Washington, D.C.: Department of Labor, 1965).

Myrdal, Gunnar, *An American Dilemma* (New York: Harper, 1944).

North, Robert D., "The Intelligence of American Negroes," *Research Reports of Anti-Defamation League*, 3(1956), pp. 2–8.

Ohlendorf, George W., and William P. Kuvlesky, "Racial Differences in the Educational Orientations of Rural Youth," *Social Science Quarterly*, 49 (Sept., 1968), pp. 274–283.

Osofsky, Gilbert, *Harlem: The Making of a Ghetto* (New York: Harper, 1965).

Parenti, Michael, "Ethnic Politics and the Persistence of Party Identification," *American Political Science Review*, 61 (Sept., 1967), pp. 717–726.

Parker, Seymour, and Robert J. Kleiner, "Status Position, Mobility and Ethnic Identification of the Negro," *Journal of Social Issues*, 20 (April, 1964), pp. 85–102.

Pettigrew, Thomas F., *A Profile of the Negro American* (Princeton: Van Nostrand, 1964).

Pettigrew, Thomas F., and Rosalind B. Spier, "The Ecological Structure of Negro Homicide," *American Journal of Sociology*, 67 (May, 1962), pp. 621–629.

Pettigrew, Thomas F., "Race and Equal Educational Opportunity," *Harvard Educational Review*, 38 (June, 1968), pp. 66–76.

Pope, Liston, "The Negro and Religion in America," *Review of Religious Research*, 5 (Spring, 1964), pp. 142–152.

Powdermaker, Hortense, *After Freedom: A Cultural Study of the Deep South* (New York: Viking, 1939).

Price, Hugh D., *The Negro and Southern Politics* (New York: New York University Press, 1957).

Prothro, James W., and Charles U. Smith, "Ethnic Differences in Authoritarian Personality," *Social Forces*, 35 (May, 1957), pp. 334–338.

Purcell, Theodore V., "The Hopes of Negro Workers for Their Children," in Arthur B. Shostak and William Gomberg (editors), *Blue-Collar World* (Englewood Cliffs: Prentice-Hall, 1964).

Rainwater, Lee, "Crucible of Identity: The Negro Lower-Class Family," *Daedalus* (Winter, 1966).

Rainwater, Lee, and William L. Yancey, "Black Families and the White House," *Trans-action*, 5 (July-August, 1966), pp. 6–11.

Rainwater, Lee, and William Yancey, *The Moynihan Report and the Politics of Controversy* (Boston: MIT Press, 1967).

Rapkin, Chester, and William G. Grigsby, *The Demand for Housing in Racially Mixed Areas: A Study of Neighborhood Change* (Berkeley: University of California Press, 1960).

Record, Wilson, *The Negro and the Communist Party* (Chapel Hill: University of North Carolina Press, 1951).

Record, Wilson, *Race and Radicalism: The NAACP and the Communist Party in Conflict* (Ithaca: Cornell University Press, 1964).

Record, Wilson, "Social Stratification and Intellectual Roles in the Negro Community," *British Journal of Sociology*, 8 (Sept., 1957), pp. 235–255.

Reiss, Ira L., "Premarital Sexual Permissiveness among Negroes and Whites," *American Sociological Review*, 29 (Oct., 1964), pp. 688–698.

Reitzes, Dietrich C., *Negroes and Medicine* (Cambridge: Harvard University Press, 1958).

Report of the National Advisory Commission on Civil Disorders (New York: Bantam Books, 1968).

Riessman, Frank, *The Culturally Deprived Child and His Education* (New York: Harper, 1962).

Robins, Lee, "Negro Homicide Victims—Who Will They Be?" *Trans-action*, 7 (June, 1968), pp. 15–19.

Rohrer, J. H., and M. S. Edmunson, *The Eighth Generation* (New York: Harper, 1960).

Rosen, Bernard C., "Race, Ethnicity and the Achievement Syndrome," *American Sociological Review*, 24 (Feb., 1959), pp. 47–60.

Ross, Arthur M., and Herbert Hill (editors), *Employment, Race and Poverty* (New York: Harcourt, 1967).

Rudwick, Elliott M., *W. E. B. DuBois* (Philadelphia: University of Pennsylvania Press, 1960).

Sawyer, Broadus E., "An Examination of Race as a Factor in Negro-White

Consumption Patterns," *Review of Economics and Statistics*, 44 (May 1962), pp. 217–220.

Schnore, Leo F., and Harry Sharp, "Racial Changes in Metropolitan Areas, 1950–1960," *Social Forces*, 41 (March, 1963), pp. 247–252.

Schultz, Theodore W., "Investment in Human Capital," *American Economic Review*, 41 (March, 1961), pp. 1–17.

Scoble, Harry, *Negro Politics in Los Angeles: The Quest for Power* (Los Angeles: Institute of Government and Public Affairs, University of California, 1967).

Scoble, Harry, "Effects of Riots on Negro Leadership," in Louis H. Masotti and Don R. Bowen (editors), *Riots and Rebellion* (Beverly Hills: Sage Publications, 1968).

Sexton, Patricia Cayo, *Education and Income: Inequities in the Public Schools* (New York: Viking, 1961).

Shuey, Audrey M., *The Testing of Negro Intelligence*, second edition, (New York: Social Science Press, 1966).

Siegel, Paul M., "On the Cost of Being a Negro," *Sociological Inquiry*, 35 (1965), pp. 41–58.

Silberman, Charles E., *Crisis in Black and White* (New York: Random House, 1964).

Simpson, George E., and J. Milton Yinger, *Racial and Cultural Minorities: An Analysis of Prejudice and Discrimination*, third edition (New York: Harper, 1965).

Sprey, Jetse, "Sex Differences in Occupational Choice Patterns among Negro Adolescents," *Social Problems*, 10 (Summer, 1962), pp. 11–23.

Street, David, and John C. Leggett, "Economic Deprivation and Extremism: A Study of Unemployed Negroes," *American Journal of Sociology*, 67 (July, 1961), pp. 53–57.

Sutherland, Robert L., *Color, Class and Personality* (Washington, D.C.: American Council on Education, 1942).

Taeuber, Karl E., "The Problem of Residential Segregation," in *Urban Riots: Violence and Social Change* (New York: Academy of Political Science, 1968).

Taeuber, Karl E., "Residential Segregation," *Scientific American*, 213 (Aug., 1965), pp. 12–19.

Taeuber, Karl E., and Alma F. Taeuber, "Changing Character of Negro Migration," *American Journal of Sociology*, 70 (Jan., 1965), pp. 429–441.

Taeuber, Karl E., and Alma F. Taeuber, "The Negro as an Immigrant Group: Recent Trends in Racial and Ethnic Segregation in Chicago," *American Journal of Sociology*, 69 (Jan., 1964), pp. 374–382.

Taeuber, Karl E., and Alma F. Taeuber, *Negroes in Cities: Residential Segregation and Neighborhood Change* (Chicago: Aldine, 1965).

Tannenbaum, Frank, *Slave and Citizen: The Negro in the Americas* (New York: Knopf, 1947).

Thompson, Daniel C., *The Negro Leadership Class* (Englewood Cliffs: Prentice-Hall, 1963).

Tobin, James, "On Improving the Economic Status of the Negro," *Daedalus*, 94 (Fall, 1965), pp. 878–898.

United States Commission on Civil Rights, *Racial Isolation in the Public Schools* (Washington: Government Printing Office, 1967).

Vander Zanden, James W., *American Minority Relations*, second edition (New York: Ronald, 1966).

Warner, W. Lloyd, Buford H. Junker, and Walter A. Adams, *Color and Human Nature* (New York: Harper, 1941).

Weaver, Robert C., *Dilemmas of Urban America* (Cambridge: Harvard University Press, 1965).

Weaver, Robert C., *The Urban Complex: Human Values in Urban Life* (Garden City: Doubleday, 1964).

Williams, J. Allen, Jr., "Interviewer-Respondent Interaction: A Study of Bias in the Information Interview," *Sociometry*, 27 (Sept., 1964), pp. 338–352.

Williams, J. Allen, Jr., "Interviewer Role Performance: A Further Note on Bias in the Information Interview," *Public Opinion Quarterly*, 32 (Summer, 1968), pp. 287–294.

Wilson, Alan B., *The Consequences of Segregation: Academic Achievement in a Northern Community* (Berkeley: Glendessary Press, 1969).

Wilson, James Q., "The Negro in Politics," *Daedalus*, 94 (Fall, 1965), pp. 949–973.

Wilson, James Q., *Negro Politics: The Search for Leadership* (New York: Free Press, 1960).

Wish, Harvey (editor), *The Negro since Emancipation* (Englewood Cliffs: Prentice-Hall, 1964).

Wolfgang, Marvin E., *Patterns in Criminal Homicide* (Philadelphia: University of Pennslyvania Press, 1958).

Wolfinger, Raymond E., "'The Development and Persistence of Ethnic Voting," *American Political Science Review*, 59 (Dec., 1965), pp. 896–908.

Woodson, Carter G., *The History of the Negro Church*, second edition (Washington, D.C.: Associated Publishers, 1945).

Woodward, C. Vann, "The Political Legacy of Reconstruction," *Journal of Negro Education*, 26 (Summer, 1957), pp. 231–240.

Wright, William E., *Memphis Politics: A Study in Racial Bloc Voting* (New York: McGraw-Hill, 1962).

Young, Harding B., "The Negro's Participation in American Business," *Journal of Negro Education*, 32 (Fall, 1963), pp. 390–401.

Part II

WHITE REACTIONS

TO BLACKS

The contributions in this section are additions to the voluminous literature on the social and psychological bases of discrimination and prejudice. The first selection, "The American Dilemma: An Empirical Test," by Frank R. Westie, is a landmark article that reports a test of what perhaps has been the most influential hypothesis concerning Negro-white relations in the United States. Set forth in 1944 by Gunnar Myrdal in his classic book, *An American Dilemma*,[1] the hypothesis, simply stated, is that many whites in the United States subscribe to the ideal of equality of opportunity and yet advocate discrimination against Negroes—an inconsistency that is recognized by many people and yet resolved to their satisfaction by a number of rationalizations. It is hardly to the credit of social science in the United States that this hypothesis was quoted, paraphrased, and criticized in hundreds of publications for twenty years without any major research being conducted to test it. As Westie is careful to point out, his research is hardly a definitive test, but it is the best

[1] Written in collaboration with Arnold Rose and Richard Sterner (Harper and Brothers, 1944).

empirical evidence on the subject yet published. Westie's data indicate that the dilemma is indeed real but that the psychological processes by which it is resolved are more complex than Myrdal envisioned.

Perhaps the most common type of study in the field of racial and ethnic relations involves the comparison of persons "high" and "low" in measured prejudice, or of persons "liberal" and "conservative" in their racial attitudes. The two categories are often compared on nonracial attitudes of various kinds, personality traits, and socioeconomic and demographic characteristics. A similar kind of study divides people into categories on the basis of some other characteristic and compares these categories on racial attitudes or measured prejudice. From these two kinds of studies, a large number of "correlates of prejudice" have been discovered, varying from fastidiousness about personal appearance to high involvement in pleasure activities, from church membership to exaggerated masculinity (in males). Usually the studies do not make clear the causal importance, if any, of the correlations. Sometimes the correlated characteristics seem to contribute to the prejudice, but more often than not, prejudice and its correlates probably have common sources.

In "Factors Related to Willingness to Experience Desegregation among Students in Segregated Schools," M. Richard Cramer reports research similar in its correlational approach to the dozens of other studies, and its findings generally agree with those of other studies. Cramer reports, for instance, that white high-school students with good grades, with high estimates of their popularity, from cities, and from high-income families were more receptive, on the whole, to desegregation than were other students. However, the study is unusual in that the number of subjects is exceptionally large, and the attitudes of blacks as well as of whites are treated. It is important, furthermore, because it reveals that some of the relationships differ markedly between the "Deep South" and the "Upper South"—an indication that social and cultural factors associated with region mediate the influence on racial attitudes of many other factors.

Cramer found in 1963–1964 that four-fifths of the white students in his "Deep South" sample were totally opposed to desegregation. This finding attests to an amazing insularity of the region at a time when all parts of the country were saturated with common stimuli from the national media of communication. Evidently, social commentators who wrote about "the end of the sectional South" during the early 1960's did so prematurely.

The next selection, "Altruism, Egoism, and Antagonism toward Negroes," by Vincent Jeffries and Richard T. Morris, also utilizes the conventional correlational approach, but the independent variable makes the study unusual. In view of the obvious relevance of the concepts of altruism and egoism to intergroup and interpersonal relations, it is surprising that they have been utilized relatively little in the research and theories of modern social science. The word "altruism" is not in the index of any current United States textbook on racial and ethnic relations, nor is it mentioned in most principles-of-sociology textbooks. Yet, one would expect general altruistic or egoistic orientations to be associated with attitudes and actions toward racial and ethnic minorities. Jeffries and Morris present evidence that what is expected is indeed the case.

This line of inquiry should prove fruitful for the understanding of intergroup relations. As Jeffries and Morris assume, some people undoubtedly are generally more altruistic than others, and greater knowledge of the sources of variation in altruism would be useful. Furthermore, we need to know under what conditions a general altruistic orientation is translated into beneficent action toward blacks and other minorities and under what conditions it is not. Many decisions involve not assigning priorities to one's own interests and the interests of others but rather assigning priorities to the interests of different others. In such cases, there seems to be a tendency to assign priorities on the basis of the closeness of affiliation of the others to oneself. For instance, the parent who perceives a conflict of interests between his child and a stranger is likely to act to further the interests of his child. This being the case, altruistic impulses expressed within solidary social groupings may be consistent with, and in fact the basis of, a collective selfishness of the group *vis-à-vis* outsiders. Therefore, one might hypothesize that the generally altruistic whites most likely to express their altruism toward blacks are those relatively lacking in close ties and obligations to other whites. More specifically, one might hypothesize that favorable action toward blacks is relatively frequent among unmarried and childless young adults. Empirical evidence might not support these hypotheses, but they suggest the kind of research that should prove fruitful.

Students of prejudice and discrimination have long debated the relationship between these phenomena and such dimensions of social stratification as education, income, and occupational prestige. In general, opinion polls and paper-and-pencil tests of prejudice have indicated that prejudice and the tendency to discriminate are more common among the poor, the poorly educated, and manual workers. However, the validity of these findings has been questioned, for it is possible that higher-status persons appear to be less prejudiced only because they are better able to perceive the purpose of questions designed to measure prejudice and therefore are less likely to give honest responses.

Voting would probably be a more valid measure of prejudice in any election in which the candidates were distinguished largely by their stands on racial issues. The 1964 Democratic primaries in Wisconsin, Indiana, and Maryland, in which a substantial proportion of the votes were cast for segregationist George Wallace, have been viewed as such elections, and the voting patterns have been analyzed to cast light on the distribution of prejudice. Undoubtedly, there will be similar studies of the votes for George Wallace in the 1968 presidential election.

However, in "The White Backlash Re-examined: Wallace and the 1964 Primaries," M. Margaret Conway casts doubt on the utility of such studies for the purpose of studying the distribution of prejudice among the social levels. In Maryland, the vote for Wallace was heavier in working-class districts, when percent nonwhite was controlled, but in Wisconsin the

Wallace vote was more characteristic of middle-class districts. The vote pattern in Indiana was more ambiguous but resembled the pattern in Maryland more than that in Wisconsin. Conway suggests that the main appeal of Wallace in Wisconsin was his general political conservatism, whereas racial issues were more salient in Indiana and Maryland. If so, previous studies of the Wallace vote in Wisconsin have given a misleading picture of the distribution of prejudice.

An important aspect of white reactions to blacks is the portrayal of blacks by the white-controlled media of communication, especially movies and television. The appearance of many Negroes in television programs and commercials during the past few years may or may not have had much effect on the racial attitudes of viewers, but it indicates that those who control casting have come to believe it is desirable, and perhaps in their self-interest, to have blacks appear in nonstereotypical roles. In "The Death of Rastus: Negroes in American Films Since 1945," Thomas R. Cripps describes changes in the typical portrayals of blacks in the movies. He points out that the traditional stereotypical portrayals are now rare, but he believes the portrayal of the black as a paragon of virtue, as in the typical Sidney Poitier movie, is simply a substitution of a new, and totally unbelievable, stereotype for the old "Rastus" portrayal. Whether or not the new image of the black in the movies is believable enough to white viewers to create more favorable attitudes toward blacks, and believable enough to blacks to improve their self images, has not yet been demonstrated through empirical investigation.

There are two major kinds of explanations for racial and ethnic discrimination and prejudice. One attributes discrimination and prejudice to the rational pursuit of self-interest by the majority population, or by some powerful segment of that population. For instance, the Marxists regard discrimination as primarily a matter of economic exploitation, and they claim that capitalists foster animosity between working-class blacks and whites as a "divide and conquer" strategy.[2] The second major kind of explanation, in contrast, considers discrimination and prejudice to be irrational and detrimental to almost all majority people as well as to the minority. Proponents of this view often concede that prejudice may serve, rather unsatisfactorily, certain personality needs of the prejudiced person, but they regard prejudice as an obstacle to more adequate means of adjustment. In the United States in recent years, liberals, as opposed to radicals, have leaned toward the latter kind of explanation, perhaps partly because it seems useful in persuasive efforts to lessen discrimination and prejudice.

The more objective and sophisticated students of racial and ethnic relations invariably use a combination of these two kinds of explanations, but there is disagreement on their relative importance. "White Gains from Negro Subordination," by Norval D. Glenn, reports an attempt to estimate from empirical evidence the extent of any economic and occupational

[2] The Marxist view obviously does not completely neglect irrationality, because it does not consider the prejudice of working-class whites to be rational in terms of their own interests.

benefits that accrue to whites in the United States from the presence and subordination of Negroes. This contribution reports convincing, although not conclusive, evidence for substantial benefits, and this evidence lends credibility to the explanations that attribute discrimination and prejudice to the rational pursuit of self-interest.

A possible benefit to certain whites that is not directly treated by Glenn may result from exploitation of black consumers. In "Poverty, Minorities, and Consumer Exploitation," Frederick D. Sturdivant and Walter T. Wilhelm report a study designed to determine whether or not blacks must pay higher prices for products and higher charges for credit because of their race. The findings suggest that "the poor pay more" for products, regardless of their race or ethnicity, but that merchants often discriminate against blacks in assessing credit charges. The study was conducted by sending disadvantaged couples of different races and ethnicity into ghetto and nonghetto stores and is a good example of experimental social scientific research.

The last two selections deal with the relationship between religion and black-white relations in the United States. A common point of view in social science is that religion has played no distinctly creative role but has merely tended to reinforce the status quo or give ideological support to social changes already underway. Neither John L. Eighmy, author of "The Baptists and Slavery: An Examination of the Origins and Benefits of Segregation," nor Jeffrey K. Hadden, author of "Ideological Conflict between Protestant Clergy and Laity on Civil Rights," accepts this point of view, although Hadden's article does underscore the limited efficacy of Protestant religious institutions and their functionaries in effecting changes in race relations. Eighmy maintains that the Baptist religion played a creative role in the antebellum South that paved the way for separation of the black and white churches after emancipation. The white Baptists, he maintains, instituted black-white separation within the antebellum congregations so that they could pursue their ideological commitment to convert the slaves to Christianity and yet preserve the social superiority of the whites. However, the "benefits" referred to in the title of the article accrued to blacks rather than whites, according to Eighmy. He believes that the separate black churches allowed blacks to escape to some degree from white paternalism and to develop a leadership and an institution relatively free from white control. Eighmy clearly believes the Baptists exerted influence that was on balance favorable to Negroes—a view not shared by most social scientists who have written about the relationship of religion to black-white relations in the United States.[3]

Hadden deals with the contemporary rather than the historical role of the church, and his view of the creativity of religion in race relations is distinctly different, although not diametrically opposed, to that of Eighmy. Many young white Protestant clergymen have become active in civil-rights activities and have given important support to the black protest

[3] For a discussion of the views of a number of social scientists, see George E. Simpson and J. Milton Yinger, *Racial and Cultural Minorities,* third edition (New York: Harper and Row, 1965).

movement, and Hadden does not deny that religious values have been important motives for their civil-rights activities. However, he presents evidence that the views and activities of the young clergymen have had little effect on the laity in the churches, who remain considerably less favorable to civil rights, on the average, than the clergymen. In fact, laymen who do not attend church are less prejudiced on the average than those who do, and laymen in general disapprove of the involvement of the churches in civil-rights activities. Therefore, although the Protestant churches have played more than an insignificant role in the civil-rights movement, they generally have not been able to change the attitudes of their own white lay members. The influence of the Catholic church on the racial attitudes of its membership is not treated by Hadden, and it may or may not have been greater than the influence of the Protestant churches.

· 15 ·

The American Dilemma: An Empirical Test[*]

FRANK R. WESTIE[**]
INDIANA UNIVERSITY

OSCAR HANDLIN, IN HIS REVIEW ARTICLE CELEBRATING THE RECENT APPEAR-ance of the 20th-anniversary of *An American Dilemma*,[1] observes:

Few serious studies of American society have been more widely read than Gunnar Myrdal's social-science classic, *An American Dilemma*. Its analysis of the Negro problem in the United States has been a magnet to scholars and a catalyst to political groups. Its recommendations have helped shape the strategy of every organization interested in legislation and in judicial interpretations.[2]

The social impact of the theory cannot be questioned, but the degree to which it describes empirical events has yet, after 20 years to be determined. In the study reported here I have attempted to test empirically the basic propositions, postulates and assumptions of the dilemma theory.

Many criticisms of the Myrdal theory have appeared in the sociological literature.[3] Not only did Myrdal and his associates fail to test the dilemma theory, but the main critics have also failed to test the basic assumptions about the world of events on which their criticisms are based.[4]

[*] Reprinted by permission of the American Sociological Association from the *American Sociological Review*, 30 (August, 1965), pp. 527-538.

[**] This study is one of a series supported, at various times, by the Human Ecology Fund, the Social Science Research Council, and the Graduate School of Indiana University. The support of these organizations is gratefully acknowledged. The invaluable assistance and collaboration of Marcia T. Segal, Frederick L. Whitam and Joseph W. Scott is greatly appreciated.

[1] Gunnar Myrdal, with the assistance of Richard Sterner and Arnold Rose, *An American Dilemma*, New York: Harper, 1944.

[2] Oscar Handlin, Review of 20th-Anniversary Edition of *An American Dilemma*, *New York Times Book Review*, April 21, 1963, p. 1.

[3] Among the more important critiques are Leo F. Crespi, "Is Gunnar Myrdal on the Right Track?" *Public Opinion Quarterly*, 9 (1945), pp. 201–212; Gwynn Nettler, "A Note on Myrdal's 'Notes on Facts and Valuations,'" Appendix 2 of *An American Dilemma*," *American Sociological Review*, 9 (1944), pp. 686–688; Arnold Rose, Reply to Nettler's "Note," *American Sociological Review*, 10 (1945), pp. 560–562; and the following reviews of *An American Dilemma*: E. Franklin Frazier in *American Journal of Sociology*, 50 (1945), pp. 555–557; Howard W. Odum, in *Social Forces*, 23 (1944), pp. 94–98; and Kimball Young, in *American Sociological Review*, 9 (1944), pp. 326–330.

[4] Empirical evaluations of the theory of the American dilemma include Ernest Q. Campbell, "Moral Discomfort and Racial Segregation—An Examination of the Myrdal Hypothesis," *Social Forces*, 39 (1961), pp. 228–234, and R. W. Friedrichs, "Christians and Residential Exclusion: An Empirical Study of a Northern Dilemma," *Journal of Social Issues*, 15 (1959), pp. 14–23. While few investigations have focused specifically on the American dilemma, any number of other studies have important implications for the theory. Perhaps most relevant are those dealing with verbally expressed attitudes and overt acts, e.g., Richard T. LaPiere, "Attitudes vs. Actions," *Social Forces*, 13

THE THEORY STATED

According to Myrdal,[5] Americans suffer from a basic ambivalence because they embrace, on the one hand, the Christian-democratic tenets of the "American Creed" and, on the other, any number of unChristian and undemocratic valuations defining relations between Negroes and whites. The theory is, essentially, an analysis of how Americans live with themselves in the face of this dilemma.

Myrdal's two basic concepts are *valuations* and *beliefs*. Valuations are conceptions of "what ought to be." Beliefs are conceptions of "what is" or "what was." Beliefs may be bizarre products of the imagination or they may be empirically valid.

Valuations may be placed along a continuum from the most general to the most specific. The American Creed valuations are very general, and their adherents consider them applicable to all Americans if not to all mankind. The valuations defining relations between Negroes and whites, on the other hand, are frequently quite specific, referring to "my kids," "my family," "our school," "our neighborhood," etc. For most Americans, Myrdal avers, the specific valuations are quite inconsistent with the general.

Americans, Myrdal maintains, want to present a rational picture of themselves to the world, but particularly to themselves. Given their desire to maintain an image of themselves as rational creatures on the one hand, and the irrationality inherent in their valuational inconsistencies on the other, Americans are faced with a dilemma. How do they live with themselves under these circumstances? According to Myrdal, they opportunistically call forth beliefs about reality to rationalize their valuation-inconsistencies. These beliefs exist ready-made in the form of culturally shared myths. For example, a particular American agrees with the general valuation in the American Creed which says that Americans ought to work toward achieving greater equality of opportunity for all. The same person also feels that Negroes ought not to go to the same school his children attend (a specific valuation). In order to rationalize this inconsistency, this person calls forth beliefs such as the following: a) "Negroes are inherently less capable intellectually than whites," therefore b) "Negro children would be frustrated in competition with white children," or, c) "The white children would be held back to the level of the slower Negro children."

(1934), pp. 230–237; Joseph D. Lohman and Dietrich C. Reitzes, "Note on Race Relations in Mass Society," *American Journal of Sociology*, 58 (1952), pp. 240–246; Bernard Kutner, Carol Wilkins and P. R. Yarrow, "Verbal Attitudes and Overt Behavior Involving Racial Prejudice," *Journal of Abnormal and Social Psychology*, 51 (1952), pp. 649–652; Melvin L. DeFleur and Frank R. Westie, "Verbal Attitudes and Overt Acts: An Experiment on the Salience of Attitudes, *American Sociological Review*, 23 (1958), pp. 667–673; Martin Fishbein, "An Investigation of the Relationship Between Beliefs About an Object and Attitudes Toward That Object," *Human Relations*, 16 (1963), pp. 233–240.

[5] This statement of the theory is my own conception of what Myrdal means. The

This dilemma may be conceived as existing on a societal level, as a part of culture. Myrdal emphasizes, however, that it ultimately resides in the consciences of particular individuals.

Myrdal's theory contains a number of assumptions about empirical reality which need to be tested. Ralph Turner was probably correct when he observed that

. . . it does not necessarily follow from the logical contradiction that most people in American society perceive any dilemma here. In fact, the over enthusiastic student of race relations may be distressed to find how many people and groups sincerely feel no disloyalty to democratic ideals in their support of segregation and discrimination.[6]

The empirical questions[7] this study seeks to answer are as follows:[8]

1. Do people endorse such conflicting valuations?
2. Do they recognize the inconsistency involved?
3. Do they, in fact, rationalize this inconsistency, and, if so, do such rationalizations take the form of beliefs?
4. Are psychological mechanisms other than rationalization employed? For example, are conflicting values repressed?
5. Where one or the other of the conflicting valuations is "adjusted" (i.e., changed or qualified), which of the valuations does the respondent alter or qualify, the general or the specific?
6. To what extent are people aware of, or oriented in terms of, the idealistic tenets of democracy and Christianity?

THE FORM OF THE EMPIRICAL TEST

The 103 cases comprising the sample were selected in 1957 from 40 residential blocks in the city of Indianapolis.[9] Within each household, we

---

interested reader should consult Appendix I, "The Mechanism of Rationalization," for Myrdal's original statement.

[6] Ralph H. Turner, "Value Conflict in Social Disorganization," *Sociology and Social Research*, 38 (1954), p. 304.

[7] The research is designed to answer empirical questions rather than test hypotheses *per se*; the questions serve the same basic research purpose without implying the degree of theoretical coherence and guidance hypotheses necessarily presume. See Frank R. Westie, "Toward Closer Relations Between Theory and Research: A Procedure and An Example," *American Sociological Review*, 22 (1957), pp. 149–154.

[8] I have also analyzed the relations between social class and the American dilemma, testing the hypothesis that persons of lower status are less troubled by it. The results will be presented in a separate paper (in preparation).

[9] A living-standard area map constructed by a commercial market analysis agency was used as the sampling base. This map demarcates three living-standard levels in the city. Numbers were assigned to the blocks on each level, and the blocks were selected for the sample through the use of a table of random numbers. The middle- and upper-class areas were combined to obtain a two-class rather than a three-class sample. An equal number of blocks were drawn from the lower living-standard level and the combined middle-upper level. Blocks in which any Negroes were known to reside were excluded from the sample. Within blocks, every nth house was selected, yielding five houses per block. Adjacent houses were used as alternates. For the lower-class sample N=52; for the upper-class sample N=51. The more conspicuous sources of bias in this

interviewed either the male head of the household or his spouse, but never both. Since most of the interviewing was done on Saturdays and in the evening, the sex ratio of the sample remained fairly well balanced (53 women and 50 men).

The questionnaire included three forms which were completed by all respondents. Form I, designed to assess *general valuations*, lists ten items designed to assess the degree to which the respondent endorses the general valuations subsumed under the "American Creed" (Table 1). Form II is designed to elicit specific valuations. It consists of ten social distance-type items describing hypothetical but quite plausible situations which permit the respondent to indicate the degree of social distance he prefers to maintain between himself and Negroes. Each item in Form II is matched to an item in Form I in such a way as to maximize the possibility of conflict between the general and specific valuations, and also to enhance the likelihood that respondents would recognize value conflicts where they exist (Table 1). Form III consists simply of spaces to record, at given probe levels, open-ended responses to the value conflicts elicited by the items on Form I and Form II.

In the interview each respondent was first asked to respond (in terms of five degrees of agreement and disagreement) to the items on Form I, then to the items on Form II. He was not permitted to refer back to Form I while completing Form II.

Responses on five probe levels were recorded on Form III:

Probe level −2:   Spontaneous remarks made while completing Form I.
Probe level −1:   Spontaneous remarks made while completing Form II.
Probe level 0:   Replies to the interviewer's request: "Would you now compare your response to question #1 on Form II with your response to question #1 on Form I."
Probe level +1:   Responses to interviewer's query: "Any comment?"
Probe level +2:   Responses to interviewer's query: "Do you see any contradiction?" (asked only where contradiction existed and where it was *unrecognized* on previous probe levels).
Probe level +3:   Responses to interviewer's query: "Any explanation?" (asked only where contradiction existed and was *recognized* on previous probe levels).

The probe levels were used to avoid calling contradictions to respondent's attention, and to determine the extent to which the respondent recognized contradictions without help from the interviewer. Probe +2 was used as a last resort when the respondent failed to recognize the contradictions, where such existed, on all previous levels.[10]

---

sampling procedure are 1) the use of every nth case within blocks; 2) the selection of an equal number of cases per block; and 3) the use of alternate households, in approximately one third of the cases, according to the interviewer's estimate. Inadequate records on this score made estimation necessary.

[10] This procedure was adopted after numerous other techniques were tried. Because of the difficulty involved in developing adequate items and procedures, the total number of pre-tests far exceeded the number of cases used in the final sample.

An elaborate system of rules for coding was developed to quantify the open-ended responses elicited at the various probe levels on Form III. Responses were coded not only to indicate whether valuations or beliefs had been volunteered, but also according to type of valuation, type of belief, whether the response was a rationalization, type of rationalization, likelihood of empirical validity (in the case of beliefs), etc. This system became so cumbersome as to defeat both statistical analysis and communication of findings. We thus resorted to a simplified code in which responses were classified as *valuations* where they contained any "ought to be" elements whatever, and *beliefs* where they included any statements of "what is," "what was," or conceptions of reality. Responses were also coded according to whether they were explanations of inconsistency or consistency, and the probe level at which each explanation had been evoked was also coded.

Sometimes beliefs and valuations are stated clearly and separately by the respondent, but often they are intertwined in the same remark. Not all statements included elements that could be classified as valuations or beliefs, of course, and such statements were simply rated "unclassifiable" on the valuation-belief dimension. Certain rules were specified for particular types of recurrent responses. For example, statements of *preference* for a "separate but equal" system were coded as valuations while such statements as "Negroes *want* to be separate but equal" were coded as beliefs. The coding was performed by the author and one other sociologist. The reliability of the coding on the valuation-belief dimension was tested by comparing the degree of agreement between the two coders on 27 schedules, including 236 coder-judgments on this dimension. There was agreement in 96 percent of the judgments.

RESULTS

Table 1 indicates the degree to which the sample as a whole endorsed the specific and the general valuations. Well over half the sample agreed with each of the ten general valuations statements, though agreement is considerably higher on the first seven statements than it is in the last three. The mean percentage agreeing with any given general item was 81. Virtually everyone in the sample (97 percent or more) agreed that everyone should have equal opportunities to get ahead, that all people should be treated as equals in the eyes of the law, that people should help each other in times of need, that children should have equal educational opportunities and that everyone should be judged according to his own individual worth. Over 90 percent agreed that everyone should have equal right to hold public office and endorsed the principle of brotherhood among men. Many of those who disagreed with the public office statement (item 5) wanted to append remarks about specific qualifications for public office, such as education or experience, qualifications which do not necessarily imply racial prejudice.

Agreement with Item 8, dealing with public facilities, approximated the mean (83 percent). Item 9 ("people should be allowed to live where they please") elicited least agreement—only 60 percent, and Item 10

TABLE 1

Responses to Each General and Specific Valuation*

General Valuation Statement	Percent (n=103)	Specific Valuation Statement	Percent (n=103)	Discrepancy: Percent Agreeing with General minus Percent Agreeing with Specific**
1. Everyone in America should have equal opportunities to get ahead.		1. I would be willing to have a Negro as my supervisor in my place of work.		
agreed	98	agree	60	38*
undecided	0	undecided	2	
disagree	2	disagree	38	
2. All people should be treated as equals in the eyes of the law.		2. If I went on trial I would not mind having Negroes on the jury.		
agreed	98	agree	76	22
undecided	0	undecided	5	
disagree	2	disagree	19	
3. People should help each other in time of need.		3. If a Negro's home burned down, I would be willing to take his family into my home for a night.		
agreed	99			
undecided	1			
disagree	0	agree	64	35
		undecided	6	
		disagree	30	
4. Children should have equal educational opportunities.		4. I would not mind having Negro children attend the same school my children go to.		
agreed	98			
undecided	1			
disagree	1	agree	79	19
		undecided	2	
		disagree	19	
5. Everyone should have equal right to hold public office.		5. I believe that I would be willing to have a Negro represent me in the Con- of the U.S.		
agree	91			
undecided	1			
disagree	8	agree	71	20
		undecided	6	
		disagree	23	
6. Each person should be judged according to his own individual worth.		6. I would not mind if my children were taught by a Negro school teacher.		
agree	97	agree	67	30
undecided	1	undecided	8	
disagree	2	disagree	8	

TABLE 1—Continued

General Valuation Statement	Percent (n=103)	Specific Valuation Statement	Percent (n=103)	Discrepancy: Percent Agreement with General minus Percent Agreeing with Specific**
7. I believe in the principle of brotherhood among men.		7. I would be willing to invite Negroes to a dinner party in my home.		
agree	94	agree	29	65
undecided	5	undecided	4	
disagree	1	disagree	67	
8. Public facilities should be equally available to everyone.		8. I would be willing to stay at a hotel that accommodates Negroes as well as whites.		
agree	83***	agree	61	22
undecided	4	undecided	4	
disagree	14	disagree	35	
9. Under our democratic system people should be allowed to live where they please if they can afford it.		9. I would be willing to have a Negro family live next door to me.		
agree	60	agree	35	25
undecided	6	undecided	2	
disagree	34	disagree	63	
10. I believe that all public recreational facilities should be available to all people at all times.		10. I don't think I would mind if Negro children were to swim in the same pool as my children.		
agree	63	agree	38	25
undecided	6	undecided	8	
disagree	31	disagree	54	

* The five response categories—"strongly agree" to "strongly disagree"—were collapsed to form the three categories shown here. ("Undecided" remained the middle category.)
** The percent agreeing with the general valuation is significantly higher than that agreeing with the specific valuation in all ten item pairs (p<.01).
*** Percentages do not total 100 due to rounding.

("public *recreational* facilities should be open to all") was similar—63 percent agree. The large difference between the pattern of responses to the first seven items and responses to the last three may be due to the fact that the latter are less abstract than the former, referring to specific situations rather than to general principles, though they are more general than the "specific valuation" items with which they are paired.

Responses to the specific valuations, shown in Table 1, tend to uphold the Myrdal hypothesis. There was considerably less agreement with the specific valuations than with the general valuations from which they were derived, in every one of the ten item-pair (in all cases p<.01).

Agreement with specific valuations was highest on Items 2, 4 and 5 (over 70 percent). These items refer to Negroes as jurors and congressional representatives, and to school integration. Each refers to a *fait accompli*, to the extent that integration in these areas has been achieved in the community.

At least 60 percent agreed with Items 1, 3, 6, and 8. Item 1 refers to Negro supervisors on the job, Item 6 with Negro school teachers. For some these too were facts of life as they knew it. Others saw these items as decisions to be made by the administration of the place of employment or the school. They expressed distaste for the idea, but felt they would have to resign themselves to it if it happened.

Item 3 dealt with willingness to take a Negro family whose home had burned down into the subject's own home for the night. The obligation to be charitable seemed very strong and even those who declined to take the hypothetical victims into their own homes said they would contribute money for hotel lodgings or donate food, clothing and furniture.

Item 8 asked whether the respondent would stay in a hotel serving Negroes as well as whites, and the majority said they would. Urban hotels in Indiana do accept Negro guests as they do in most of the northern and border states where the respondents might travel. Once again, they were faced with a question about which they have little choice: hotels in their experience are in fact integrated. Some added that they would not care to stay in a hotel that catered *primarily* to Negroes.

The majority disagreed with Items 7, 9, and 10. Item 7 deals with "social" integration, Item 9 with housing integration and Item 10 with integrated swimming pools. Unlike the other seven items, these deal with close personal contacts over which individuals presumably have some control.

Thus, not only were the more general, abstract American Creed valuations more readily endorsed than specific ones with situational relevance, but the degree to which a given item represents a *fait accompli* for the respondent seems to be a factor in determining whether the majority of the sample accept or reject it. This finding supports the "definition of the situation" interpretation of race relations favored by Lohman and Reitzes, Blumer, Killian, Rose and others.[11] Where the formal group structure defines a given action in clear-cut terms and where these definitions are

[11] Joseph D. Lohman and Dietrich C. Reitzes, "Note on Race Relations in Mass Society," *op. cit.*, and "Deliberately Organized Groups and Racial Behavior," *American Sociological Review*, 19 (1954), pp. 342–348; Herbert Blumer, "Attitudes and the Social Act," *Social Problems*, 3 (1955), pp. 59–65; Arnold M. Rose, "Intergroups Relations vs. Prejudice: Pertinent Theory for the Study of Social Change," *Social Problems*, 4 (1956), pp. 173–176 and "Inconsistencies in Attitudes Toward Negro Housing," *Social Problems*, 8 (1961), pp. 286–293; and Lewis M. Killian, "The Effects of Southern White Workers on Race Relations in Northern Plants," *American Sociological Review*, 17 (1952), pp. 327–331.

acted out by most of the members, then an individual's valuations (or attitudes, as the case may be) tend to "follow" even though initially he might have preferred a different state of affairs.

Table 2 summarizes the amount of agreement and disagreement for the ten item-pairs. Each person responded to ten item-pairs for a total of 1030 paired responses. Of these, 647 were consistent, the subjects agreeing or disagreeing with both sides of a given item-pair. No dilemma is indicated in these response-pairs. The remaining 383 response-pairs were inconsistent, indicating a potential dilemma. Whether a dilemma exists, however, depends on the respondent's reactions to his own inconsistencies.

Analysis of *response patterns* rather than individuals facilitates statistical treatment of the data where multiple responses are permitted, but it does raise a question as to whether the responses are primarily those of a few exceptionally verbose individuals. The data presented in Table 3 indicate that this is not the case. Relatively few are so consistent in their

TABLE 2

Frequency of Consistent and Inconsistent Responses

	Total Consistent Responses	Agree with Both General and Specific	Disagree with Both General and Specific
Frequency	647	562	85
Percent	100	86.9	13.1
Mean per Person	6.3	5.5	.8
	Total Consistent Responses	Agree with General, Disagree with or Undecided about Specific	All Others*
Frequency	383	335	48
Percent	100	87.5	12.5
Mean per Person	3.7	3.2	.5

* Disagree with general—agree with or undecided about specific; Undecided about general—agree or disagree with specific.

TABLE 3

Frequency Distribution of Response Patterns

	Number of Item-Pairs											
Pattern	0	1	2	3	4	5	6	7	8	9	10	Total
Agree with Both General & Specific	10	8	3	9	7	13	7	16	9	8	13	103
Disagree with Both General & Specific	58	21	15	4	3	2	–	–	–	–	–	103
Agree with General; Disagree with Specific	28	11	16	14	10	6	6	6	3	3	–	103
Agree with General; Undecided, Specific	75	18	7	3	–	–	–	–	–	–	–	103
All Other Patterns	65	26	10	2	–	–	–	–	–	–	–	103

responses as to be free from the possibility of experiencing a dilemma. Only 13 (12.6 percent) of the respondents agreed with all ten general valuations and their related specific valuations, and no one disagreed with both the general and the specific valuations in more than five pairs. No respondent agreed with all the general and disagreed with all the specific items. In short, most of the respondents are potentially subject to a dilemma of some sort, though relatively few are subject to it in the majority of areas about which they were questioned.

I have spoken here of "potential" conflict because it is an empirical question whether those who agree with the American Creed valuations and disagree with the specific valuations derived from them do in fact experience a dilemma in a personal sense, as Myrdal maintains. Unless an individual recognizes the contradictions in his responses no dilemma can properly be said to exist for him. Clues as to the extent to which contradictions are recognized appear in Table 4, where open-ended responses are classified according to the point in the interview at which they were made and whether they were spontaneous or elicited under probing. Nearly 60 percent of all remarks were spontaneous. These people were qualifying their structured responses to Forms I and II or commenting on the statements presented to them for consideration. The bulk of these spontaneous remarks were made while the respondents were completing Form II (specific valuations). Remarks volunteered while completing Form I tended to be situational qualifications that anticipated Form II. It is reasonable to assume that those who made spontaneous remarks clearly experienced contradiction. At this point in the interview the interviewer

TABLE 4

Degree of Spontaneity in Open-Ended Remarks

	All remarks	Spontaneous	Under Probing	
Frequency	1483.5°	884	599.5	
Percent	100	59.6	40.4	
Mean per Person	14.1	8.6	5.8	
	Total Number of Spontaneous Remarks	Form I°°	Form II°°°	After I & II
Frequency	884	233	399.5	251.5
Percent	100	26.4	45.2	28.4
Mean per Person	8.6	2.3	3.9	2.4
	Total Number of Remarks Made Under Probing	Probe Level +1 "Any Comment?"	Probe Level +2 "Any Contradiction?"	Probe Level +3 "Any Explanation?"
Frequency	599.5	116	361	122.5
Percent	100	19.4	60.2	20.4
Mean per Person	5.8	1.1	3.5	1.2

° Fractions result from grouping, for coding purposes, the responses of the relatively few people who made ten or more remarks each.

°° This column refers to few spontaneous remarks made in response to the general valuation statements.

°°° This column refers to spontaneous remarks made in response to the specific valuations.

had given no sign that he saw or was the least bit interested in contradictory responses.

The first explicit probe, "Any comment?" elicited approximately one remark per person, but the more explicit and direct "Do you see any contradiction?" produced an average of 3.5 per person, and the probe "Any explanation?" one or two additional explanatory remarks (Mean=1.2). Some of those who made remarks only under probing probably do not experience a dilemma but simply recognize contradictions when they are brought to their attention.

Of the 293 inconsistencies noted, respondents admitted approximately 42 percent (122) and recognized but denied about the same number (125) (Table 5). Nearly 16 percent of the inconsistencies remained unseen even after explicit probing. (Note that a given respondent may have admitted some inconsistencies, denied others and failed to see still others. References here are to the amount of inconsistency apparent in the responses, not to individuals.)

Table 5 presents a rather interesting finding: over 25 percent of all explanations were not explanations of inconsistency, but rather explanations of *consistency* between general and specific valuations. *Most of these explanations were justifications of democratic responses* (e.g., "It's the only Christian thing to do"). These explanations of consistency were not merely justifications of negative consistency, i.e., disagreement with both the general and specific valuations: 66 percent of the explanations of consistency were actually made by people whose responses included no negative consistencies.

Myrdal maintains that the value conflicts are rationalized by opportunistically calling forth culturally shared beliefs to explain the apparent contradiction. But a variety of other types of resolutions also occurred.

1. Most conspicuous among these alternatives was the calling forth of new valuations, that is, valuations in addition to those in conflict (e.g., "I don't think Negroes should be in politics").

TABLE 5

Types of Reactions of Respondents to Their Consistent and Inconsistent Responses

	All Explanations	Explanations of Consistency	Explanations of Inconsistency	
Frequency	1071	274	797	
Per Cent	100	25.6	74.4	
Mean Per Person	10.4	2.7	7.7	
	All Inconsistencies	Admitted	Denied*	Not Seen**
Frequency	293	122	125	46
Per Cent	100	41.6	42.7	15.7
Mean per Person	2.8	1.2	1.2	.4

* In these cases of inconsistency the respondent did in fact respond inconsistently, recognized the "apparent" inconsistency, but denied that his responses were inconsistent.

** These include all instances of inconsistency where the respondent gave no clear-cut evidence of recognizing any inconsistency.

2. Repression of one or the other of the values in conflict, or of the conflict itself (e.g., the answer "What conflict?" in response to the probe "Do you see any conflict?"). Failure to recognize a conflict could be due to repression or to limited logical abilities or both, but our method does not permit us to distinguish between these.
3. Adjustment of the general valuation as it applies to the respondent (e.g., "I guess I'm not so democratic after all").
4. Limitation of the range of applicability of the general valuation (e.g., Brotherhood refers to whites" or, "I wasn't thinking of Negroes at first").
5. Appeal to the doctrine of relativity (e.g., "There are different kinds of brotherhood").
6. Apparent projection of one's own attitudes to others (e.g., "I wouldn't mind having a Negro dinner guest in my home but we must consider the other guests," or, referring to the same situation, "My husband wouldn't like it.") Often the burden of the conflict is shifted to the Negro, "A Negro [juror] would be prejudiced."
7. Compartmentalization of conflicting valuations (e.g., "You can believe in brotherhood and not invite certain people to your home"). This is to be distinguished from repression because in this instance the person is clearly aware of his values on both ends of the continuum, but does not see any necessary connection between the two.

These alternative resolutions of value conflict are sometimes quite difficult to distinguish from each other. In addition, other solutions were offered which, though typically less logical, were frequently more candid than any of those listed (e.g., "He [a Negro] has a right to hold public office, but I just wouldn't vote for him," or, "I'm prejudiced").

To test the Myrdal theory on the most general level, it seemed expedient to ignore many of the subtle differences observed among the response-types listed. Most responses given could be reduced to variations within the general categories beliefs and valuations. The findings in Table 6 clearly indicate that Myrdal's analysis of how people respond to value conflict is limited, for in this sample people invoke valuations as frequently as they do beliefs in attempting to resolve the conflict. *There was no significant difference between the number of beliefs and the number of valuations invoked by respondents in explaining the discrepancies in their responses.* Again the possibility occurs that this finding might be characteristic of a handful of verbose subjects rather than typical. The frequency

TABLE 6

Beliefs Versus Valuations: Types of Explanations Invoked by Respondents

	All Explanations*	Beliefs	Valuations
Frequency	1149	618	531
Percent	100	53.8	46.2
Mean per Person	11.2	6.0	5.2

* The term "explanation" refers to respondents' open-ended remarks, classifiable as beliefs or valuations, at any probe level. Some respondents made more than one such remark about a discrepancy between a given pair of valuations.

distribution of beliefs and valuations in Table 7 indicates that this finding is not simply an artifact of method. While 15 subjects invoked more than ten beliefs each, the distribution of the majority in the one-to-ten range is fairly even. Some 84 percent of the respondents fell within the one-to-ten range and accounted for 66 percent of the total number (618) of beliefs invoked. The distribution of valuations is quite similar.

Each explanation, whether it involved a valuation or a belief, was in fact a compromise of either the general or the specific standard. Those who are bothered by the conflict must either change or qualify at least one position to resolve the conflict. Table 8 compares the frequency of *adjustments of general valuations* with the frequency of *adjustments of specific valuations*. If a person says, upon recognizing a conflict, "I wasn't thinking of Negroes when I said people should have equal opportunities," this qualifies as an adjustment (i.e., change or qualification) of a general valuation. If, on the other hand, upon seeing the conflict between his endorsement of equal opportunity and his rejection of the idea of a Negro as his supervisor, he says, for example, "Well, I guess it might be all right for a Negro to be supervisor if he were unusually qualified," this would be an adjustment of a specific valuation.

In most cases the respondent adjusted the specific valuation so that his disagreement with the specific item did not really seem, to him at least, to violate the precept set forth in the general form. Some adjustments were made in the general valuations, as well, however. Nearly 82 percent of all responses were adjustments of specific valuations; 18.4 percent were adjustments of the tenets of the American Creed (See Table 8).

TABLE 7

Distribution of Respondents by Number of Beliefs and Number of Valuations

Number of Beliefs*	Number of Respondents	Number of Valuations**	Number of Respondents
0	5	0	15
1	9	1	8
2	14	2	7
3	8	3	13
4	10	4	9
5	10	5	6
6	9	6	8
7	4	7	10
8	7	8	6
9	6	9	7
10	6	10	4
11	1	11	2
12	4	12	2
13	3	13	1
14–20	7	14–20	5
	103		103

* Total number of beliefs invoked=618.
** Total number of valuations invoked=531.

Summary of Empirical Relationships

1. A substantial majority of the sample subscribe, at least verbally, to the American Creed: the mean percent of agreement with the ten general valuation statements is 81.1 percent.

2. Respondents were considerably less likely to endorse the specific valuations than the general valuations; the mean percentage agreeing with the specific valuations was 56 percent. Thus, as Myrdal emphasizes, a considerable discrepancy exists between specific and general valuations.

3. Respondents tended to recognize the conflict between their general and specific valuations without comment from the interviewer. The majority (59.6 percent) of explanations of conflict were volunteered spontaneously.

4. There is a tendency to explain consistency as well as inconsistency. Of the total number of "explanations" given by our sample, 25.6 percent were explanations of consistency.

5. To resolve conflicts between the specific and the general valuations presented to them in the interview, the respondents invoked additional valuations (other than the two in conflict) almost as frequently as they did beliefs.

6. In resolving the dilemma, the general pattern is for the respondent to adjust to specific valuations so that it does not appear to conflict with the general, though some adjustments were also made in the general valuations.

7. When the specific valuations refer to legal, political, and educational relationships, conflict between the general and specific valuations is appreciably less likely. This is due to the fact that non-discriminatory behavior is most likely to be endorsed in these areas.

Interpretations

The possibilities for interpretation in a study such as this are almost infinite. Space limitations make it necessary to ignore many alternative interpretations[12] and to limit analysis to a few of the more significant findings.

[12] For instance, the relevance of theories of cognitive dissonance is readily apparent. See Leon A. Festinger, *A Theory of Cognitive Dissonance*, Evanston, Ill.: Row, Peterson, 1957, and Jack W. Brehm and Arthur R. Cohen, *Exploration in Cognitive Dissonance*, New York: Wiley, 1962.

TABLE 8

Types of Adjustment of Conflicting Valuations

	All Adjustments	Adjustment of General Valuations	Adustment of Specific Valuation
Frequency	1345	248	1097
Per Cent	100	18.4	81.6
Mean per Person	13.1	2.4	10.6

Empirical relationship #5 is worthy of discussion. Myrdal theorized that when people find their racial prejudices in conflict with their democratic ideals, they find *logical* ways to deny the conflict. Our findings indicate that people frequently do follow the type of logical procedure Myrdal expected. Thus, when people who think of themselves as democratic say that they would not want a Negro as their supervisor in their place of work, not all of them invoke a belief such as "Negroes are inherently less capable than whites." Instead, a common reaction is to assert an additional valuation to the ones in conflict, or to repeat, in slightly altered form, one of the valuations in conflict.

A wealth of sociological evidence suggests that in many social situations in America, it is not the person who behaves in a prejudiced manner who is deviant, but rather the non-prejudiced person who refuses to discriminate. Empirical relationship #4 appears to support this contention, for 274 of the explanations were *explanations of consistency*. In other words, many people who endorse the tenets of the American Creed found it necessary to rationalize, explain, or otherwise justify their *democratic* choices regarding specific areas of race relations. Thus, people with no dilemma in Myrdal's sense seem to experience another type of dilemma: a conflict between their endorsement of democratic action and yet *another normative system*, which exists in the majority of American local communities: the system which says that one ought to be prejudiced and one ought to discriminate.

Empirical relationship #6 is of some social significance, though it contradicts neither Myrdal's nor widespread sociological expectations. Myrdal predicts that in the long run the general tenets of the American Creed will win out over the contradictory valuations defining American race relations. We had thought (after pre-tests) that we might find that many people would alter the general to fit the specific. Actually, 81.6 percent of the "explanations" were adjustments of specific valuations. This suggests that Myrdal's optimism is not unjustified, and lends little support to the fear that people might react to the dilemma by renouncing their allegiance to the democratic tenets of the American Creed. This conclusion must be qualified, however, by the finding that many people feel constrained to justify their egalitarian specific valuations, again suggesting that another, undemocratic normative order co-exists with the more general democratic normative order.

The finding (#7) that conflict is appreciably less when the specific valuation refers to legal, political, and educational institutions (largely integrated in the community studied), is relevant to a number of theories. A most plausible interpretation is that people tend to go along with intergroup arrangements that are *faits accomplis*. Unambiguous democratic definitions of the situation are implied by the fact of integration in these areas, and they may well assume the status of normative imperatives more effective in guiding behavior than the private preferences of those who would prefer less democratic arrangements.

In broadest outline, then, this study supports the Myrdal theory. People do experience a conflict[13] and do try to resolve it. Myrdal does not, however, adequately describe the process whereby people seek resolution.

As a test of Myrdal's theory, this research must be considered preliminary. As a pilot study it supports the Myrdal theory sufficiently to justify test on a nationwide basis. If it is true, as Handlin says, that *An American Dilemma* is "a book that changed American life,"[14] then surely Myrdal's primary theory deserves such a test.

[13] An important qualification of the present findings is in order. We do not know 1) whether the conflict our respondents experienced in the interview situation exists for them outside the interview situation, or 2) whether it exists on an affective as well as a verbal or intellectual level. Other-directed, compartmentalizing people responding to the demands of specific situations may not be particularly upset by the fact that what they do in one situation contradicts what is expected in another. As for the nature of the conflict experience, many of our respondents manifested considerable anxiety when the contradiction became apparent to them. I hope one day to combine the techniques used in a previous study of the relation between autonomic responses and attitudes. A recording of autonomic responses in the conflict situation might reveal the extent to which the conflict is affectively experienced in the interview. Cf. Frank R. Westie and Melvin DeFleur, "Autonomic Responses and Their Relationship to Race Attitudes," *Journal of Abnormal and Social Psychology*, 58 (1959), pp. 340–347.

[14] Review of *An American Dilemma, op. cit.*

Factors Related to Willingness to Experience Desegregation among Students in Segregated Schools[1]

M. RICHARD CRAMER
UNIVERSITY OF NORTH CAROLINA

CONGRESS AND THE COURTS HAVE DECREED THE END OF RACIAL SEGREGATION in public institutions. With this, our nation has officially dedicated itself to what has been termed a "great social experiment"—to see whether its largest racial minority can be assimilated into the mainstream of American life.

If such an experiment is occurring, it must be described as a *natural* one in which scientists have little to do with manipulating the major independent variables (such as the rate and form of desegregation); instead, they observe and record the possible effects of these variables and specify the conditions under which these effects may occur.

The following report claims no broader scope than the above. It is concerned with the measurement at one point in time of a single index of a key dependent variable in the desegregation process: attitudes about desegregation. It also attempts to use a group of other factors as predictors of differentiation in these attitudes.

In the great social experiment under discussion, young people are particularly interesting subjects. They have been intensely involved in important aspects of racial change, especially in the South, where a focal point has been the desegregation of schools. Also, they constitute tomorrow's adult population; the attitudes and behavior patterns young people develop from current experiences promise to affect the future of race relations.

This effect on future conditions would be expected especially for youth who, according to their aspirations and plans, will probably assume upper- and middle-status positions in the society. Such a group is examined in this paper: a sample of about 11,000 Southern high school students *with at least some intention of attending college*. They are a part of a larger sample of nearly 16,000 students whose schools had been purposely selected to represent urban and rural, white and Negro, and Deep and Upper South populations in grades 9–12.[2] At the time of the survey, com-

---

[1] A revised version of this paper was read at the Society for the Study of Social Problems meeting in San Francisco, August, 1967.

[2] The research from which this paper derives was originally designed to focus on Negro youth. For this reason an additional criterion for sample selection was the level of educational performance in each county by Negroes, as measured by college entrance, truancy, dropout rates, etc. Also for this reason, more Negroes (N = 10,274) than whites (N = 5,604) were surveyed. An attempt was made to administer questionnaires to all Negro high school students in the chosen counties but to only about a quarter of the whites. Altogether 17 counties and 52 schools were involved in the study.

♦ First published in *Social Science Quarterly* 49, No. 3 (December, 1968).

plete or virtually complete segregation was still the rule in all of the high schools studied.

The students were administered questionnaires in their classrooms in late 1963 and early 1964. The central concern of the questioning was the educational and occupational aspirations and plans of respondents and the possible determining factors of these aspirations and plans.[3] Those students possibly planning to attend college were asked their preference on racial composition at college. The three fixed-alternative choices were a college that had (1) "only students of my own race," (2) "mostly students of my race," and (3) "students accepted without regard to race." These alternatives will be referred to, respectively, as preferences for "total segregation," "substantial segregation," and "nonsegregation."[4]

As suggested earlier, the interest in responses to this question is twofold: (1) to help document the state of feeling along a key attitudinal dimension at one point in the recent history of race relations in the South, and (2) to treat these responses (very tentatively) as indicators of more general racial attitudes, the correlates of which can be used to aid in predicting those who are more likely to support, or oppose, future integration.

In this latter regard, personal characteristics relevant to the future status and behavior of respondents will be examined. A chief aim is to obtain some clue, if possible, to the relative influence that racial liberals and conservatives are likely to have when the subjects under study reach adulthood. It will be useful to focus first on the relationships between several indicators of "leadership potential" and the measure of racial attitudes. The indicators are as follows:

1. Self-reported grade average in school
2. Self-reported extent of participation in extracurricular activities

[3] This study was done under the direction of Professors Charles E. Bowerman (University of North Carolina) and Ernest Q. Campbell (Vanderbilt University) and was supported by the Cooperative Research Program of the U.S. Office of Education. For a full report, see M. Richard Cramer *et al.*, *Social Factors in Educational Achievement and Aspirations among Negro Adolescents* (Chapel Hill: Institute for Research in Social Science of the University of North Carolina, 1966).

[4] In any question on a sensitive issue such as racial attitudes, there is always danger of response bias. If subjects perceive that a certain answer is most appropriate in the context in which the questioning is conducted, and if they perceive that they may be identified with their answer, they will tend to give the "appropriate" response, even if it does not reflect their own true feelings. Among the steps taken by the researchers to minimize this danger were the following:

1. The questionnaire was designed so that the few "sensitive" items were dispersed among nonsensitive, relatively objective, yet interesting items that evoked respondents' attention to the content matter of questions, rather than to the implications of response alternatives.
2. Questionnaires were distributed by regular teachers in classroom settings to reduce possible effects of the outside "liberal white" auspices of the study.
3. Rather elaborate steps were taken to assure subjects that their responses were confidential: no names were placed on the questionnaires, and no one inspected the completed forms before they were placed in envelopes which were immediately sealed before being taken to the university where the data were to be analyzed.

3. Self-reported popularity of respondent and of his group of friends in school

4. Level of the respondent's occupational goals

In different contexts, and with different measures, it has been found that higher-status persons tend to have more liberal attitudes on questions of civil liberties and race relations.[5] The present study will investigate whether this generalization can be applied to youth in the South, where it might be expected that all status levels of whites would share a relatively conservative viewpoint and all levels of Negroes would share a liberal position. By looking only at the college-bound, this study will apply a stringent test of the generalization, since it will attempt to draw a distinction between groups within the upper-status portion of the total population. The distinction might be thought of as one between the upper-status leaders and the upper-status rank and file.

In addition to the cluster of indices under "leadership potential," two other measures will also be examined in discussing correlates of racial attitudes. These, too, are thought to represent an underlying personality dimension which could affect both current attitudes and future social significance of the respondent. The measures concern preference for "the new" versus "the customary" and the respondent's expected geographical place of residence as an adult. The postulated underlying dimension for both items is innovation potential; this study predicts that receptivity to desegregate is positively related both to receptivity to new things in general and to the expectation of living outside the South in the future.[6] It is to be expected that within each race, the more innovative student would be more willing to explore interracial contact beyond this current experience.

Receptivity to College Desegregation in 1963–1964

While the leadership- and innovation-potential dimensions provide the focus for this paper, the presentation of findings begins by simply reporting the frequency distribution of high school students' responses to the question on college racial preference. Here one needs to keep in mind the "snapshot" quality of these observations; the data suggest attitudes during the 1963–1964 academic year. Data for other times are unavailable, although, as noted below, there are reasons why one should expect attitudes toward college desegregation to have changed from year to year in the recent past.

Also in this section, we wish to establish the degree to which certain

[5] For example, see Samuel A. Stouffer, *Communism, Conformity, and Civil Liberties* (Garden City, N.Y.: Doubleday and Co., 1955); Robin M. Williams, Jr., *Strangers Next Door* (Englewood Cliffs, N.J.: Prentice-Hall, 1964); and George E. Simpson and J. Milton Yinger, *Racial and Cultural Minorities*, 3rd ed. (New York: Harper and Row, 1965), pp. 103–108.

[6] In considering regional preference as an index of some underlying factor of "innovational potential" that may affect racial attitudes, we do not wish to ignore the probability that racial attitudes may help determine regional choice, too. Thus the influence may well operate in both directions.

background factors account for the choice of attitudinal response. Thus, students in various demographic and socioeconomic categories are compared regarding their preferences on college racial composition.

Not surprisingly, Negro and white high school students differed markedly in the 1963–1964 survey in their degree of favorability toward racial composition at college (Table 1).[7] Fully three-quarters of the Negroes preferred desegregation, while over half of the whites chose complete segregation. This finding reinforces the observation that "desegregation" has different meanings for members of the two races. While the espousal of "black separatism" by some Negro militants could eventually lead as large a proportion of Negroes as whites to favor segregation, all studies to date have shown members of the two races to differ widely in their attitudes.[8] We would expect this to be especially true of Southerners on the issue of school segregation. Here the separation of races has remained both a symbol of Negro subordination and a means of providing whites with superior educational opportunities and, concomitantly, greater access to other highly valued goals in the society.

One might expect perceptions of the nearness and inevitability of desegregation to affect preference for a particular college racial composi-

TABLE 1

Relationship between College Racial Preference
and Race of Respondent

	Race of Respondent	
College Racial Preference	Negro (Per Cent)	White (Per Cent)
Total segregation	9.7	51.4
Substantial segregation	14.6	23.4
Nonsegregation	75.7	25.2
Total	100.0	100.0
N =	(7,495)	(3,748)

[7] In the data analysis for this paper, tests for statistical significance were not used. If these were used, we would have to ignore the requirement of probability sampling—a requirement that is, admittedly, often ignored in statistical analysis. In addition, with N's as large as those reported here, minute differences can be statistically significant—that is, unlikely to occur by chance more than one or five per cent of the time if a null hypothesis of no difference is correct. Rather than use the statistical-test criterion for identifying relationships between variables, we have chosen instead to rely on percentage comparisons. In general we shall consider any difference of more than five percentage points as indicative of at least a relational tendency—most differences such as these would prove to be statistically significant with samples as large as ours.

[8] Recent studies reporting these findings include Williams, *Strangers Next Door*; William Brink and Louis Harris, *Black and White* (New York: Simon and Schuster, 1967); and Donald R. Matthews and James W. Prothro, *Negroes and the New Southern Politics* (New York: Harcourt, Brace and World, 1966).

tion.[9] At least among those predisposed to favor segregation (whites, usually), such perceptions might weaken the insistence on total segregation at college. While segregation was the rule in the survey schools in 1963–1964, respondents from the Upper South were undoubtedly more aware, in general, than those from the Deep South that school desegregation was inevitable. At the time of the research, some desegregation had already occurred at the public school level elsewhere in the two Upper South states—Virginia and North Carolina—in the study. But it had not yet occurred at this level anywhere in Mississippi and Alabama, the two Deep South states in the study. Moreover, public college desegregation had been in effect, to a small degree, in North Carolina and Virginia for over a decade, while it was new and still strongly contested in the other two states during the 1963–1964 academic year.

The above suggests that, at least among whites, a subregional difference would influence receptivity to college desegregation, regardless of whether there was any original difference in racial attitudes in the two areas. This line of reasoning is supported rather strongly by the data in Table 2.[10] Among white students from the Deep South, the percentage was 39 points higher for those favoring total segregation and 24 points lower for those favoring desegregation. The subregional difference prac-

TABLE 2

Relationship between College Racial Preference and
Race and Subregion of Respondent[a]

College Racial Preference	Race and Subregion of Respondent			
	Negro		White	
	Upper South (Per Cent)	Deep South (Per Cent)	Upper South (Per Cent)	Deep South (Per Cent)
Total segregation	8.8	10.4	40.2	79.0
Substantial segregation	13.2	15.7	27.7	12.7
Non-segregation	78.0	73.9	32.1	8.3
Total	100.0	100.0	100.0	100.0
N =	(3,258)	(4,236)	(2,663)	(1,085)

[a] Upper South refers to Virginia and North Carolina; Deep South refers to Alabama and Mississippi.

[9] Two particularly relevant studies are Morton Deutsch and Mary E. Collins, *Interracial Housing* (Minneapolis: University of Minnesota Press, 1951), and Herbert H. Hyman and Paul Sheatsley, "Attitudes Toward Desegregation," *Scientific American*, 211 (July, 1964), pp. 16–23. In both, dramatic changes in attitudes are observed as a result of increased exposure to racial desegregation.

[10] In this and succeeding tables, a control for race is always applied. Race obviously influences responses to the attitudinal question; but, how much can other factors account for variations in these responses within each race? In later tables we could also display the effects of controlling for subregion and for other background factors. In the interest of brevity, however, these results will be reported in the text only when they indicate a major deviation from the overall findings.

tically disappeared among Negroes, though, whose commitment to desegregation was relatively strong in both areas at the time of the survey.

Relationships between three other background variables and college racial preference are presented in Table 3. These variables have been linked to racial attitudes in previous research,[11] but they met with mixed success in predicting attitudes toward college desegregation among our respondents.

With race held constant, sex has little relationship to desegregation attitudes; but moderate relationships do appear between these attitudes and both socioeconomic status (as measured by an index of material possessions) and place of residence. The urban students of each race were most receptive to desegregation, with those living on farms were least

TABLE 3

Relationship between Other Background Factors and
College Racial Preference

Background Variable	College Racial Preference			
	Total Segregation (Per Cent)	Substantial Segregation (Per Cent)	Non-Segregation (Per Cent)	N
Race and Sex				
Negro male	8.5	14.5	77.0	3,237
Negro female	10.7	14.7	74.6	4,258
White male	53.7	22.2	24.1	1,937
White female	49.0	24.5	26.5	1,807
Race and Socioeconomic Status[a]				
Negro high SES	5.1	10.2	84.8	2,892
Negro low SES	12.0	19.0	68.9	4,045
White high SES	46.8	25.1	28.1	2,483
White low SES	60.8	19.9	19.2	1,123
Race and Place of Residence				
Nebro urban	6.8	11.7	81.4	3,944
Negro rural non-farm	10.2	14.8	74.9	1,552
Negro farm	15.1	19.8	65.1	1,865
White urban	41.9	25.3	32.8	2,186
White rural non-farm	55.7	21.9	22.4	688
White farm	72.1	19.5	8.4	850

[a] For Negroes, high SES refers to a score of 5 or 6 on a 6-point material-possessions index; for whites, high SES means a score of 6. The different cutting point is necessitated by the great racial disparity in the distribution of scores on this index.

[11] For recent summaries of such findings, see relevant sections in Williams, *Strangers Next Door*; Brink and Harris, *Black and White*; Simpson and Yinger, *Racial Minorities*; and James W. Vander Zanden, *American Minority Relations*, 2nd ed. (New York: Ronald Press, 1966).

receptive. At the same time, those from more prosperous families were more likely to favor desegregation.[12] The results in Table 3 are essentially the same in both subregions, but place of residence and socioeconomic status were better predictors of white attitudes in the Upper South. In the Deep South, the urban and rural and the prosperous and poor whites all were less differentiated in their resistence to integration.

At this time, then, as school desegregation was moving very slowly (before the 1964 Civil Rights Act and subsequent prodding by the Department of Health, Education, and Welfare to accelerate the pace) most white high school students from segregated schools wished to attend segregated colleges. Somewhat greater receptivity to attending integrated colleges, however, was found among respondents from the Upper South —especially among those from the cities and from relatively comfortable economic backgrounds. In contrast, Negroes preferred nonsegregation, with only minor subregional variation, but the poorer and rural respondents shared this preference less frequently.

None of the above observations will surprise those who have followed the desegregation process in the South; but the findings are an indicator of the exact level of desegregation receptivity in 1963–1964, and they are a useful baseline for future measures of racial attitudes of Southern high school students.

DESEGREGATION ATTITUDES AND LEADERSHIP POTENTIAL

As we turn to examine the way leadership and innovation potential relate to racial attitudes, the validity of the college-racial-preference measure as a general index of racial attitudes must be questioned. Only if its validity can be assumed, may the measure be used to determine which Southern youths are more likely to be racial liberals or conservatives in contexts other than choice of colleges.

The justification for this assumption is as follows: used as a measure of college racial preference, the item in question is time-bound; the frequency distribution of responses to this particular item may have changed since 1963 because of the increasing inevitibly of some desegregation for college-goers. In 1963–1964, however, rejection of total school segregation by the respondents indicated a favorable attitude toward integration beyond the current community level. As such, the item has some utility as an indicator of racial liberalism in general.[13]

---

[12] The relationship between socioeconomic status and college desegregation attitudes is not as strong as the association between these attitudes and place of residence. The relationship is further diminished when place of residence is applied as a control variable. For example, among white farm residents, even of high SES, only 32.2 per cent favor some degree of college desegregation. This is 7.3 percentage points more than among lower SES white farm residents, but fully 26.6 percentage points *less* than among high SES students from the towns and cities. Similar patterns occur among Negroes and for other urban-rural and class comparisons.

[13] In further defense of our resort to a single-item indicator of racial attitudes, it must be repeated that the central concern of the research was with a completely different topic, and any stress on race-relations questions would have jeopardized the excellent cooperation of participating school administrators.

While this justification may not be totally convincing, it sufficiently satisfies the author to permit at least a tentative examination of some interesting and relatively unexplored matters in the area of correlates of racial attitudes. Specifically, the study asks whether potential leaders and innovators are more likely to be racial liberals. If this is found, the study will speculate briefly on what it might imply for the future.

Table 4 reveals a rather consistent pattern of greater pro-integration sentiment for Negroes with leadership characteristics, but the picture is not so clear for whites.

Eighty-four per cent of Negro students with grades of B+ or better wanted to go to a college where race was not considered in admissions, as compared to just over 70 per cent of those with C averages or lower. All control categories show at least a 10 percentage-point difference between top and mediocre students, with the greatest difference occurring among those from farms. Whereas 77 per cent of the best Negro students from farms favored nonsegregation, only 54 per cent of the poorer students from farms felt this way.

Whites with poorer grades also showed a general trend of greater resistence to desegregation. The percentage preferring total segregation varies by 9.3 points between students with B+ or better grades and those with C or poorer averages. When controls were introduced, however, one finds that this trend remained true only for the Upper South and for urban areas. The Upper South, in fact, showed a percentage difference of 19 points—29.1 versus 48.0—between the good and poor students. But whites from the more traditional Deep South and rural areas showed higher, and practically unvarying, rates of opposition to any integration at the college level. Academic leaders were as likely to follow the norm as were the less successful students.

It might be argued that wherever there is support for nonsegregation among the brighter students, it does not so much indicate basic liberalism on matters of race as it does a realistic appraisal of conditions at the better colleges and universities to which these students would be attracted. One can reply, however, that whether the liberal response is due to basic attitudes or to expediency, it suggests a willingness to accept increasing desegregation in public life. In other words, for purposes of this analysis, one assumes the "expedient" liberal will be as liberal in practice as the "principled" liberal.

Moving on to other results, one finds that the general hypothesis that student leaders are more receptive to desegregation is even less supported among whites when participation in extracurricular activities is used as the indicator of leadership. At the same time, consistent, though unspectacular, confirmation of the hypothesis appears again among Negroes, even with controls applied. The measure, a simple count by the respondent of the number of his activities, is very crude and may be at fault for the inconclusive findings. It seems, though, that among whites, the more active person is somewhat more likely to prefer a segregated college, while the least active student is the most willing to attend a nondiscriminating school.

TABLE 4

Relationship between Indices of Leadership Potential
and College Racial Preference, Controlling for Race

| | College Racial Preference | | | | | | | |
Independent Variable	Total Segregation (Per Cent)	Negro Substantial Segregation (Per Cent)	Non-Segregation (Per Cent)	N	Total Segregation (Per Cent)	White Substantial Segregation (Per Cent)	Non-Segregation (Per Cent)	N
Grades in School								
A, A−, B+	7.0	8.7	84.3	1,461	46.1	25.6	28.3	1,050
B, B−, C+	9.0	14.3	76.8	3,668	52.5	23.5	24.0	1,610
C, C−, D, F	10.9	18.1	71.0	1,943	55.4	20.3	24.3	1,040
Number of Extra-curricular Activities								
2 or more	7.3	12.3	80.5	3,665	52.8	23.7	23.4	2,257
1	9.5	14.3	76.2	1,614	49.5	24.7	25.9	661
0	11.5	13.3	75.2	723	48.2	20.0	31.9	571
Within-Clique Status								
Leader	7.9	9.5	82.6	1,654	47.8	24.2	28.0	986
Popular, non-leader	8.0	14.3	77.7	2,558	53.7	23.7	22.5	1,979
Accepted	12.6	16.7	70.8	708	53.8	21.5	24.7	288
Outsider	15.2	19.2	65.6	151	54.1	5.4	40.5	37
Status of Respondent's Clique								
Leading group	8.8	11.8	79.3	566	50.0	24.1	25.9	398
Above average	7.9	12.0	80.1	3,080	51.4	23.2	25.5	2,072
Average	9.8	14.7	75.5	2,343	53.2	23.0	23.8	965
Below average	16.6	15.0	68.4	373	41.7	25.9	32.4	108
General Popularity of Respondent								
Popular, well-liked	8.7	12.3	79.0	3,851	49.8	24.1	26.2	2,156
Average	8.8	13.7	77.4	2,177	53.6	22.4	24.0	1,329
Not well-liked	13.0	17.6	69.5	239	59.0	18.0	23.0	61
Status of Expected Occupation[a]								
White collar	4.9	9.1	86.0	955	47.1	25.3	27.5	904
Glamour	6.0	14.3	79.7	266	55.2	19.5	25.3	87
Blue collar; military	9.1	14.2	76.7	1,173	55.6	17.8	26.6	421
Farming	12.0	16.3	71.7	92	72.1	17.7	10.2	147

[a] Males only.

A control for subregion further complicates the picture, at least in the Upper South, where the inactive students have not only the highest preference for nonsegregation but also the highest percentage favoring total segregation. Thus, slight curvilinearity describes the relationship between pro-integration attitudes and extent of participation in activities among Upper South whites. All other control categories follow the weak pattern seen in the overall white sample, except that there is virtually no relationship among rural–non-farm students.

The most direct measures of leadership in this study involve the respondent's evaluation of his own popularity both within his clique and in the whole student body and his evaluation of the status of his clique in the school. With these measures, a moderate tendency for leadership status to be positively related to desegregation receptivity is found among Negroes. For example, 82.6 per cent of the self-reported "leaders" desire nonsegregation in college, as compared to only 65.6 per cent of those who consider themselves "outsiders."[14] About 80 per cent of those Negroes in "leading" or "above average" groups at school prefer nonsegregation, as compared to 68.4 per cent of those whose groups rate "below average." Those who see themselves as generally popular or well-liked at school show 79 per cent opposing any racial criterion in college admissions, while 69.5 per cent of the "not well liked" have similar attitudes. Among Negroes, then, there is at least a 9 percentage-point difference on all measures between the top and bottom status groups in their preference for nondiscriminating colleges. None of the controls changes the basic conclusion that there is greater willingness to attend an integrated college among those Negroes with greater popularity or status in high school.

Such a generalization is more tenuous for whites. The preference for total segregation is somewhat greater for the "outsider," the person of "average status" and for the person who is "not well liked" than it is for those individuals having greater status. But the "outsider" is also somewhat more likely to favor total nonsegregation, and members of "below average" groups are more liberal toward desegregation than those in "average" groups. For that matter, they are more liberal than those in higher status groups, as well. Moreover, there are frequent exceptions to the overall trends in certain categories of the control variables. Most noteworthy among these exceptions are the lack of any relationship between racial attitudes and within-clique status for farm whites; the generally negative relationship between racial liberalism and status of clique for Deep South whites; and the lack of relationship between racial attitudes and general popularity for those with low socioeconomic status, those from rural–non-farm homes, and those within either subregion once that control is applied. In short, the key hypothesis of a direct status-

---

[14] The response "no special friends," chosen by 1,395 Negroes and 284 whites is excluded from Table 4 because of its ambiguous placement with the other responses on an ordinal scale. As opposed to the "outsider," the person who gives this answer apparently is not alienated from the school; he may simply perceive himself as not limited in his friendships. As a group, respondents giving this answer were intermediate, within each race, in their desegregation attitudes.

liberalism relationship is not supported among whites when social position in the school serves to define status.

There is greater success with the use of the final indicator of "leadership potential"—expected occupation of respondents—in Table 4. The data here are for males only, and about 20 per cent of the college-bound did not answer or gave unclassifiable answers. Here the data show that in both races students with white-collar ambitions—who are assumed to include a disproportionate share of future leaders—are more likely to be receptive to desegregation than those who aspired to glamour, blue-collar, military, or farming jobs. The last goal—farming—is generally associated with the greatest resistance to desegregation. These findings are most clearly seen for Negroes by comparing key percentages: 86 per cent of those with white-collar expectations, versus slightly less than 80 per cent of those with glamour, blue-collar, or military aims, and only 71.7 per cent of those planning to be farmers favored total nonsegregation. For whites, the clearest picture appears with use of the percentage preferring complete segregation as a means of comparison: 72 per cent of those with farming ambitions, about 55 per cent with intermediate job goals, and only 47 per cent with white-collar plans preferred total segregation.

Only one important qualification to the above findings is indicated after controls are introduced. Among farm students in both races, the person with glamour-job ambitions is most unwilling to attend a desegregated college; otherwise, there is little variation by occupational goal among students from farms, as all of them are generally unfavorable toward desegregation, compared to others of the same race.

In sum, Table 4 shows that receptivity to integration is more consistently associated with high leadership potential among Negroes than among whites. The most alert, most ambitious, most active, and most admired Negroes (according to their own reports) are generally more likely than their peers, even among those with similar educational goals, to prefer nonsegregation.

In the white sample, academic success and vocational ambition act in the same way that all of the leadership potential variables act in the Negro sample. That is, those students with top grades and high job goals are more favorable toward desegregation, except possibly in situations where normative controls are strong enough to minimize variations in attitudes, as in rural areas and the Deep South.

There may be two conflicting trends, however, which serve to prevent the determining of any overall relationship between desegregation attitudes and present leadership status in school. First, there is the initially hypothesized combination of leadership and liberalism, which may occur in many students. In contrast, some white leaders in the school, rather than being in the forefront of racial change, may have their high status associated with a superconformity to the norms of peers. Indeed, "outsiders," nonparticipants, and those in relatively unpopular groups may show their detachment to peers by being more willing to "buck" the norms and to accept desegregation at college. Thus, among whites, present social status is not a good predictor of racial attitudes. Two other important components of potential for leadership in the future—intelligence and vocational ambition—do seem, however, to have some association with the dependent variable.

DESEGREGATION ATTITUDES AND "INNOVATION POTENTIAL"

Turning from an examination of leadership potential, this study shows (in Table 5) a relatively strong, straightforward association between innovation potential and racial liberalism. First, students who anticipate leaving the South show a greater tendency to favor integration at college. This is true for the Negro sample, where there is a 12.5-percentage-point difference in the preference for nonsegregation between those who intend to leave the South and those who intend to remain. It is even more strikingly true for whites, where an 18-point difference separates those with different regional preferences in their percentage favoring total segregation. Further support for the hypothesis being examined in Table 5 lies in the fact that in all categories of the control variables in both races, the association persists between pro-integration of attitudes and an inclination to move out of the South.

Similarly, the second measure of innovation potential—preference for the new or unusual—is also consistently and positively related to desegregation receptivity in both races, even when controls are applied. The relationship is not particularly strong, however, as the more innovative respondents had generally less than a 10-percentage-point advantage over

TABLE 5

Relationship between Indices of Innovation Potential
and College Racial Preference, Controlling for Race

| | College Racial Preference | | | | | | | |
| | Negro | | | | White | | | |
Independent Variable	Total Segregation (Per Cent)	Sub-stantial Segregation (Per Cent)	Non-Segregation (Per Cent)	N	Total Segregation (Per Cent)	Sub-stantial Segregation (Per Cent)	Non-Segregation (Per Cent)	N
Expected Region of Residence								
South	12.4	18.1	69.5	1,479	56.1	22.4	21.5	2,408
non-South	7.2	10.8	82.0	4,144	38.1	24.9	37.0	860
Preference for the customary								
Always; usually	11.4	16.0	72.6	1,745	55.2	21.6	23.2	755
Sometimes; never	7.3	11.2	81.5	4,094	50.3	23.4	26.3	2,711

their peers in favoring nondiscrimination or opposing segregation at college.

The salient conclusion to be drawn from Table 5 is that those favoring change in general also favor integration. The concern here is not whether those with high innovation potential are also more likely to have general leadership positions in the future. The data do suggest, though, that those more likely to participate in the dynamic portion of societal affairs —those more likely to influence system change, as opposed to affecting system maintenance—show somewhat greater promise than do their peers of being liberal in race relations.

The last part of this paper, then, has focused on the supposed indices of two factors involved in predicting racial attitudes. Although not as "potent" in predicting attitudes as race, socioeconomic status, or type or subregion of residence, these indicators—of potential for leadership and potential for innovation—usually show an association with favorability toward desegregation, even when the background variables are controlled.

Speculation

If one can assume that the attitudes found here will stay with the students into adulthood, he can make this interpretation: that the more liberal members of this 1963–1964 Southern sample will have somewhat greater influence than their numbers would indicate on future race relations. It is questionable whether this actually foreshadows greater racial integration in the South, however, because liberals may still not dominate among whites in the region. This is especially true if emigration is selective in the way that the regional-preference responses suggest—that is, that liberals have a greater tendency to leave the South.

Altruism, Egoism, and Antagonism toward Negroes[1]

VINCENT JEFFRIES
SAN FERNANDO VALLEY STATE COLLEGE

RICHARD T. MORRIS
UNIVERSITY OF CALIFORNIA, LOS ANGELES

THIS ARTICLE PRESENTS THE RESULTS OF A STUDY OF THE RELATIONSHIP BE-tween the values of altruism and egoism, and the level of antagonism to-ward Negroes. The study is based on 583 interviews conducted in the Los Angeles metropolitan area as part of a larger study of white reactions to the Watts riots in August of 1965.[2]

Pitirim A. Sorokin's theory of solidarity and antagonism[3] provides the initial conceptual framework for the study. The major proposition of this theory is that the character of the cultural values of a society, or, in Soro-kin's terminology, its moral norms and law norms, are an "immediate" and "decisive" factor in determining the degree of antagonism or solidarity prevalent in the interaction between individuals and groups in the society. Two contrasting types of value orientation are discussed by Sorokin. The first type legitimizes such attitudes as competition, rivalry, the urge to defeat, and selfishness. The second type emphasizes the spirit of love, cooperation, mutual aid, and concern for others. A society emphasizing the first type of value orientation would be characterized by the existence of more intergroup antagonism than would a society emphasizing the second type.

Egoism and altruism were selected in the present study as cultural (or shared) values representative of the two orientations central to Sorokin's theory. They are considered here to be basically conflicting values pre-valent in American culture. The value of egoism involves a stress upon the self as the focal point of purposeful behavior. Selfishness is an ele-ment of this value. According to this view, virtue and happiness consist in the pursuit of self-interest. Altruism is in direct contrast to egoism in that the other is placed ahead of the self. Devotion to the interests and welfare of others, together with unselfishness, are elements of this value. Much of an individual's daily social interaction is oriented by a choice,

[1] Funds for this research were provided by a grant from the U.S. Office of Economic Opportunities, funded through the Institute of Government and Public Affairs, Univer-sity of California, Los Angeles. Computing assistance was obtained from the Health Sciences Computing Facility, UCLA, sponsored by NIH Grant Pr-3. An earlier version of this article was read at the American Sociological Association Meetings, San Fran-cisco, August, 1967.

[2] For a more general presentation of the entire study, see Richard T. Morris and Vincent Jeffries, "Violence Next Door," *Social Forces*, 47 (March, 1968), pp. 352–358. The present article attempts to elaborate upon the value aspects of the research.

[3] Pitirim A. Sorokin, *Society, Culture and Personality, Their Structure and Dynamics* (New York: Harper and Brothers, Publishers, 1947), pp. 119–131.

◆ First published in *Social Science Quarterly* 49, No. 3 (December, 1968).

conscious or not, between following in varying degrees one of these two values.

The choice or balance between these two values is here considered important in determining whether the attitudes of an individual (or group) toward others will be predominantly solidary or antagonistic. The value of altruism would be expected to be associated with a sense of unity, oneness, and common humanity. Also, because of the concern for others which is a basic component of this value, altruism would be likely to lead to an increased awareness of the problems, concerns, or injustices which are the lot of others. These characteristics of the value of altruism should further a general tendency toward solidarity with other groups, including Negroes. In contrast, the value of egoism implies separateness and lack of unity between the self and others. This value is therefore likely to be associated with a lack of concern for others, and a lack of awareness of their problems and grievances. Given a predominant concern with the wishes and needs of the self, others may more easily be viewed as threats or competitors for whatever the self desires. Thus, egoism is more likely than altruism to further the development of an attitude of generalized antagonism toward others, including Negroes.

This article presents an investigation of whites' attitudes toward Negroes. On the basis of Sorokin's theory the study has attempted to test the hypothesis that the value of altruism is associated with a lower level of antagonism toward Negroes than is the value of egoism. A few previous studies have indicated similar relationships between these values and antagonism toward minority groups.

Studies by Evans[4] and Gough[5] have both shown a negative relationship between anti-Semitism and high scores on the "social" value subscale of the Allport-Vernon Scale of Values.[6] The individual dominated by the social value is described as one whose "highest value is love of people" and who "prizes other persons as ends, and is therefore himself kind, sympathetic, and unselfish."[7] The social value thus appears comparable to altruism as defined in this study.

Further evidence supporting the hypothesis that altruism is related to a lower level of antagonism toward Negroes than is egoism is found in *The Authoritarian Personality*.[8] Individuals scoring low in antagonism toward minority groups were found to be characterized by a "warm and affectionate 'love-seeking' attitude,"[9] a "need to do something for peo-

[4] Richard I. Evans, "Personal Values as Factors in Anti-Semitism," *The Journal of Abnormal and Social Psychology*, 47 (Oct., 1952), pp. 749–756.

[5] Harrison G. Gough, "Studies of Social Intolerance: I. Some Psychological and Sociological Correlates of Anti-Semitism," *The Journal of Social Psychology*, 33 (May, 1951), pp. 237–246.

[6] Gordon W. Allport and Philip E. Vernon, *A Study of Values*, Manual of Directions (New York: Houghton Mifflin, 1931).

[7] *Ibid.*, p. 8.

[8] T. W. Adorno, Else Frenkel-Brunswick, Daniel J. Levinson, and R. Nevitt Sanford, *The Authoritarian Personality* (New York: Harper and Row, Publishers, 1950), esp. pp. 228–240, 400–416.

[9] *Ibid.*, p. 400.

ple,"[10] and a "genuine liking of, and warm interest and concern for people, along with belief in their essential goodness."[11] In contrast, individuals scoring high in antagonism were characterized by exploitative, manipulative, and opportunistic attitudes toward others.[12] Although the authors were not directly investigating cultural values as such, the forementioned findings strongly indicate an egoistic value orientation among those subjects who were high in antagonism toward minority groups and an altruistic value orientation among those low in antagonism.

MEASURING SOLIDARITY AND ANTAGONISM

This study distinguishes between two general types of attitude: antagonism and solidarity.[13] Antagonism is defined as a negative attitude toward others, which may vary in intensity from mild avoidance or a sense of incompatibility to such attitudes as opposition, mistrust, dislike, or enmity. Solidarity, a positive attitude toward others, may range in intensity from mild forms such as acceptance or friendliness to more intense forms such as cordiality, trust, or love.

Some facets of solidarity and antagonism toward Negroes are measured in the present study by a social distance score, an item asking about the degree of trust of Negroes, and a question pertaining to consideration of the use of firearms during the Watts riots.

The social distance score was based on the number of "yes" answers to a series of five questions asking whether the respondents would "ever find it distasteful" to engage in a variety of social interactions with Negroes.[14] The situations involving Negroes presented in the questions were eating at the same table, working on the same job, going to the same party, living in the same neighborhood, and sanctioning a Negro's marriage to someone in the respondent's family. Those who answered "yes" to two or more of these questions were classified as showing high social distance, or antagonism. Those who answered "yes" to only one question, or to none of the questions, were classified as showing low social distance, or solidarity. On this basis, 44 per cent (257) of the sample were antagonistic toward Negroes, while 56 per cent (326) showed attitudes of solidarity.

The second measure of antagonism toward Negroes was trust, which was measured by responses to the following question:

> As far as Negroes are concerned, do you feel you can trust most of them, some of them, or none of them?

Forty-five per cent (259) felt they could trust most Negroes, 49 per cent (286) some, and 5 per cent (31) none. One per cent (7) declined

10 *Ibid.*, p. 416.

11 *Ibid.*, p. 412.

12 *Ibid.*, pp. 400, 415–416.

13 The use of these two terms is based upon the writings of Pitirim A. Sorokin, *Society, Culture and Personality*, pp. 93–98.

14 The items used to measure social distance were derived from Robin M. Williams, Jr., *Strangers Next Door* (Englewood Cliffs, N.J.: Prentice Hall, 1964), pp. 28–29.

to express an opinion. This study has classified "trusting most Negroes" as a solidary response, "trusting some or no Negroes" as an antagonistic response.

The willingness of respondents in the survey to use firearms against Negroes during the Watts riot in August of 1965 was determined by responses to this question:

> Did you at any time consider using firearms to protect yourself or your family?

Twenty-nine per cent (167) of the respondents had considered using firearms, while 69 per cent (404) had not done so. Two per cent (12) did not answer. The first response regarded as a manifestation of antagonism, the second, more indirectly, as an indication of solidarity.

MEASURING ALTRUISM AND EGOISM

Three forced-choice questions were used to determine the values of respondents in the survey. They were asked to indicate for each question, which of the two statements they believed to be more nearly true. In each of the paired statements which follow, the first statement represents the value of altruism, the second that of egoism.

I. A. Most of the time a person should look out for others first, even when it may put him at a disadvantage.

    B. Most of the time a person should look out for himself, even when it may put others at a disadvantage.

II. A. A person's first concern should be for others.

    B. A person's first concern should be for himself.

III. A. The best way to find happiness in life is to forget yourself and try to help others.

    B. The best way to find happiness in life is to look out for your own self-interest first.

For item I, 46 per cent (269) of the respondents selected altruism, 49 per cent (285) egoism. For item II, 42 per cent (248) selected altruism, 53 per cent (308) egoism. For item III, 61 per cent (358) selected altruism, 35 per cent (203) egoism. For both items I and II, 5 per cent (29, 27) declined to make a choice; for item III, 4 per cent (22) declined. Since the individual items proved to be highly correlated with each other, an index, or score, was constructed.[15] Twenty-seven per cent (159) of the

---

[15] The correlation (gamma) between item I and item II is .82; between I and III it is .65. The correlation between items II and III is .68. The Coefficient of Reproducibility of the three items for Guttman Scaling using the Goodenough technique is .87. The Coefficient of Scalability is .70. A Coefficient of Reproducibility of .85–.89 is usually considered a quasi-scale while .90–1.00 is a scale. The level of acceptability for the Coefficient of Scalability is a minimum between .60 and .65, perfect scalability being indicated by a value of 1.00. Since the minimum number of items necessary for a reliable scale is usually considered to be four or five, the above coefficients are only suggestive of scalability, and do not indicate the existence of a scale. See Allen L. Edwards, *Techniques of Attitude Scale Construction* (New York: Appleton-Century-Crofts, Inc., 1957), pp. 172–200; Herbert Menzel, "A New Coefficient for Scalogram Analysis,"

sample endorsed altruism for all three items, 19 per cent (110) chose altruism twice and egoism once, 23 per cent (131) chose egoism twice and altruism once, 21 per cent (125) endorsed egoism for all three items, and 10 per cent (58) of the sample gave one or more "no answer" responses. Respondents were classified as altruistic or egoistic according to their majority response, while those with "no answer" responses were excluded from the analysis employing the index.

It is interesting to note at this point that one of the most serious criticisms received about the use of the value items, before going into the field, was that the results would not show a reasonable distribution of responses. Critics said the way the questions were worded would make quite obvious which choice was the "good" one, and thus all, or nearly all, of the respondents would choose the culturally approved value of altruism, rather than admit selfishness or self-centeredness. In the present sample, there seemed to be no hesitancy in expressing either value, and only a very small proportion of respondents could not, or would not, make the choice.

The use of forced-choice questions was based on the assumption that this method would provide a more valid measure of the respondent's values than would questions involving acceptance or rejection of a single value. The forced-choice technique was also more in line with Kluckhohn's conceptualization of values as justified *preferences*.[16] The difficulty in using an "agree-disagree" format is that in the case of "disagree" responses, one is never quite sure what value *is* espoused.

The Sample

Data for the study consist of a sample of 583 interviews with white respondents selected from six communities in the Los Angeles metropolitan area. Between 92 and 100 interviews were conducted in each community during a three-month period from November 18, 1965, to February 4, 1966. The sample was stratified according to socioeconomic status, ethnic and racial composition, sex, and age. Two communities, one integrated and one white, were selected, each one representing the three levels of socioeconomic status: high, middle, and low.[17] Age quotas provided for selecting 25 per cent of the sample between the ages of 20 and 24, 50 per cent between the ages of 25 and 54, and 25 per cent aged 55 and over. Sex quotas provided for an equal number of males and females for each of these age categories. The forementioned age quotas were approximate-

---

Public Opinion Quarterly, 17 (Summer, 1953–1954), pp. 268–280; Samuel A. Stouffer *et al.*, *Measurement and Prediction* (New Jersey: Princeton University Press, 1950).

16 Clyde Kluckhohn and others, "Values and Value-Orientations in the Theory of Action," in Talcott Parsons and Edward A. Shils, eds., *Toward a General Theory of Action* (New York and Evanston: Harper and Row, Torchbook Edition, 1962), pp. 394–405.

17 The socioeconomic status and racial composition of the six communities were based on 1960 Census figures as presented by Marcia Meeker and Joan R. Harris, *Background for Planning* (Research Department, Welfare Planning Council, Los Angeles Region, 1964), pp. 80–84.

ly similar to the age distribution of the general population of voting age in the Los Angeles metropolitan area.

RESULTS

The first part of this section presents the relationship between the values of altruism and egoism and the three measures of antagonism toward Negroes: social distance, trust, and consideration of using firearms. The results are shown for each of the three altruism-egoism forced-choice items and for the index or score based on responses to these items. These basic cross tabulations are then controlled for sex, age, education, and occupation. In this case, only the index is used to measure value orientation. For each cross tabulation the statistic gamma,[18] is presented as a measure of the strength of the association. Probability levels for chi-square up to .20 are recorded under each table, while levels greater than this are designated as not significant, as indicated by the abbreviation NS.[19]

Table 1 shows the relationship between values and antagonism toward Negroes, using the social distance score as a measure. The data indicate that altruistic respondents are less antagonistic toward Negroes than are egoistic respondents, the percentage difference ranging from 13 to 20 per cent, depending upon the measure of values. The statistical association between values and social distance is of moderate strength, ranging between .27 and .38.

Table 2 shows that altruistic respondents are also more likely to trust Negroes than are egoistic respondents. The percentage difference in antagonism according to values ranges between 12 and 16 per cent, and the statistical association between .24 and .36.

Table 3 presents the relationship between values and consideration of using firearms against Negroes. Respondents endorsing altruism are less

[18] Gamma is a symmetrical statistic, ranging in value from plus 1 to minus 1. This statistic may be interpreted as a proportional reduction in error measure, the value of gamma indicating the proportion by which error in estimating the order of pairs can be reduced by shifting from a random device to the estimation rule specified in the statistic. A positive gamma indicates that order on the dependent variable is the same as the order on the independent variable, while a negative gamma indicates that order on the dependent variable is the opposite of that on the independent variable. See Herbert L. Costner, "Criteria for Measures of Association," *American Sociological Review*, 30 (June, 1965), pp. 341–353.

[19] The consistency of the relationship between the independent and the dependent variable in the partial relationships, and the degree of statistical association. as indicated by the value of gamma, are the primary criteria used in evaluating the findings in this study. A gamma of .40 or greater is considered to indicate a "strong" relationship; .20 to .39 a "moderate" one; and .10 to .19 a "weak" one. A value of gamma less than .10 is considered to indicate that a relationship does not hold. In view of this criteria and the high degree of dependency of chi-square probabilities upon the number of cases, probabilities were recorded up to the .20 level, rather than the traditional .05. For a discusssion of the suitability of using such higher levels of significance, see James K. Skipper, Jr., Anthony T. Guerther, and Gilbert Nass, "The Sacredness of .05: A Note Concerning the Uses of Statistical Levels of Significance in Social Science," *American Sociologist*, 2 (Feb., 1967), pp. 16–18.

TABLE 1

Altruism and Egoism by Social Distance from Negroes

	Value	Low Social Distance (solidarity) Per Cent		High Social Distance (antagonism) Per Cent	N
Item I					
	Altruism	63		37	269
"Self *or* others					
at disadvantage"	Egoism	50		50	285
			P .01		
			gamma .27		
Item II					
	Altruism	63		37	248
"Concern for					
others *or* self"	Egoism	49		51	308
			P .01		
			gamma .27		
Item III					
	Altruism	64		36	358
"Happiness in					
helping others *or*					
self-interest"	Egoism	44		56	203
			P .001		
			gamma .38		
	Altruism	64		36	269
Index					
	Egoism	49		51	256
			P .001		
			gamma .30		

likely to have considered using firearms, although the percentage difference is only 4 per cent for item II. The statistical association between
value orientation and the use of firearms ranges from .10 to .31.

The relationship between altruism-egoism and antagonism, controlled
for sex, is presented in Table 4. The data show that there is little change
in the original relationship between values and social distance or trust.
In the case of this third measure of antagonism—consideration of the
use of firearms—the original relationship is stable for males, but does not
hold for females.

Table 5 shows that the relationship between values and antagonism
holds when controls for age are applied. For social distance and trust,
the original relationship decreases in strength for the young, while increasing for the middle-aged. The relationship between values and use

of firearms increases appreciably for the young, but decreases for both the middle-aged and old.

The controls for education are presented in Table 6. The original relationship between egoism and antagonism holds for all of the partials for social distance and trust, but is weak in the case of respondents who have not completed high school. The relationship between egoism and consideration of using firearms does not hold for respondents who had not completed high school or for college graduates, but increases noticeably among high school graduates.

Table 7 presents the controls for occupation. For social distance, the original relationship between values and antagonism is reversed among clerical and sales workers, while holding for the other two occupational categories. In the case of trust in Negroes, the original relationship holds but tends to become weaker. The relationship between egoism and use

TABLE 2

Altruism and Egoism by Trust in Negroes

	Value	Trust Most (solidarity) Per Cent		Trust Some or None (antagonism) Per Cent	N
Item I					
	Altruism	53		47	267
"Self *or* others					
at disadvantage"	Egoism	39		61	282
		P	.001		
		gamma	.28		
Item II					
	Altruism	56		44	245
"Concern for					
others *or* self"	Egoism	37		63	306
		P	.001		
		gamma	.36		
Item III					
"Happiness in	Altruism	50		50	355
helping others *or*					
self-interest"	Egoism	38		62	201
		P	.01		
		gamma	.24		
	Altruism	53		47	267
Index					
	Egoism	40		60	255
		P	.01		
		gamma	.25		

TABLE 3

Altruism and Egoism by Consideration
of Using Firearms against Negroes

	Value	Consider Using Firearms No (solidarity) Per Cent		Consider Using Firearms Yes (antagonism) Per Cent	N
Item I "Self *or* others at disadvantage"	Altruism	76		24	263
	Egoism	67		33	279
		P	.02		
		gamma	.23		
Item II "Concern for others *or* self"	Altruism	73		27	240
	Egoism	69		31	304
		P	NS		
		gamma	.10		
Item III "Happiness in helping others *or* self-interest"	Altruism	76		24	351
	Egoism	62		38	198
		P	.001		
		gamma	.31		
Index	Altruism	75		25	261
	Egoism	67		33	252
		P	.05		
		gamma	.20		

of firearms is particularly strong among blue-collar workers, does not hold among clerical and sales workers, and is reversed among professional and managerial workers.

In summary, the application of controls shows that the relationship between egoism and high social distance holds except among clerical and sales workers, while the relationship between egoism and lack of trust is maintained for all of the partials. The relationship between egoism and willingness to use firearms is less consistent, and is of moderate strength only among men, high school graduates, and blue-collar workers. This is perhaps due to the uneven distribution of responses on this item, and the fact that proximity to the riot area and the degree of fear experienced are both strongly related to willingness to use firearms against Negroes.

TABLE 4

Altruism and Egoism by Social Distance, Trust, and Consideration of Using Firearms, Controlling for Sex

| | MALE | | | | | | FEMALE | | | | | |
| | Social Distance High | | Trust Some or None | | Consider Using Firearms | | Social Distance High | | Trust Some or None | | Consider Using Firearms | |
Value (Index)	Per Cent	N	Per Cent	N	Per Cent	N	Per Cent	N	Per Cent	N	Per Cent	N
Altruism	37	99	47	99	31	96	35	170	47	168	21	165
Egoism	50	153	59	152	41	150	52	103	61	103	23	102
P	.05		.10		.20		.01		.05		NS	
gamma	.26		.23		.20		.34		.28		.04	

TABLE 5

Altruism and Egoism by Social Distance, Trust and Consideration of Using Firearms, Controlling for Age

| | Age 18–29 | | | | | | Age 30–54 | | | | | | Age 55–98 | | | | | |
| | Social Distance High | | Trust Some or None | | Consider Using Firearms | | Social Distance High | | Trust Some or None | | Consider Using Firearms | | Social Distance High | | Trust Some or None | | Consider Using Firearms | |
Value (Index)	Per Cent	N	Per Cent	N	Per Cent	N	Per Cent	N	Per Cent	N	Per Cent	N	Per Cent	N	Per Cent	N	Per Cent	N
Altruism	38	98	53	98	29	96	29	112	40	112	26	107	46	59	51	57	16	58
Egoism	46	76	61	76	45	75	48	108	60	107	34	106	62	71	59	71	19	70
P	NS		NS		.05		.01		.01		NS		.10		NS		NS	
gamma	.17		.15		.34		.38		.38		.18		.32		.17		.11	

TABLE 6
Altruism and Egoism by Social Distance, Trust, and Consideration of Using Firearms, Controlling for Education

Value (Index)	0–11 Yrs.						High School Grad.						Some College						College Grad. and Graduate School					
	Social Distance High		Trust Some or None		Consider Using Firearms		Social Distance High		Trust Some or None		Consider Using Firearms		Social Distance High		Trust Some or None		Consider Using Firearms		Social Distance High		Trust Some or None		Consider Using Firearms	
	Per Cent	N	Per Cent	N	Per Cent	N	Per Cent	N	Per Cent	N	Per Cent	N	Per Cent	N	Per Cent	N	Per Cent	N	Per Cent	N	Per Cent	N	Per Cent	N
Altruism	45	60	59	59	35	57	34	68	51	68	21	67	39	76	38	76	23	75	19	53	38	53	25	51
Egoism	53	64	67	64	35	63	60	70	64	69	35	68	49	65	58	65	29	65	39	44	45	44	25	44
P	NS		NS		NS		.01		.20		.10		NS		.02		NS		.05		NS		NS	
gamma	.16		.17		.04		.45		.25		.35		.20		.39		.17		.46		.16		.01	

TABLE 7
Altruism and Egoism by Social Distance, Trust, and Consideration of Using Firearms, Controlling for Occupation

Value (Index)	Craftsmen, Operatives, Service, Labor						Clerical and Sales						Professional and Managerial					
	Social Distance High		Trust Some or None		Consider Using Firearms		Social Distance High		Trust Some or None		Consider Using Firearms		Social Distance High		Trust Some or None		Consider Using Firearms	
	Per Cent	N	Per Cent	N	Per Cent	N	Per Cent	N	Per Cent	N	Per Cent	N	Per Cent	N	Per Cent	N	Per Cent	N
Altruism	48	31	57	30	29	31	37	35	34	35	31	35	25	48	46	48	36	44
Egoism	55	44	67	43	51	43	27	26	42	26	35	26	42	57	53	57	35	57
P	NS		NS		.10		NS		NS		NS		.10		NS		NS	
gamma	.12		.23		.44		.23		.17		.07		.37		.14		.03	

SUMMARY AND IMPLICATIONS

The data support the hypothesis that altruism is associated with a lower level of antagonism and a higher level of solidarity toward Negroes than is egoism. This is true for all three measures of antagonism used in the study, and in most instances remains true when this relationship is controlled for spuriousness.

Another criticism raised by colleagues of the authors after the completion of the study was that the findings merely represent a tautology: that egoism is the same as antagonism, and altruism the same as solidarity. The argument goes on to state that it is conceptually, or operationally, impossible to separate values from attitudes, and that the study simply relates one set of attitudes to another very similar set and, naturally, shows a strong correlation.

There are two answers to this criticism, one involving the problem of generality-specificity in the organization of attitudes, the other involving differential correlates of attitudes and values.

In our judgment, and following an old tradition,[20] one can distinguish conceptually between general orientations (which we call values) and specific object-bound views (which we call attitudes). Presumably, every member of a culture learns and organizes his views of the world and of himself according to some set of basic principles which guide him in his everyday decisions on specific problems. What is not clear, and what we need to discover through research, is what this organization is and which general orientations lead to which specific attitudes about which specific issues. It is by no means clear or self-evident that a person who says he looks out for himself first will consider using firearms to protect himself in a riot, or will find it distasteful to live in the same neighborhood with Negroes.

The second point, even granting that we are dealing with two sets of attitudes, is that if they are identical or even very similar, we should find that they are related to other variables in the same way. This, however, is definitely not the case with egoism-altruism and antagonism toward Negroes. For example, almost no sex difference emerges in antagonism toward Negroes on two of the three measures (more men consider using firearms than do women), but there is a marked difference on values according to sex (women are much more apt to be altruistic). As another example, a strong relationship exists between education and antagonism toward Negroes, as found in other studies,[21] but there is almost no relationship between education and egoism-altruism. In short, it appears that

---

[20] See Gordon W. Allport, "Attitudes," in C. M. Murchison, ed., *Handbook for Social Psychology* (Worcester, Mass.: Clark University Press, 1935), pp. 798–844; Bernard Berelson and Gary A. Steiner, *Human Behavior* (New York: Harcourt, Brace, and World, Inc., 1964), pp. 557–558; and M. B. Smith, "The Personal Setting of Public Opinions: A Study of Attitudes Toward Russia," *Public Opinion Quarterly*, 11 (Winter, 1947), pp. 507–523.

[21] See Gordon W. Allport, *The Nature of Prejudice* (New York: Doubleday and Company, 1958), pp. 404–407; and Robin M. Williams, Jr., *Strangers Next Door*, pp. 54–55.

general value orientations are learned very differently from specific attitudes toward minorities. The way in which these socialization processes take place is still far from clear, but we maintain that we are dealing with two very different and distinct kinds of phenomena.

Two major implications of this study may influence future theory and research. The first of these concerns the cultural approach to the study of prejudice toward minority groups. This study indicates the need to broaden the scope of investigation of the cultural sources of prejudice to include values such as egoism and altruism or other general value orientations prevalent in our culture which are not manifestly related to majority-minority relations.

A second implication of the study pertains to the development of a general theory of the cultural sources of solidarity and antagonism. This study has dealt only with attitudes toward Negroes, but it is likely that both egoism and altruism, as well as other values investigated (but not reported) here, are similarly associated with interpersonal and intergroup solidarities and antagonisms of other kinds. Such a more general relationship is clearly suggested by Sorokin's theory.[22]

[22] Sorokin, *Society, Culture and Personality*, pp. 119–131.

The White Backlash Re-examined: Wallace and the 1964 Primaries

M. MARGARET CONWAY

UNIVERSITY OF MARYLAND

SUBSEQUENT TO THE 1964 NORTHERN DEMOCRATIC PRESIDENTIAL PRIMARIES, much attention has been focused on the bases of political support for Alabama Governor George Wallace. Contradictory evaluations have been made of the voting results in the Maryland, Indiana, and Wisconsin primaries. In a recent article, Rogin interpreted support for Wallace as being primarily an expression of racial prejudice on the part of middle- and upper-class, conservative, native-stock Republicans.[1] Using aggregate data to examine the social composition of Milwaukee suburbs and comparing their support for Wallace, he concluded that the more middle-class suburbs, and therefore middle-class voters, supported Wallace to a greater degree than those he characterized as working class.[2] Rogin also related votes by county for Wallace to votes for Republican candidates in previous elections and characterized the Wallace vote as corresponding to a normal Republican vote.[3] He argued that support for Wallace came from predominantly middle-class areas, including the middle-class suburbs, the counties heavily populated by German immigrants and their descendents, and areas with a large proportion of residents in managerial, professional, and other white-collar occupations.[4]

---

[1] Michael Rogin, "Wallace and the Middle Class: The White Backlash," *Public Opinion Quarterly*, 30 (Spring, 1966), pp. 98–108.

[2] However, in a footnote he also cautions that "the middle class suburbs may have supported Wallace more than the working class suburbs, but that does not necessarily mean that most of Wallace's vote came from the middle class." Rogin, "Wallace and the Middle Class," footnote 11, p. 102. Rogin argues that the greater support of Wallace by Republican middle class voters is evidenced by the percentage of the Democratic primary vote received by Wallace in the middle class suburbs. However, he does not present data indicating what the per cent of voting participation in the Democratic primary was of the total voting turnout in each suburb. If only a small proportion of the total number voting voted in the Democratic primary in middle class suburbs and a large proportion of them voted for Wallace, it would appear when simply comparing the per cent in the Democratic primary voting for Wallace in the middle class and in the lower suburbs that a sizeable proportion of Wallace support is coming from the higher status suburbs. Perhaps only a very small proportion of the votes received by Wallace came from those suburbs and that proportion could have been contributed by the working class voters residing in those suburbs.

[3] Rogin, "Wallace and the Middle Class," p. 104. Rogin fails to present correlations between county socioeconomic characteristics and vote for Wallace.

[4] Rogin argues that when one controls for education "the lower class is less discrimination minded than the upper class" (p. 99) although, as Rogin points out, among the lower class the less educated predominate. Rogin cites a work by Stember as providing evidence that when education is controlled lower class members are more likely to favor educational and job equality and less likely to object to equal access to public accommodations for Negroes. (C. Stember, *Education and Attitude Change* [New York: Institute of Human Relations Press, 1961], pp. 84–87). While Stember argues that the lower economic groups are less discrimination minded when education is controlled,

♦ First published in Social Science Quarterly 49, No. 3 (December, 1968).

Contrasting Rogin's conclusions, Lipset, in analyzing the voting behavior in the three northern primaries, concluded that Wallace received
his greatest support from the predominantly Catholic, working-class
areas of the major industrial centers such as Milwaukee, Gary, and Baltimore.[5] In an earlier study, Key suggested the working class would be
more opposed to extension of desegregation, because working-class members would be most directly affected by desegregation.[6]

Other studies have presented conflicting evidence. Lipset delineated
patterns of both middle-class and working-class support for anti-liber-
tarians.[7] Lenski noted that on civil rights dimensions, the working class
was more conservative than the middle class, while the middle class was
more conservative on welfare state issues.[8] Key found conflicting evidence of middle-class support for liberal issue stands in a secondary
analysis of Survey Research Center data.[9]

The purpose of this paper is to determine which hypothesis is most
appropriate in analyzing patterns of support for Wallace in the 1964
Northern primaries.

METHOD

As Ranney pointed out, one can use aggregate data to establish generalizations about voting behavior of electorates with certain characteristics.[10] The study of a population of elections approach was used here
with the analysis examining the relationships existing between county
political and social characteristics and each county electorate's voting
behavior in the three states. Each state is analyzed separately, with each
county being treated as an electorate and with the nature of the electorate being indicated by the socioeconomic and political characteristics
of the county's population.[11]

---

in several areas his data do not warrant that conclusion, such as support for Negro
candidates for public office, approval of school integration, and general approval of
intergration. Furthermore, a number of problems exist in Stember's analysis. His data
are drawn from a number of public opinion polls conducted over a considerable period
of time, but possible shifts in opinion among sub-groups in society are not examined.
The sources of the data on specific issues are not given, the size of sample or number of
respondents in specific categories is not indicated, and no tests for significance of difference between proportions in the different social classes are used. One suspects that
many differences found by Stember between different social classes are so small as to
be very probable by chance.

[5] Seymour Martin Lipset, "Beyond the Backlash," *Encounter*, 23 (Nov., 1964), p. 22.

[6] V. O. Key, Jr., *Public Opinion and American Democracy* (New York: Alfred A.
Knopf, 1964), pp. 137–138.

[7] Seymour Martin Lipset, *Political Man* (New York: Doubleday and Company,
1959), Chs. 4 and 5.

[8] Gerhard Lenski, *The Religious Factor* (Garden City, N.J.: Doubleday and Company, 1961), pp. 188–189.

[9] Key, *Public Opinion and American Democracy*, pp. 135–149.

[10] Austin Ranney, "The Utility and Limitations of Aggregate Data in the Study of
Electoral Systems," *Essays on the Behavioral Study of Politics*, ed. A. Ranney (Urbana:
University of Illinois Press, 1962), pp. 99–101.

[11] This type of data has been used in both cross sectional and longitudinal analyses
by political scientists. See, for example, V. O. Key, *American State Politics* (New

Eight types of census data from the 1960 population census have been selected as descriptive of characteristics perhaps related to prejudicial voting behavior among the electorates studied: median education of persons over 25, per cent of the labor force employed in white collar occupations, per cent of home owner occupied dwellings, per cent of the labor force employed in manufacturing, median family income, per cent of the country's population residing in urban areas, per cent nonwhite population, and per cent of the native population of foreign or foreign and native parentage.[12] These are used as indicators of the educational, occupational and income levels, life style, degree of ethnicity, and minority group composition of the electorate.

Also used as independent variables are two indicators of previous voting behavior by the counties' electorates: the per cent of the county's total gubernatorial vote received by the Republican candidate in the most recent general election prior to the 1964 primary, and the per cent of the county's general election vote received by a prominent conservative candidate for the United States Senate. The gubernatorial elections used were held in 1962 in Wisconsin and Maryland and in 1960, in Indiana. Indicators of conservative voting in the respective states are the per cent of each Wisconsin county's total vote received by Senator Joseph McCarthy in 1952, the per cent of the vote received by John M. Butler in his contest with Senator Millard Tydings in Maryland in 1954, and the per cent of the vote received from the various Indiana counties by Senator William Jenner in 1952. All three conservative candidates were Republicans.

A question might be raised as to whether findings from the three states may be influenced by the nature of the Democratic primaries. Wisconsin operates its primaries under an open primary system; any voter may vote in either party's primary. In Indiana's primary system, a registered voter of one party may ask for the opposition party's ballot; if challenged, the voter merely signs an affidavit signifying he will vote for that party's candidates in the general election. Many observers believe a considerable amount of this type of crossing over into the Indiana Democratic party's primary occurred in the 1964 election. Maryland operates on a closed

---

York: Alfred A. Knopf, 1956); V. O. Key, *Southern Politics* (New York: Vintage Books, 1949); Milton C. Cummings, Jr., *Congressmen and The Electorate* (New York: The Free Press, 1966).

The census data are not directly descriptive of the characteristics of the electorate for two reasons: the time differential between the census data collection and the election and the electorate's being only a portion of the population residing within the county. To be technically correct, reference is to these socioeconomic and political characteristics as being descriptive of the social environment of the electorate, rather than of the electorate. This distinction is not generally made explicit in research using census data to evaluate electoral behavior.

[12] Source of the census data used is the *U.S. Census of Population, 1960*, Vol. 1, Parts, 16, 22, and 51. Data on the vote for Wallace are expressed as a per cent of the total Democratic primary vote and were obtained from the following sources: *1966 Wisconsin Blue Book*, p. 726; "General Election Returns, November 3, 1964," p. 1, Office of the Secretary of State, Annapolis, Maryland, mimeo; 1964 election returns, Office of the Secretary of State, Indianapolis, Indiana, Xerox.

primary system; only persons registered for six months as members of a particular party may vote in that party's primary. Maryland's registration figures, however, indicate that 70.8 per cent of the voters were registered as Democrats in the 1964 primary; many voters supporting Republicans at the national level register as Democrats to participate in selecting majority party nominees for local and legislative offices (securing the Democratic party's nomination has normally guaranteed a candidate's election). The state's different economic and social groups, therefore, are widely represented in the Democratic party. The three states appear to operate under nonequivalent primary systems, but the differences in composition of the primary electorate may not be as large as the formal structure would indicate.

FINDINGS

Table 1 presents the simple and multiple correlations between vote for Wallace and the independent variables for Wisconsin, Maryland, and Indiana. The variables used in the analysis account for 77 per cent of the variance in support for Wallace in Maryland, 53 per cent in Wisconsin, and 33 per cent in Indiana. In general, the correlation coefficient patterns appear to differ between the states, although some similarities in size, direction and level of significance exist.

TABLE 1

Simple and Multiple Correlations between
Vote for Wallace and the Independent
Variables, by State

	Maryland	Indiana	Wisconsin
Per cent white collar	−.351[a]	.043	.196[a]
Per cent urban	−.366[a]	.261[b]	.137
Per cent employed in manufacturing	.066	.138	.322[b]
Median family income	−.353[a]	.339[b]	.263[a]
Per cent nonwhite	.699[b]	.483[b]	.315[b]
Median education	−.210	.034	.260[a]
Per cent home owner occupied dwellings	−.192	.082	−.133
Per cent foreign parentage	−.333[a]	.247[b]	−.213[a]
Per cent of vote for Republican gubernatorial candidate	−.540[b]	−.088	.526[b]
Per cent of vote for conservative candidate	−.504[b]	−.356[b]	.270[a]
Multiple correlation	.882	.577	.730
Coefficient of determination	.778	.333	.532

[a] Significant at the .05 level.
[b] Significant at the .01 level.

In Indiana and Maryland negative (and in three instances, significant) correlations exist between support for Wallace and previous Republican and conservative support.[13] In contrast, positive and significant correlations were found between these sets of variables in Wisconsin. The pattern of association found by Rogin in Wisconsin between support for Wallace and the political variables may not have been present in Maryland and Indiana. In all three states, significant and strong positive correlations exist between support for Wallace and per cent of nonwhite population in the county. No other socioeconomic variables have a common pattern of association with support for Wallace. In summary, examination of the simple correlations shows dissimilarities exist in the pattern of association between support for Wallace and the political and socioeconomic variables.

Tests of significance were used to determine if differences in strength of association between support for Wallace and the socioeconomic and political characteristics of the electorates in the three states occurred by chance. The null hypothesis was tested by the use of z scores[14]; the z values and their probabilities are presented in Table 2. For three comparisons the null hypothesis of no difference in the degree of association between the vote for Wallace and selected characteristics in the states of Indiana and Wisconsin is rejected; however, two of these three are electoral factors—vote for a Republican in the previous gubernatorial election and vote for a conservative candidate for United States Senate. The other correlation set in which the difference in degree of association is significant is that between vote for Wallace and white-collar employment. These are crucial comparisons, as Rogin has argued that the middle-class, Republican voters were more likely to support Wallace in Wisconsin and therefore the so-called backlash vote in 1964 was more a middle-class than a lower-class phenomenon. The sign and size of the correlations differ to such a degree that the electorates ranking high in these political and socioeconomic characteristics exhibit quite different patterns of support in the two midwestern states. In Wisconsin, support for the middle-class electorate hypothesis can be found, but the Indiana data do not support the hypothesis.

[13] Use of tests of significance in analyzing data from a population is a questionable practice. However, one can use it to evaluate the likelihood of obtaining correlations of a given magnitude if a set of columns of random numbers had been correlated. For a discussion of this, see Thomas R. Dye, "Malapportionment and Public Policy in the Fifty States," *Journal of Politics*, 27 (Aug., 1965), footnote 15, p. 593; Thomas R. Dye, *Politics, Economics, and The Public* (Chicago: Rand McNally, 1966), p. 39.

[14] The hypotheses may be tested by converting the simple correlations to z scores and using the formula $Z = \dfrac{(Z_1 - Z_2) - O}{\sigma_{z_1 - z_2}}$. We can then check the values of the resultant Z in the normal table, obtaining an estimate of the probability of occurrence of that value of Z. If the probability is low (usually the standard of .05 or less is used) we can reject the null hypothesis that $r_1 = r_2$ and conclude that in one state a significantly stronger degree of association exists between the two variables than is found in the other. For a discussion of this method of making comparisons between correlations based on independent samples, see H. M. Blalock, *Social Statistics* (New York: McGraw Hill, 1960), pp. 310–311.

TABLE 2

Comparison of Degrees of Relationship
between Variables in Three States[a]

Degree of Relation-ship between Vote for Wallace and:	Maryland–Indiana $P_1=P_2$ z Score Probability		Indiana–Wisconsin $P_2=P_3$ z Score Probability		Maryland–Wisconsin $P_1=P_3$ z Score Probability	
Per cent white collar	1.68	.09	3.43	.0006[b]	2.27	.02[b]
Per cent urban	2.67	.007[b]	.79	.43	2.09	.02[b]
Per cent employed in manufacturing	.29	.76	1.12	.26	1.06	.29
Median family income	2.97	.003[b]	.51	.61	2.57	.01[b]
Per cent nonwhite	2.15	.03[b]	.84	.40	2.14	.03[b]
Median educational attainment	.89	.37	1.60	.11	1.93	.05[b]
Per cent home owner occupied dwellings	1.13	.25	1.31	.19	.24	.81
Per cent foreign parentage	2.45	.002[b]	.52	.60	2.85	.004[b]
Per cent vote for Republican guber-natorial candidate	3.21	.001[b]	2.46	.02[b]	4.72	.00006[b]
Per cent vote for conservative senato-rial candidate	1.07	.28	2.76	.005[b]	3.30	.001[b]

[a] The null hypothesis is tested; i.e., there is no greater association between percentage nonwhite population in the counties and vote for Wallace in either of the two states compared than in the other. Those z scores which are statistically significant indicate that rejecting the null hypothesis is appropriate. For a discussion of this statistical method, see H. M. Blalock, *Social Statistics, loc. cit.* $P_1=P_2$ can be read as the strength of association between the variables compared as equal in Maryland to the strength of association between the variables compared in Indiana; $P_2=P_3$ as the strength of association between variables in Indiana is equal to the strength of association between variables in Wisconsin; $P_1=P_3$ as the strength of association between the two variables in Maryland is equal to the strength of association between the two variables in Wisconsin.

[b] Statistically significant.

For five of the ten comparisons the strength of association between variables differs significantly when comparing Maryland and Indiana, and in eight of the ten comparisons significant differences exist between Maryland and Wisconsin.

In Maryland a negative correlation significantly different from the positive correlations found in Wisconsin existed between electoral support for Wallace and white-collar employment, support for the Republican gubernatorial candidate, and support for the conservative Senate candidate. It

TABLE 3

Summary Table: Rejection of Null Hypothesis
of No Difference in Degree of Association
between Variables

Variables Vote for Wallace and:	Reject Null Hypothesis		
	Md.–Ind. $P_1 = P_2$	Ind.–Wis. $P_2 = P_3$	Mid.–Wis. $P_1 = P_3$
Per cent employed as white collar	no	yes	yes
Per cent urban	yes	no	yes
Per cent employed in manufacturing	no	no	no
Median family income	yes	no	yes
Per cent nonwhite	yes	no	yes
Median education	no	no	yes
Per cent home owner occupied dwellings	no	no	no
Per cent one parent foreign born or foreign born	yes	no	yes
Per cent vote for Republican gubernatorial candidate	yes	yes	yes
Per cent vote for conservative senate candidate	no	yes	yes

appears that in Indiana and Maryland the counties more Republican, middle class, and conservative were not the high backlash electoral units.[15]

These findings could be a consequence of one or a combination of several factors. The primary systems of Maryland and Indiana may exclude Republicans, who tend to be heavily drawn from the middle-class groups in society, from voting in the Democratic primaries to such a degree that the true picture of the middle-class electorate's contribution to backlash voting cannot emerge in this analysis.

Another explanation may be that backlash voting occurs in areas having a concentration of Negro population. The states differ in their distribution patterns of the black population, thus different patterns of correlations between vote for Wallace and other variables may be a function of the dis-

[15] Analysis of precinct voting patterns in the populous electoral units in Maryland (Montgomery, Prince Georges, Anne Arundel, Baltimore, and Howard counties and city of Baltimore) indicates that Wallace support tended to come disproportionately from low-income, white, ethnic precincts in these predominately urban and suburban electorates, and the same pattern of support existed in the 1966 Maryland Democratic gubernatorial primary and general election contests for Democratic candidate George Mahoney. See Robert D. Loevy, "Computer Analysis of 1966 Gubernatorial General Election," Nov., 1966, and "Computer Analysis of 1966 Democratic Gubernatorial Primary in Baltimore City and Baltimore County," Oct. 3, 1966 (Field Politics Center, Goucher College, mimeo); B. Engleberg, "Demographic and Comparative Analysis of the Baltimore Vote for Governor George C. Wallace: 1964 Maryland Democratic Primary," (College Park. Md.: May 11, 1967, mimeo).

tribution of that population.[16] Rogin asserted that the Wallace vote in the Northern states repeats the Southern black belt pattern, with whites in counties with large numbers of Negroes being more supportive of his candidacy. Anti-Negro sentiment was viewed as being more salient in urban areas and particularly among the urban middle class.[17]

This explanation can be tested by use of partial correlations to see what relationships exist between support for Wallace and certain characteristics of the countries after controlling for the per cent nonwhite population in each county. As Table 4 indicates, the explanation that Wallace's voting support was a function of the distribution of nonwhite population appears more appropriate for Indiana and Maryland than for Wisconsin.[18] In Indiana and Maryland, a very low partial correlation occurs between per cent of the total Democratic primary vote received by Wallace and white-collar employment, with the partial correlation being negative for Maryland and neither being statistically significant. There are positive partial correlations between per cent employed in manufacturing and support for Wallace in Maryland and Indiana, but only in Indiana is there a significant partial correlation between manufacturing employment and support for Wallace. In Wisconsin, the partial correlation is almost nil.

Even more interesting is the relationship between vote for Wallace and the two political indices, vote for the most recent Republican gubernatorial candidate and vote for a well-known conservative senatorial candi-

---

[16] The degree to which desegregation could be perceived as a threat might be a function of the proportion of nonwhite persons residing in the area. An area with greater percentage of Negroes has greater demand potential for integrated schools, housing, public accommodations, and for job opportunities. The saliency of desegregation may also be a function of relative status security.

Immigrants or children of immigrants who have only recently attained a higher status might feel more threatened by the demands of a more disadvantaged group.

However, the threat could be less salient to the working class, in part as a result of the greater degree of political apathy on its part and the relative abstractness of the threat. Democratic party organization activities in mobilizing support for official party candidates in opposition to Wallace may also have had greater effects on the working class.

The possible causes of middle-class opposition to the extension of Negro civil rights are discussed by Rogin, "Wallace and the Middle Class," p. 107. The urban middle class may also perceive the extension of desegregation as a threat to the integrity of their communities, integrity defined in terms of social rank and life style. See Scott Greer, *The Emerging City* (New York: The Free Press, 1962).

[17] Rogin, "Wallace and the Middle Class," p. 106.

[18] In effect we are examining several simple causal models, in which the correlation between Wallace support and each of the independent variables is viewed as a spurious correlation produced by its relationship to per cent nonwhite population. For example,

Per Cent Nonwhite Population

Per Cent Employed in   Per Cent Support for
Manufacturing   Wallace

No causal arrow exists between percentage employed in manufacturing and support for Wallace, indicating no causal relationship in the model. If the partial correlation between manufacturing employment and support for Wallace is less than .10, we would be justified in retaining this model. Otherwise, we would revise the model by drawing a causal arrow from percentage employed in manufacturing to support for Wallace.

TABLE 4

Partial Correlation between Vote for Wallace and
Selected Variables, Controlling for Per Cent
Nonwhite Population, by State

Partial correlation between vote for Wallace and vote for Republican gubernatorial candidates, controlling for per cent nonwhite population

Indiana	−.040
Maryland	−.304[a]
Wisconsin	.565[b]

Partial correlation between vote for Wallace and vote for conservative senatorial
candidate, controlling for per cent nonwhite population

Indiana	−.174[a]
Maryland	−.382[a]
Wisconsin	.303[b]

Partial correlation between vote for Wallace and white-collar employment, controlling for per cent nonwhite population

Indiana	.068
Maryland	−.069
Wisconsin	.143

Partial correlation between vote for Wallace and manufacturing employment,
controlling for per cent nonwhite population

Indiana	.331[b]
Maryland	.217
Wisconsin	.050

---

[a] Significant at .05 level.
[b] Significant at .01 level.

date. Once again Maryland and Indiana exhibit a similar political pattern
with Wisconsin being distinctly different. In Maryland and Indiana there
are negative partial correlations, while in Wisconsin both partials are
positive, large, and statistically significant at the .01 level. In Indiana and
Maryland the electorate's support for Wallace appears strongly influenced
by the proportion of nonwhites in the county and that support was not
drawn disproportionately from the electorates which were more middle
class, Republican, and conservative.

The nonwhite category includes American Indians, and Wisconsin has
a number of counties with a significant proportion of Indian residents
while Indiana and Maryland do not. Therefore, additional partial correlations were calculated for Wisconsin, controlling just for the proportion of
Negro population in the counties. The results are presented in Table 5.
The pattern is the same as previously found when controlling for per cent
nonwhite population except for the relationship between manufacturing
employment and vote for Wallace, the partial correlation now approxi-
mating that found in Indiana and Maryland.

Wallace support in Wisconsin could have been based on economic and
political conservatism not connected with civil rights. Speeches by Wallace in the three states emphasized the allegedly unwarranted expansion

TABLE 5

Wisconsin: Partial Correlations, Controlling for Per Cent Negro,
between Vote for Wallace and Selected Variables

Partial correlation, vote for Wallace and:	
Republican gubernatorial candidate	.583[b]
conservative senatorial candidate	.363[b]
white-collar employment	.145
manufacturing employment	.276[a]

[a] Significant at .05 level.
[b] Significant at .01 level.

of the federal government into a number of policy areas, with the civil rights field being just one of his examples; this larger federal role theme may have been more salient in Wisconsin than in the other states.

Another influence may have been a result of the interrelationship of the timing of the primaries and the coverage given the Wallace candidacy by the mass media; repetition of certain themes may have caused Wallace to be symbolized in the two later primaries as an anti-black candidate, whereas the more limited exposure provided by the mass media in the Wisconsin primary may have presented his candidacy in terms of a more conservative appeal.[19]

Summary

This analysis began with two alternative hypotheses about the association of political and socioeconomic characteristics with electoral support for Wallace. The middle-class electorate hypothesis appears more appropriate for Wisconsin, but the patterns of voting in Wisconsin may have reflected also a broader conservative appeal. In Maryland and Indiana voting patterns appear to represent a pattern of working-class electorate backlash, with negative or low positive partial correlations found between the independent variables of white-collar employment, Republican gubernatorial support, and support for a Republican conservative senatorial candidate when controls for the proportion of black population in each county are applied. A black belt voting pattern also appears to have been present.

[19] The Wisconsin primary was held on April 7; the Indiana primary on May 5; and the Maryland primary on May 19. The voting studies based on attitude-opinion surveys have focused on general elections; hopefully these studies will be expanded to studies of primaries and of the role of mass media in shaping the potential voter's perceptions of candidates and definition of salient issues when the mediating effects of political party identification are inoperative because of the nature of the election itself.

19

Poverty, Minorities, and Consumer Exploitation

FREDERICK D. STURDIVANT
THE UNIVERSITY OF TEXAS AT AUSTIN

WALTER T. WILHELM
UNIVERSITY OF SOUTHERN CALIFORNIA

A NUMBER OF REPORTS, RANGING FROM INFORMAL STUDIES BY JOURNALISTS to carefully researched investigations, have provided evidence that residents of ghettos pay more for their consumer goods than do other Americans.[1] For example, David Caplovitz' study of 464 families living in three New York settlement houses revealed a consistent pattern of high prices, poor quality, high interest charges, and unethical merchandising techniques being inflicted on them. He concluded that "the problems of low-income consumers stem from the same set of forces that have created that special system of sales-and-credit—the quasi-traditional economy—catering to their wants."[2] In California, the Governor's Commission on the Los Angeles Riots tended to reinforce this view. Following three months of investigation into the causes of the Watts riots, the Commission reported, "our conclusion, based upon an analysis of the testimony before us and on the reports of our consultants is that consumer problems in the curfew area are not due to systematic racial descrimination but rather result from the traditional interplay of economic forces in the market place, aggravated by poverty conditions."[3] These studies suggest, therefore, that the market system works to the disadvantage of the poor simply because they are poor, not because of their race or ethnicity. Any correlation between minority status and exploitation is, according to these studies, attributable to the high incidence of poverty among minorities rather than to some insidious form of discrimination.

The studies reported to date have not, however, provided adequate proof to support this conclusion. The Governor's Commission, for example, reached its conclusion without conducting a series of comparative shopping analyses between ghetto and non-ghetto stores, utilizing shoppers of various racial and ethnic backgrounds. Instead, staff consultants and their research assistants "spot checked" prices in various locations throughout central Los Angeles.[4] Caplovitz did analyze certain of his data utilizing the variable of minority status. His findings in this area, however, were unclear. On the one hand he noted, "The amount paid for appli-

[1] For examples of the former, see *The Wall Street Journal*, August 16, 1966; *Women's Wear Daily*, July 6, 1966; *Los Angeles Times*, October 8, 1967; and *Los Angeles Herald-Examiner*, October 11, 1966.

[2] David Caplovitz, *The Poor Pay More* (New York: The Free Press, 1963), p. 179.

[3] The Governor's Commission on the Los Angeles Riots, "Violence in the City—An End or a Beginning?" (Los Angeles, Dec., 1965), p. 63.

[4] Interview with Gerald L. Rosen, Staff Attorney, Governor's Commission on the Los Angeles Riots, January 18, 1966.

♦ First published in *Social Science Quarterly* 49, No. 3 (December, 1968).

ances differs greatly among the racial [sic] groups. Whites pay the least,
Puerto Ricans the most, with Negroes in between."[5] He then noted, however, that nonwhites tended to pay lower prices when the purchase was
made in cash. In fact, his data suggested that nonwhites paid less than
whites when buying on credit in large stores outside the ghetto. This conflicting evidence was derived from the shopping experiences of the 464
cooperating families. The variables of method of payment, minority status,
and type of store were considered. However, brand and model variations
were not taken into account. Thus, one does not know if whites generally
selected more expensive models and brands or if this shopping behavior
was perhaps characteristic of either the Negroes or Puerto Ricans studied.
If the variable of product brand and model is held constant, meaningful
price comparisons cannot be made unless one subscribes to the rather
risky assumption that brand or product quality selection is randomly distributed among the various ethnic and racial groups. In essence, the statement that exploitation in the marketplace is a function of economic status
rather than minority status is still untested.

RESEARCH DESIGN AND METHODOLOGY

The present study was conducted in Los Angeles and involved the use
of three couples and three shopping areas. The three couples represented
the major populations of the city—Negro, Mexican-American, and Anglo-
white. The shopping districts were in the predominately Negro south
central section of Los Angeles (which includes Watts), the Mexican-
American section of east Los Angeles, and Culver City, which is a middle-
class Anglo-white community.

The criteria used in selecting the couples included not only minority
group status, but also comparable "credit profiles." The similarity of their
profiles was designed to neutralize any price or credit differentials based
on alleged risk. The characteristics of the shoppers' credit profiles are
given in Figure 1.

FIGURE 1
Shoppers' Credit Profile

Family status	Married, 1–2 children
Age of head of household	25–30 years
Employment	Employed full-time for 1–2 years on present job
Gross income	$2,850–$3,250
Savings	$0–$100
Total assets	$300–$450
Indebtedness	$200–$500
as per cent of gross income	6.6–16
as per cent of assets	67–111

[5] Caplovitz, *The Poor Pay More*, pp. 90–91.

The stores selected for comparative shopping in the Negro and Mexican sections were determined, in part, on the basis of detailed studies of consumer shopping patterns in those areas. Appliance and furniture stores in the two areas were arrayed on the basis of shopping frequency patterns determined from nearly 2,000 consumer interviews conducted in an earlier study of Watts and east Los Angeles.[6] Stores were then either included or eliminated from the sample, depending on the presence or absence of the same brands and models available in the control area. Culver City was selected as the non-poverty shopping area because the composition of its retailing community and price structure typified shopping conditions for suburban Los Angeles area communities.

The attrition rate for stores to be included in the study was rather high because of the difficulty of finding the same brands and models in the disadvantaged areas as were found in Culver City. Comparative pricing analyses involving poverty areas and more prosperous sections in a city are very difficult because of variations in merchandise. When national brands are carried by a ghetto appliance dealer, he generally stocks only the lower end of the line. Retailers in higher-income areas usually concentrate on the middle and upper price ranges of the product line. Furthermore, off-brand merchandise makes up a substantial part of the ghetto dealer's stock. Since these lines generally are not carried in other areas, direct price comparisons are impossible. Among the stores frequented by the residents of the two poverty areas, therefore, only six carried brands and models capable of direct price comparisons with those in stores in the outside community. The stores selected in the outside area were comparable to the ghetto stores in terms of size and estimated sales volume.[7]

The shopping procedure involved the selection of a 19-inch, black-and-white, portable TV set by each couple in each of the nine stores. Each couple (the order was determined randomly) selected a predetermined TV set and did everything necessary to obtain price data, except sign the contract. The shopping trips to each store were separated by a minimum of three days to avoid any suspicion by the sales clerks or management. The shopping was conducted during the last two weeks of July and the first week of August, 1967. A final briefing was given the similarly attired couples before they entered each store to make certain they selected the correct model TV. A typical dialogue in the store is as follows:

SALESMAN: May I help you?

SHOPPERS: Yes, we would like to see your portable TV's.

SALESMAN: They are right over here. Did you have anything special in mind? Color?

[6] Frederick D. Sturdivant, "Better Deal for Ghetto Shoppers," *Harvard Business Review*, 46 (March–April, 1968), pp. 130–139.

[7] The reader may be disturbed initially by the small size of the sample. However, it should be noted that *every* television dealer in the two low-income areas that met the comparability criteria for the test was included in the study. The comparability criteria could have been relaxed and thus the sample size increased, but such a step would have made it impossible to test the hypothesis.

SHOPPERS: No, we want a black-and-white set. (*The shoppers look at several sets and then ask about the preselected set.*)

SHOPPERS: This is a nice set. It is the type we had in mind.

SALESMAN: It is a very nice set. We could deliver it today. (*Salesmen often attempted to get the shoppers interested in a more expensive model*).

SHOPPERS: How much does it cost?

SALESMAN: (*Quotes the price.*)

SHOPPERS: How much would it run us a month? (*The salesman figures out the credit terms. The couple specifies that they want the smallest down-payment and the lowest possible payments. Upon being told the monthly payment figure, the wife says they should think it over and asks the salesman to write down the credit terms. Only one store refused this request, saying that such information was "confidential and not allowed out of the store."*)

In summary, the method included the selection of six of the most frequently used furniture and appliance stores in the two major poverty areas of Los Angeles for comparison with three stores (selected on the basis of comparable brand and model availability) from an average suburban community. Fundamental to the method was the use of three disadvantaged couples representing the three major population groups in the area, with basically the same credit characteristics. The three couples dressed in basically the same mode, shopped in the same stores, and priced exactly the same products. They obtained a price based on cash payment and the price for an 18-month installment contract. Thus, the only relevant variable not held constant was minority status.

FINDINGS

In the process of testing for discrimination in the marketplace, data was collected which again confirm the presence of higher prices in ghetto stores. Ignoring the question of minority status for the moment, Table 1 indicates that the average price asked of the three couples for a given product was always higher in the disadvantaged-area stores than in the control area (Culver City). The total cost, or the credit price (shown in parentheses), averaged higher in the poverty areas as well.

While there were notable differences in prices between areas, there was an observable consistency in retail prices within the stores.[8] Among the prices recorded in Table 2, 19 of the 24 retail prices asked for the four models of TV sets were the same, regardless of the purchasers' minority status. The prices asked the couples in the three Watts area stores were identical. In the control area, store #1 increased the price by $10 for both the Negro and Mexican couples. In this case, the Negro couple shopped at the store first and was asked $119 for the RCA Model AH0668

[8] This consistency in retail prices was not attributable to the presence of price tags. In five of the six ghetto stores and in one of the control area stores, the customers had to rely on sales personnel for price information.

TABLE 1

Average Retail and Credit Price for Portable TV Sets, by Area and by Brand

Product	Watts Area	Average Price[a] East L.A. Area	Control Area
Zenith	$170	—	$130
X1910	($194)		($146)
Olympic	$270	$230	—
9P46	($448)	($277)	
RCA	$148	—	$115
AH0668	($174)		($154)
Zenith	—	$208	$140
X2014		($251)	($190)

[a] Prices are averages computed from the shopping experiences of the three couples in each of the stores selected. Retail prices refer to the price asked for the product before adding on sales tax and credit charges. Credit prices, *shown in parentheses*, are the total of retail prices, sales tax and interest charges.

TV. Four days later, the white couple was offered the same set for $109. After a wait of another three days, the Mexican couple shopped at the store and was asked $119 for the set. The other six shopping trips in the control area produced identical prices for all three couples. The Mexican area showed the greatest variation in prices. In part, this practice may be attributable to cultural patterns in the Mexican community where higgling and haggling is more common. There was no pattern of discrimination. In store #1 the Mexican couple was asked the highest price while in store #3 the Mexican and Negro couples were charged slightly higher prices than was the Anglo couple.

When credit prices are considered, however, it becomes clear that credit and carrying charges are the devices most commonly used for exploitation. In the two east Los Angeles stores, for example, the white couple was not quoted the highest retail prices, but they were quoted the highest credit prices. In all nine cases in the control area there were differences in credit charges even though the retail price differed in only store #1. The most blatant case of discrimination occurred in Culver City store #1. While the legal limit on interest is 15 per cent on an 18-month installment contract in California, the Mexican and Negro couples were asked to pay 42 and 44 per cent, respectively.[9] The white couple was asked the legal rate. In store #3 in Culver City, the two minority group couples

[9] The Unruh Retail Installment Sales Act sets the maximum rate a dealer may charge on time contracts in California. A dealer may charge less, of course, but no evidence of this practice was found in the study. For most installment contracts under $1,000 the maximum service charge rate in 5/6 of 1 per cent of the original unpaid balance multiplied by the number of months of the contract. In revolving charge accounts, such as those used by most department stores, the legal limit is 1½ per cent per month on the first $1,000 and 1 per cent per month on the balance over $1,000.

TABLE 2

Retail[a] and Credit[b] Prices for Portable TV Sets by Area, Store, Brand, and Race

Area and Store	Zenith—X1910			Olympic—9P46			RCA—AH0668			Zenith—X2014		
	Negro	M-A	Anglo	Negro	M-A	Anglo	Negro	M-A	Anglo	Negro	M-A	Anglo
East L.A.												
Store 1				$200 ($265)	$240 ($281)	$230 ($284)						
Store 2[c]												
Store 3										$210 ($245)	$210 ($250)	$204 ($258)
Watts												
Store 1	$170 ($194)	$170 ($194)	$170 ($194)									
Store 2							$148 ($178)	$148 ($169)	$148 ($174)			
Store 3				$270 ($421)	$270 ($507)	$270 ($418)						
Culver City												
Store 1							$119 ($172)	$119 ($169)	$109 ($122)			
Store 2										$140 ($183)	$140 ($183)	$140 ($203)
Store 3	$130 ($145)	$130 ($152)	$130 ($140)									

[a] Retail prices refer to the price asked for the product before adding sales tax and interest charges.
[b] Credit prices, *shown in parentheses*, are the total of retail prices, sales tax, and interest.
[c] The model preselected for this store was sold before the experiment was completed.

were asked a higher (and illegal) rate of interest. In store #2 all three couples were asked an illegal rate with the white couple being asked the highest amount.

In the predominately Negro area stores, where all three couples had been asked identical retail prices, only one store charged the same legal rate of interest on its 18-month installment contracts. There were minor variations in the charges assigned by store #2, with the Negro couple being quoted the highest amount and the Mexican shoppers the lowest. At store #3 the retail price was quoted at $270 before tax. Adding tax at 5 per cent, which was a constant percentage in all credit prices noted, the total retail price before financing should have been $283.50. Deducting the required minimum down payment of $15.80, the total to be financed was $267.70. At the legal rate of 15 per cent for an 18-month contract, interest charges would have amounted to $40.16 for a total price of $322.66. However, the total price quoted to the Anglo and Negro couples was approximately $420, which means an interest rate of nearly 50 per cent. The total cost quoted to the Mexican couple was $506.62 with interest charges of 82 per cent.[10]

SUMMARY AND CONCLUSIONS

In spite of the difficulties associated with finding identical products in ghetto and non-ghetto stores, this study has attempted to determine the basis of price discrimination experienced by disadvantaged shoppers. The research question was, "Is exploitation in the marketplace a function of low income or minority status?" By selecting three pairs of disadvantaged shoppers whose only significant difference was race and ethnic origin and then having these couples shop in the same stores for identical merchandise, the research design attempted to answer the question.

The findings demonstrate that installment purchases, which especially characterize the purchasing behavior of the disadvantaged, produce major variations in the prices paid by the poor. While no perfect pattern of discrimination based on minority status emerged from the study, it was common for the couples to be asked higher credit rates when shopping outside their own areas. In east Los Angeles, the white couple received the highest price quotations. In the Watts area, the store charging the highest and most varied prices asked a substantially higher price of the Mexican couple. In two of the non-ghetto stores the minority shoppers were charged higher, and illegal, amounts.

The findings indicate that merchants find credit charges an excellent vehicle for exercising economic and racial or ethnic discrimination, but Table 2 demonstrates that however substantial and illegal many of these charges may be, they are not as significant as price variations between disadvantaged and prosperous areas. While the minority couples were subjected to discriminatory pricing in two of the three control area stores, in no case would they have paid more than in the ghetto stores for the

---

[10] This model Olympic TV set wholesales for $104. Thus, with a retail price of $270 the dealer was already profiting from a markup of 160 per cent.

same merchandise. In most instances the prices were substantially less. It might be concluded that disadvantaged minority shoppers pay more, especially in the ghetto.

The presence of high business costs, parasitic retailers, and the dominance of inefficient "mom-and-pop" firms in the ghetto underline the need of comparative shopping by the disadvantaged. At the same time, the willingness of certain outside retailers to take advantage of the poor, especially members of minority groups, suggests that the disadvantaged are subject to economic exploitation even when shopping beyond the boundaries of the ghetto.

Notwithstanding the difficulties of designing a test of minority groups and economic exploitation (a parallel study of automobile prices had to be abandoned in this project), additional studies should be undertaken. Experiments involving this phenomenon in other major American cities would provide a more complete understanding of these practices. Doubtless, the situation is not unique to Los Angeles, and the extent to which it reflects a national pattern of discrimination against the minorities and the poor shows that it deserves further analysis and correction.

20

The Death of Rastus: Negroes
in American Films Since 1945*

THOMAS R. CRIPPS
MORGAN STATE COLLEGE

Students of the film have been divided over the issue of just what movies communicate. Those closer to the era of the behaviorists such as Lenin and Jane Addams believed that movies molded opinion. They held that films have a proven effect upon behavior because the experience of movie-going, unlike theater, is "extrasocial" and thus a clear identification takes place between filmed image and the mind of the viewer.[1]

More recent observers argue that the film is a kind of reflector of values. Siegfried Kracauer postulates a cinema as a social communicator of deep layers of Jungian collective meanings and psychological dispositions.[2] Given this assumption, each viewer's background determines what he gets from a film; that is, he captures what is usable to himself. "He utilizes the pictured situation," as Franklin Fearing puts it, "in the process of coming to terms with the larger environments."[3] Thus movies form attitudes in a chance way, depending on biases already held by the audience members individually. They have residues of imagery from older movies through which they view new images. Thus they may evade, misinterpret, or miss the point of a film's persuasion. In some cases a boomerang effect is

---

* Reprinted by permission from *Phylon*, 28 (Fall, 1967), pp. 267–275.

[1] Paul G. Cressey, "The Motion Picture Experience as Modified by Social Background and Personality," *American Sociological Review*, III, 4 (August, 1938), 516–525. For brief comments by earlier observers, see Thomas R. Cripps, "The Negro Reaction to the Motion Picture 'Birth of a Nation,'" *Historian*, XXV, 3 (May, 1963), 344–362.

[2] For various shades of opinion on the effects of motion picture viewing, see Hortense Powdermaker, "An Anthropologist Looks at the Movies," 80–87; Norman Woelfel, "The American Mind and the Motion Picture," 88–94; Allan A. Hunter, "A Clergyman Looks at the Movies," 95–97; Leo C. Rosten, "Movies and Propaganda," 116–124, all in *Annals of the American Academy of Political and Social Science*, CCLIV (November, 1947). For estimates of value transmission to various audiences, see Mildred J. Wiese and Stewart G. Cole, "A Study of Children's Attitudes and the Influence of a Commercial Motion Picture," *Journal of Psychology*, XXI (January, 1946), 151–171 (in which the authors found that a movie gave support to "their uncritical conception of an idealized America," 170); Siegfried Kracauer, "Those Movies with a Message," *Harper's*, CXCVI, 1777 (June, 1948), 567–572, who warns that message movies may show the fragility of that which they wish to promote. See also Frederick Elkin, "Value Implications or Popular Films," *Sociology and Social Research*, VIII, 5 (May–June, 1954), 320–322, who more recently and scientifically argues that even an Abbott and Costello comedy may have an unconscious "social function" of suggesting values, though less obviously with a problem or message film.

[3] Franklin Fearing, "Influence of the Movies on Attitudes and Behavior," *Annals of the American Academy of Political and Social Science*, CCLIV (November, 1947), 70–79.

achieved: that is, the viewer comes away believing more strongly in the attitude opposite to the one presented by a film. German audiences, for example, missed the point of the problem movie, *Blackboard Jungle*, taking it to be a documentary with Glenn Ford the only professional actor.[4]

At least one critic, after seeing Stanley Kramer's movie about the hysterical paralysis of a Negro soldier, concluded that *"Home of the Brave* will convert no one; in some observers (because of the unintentionally implied cowardice of the Negro), it could have the effect of confirming prejudice." A social scientist who studied the attitude creation of the movie biography of Sister Kenny found it a weak propaganda agent simply because the audience respondents did not attribute accuracy and seriousness of purpose to motion pictures. Other critics have pointed to ethnic and national attitudes and minority relationships as other factors in the successful transmission of images by the film. As Kracauer has put it:

Hollywood and any national film industry for that matter is both a leader and a follower of public opinion. In portraying foreign characters it reflects what it believes to be the popular attitudes of the time, but it also turns these often vague attitudes into concrete images.[5]

Thus in American motion pictures in-group self-images will become the norm of behavior and all the jangling diversity of ethnic groups will round off into a broadly based white Anglo-Saxon Protestant type. Some minority groups have contributed to this kind of negative stereotyping by their protests against reprehensible typing. Witness protests by Italians

[4] Russell Middleton, "Ethnic Prejudice and Susceptibility to Persauasion," *American Sociological Review*, XXV, 5 (October, 1960), 679–686. For arguments for the persuasiveness of propaganda films, see, among others, Albert L. Goldberg, "The Effects of Two Types of Sound Motion Pictures on the Attitudes of Adults Toward Minorities," *Journal of Educational Psychology*, XXXIX (May, 1956), 386–391; L. E. Raths and F. N. Trager, "Public Opinion and 'Crossfire,' " *Journal of Educational Sociology*, XXI (February, 1948), 345–348; Irwin C. Rosen, "The Effects of the Motion Picture 'Gentleman's Agreement' on Attitudes toward Jews," *Journal of Psychology*, XXVI (October, 1948), 525–536; and C. I. Hovland *et al, Experiments on Mass Communication* (Princeton, 1961). For statements critical of the efficacy of firm propaganda, see, among others, Eunice Cooper and Helen Dinerman, "Analysis of the Film 'Don't Be a Sucker': A Study in Communication," *Public Opinion Quarterly*, XV (Summer, 1951), 243–264; Eunice Cooper and Marie Jahoda, "The Evasion of Propaganda: How Prejudiced People Respond to Anti-Prejudice Propaganda," *Journal of Psychology*, XXIII (January, 1947), 15–25; S. H. Flowerman, "Mass Propaganda in the War against Bigotry," *Journal of Abnormal and Social Psychology*, XLII (October, 1947), 429–439; Herbert Hyman and Paul B. Sheatsley, "Some Reasons Why Information Campaigns Fail," *Public Opinion Quarterly*, XI (Fall, 1947), 413–423; J. E. Hulet, Jr., "Estimating the Net Effect of a Commercial Motion Picture upon the Trend of Local Public Opinion," *American Sociological Review*, XIV (April, 1949), 263–275; Hans Zeisel, "A Note on the Effect of a Motion Picture on Public Opinion," *American Sociological Review*, XIV (August, 1949), 550–551 (cited in Middleton). For the reaction to "Blackboard Jungle," see Joseph Axelrod, "German and Austrian Reaction to the 'Blackboard Jungle,' " *School and Society*, LXXXV, 2105 (February 16, 1957), 57–59.

[5] Robert Hatch, "Movies: Good Intention," *New Republic* (May 16, 1949), 22–23; *Hulet, op. cit.*, 263–275; Siegfried Kracauer, "National Types as Hollywood Presents Them," *Public Opinion Quarterly*, XIII, 1 (Spring, 1949), 53–72.

against *The Untouchables* and protests by Negroes against *Birth of a Na-* *tion.* The result is not an elimination of the stereotpyes but instead the continuation of the least objectionable of them. As Terry Ramsaye stated: "the multitude can chuckle at Step'n Fetchit and laugh with Rochester, but they will woo and win with the Gables, the Taylors and the Coopers." Thus villainous Negroes stay off the screen at the price of making "the negro [sic] so amusing and agreeable that an audience is always pleased at the appearance of a black face."[6]

The combination of these two factors produces a kind of selective censorship. The history of film censorship in America is a long, tedious tale of the suppression of the sins of the Puritans. As Sterling Brown has pointed out, seven stereotypes of Negroes can be isolated: the contented slave, the wretched freeman, the comic Negro, the brute Negro, the tragic mulatto, the local color Negro, and the exotic primitive. The elements of these types include laziness, filth, sensuality, and crime, so that it is as though white America is torn between two conclusions: Negroes are America's anti-democratic nightmare and Puritan conscience and must be suppressed, or they must be depicted publicly as the stereotype because it sustains the myth of Anglo-Saxon purity.[7]

In practice a compromise has been struck. The private censorship code of the motion picture producers of America proscribes all the vicious elements of the stereotype and tolerates the ridiculous elements. Thus, through the 1930's and 1940's, only racial comics such as Rochester, Willie Best, and Mantan Moreland (as Charlie Chan's valet) crept into American films.[8] The effect in recent films has been that Negroes must still remain segregated even as the imperatives of segregation diminish in reality. A normal sexual role, for example, continues to be denied to Negroes. Sidney Poitier, in the widely acclaimed *Lilies of the Field*, is as effectively denied a full characterization by the presence of the nuns as co-stars as, say, Lena Horne was in the musicals in which she was consigned to a vaudeville act that bore no relation to the plot line.

In a sense the producers' code makes movies a technological equivalent of folk art. Their dependence on the box office makes them, at the same time, a reflection, a distortion, and an exaggeration of American life. If

---

[6] Margaret Farrant Thorp, *America at the Movies* (New Haven, 1939), 130; for other popular criticisms of unintentioned stereotyping in message movies, see Kracauer, *op. cit.*, 567; Dore Schary, "Our Movie Mythology," *Reporter*, XXII, 5 (March 3, 1960), 39–42; Hollis Alpert, "D for Effort," *Saturday Review*, XLII (October 3, 1959), 29.

[7] Sterling A. Brown, "Negro Characters as Seen by White Authors," *Journal of Negro Education*, II, 2 (April, 1933), 179–203. For the most recent of studies of censorship and its effects, see Murray Schumach, *The Face on the Cutting Room Floor* (New York, 1964), pp. 279 ff, Appendix III.

[8] See Cripps, *op. cit.*, for an earlier example of the striking of the bargain. For a copy of the Hollywood motion picture producers' code, see Schumach, *op. cit.*, Appendices. For a recognition of the compromise in advice given to young screenplay writers, see Walter B. Pitkin and William M. Marston, *The Art of Sound Motion Pictures* (New York, 1930), pp. 25, 62, one of several "how-to" books in which the authors advise young writers to "study closely the vogue in pictures" in order to determine what sells. A handy chart delineating the various radical taboos is appended.

"Hollywood is the mass unconscious," the theater is the place where wishes are gratified, where (according to Marlon Brando) "people . . . correlate what happens on the screen with their own experience." One of Walker Percy's characters expresses this mythical quality:

Our neighborhood theater in Gentilly has permanent lettering on the front of the marque reading: Where Happiness Costs So Little. The fact is I am quite happy in a movie, even a bad movie. Other people, so I have read, treasure memorable moments in their lives. . . . What I remember is the time John Wayne killed three men with a carbine as he was falling to the dusty street in *Stagecoach*, and the time the kitten found Orson Welles in the doorway in *The Third Man*.[9]

It can be seen that although movies are a "symbolic expression of life," they can shape "value patterns" to a degree only and then not in the efficient way assumed by the earlier observers.[10]

Socially conscious Hollywood producers have accepted this view to some extent. Many are self-conscious and guilty about the charge that Hollywood's achievements in race relations over the long run have been anti-Negro from *Birth of a Nation* to *Gone With the Wind*. But it would be difficult to imagine a different condition in view of the social scientists' vision of moviemakers as essentially followers of rather than creators of mores. They would have had to crusade, "which Hollywood seldom does except for the most certain and established causes."[11] What is basically a scientific argument has its layman's equivalent: that is the liberal position that movies should "both symbolize and effectuate a revolution in the imagination and behavior"; as opposed to the conservative notion that because movies are one of the "principal influences of the modern world in the determination of the character of our people and our society" producers have a moral responsibility to seek what is right—a consensus. Thus to the conservative "controversial pleading and the pursuit of theoretical and experimental causes should have no place in the theatrical film."[12]

[9] For development of the concept of the mass unconscious, see Siegfried Kracauer, *From Caligari to Hitler* (Princeton, 1947); the cinema criticism of Parker Tyler, especially *Hollywood Hallucination* (New York, 1944), pp. 231–238, 244; for the Brando comment, see Richard Dyer McCann, *Hollywood in Transition* (Boston, 1962), p. 187; for less technical comments, see Jean Benoit-Levy, *The Art of the Motion Picture* (New York, 1946), pp. 196–201, 217–218; Robert Hughes, *Film: Book 1* (New York, 1959), pp. 3–24, 35–60; Gilbert Seldes, *The Public Arts* (New York, 1956), pp. 191, 210, 298; Henry James Forman, *Our Movie Mad Children* (New York, 1935), *passim*; Walter Percy, *The Moviegoer* (New York, 1962), pp. 12–13.

[10] For fairly recent statements of the efficacy of film propaganda see J. P. Mayer, *Sociology of the Film* (London, 1946), pp. 167–168, 49, 17–18, 25; Martha Wolfenstein and Nathan Leites, *Movies: A Psychological Study* (Glencoe, Illinois, 1950), p. 307.

[11] Dore Schary, "Censorship and Stereotypes," *Saturday Review of Literature*, XXXII, 18 (April 30, 1949), 9–10; Louis Kronenberger and John T. McManus, "Motion Pictures, the Theater, and Race Relations," *Annals of the American Academy of Political and Social Science*, CCXLIV (March, 1946), 152–158.

[12] Martin S. Dworkin, "The New Negro on the Screen," *Progressive*, XXIV, 11–12 November–December, 1960), 33–36; Martin Quigley, "Importance of the Entertain-

Censorship has been one of the most persistent influences on the maintenance of stereotypes. Southern censorship has taken the most exaggerated stances. In Atlanta, *Lost Boundaries* and *Imitation of Life* were banned *in toto* as inciting to violence or lawbreaking. Of all the movies in the 1940's about Negroes only Faulkner's *Intruder in the Dust* was uncut. In 1945 *Brewster's Millions* was banned in Memphis because Eddie Anderson stood too close to, and seemed too friendly with, Helen Walker. Even an innocuous film such as *Island in the Sun* was either protested or banned in Memphis, New Orleans, Jacksonville, and Montgomery, because White Citizens Councils and the Ku Klux Klan saw it as "immoral and indecent" because of the implied equality of the characters of Harry Belafonte and Joan Fontaine.[13] Where there is no censorship on racial grounds, producers, sensitive to protest from both Negroes and whites, have reduced Negro roles to ambivalent ciphers. Otto Preminger's *Carmen Jones*, as James Baldwin has pointed out, is not believable precisely because the role of Joe (played by Belafonte) is reduced to a nullity for fear of stereotyping Negro sexuality. Typically, any breaking of the color line, perhaps expressing the unconscious reservations of liberal moviemakers, is met by violence. In Robert Wise's *Odds Against Tomorrow*, Belafonte is burned to death unrecognizably along with racist (played by Robert Ryan) whom he fought, the obvious implication being that to resist segregation is to die. In *Broken Lance*, Spencer Tracy dies pointlessly after his interracial marriage to Katy Jurado.[14]

Tragedy can be barely averted only when non-Negroes are involved, as in *Broken Arrow* (American Indians), *Bhowani Junction* (East Indians), and *Love Is a Many-Splendored Thing* (Chinese); or when Negroes are saved by the sacrifice of a white friend, a kind of symbolic atonement for lynching, as in *Home of the Brave* and *Intruder in the Dust*; or when white actresses play Negro roles, as in, most recently, *Kings Go Forth*.[15]

The story of Negroes in American films since 1945, therefore, is not only the story of the death of Rastus, or Sambo, or Uncle Tom, but the rebirth of a complete man as yet unnamed. The story, so far, has three parts: up to 1954, Negroes as a social problem; through the 1950's, Negroes as emerging characters yet bearing the vestiges of Rastus; and fiinally from the varied themes of the 1960's, the beginnings of the fully articulated character. The first intimations of the end of the Negro stereo-

---

ment Film," *Annals of the American Academy* . . . , CCLIV (November, 1947), 65–69.

[13] Gerald Weales, "Pro-Negro Films in Atlanta," *Phylon*, XIII, 4 (Winter, 1952), 298–304 (reprinted from *Films in Review*, November, 1952); Philip T. Hartung, "Trillions for Brewster," *Commonweal*, XLII, 4 (May 11, 1945), 94–95; *New York Times*, July 4, 18; August 17, 1957; November 25, 1949.

[14] James Baldwin, "Life Straight in de Eye," *Commentary*, XIX, 1 (January, 1955), 74–79; Martin S. Dworkin, "The New Negro on the Screen," *Progressive*, XXV, 1 (January, 1961), 38.

[15] Henry Popkin, "Hollywood Tackles the Race Issue," *Commentary*, XXIV, 10 (October, 1957), 354–357; Martha Wolfenstein and Nathan Leites, "Two Social Scientists View 'No Way Out,'" *Commentary*, X, 4 (October, 1950), 388–391; Albert Johnson, "Beige, Brown, or Black," *Film Quarterly*, XIII, 1 (Fall, 1959), 38–43.

type were seen in the anti-fascist war movies: Dooley Wilson's wise piano player in Warner Brothers' *Casablanca*; Rex Ingram's Senegal soldier in *Sahara*; and Canada Lee in Alfred Hitchcock's *Lifeboat*.[16]

Shortly after the vogue of war movies ended, the cycle of racial message movies began. Stanley Kramer's *Home of the Brave*, adapted from Arthur Laurents' polemic against anti-Semitism, was the first in 1948, followed by Louis de Rochemont's *Lost Boundaries* and Elia Kazan's *Pinky*. By 1952, with Clarence Brown's *Intruder in the Dust* the cycle had spent itself, not so much departing from the old stereotypes but creating a new one: that of Negroes who cannot be fulfilled without the sacrifice of or the support of white men. As a case in point, James Edwards, the Negro in *Home of the Brave*, goes on a mission to a Japanese-held island where his best friend, a white man, is killed. Edwards feels a dual guilt at his friend's death first, because he is glad that he personally survived and second, because he had wished his friend dead after an argument in which he had been called a racial epithet. Falling victim to hysterical paralysis, he is taken to the base psychiatrist who induces Edwards to walk again by hurling the same epithets at him, symbolically implying that Negroes can be fulfilled only on white men's terms. At the end of the film the audience sees a fraternal scene in which Edwards and a one-armed white man depart, suggesting Negro-white equality only as long as the whites are not complete. In *Pinky*, *Lost Boundaries*, and *Intruder in the Dust* the problems by Negroes are resolved in each case at the pleasure of upper-class white society. So little came from the cycle of problem movies that Negroes nearly disappeared from the screen completely in the early 1950's.[17]

By the mid-1950's the cycle had achieved only a few side effects. The all-Negro exploitation films such as Robert Gordon's *Joe Louis Story* and James Wong Howe's *Go Man Go*, a cheap program movie about the Harlem Globe Trotters, declined in numbers. The South's romantic "lost cause" mystique became tarnished and its decadence in the manner of Tennessee Williams was emphasized in a rash of movies. Indians began to get sympathetic treatment in several Westerns.

After 1954, cinema Negroes became, not a problem for whites to comprehend, but symbolic figures of the struggle against oppression. In the strident *Blackboard Jungle*, only Sidney Poitier is allowed to struggle successfully against the tide of urban poverty. In Darryl Zanuck's movie of Alec Waugh's *Island in the Sun*, it is Harry Belafonte, until then a popular nightclub singer, who plays the dynamic labor leader; and in

[16] Dorothy B. Jones, "Tomorrow the Movies: IV. Is Hollywood Growing Up?" *New Republic*, CLX, 5 (February 3, 1945), 123–125; Dworkin, *Progressive*, XXIV, 10, 39–41.

[17] See Dworkin, *ibid*. Except for this series of articles there is no treatment of Negroes in films after 1948. For an inadequate survey of the years before 1948, see Noble, *The Negro in Films* (London: Skelton Robinson [1948?]; for rather doctrinaire-Marxist comment on history and propaganda, see V. J. Jerome, *The Negro in Hollywood Films* (New York, 3rd printing, 1952); John Howard Lawson, *Film in the Battle of Ideas* (New York, 1953); and Gordon Kahn, *Hollywood on Trial: The Story of the 10 Who Were Indicted* (New York, 1948).

Robert Wise's tightly directed crime thriller, *Odds Against Tomorrow*, it is again Belafonte who is the criminal at war with both society and his Southern racist accomplice.[18] Only occasionally did the old Negro intrude upon the new Negro tragic hero-as-victim, as in Otto Preminger's gaudy production of *Porgy and Bess* in 1959.

By the 1960's, institutional racial equality had become socially acceptable behavior in many areas of America. One heard occasional liberal voices even from a closed society such as Mississippi.[19] Churches began to break their long silence on the issue of race.[20] Professional associations opened their doors to Negroes. No longer news was the marriage of the famous Negro actor, Sammy Davis, Jr.; nor Lyndon Johnson, late of Texas, dancing at his inauguration with the wives of the various darker-skinned men in attendance. Such rapid change was accepted in varying degrees. The intellectuals and the well-to-do had nothing to fear from it. The middle-class houseowner nervously accepted it in every neighborhood but his own. Older people and working-class people tended to not accept it at all. These varying degrees of acceptance of change were reflected in a tripartite cinema of the 1960's. A comparable case can be seen in the film treatment of juvenile behavior in the highly literate *David and Lisa* by Frank and Eleanor Perry; the middle-brow, guilt-evoking *Rebel Without a Cause*; and the sensational exploitation movie, *Untamed Youth;* each one dealing with the same subject, but in three distinct styles. Similarly, as Negroes intrude upon the collective consciousness of America they evoke a similar set of divergent images.[21]

At the lowest level of exploitation of racial themes is Stephen Borden's *My Baby is Black*, which depicts a love affair between a Negro medical student in Paris and his white girl friend. The audience is titillated by shots of the two in embrace alternated with scenes of vicious rejection of the Negro by the girl's parents. Another cheap exploitation film of the 1960's was Larry Buchanan's *Free, White, and 21*, in which a Negro, Frederick O'Neal, is accused of rape and acquitted. The film's gimmick is that, near the end, the audience is asked to "vote" as jurors to determine O'Neal's guilt or innocence, after watching a plot that clearly shows him innocent. After he is acquitted, a lie detector test showing the jury wrong is introduced into the film. The prosecutor, playing every string of the lurid rape theme, asks rhetorically whether we do not "love the Negro too much." Both films express clearly the undercurrent of white proletarian reservations toward the assimilation of Negroes into American life.

[18] Dworkin, *Progressive*, 36–38.

[19] For a recent example of liberal Southern comment, see James W. Silver, *Mississippi: the Closed Society* (New York, 1964).

[20] For a criticism of the silence of the churches on social issues, see Peter Berger, *The Noise of Solemn Assemblies* (Garden City, 1961).

[21] In dealing with the films of the 1960's, I have not supplied complete information about producers, releasing companies, and directors because they would be of little bibliographic value. Typically, in periodical indexes, firms are listed by title, then journal in which a review or article appeared. Those few libraries which keep active files of film reviews also catalogue by title, as do the various Library of Congress film copyright volumes.

In the middle-brow movies of the 1960's, many New Negro social roles are depicted, usually no more than one in each film. In Hubert Cornfield's *Pressure Point*, Sidney Poitier plays a prison psychiatrist whose patient is a racial psychotic played by Bobby Darin, who is an anti-Roosevelt, anti-Semitic fascist. Thus the audience is led to accept a Negro as a doctor, if for no other reason than that the psychotic cannot. Another break from the stereotype is even more literally stated in Millard Kaufman's *Convicts Four*. The standard blues-humming Negro convict gives way to a prepossessing, aggressive convict played by Sammy Davis, who upon being assigned a new cellmate, a murderer, announces that he is not to be called "shine," that he is never to be asked to sing or dance, and finally that it is he to whom tribute is owed if the new man wishes to be protected from the hazing by the other inmates. The result is a unilateral white paper announcing that hereafter Rastus is dead.

In many movies small chips have been made in the stereotype. In Robert Aldrich's psychological murder mystery, *Whatever Happened to Baby Jane?*, all the whites are afraid, psychotic, or cheap crooks. Only the Negro maid is a balanced human being. She is like an enduring Faulkner Negro moved to a Northern city. In John Frankenheimer's *Manchurian Candidate*, dignified middle-class Negroes appear as window dressing. Warner Brothers announced that forty Negro extras appear in their comedy, *Kisses for My President*. In Gordon Douglas' *Rio Conchos*, Jim Brown plays a courageous Negro soldier immediately after the Civil War. The only racial stereotype is a lazy, serio-comic Mexican played by Tony Franciosa. All of the Southerners in the film are outlaws whose commander is insane and lives in a mock-up facade of a Southern mansion which symbolically burns to the ground in the last scene in the picture.

Occasionally the old stereotypes recur. In John Ford's *Man Who Shot Liberty Valence*, Woody Strode plays an Uncle Tom who shuffled off camera after being hit with a bucket of whitewash. In three Frank Sinatra comedies, Sammy Davis has played comic Negro Sambo types, especially in John Sturges' *Sergeants Three*, in which he plays Kipling's Gunga Din renamed Jonah and moved to the American frontier.

It is in the so-called art movie, independently produced on a low budget for limited distribution in small urban theaters, where one finds the most sensitive view of Negroes in American life. Artistically, this kind of film attempts to deal with reality seriously, with little concession being made to market conditions, profits, or mass taste. The first limited success of this genre was John Cassavetes' *Shadows* (1960). Using unknown actors, Ben Maddow's script attempted to show the world of Negroes as closed and esoteric by juxtaposing it with the world of whites through the medium of the anxieties of a young girl who has been passing. On the surface, it would seem that Lela Goldoni's role is simply a repeat of many other white actresses who have played Negroes, including Jeanne Crain's *Pinky*, Flora Robson in *Saratoga Trunk*, and Yvonne de Carlo in *Band of Angels*. There is not the cheap sexually charged situation of the earlier films, but only the contrast of two worlds and the need, in American society, to choose one or the other. Similar to *Shadows* was Shirley Clarke's *Cool World* which also used unknown or amateur actors and which was shot on location in Harlem from various concealed angles. The result is a fast-paced film about the habitués of the cool world of small time gangsters, junkies, and prostitutes. The movie is not a racial message or a plea to white America to send aid, but a story that uses a real part of Negro America without apology. There are sensual scenes, shots of narcotics addiction, drinking, wrecked and poor families, but the film does not piously say "look at the way these Negroes behave." It is a film about poor people who live in a city. The failure of the film, if it has one, is that few people saw it, even though in the Negro neighborhoods it was retitled *Cool World in Harlem* and luridly advertised.

The best evidence of the death of Rastus is Michael Roehmer's 1965 production, *Nothing But a Man*, the story of a marriage of a Negro railroad worker played by Ivan Dixon and a Negro school teacher played by Abbey Lincoln. They live in a small Southern town which is seen as a physical, unnamed presence pressing upon them in dozens of small ways. The pressures seem about to destroy the marriage as they destroyed the life of the railroad worker's father. The theme is not what are Negroes like, which would be a return to the stereotype, but rather, how do people behave under strain; how do they survive; how do they live as persons when the society sees them as types.

Social change has thus compelled a comparable change in some artfully made movies about Negroes; while a few other movies still deal in the old sensationalism of the contradictory stereotypes of comedy, sexuality, brutality, and laziness. Neither is the norm for American movie-going behavior. In most middle-brow films of the 1960's, Negro characters had changed into perfectly abstinent, courageous paragons of virtue as stifling and destructive of mature characterization as the old Rastus stereotype. This new unreality is evident in the absence of adult sexual behavior in the films of Sidney Poitier. In *Blackboard Jungle* women characters were carefully segregated from Poitier; in *The Defiant Ones* he is chained to a male character and confronts no women; in *Raisin in the Sun*, he is married, but residing in his mother's crowded apartment; in *Lilies of the Field* his co-stars are a gaggle of nuns; in *The Long Ships*, he is an African prince who, despite his large harem, has taken an oath of chastity. One can still wonder when a commercial film will put all the parts of *the* Negro together into a whole man.

21

White Gains from Negro Subordination[*]

NORVAL D. GLENN[**]
UNIVERSITY OF TEXAS AT AUSTIN

A QUESTION OF CONSIDERABLE THEORETICAL AND PRACTICAL IMPORTANCE IS the extent of any occupational and economic benefits that whites in the United States derive from the subordination of Negroes. Certainly the initial subordination, through slavery, was for economic gain, and almost as certainly economic considerations were among the primary motives for continued Negro subordination after Emancipation. Many students of contemporary American race relations believe that economic functions of discrimination to a large extent account for its perpetuation. Others, however, believe that noneconomic motives now largely determine white policy and action toward Negroes. Two sociologists recently claimed that the economic need for the Negro is virtually gone, that if he disappeared tomorrow, he would hardly be missed.[1]

In spite of the importance and controversy attached to the question, it has been subjected to little empirical investigation,[2] probably because of the difficulty in ascertaining that whites would be more prosperous and have more favorable occupations if Negroes were not present and sub-

---

[*] Reprinted by permission of the Society for the Study of Social Problems, from *Social Problems*, 14 (Fall, 1966), pp. 159-178.

[**] A grant from the University of Texas Research Institute financed the research reported here. The author is indebted to S. Dale McLemore for a critical reading of the manuscript.

[1] Sidney M. Wilhelm and Edwin H. Powell, "Who Needs the Negro?" *Trans-Action*, 1 (September-October, 1964), pp. 5-6.

[2] To the author's knowledge, the only recent studies designed specifically to investigate this question are reported in Norval D. Glenn, "Occupational Benefits to Whites from the Subordination of Negroes," *American Sociological Review*, 28 (June, 1963), pp. 443-448; and Philips Cutright, "Negro Subordination and White Gains," *American Sociological Review*, 30 (February, 1965), pp. 110-112. See also Norval D. Glenn, "Reply to Cutright on Negro Subordination," *American Sociological Review*, 30 (June, 1965), p. 416. The classic statement of the alleged white economic gain from Negro subordination is in John Dollard, *Class and Caste in a Southern Town*, New Haven: Yale University Press, 1937, ch. 6. However, Dollard's conclusions are impressionistic and are based primarily on observations in one small Southern community. Several authors give data that relate to but do not systematically test the hypothesis of white benefits. For instance, Myrdal noted in the early 1940's that the occupational status of Southern whites was somewhat higher, in certain respects, than that of Northern whites, and he attributed the difference to the whites' near monopoly on higher jobs in the South (Gunnar Myrdal, *An American Dilemma*, New York: Harper and Row, 1944, p. 297). However, this white gain noted by Myrdal plays no important role in his theory of discrimination and prejudice. Blalock reports that in 1950 certain aspects of white status were higher in those Southern counties with higher concentrations of Negroes, but he does not conclude that the higher white status resulted from the subordination of the numerous Negroes. See Hubert M. Blalock, Jr., "Per Cent Non-White and Discrimination in the South," *American Sociological Review*, 22 (December, 1957), p. 681.

ordinated. Published data on the subject do not allow conclusions of maximum certainty. In general, they support the view that whites derive appreciable occupational and economic benefits from the low status of Negroes, but since the data are for 1950 and earlier, one cannot be confident that recent changes in the economy and in the demand for different kinds of labor have not ended any previous white benefits.

The present study, though not definitive, is designed to supply more recent and more nearly conclusive data. Based on 1960 census data, it is similar to a study the author did with 1950 data,[3] but the analysis is modified and extended.

THE PROBLEM AND METHODS

Negro subordination, as the term is used here, refers to the disparity between Negroes and whites in such stratification variables as power, income, and occupation, and therefore it is not synonymous with discrimination. Subordination of Negroes results from both present discrimination and the remaining effects of past discrimination, including the poorer average qualifications of Negro workers. The most extreme subordination would exist if all Negroes were below all whites with respect to the stratification variable being considered, and there would be no subordination if Negro and white status were equal. Overlapping of the Negro and white distributions constitutes intermediate subordination; the greater the overlap, the smaller the subordination. The question of whether or not whites benefit from Negro subordination is, then, a question of whether or not white status is absolutely higher than it would be if Negroes were not below whites. If the answer is yes, then rational consideration of self interest could lie behind white resistance to Negro advancement.

The manner in which whites are assumed to benefit from Negro subordination is simple: the concentration of Negroes near the bottom of the occupational and economic hierarchies allegedly keeps whites up. For instance, to the extent that Negroes do low-paying and unpleasant work, whites are assumed able to escape such work. Discrimination and relatively low qualifications handicap Negroes in the competition for high-paying jobs, thus supposedly making it easier for whites to rise into and keep these jobs. In addition, it is believed that the concentration of Negroes in unskilled and semi-skilled work increases the supply of labor at those levels and thus decreases labor costs—a possible detriment to unskilled and semi-skilled white workers but a benefit to white employers.

It is not inevitable or obvious that any of these gains accrue to whites. For instance, the concentration of Negroes in low-level jobs could simply increase the proportion of such jobs and/or increase unemployment instead of helping whites to rise and stay up in the job hierarchy. An abundance of unskilled Negro labor might retard mechanization and prevent the most efficient utilization of labor rather than appreciably reducing the

---

[3] Glenn, "Occupational Benefits to Whites from the Subordination of Negroes," *op. cit.*

costs of employers. Even if sizable occupational gains do accrue to whites, these gains could be offset by detrimental economic consequences of Negro subordination. Inefficient use of Negro talent undoubtedly reduces the productivity of the economy, perhaps by several billions of dollars annually.[4] This waste of productive potential primarily hurts Negroes, but it also hurts whites to some extent. For instance, Negro poverty hurts white-owned businesses that offer goods and services to the Negro market, and the direct and indirect consequences of the Negro disadvantage cost white taxpayers an incalculable amount in welfare, relief, and law-enforcement expenses. Although discrimination and the effects of past discrimination give whites a larger proportion of the total wealth, they do not necessarily increase the absolute size of the white share.[5]

Determining the exact extent of beneficial and detrimental consequences to whites from Negro subordination seems impossible. The detrimental effects are particularly hard to measure. It would be very difficult if not impossible to arrive at even a defensible rough estimate of the extent to which Negro subordination lowers total productivity, increases the tax burden, increases unemployment, and affects the occupational structure. About the best that one can hope to do is estimate the extent and nature of benefits and detriments to particular segments of the white population. Such estimates can have considerable theoretical and practical utility even if one cannot estimate with comparable accuracy the balance of gains and losses to the total white population. For example, the knowledge that whites in certain occupations in certain parts of the country benefit in some ways from Negro subordination can help explain prejudice, discrimination, and interracial conflict, irrespective of what the overall consequences of the Negro disadvantage may be.

Probably the most fruitful approach to discovering the partial consequences of Negro subordination is ecological analysis. Most of any white benefits and some of the detriments that result from low Negro status are not evenly distributed geographically but are primarily in localities in which Negroes are a large percentage of the population. For instance, the white workers who are likely to benefit from the competitive handicap of Negroes are those who actually are, or who in the absence of discrimination would be, competing against Negroes. Competition for jobs is not strictly local, of course, but for many kinds of jobs it is largely so, and therefore any positive effects of the Negro handicap would be primarily upon whites who live near large Negro populations. Consequently, if whites do gain appreciably in occupational and income status from Negro subordination, one would expect, in the absence of offsetting influences, a positive ecological association of the percentage of the population that is Negro and measures of white status. If there were no other plausible ex-

[4] George Eaton Simpson and J. Milton Yinger, *Racial and Cultural Minorities: An Analysis of Prejudice and Discrimination*, New York: Harper and Row, 1965, p. 187.

[5] See Simpson and Yinger, *op. cit.*, pp. 187–190, and Norval D. Glenn, "The Role of White Resistance and Facilitation in the Negro Struggle for Equality," *Phylon*, 26 (Summer, 1965), pp. 110–111.

planations, such an association would suggest that Negro subordination benefits at least some of the whites in the localities with the larger percentages of Negroes.

The extent of any white occupational and economic gains depends not only upon the relative size of the Negro population but also upon the degree of subordination. If whites do benefit in the manner that is often assumed, the extent of white gains will be greater if most Negroes are below most whites than if the Negro and white distributions overlap considerably. However, it is not necessary in a study such as this one to investigate the relationship between degree of subordination and white status variables. Degree of subordination and percentage of the population Negro are positively correlated,[6] and therefore the effects of both are reflected in the association of percentage Negro with white status.

A positive ecological association of percentage Negro and white status variables is, of course, not conclusive evidence of white gains from Negro subordination. There are several alternative explanations, the most plausible of which are discussed in some detail below. High Negro population concentration and high white status could commonly result from other factors. Ideally, then, one would ascertain the partial association between percentage Negro and white status with all other probable influences upon white status held constant. Unfortunately, however, it is not possible to identify, measure, and hold constant all or most of the numerous other influences. One can only control as many of the relevant variables as possible and bring extra-statistical reasoning and as much empirical evidence as possible to bear upon the alternative explanations.

The localities used for this study are 179 of the 213 Urbanized Areas designated in the 1960 census reports. Since the census reports give occupational and income data for Urbanized Areas for nonwhites rather than specifically for Negroes, those Urbanized Areas in which a substantial proportion of the nonwhites are not Negroes are excluded.[7] In addition, a few Urbanized Areas are excluded because they had so few nonwhites in 1960 that the Census Bureau did not tabulate data by color.[8] Of the remaining Urbanized Areas, 102 are in the North and West, 52 are in the South, and 25 are in the Border Region.[9]

[6] When the absolute difference between measures of white and nonwhite status is used as a crude index of Negro subordination, the correlation between percentage nonwhite and the index among the Urbanized Areas in each region is either nil or positive. For instance, in the South the product moment correlation between percentage nonwhite in 1960 and the absolute difference between the white and nonwhite percentages of family with income below $3,000 in 1959 is +.59. In the North and West and in the Border Region the correlations are also positive but are smaller.

[7] These are the California Urbanized Areas and Honolulu, Hawaii.

[8] These are Meriden, Connecticut; Dubuque, Iowa; Lewiston-Auburn and Portland, Maine; Fall River, Fitchburg-Leominster, Lawrence-Haverhill, Lowell, and Pittsfield, Massachusetts; Bay City, Michigan; Billings and Great Falls, Montana; Manchester, New Hampshire; Fargo-Morehead, North Dakota; Eugene, Oregon; Altoona and Scranton, Pennsylvania; Sioux Falls, South Dakota; Harlingen-San Benito and Laredo, Texas; Provo-Orem, Utah; and Green Bay, Wisconsin.

[9] The Southern Urbanized Areas are those in Florida, Georgia, South Carolina, North Carolina, Virginia, Tennessee, Alabama, Mississippi, and Louisiana, plus Little Rock-

Limiting the study to Urbanized Areas very roughly controls those influences upon white status that vary by community size, and separate analyses by region are performed to control those influences that vary by region. Several additional control variables, including the percentage of the labor force in manufacturing industries (an index of industrialization), were at first used, but none of these controls appreciably altered the relationship between percentage nonwhite and white status.

The measures of white status used here are a summary index of occupational status of employed males (abbreviated IOS),[10] percentage of employed males in nonmanual and skilled occupations, percentage of families with annual income of $10,000 or more, percentage of families with income below $3,000, and percentage of the male civilian labor force unemployed. It is hypothesized that, in the Urbanized Areas in each region, the first three of these measures vary directly with percentages of the population nonwhite and the last two vary inversely. The relationships between percentage nonwhite and measures of status applied to people of all races in the Urbanized Areas also are investigated, so it can be discerned when a positive relationship between percentage nonwhite and

North Little Rock, Arkansas; Texarkana, Texas-Arkansas; and Beaumont, Galveston-Texas City, Houston, Port Arthur, and Tyler, Texas. The Border Urbanized Areas are those with central cities in Oklahoma, Kentucky, West Virginia, and Maryland, plus Fort Smith, Arkansas; Springfield, Missouri; and Abilene, Amarillo, Austin, Corpus Christi, Dallas, Fort Worth, Lubbock, Midland, Odessa, San Angelo, San Antonio, Waco, and Wichita Falls, Texas. All other Urbanized Areas included in the analysis are classified as Northern or Western.

[10] The IOS is computed by assigning a value to each of the census "occupational groups," assigning to each worker the value of his occupational group, and taking the average of the individual values of all workers in an Urbanized Area or a category of Urbanized Areas. The values for the occupational groups are arrived at by the following formula:

$$\text{IOS for an occupational group} = (a/A + b/B) \times 100/2$$
$$= (a/A + b/B) \times 50$$

when:

a = median earnings of experienced male civilian workers in the occupational group in 1959.

A = median earnings of all experienced male civilian workers in 1959.

b = median years of school completed by experienced male civilian workers in the occupational groups as of 1960.

B = median years of school completed by all experienced male civilian workers as of 1960.

The value is above 100 if both the earnings and education of the workers in the occupational group were above the medians for all workers, and the value is below 100 if both earnings and education were below parity. The values for the occupational groups are as follows: professional, technical, and kindred workers (146); farmers and farm managers (63); managers, officials, and proprietors, except farm (129); clerical and kindred workers (108); sales workers (111); craftsmen, foremen, and kindred workers (104); operatives and kindred workers (88); service workers, including private household (77; farm laborers and foremen (43); laborers, except farm and mine (70). A similar but more refined measure is Duncan's Socio-Economic Index for the occupational groups, but the IOS has the advantage of being based on 1960 rather than 1950 census data. Both the SEI and IOS were used for parts of this study with virtually the same results.

white status is simply a function of more favorable total status where non-whites are more numerous. In such cases, the more favorable total status is not likely to be a result of the large nonwhite population (the presence and subordination of large numbers of Negroes apparently *lower* total status),[11] and therefore no white benefits from Negro subordination are indicated.

In addition, an attempt is made to detect benefits to white employers. The relationship between percentage of the population that is nonwhite and number of employed private household workers per 1,000 families is studied to help determine whether or not Negro subordination appreciably increases the availability of domestic help. The relationship between percentage nonwhite and median earnings of males in different classes of occupations is investigated to throw light upon the effects of Negro subordination on labor costs and the earnings of different classes of white workers.

Two methods of analysis are used. First, the Urbanized Areas are divided into four classes according to percentage nonwhite, and the populations of the Urbanized Areas within each class are examined collectively.[12] The Urbanized Areas in the North and West and in the South are dichotomized by percentage nonwhite and the collective populations in the two classes are compared. Then, product moment coefficients of correlation between percentage nonwhite and each of the dependent variables are computed for the Urbanized Areas in each region.

FINDINGS

The signs of the coefficients of correlation are all in the expected direction, although some of the values are negligible (Table 1). The aggregate data for the North and West and for the South also consistently show the hypothesized associations (Table 2), and white occupational status and employment vary directly with percentage nonwhite in the absence of controls for region (Tables 3 and 4). Some of these data need to be examined in detail, but first it is well to consider whether or not they can be explained on some basis other than white gains from Negro subordination.

Generally speaking, associations between percentage nonwhite and the status measures for persons of all races do not account for the associations between percentage nonwhite and the white status variables. In the South,

[11] See the associations between percentage nonwhite and the status variables for people of all races in Tables 1 through 5.

[12] When this is done, the Washington Urbanized Area is excluded, because its population was a large percentage of the total population in the class of 20 through 29.9 per cent nonwhite, and the very favorable status of its whites undoubtedly results more from its unusual economic base than from the subordination of its numerous Negroes. The class of zero through 9.9 per cent nonwhite includes 80 Urbanized Areas in the North and West, 14 in the Border Region, and one in the South (St. Petersburg, Florida). The class of ten through 19.9 per cent nonwhite includes 21 Urbanized Areas in the North and West, nine in the Border Region, and 12 in the South. The class of 20 through 29.9 per cent nonwhite has one Urbanized Area in the North (Atlantic City, New Jersey), one in the Border Region (Baltimore), and 23 in the South. All of the 16 Urbanized Areas with 30 percent or more of nonwhites were in the South.

TABLE 1

Product Moment Coefficients of Correlation Between Percentage
Nonwhite and Status Variables[*]

Dependent Variable	North and West		Border		South	
	Whites	All Races	Whites	All Races	Whites	All Races
Index of occupational status	+ .14	+.10	+.65	+.36	+.33	−.23
Percentage of male civilian labor force unemployed	−.19	+.02	−.45	−.30	−.42	−.10
Percentage of families with income below $3,000	−.22	+.01	−.56	−.10	−.55	+.44
Percentage of families with income of $10,000 and up	+.34	+.22	+.62	+.54	+.27	−.06
Number of employed private household servants (all races) per 1,000 families		+.25		+.27		+.72

[*] Units of analysis are Urbanized Areas.

only the negative association of percentage nonwhite with white unemployment can be partially explained in this manner, and even in this case, the association with the white measure is considerably stronger. Percentage nonwhite explains 18 per cent of the variance of white unemployment but only one per cent of the variance of total unemployment. In the Border Region, all of the associations between percentage nonwhite and white status are accompanied by like-signed associations between percentage nonwhite and the status variables for all races, but all of the latter associations are weaker. For instance, percentage nonwhite explains 31 per cent of the variance of percentage of white families with incomes below $3,000 but only one per cent of the variance of percentage of all families below the poverty line. Likewise, the explained variance is 42 per cent with the white IOS and only 13 per cent with the total IOS. On the other hand, the lower white unemployment and the larger percentage of white families with income of $10,000 or more can be explained largely by more favorable conditions for people of all races in the Border Urbanized Areas with large nonwhite populations. In the North and West, the associations of percentage nonwhite with the white IOS and with percentage of white families with income of $10,000 or more can be explained largely by associations with the comparable status measures for all races. However, the aggregate data in Table 2 show a positive association of percentage nonwhite with white occupational status and a negative association with total occupational status.

Although in most cases higher total status does not account for the higher white status in Urbanized Areas with large nonwhite populations, one must consider the possibility that high percentage nonwhite and favorable white status are commonly caused by influences that do not pro-

TABLE 2

Status Variables by Percentage Nonwhite, for the North and West and for the South

Percentage Nonwhite	Percentage of Employed Males in Nonmanual and Skilled Occupations		Percentage of Male Civilian Labor Force Unemployed		Percentage of Families with Income below $3,000		Percentage of Families with Income of $10,000 and up		Number of Employed Private Household Workers per 1,000 Families
	Whites	All Races	Whites	All Races	Whites	All Races	Whites	All Races	All Races
North and West									
0=9.9	65.8	64.7	4.6	5.0	11.9	12.7	19.3	18.0	26
10 and up	67.6	63.9	4.0	4.8	10.3	12.6	23.9	21.8	30
South									
0=24.9	73.0	65.1	4.4	4.8	18.7	23.1	15.6	13.6	61
25 and up	76.3	62.1	3.5	4.6	14.2	24.5	17.7	13.5	85

TABLE 3

Occupational Distribution of Employed Male Workers in Urbanized Areas, by Percentage of the Population Nonwhite, 1960

Occupational Group	Whites Percentage Nonwhite				All Races Percentage Nonwhite			
	0-9.9	10-19.9	20-29.9	30 & Up	0-9.9	10-19.9	20-29.9	30 & Up
Professional, technical, and kindred workers	13.4	13.7	13.6	13.4	13.1	12.7	11.6	10.6
Farmers and farm managers	0.2	0.1	0.2	0.1	0.2	0.1	0.2	0.2
Managers, officials, and proprietors, except farm	12.3	13.2	16.1	17.9	11.9	12.1	13.2	13.3
Clerical and kindred workers	8.9	10.1	9.8	10.3	8.8	10.0	9.0	8.6
Sales workers	8.8	9.3	11.2	11.2	8.6	8.5	9.2	8.5
Craftsmen, foremen, and kindred workers	22.6	21.9	23.4	22.8	22.2	20.9	20.9	19.8
Operatives and kindred workers	20.7	19.9	17.2	16.4	21.0	21.1	19.2	20.4
Private household workers	0.1	0.1	0.0	0.0	0.1	0.2	0.2	0.2
Service workers, except private household	6.4	6.7	4.6	4.6	6.9	7.9	7.8	7.8
Farm laborers and foremen	0.3	0.2	0.1	0.1	0.3	0.2	0.2	0.2
Laborers, except farm and mine	6.2	4.7	3.8	3.3	6.8	6.2	8.4	10.3
Total	100.0	100.0	100.0	100.0	100.0	100.0	100.0	100.0
Percentage in nonmanual and skilled occupations	66.0	68.3	74.1	75.6	64.6	64.2	63.0	60.8
IOS	106.1	107.2	109.5	110.3	105.5	105.4	104.8	103.5

TABLE 4

Percentage of the Civilian Male Labor Force Unemployed, in Urbanized
Areas, by Percentage of the Population Nonwhite, 1960

Percentage Nonwhite	Whites	All Races
0–9.9	4.7	5.0
10–19.9	4.0	4.7
20–29.9	3.7	4.4
30 and up	3.6	5.2

TABLE 5

Percentage of Families in Urbanized Areas at Low and at High Income Levels,
by Percentage of the Population Nonwhite, 1959

Percentage Nonwhite	Income Less Than $3,000		Income of $10,000 or More	
	White	All Races	White	All Races
0–9.9	12.8	13.7	18.7	17.5
10–19.9	11.2	13.7	22.9	20.9
20–29.9	13.8	20.6	18.2	15.0
30 and up	14.0	26.1	17.3	12.6

duce favorable total status. A high rate of economic growth could be such
an influence. The greatest opportunities for whites to advance occupationally and economically and to avoid unemployment are almost certainly in
the Urbanized Areas with the most rapidly expanding economies, and
these same localities may be most likely to attract large numbers of Negro
migrants. The large influx of Negroes, in turn, might reduce the status
measures for the total populations of these Urbanized Areas below the
measures for less rapidly developing localities.

This alternative explanation cannot be ruled out for the North and
West. Rate of population growth is a fairly good index of rate of economic
expansion, and the average population increase from 1950 to 1960 was
28.2 per cent in the Urbanized Areas with less than ten per cent of nonwhites and 31.7 per cent in those with larger proportions of nonwhites.
Furthermore, earnings within broad occupational classes averaged higher
in the Urbanized Areas with the larger Negro population concentrations
(Table 8). This suggests that certain influences for prosperity were greater in these communities and that in the absence of the large numbers of
Negroes some of the measures of total status might have been higher.[13]
Some of the whites in the Urbanized Areas in the North and West with

[13] The Urbanized Areas with the larger proportions of nonwhites had larger populations on the average (2,104,560 compared with an average of 305,375 in the other
Northern and Western Urbanized Areas), and population size is positively associated
with occupational and economic status. See Leo Schnore, "Some Correlates of Urban
Size: A Replication," American Journal of Sociology, 69 (September, 1963), pp. 185–
193.

the larger numbers of Negroes may benefit from Negro subordination, but the data of this study do not in themselves prove any benefits.

The South is a different story. The more favorable white status in the Urbanized Areas with 25 per cent or more of nonwhites cannot be explained by recent more rapid economic growth in those localities. On the average their populations increased 36.9 per cent from 1950 to 1960, compared with an average growth of 65.1 per cent in the other Southern Urbanized Areas. Nor is there any other apparent reason why the Southern whites in the localities with the larger percentages of nonwhites should have had greater opportunities for advancement in recent years. In 1960 these Urbanized Areas were very similar to others in the South in average population size, percentage of workers in manufacturing and earnings within broad occupational classes (Table 8).[14] The percentage of nonwhites in the Southern Urbanized Areas apparently depends more upon the historical Negro density in their hinterlands than upon economic factors that have made them relatively attractive or unattractive to Negro migrants. The fact that whites in the Southern Urbanized Areas with large Negro populations have unusually favorable occupational status and employment rates and higher incomes than other Southern whites is very likely the consequence of the presence and subordination of the Negroes.

Assuming that this conclusion is correct, it would not follow from this fact alone that any of the whites in these Urbanized Areas benefit from Negro subordination. If Negroes did not fill a large proportion of the low-level jobs in these communities, one might guess that the work done by Negroes would be done by machines and whites recruited from nearby rural areas rather than by the present white residents. However, it seems that neither machines nor rural whites nor both together could now adequately replace Negroes in the Southern economy. Machines cannot now replace such service workers as janitors and waiters nor as yet even most laborers and operatives, and rural whites simply are not numerous enough. In 1960 there were 1,249,326 Negro males employed at unskilled and semi-skilled nonfarm work in the South, and only 527,000 of these could have been replaced by all Southern white farmers, farm managers, and farm laborers who had income below $3,000 in 1959. Although much (perhaps most) of the Southern low-income farm labor force could be spared, some of these workers would be needed on the farms, especially if the Negro farm labor force were depleted. Furthermore, many of the rural whites are too old or simply too committed to a rural way of life to make the transition to low-level urban occupations. In addition to creating a labor shortage at the lower levels, rapid out-migration of all or almost all Southern Negroes would reduce the total population of the South and thus reduce the need for workers at the higher levels. Therefore, downgrading or out-migration of a considerable number of whites would seem inevitable.

If all or most Negroes had moved away more slowly several years or

[14] The average population size of Urbanized Areas with 25 per cent or more of nonwhites was 240,498, and other Southern Urbanized Areas averaged 231,347. Average percentage of workers in manufacturing industries was 21.3 and 23.1 respectively in the two classes of Urbanized Areas.

TABLE 6

Estimated White Bonus Jobs in 8 Southern Urbanized Areas with
35 Percent or More of Nonwhites, 1960

Occupational Group	Percentage Distribution of All Employed Males in 8 Northern and Western Urbanized Areas	Percentage Distribution of Employed White Males in 8 Southern Urbanized Areas	Difference	Estimated Percentage Of White Males in Bonus Jobs in Southern Urbanized Areas	Estimated Number of White Males in Bonus Jobs in Southern Urbanized Areas
Professional, technical, and kindred workers	14.2	12.3	−1.9	—	—
Farmers and farm managers	0.3	0.2	−0.1	—	—
Managers, officials, and proprietors, except farm	13.4	18.0	+4.6	25.6	12,189
Clerical and kindred workers	9.5	9.8	+0.3	3.1	803
Sales workers	9.6	12.6	+3.0	23.8	7,919
Craftsmen, foremen, and kindred workers	21.0	23.1	+2.1	9.1	5,570

Occupational Group	Percentage Distribution of All Employed Males in 8 Northern and Western Urbanized Areas	Percentage Distribution of Employed White Males in 8 Southern Urbanized Areas	Difference	Estimated Percentage Of White Males in Bonus Jobs in Southern Urbanized Areas	Estimated Number of White Males in Bonus Jobs in Southern Urbanized Areas
Operatives and kindred workers	18.1	17.0	–1.1	–	–
Private household workers	0.1	0.03	–0.1	–	–
Service workers, except private household	6.9	4.0	–2.9	–	–
Farm laborers and foremen	0.4	0.1	–0.3	–	–
Laborers, except farm and mine	6.5	2.8	–3.7	–	–
Total	100.0	100.0		10.0	26,481

Each Southern Urbanized Area is matched with a Northern or Western Urbanized Area with the same percentage of its workers (within one percentage point) employed in manufacturing but with less than five percent of its population nonwhite. The Southern Urbanized Areas are Albany, Georgia; Birmingham, Alabama; Durham, North Carolina; Jackson, Mississippi; Macon, Georgia; Memphis, Tennessee; Monroe, Louisiana; and Savannah, Georgia. The Northern and Western Urbanized Areas are Albany-Schenectady-Troy, New York; Denver, Colorado; Minneapolis-St.Paul, Minnesota; Portland, Oregon-Washington; Reading, Pennsylvania; Salt Lake City, Utah; Sioux City, Iowa-Nebraska-South Dakota; and Spokane, Washington.

The Northern and Western Urbanized Areas were larger on the average (515,215) than the Southern ones (215,113). Since occupational status is generally somewhat more favorable in larger communities (Schnore, *op. cit.*), any basis introduced by the larger Northern and Western Urbanized Areas is toward underestimating the white bonus jobs.

several decades ago, the consequences might have been different. Some of the whites who have moved from the South might have been retained to fill low-level jobs vacated by Negroes. However, there is little or no evidence that the presence and subordination of large numbers of Negroes in the South have driven many unskilled and semiskilled whites from the region. Negroes have rarely been preferred for any kind of work when qualified whites have been available, and therefore failure to compete successfully against Negroes has motivated whites to leave the South. White migrants from the region have been disproportionately well-educated in comparison with the remaining Southern whites,[15] and the well-educated whites have faced practically no competition from Negroes. The lower wages and salaries in the South have impelled many whites at all occupational levels to leave. However, average pay is low in Southern localities with few Negroes as well as in those with many Negroes, and this apparently results mainly from the lag in industrialization and urbanization of the South, weakness of the Southern labor movement, soil erosion, subsistence farming, lingering effects of the traditional one-crop commerical agriculture, and the like—factors related to Negro subordination but not direct results of it.

Therefore, it seems unlikely that the absence of the numerous Negroes in the South during recent decades would have prevented very much white out-migration. The primary consequence, it seems, would have been to reduce or prevent the advancement of many whites who have risen to high- and intermediate-level jobs because they were competing on very favorable terms against a large handicapped segment of the labor force. And certainly if the numerous Negroes were present but not handicapped in the competition, some Southern whites in high- and intermediate-level jobs would be lower in the occupational hierarchy.

The concept of "white bonus jobs" introduced by Cutright is useful in assessing the probable extent and nature of white occupational gains in the Southern Urbanized Areas.[16] White bonus jobs are high-level jobs available to whites because Negroes are present and subordinated. In other words, they are jobs filled by whites that would be filled by Negroes if the Negroes were not subordinated and that would not exist if the Negroes were not present. Unfortunately, Cutright uses a measure that almost certainly overstates the number of bonus jobs. It is based upon the assumption that the disparity between the proportion of all employed workers in upper-level occupations and the proportion of white employed workers in these occupations is the proportion of whites in bonus jobs. That is, it is based upon the assumption that the total occupational structure is unaffected by the presence and subordination of Negroes. In fact, the data in Table 3 show that in 1960 the proportion of upper-level jobs

[15] Elizabeth M. Suval and C. Horace Hamilton, "Some New Evidence on Educational Selectivity in Migration to and from the South," *Social Forces*, 43 (May, 1965), pp. 536–547.
[16] Cutright, *op. cit.*

varied inversely with percentage nonwhite—an association that very likely reflects the effects of Negro subordination.[17]

Given the apparent invalidity of Cutright's "zero-sum" assumption, the number of white bonus jobs can only be estimated. In this study, the number and nature of these jobs in the eight Southern Urbanized Areas with 35 percent or more nonwhites are estimated by guessing what the total male occupational distribution would be if Negroes were not present or subordinated. This is done by matching these Urbanized Areas with eight non-Southern Urbanized Areas that had the same proportions of their employed labor forces in manufacturing industries but had no more than five percent of nonwhites. Since degree of industrialization is a major determinant of occupational structure, it is assumed that the occupational structure in the Southern communities would resemble that in the matched non-Southern communities if the former had few or no Negroes. The estimated proportion of whites in bonus jobs in the Southern Urbanized Areas is calculated by subtracting the proportion of workers in each class of high-level occupations in the estimated total distribution from the proportion in that occupational class in the real white distribution (Table 6).

The greatest apparent numbers of white bonus jobs were as managers, officials, and proprietors, and as sales workers—precisely the occupations in which Negro representation is smallest and in which the greatest numbers of white bonus jobs would be expected.[18] There also were apparently a sizable number of bonus jobs as craftsmen and foremen and a smaller number as clerical workers—a pattern again congruent with Negro representation in these occupations. An estimated ten percent of the employed white males in the eight Urbanized Areas were in bonus jobs, but this apparent gain was partially offset by a smaller-than-normal proportion of whites in professional and technical work. On the other hand, probably many more than ten percent of the whites in these Urbanized Areas benefited from the unusually high white occupational distribution. If the whites in the bonus jobs had not been in them, it is unlikely that they would have been at the very lowest levels, where there was the greatest deficit in white jobs. Rather, they would have been at only slightly lower levels, where they would have displaced other whites to slightly lower levels, and so on. Therefore, whites in almost all occupations except the very lowest ones and the professions may have benefited from Negro subordination. Whatever white gains there were may have accrued in some small measure to a majority of the whites in these communities.

The pattern of occupational variation by percentage nonwhite shown in Table 3 is additional evidence for the view that the greatest numbers of

[17] An alternative explanation is that Negroes may tend to migrate to localities where unusually large numbers of low-level jobs are available. However, since most of the Negroes in the South are indigenous to the region, this explanation could hardly account for the larger proportion of low-level jobs in the South than in the North and West.

[18] For data on Negro representation in the occupational groups in 1960, see Leonard Broom and Norval D. Glenn, *Transformation of the Negro American*, New York: Harper and Row, 1965, p. 110.

white bonus jobs are as managers, officials, and proprietors, and as sales workers. These data also suggest that white opportunities in professional and technical work are not increased by Negro subordination. Since impoverished Negroes provide relatively little effective demand for professional services, and since Negroes provide much professional service for themselves, the lack of white bonus jobs as professionals is not surprising.

Any occupational gains to whites from Negro subordination would be offset if the subordination appreciably increased white unemployment. However, there is no evidence that Negro subordination increases white unemployment, and the data indicate that it may substantially reduce white unemployment in some Southern Urbanized Areas. In 1960 white unemployment varied inversely with percentage of nonwhites, overall and in each region (see Tables 1, 2, and 4). For reasons given above, it would be hazardous to infer white employment gains from the data for the North and West and the Border Region. In the South, however, the inverse relationship is only to a small degree explained by a slight tendency for percentage nonwhite and total unemployment to vary inversely, and there is no other apparent reason for it aside from the effect of Negro subordination. In many Southern Urbanized Areas, unusually high total unemployment occurred with unusually low white unemployment. For instance, total unemployment was higher and white unemployment was lower in the Urbanized Areas with 30 percent or more of nonwhites (all in the South) than in any other class of Urbanized Areas (Table 4). Since Negro workers are usually the "last hired and first fired" and are highly concentrated in the jobs most susceptible to elimination by recessions and technological change, a large proportion of Negro workers in a locality apparently makes

The evidence for white income gains is more tenuous than that for occupational and employment gains. White family income in 1959 was generally lowest in the Urbanized Areas with numerous nonwhites (see Table 5). However, this was merely a reflection of the lesser prosperity of the South. In each region, percentage nonwhite and white family income were positively associated (Tables 1 and 2). As is pointed out above, the positive associations in the North and West and in the Border Region can to a large extent be explained by positive associations between percentage nonwhite and total family income—associations that probably result from the attraction of Negro migrants to the larger and more prosperous cities. In the South, on the other hand, the evidence for white income benefits from Negro subordination is strong. Whites in the communities with many nonwhites were considerably more prosperous than whites in other Southern Urbanized Areas, in spite of greater overall poverty in the former communities. The difference in the white income distributions was greater at the lower than at the higher income levels. The percentage of white families with income below $3,000 was 4.5 percentage points lower in the Urbanized Areas with 25 percent or more of nonwhites, but the percentage of families with income of $10,000 or more was only 2.1 points higher in those communities. This suggests that Negro subordination may have helped many Southern whites escape poverty but that it probably helped fewer attain very high income.

Any income gains to whites may not be as great as the data suggest. Since the relatively low level of prosperity in the South probably results partly from Negro subordination, discrimination against Negroes may simply help Southern whites overcome an economic handicap that the discrimination partly causes. For instance, the entire Southern economy probably suffers from the inefficient utilization of human resources that discrimination causes and from the low average buying power of the Negro consumer. However, unless the economic lag of the South is almost entirely the result of Negro subordination, the data presented here suggest white economic gains. And, in fact, several additional factors almost certainly help account for the relatively low prosperity in the South: the lag in industrialization, persistence of subsistence farming and (until recently) one-crop commercial agriculture, poor educational institutions, and the like. As is pointed out above, some of these are related to Negro subordination, but none is solely the result of it. The South would almost certainly be poorer than the other regions even without the presence or subordination of its numerous Negroes. Yet in spite of the greater overall poverty in the South, whites in Southern Urbanized Areas are almost as prosperous as whites in Urbanized Areas in other parts of the country. This probably would not be possible without Negro subordination.

The data of this study indicate that labor costs probably are reduced somewhat but not necessarily very steeply by Negro subordination. The correlations between percentage nonwhite and the median earnings of male workers in broad occupational classes are all either small or negligible; variation in percentage nonwhite explains only a minute proportion of the variation in earnings within occupations in each region (Table 7). In the North and West, all of the correlations are positive, presumably because Negroes have migrated primarily to cities with relatively high wages, and the correlations are almost as high with the low-level occupations as with the others.

The data in Table 8 are stronger evidence that earnings within occupations are reduced by Negro subordination. Although average median earn-

TABLE 7

Product Moment Coefficients of Correlations Between Percentage Nonwhite and Median Earnings of Males in Broad Occupational Classes, by Region, 1959*

Occupational Class	North and West	Border	South
Professional, managerial, and kindred workers	+.33	+.37	+.05
Craftsmen, foremen, and kindred workers	+.33	+.19	−.01
Operative and kindred workers	+.19	−.06	−.17
Laborers	+.25	+.16	−.16

* Units of analysis are Urbanized Areas.

TABLE 8

Average Median Earnings of Males in Broad Occupational Classes in Urbanized Areas, by Region and Percentage Nonwhite, 1959

Occupational Class	North and West			South		
	Less Than 10% Nonwhite	10% or More Nonwhite	Percentage Difference	Less Than 25% Nonwhite	25% or More Nonwhite	Percentage Difference
Professional and managerial workers	$6,813	$7,157	+5.0%	$6,302	$6,352	+0.8%
Craftsmen and foremen	5,499	5,710	+3.8	4,584	4,547	−0.8
Operatives and kindred workers	4,719	4,787	+1.4	3,530	3,333	−5.6
Laborers	3,474	3,552	+2.2	2,335	2,231	−4.5

ings in all occupational classes were higher in the Northern and Western Urbanized Areas with larger percentages of nonwhites, the difference was smaller in low-level occupations, in which Negroes were highly concentrated. Any gain to employers apparently was not very great, but the higher proportion of nonwhites in the Urbanized Areas with ten percent or more nonwhites may have reduced the cost of operatives and laborers by two to three percent. In the South, the gain to employers may have been greater. Average median earnings of upper-level workers were about the same in the two classes of Urbanized Areas, but median earnings of laborers averaged nearly five per cent greater in the communities with less than 25 percent nonwhites, and median earnings of operatives averaged nearly six per cent higher.

Since employers probably benefited considerably from Negro subordination in many Urbanized Areas with less than 25 percent nonwhites, it is not possible to estimate with confidence the extent of the probable benefit in communities with the greater number of nonwhites. However, a reduction in the cost of operatives and laborers of around ten percent seems a conservative estimate, and certainly such a benefit would be great enough to provide incentive for continued Negro subordination. The cost of unskilled and semiskilled labor was lower by a great deal more than ten percent in the South than elsewhere,[19] but since wages were low even in Southern Urbanized Areas with few Negroes, such conditions as a relatively low level of industrialization, depressed agriculture, and lack of a strong labor movement probably are the primary reasons rather than the size and subordination of the Negro population.

The data on earnings within occupational classes are not strong evidence that Negro subordination keeps down the earnings of white workers. In the South, the nonwhite occupational distribution was generally more favorable in the Urbanized Areas with larger proportions of nonwhites, but nonwhite family income was generally lower in those communities.[20] These differences indicate that nonwhite earnings within occupations were lower where Negroes were more numerous relative to whites, and they suggest that white earnings may have been, if any different, higher in those localities.

The employers who probably benefit most from Negro subordination are Southern white housewives who employ domestic help. The number of employed household workers per 1,000 families was three times greater in the Urbanized Areas with 30 percent or more nonwhites than in those

[19] For instance, the average median earnings of laborers in 1959 were only $2,278 in the Southern Urbanized Areas, compared with $3,491 in the Northern and Western Urbanized Areas.

[20] The percentage of employed nonwhite males who were in nonmanual and skilled occupations was 23.6 in the Urbanized Areas with at least 25 percent nonwhites but was only 20.7 in the other Southern Urbanized Areas. The percentage of nonwhite families with income less than $3,000 was 52.2 in the former and 48.4 in the latter Urbanized Areas. Since nonwhite unemployment was only slightly higher in the Urbanized Areas with many nonwhites (8.1 percent compared with 7.1 percent in the other communities), the difference in income apparently resulted from a difference in average pay within low-level occupations.

with less than ten percent nonwhites (Table 9). However, the data by region (Tables 1 and 2) do not strongly indicate that Negro subordination increases the availability of domestic help except in the South. In the North and West and the Border Region, the small positive associations between percentage nonwhite and number of household workers are explained partly by a larger proportion of high-income families in the Urbanized Areas with many nonwhites.[21] In the North and West, Negro women are more likely to find other kinds of work, and therefore a fairly large Negro population does not assure a large supply of inexpensive domestic help. In the Border Region, the lack of a strong association between percentage nonwhite and the availability of domestic help reflects partly the fact that several of the Urbanized Areas with few Negroes had large Latin-American populations that provided many domestic workers. In the other Border Urbanized Areas, Negro subordination probably did greatly increase the supply of household help.

CONCLUSIONS AND IMPLICATIONS

The evidence is convincing though not conclusive that many whites in Southern Urbanized Areas benefit occupationally and economically from the presence and subordination of a large disadvantaged Negro population. The primary beneficiaries apparently are middle-class Southern housewives and white workers in proprietary, managerial, sales, and upper-level manual occupations. A majority of these beneficiaries apparently have intermediate rather than high incomes. A good many whites may escape poverty but few seem to receive very high income as the result of the presence and subordination of numerous Negroes.

This study reveals little evidence for the alleged economic dysfunctions of Negro subordination to low-level whites. In 1959 earnings within low-level occupations were somewhat lower in the Urbanized Areas with the greater proportions of nonwhites than in other Southern Urbanized Areas,

TABLE 9

Number of Employed Private Household Workers (Both Sexes) Per 1,000 Families (All Races) in Urbanized Areas, by Percentage of the Population Nonwhite, 1960

Percentage of Nonwhite	
0–9.9	28
10–19.9	33
20–29.9	67
30 and up	91

[21] When the percentage of families with income of $10,000 or more is held constant, the correlation between percentage nonwhite and number of employed private household workers per 1,000 families is reduced to +.19 in the North and West and to +.10 in the Border Region. In contrast, the partial and zero-order correlations in the South are identical (+.72).

but this difference probably reflects lower earnings of nonwhites rather than of whites. Therefore, the findings of this study do not support the Marxist view that discrimination against Negroes benefits the "capitalist class" but hurts white workers.

The data of this study by themselves are not an adequate basis for conclusions concerning the balance of beneficial and detrimental economic influences of Negro subordination upon the total white population. The detriments may well outweight the benefits, but the benefits suggested by the data are important nevertheless. However great the detrimental effects may be, they are probably rather widely distributed and may be incurred in some measure by almost all whites. Taxpayers throughout the country help pay the costs of Negro poverty, and almost everyone is indirectly affected by the relatively low level of Negro buying power. The detrimental effects may be so diffuse and widely distributed that few people are aware of them or are greatly concerned if they are aware of them. Therefore, the detrimental consequences of Negro subordination probably have little effect upon the attitudes and actions of most whites toward Negroes. Any beneficial consequences, by contrast, seem to be concentrated upon relatively few whites, and these whites are more likely to be aware of the effects of Negro subordination. Even those whites who are unaware of the benefits they receive may act in accordance with their self interest, since they may adhere to a racial ideology shaped by the interests of earlier generations of whites. If the traditional Southern racial ideology continues to be congruent with white economic interests, as the data presented here suggest, the interests will tend to reinforce and perpetuate it, even if many whites who gain from Negro subordination fail to perceive their gain.[22]

It is unlikely that any present white gains from Negro subordination will soon disappear.[23] In time, much lower-level work now performed by Negroes will be done by machines, and Negroes will not be needed to relieve whites of menial tasks. However, there will always be a job hierarchy; intermediate-level jobs of today will become low-level jobs of tomorrow, and so long as most Negroes are employed and subordinated, they will probably continue to reduce the proportion of white workers at the lowest levels. Since the nonwhite unemployment rate in the summer of 1965 was virtually the same as it was 15 years earlier, the unemployment of a majority of Negroes does not seem imminent.[24] And at recent

[22] For fuller discussion of the ways in which the interests of whites may affect their action toward Negroes, see Glenn, "The Role of White Resistance and Facilitation in the Negro Struggle for Equality," *op. cit.*

[23] The white gain apparently declined little from 1950 to 1960. In his study with 1950 data, the author found that the percentage of employed white nonagricultural males in nonmanual and skilled work was 61.2 in Standard Metropolitan Areas with less than three percent Negroes and that it was 73.8 in SMA's with 25 percent or more Negroes—a spread of 12.6 percentage points. The present study reveals that 64.8 percent of the employed white males in Urbanized Areas with less than three percent nonwhites were in nonmanual and skilled occupations, compared with 76.3 percent in Urbanized Areas with 25 percent or more nonwhites—a spread of 11.5 percentage points.

[24] Nonwhite unemployment was near eight percent at both dates, but it was some-

rates of closure of the Negro-white occupational and income gaps, Negro subordination will remain considerable for many decades.[25]

Therefore, it seems that Negro-white antagonism in the United States is and will long remain partly a matter of realistic conflict. Negroes cannot advance without the loss of traditional white benefits, and it is unlikely that most of the whites who benefit from the inferior status of Negroes will willingly allow Negro advancement.[26] This is not to say that race prejudice and social discrimination against Negroes are strictly or even largely an expression of economic rationality. However, white economic interests and whites' perceptions of these interests very likely play a major role in prompting white resistance to the so-called "Negro revolt."

---

what higher (near ten percent) during much of the early 1960's. Eventually, automation may rapidly increase nonwhite unemployment, as Willhelm and Powell predict (*op. cit*).

[25] See Leonard Broom and Norval D. Glenn, "When Will America's Negroes Catch Up?" *New Society*, March 25, 1965, pp. 6–7.

[26] However, as the author has pointed out elsewhere, white resistance to Negro advancement is almost certainly reduced in periods of rapid economic growth and rapid upward shifts in the occupational structure, when Negroes can advance without whites incurring any absolute losses in income or occupational status. Even at such times, closing the Negro-white gap entails loss of a white competitive advantage, but whites who nevertheless are moving up are likely to be less aware of and less concerned about this loss. See Norval D. Glenn, "Changes in the American Occupational Structure and Occupational Gains of Negroes," *Social Forces*, 61 (December, 1962), pp. 188–195, and "Some Changes in the Relative Status of American Nonwhites, 1940 to 1960," *Phylon*, 24 (Summer, 1963), pp. 109–122.

22

The Baptists and Slavery: An Examination of the Origins and Benefits of Segregation

JOHN LEE EIGHMY

OKLAHOMA BAPTIST UNIVERSITY

ONE OF THE MOST WIDELY RECOGNIZED CHARACTERISTICS OF SOUTHERN RE-
ligion in the antebellum period is that the churches gave moral endorsement to that system of ideas and institutions which distinguished the
slave states from the rest of the Union and set that region on the tragic
course of secession and war.[1] The church's loyalty to the Southern cause
is hardly disputable, but the very solidarity of this support can easily become the basis for a misreading of both the church's record on slavery
and its contribution to the Negro's social progress in the century or more
before emancipation. The purpose of this article is to re-examine the
record with specific attention to the Baptist denomination, the South's
largest religious body.

The first contention of this study is that the attitudes of Southern Baptists regarding slavery were more than a reflection of the ideology of a
society based on human servitude. Certainly, the Baptists as much as any
group eventually sanctioned slavery, but not without debating for more
than a century the morality of the institution. The earliest known Baptist
action on slavery occurred in 1710, when a South Carolina church questioned the cruelty of punishments allowed by the slave code.[2] At the time
of the American Revolution, many Baptists freed their slaves while
churches vigorously entered into the antislavery debate.[3] A Georgia association opposed future importation of slaves in 1793. Some Baptists in the
Carolinas considered slavery to be incompatible with Christianity. Opposition to slavery appeared in nearly every association in Virginia. The
General Committee, representing the state's six district bodies, condemned slavery as a "violent deprivation of the rights of nature" and then
advised Baptists to "make use of every legal measure to extirpate the hor-
rid evil from our land."[4] Slavery became an even livelier issue farther

[1] William B. Hesseltine and David Smiley, *The South in American History*, 2d ed.
(Englewood Cliffs, N.J.: Prentice-Hall, 1960), pp. 209–210; Francis B. Simkins, *A History of the South*, 3d ed. (New York: A. A. Knopf, 1963), p. 164; William S. Jenkins,
Pro-Slavery Thought in the Old South (Gloucester, Mass.: Peter Smith, 1960), pp.
200–218; Wilbur J. Cash, *The Mind of the South* (New York: A. A. Knopf, 1941), p.
80.

[2] William G. McLaughlin and Winthrop D. Jordan, "Baptists Face the Barbarities of
Slavery in 1710," *The Journal of Southern History*, 29 (Feb.-Nov., 1963), pp. 495–
501.

[3] William W. Sweet, ed., *The Baptists, 1783–1830* (New York: Henry Holt, 1931),
p. 79; B. D. Ragsdale, *Story of Georgia Baptists* (Atlanta: published by the author,
n.d.), 3, p. 72; George W. Paschal, *History of North Carolina Baptists* (Raleigh: North
Carolina Baptist Convention, 1955), 2, p. 237; Leah Townsend, *South Carolina Baptists, 1670–1805* (Florence, S.C.: Florence Printing Co., 1935), pp. 257–258.

[4] Robert B. Semple, *A History of the Rise and Progress of the Baptists in Virginia*
(Richmond: published by the author, 1810), pp. 10, 304; Garnett Ryland, *The Baptists*

west. Some pioneer preachers in Kentucky made opposition to slavery a matter of dogma. When the regular associational bodies would not adopt an antislavery position, emancipationists David Barrow, Carter Tarrant and others led 12 churches to organize a separate antislavery association.[5]

NEUTRALITY ON SLAVERY

The Baptist majority throughout the South disapproved of the divisive antislavery agitation. When an investigation of emancipation by one Virginia association "excited considerable tumult" among the churches, the assembly decided that the issue was an "improper subject" for examination by a religious body. Local protests also forced the General Committee to drop emancipation from its deliberations.[6] Kentucky Baptists reacted in a similar fashion. The Elkhorn Association had to repudiate an antislavery statement when opposition to the action developed in member churches. This body then admonished ministers and churches not to "meddle with emacipation [sic] from slavery or any other political subject."[7]

Neutrality on the "political" issue of slavery gave way to a defense of the institution early in the nineteenth century. David Benedict, a New Englander who toured the South in 1813, reported that most Baptists accepted slavery as an inherited system supported by history and scripture.[8] Richard Furman, a pastor in Charleston, delivered the first formal apology for slavery by a Baptist. Writing in 1823 to protest laws restricting religious instruction for slaves, Furman argued that such instruction could not endanger the institution because the Bible supported slavery. He concluded that slavery "when tempered with humanity and justice, is a state of tolerable happiness; equal, if not superior, to that which many poor enjoy in countries reputed to be free."[9] Furman's arguments became a standard part of proslavery thought during the next 40 years. Richard Fuller, another distinguished South Carolinian, prepared the most comprehensive defense of slavery to that date when he debated the question with Francis Wayland, president of Brown University. The lengthy exchange between these two eminent divines appeared in Baptist papers in both sections and was later published as a book.[10]

All the Baptist periodicals in the South discussed slavery. Although the

of Virginia, 1699–1926 (Richmond: Board of Missions and Education, 1955), pp. 153–154.

[5] Walter B. Posey, The Baptist Church in the Lower Mississippi Valley, 1776–1845 (Lexington: University of Kentucky Press, 1957), p. 90; David Benedict, A General History of the Baptist Denomination in America (Boston: published by the author, 1813), 2, pp. 231–245; Sweet, Religion on the Frontier, p. 83.

[6] Semple, History of Baptists in Virginia, p. 304; Ryland, Baptists of Virginia, pp. 152, 154.

[7] J. H. Spencer, A History of Kentucky Baptists from 1769 to 1885 (n.p.: published by the author, 1886), 1, pp. 183–185.

[8] Benedict, Baptist Denomination in America, pp. 206–213.

[9] Richard Furman, Exposition of the Baptists . . . (Charleston: A. E. Miller, 1823), p. 17. Jenkins, Pro-Slavery Thought, p. 72, said this document was the "most significant pro-slavery statement in the early twenties."

[10] Richard Fuller and Francis Wayland, Domestic Slavery Considered as a Scriptural Institution (New York: Lewis Colby, 1845).

editors unanimously upheld the lawfulness of the institution, they often criticized certain abuses, and some entertained the hope that it eventually would be abolished. Editors in Virginia, Georgia, North Carolina, and Kentucky strongly supported the American Colonization Society.[11] A few Upper South editors expressed opinions on slavery that were even less orthodox, by Southern standards. James Pendleton, having once voiced antislavery views, lost his editorial post on a Tennessee paper in 1861.[12] W. C. Buck, a Kentucky editor during the 1840's, often criticized slavery. He argued that the servitude sanctioned in the Bible benefited the slave, whereas the American slave system operated for the "luxury of the master."[13] Thomas Meredith, a North Carolina editor from 1833 to 1850, called the "American system" of slavery an "evil of great magnitude which we cannot but hope will sooner or later be banished from the earth."[14]

Religious Origins of Segregation

This article has tried to show thus far that Southern Baptists expressed some independence of mind on the question of slavery. Stronger evidence of a capacity for self-direction in matters of race may be seen in their efforts to Christianize the slave population. A survey of the Baptist mission to the enslaved reveals the church serving as a creative social force of far-reaching significance for the progress of the Negro. More precisely, the church engaged in social invention when, after evangelizing the slaves, it formalized the social relationships between two races brought together by a common faith. The churches, having proclaimed a spiritual brotherhood, found it necessary to institute a pattern of behavior that would respect racial distinctions in social intercourse.

The way in which the church dealt with the problem of race relations raises a question about the origins of segregation. Comer Vann Woodward, in a widely celebrated study, has argued recently that segregation originated in the Jim Crow laws of the 1890's. Woodward sheds much-needed light on the history of racial separation, but his central thesis is somewhat misleading, even when it admits that church segregation began during Reconstruction. The argument advanced in the present article is that the origins of segregation are to be found in the rather systematic separation of the races in the churches while the Negro was still enslaved.[15]

11 Roger H. Crook, "The Ethical Emphasis of the Editors of Baptist Journals Published in the Southeastern Region of the United States up to 1865" (Th.D. diss., Southern Baptist Theological Seminary, 1947), pp. 139–227; *The Christian Index* (Atlanta), June 15, 1837, pp. 272–273; *The Religious Herald* (Richmond), January 20, 1832, p. 2.

12 James M. Pendleton, *Reminiscences of a Long Life* (Louisville: Baptist Book Concern, 1891), pp. 92–113; Crook, "Ethical Emphasis," pp. 160, 194–195.

13 *Ibid.*, p. 170.

14 *The Biblical Recorder* (Raleigh), November 9, 1844.

15 See Woodward's *The Strange Career of Jim Crow* (New York: Oxford University Press, 1957), pp. vii–xvii; and Charles E. Wynes' supporting monograph *Race Relations in Virginia, 1870–1902* (Charlottesville: University of Virginia Press, 1961), pp. vii–viii. Woodward's thesis is challenged by Kyle Haselden, *The Racial Problem in Christian Perspective* (New York: Harper and Row, 1964), p. 28; and by David Reimers, *White Protestantism and the Negro* (New York: Oxford University Press, 1965), pp. 18, 25.

That segregation should have its origin in religion becomes understandable when it is remembered that the church, by the very act of preaching
a gospel of brotherhood, established a demonstrable basis for equality. It
thereby created the need for a system of racial separation that would prevent social expressions of equality. Since religion afforded the one common experience in which the races met on any kind of equal ground,
the churches were under a special compulsion to attend to the problem
of the social relations between bond and free. At first slaves took special
religious instruction from their masters or worshipped with whites in separately assigned seats in the churches. Undoubtedly social intercourse
was freer at that time than it would be after the passage of the Jim Crow
laws, but the physical proximity of the races did not itself alter the fundamental distinctions between them. The terms under which the slave
participated in church life suggests that separation, not integration, was
the ruling consideration. Churches not only practiced separation within
their congregations, but they increasingly turned to separate religious exercises for the slave communicants. As shall be seen, the final stage in religious separation, church life conducted by the Negroes themselves, became a firmly established practice in the antebellum period.[16]

When separation is recognized as the emerging pattern for religion under slavery, then the role of the church in preparing the slaves for emancipation can be appreciated. Separation, which re-enforced the supremacy of the dominant race, served an almost contrary purpose for the enslaved. To begin with, the understanding that the church would respect
racial differences cleared the way for the massive ingathering of slave
converts. In view of the actual social distinctions between the races, it
would seem that a large measure of separation was almost necessary for
a flourishing church life among a dispossessed people. But beyond the
strictly religious gains, separation benefited those in bondage because it
offered them an early escape from paternalism and an initial experience
in self-determination.

The Baptist Mission to the Enslaved

The evidence supplied by the Baptists on race relations in religion is of
first importance because eventually they enlisted more Negroes than any
other denomination. Several reasons account for the Baptist success: an
emphasis on personal conversion, baptism by immersion, and congregational participation in church life all offered special attractions to the enslaved. Belief in the liberty of the soul allowed no racial barrier to confine
the Baptist movement.

Historians of the Negro church have also emphasized the close parallel
between the slave conversions and the religious revivals, in which the
Baptists played a leading role. Baptist preachers, laboring without benefit
of formal training, offered a simple but fervent gospel which attracted
the unlettered, regardless of race. Baptist gatherings gave the penitent
slave a joyous release from plantation rigors as well as an otherworldly

16 *Ibid.*, p. 18; Haselden, *Racial Problem*, pp. 28–29.

hope. Slaveowners welcomed and sometime paid for such preaching because it did more to strengthen than to undermine slavery.[17]

Of course, the conversion of slaves ultimately depended on the missionary enterprise of whites. From their founding, Baptist conventions viewed the slave population as a mission field of special importance, and missionaries under their appointment regularly gave time to the slaves.[18] However, the mission boards always placed the primary responsibility for this work on the local churches. Such well-known pastors as Basil Manly, James C. Furman, Richard Fuller, and Isaac Taylor Tichenor held separate services for the people of color. Most outstanding was the work of Robert Ryland, president of Richmond College and pastor of the African Baptist Church in Richmond, Virginia, from 1841 to 1866. Ryland baptized 3,832 converts and prepared a special catechism for their instruction.[19]

The desire to evangelize sometimes conflicted with slave code restrictions. South Carolina Baptists in 1801 and 1823 tried to alter legislation against religious instruction. The 1848 Virginia Convention appealed for the right of slaves to assemble for religious purposes. Mercer University President Nathaniel Crawford declared a Georgia law forbidding slaves to read an "outrage upon humanity . . . and a disgrace to Christianity and the civilization of our people." Even during the Civil War, Georgia Baptists had a hand in modifying a law denying licenses to colored ministers.[20]

SEPARATION OF THE RACES

Since the Baptists were highly successful evangels to the colored, it is particularly important to examine how they handled the problem of social intercourse. There has been some confusion on the matter because of the ambiguity that characterized the Negro's status in biracial churches. Slaves commonly worshipped with whites in the same congregation.[21] The Baptists, indeed, seem to have gone farther than others in allowing Negro par-

[17] Carter G. Woodson, *The History of the Negro Church,* 2d ed. (Washington: The Associated Publishers, 1945), p. 22; Workers of the Writers' Program, *The Negro in Virginia* (New York: Hastings House, 1940), pp. 99, 103; Wesley M. Gewehr, *The Great Awakening in Virginia, 1740–1790* (Durham: Duke University Press, 1930), pp. 235–241.

[18] *Proceedings of the General Association of Virginia, 1835* (n.p., n.d.), p. 3, and *1850,* p. 6; *Minutes of the Baptist State Convention of Texas, 1852* (Washington, Tex., n.d.), pp. 13, 15; James B. Sellers, *Slavery in Alabama* (University; University of Alabama Press, 1950), pp. 304–305; Orville W. Taylor, *Negro Slavery in Arkansas* (Durham: Duke University Press, 1958), pp. 181–182; *Proceedings of the Southern Baptist Convention, 1845* (Nashville, 1845), p. 15; Mary Emily Wright, *The Missionary Work of the Southern Baptist Convention* (Philadelphia: American Baptist Publication Society, 1890), pp. 313–322.

[19] Simkins, *History of the South,* p. 165; Walter L. Fleming, *Documentary History of Reconstruction* (New York: Peter Smith, 1950), 2, p. 247; Woodson, *Negro Church,* pp. 140–145; *The Religious Herald* (Richmond), July 1 and 8, 1880.

[20] *Proceedings, Southern Baptist Convention, 1849,* p. 39; *Proceedings, General Association of Virginia, 1835,* p. 3, and *1848,* p. 7; *Baptist Home Missions in North America* (New York: Baptist Home Mission Rooms, 1883), p. 390; Richard Furman, *Exposition of the Baptists;* Ragsdale, *Georgia Baptists,* p. 80; *History of the Baptist Denomination in Georgia* (Atlanta: Jas. P. Harrison, 1881), p. 264.

[21] Haselden, *Racial Problem,* p. 24, argues that W. D. Weatherford's *American*

ticipation in church life. They ordained colored deacons and preachers who exercised some disciplinary supervision over the members of their race. But the mere presence of slaves in white congregations can easily obscure the racial distinctions carefully observed within the churches. The Baptists did not allow their faith to effect a social brotherhood in any practical sense. On the contrary, their conduct reflects the white man's determination to keep the races separate in social life. Negro members never enjoyed an equal voice in church affairs, and when biracial congregations assembled, the slaves normally sat in a segregated section.[22]

The desire for separation did not stop with the etiquette of distinction practiced when the races worshipped together. White Baptists made perfectly clear their preference for complete separation in religious life. State conventions often studied the problem of how best to give religious instruction to the colored. One theme runs through these reports: the method most highly recommended called for separate meetings and, whenever possible, the use of separate quarters. The Virginia Convention praised the establishment of Negro churches. Arkansas Baptists were urged to set aside a special section of the church for the use of slaves. The Mississippi and Kentucky conventions recommended separate meeting houses. A report to the Tennessee Convention complained about the unsuitability of religious instruction in mixed congregations. A Texas committee report in 1851 boasted that almost every pastor held separate meetings for the slave members.[23]

To the whites, separation befitted the slave's subordinate status, but the practice brought unexpected benefits to the Negro race. A separated church was but one step away from a religion conducted by the Negroes themselves. The simplicity, informality, and evangelistic emphasis of the Baptist faith encouraged an independent church life among the slaves. One study of Virginia slave life reveals a dynamic religious community. Slaves held religious exercises in their own quarters or else fled to secret "hush harbors" in the woods and fields to escape white surveillance.[24] The slave's

---

Churches and the Negro (Boston: Christopher Publishing House, 1957), p. 17, is misleading in stressing the evidence of antebellum integration.

[22] The Religious Herald (Richmond), July 8, 1880; Proceedings of the Mississippi Baptist State Convention, 1850 (Jackson, 1850), p. 23; Minutes of the Alabama Baptist State Convention, 1846 (n.p., n.d.), p. 19; W. Harrison Daniel, "Southern Protestantism and the Negro, 1860–1865," The North Carolina Historical Review, 41 (July, 1964), pp. 340–342; Sellers, Slavery in Alabama, pp. 299–300, 321; Taylor, Slavery in Arkansas, pp. 178–180; Writers' Program, Negro in Virginia, pp. 100–109, 143–147; Everett Dick, The Dixie Frontier (New York: A. A. Knopf, 1948), pp. 96, 185, 188.

[23] Proceedings, General Association of Virginia, 1845, p. 5, and 1863, Appendix E, pp. 76–77; Proceedings of the Arkansas Baptist State Convention, 1848 (Little Rock, 1848), p. 7, and 1850, p. 6; Proceedings, Mississippi Baptist Convention, 1850, p. 22; Minutes of the General Association of Baptists in Kentucky, 1860 (Louisville, 1860), p. 24; Proceedings of the General Association of the Baptists of Tennessee, 1848 (Nashville, 1849), p. 13; Proceedings of the West Tennessee Baptist Association, 1849 (Nashville, 1850), Appendix E, pp. 41–42; also 1857, p. 11; 1858, p. 7; 1861, pp. 7–8; Minutes, Baptist Convention of Texas, 1851, Appendix E, p. 14; also 1853, pp. 19–20; 1856, p. 15; 1857, p. 17.

[24] Writers' Program, Negro in Virginia, pp. 143–147; Sellers, Slavery in Alabama, p.

informal church life—sometimes called the "invisible institution"—went, largely unrecorded. It flourished nonetheless, producing some outstanding leaders, both slave and free, and many all-Negro congregations. Historians have recorded some of the work of George Leile and Andrew Bryan of Georgia; Harray Cowan and Joseph Baysmore of North Carolina; William Moses and John Jasper of Williamsburg and Richmond, Virginia; and missionaries Collin Teague and Lott Carey. These men and others built Negro Baptist churches in many cities, towns, and rural districts in the seaboard states. In early nineteenth century Kentucky and Tennessee, Negro historian Carter Woodson has estimated that one-fourth or more of the Baptist congregations were Negro.[25]

RELIGIOUS RECONSTRUCTION

The Negro's conduct of his own church life under slavery goes far toward explaining the development of a completely segregated church shortly after Appomattox. Religious reconstruction, it turned out, was to be largely the work of the freedmen themselves. The help of Northern Baptists bore fruit in education later in the century. White Baptists of the South, suspicious of carpetbag missionaries, gave little support to this work; furthermore, their own organizations made an almost negligible contribution to the freedmen's religious needs. Perhaps it is too much to have expected from the defeated South an immediate show of generosity and initiative in elevating the status of former slaves. Southern Baptist agencies were all near bankruptcy. Unfortunately, emancipation raised an issue that would not wait for better times. Would the freedmen worship in white churches where many Negroes held membership or carry on separately as many others had been doing?[26]

As soon as the war ended, the white Baptists seemed to anticipate the eventual departure of colored members. The Alabama Convention of 1865 affirmed the right of Negroes to withdraw. The Virginia Convention advised churches to encourage separation. James C. Furman urged South Carolina Baptists to assist the Negroes in organizing their own churches. More important in determining racial division than any announced church policy was the fact that both races saw their highest interests to be served

294; J. A. Whitted, *A History of the Negro Baptists of North Carolina* (Raleigh: Edwards and Broughton, 1908), p. 10.

[25] E. Franklin Frazier, *The Negro in the United States* (New York: Macmillan, 1949), p. 343; Writers' Program, *Negro in Virginia*, pp. 100–109; John L. Bell, Jr., "Baptists and the Negro in North Carolina during Reconstruction," *The North Carolina Historical Review*, 43 (Oct., 1965), p. 402; Woodson, *Negro Church*, pp. 35–36, 97–104; *Baptist Home Missions*, pp. 387–390; Sellers, *Slavery in Alabama*, p. 300; Benedict, *Baptist Denomination*, pp. 189–194.

[26] Robert A. Baker, *Relations between Northern and Southern Baptists* (n.p.; published by the author, 1848), pp. 104–116, 171–173; Charles L. White, *A Century of Faith* (Philadelphia: Judson Press, 1932), pp. 104–106; *Baptist Home Missions*, pp. 438–466; *Proceedings, Southern Baptist Convention, 1866*, p. 86; and *1868*, pp. 15, 17–20; *1870*, p. 36; *1875*, pp. 73–75; *1879*, pp. 14, 26; Alratheus Ambush Taylor, *The Negro in South Carolina During Reconstruction* (Washington: The Association for the Study of Negro Life and History, 1924), p. 117; Winfred E. Garrison, *The March of Faith* (New York: Harper and Brothers, 1933), p. 21.

by separation. Negroes wanted above all to escape white control. If they remained in biracial churches, they were not likely to exercise a real voice in church affairs. A North Carolina Baptist official insisted that no new privileges should be given to the freedmen. A Virginia editor confessed the greatest fear among white men when he warned that the continuation of biracial churches would inevitably lead to the "mongrelization of the noble Anglo-Saxon race."[27]

Since both races preferred separation, the development of the Negro church came about amicably and rapidly. Baptist congregational government facilitated the transition. Local white churches ordained Negro leaders, organized new churches, and granted letters of dismissal. In some instances, whites helped build Negro churches. But most of the credit for the separate religious establishment must go to the Negroes themselves. Mainly it was their own initiative that created a whole new ecclesiastical edifice within a few years. Statewide organizations appeared in North Carolina in 1866 and in Alabama and Virginia in 1867. By 1882 the separated Negro Baptists numbered 800 thousand. They had conventions in every Southern state and were publishing eight religious papers. In 1886 they established their first national body, the American National Baptist Convention.[28]

The growth of the Negro church certainly must stand as one of the most enduring accomplishments of the Reconstruction period. This achievement suggests a final observation concerning the contribution of segregation to the Negro race. Despite all the injustice that can be attributed to segregation in American experience, the operation of this policy in the nineteenth century was not altogether oppressive. In a situation in which the full exercise of equality was not permitted, segregation afforded opportunities, not otherwise available, for the social advancement of Negroes within their own community. Religious separation in slavery provided a socializing experience which helped prepare the slaves for the direction of their own affairs as free men. Without this experience, the race's progress would have been retarded much more than it was. After emancipation, the segregated church became the central institution in the Negro community— for all a haven in a discriminatory society, for many the only forum in which to display talents for leadership.[29]

[27] *Minutes, Alabama Baptist Convention, 1865*, p. 16; *Proceedings, General Association of Virginia, 1866*, p. 26; *Minutes of the Baptist Denomination in South Carolina, 1865–1866* (Greenville, 1866), p. 240; Writers' Program, *Negro in Virginia*, p. 248; Rufus Spain, "Attitudes and Reactions of Southern Baptists to Certain Problems of Society, 1865–1900" (Ph.D. diss., Vanderbilt University, 1961), p. 37; Bell, "Baptists and the Negro," pp. 397–398.

[28] Writers' Program, *Negro in Virginia*, p. 248; Taylor, *Slavery in Arkansas*, pp. 118–119; Charles T. Rankin, "The Rise of Negro Baptist Churches in the South through the Reconstruction Period" (Th.M. thesis, Southern Baptist Theological Seminary, 1955), pp. 1, 52–60; *Baptist Home Missions*, p. 421; B. F. Riley, *A History of the Baptists in the Southern States East of the Mississippi* (Philadelphia: American Baptist Publication Society, 1898), p. 323; Bell, "Baptists and the Negro," pp. 402–404.

[29] Benjamin E. Mays and Joseph W. Nicholson, *The Negro's Church* (New York: Institute of Social and Religious Research, 1933), pp. 6–8.

23

Ideological Conflict between Protestant Clergy and Laity on Civil Rights

JEFFREY K. HADDEN
CASE WESTERN RESERVE UNIVERSITY

I N RECENT YEARS THE MASS MEDIA HAVE ABOUNDED WITH STORIES OF CONflict between clergy and laity over the direct-action involvement of the former in the civil rights struggle. However, there is a dearth of systematic data on the extent, nature, and implications of this conflict.

The purpose of this paper is to explore two central issues in the conflict: (1) the attitudes of Protestant clergy and laity toward civil rights, and (2) the attitudes of laity toward the involvement of clergy in civil rights. The data for this paper came from two principal sources. The first is a national mail survey of Protestant ministers in six major denominations which was conducted early in 1965.[1] The second is a national survey of the

[1] The data presented here on clergy attitudes toward civil rights issues were gathered as only one part of a more comprehensive study of Protestant clergy. In all, the questionnaire contained 524 questions. For a general description of the study see Jeffrey K. Hadden, "A Study of the Protestant Ministry of America," *Journal for the Scientific Study of Religion*, 5 (Fall, 1965), pp. 10–23.

The data were gathered in early 1965 by a mail questionnaire which was sent to a probability sample of more than 10,000 parish and campus clergymen in six major Protestant denominations: American Baptist, American Lutheran, Episcopalian, Methodist, Missouri Synod Lutheran, and Presbyterian, U.S.A. The overall response rate was 62 per cent.

The data presented in this paper are based on 7,441 returns from parish clergy. Subjects were asked to respond to attitude statements on a six-point continuum. The response categories were as follows: "strongly agree," "agree," "probably agree," "probably disagree," "disagree," and "strongly disagree." In previous reports I have combined the first two categories ("strongly agree" and "agree"). In this article the "probably agree" category is combined with the other two "agree" categories to make the data as nearly comparable as possible with the data for laity.

Two additional observations should be made regarding the context of the data presented here. First, in previous papers I have demonstrated that theological orientations vary significantly across, as well as within, denominations and that theological orientation is significantly related to measures of political ideology. See Jeffrey K. Hadden, "A Protestant Paradox—Divided They Merge," *Trans-Action*, 4 (July–Aug., 1967), pp. 63–69; and Jeffrey K. Hadden, "The Relationship between Theological Position and Political Ideology among Protestant Ministers," a paper presented at the Annual Meetings of the Society for the Scientific Study of Religion, Chicago, Oct., 1966. Therefore, the data presented here are analyzed by denomination rather than by a simple group of all the clergy together.

A second observation concerns the time lag since the data were gathered. Brink and Harris have observed rather significant changes in the attitudes of the American public on the race issue between 1963 and 1966. See William Brink and Louis Harris, *Black and White* (New York: Simon and Schuster, 1967). In brief, they report a more conservative mood, which they attribute to riots, greater militancy on the part of Negro leaders, and the growing realization that integration may mean "next door." If this is true for the nation as a whole, then researchers must at least entertain the possibility that clergy attitudes toward civil rights have also become more conservative since the present data were gathered in early 1965. My continuing studies of clergy, however, do not support this contention. During the period from June, 1966 through October,

American lay public's attitudes toward civil rights and the involvement of clergy in the civil rights struggle, which was conducted early in 1967.[2]

Comparison of Clergy and Lay Attitudes on Civil Rights

Clergy in the six denominations studied were, as a group, overwhelmingly sympathetic to the general principle of achieving social justice for Negroes in America. Only 10 per cent of the clergy responded affirmatively to the statement, "I basically disapprove of the civil rights movement in America." Table 1 shows the response of clergy to this item by denomination, theological position, and age. The range of agreement with this proposition was from 6 per cent among Presbyterians to 14 per cent among Missouri Synod Lutherans. The theologically conservative were considerably more likely to disapprove of the civil rights movement than were those of more liberal theological persuasion. Also, the older clergy were more likely to disapprove than were the younger. Because of the limitations of space, denominational data are not presented in subsequent tables, but the general pattern holds for the other items. In fact, differences by denomination are even more marked on other items.[3]

The clergy expressed deep concern that the churches and Christians have not understood and faced the implications of the civil rights struggle. Eighty-three per cent agreed with the strongly worded statement, "For the most part, the churches have been *woefully inadequate* in facing up to the civil rights issue." Ninety-three per cent agreed that "many whites pretend to be very Christian while in reality their racial attitudes demonstrate their lack of understanding or misunderstanding of Christianity."

Only one of these three items was included in the national lay sample, but as indicated in Table 2, it reveals a dramatic contrast in the views of clergy and laity. While only 10 per cent of the clergy expressed basic disapproval of the civil rights movement, 44 per cent of the lay public felt

---

1967, I conducted interviews with probability samples of clergy in Cleveland, Ohio; Grand Rapids, Michigan; and Milwaukee, Wisconsin. In none of these cities did I detect a more conservative mood among clergy, but rather a growing concern that the church and the government have not been adequate in their responses to the civil rights crisis.

[2] The data on the public's response to clergy involvement in civil rights were gathered for the author in the National Opinion Research Center's AMALGAM SURVEY, January, 1967. The data were gathered by personal interviews and constitute a representative national sample of 1,504 respondents. Two hundred Negroes in the sample are eliminated from the analysis presented here.

Subjects were asked to respond to attitude statements on a four-point continuum, because the NORC field director felt that the six-point continuum would be awkward in a personal interview. The response categories were as follows: "definitely agree," "probably agree," "probably disagree," and "definitely disagree." The percentages reported here combine the first two categories, "definitely agree" and "probably agree."

Finally, it should be noted that inadequate research funds severely restricted the number of questions that could be included in this survey. Parallelism with the clergy survey was sacrificed in order to include questions on the public's attitudes toward clergy involvement in civil rights. Three parallel items do, however, provide a basis for comparing clergy and laity.

[3] For a more detailed analysis of the relationship between denomination, age, theological position, and beliefs, see Hadden, "Protestant Paradox."

TABLE 1

Per Cent of Clergy Disapproving of the Civil Rights Movement

		Total	American Baptist	American Lutheran	Episcopalian	Methodist	Missouri Synod Lutheran	Presbyterian
N=		7,441	654	908	1,271	2,515	895	1,198
"I basically disapprove of the civil rights movement in America." (per cent agreeing)								
Total	(N=7,441)	10	10	9	7	12	14	6
Theological position								
Fundamentalist	(N=342)	23	35	16	—a	39	19	6
Conservative	(N=3182)	13	11	9	11	19	14	11
Neo-orthodox	(N=2032)	5	2	4	5	7	5	4
Liberal	(N=1560)	7	3	15	4	8	—a	5
Age								
Under 35	(N=2066)	6	6	7	4	9	10	2
35–44	(N=2312)	9	9	9	6	12	12	6
45–54	(N=1683)	11	9	8	9	12	16	10
55 and over	(N=1380)	18	17	17	8	17	12	8

a N was too small to compute statistically reliable percentages.

this way. Protestants were more likely (47 per cent) than Catholics (40 per cent) to report disapproval, and Jews were considerably less likely (24 per cent) to disapprove of the civil rights movement. Several Protestant denominations had too few cases to permit reliable comparisons. However, religious involvement in Protestantism, as measured by frequency of attendence, was *not* systematically related to response on this item. The one notable point was that those who reported that they *never* attended church were the *least* likely to disapprove of the civil rights movement (36 per cent). Age, although related to clergy attitudes, was not significantly related to lay response on this question. Again, because of space limitations, detailed tabular data will not be presented by church involvement and age. However, the same pattern of response existed on other items: neither age nor frequency of church attendance bore any substantial relationship to attitudes toward civil rights issues.

Thus the overwhelming majority of clergy expressed approval for civil rights as well as concern that the churches and their membership have been inadequate in their response to the problem. In contrast, a substantial proportion of laity, regardless of age or extent of involvement in religious activity, expressed disapproval of the civil rights movement.

One must be cautious about concluding from a single item that clergy

TABLE 2

Per Cent of Laymen Disapproving Civil Rights Movement[a]

"I basically disapprove of the civil rights movement in America." (per cent agreeing) Total	N 1,304	Per Cent 44
Religious group		
Protestant	824	47
Catholic	434	40
Jew	46	24
Frequency of church attendance (Protestant only)		
Every week	253	48
Nearly every week; 2–3 times a month	179	45
About once a month; several times a year	182	51
About once or twice a year;		
less than once a year	165	49
Never	44	36
Age (Protestant only)		
Under 35	219	43
35–44	160	44
45–54	140	40
55 and over	304	48

[a] Negro respondents were eliminated from sample.

and laity are irreconcilably divided on the civil rights issue. A different phrasing of questions or a more specific content might reveal more agreement than would appear on the basis of this single item. Moreover, the overwhelming sympathy that clergy expressed for the *general principle* of civil rights may not be sustained when the *specific* implications of these principles are explored. These possibilities are investigated next.

Four items in the clergy questionnaire attempted to tap some of the "simplistic" solutions to the racial crisis. These items, presented in Table 3, do not measure overt racial prejudices; in fact, they may actually be partially true.

All of these items reflect an element of stereotyping or scapegoating. By pointing to the government or the Negro in rather condescending terms, they tend to remove the responsibility of the racial crisis from the broader society and from the individual respondent. In short, they seem to reflect a lack of understanding of the complexity of the racial crisis in America.

As a group, clergy were more likely to agree with these statements than they were to disavow the legitimacy of the civil rights movement. Still, the large majority did reject the solutions to the racial crisis implied in these statements. Moreover, theological position and age were strongly associated with response to these items. For example, while 41 per cent of the fundamentalists believed that the racial crisis would have been less serious if the federal government had not intervened, only 9 per cent of the neo-orthodox and liberal clergy agreed with this position. On the same item, 10 per cent of those under age 35, as compared with 31 per cent of those over 55, agreed.

Considerably larger proportions agreed with the statements which placed responsibility with Negroes than agreed with statements indicting the government and political leadership. This may reflect a nonprejudicial sentiment that Negroes must share in the task of solving the racial problem. This interpretation would seem to be supported by the fact that approximately half of those indicating agreement with these statements checked the "probably agree" rather than the "agree" or "definitely agree" categories in the questionnaire, i.e., their position was held with some degree of tenuousness. However, the fact that the more theologically liberal and the younger were significantly less likely to agree with these statements would seem to argue for interpreting agreement as a manifestation of latent or subtle prejudice.

Only one item from this group is available in parallel form for the lay survey, but again, the results revealed dramatic disparities in response. While only 35 per cent of the Protestant clergy believed that "Negroes would be better off if they would take advantage of the opportunities that have been made available rather than spending so much time protesting," 89 per cent of the Protestant laity agreed with this statement. Again, neither frequency of church attendance nor age is systematically related to the layman's response to this statement.

The data form a consistent pattern. While clergy are extremely sympathetic toward civil rights and express considerable understanding of the complexity of the problem, a large proportion of laity neither approve of

TABLE 3

Per Cent of Clergy Agreeing that Responsibility for Civil Rights Rests with Government and Negroes

| | Total | Theological Position | | | | Age | | | |
		Funda-mentalist	Con-servative orthodox	Neo-orthodox	Liberal	Under 35	35–44	45–54	55 and over
"The real obstacle to integration in this nation is political leadership and not the people selves." (per cent agreeing)	24	43	25	20	21	18	21	27	35
"The racial crisis in this country would probably be less serious if the federal government had not intervened." (per cent agreeing)	17	41	22	9	9	10	14	19	31
"Negroes would be better off if they would take advantage of the opportunities that have been made available rather than spending so much time protesting." (per cent agreeing)	35	59	43	21	21	25	29	40	51
"Negroes could solve many of their own problems if they were not so irresponsible and carefree about life." (per cent agreeing)	42	70	51	27	26	30	37	47	64

the civil rights struggle, nor do they share the sense of its seriousness and complexity. Moreover, neither age nor involvement in church life seem to make much difference in the layman's attitudes.

This latter point is corroborated by other studies and is consistent with the cries of church critics who contend that there is as much racial prejudice among church members as there is among people who do not attend church. For example, in a recently published study of Episcopalians, Glock, Ringer, and Babbie concluded that ". . . involvement . . . [in the life of the church] . . . is not related in any way to parishioner's social ideologies."[4] Similarly, Greeley and Rossi, in a comprehensive national study of the impact of Catholic education, concluded that those who have received all or some of their education in Catholic institutions are not essentially different in their attitudes toward other groups and social issues than are those Catholics who received none of their education in Catholic institutions.[5] Also, a 1963 National Opinion Research Center (NORC) survey failed to find any strong relationship between the intensity with which people hold religious beliefs and their response on an integration scale.[6]

In short, the evidence points to the conclusion that church involvement and the intensity of religious beliefs are not related to attitudes toward the racial situation. If the most actively involved laymen held more favorable attitudes toward civil rights than those who were less involved, the clergy would have a stronger base of support for their liberal views on the civil rights issue. But this is not the case; and herein lies an important source of conflict between clergy and laity.

ATTITUDES TOWARD CLERGY INVOLVEMENT IN CIVIL RIGHTS ACTIVITY

If a significant proportion of laity disapprove of the civil rights movement, does it not follow that they will have serious misgivings about the involvement of clergy in this struggle? The answer is yes, but the data present an interesting paradox. Table 4 indicates that the large majority of American Protestants believe that religion is a source of moral strength and concern in society. Eighty-nine per cent agreed that "the best mark of a person's religiousness is his degree of concern for others." Moreover, they felt that clergymen have an important role to play as moral leaders. Eighty-four per cent felt that "clergymen have a responsibility to speak out as the moral conscience of this nation."

Yet, in spite of this general affirmation of religion as a source of moral strength and concern for others and of clergy as spokesmen on moral issues, a significant proportion rejected a variety of ways in which clergy might actually exercise moral leadership. Fifty per cent of the Protestants felt that "clergymen should stick to religion and not concern themselves with social, economic, and political questions." But as the statements be-

---

[4] Charles Y. Glock, Benjamin B. Ringer, and Earl R. Babbie, *To Comfort and to Challenge* (Berkeley: University of California Press, 1967), p. 171.

[5] Andrew M. Greeley and Peter H. Rossi, *The Education of Catholic Americans* (Chicago: Aldine Publishing Company, 1966), pp. 114–137.

[6] Paul B. Sheatsley, "White Attitudes toward the Negro," *Daedalus*, 95 (Winter, 1966), pp. 217–237.

TABLE 4

Protestant Lay Attitudes toward Involvement of
Clergy in Civil Rights

	Per Cent Agreeing
"The best mark of a person's religiousness is his degree of concern for others."	89
"Clergy have a responsibility to speak out as the moral conscience of this nation."	84
"Clergy should stick to religion and not concern themselves with social, economic, and political questions."	50
"Clergy who participate in demonstrations and picketing do more harm than good for the causes they support."	77
"I would be upset if my minister were to participate in a picket line or demonstration."	77
"Martin Luther King is an outstanding example of making Christianity relevant and meaningful for our day."	27
"I am in basic sympathy with Northern ministers and students who have gone south to work for civil rights."	33

came even more specific as to the nature of involvement, the proportion who disapproved increased to approximately three-quarters. Seventy-seven per cent believed that "clergymen who participate in demonstrations and picketing do more harm than good for the causes they support." The same percentage said that they would be upset if their own minister were to participate in picket lines or demonstrations.

While Martin Luther King, Jr., was widely acclaimed as a responsible civil rights leader, as evidenced by his receipt of the Nobel Peace Prize and the national mourning following his assassination, the large majority of Protestant laity in 1967 had serious reservations about his role as a spiritual leader. Only 27 per cent agreed with the statement, "Martin Luther King is an outstanding example of making Christianity relevant and meaningful for our day."

Interestingly, a somewhat larger proportion, 33 per cent, reported that they were basically sympathetic toward Northern ministers and students who had gone south to work for civil rights. Response to this item varied considerably by region, with only 24 per cent in the South as compared with 45 per cent in the rest of the country reporting sympathy.

This finding suggests that Americans are not nearly so opposed to clergy protesting against the prejudices of others as they are against having the issue brought home. The fact that Dr. King moved into Northern cities in recent years and thus threatened the complacency of Northerners may explain why his approval index was lower than that of clergy who went south and were visible only to Southerners.

This same question was asked of clergy, and again, the comparison of clergy and laity is dramatic. Sixty-five per cent of the clergy were sympathetic toward Northern ministers and students who had gone south to work for civil rights.

INTERPRETATION

These data present a perplexing and troublesome dilemma. The large majority indicate that they believe that concern for others is a good indicator of one's religiousness. Similarly, a large majority assent to the abstract idea that clergy should speak out as the moral conscience of the nation. Yet, in their attitudes toward the civil rights movement and its leadership and in their feelings about clergy involvement, they seem in large part to contradict these general beliefs about the role of religion and the clergy in the achievement of a moral and just society.

A theoretical understanding of this problem was suggested by Myrdal almost a quarter of a century ago in his classic study of race relations, *An American Dilemma*.[7] Myrdal's central thesis is that Americans live with two contradictory belief systems. On the one hand, they believe in the tenets of the "American Creed" which embraces the principles of democracy, equality, and Christian brotherhood. On the other hand, they also hold views about Negroes which are in sharp contrast to these principles. In order to cope with these contradictory beliefs, Myrdal argues, Americans tend to introduce a third set of beliefs, which he calls "mechanisms of rationalization," that have the effect of reducing the inconsistency. More recent developments in social psychology have underscored the theoretical soundness of Myrdal's argument.[8] From this theoretical perspective, it would seem that laymen approve of the general principle that clergy should be moral spokesmen, but they disapprove of the clergyman's involvement in the civil rights struggle precisely because the clergyman's involvement dramatizes the dissonance between the layman's general beliefs about brotherhood and his specific beliefs about Negroes. The clergyman's involvement challenges the layman's mechanisms of rationalization by pointing out the specific ways in which the implications of the Christian faith have not been understood.

SUMMARY

The role of religion in the racial crisis in America has been a topic of increasing public concern. On the one hand is a public awareness of clergy involvement in the struggle. On the other hand, the intensification of the racial crisis during the past few years has caused many to take a critical look at the effect of religion on prejudice. Many social critics are claiming that racial prejudice is no less a problem within the church than outside it. Heretofore, these charges have been largely a matter of speculation.

The data presented here permit several conclusions:

1. Clergy in the six denominations studied are, as a group, sympathetic toward the movement to achieve social justice for Negroes.

2. Clergy, however, are not unanimous in expressing this sentiment. Older clergy and theologically conservative clergy express

[7] Gunnar Mrydal, *An American Dilemma* (New York: Harper & Row, 1944).
[8] See, for example, Leon Festinger, *A Theory of Cognitive Dissonance* (New York: Harper & Row, 1957).

greater prejudicial sentiment than the younger and theologically liberal.

3. Laymen, as a group, express much greater prejudicial sentiment than clergy.

4. The extent of involvement is the life of the church (as measured by frequency of church attendance) does not affect their racial views.

5. Those who never attend church express somewhat less prejudicial sentiment than those who do attend.

6. In general, laity believe that clergy should speak out on moral issues, but specifically, they reject clergy involvement in the civil rights struggle.

These findings, obviously, do not resolve all the questions related to the role of the church in the civil rights struggle. Indeed, they serve to focus attention on a number of additional questions that are extremely important. If clergy and laity are widely divided on the civil rights issue, how is the conflict managed? Do clergy maintain a private and public posture on civil rights, or do they manage to get involved in activities that are more tolerable to their laity than are picketing or protesting? What are the historical antecedents of this conflict? What are the implications of this conflict for the organizational structure and authority of the church? Does the emergence of a new breed of clergy represent hope for reducing prejudice in the churches and society, or will their presence result in intensified internal conflict over the meaning and purpose of the institutional church? Obviously, these questions go beyond the scope of this paper. The data presented here, however, suggest that these are important questions that social scientists should be examining.

A Selected Bibliography on White Reactions to Blacks

Aiken, Michael, and N. J. Demerath, III, "The Politics of Tokenism in the Mississippi Delta," *Trans-action*, 5 (April, 1967), pp. 26–34.

Allport, Gordon W., *The Nature of Prejudice* (Boston: Beacon, 1954).

Baron, Harold M., "Black Powerlessness in Chicago," *Trans-action*, 6 (Nov., 1968), pp. 27–33.

Becker, Gary S., *The Economics of Discrimination* (Chicago: University of Chicago Press, 1957).

Berger, Curtis J., "Law, Justice and the Poor," in *Urban Riots: Violence and Social Change* (New York: Academy of Political Science, 1968).

Blalock, H. M., Jr., "Economic Discrimination and Negro Increase," *American Sociological Review*, 21 (Oct., 1956), pp. 584–588.

Blalock, H. M., Jr., "Occupational Discrimination: Some Theoretical Propositions," *Social Problems*, 9 (Winter, 1962), pp. 240–247.

Blalock, H. M., Jr., "Per cent Non-White and Discrimination," *American Sociological Review*, 22 (Dec., 1957), pp. 677–682.

Blalock, H. M., Jr., "A Power Analysis of Racial Discrimination," *Social Forces*, 39 (Oct., 1960), pp. 53–59.

Blalock, H. M., Jr., *Toward a Theory of Minority Group Relations* (New York: Wiley, 1967).

Bowles, Samuel, "Towards Equality of Educational Opportunity," *Harvard Educational Review*, 38 (Winter, 1968), pp. 89–99.

Brink, William, and Louis Harris, *Black and White: A Study of U.S. Racial Attitudes Today* (New York: Simon and Shuster, 1967).

Broom, Leonard, and Norval D. Glenn, *Transformation of the Negro American* (New York: Harper, 1965).

Campbell, Ernest Q., "Moral Discomfort and Racial Segregation—An Examination of the Myrdal Hypothesis," *Social Forces*, 39 (March, 1961), pp. 228–234.

Cash, Wilbur J., *The Mind of the South* (New York: Knopf, 1941).

Clark, Kenneth B., *Dark Ghetto* (New York: Harper, 1965).

Cloward, Richard A., and Frances Fox Piven, "The Urban Crisis and the Consolidation of National Power," in *Urban Riots: Violence and Social Change* (New York: Academy of Political Science, 1968).

Coleman, A. Lee, "Race Relations and Developmental Change," *Social Forces*, 47 (Sept., 1967), pp. 1–8.

Cox, Oliver C., *Caste, Class and Race* (Garden City: Doubleday, 1948).

Crain, Robert L., *The Politics of School Desegregation: Comparative Case Studies of Community Structure and Policy Making* (Chicago: Aldine, 1967).

Cramer, M. Richard, "School Desegregation and New Industry: The Southern Community Leader's Viewpoint," *Social Forces*, 41 (May, 1963), pp. 384–389.

Curtis, Richard F., Dianne M. Timbers, and Elton F. Jackson, "Prejudice and Urban Social Participation," *American Journal of Sociology*, 73 (Sept., 1967), pp. 235–244.

Davis, Allison, Burleigh B. Gardner, and Mary R. Gardner, *Deep South* (Chicago: University of Chicago Press, 1941).

Deutsch, Morton, and Mary Evans Collins, *Interracial Housing: A Psychological Evaluation of a Social Experiment* (Minneapolis: University of Minnesota Press, 1951).

Dollard, John, *Caste and Class in a Southern Town*, third edition (Garden City: Doubleday, 1957).

Edwards, G. Franklin, "Community and Class Realities: The Ordeal of Change," *Daedalus*, 95 (Winter, 1966), pp. 1–23.

Erskine, Hazel, "The Polls: Demonstrations and Race Riots," *Public Opinion Quarterly*, 31 (Winter, 1967), pp. 655–677.

Erskine, Hazel, "The Polls: Negro Employment," *Public Opinion Quarterly*, 32 (Spring, 1968), pp. 132–153.

Fleming, Walter L., *Documentary History of Reconstruction* (New York: Peter Smith, 1950).

Franklin, John Hope, "History of Racial Segregation in the United States," *Annals of the American Academy of Political and Social Science* (March, 1956), pp. 1–9.

Franklin, John Hope, "The Two Worlds of Race: A Historical View," *Daedalus*, 94 (Fall, 1965), pp. 899–920.

Fukuyama, Yoshio, "Parishioners' Attitudes toward Issues in the Civil Rights Movement," *Sociological Analysis*, 29 (Summer, 1968), pp. 94–103.

Gans, Herbert J., "The Failure of Urban Renewal," *Commentary*, 39 (April, 1965), pp. 29–37.

Gans, Herbert J., "The Ghetto Rebellions and Urban Class Conflict," in *Urban Riots: Violence and Social Change* (New York: Academy of Political Science, 1968).

Ginzberg, Eli (editor), *The Negro Challenge to the Business Community* (New York: McGraw-Hill, 1964).

Ginzberg, Eli, and Alfred S. Eichner, *The Troublesome Presence: American Democracy and the Negro* (New York: Free Press, 1964).

Glenn, Norval D., "The Role of White Resistance and Facilitation in the Negro Struggle for Equality," *Phylon*, 26 (Summer, 1965), pp. 105–116.

Goodman, Mary Ellen, *Race Awareness in Young Children*, revised edition (New York: Collier, 1964).

Gossett, Thomas F., *Race: The History of an Idea in America* (Dallas: Southern Methodist University Press, 1963).

Grimes, Alan P., *Equality in America: Religion, Race and the Urban Majority* (New York: Oxford University Press, 1964).

Grimshaw, Allen D., "Lawlessness and Violence in the United States and Their Special Manifestations in Changing Negro-White Relationships," *Journal of Negro History*, 44 (1959), pp. 52–72.

Grimshaw, Allen D., "Relationships among Prejudice, Discrimination, Social Tension and Social Violence," *Journal of Intergroup Relations,* 2 (1961), pp. 302–310.

Grimshaw, Allen D., "Urban Racial Violence in the United States: Changing Ecological Considerations," *American Journal of Sociology,* 66 (Sept., 1960), pp. 109–119.

Gunterman, Stanley E., "A Bibliography on Violence and Social Change," in *Urban Riots: Violence and Social Change* (New York: Academy of Political Science, 1968).

Hadden, Jeffrey K., and Raymond C. Rymph, "Social Structure and Civil Rights Involvement: A Case Study of Protestant Ministers," *Social Forces,* 45 (Sept., 1966), pp. 51–61.

Handlin, Oscar, *Fire-Bell in the Night: The Crisis in Civil Rights* (Boston: Little, Brown, 1964).

Handlin, Oscar, *Race and Nationality in American Life* (Boston: Little, Brown, 1950).

Harlan, Louis R., *Separate and Unequal: Public School Campaigns and Racism in the Southern Seaboard States, 1901–1915* (Chapel Hill: University of North Carolina Press, 1958).

Harper, Dean, "Aftermath of a Long, Hot Summer," *Trans-action,* 2 (July–August, 1965), pp. 7–11.

Heer, David M., "The Sentiment of White Supremacy: An Ecological Study," *American Journal of Sociology,* 64 (May, 1959), pp. 592–598.

Hesseltine, William B., *The South in American History,* second edition (Englewood Cliffs: Prentice-Hall, 1960).

Hill, Herbert, "Racial Inequality in Employment: The Patterns of Discrimination," *Annals of the American Academy of Political and Social Science,* 357 (Jan., 1965), pp. 30–47.

Hodge, Robert W., and Donald J. Treiman, "Occupational Mobility and Attitudes toward Negroes," *American Sociological Review,* 31 (Feb., 1966), pp. 93–102.

Hyman, Herbert H., and Paul B. Sheatsley, "Attitudes toward Desegregation," *Scientific American,* 195 (Dec., 1956), pp. 35–39.

Hyman, Herbert H., and Paul B. Sheatsley, "Attitudes toward Desegregation—Seven Years Later," *Scientific American,* 211 (July, 1964), pp. 16–23.

Jacobs, Paul, *The State of the Unions* (New York, Atheneum, 1963).

Jacobson, Julius (editor), *The Negro and the American Labor Movement* (Garden City: Doubleday, 1968).

Jenkins, William S., *Pro-Slavery Thought in the Old South* (Gloucester, Mass.: Peter Smith, 1960).

Johnson, David W., "Racial Attitudes of Negro Freedom School Participants and Negro and White Civil Rights Participants," *Social Forces,* 45 (Dec., 1966), pp. 266–273.

Jordan, Winthrop D., *White Over Black: The Development of American Attitudes toward the Negro, 1550–1812* (Chapel Hill: University of North Carolina Press, 1968).

Katz, Shlomo (editor), *Negro and Jew* (New York: Macmillan, 1967).

Killian, Lewis M., and Charles Grigg, *Racial Crisis in America: Leadership in Conflict* (Englewood Cliffs: Prentice-Hall, 1964).

Krueger, A. O., "The Economics of Discrimination," *Journal of Political Economy*, 71 (Oct., 1963), pp. 481–486.

Levy, Burton, "Cops in the Ghetto: A Problem of the Police System," in Louis H. Masotti and Don R. Bowen (editors), *Riots and Rebellion* (Beverly Hills: Sage Publications, 1968).

Lieberson, Stanley, "A Societal Theory of Race and Ethnic Relations," *American Sociological Review*, 26 (Dec., 1961), pp. 902–909.

Logan, Rayford W., *The Negro in the United States: A Brief History* (Princeton: Van Nostrand, 1957).

Maranell, Gary M., "An Examination of Some Religious and Political Attitude Correlates of Bigotry," *Social Forces*, 45 (March, 1967), pp. 356–362.

Marden, Charles F., and Gladys Meyer, *Minorities in American Society*, third edition (New York: American Book, 1968).

Marshall, Ray, "The Negro and Organized Labor," *Journal of Negro Education*, 32 (Fall, 1963), pp. 375–389.

Martin, James G., *The Tolerant Personality* (Detroit: Wayne State University Press, 1964).

Matthews, Donald R., and James W. Prothro, "Southern Racial Attitudes: Conflict, Awareness, and Political Change," *Annals of the American Academy of Political and Social Science*, 344 (Nov., 1962), pp. 108–121.

Meer, Bernard, and Edward Freedman, "The Impact of Negro Neighbors on White Home Owners," *Social Forces*, 45 (Sept., 1966), pp. 11–19.

Mendelson, Wallace, *Discrimination* (Englewood Cliffs: Prentice-Hall, 1962).

Merton, Robert K., *Social Theory and Social Structure* (New York: Free Press, 1957), pp. 131–160.

Middleton, Russell, "The Civil Rights Issue and Presidential Voting among Southern Negroes and Whites," *Social Forces*, 40 (March, 1962), pp. 209–215.

Moore, Barrington, Jr., "Thoughts on Violence and Democracy," in *Urban Riots: Violence and Social Change* (New York: Academy of Political Science, 1968).

Morris, Richard T., and Vincent Jeffries, "Violence Next Door," *Social Forces*, 46 (March, 1968), pp. 352–358.

Myrdal, Gunnar, *An American Dilemma* (New York: Harper, 1944).

Noel, Donald L., and Alphonso Pinkney, "Correlates of Prejudice: Some Racial Differences and Similarities," *American Journal of Sociology*, 69 (May, 1964), pp. 609–622.

Parker, James H., "The Interaction of Negroes and Whites in an Integrated Church Setting," *Social Forces*, 46 (March, 1968), pp. 359–366.

Quinn, Olive Westbrooke, "The Transmission of Racial Attitudes among White Southerners," *Social Forces*, 33 (1954), pp. 41–47.

Rainwater, Lee, "Open Letter on White Justice and the Riots," *Transaction*, 9 (Sept., 1967).

Reimers, David, *White Protestantism and the Negro* (New York: Oxford University Press, 1965).

Rogin, Michael, "Wallace and the Middle Class: The White Backlash in Wisconsin," *Public Opinion Quarterly*, 30 (Spring, 1966), pp. 98–108.

Rose, Peter I., *They and We: Racial and Ethnic Relations in the United States* (New York: Random House, 1964).

Rossi, Peter H., and Robert A. Dentler, *The Politics of Urban Renewal: The Chicago Findings* (New York: Free Press, 1961).

Rudwick, Elliott M., *Race Riot at East St. Louis, July 2, 1917* (Carbondale: Southern Illinois University Press, 1964).

Sheatsley, Paul B., "White Attitudes toward the Negro," *Daedalus*, 95 (Winter, 1966), pp. 217–237.

Silberman, Charles E., *Crisis in Black and White* (New York: Random House, 1964).

Simpson, George E., and J. Milton Yinger, *Racial and Cultural Minorities: An Analysis of Prejudice and Discrimination*, third edition (New York: Harper, 1965).

Singer, Dorothy G., "Reading, Writing, and Race Relations," *Trans-action*, 7 (June, 1967), pp. 27–31.

Stampp, Kenneth M., *The Peculiar Institution: Slavery in the Ante-Bellum South* (New York: Knopf, 1956).

Stember, C., *Education and Attitude Change* (New York: Institute for Human Relations Press, 1961).

Stouffer, Samuel A., *Communism, Conformity and Civil Liberties* (Garden City: Doubleday, 1955).

Sturdivant, Frederick D., "Better Deal for Ghetto Shoppers," *Harvard Business Review*, 46 (March–April, 1968), pp. 130–139.

Tumin, Melvin, *Desegregation: Resistance and Readiness* (Princeton: Princeton University Press, 1958).

Vander Zanden, James W., *American Minority Relations*, second edition (New York: Ronald, 1966).

Vander Zanden, James W., "The Klan Revival," *American Journal of Sociology*, 65 (March, 1960), pp. 456–462.

Vander Zanden, James W., *Race Relations in Transition: The Segregation Crisis within the South* (New York: Random House, 1965).

Vander Zanden, James W., "Voting on Segregationist Referenda," *Public Opinion Quarterly*, 25 (Spring, 1961), pp. 92–105.

Vanfossen, Beth E., "Variables Related to Resistance to Desegregation in the South," *Social Forces*, 47 (September, 1968), pp. 39–44.

Von Eckart, Wolf, "Black Neck in the White Noose," *New Republic*, 149 (Oct. 19, 1963), pp. 14–17.

Weatherford, W. D., *American Churches and the Negro* (Boston: Christopher Publishing House, 1957).

Westie, Frank R., "Racial and Ethnic Relations," in Robert E. L. Faris (editor), *Handbook of Modern Sociology* (Chicago: Rand McNally, 1964).

Whitam, Frederick L., "Subdimensions of Religiosity and Race Prejudice," *Review of Religious Research*, 3 (Spring, 1962), pp. 166–174.

Willhelm, Sidney M., and Edwin H. Powell, "Who Needs the Negro?" *Trans-action*, 1 (Sept.–Oct., 1964), pp. 3–6.

Williams, J. Allen, Jr., "Reduction of Tension through Intergroup Contact: A Social Psychological Interpretation," *Pacific Sociological Review*, 7 (1964), pp. 81–88.

Williams, J. Allen, Jr., and Paul L. Wiener, "A Re-examination of Myrdal's Rank Order of Discriminations," *Social Problems*, 14 (Spring, 1967), pp. 443–454.

Wood, James R., and Mayer N. Zald, "Aspects of Racial Integration in the Methodist Church: Sources of Resistance to Organizational Policy," *Social Forces*, 45 (December, 1966), pp. 255–265.

Williams, Robin M., Jr., with the collaboration of John P. Dean and Edward A. Suchman, *Strangers Next Door: Ethnic Relations in American Communities* (Englewood Cliffs: Prentice-Hall, 1964).

Woodward, C. Vann, *The Strange Career of Jim Crow*, third edition (New York: Galaxy, 1966).

Part III

BLACK RESPONSES
TO WHITE REACTIONS

During the 1960's, a very large proportion of the literature published on black-white relations in the United States has dealt with recent changes in the responses of blacks to discrimination and prejudice. Few social scientists predicted the great increase in black protest early in the decade, although there were theoretical perspectives in sociology, social psychology, and political science that would have allowed relatively accurate prediction. But once the increase occurred, social scientific analyses of it abounded, and few serious students of black-white relations failed to predict the developments of the middle and late 1960's, including the escalation of ghetto violence and the renunciation of the goal of integration by many blacks.

The articles in this section are representative of recent publications on this topic. They demonstrate how much progress social scientists have recently made toward understanding black protest and similar activities, but they also demonstrate how much is left to be understood. The reader will soon learn that several of the contributions which follow raise more questions than they answer.

Much literature on recent black protest activity suffers from a lack of historical perspective, with the consequence that current conditions and recent developments are often misunderstood and misinterpreted. Although the contributions in this anthology generally do not suffer from this defect, the lay reader needs greater knowledge of the background of recent developments than most of these papers give. "The Historical Development of the Black Protest Movement," by Bryan T. Downes and Stephen W. Burks, should help to provide the needed perspective. The authors' primary task is to describe rather than to explain, and therefore they do not attempt to deal with all the social, cultural, demographic, and economic changes in society as a whole that would have to be used to explain fully the origin and evolution of black protest in the United States. Nevertheless, their description yields clues as to reasons for recent developments. They also discuss in some detail the present state of relations between blacks and whites in the United States and predict some trends and developments.

"Social Structure and the Negro Revolt: An Examination of Some Hypotheses," by James A. Geschwender, is one of the better attempts to explain the increase in black protest. Each hypothesis examined by Geschwender has been treated at greater length by other authors, but Geschwender is the only one who has examined all of them and weighed their relative explanatory utility in one concise article. He concludes that the hypotheses based on the concept of relative deprivation are best supported by his data.

Some Negroes have devoted more time and energy to protest activity than others, and many studies have been conducted to explain this variation. Two of these are reported in "Class and Status Bases of Negro Protest" by Anthony and Amy Orum, and "Religion: Opiate or Inspiration of Civil Rights Militancy among Negroes," by Gary T. Marx.

The Orums test some of the same hypotheses tested (in contribution 25) by Geschwender, but they use attitudinal as well as demographic data and study only a sample of college seniors. In contrast to Geschwender's data, their findings support none of the hypotheses, but on the other hand, neither do they refute any. Whereas earlier studies found that Negro college students from the higher social levels were more likely to participate in protest activities, the Orums found no relationship between social level and participation in civil-rights action. Furthermore, they found that the students who perceived the greatest amount of discrimination were the least likely to participate. These findings indicate that some currently popular theories used to explain protest activity need modification and refinement.

Gary T. Marx is concerned with the relationship of religion to blacks' tendency to engage in protest activities. An earlier Marx, Karl, claimed that religion is an opiate to oppressed people that inhibits collective action to better their conditions. More recently, scholars have suggested that the religiosity of rural southern blacks in the United States and the anticipation of a glorious afterlife it provides diverts attention from worldly conditions and encourages a submissive posture *vis-à-vis* whites. The study by Marx indicates that this impression is correct, in that otherworldly religiosity and civil-rights militancy are found to be inversely related. However, he emphasizes that the effects of religion on black responses to subordination have not been simple and have not been always in one direction. At present, for instance, a "temporal" kind of religiosity seems at least not to inhibit protest, and it may often facilitate it.

In "Negro Political Strategy: Coalition or Independent Power Politics," Harry Holloway points out that Negro political activity has increased substantially in the past few years but that the Negro political potential has not nearly been realized. In spite of some disillusionment among blacks with the political approach to Negro advancement,[1] political responses to domination are likely to remain a salient aspect of the Negro struggle for equality. However, Holloway points out some inherent limitations of black politics. He examines, through case studies of Atlanta, Houston, and Memphis, three types of political strategy: a coalition with conservatives, a coalition with liberals, and independent power politics. Without some kind of coalition, the Negroes have less political power, but in both kinds of coalitions, whites dominated the blacks.

Contributions 29, 30, and 31 treat a type of black response that historically was rare but which has become increasingly frequent since 1964. Until the last few years, violent responses from blacks were either by isolated individuals or else were directly provoked by white attacks. Recently, however, collective black violence, not so obviously provoked by white violence, has become more common.[2]

Most social scientists who have studied the violence in urban black ghettos in the 1960's have observed that the outbreaks differed in several respects from earlier "race riots" in the United States, and some have claimed that they were not riots at all, strictly speaking, but rather were insurrections. (Many political activists in the "New Left" also hold this view.) To these scholars, the outbreaks were purposeful, deliberate efforts to effect social change. However, there is considerable disagreement concerning the extent to which the violent behavior was instrumental and goal-directed and the extent to which it was merely expressive—a release of hostile impulses generated by the frustrations of ghetto life. The scholars who have viewed the violence from a conventional "collective-behavior" perspective have tended to view the outbreaks as almost entirely expressive and irrational. In "Civil Rights Protests and Riots: A Disappearing Distinction," James A. Geschwender maintains that since 1964 the outbreaks have become more purposeful and less completely expressive (although he does not term them insurrections) and have become "creative violence"—an instrument of the civil-rights movement.

[1] See Jewel Prestage, "Black Politics and the Kerner Report: Concerns and Directions," contribution 41 in this anthology.

[2] To be sure, the recent ghetto riots were usually precipitated by some kind of white action, ranging from the assassination of Martin Luther King to a real or alleged case of police brutality. However, the black violence was not usually caused by white attacks on the black rioters.

David O. Sears and T. M. Tomlinson, in "Riot Ideology in Los Angeles: A Study of Negro Attitudes," present evidence that supports Geschwender's conclusion. They found that a substantial proportion, although not a majority, of the residents in the area where the 1965 violence occurred approved of it, and a majority said that the violence had a purpose or goal, that it was Negro protest, and that its targets deserved to be attacked. Furthermore, more of the residents thought it helped the Negro cause than thought hurt it.

Although most social scientists who addressed themselves to black violence in the early 1960's anticipated the increase in outbreaks during the latter part of the decade, they were less able to predict where the violence would occur. Although the probability of outbreaks has been high in all cities with large ghettos, the cities experiencing the major disruptions have not differed conspicuously from the others in their economic, demographic, and political characteristics. Some observers have suggested that the random occurrence of precipitating events or incidents has largely determined where the violence has occurred. However, careful study has shown that the occurrence of violence was not random and that the riot cities differed on the average from the nonriot cities in several respects. In "The Social and Political Characteristics of Riot Cities: A Comparative Study," Bryan T. Downes reports that riot cities generally had larger and more dense populations, a higher proportion of nonwhites, more rapidly growing nonwhite populations, lower median educational attainments, lower median family incomes, higher unemployment rates, and higher proportions of their workers in blue-collar jobs. These same characteristics were generally correlated with the intensity of the hostile outbreaks in the riot cities.

Downes's analysis is only a needed first step, and he indicates his intentions to proceed to more sophisticated analyses. Without data on the intercorrelations among the characteristics associated with violence, it is impossible to determine their probable causal importance. For instance, low median incomes and low educational attainments may be associated with violent outbursts only because they are also associated with percent nonwhite. Furthermore, the reader must be cautioned in regard to the ecological fallacy—that is, he should not equate these data for population aggregates (cities) with data for individuals. Although riots are more likely to occur in cities with low median incomes and low educational attainments, the ghetto residents most likely to engage in violence are not those with the lowest incomes and least education.[3] Additionally, although riots are more likely to occur in cities with rapidly growing nonwhite populations, migrant blacks are less likely to participate in violence than lifelong residents of the cities.

One of the more conspicuous developments in the black protest movement during the middle and late 1960's has been the emergence of "black-power" ideology and similar orientations, such as that of the Black Pan-

---

[3] See the *Report of the National Advisory Commission on Civil Disorders* (Washington: United States Government Printing Office, 1968), pp. 73–77. The summary of this report is included as contribution 33 of this anthology.

thers. In general, white liberals, committed to the ideals of integration and interracial harmony, have reacted to the concept of "black power" with disillusionment and perhaps no small amount of fear. As whites have been expelled from roles of policymaking and leadership in the Student Nonviolent Coordinating Committee, many have felt rejected by those they were trying to help.

Joyce Ladner, in "What Black Power Means to Negroes in Mississippi," explains some reasons for the black-power movement and some benefits that are to be gained from it. She emphasizes that blacks cannot gain self-respect and a feeling of true equality as long as they are subordinated to whites—even in the black protest movement. Her views are consistent with the conclusion recently made by several black leaders (as well as by several social scientists) that a temporary separation of blacks and whites in some spheres of activity may be necessary before much greater integration can be achieved.[4]

A large body of literature deals with the effects of Negro-white interaction on the attitudes of whites toward Negroes. In "The Prejudice-Interaction Hypothesis from the Point of View of the Negro Minority," Ernest Works reports the findings of a study of the effects of interracial interaction on the attitudes of Negroes toward whites. In general, living in integrated housing seems to have the same effect on Negroes as on whites. Members of each race seem to develop more favorable attitudes toward the other, although undoubtedly there are circumstances in which living in integrated housing would not have this effect.

If recent developments in black-white relations have dismayed those whites active in the civil-rights movement, they have obviously created even more consternation among more conservative whites. Especially to the latter, the increase in racial conflict constitutes a "deterioration" of race relations. However, in "The Functions of Racial Conflict," Joseph Himes suggests that the conflict has and will have many beneficial consequences to black Americans, especially in the long run. He maintains that it has strengthened the in-group identity of blacks and may eventually lead to greater identification with the larger social system. Other observers agree with Himes and would add that conflict, perhaps violent conflict, is the inevitable cost of significant black progress in United States society. Many blacks are now willing to risk the costs, and much of the recent disunity between blacks and white liberals grows out of the fact that the latter tend to value peace and harmony more than they value black advancement.

[4] From a historical perspective, a similar interpretation is suggested by Eighmy in contribution 22 of this anthology.

24

The Historical Development of the Black Protest Movement*

BRYAN T. DOWNES
MICHIGAN STATE UNIVERSITY

STEPHEN W. BURKS
MICHIGAN STATE UNIVERSITY

Of THE VARIOUS FORMS OF BLACK PROTEST WHICH HAVE EVOLVED IN THE last decade, nonviolent direct action or "creative disorder"[1] has been one of the most widespread, disruptive, and successful. First used in the Montgomery Bus Boycott of 1955, direct action gained real momentum in the late 1950's and early 1960's with the development of a sustained and determined effort to desegregate nonviolently all public facilities, particularly in the South. However, growing out of this more militant direct action strategy has been a violent "Black Revolt." Although this black revolt has been basically anomic and unorganized, at least until the summer of 1968, it has become an integral part of the black protest movement and is being perceived by a growing number of blacks (and whites) as a legitimate means for increasing the rate of social and political change.[2]

The marked change in the nature of the black protest movement since the Birmingham riot of 1963 is indicated most dramatically by the fact that between January 1, 1964 and January 1, 1968 there were more than 200 separate instances of racial violence.[3] These ranged in intensity from minor clashes between groups of Negroes and whites to the major conflagations of Watts, Newark, and Detroit. In each year since 1964, the number of such incidents has increased, and in each year the amount of economic loss due to looting and arson has also increased. The resort to violence by black Americans is thus an indication of the change which

---

* First published in this volume. The authors are indebted to the Political Science Department of Michigan State University for support. Portions of this paper have been drawn from "The Black Protest Movement and Urban Violence," a paper prepared for delivery at the 1968 Annual Meeting of the American Political Science Association, Washington, D.C., September, 1968.

[1] For a discussion of the meaning of this term see: Arthur I. Waskow, *From Race Riot to Sit-In, 1919 and the 1960's* (Garden City: Doubleday, 1966), pp. 276–290.

[2] For a discussion of these attitudes see: William Brink and Louis Harris, *Black and White: A Study of U.S. Racial Attitudes Today* (New York: Simon and Schuster, 1966); and Angus Campbell and Howard Schuman, "Racial Attitudes in Fifteen American Cities," in *Supplemental Studies for the National Advisory Commission on Civil Disorders* (Washington, D. C.: United States Government Printing Office, July, 1968), pp. 1–67.

[3] See the discussion in: Bryan T. Downes, "The Black Protest Movement." See also: Daniel C. Thompson, "The Rise of the Negro Protest," in Arnold M. Rose (ed.), *The Negro Protest, The Annals*, vol. 357 (January, 1965), p. 18. Other articles in this issue of *The Annals* provide a great deal of interesting information on the black protest movement.

has taken place in the tactics and general philosophy of the Negro protest movement. These bear further discussion.

THE HISTORICAL PERIODS

Most Americans feel that miltant civil-rights activity began with the Supreme Court desegregation decision (*Brown v. Board of Education*) of 1954. If one examines the historical experience of the Negro, however, it is apparent that the present period of protest is the most recent phase in a reform-oriented movement which began several hundred years ago.[4] It simply represents a more vigorous continuation of earlier protest activity on the part of Negroes.

In this paper it is our purpose to briefly describe the development of the black protest movement from the period of slavery to the present. We discuss six major periods in race relations in the United States, the social forces which defined them, and the types of violence which characterized each period. In so doing we are attempting to place current racial violence in a somewhat broader historical perspective by indicating how it is only the most recent phase in a much older struggle for racial equality.

Although our classification scheme is somewhat arbitrary, the history of Negro protest activity can be broken down into six rather distinct periods: (1) Slavery, Subjugation, and Resistance, 1610–1860; (2) Civil War and Reconstruction, 1861–1877; (3) Repression and Segregation, 1878–1914; (4) Two World Wars, the Depression and Racial Readjustment, 1915–1945; (5) Consolidation and Change, 1946–1954; and (6) Creative Disorder, Militancy, and the Resurgence of Racial Violence, 1955–1968.[5]

SLAVERY, SUBJUGATION, AND RESISTANCE (1610–1860)

The position in which the Negro was placed when first brought to the United States from Africa in 1610, and the systematic and brutal perpetuation of that position until 1860, represents a unique period in the history of race relations. Never before had such a large group of people been so thoroughly subjugated for such a long period with such permanent effects. Today we are still reaping the consequences of the racial attitudes,

[4] For example see: Benjamin Quarles, *The Negro in the Making of America* (New York: Collier Books, 1964); Samuel Lubell, *White and Black: Test of a Nation* (New York: Harper and Row, 1964); Charles E. Silberman, *Crisis in Black and White* (New York: Random House, 1964); Louis E. Lomax, *The Negro Revolt* (New York: Signet Books, 1962); *Report of the National Advisory Commission on Civil Disorders* (New York: Bantam Books, 1968); Joanne Grant (ed.), *Black Protest: History, Documents, and Analyses, 1619 to the Present* (Greenwick, Conn.: Fawcett Publications, 1968); C. Eric Lincoln, "The American Protest Movement for Negro Rights," in John P. Davis (ed.), *The American Negro Reference Book* (Englewood Cliffs: Prentice-Hall, 1966), pp. 458–483; and Waskow, *From Race Riot to Sit-In*.

[5] This classification draws heavily upon: Allen D. Grimshaw, "Lawlessness and Violence in America and Their Special Manifestations in Changing Negro-White Relationships," *Journal of Negro History*, vol. 64, no. 1 (January, 1959), pp. 52–72. See also the discussion of various books written about these periods in: John Hope Franklin, "Rediscovering Black America: A Historical Roundup," *The New York Times Book Review* (September 8, 1968), pp. 48, 50, 52.

fears, and behavioral patterns which were engendered during that period.[6]

The period of slavery in America was not as thoroughly dominated by racial concerns as is commonly believed. Although slave rebellions and other forms of violent and nonviolent protest by Negroes forced whites to maintain a harsh system of order, interracial violence was initially interpreted less in racial than in class or social terms, particularly in terms of the master-servant relationship. During the period from 1610 to approximately 1800 the Negro was treated more like an economic commodity, as a servile class, than as a distinct racial group presenting a threat to the existing social order. Oppression was based more on the principle of "minimizing one's return on an investment" than on racial considerations.[7]

However, during the early 1800's the relationship between Negroes and whites, particularly in the South, began to take on increasingly racial overtones. This stemmed from two developments. First, the ratio of blacks to whites had reached the point in some Southern states where widespread insurrection represented a real threat. As the black slave's real or imagined ability to disrupt the system increased, so did the importance which whites attached to "keeping him in his place." The second development is what Kenneth B. Clark refers to as "moral schizophrenia," the basic incompatibility between the practical need for slave labor in the South on the cotton plantations and the moral aspects of black servitude.[8]

As some white Northerners began to challenge the legitimacy of slavery, white Southerners reacted by enforcing the system even more strongly. Slave protests, in turn, assumed a distinctly racial character. The rebellions led by Gabriel Prosser in 1800, Denmark Vesey in 1822, and Nat Turner in 1831, the best known and most successful slave revolts of the period, were all generalized attacks on white people rather than specific attacks on particular repressive slave owners.[9] The attacks, however, were indicative of the growing strains within the South between the two races, strains which ultimately culminated in the Civil War.

In the North support for the Negro cause was by no means uniform. The few liberals and intellectuals who had brought the issue of slavery to the attention of the nation were in most instances simply challenging the legality of slavery and not the premise of racial inferiority upon which it rested. Although Negroes were not numerous in the North and therefore did not arouse the degree of uneasiness and dread among whites as they did in the slave states, the North was no paradise for blacks. Benja-

[6] For example, see the text of the report on the Negro family prepared by Daniel P. Moynihan in: Lee Rainwater and William Yancey, *The Moynihan Report and the Politics of Controversy* (Cambridge: M.I.T. Press, 1967).

[7] See the discussion in: Benjamin Quarles, *The Negro*, pp. 15–61.

[8] Discussed in: Mary H. Hall, "A Conversation with Kenneth B. Clark, *Psychology Today* (June, 1968), pp. 19–25.

[9] See the discussion of these revolts in: Herbert Aptheker, *American Negro Slave Revolts* (New York: Columbia University Press, 1943). Aptheker documents some 250 slave conspiracies and revolts, some dating back to colonial times.

min Quarles notes that even though "by 1830 slavery had been virtually abolished in the North, the Negro bore the indelible mark of a degraded inferior; he was regarded as a threat to the general welfare, if not an outright liability."[10] Many Northerners, particularly the increasing number of European immigrants who had recently settled in the cities, perceived blacks as a direct threat to their precarious economic situation and were generally unreceptive to the idea of a major confrontation between North and South over the issue of slavery. So too were most political leaders, including Abraham Lincoln. Their solution to the growing problem of the increased antagonism between the races was either to ship Negroes back to Africa or give them a separate state in the West.

Thus, as was the case in the South, conflicts between whites and blacks in the North were increasingly interpreted in racial terms, with fear of economic competition from Negro migrants being an important determinant of early racial conflict. Furthermore, racial violence did break out in various Northern cities in the 1830's, and again in 1863 when the Irish in New York precipitated a pogrom against Negroes. This outburst of violence resulted in hundreds of Negroes being killed and businesses and homes being burned by Irish-Americans who were enraged at being conscripted to fight in a war to free Negroes while Negroes stayed at home.[11] In total, these incidents were indicative of the ambivalence of many Northerners on the race question, and of how little the Civil War would alleviate basic racial antagonisms in the North.

CIVIL WAR AND RECONSTRUCTION (1861–1877)

If the Civil War served to settle permanently the issue of slavery in the United States, it only aggravated the growing hostility between the races.[12] In Northern cities, the poor, who felt their jobs and housing most directly threatened by Negroes, were forced to fight a war they did not support. In both armies, Negro soldiers were treated more as obstacles to victory than as the central group over whom the war was being fought. In fact blacks were not allowed to enlist in the northern army until manpower shortages forced conscription measures to be enacted. In the South slaves were used only as military laborers.[13] Furthermore, the devastation caused by the war in the South only broadened and intensified the antagonisms of whites toward blacks. Thus by the end of this period the relationship between whites and blacks would be clearly defined in interracial terms with interclass concerns becoming secondary.

The punitive nature of Reconstruction in the South completed the polarization process begun by the war. The well-known excesses of the "carpetbaggers" in exacting tribute from the defeated Southerners, coupled with the "instant enfranchisement" of tens of thousands of former slaves, and

---

[10] Quarles, *The Negro*, p. 92.
[11] Waskow, *From Race Riot to Sit-In*, p. 9. These figures differ quite sharply from those presented in Grimshaw, *op. cit.*, p. 60.
[12] *Ibid.*, pp. 59–63.
[13] Quarles, *The Negro*, pp. 109–125.

the political confusion which resulted, served only to reinforce the Southerner's belief that the Negro was incapable of governing himself.

With the issue of slavery successfully resolved, Negro leaders now focused their attention on the economic and social inequities which prevented their people from exercising their new freedom. Numerous Negro organizations sprang up throughout the country to discuss ways of combattling discrimination, but by the late 1870's the country had shifted its attention elsewhere, and attempts to bring about social change through channels of organized protest went largely unheeded.

REPRESSION AND SEGREGATION (1878–1914)

Given the bitterness of white southerners over losing the War and over the vindictive way in which Reconstruction was carried out, one could have expected a wave of retaliation to occur throughout the South when federal troops were withdrawn in 1877.[14] Surprisingly, however, the 1880's was a period of comparative racial calm. A wave of populism in the country was able to refocus racial conflict temporarily along class lines. Negroes and poor white farmers forged an uneasy alliance against the "common enemy," the wealthy capitalistic aristocracy. With the decline of populism in the 1890's this alliance quickly dissolved. Poor whites, seeking a scapegoat, blamed the Negro for the downfall of the movement and once again insisted on their social superiority over the Negro. The stage was set for the reinstitution of white supremacy in the South.

The preoccupation of the North with the problems of industrialization and the unwillingness of Southern state governments to enforce the new legal rights of Negroes created a situation in which the Negro in the South was systematically deprived of the political, social, and legal gains he had made as a result of the Civil War and Reconstruction. These changes were institutionalized in the form of "Jim Crow," or segregation laws, which effectively returned the Negro to a condition of servitude in the South. Although at first southern states had hesitantly begun to enact segregation laws, such policies were given national sanction in 1896 with the *Plessy v. Ferguson* decision of the United States Supreme Court. With this decision, the "separate but equal" doctrine became national policy, and this policy was to remain largely unaltered for 58 years.

The institutionalization of segregation was accompanied by a wave of terror, by whites against blacks.[15] Lynchings became a common method used by white supremacists to "keep the nigger in his place," with over 1100 lynchings occurring between 1900 and 1915. With little hope of improving his life in the South, the Negro began to look northward for new opportunities in the rapidly industrializing cities. The migration of blacks northward began after the Civil War, and by the turn of the century sizable Negro populations lived in many large Northern cities. According to the President's Commission on Civil Disorders, "the movement

---

[14] *Ibid.*, pp. 109–155; and Grimshaw, *op. cit.*, pp. 63–65.

[15] *Ibid.*, p. 64. See also the discussion in: Waskow, *From Race Riot to Sit-In*, pp. 105–142.

of Negroes out of the rural South accelerated during World War I, when floods and boll weevils hurt farming in the South, and the industrial demands of the war created thousands of new jobs for unskilled workers in the North."[16] For example, during the period 1910 to 1920, 454,000 blacks left the South. However, 91 percent of the nation's 9.8 million Negroes still lived in the South in 1910 and only 27 percent of American Negroes lived in cities of 2,500 persons or more, as compared to 48 percent of the nation's white population.[17] Although the number of blacks leaving the South and migrating northward appears small when compared to the 14.5 million whites who immigrated from Europe from 1901 to 1920, white intimidation in the South expanded to include not only the enforcement of segregation but also the prevention of "escape" to the North. Many Southerners felt that continued migration of blacks would ultimately lead to a depleted labor force and pose a threat to the agrarian economy of the South.

Analyses of the Negro protest movement during the late 1800's and early 1900's generally focus on the influence of the two most eminent Negro leaders of the period, Booker T. Washington and W. E. B. DuBois. Although Washington's and DuBois's philosophies toward protest were quite different, each assumed the stewardship of the Negro cause at a time in history when the objective situation and the "mood" of the Negro were conducive to their respective appeals. To study either man independently of this broader context is to give undue credit (or blame) to his influence on history.

Washington's conservative accommodationist philosophy placed primary emphasis on individual self-improvement and character building. Through patience and persistence, according to Washington, any Negro could learn those occupational and social skills which would make him acceptable to white society. Diligence and acceptance of white guidance were prerequisites to this end. This approach represented a very pragmatic attempt to change the objective situation of the Negro in both the North and South, particularly the latter. In fact it has been argued that Washington became the preeminent leader of this period precisely because he espoused the only realistic mode of adaptation to that situation.

In contrast, DuBois's "radical" philosophy grew out of anger and indignation over the degraded position of the Negro in American society. Emphasizing racial pride and solidarity, DuBois called for active protest against segregation, discrimination, and violence against blacks. During this period, however, DuBois was never able to generate the necessary support to challenge existing institutions successfully.

Booker T. Washington's career coincided with the abandonment of Reconstruction and the institutionalization of segregation throughout the South. An ex-slave whose early life was marked by adversity, he had educated himself and risen to the presidency of the leading Negro college in the country, Tuskegee Institute. Washington was thus one of a small

---

[16] *Report of the National Advisory Commission on Civil Disorders*, p. 239.
[17] *Ibid.*

Negro élite regularly consulted by whites on matters of race relations. It was in a speech at the Atlanta Exposition of 1895 that Washington attained nationwide prominence. To a largely white audience, he characterized his race as "the most patient, faithful, law-abiding, and unresentful people that the world has even seen," and the appealed to whites to assist Negroes in bettering their condition.[18] On the other hand, he exhorted his followers to till the soil and obediently learn the ways of the white man as a means of improving their lives. In dealing with the growing issue of segregation, he concluded with the now famous phrase:[19]

In all things that are purely social we can be as separate as the five fingers, yet one as the hand in all things essential to mutual progress.

The Atlanta compromise, as it came to be called, was acclaimed as a practical, moderate program for Negro advancement. Perhaps more importantly, it provided psychological reassurance to whites that Negroes themselves supported segregation. Washington found himself courted by the nation's most powerful industrial and political figures, and he skillfully parlayed this support into an almost impregnable position of leadership over the Negro movement. It is said that at the height of his power, every Negro appointment of any significance in the federal government was cleared through him. Further, he had an important influence on the nature and direction of philanthropic support to Negro business and educational enterprises.[20]

Because of his access to powerful whites, his support among a growing Negro middle class, and the absence, at least in the early 1900's of an effective counterforce of disillusioned and angry blacks, Washington was able to influence the relatively peaceful and accommodating form which the Negro protest movement took during this period. According to John Hope Franklin, however, as Washington became not only the leading exponent of industrial education for blacks but also the spokesman for millions of Negroes, opposition among his own people increased.[21] A small group of men began to take serious exception both to the point of view of the Washington approach and to the techniques employed to elevate his people. Foremost among such opponents was W. E. B. DuBois.

Born and raised in a small Massachusetts town, free of slavery and relatively untouched by discrimination, DuBois grew up without experiencing many of the hardships that had characterized Washington's youth. Intellectually gifted, he attended Fisk and Harvard Universities, and returned after a period of study in Europe to receive the first Ph.D. awarded by Harvard to a Negro. Background, education, and travel thus com-

[18] Booker T. Washington, "A Moderate Negro View," in Leslie H. Fishel, Jr. and Benjamin Quarles (eds.), *The Negro American, A Documentary History* (Glenview, Illinois: Scott, Foresman, 1967), p. 343.

[19] *Ibid.*, p. 344.

[20] Quarles, *The Negro*, pp. 166–172. See also: John Hope Franklin, *From Slavery to Freedom: A History of Negro Americans* (New York: Alfred A. Knopf, 1967), pp. 382–412; and E. Franklin Frazier, *The Negro in the United States* (New York: Macmillan, 1957), pp. 540–563.

[21] Franklin, *From Slavery*, p. 393.

bined to produce a militant intellectual who rebelled against racial subservience.

DuBois was a self-proclaimed aristocrat, and he called upon the "talented tenth" of the Negro population to unite and provide active leadership in opposition to racial discrimination. In 1905 he and a group of prominent Negro intellectuals formed the Niagara Movement, an effort to draw attention to the dangers of accommodationism and to provide a base for greater militancy in Negro protest activity. His speech at the first convention of this group reflected this mood:[22]

We want full manhood suffrage and want it now. . . . We want discrimination in public accommodations to cease. . . . We want the Constitution of the country enforced. . . . We want our children educated. . . . We are Men! We will be treated as men. And we shall win.

Although it continued to meet for a number of years, the Niagara Movement failed to develop widespread support. Faced with growing debts, it began to break apart in 1909.

It was during the same year that a group of white liberals, alarmed at the growing rate of lynchings and generalized violence against Negroes, formed the National Negro Committee. The Committee's comparatively militant position toward the protection of Negro rights made it a logical ally of the Niagara Movement, and the two merged in 1910 to become the National Association for the Advancement of Colored People (NAACP). DuBois was appointed managing editor of its magazine, *Crisis*. He aggressively expanded its circulation to 22,000 by 1912, 35,000 by 1915, and 104,000 by 1919.[23] Finally provided with a solid financial base and a vehicle for the expression of his beliefs, DuBois boldly challenged Washington's philosophy with attacks on segregation and ridicule of accommodationism. While DuBois's influence never equaled that of Washington, the latter's career was on the decline until his death in 1915.[24] DuBois and the NAACP now became the dominant force in Negro protest.

Since its inception, the NAACP has been the backbone of the Negro protest movement.[25] Utilizing the channels of "litigation, legislation, and education," it has figured prominently in such important civil rights advances as *Brown v. Board of Education* (the Supreme Court decision of 1954 which overturned the "separate but equal" doctrine) and the 1964 and 1965 Civil Rights Acts. Another area in which it has been instrumental in protecting Negro rights has been in providing financial and legal assistance to Negroes arrested during demonstrations and incidents of racial violence. With its professional staff, solid financial base, and reputation for responsible protest, the NAACP has traditionally been recognized as the most legitimate spokesman for the Negro protest movement. Nonethe-

[22] Lincoln, *op. cit.*, p. 465.

[23] Francis L. Broderick, "W. E. B. DuBois: Entente with White Liberals, 1910–1920," in Melvin Drummer (ed.), *Black History: A Reappraisal* (Garden City. Doubleday, 1968), p. 366.

[24] August Meier, "Booker T. Washington: An Interpretation," *Ibid.*, pp. 338–355.

[25] Lincoln, *op. cit.*, pp. 465–467.

less, its biracial composition and moderate, legalistic orientation has restricted the amount of influence it has had on the Negro masses, particularly younger Negroes living in urban ghettos.[26]

When Negroes moved from the rural South to Northern cities they encountered many new problems, such as poor jobs, housing, education, and health conditions. As the influx of migrants increased through the "pull" of wartime job opportunities and the "push" of "Jim Crow" or segregation laws, these problems grew. In order to assist blacks in more effectively making the adjustment of urban living, the National League on Urban Conditions among Negroes was formed in 1911, and soon after became known as the Urban League.[27]

The Urban League has traditionally limited its activities to improving conditions of Negroes living in cities by helping them find jobs and housing and in adjusting to the unfamiliar urban milieu. In its moderate, middle-class, biracial composition and nonmilitant orientation, the Urban League is similar to the NAACP. The two organizations have worked together and have become leaders of the more traditional or conservative wing of the Negro protest movement.

Two World Wars, the Depression, and Racial Readjustment (1915–1945)

The Depression slowed the migration of blacks northward, but the migratory flow was set in motion again by World War II. From 1910 to 1950 the number of blacks living outside the South increased from 1,899,654 to 5,989,543.[28] As Table 1 indicates, this change meant that by 1950 about 32 percent of all Negroes lived outside the South. This migration created as many new problems for the Negro as it solved. Congested ghettos replaced rural shacks, sweat shops replaced the cotton fields, and uniformed police replaced the night-riding lynching vigilantes.

This movement of blacks northward also had a significant effect on the development of the Negro protest movement. Heavily concentrated in ghetto areas, Negroes now gained a potential for mass action which they had not known in the rural South. In the period 1910–1920, a number of factors combined to trigger this potential.[29] First, many cities were simply not able to absorb the large influx of Negroes. Blacks spilled over ghetto boundaries, confronting and displacing whites, increasing the hostility between the two groups. Second, unemployment and job insecurity were high, particularly after the economic cutback following World War I. Competition for jobs took on an increasingly racial tone. Third, by Presi-

[26] John A. Morsell, "The National Association for the Advancement of Colored People and Its Strategy," in Rose (ed.), *The Negro Protest*, pp. 97–101.

[27] Whitney M. Young, Jr., "The Urban League and Its Strategy," *Ibid.*, pp. 102–107. Young has recently "embraced" the idea of black power in a sharp reversal of his previous position.

[28] See the discussion of this period in: Lubell, *White and Black: Test of a Nation* (New York: Harper and Row, 1964), pp. 34–49; and Quarles, *The Negro*, pp. 156–214.

[29] Waskow, *From Race Riot to Sit-In*. See also: Elliott M. Rudwick, *Race Riot at East St. Louis July 2, 1917* (Cleveland: Meridian Books, 1964).

Table 1

Rise in Negroes Outside the South*

Year	Percent of Total Negro Population	Number of Negroes Outside the South
1900	10	1,647,377
1910	11	1,899,654
1920	15	2,407,371
1930	21	3,483,746
1940	23	3,986,606
1950	32	5,989,543
1960	40	9,009,470
1966**	45	9,700,000

* Source: Samuel Lubell, *White and Black*, p. 36.
** Source: *Report of the National Advisory Commission on Civil Disorders* (New York: Bantam Books, 1968), p. 239.

dential order, segregation was adopted by all federal agencies as official policy, removing the one area in which Negroes had been able to make significant advances after the Civil War. This action rapidly accelerated the diffusion of segregationist policies throughout American society. Fourth, participation in World War I gave thousands of Negroes an exposure to foreign cultures which made them aware of the glaring inequities and injustices in their own system. Rigid segregationist practices and assignment to only the most menial tasks while in military service only served to heighten the bitterness of blacks. Fifth, the maintenance of a large standing army following World War I kept sizeable concentrations of battle-oriented white troops on bases near major cities, and thus near ghetto areas, increasing the probability of racial incidents. Finally, law enforcement agencies were openly discriminating in their treatment of blacks, and in the absence of protection from either civilian or military police Negroes were forced to protect their own rights.

In 1919, racial violence erupted in twenty-seven cities throughout the country.[30] Seven of these were considered full-scale riots in which large numbers of whites and blacks engaged in open warfare against each other. These violent hostile outbursts occurred between May 19 and September 30 in Charleston, South Carolina; Longview, Texas; Washington, D.C.; Chicago, Illinois; Knoxville, Tennessee; Omaha, Nebraska; and Philips County, Arkansas. These outbursts represented the first time that large numbers of blacks fought back against whites and even took the initiative in attacking whites. This was quite different from the pattern of many earlier hostile outbursts, such as the one which occurred in New York in 1863. In these "southern-style riots" or pogroms, whites invaded Negro neighborhoods, attacking, killing, and burning, with blacks offering little or no resistance.[31]

[30] Waskow, *From Race Riot to Sit-In*, pp. 1–218.
[31] Grimshaw, *op. cit.*, pp. 67–68.

Surprisingly, the outbursts of 1919 were the last extensive incidents of collective violence to occur for almost twenty-four years. Although a large riot did occur in 1935 in Harlem (New York City) and smaller incidents were recorded throughout the period, it was not until 1943 that extensive racial violence broke out again, this time in Harlem and Detroit.[32] All of these hostile outbursts were basically urban phenomena with the most violent ones occurring during or just at the close of one of the world wars. Why the violent outbursts of 1919 and 1943 were not followed by increasing number of incidents of racial violence, as current outbursts have tended to be, is unclear. Perhaps, as James Q. Wilson has observed in a recent *New York Times* article, "the climate of opinion, the mood of a generation, or the drift of sentiments," were not right.[33] Others have attributed the lack of further outbursts to mediating efforts of the NAACP, the Urban League, and other such Negro organizations and conversely to the lack of militant "black power" groups; others to the biracial commissions on race relations which were established in many cities to investigate the causes of rioting and generally to aid in the Negro quest for equality; and still others to the increased neutrality of law-enforcement agencies in administering justice.

One of the first Negro mass movements, the Universal Negro Improvement Association, was organized in the 1920's by a West Indian named Marcus Garvey. This organization gained some prominence among approximately three million Negroes in the United States who were opposed to integrating themselves into white society. Most of these individuals did not believe that whites could ever accept them on equal terms. Instead, they adopted Garvey's solution, "return to Africa," where they could establish their own advanced civilization. Although his goals were somewhat unrealistic and the movement ultimately failed, Garvey was important because "he left a legacy of attitudes and beliefs which continue to motivate, or at least influence the behavior of a Negro protest segment which is as yet outside the mainstream of Negro protest. Garvey taught his followers to distrust the white man and to rely solely upon their own efforts to better their conditions."[34] Furthermore, he exalted his followers to take pride in being black and to develop solidarity as a race. Today, much of the opposition among Negroes to the whole notion of integration comes from black nationalists groups, who like Garvey, believed that the Negro must be the source of his own "salvation."

During this period, Negroes did not make very extensive use of the ballot box to carry forward their protest movement. Instead, Negro voting appeared more as a response to favorable civil-rights activity than as an attempt to bring such activity about. Although as a group they suffered greatly from the effects of the Depression, Negroes retained a strong loyalty to the party of Lincoln in 1932, and only shifted to Roosevelt after they

[32] For an excellent discussion of the Detroit race riot of 1943 see: Alfred M. Lee and Norman Humphrey, *Race Riot* (New York: Dryden Press, 1943).

[33] James Q. Wilson, "Why Are We Having a Wave of Violence," *The New York Times Magazine* (May 19, 1968), pp. 23–24, 116–120.

[34] Lincoln, *op. cit.*, p. 477.

had begun to experience the fruits of the New Deal. This same pattern occurred in 1952 with Eisenhower.[35] Negroes did not switch to him in large members until 1956 after he had responded favorably on civil rights issues.

The education and economic advances made by Negroes both immediately prior to and during World War II were considerable, although hard won.[36] For example, only after A. Philip Randolph confronted President Roosevelt with the threat of a massive Negro protest march on Washington in 1941 did he issue Executive Order 8802 prohibiting discriminatory hiring practices in defense industries or government.[37] Industry complied with the new order reluctantly, but sustained pressure from the newly created Fair Employment Practices Commission gradually brought about the hiring of Negroes on an unprecedented scale.[38] However, rapid population growth in industrial areas, particularly in northern and western cities, created new racial tensions, and violence occurred in a number of cities.[39]

In the military, Negroes played a more important role than they had in World War I. All branches of the service accepted them, and they served commendably in a broad range of units. For the most part, however, the units were segregated, and the existence of overt discrimination against Negro officers and enlisted men created considerable frustration and bitterness, and it provoked numerous racial incidents on bases both at home and abroad.[40]

In sum, World War II differed from World War I in that Negroes demanded and were granted greater participation in the war effort. At home Negro unemployment dropped and improvements in Negro occupational status were reflected in higher earnings. Educational opportunities, particularly technical and vocational, also increased. In addition, the war exposed many more Negores to foreign cultures, giving them a greater understanding of the inequities in their own system. It also forced the United States into a position of world leadership, making it more difficult to espouse democracy and freedom for other nations without paying greater attention to its own domestic racial problems. However, the two wars were similar in the clearly defined segregated and subordinate role which blacks

[35] Lubell, *White and Black*, pp. 50–93.

[36] These advances appear even more impressive when compared with the very limited occupational and income gains made by Negroes during World War I. See the discussion of these advances in: Abram L. Harris, "Education and the Economic Status of Negroes in the United States," in Robert A. Goldwin (ed.), *100 Years of Emancipation* (New York: Rand McNally, 1963), pp. 129–157.

[37] For a careful analysis of the events leading up to the nondiscrimination order see: Herbert Garfinkle, *When Negroes March* (New York: Free Press, 1959).

[38] Employment figures and other factual material concerning the Negro in industry during the wartime years are found in: Franklin, *From Slavery*, pp. 592–596; and Quarles, *The Negro*, pp. 216–218.

[39] Franklin, *From Slavery*, pp. 597–598.

[40] *Ibid.*, pp. 580–591. William H. Hastie, a prominent Negro jurist and former federal judge, was appointed civilian aide to the Secretary of War for racial matters at the beginning of the war. In 1943, he resigned in frustration over his inability to reduce segregation or discrimination in the armed services. See his letter of resignation in: Fishel and Quarles (eds.), *The Negro American*, pp. 473–476.

were forced to accept, particularly in the armed forces, and in the amount of racial hostility and violence which occurred.

CONSOLIDATION AND CHANGE (1946–1954)

Very little needs to be said about the postwar period 1946–1954, other than to note the surprising lack of racial conflict or Negro protest activity, except in the courts. Given the similarities in the conditions after both world wars, that is, the steady northward and westward migration of blacks and the fluctuations in the economy, it is difficult to understand why after World War II there was neither racial violence on a major scale nor any marked increase in protest activity among Negroes. One explanation offered for this period of relative calm is that blacks were resigned to segregation in 1946 in a way that they had not been in 1918. In the intervening 28 years they had been socialized into a certain role, and there was less prospect of changing the *status quo* than there seemed to have been in 1918. Some of the reasons noted previously for the long period of relative racial peace may also apply to the immediate post-World War II period. This was the lull before the gathering storm.

As Table 2 indicates, Negroes left the South in increasing numbers in the 1940's, 1950's, and 1960's. By 1966, the black population had increased to 21.5 million, with two significant geographical shifts taking place.[41] First, the proportion of Negroes living in the South had dropped to 55 percent, and about 69 percent of all Negroes lived in metropolitan areas compared to 64 percent for whites. Second, although the total Negro population more than doubled from 1910 to 1966, the number of blacks living in cities rose fivefold (from 2.6 million to 14.8 million) and the number outside the South rose elevenfold (from 880,000 to 9.7 million).

CREATIVE DISORDER, MILITANCY, THE RESURGENCE OF RACIAL VIOLENCE (1955–1968)

CREATIVE DISORDER AND MILITANCY (1955–1963). The 1954 Supreme Court decision which reversed the "separate but equal" doctrine in public

Table 2

Out-Migration of Negroes from the South[*]

Period	Net Negro Out-Migration from the South	Average Annual Rate
1910–1920	454,000	45,400
1920–1930	749,000	74,900
1930–1940	348,000	34,800
1940–1950	1,597,000	159,700
1950–1960	1,457,000	145,700
1960–1966	613,000	102,000

[*] Source: *Report of the National Advisory Commission on Civil Disorders* (New York: Bantam Books, 1968), p. 240.

[41] *Report of the National Advisory Commission on Civil Disorders*, p. 239

schooling is regarded by Negroes and students of the black protest movement alike as an extremely important landmark in the struggle for full equality for blacks in America. This decision was the result of careful preparation by the NAACP legal staff, It was a product of a well-developed sense of timing, born of over forty years of probing the strengths and weaknesses of segregation. *Brown v. Board of Education* represented a major step in the long-range strategy of the NAACP leadership to integrate Negroes into American life. This strategy had been one of "measured protest," in which legal and moral persuasion were key elements. While such protest lacked the drama and success of later efforts, it was attuned to white attitudes in a way that prevented wholesale reversals in white attitudes.

A steady and increasingly militant stream of group protest activity appears to have been generated by that decision. The initial phase of this period (1954–1963) has been refered to as one of "creative disorder" because of the reliance on ostensibly nonviolent direct action to bring about social and political change.[42] This period really began in 1955, with the refusal of Mrs. Rosa Parks, a Negro woman in Montgomery, Alabama, to yield her seat on a bus to a white passenger. The arrest of Mrs. Parks subsequently led to an organized black boycott of the bus company. The outcome of the boycott was a federal ruling prohibiting segregation on buses. This success prompted the formation of the Southern Christian Leadership Conference (SCLC) in 1957, headed by Dr. Martin Luther King, Jr. Another significant milestone in the civil-rights movement also occurred in 1957, when President Eisenhower ordered federal troops into Little Rock, Arkansas to enforce the Supreme Court ruling on school segregation. This was the first time that the federal government had unilaterally intervened to protect the rights of Negroes in the South. As such, it set a precedent which permanently disposed of the supremacy of the states in policies regarding race relations by making it quite clear to the states that the federal government would intervene with force if necessary, to protect the civil rights of black Americans.

In contrast, the period 1958–1960 was one of relative calm, with Negro organizations concentrating on building membership and systematically testing white reactions to the Court decision. After the federal-state "showdown" in Little Rock, Southern tactics switched from overt to covert defiance. School systems were shut down to prevent compulsory compliance with the order and "private" schools for white children were established to take their place. Resistance was not uniform, however. Some states reluctantly accepted the inevitability of change and took steps to integrate their schools gradually. This was particularly true in the border states.

Although the desegregation decision triggered a wave of protest activity, it was an activity which for the first five years was concentrated in the courts. Test cases were necessary to establish both how far the government was willing to go to protect Negro rights, and to assess the nature and extent of white resistance to change in the South. With the sixties came a

[42] See the discussion of the initial phase in this period in: Lomax, *The Negro Revolt.*

new phase in the protest movement. Because of the inability to achieve rapid change in the *status quo* through the courts, a determined effort was launched by blacks to bring about a variety of changes in the position of the Negro in the south by directly confronting white society.

In February 1960, four black college students sat down at a segregated lunch counter in Greensboro, North Carolina, and refused to leave until they had been served. This marked the first "sit-in," and it signaled the arrival of organized militant youth into the ranks of the protest movement. Louis E. Lomax has observed that the sit-ins involved more people than any other civil-rights movement in history, with some seventy thousand black and white persons staging over eight hundred sit-ins in more than one hundred cities.[43] In addition, it has been estimated that upwards of four thousand persons, most of them black students, were arrested before the sit-ins came to a halt.[44] At the end of two years, lunch counters had been desegregated in many southern cities.

Responsibility for organizing the sit-ins and for effectively channeling the energies of individual protest groups on college campuses throughout the country fell to the Student Nonviolent Coordinating Committee (SNCC).[45] SNCC has been the most militant of the so-called nonviolent protest groups since its inception in 1960. Although it began as a biracial movement, since 1965 it has been the primary force behind the concept of "black power," which one of its former leaders, Stokely Carmichael, first introduced. As a result of SNCC's emphasis on the need for the Negro to develop a positive image of himself and a positive black consciousness, independent of white control or influence, the white membership of SNCC has moved to the periphery of the organization or has left it altogether. White financial support has also diminished as SNCC has become more separatist in its orientation. This has left it with a small but dedicated staff which concentrates on those means by which "black power" can best be attained.

A second group which came into prominence in the early 1960's was the Congress of Racial Equality (CORE).[46] Although organized in 1942 as the first of the nonviolent direct-action protest groups (concerning itself with problems of discrimination against Negroes), the organization remained relatively obscure until 1961, when it organized and gained nationwide support for a series of "freedom rides" designed to desegregate bus facilities in the Southern states. These rides consisted of groups of blacks and whites who took bus trips to various southern cities, with the objective of openly violating the "Jim Crow" laws regarding segregated bus terminals. The initial rides gave rise to considerable violence, with riders being beaten by white mobs and buses being set afire in several cases. Federal marshals were called in to restore order when buses were attacked in Montgomery, Alabama. Gradually, however, the discipline

[43] *Ibid.*, p. 136.
[44] *Ibid.*
[45] Howard Zinn, *SNCC, The New Abolitionists* (Boston: Beacon Press, 1964).
[46] Lomax, *The Negro Revolt*, pp. 133–143. See also: Inge Powell Bell, *CORE and The Strategy of Non-Violence* (New York: Random House, 1968).

and persistence of the riders prevailed. By the end of 1961, more than a thousand riders had openly challenged the legality of segregated public facilities. These actions were directly responsible for the desegregation of over 120 bus stations in the South and they set the stage for an Interstate Commerce Commission ruling prohibiting interstate carriers from using segregated terminals or from discriminating in the seating of passengers.[47]

VIOLENCE AND REYOND (1964–?). In the Spring of 1963, Birmingham, Alabama, long considered the heart of segregationalist feeling in the South, was selected by the SCLC leadership for a prolonged series of non-violent demonstrations aimed at desegregating lunch counters and other facilities. After five weeks of demonstrations, a truce was arranged and talks began. The truce was broken several days later when a bomb exploded in a Negro church on a Sunday morning, killing four young Negro girls attending Sunday School. The restraint and discipline which had been maintained during the five weeks of harassment and intimidation collapsed. The two days of rioting which followed, and the brutality with which it was suppressed, can be seen as the beginning of the second phase of this period, one increasingly characterized by collective racial violence, a phase of disillusionment and revolt.[48]

As leaders of the black protest movement continued pressing their demands in the South, violence continued. However, the Negro revolt soon spread northward and with it the violent hostile outbursts which had been initiated in Birmingham in 1963. As the protest movement moved North, many leaders soon realized that the fundamental problem confronting blacks in the North was the achievement of equality and not simply the removal of legal barriers to full opportunity as it had been in the South.

Bayard Rustin has observed:[49]

From sit-ins and freedom rides we have gone into rent strikes, boycotts, community organization, and political action. As a consequence of this natural evolution, the Negro today finds himself stymied by obstacles of far greater magnitude than the legal barriers he was attacking before: automation, urban decay, de facto segregation. These are problems which, while conditioned by Jim Crow, do not vanish upon its demise. They are more deeply rooted in our socio-economic order; they are the result of the total society's failure to meet not only the Negro's needs, but human needs generally.

Thus, the movement entered a more revolutionary phase in which legal changes were no longer perceived as sufficient. Many blacks now felt that fundamental changes in institutions and institutional practices were necessary in order to bring about a radical upgrading of the position of black

---

[47] Lincoln, op. cit., p. 474.

[48] For a discussion of the racial violence which occurred during the second phase of this period see: Bryan T. Downes, "Social and Political Characteristics of Riot Cities: A Comparative Study," Social Science Quarterly, vol. 49, no. 3 (December, 1968), reprinted in this volume.

[49] Bayard Rustin, "From Protest to Politics: The Future of the Civil Rights Movement," in Raymond Murphy and Howard Elinson (eds.), Problems and Prospects of the Negro Movement (Belmont: Wadsworth Publishing Company, 1966), p. 412.

Americans.[50] Although most blacks remained committed to integration and to bringing it about by working within the established system through legitimate political channels, some rejected this approach. A vocal minority, composed mainly of younger blacks, wanted to disengage from white society and create a separate black nation. Many of these militant individuals were also convinced they could only bring about this change through violence.[51]

Just as the legalistically oriented NAACP had been displaced by the direct nonviolent confrontation tactics of Martin Luther King, Jr., so King too was challenged and partially eclipsed by younger, more militant blacks. Stokely Carmichael, Floyd McKissick, and H. "Rap" Brown led a growing number of militants who appealed to the impatience and frustration of ghetto Negroes. Although the term "black power" was roundly condemned by King and other Negro leaders when it was first introduced in 1965, the popular response to the concept forced them to first rationalize and then embrace it as a means of maintaining some degree of control over the civil rights movement. The base of black protest was broadening, and with it came a concomitant loss of discipline and restraint. What had begun as a moderate middle-class oriented challenge to "Jim Crow" in the South now became a series of violent rebellions among the ghetto dwellers of the North.

Despite the continuous trend since 1944, in both the North and South, toward white acceptance of racial integration, there has developed in recent years a growing uneasiness among whites about the form which the black protest movement has taken. As Paul B. Sheatsley has observed, "Though large majorities have expressed approval of civil rights legislation and disapproval of racial discrimination, equally large majorities have declared themselves opposed to demonstrations, protests, and especially to rioting and violence."[52] Most whites now recognize the legitimacy of black protest. However, they are becoming increasingly concerned about the nature of such protest and that the pace of civil-rights progress has been "too fast."

As the tactics of the Negro protest movement have become more militant, white atitudes have hardened in fear and resentment. As whites have become more alarmed over the tactics employed by black protest groups many also have become less committed to Negro advancement. The attachment of an "anti-riot" rider to the Civil Rights Bill of 1966 and the subsequent rejection of the entire bill by the House of Representatives suggests a growing antipathy in Congress toward support of the civil-

[50] See the discussion in: Stokely Carmichael and Charles V. Hamilton, *Black Power, the Politics of Liberation in America* (New York: Random House, 1967).

[51] See: C. Eric Lincoln, *Black Muslims in America* (Boston: Beacon Press, 1961); copyright volumes.

[52] Paul B. Sheatsley, "American Attitudes on Race and Civil Rights." A model lecture prepared for the United States Information Agency (National Opinion Research Center, University of Chicago, September, 1965), pp. 9–10. See also: Paul B. Sheatsley, "White Attitudes toward the Negro," in Talcott Parsons and Kenneth B. Clark (eds.), *The Negro American* (Boston: Beacon Press, 1965), pp. 303–324.

rights movement. The surprisingly popular response to the candidacy of George Wallace is an even stronger demonstration of the same trend. While the evidence is not conclusive, it is sufficient to suggest that an inexorable polarization is occurring in which Negroes are turning to increasingly strident and militant leadership for direction, while whites are retrenching and falling back on "law and order" as a solution to the problem of Negro militancy. This self-reinforcing cycle would appear to be irreversible, for the moderation and restraint which whites demand of Negroes is the very thing which many blacks perceive as having prevented their progress, and the kinds of concessions Negroes are demanding from whites impringe directly on those things which whites are most determined to protect for themselves.

Negro interests have traditionally been "protected" by whites who have interceded on their behalf in an otherwise indifferent or hostile society. Paternalism, however, is no substitute for participation.[53]

. . . No man can be truly free whose liberty is dependent upon the thought, feeling, and actions of others, and who has himself no means in his own hands for guarding, protecting, defending, and maintaining that liberty. . . . The law on the side of freedom is of great advantage only where there is power to make that law respected. I know no class of my fellow-men, however just, enlightened, and humane, which can be wisely and safely trusted absolutely with the liberties of any other class.

Although the above statement is fully applicable as an explanation of the black protest movement of the 1960's, it was written by Frederick Douglass in 1881. In the wake of their abandonment by Northern liberals after the burst of progress immediately following the Civil War, Negroes soon recognized that their destinies were again subject to the vicissitudes of white politicians. The frailty of moral commitment among whites was demonstrated by the invalidation in 1883 of the Civil Rights Act of 1875 by the United States Supreme Court. As industrial interests in the North secured their control of Congress during the same period, the votes of Negro legislators became less important in securing favorable legislation. Once the industrial coalition between North and South had been reestablished, black legislators and their interests became irrelevant, if not an impediment, to the tasks of industrialization which lay ahead. Lacking the power to effectively challenge their betrayers, Negroes succumbed to segregation.

The United States is currently entering a similar period, a second post-Reconstruction if you wish, in which many white Americans have become more concerned with "law and order" and less with justice and equal opportunity for blacks. While it is possible that in the near future the Supreme Court could rule unconstitutional or seriously hobble existing civil-rights legislation, while an increasingly conservative Congress could withdraw vital support from programs for education, housing, and job

[53] Frederick Douglass, *The Life and Times of Frederick Douglass* (New York: Collier Books, 1962), p. 539.

training and while white Americans could grow increasingly intolerant of protest activities, it is impossible to expect or assume that such actions will force blacks into submission or compliance of a type that has occurred in the past.

Confrontations are likely to continue between blacks and whites as leaders of the black community press their demands through direct action. However, expectations are beginning to outdistance the concrete accomplishments of programs designed to bring about black equality. Although Congress has begun to respond to Negro demands, the pace has been too slow for many militant black leaders. Programs have been forthcoming but the allocation of funds for these programs has been limited when compared to the immensity of the problem of bringing about Negro equality.[54] The scarcity of resources even in a nation as rich as ours is underlined, for we have found it difficult to fight a war in Vietnam and adequately cope with the problems of the poor and disadvantaged in our own society.

Since 1963 over 300 outbursts of collective racial violence have occurred in many of our major cities.[55] These incidents have involved rock throwing, fighting, looting, burning, and killing. In contrast to earlier outbursts of racial violence, blacks have been the primary participants, many of whom have been bent upon attacking police and merchants, objects they consider responsible for a great deal of racial injustice in the ghetto. Thus it would appear that the black man's dream of integration, social justice, and equality can be deferred no longer, for it has exploded in violence and destruction which have wrecked havoc on many of our urban ghettos.

CONCLUSION

Given the increased militancy and resort to violence by black Americans, what is likely to be the future form which black protest will take in the United States?

First, blacks are likely to continue to wreak havoc and destruction upon many of our cities in the near future. There are good historical reasons for assuming that in a country like the United States, with its history of collective racial violence, violence becomes an accepted way of responding to deprivations.[56] Historically, violence has often been associated with the black protest movement, and as we have indicated, a new pattern of racial violence has emerged from this movement since 1963. When these latest outbursts are taken into account, in conjunction with the growth of ex-

---

[54] For a discussion of this problem see: Michael Harrington, *The Other America: Poverty in the United States* (New York: The Macmillan Company, 1962); and Kenneth B. Clark, *Dark Ghetto, Dilemmas of Social Power* (New York: Harper and Row, 1965). For a discussion of one attempt at resolution see: John C. Donovan, *The Politics of Poverty* (New York: Pegasus Press, 1967).

[55] Bryan T. Downes, "The Black Protest Movement and Urban Violence," *op. cit.*

[56] Ted Gurr, "Urban Disorder: Perspectives from the Comparative Study of Civil Strife," *American Behavioral Scientist*, vol. 2, no. 4 (March-April, 1968), p. 54. Other articles in this issue on urban violence and disorder also discuss the current outbursts of racial violence which have been occurring in many of our cities.

tremist organizations that advocate covert and violent protest, the infer-
ence is that hostile outbursts will continue in the future.[57]

Second, as recent studies have shown, participation in and support for
violent outbursts is by no means limited to a tiny minority of malcontents
in the black community. In the eyes of a growing number of Negro citizens, hostile outbursts represent legitimate protest against the actions of
whites. They are also perceived as bringing about long-delayed action, by
government and the private sector, designed to improve the life of black
Americans.[58]

Furthermore, there has been a tendency to radicalize the Negro masses
in the North through a "competition of militancy" among Negro leaders.[59]
The bolder demands of newer, younger militant blacks have forced more
conservative civil-rights organizations like the NAACP and the Urban
League, particularly the latter, to assume a more militant stance. As we
now know, these militants "are the cream of urban Negro youth in particular and urban Negro citizens in general."[60] They are better educated,
hold a more positive image of themselves, and tend to be far more sophisticated politically than nonmilitants.

One of the tragedies of the struggle against racism in our society is that
up to this point in the black protest movement there has been no broadly
based national organization which has spoken for the growing militancy
of young black people in our urban ghettos and the black belt South. Outside of CORE, SNCC, and few other more militant groups, there has only
been a "civil-rights" movement whose tone of voice was adapted to a
middle-class white audience and which served as a sort of buffer between
this audience and angry young blacks. Although this movement "claimed
to speak for the needs of a community, it did not speak in the tone of that
community."[61] For this reason most civil-rights activists and social scientists underestimated the amount of rage Negroes were suppressing prior
to 1964 and correspondingly the amount of bigotry the white majority was
disguising.[62]

Third, the continued failure of nonviolent creative disorder to bring
about desired changes, particularly in the North, has disillusioned and
discouraged large numbers of younger urban blacks, who are now more

[57] *Ibid.*

[58] T. M. Tomlinson, "The Development of a Riot Ideology among Urban Negroes,"
American Behavioral Scientists, op. cit., p. 28. See also: A *Survey of Attitudes of Detroit Negroes After the Riot of 1967* (Detroit: Detroit Urban League, 1967); and
Kurt and Gladys Lang, "Racial Disturbances as Collective Protest," *American Behavioral Scientist, op. cit.,* pp. 11–13; and David Sears and T. M. Tomlinson, "Riot Ideology among Los Angeles Negroes," *Social Science Quarterly,* 49 (December, 1968),
reprinted in this volume.

[59] Lubell, *White and Black,* p. 134.

[60] Tomlinson, *op. cit.*

[61] Carmichael and Hamilton, *Black Power,* p. 50. See also: Lewis Killian and
Charles Grigg, *Racial Crisis in America: Leadership in Conflict* (Engelwood Cliffs:
Prentice-Hall, 1964).

[62] Martin Luther King, Jr., "The Role of the Behavioral Scientist in the Civil Rights
Movement," *American Psychologist,* vol. 23, no. 3 (March, 1968), p. 181; also reprinted in this volume.

than ever prone to become "ready tinder for a spark of riot."[63] Given such failures, what is likely to be the future of the politics of nonviolent confrontation? The answer depends on at least two factors: (1) the degree of inventiveness and self-discipline in the Negro community as it tries to create new techniques to cope with failures which have already occurred using direct action, and (2) the response of political authorities to the use of creative disorder as not only a means of attracting public attention but also as a means of articulating demands and grievances.[64] Thus far Negro leaders have not been very inventive nor have political authorities paid much attention to the demands articulated. Largely because of this, those individuals and groups making use of direct action are being forced to turn to more threatening and violent techniques, such as civil disobedience and threats of violence.[65]

Fourth, if past experience is any indication, governmental action is not likely to be forthcoming unless it is systematically and consistently demanded by blacks.[66] Until recently, however, Negroes have remained largely unorganized and as a result have not been strong enough politically to exert the leverage necessary to bring about change through the political process. Thus they have resorted to varying strategies of protest. The fact that Negroes now constitute such a large and rapidly growing proportion of the population in our largest cities provides them with an excellent opportunity to acquire political power.[67] However, as Bayard Rustin has so persuasively argued, neither protest nor the country's 21.5 million black people can win political power alone, except perhaps in a few cities.[68] Blacks need allies! In fact, the future of the nonviolent Negro struggle for equality depends on whether contradictions in this society can be resolved peacefully by a coalition of progressive forces which become the effective political majority in the United States.[69]

Fifth, for whites the choices obviously get harder as the black revolution penetrates deeper into their world. A great many whites already feel that Negroes have pressed too far.[70] But they have missed the essential point—the revolution is one of ever-rising expectations. A victory here simply whets the appetite for further victories, therefore, the revolt will

63 Waskow, *From Race Riot to Sit-In*, p. 284.

64 *Ibid.*, p. 283. For a pessimistic discussion of the problems facing Negroes in effectively challenging the existing white "power structure" see Lewis M. Killian, *The Impossible Revolution?* (New York: Random House, 1968).

65 For an enlightening discussion of the position of one Supreme Court jurist on civil disobedience see Abe Fortas, *Concerning Dissent and Civil Disobedience* (New York: The New American Library, 1968).

66 Waskow, *From Race Riot to Sit-In*, pp. 282–283.

67 Silberman, *Crisis in Black and White*, p. 194. For a discussion of the changing population patterns of Negroes in our urban areas see: Karl E. and Alma F. Taeuber, *Negroes in Cities: Residential Segregation and Change* (Chicago: Aldine Publishing Company, 1965).

68 Rustin, *op. cit.*, p. 415.

69 *Ibid.*, p. 416.

70 Campbell and Schuman, *op. cit.*; and Peter H. Rossi, *et al.*, "Between Black and White—The Faces of American Institutions in the Ghetto," in *Supplemental Studies for the National Advisory Commission on Civil Disorders*, pp. 69–215.

not stop on some convenient plateau of half-accommodation or half-integration.[71] Certainly there is no evidence to indicate the majority of white Americans eagerly look forward to integration.[72] Most are quite comfortable in a segregated society and would prefer the demonstrations and hostile outbursts to cease, so problems could be worked out more gradually.

But most whites recognize the legitimacy of Negro protest. Although people do respond to immediate events, such as, demonstrations and collective racial violence, and often have very strong opinions about them, the evidence we have indicates that white attitudes toward such basic issues as school and residential integration, social mixing, and the use by Negroes of public accommodations, are not subject to sudden and dramatic shifts.[73] As Paul Sheatsley has observed, "if all the events in the months and years preceding December 1963 did not halt the rising trend toward acceptance of integration, it is doubtful that recent events will produce any major change in basic attitudes toward integration."[74]

Finally, when violent racial outbursts are brought under control by political authorities, some time in the next several years, there will probably be a retrenchment by both blacks and whites.[75] If at this point nothing has been done to relieve the basic conditions which give rise to hostile outbursts, then, it is entirely conceivable that both public and clandestine black organizations may actively foment civil disobedience and guerilla warfare in our cities.[76] Furthermore, competition for leadership among the largely unorganized black protest groups will inevitably generate even more extreme demands faster than moderate requests can be met.[77]

Is there any hope of averting such an outcome? Averting it would require a number of changes, including the following ones suggested by T. M. Tomlinson.[78] First, belatedly (and perhaps too late) there must be a "massive infusion" of public and private fiscal and intellectual resources into our ghettos. We can also no longer tolerate a random infusion; instead, it must be guided by well-thought-out, comprehensive programs designed to meet black demands. Second, there must be a general strengthening of Negro leadership through a unification of younger militants and more conventional leaders of the Negro middle class in the common cause of Negro development. The key to such a merger could be the notion of "black power." Third, "whites must demonstrate faith in the concept of Negro equality" by indicating that they are "truly willing for Negroes, as Negroes, to enter into a society which is black and white." Furthermore,

---

[71] Brink and Harris, *Black and White*, p. 178. See also: Gary T. Marx, *Protest and Prejudice: A Study of Belief in the Black Community* (New York: Harper and Row, 1967).

[72] Paul B. Sheatsley, "White Attitudes Toward the Negro," *op. cit.*, p. 322.

[73] *Ibid.*, p. 320.

[74] *Ibid.*

[75] Tomlinson, *op. cit.*, p. 30.

[76] *Ibid.* During the summer of 1968, blacks precipitated a number of violent racial outbursts by systematically ambushing and attempting to kill police. This is very different from the anomic (unorganized) patterns of most post-1963 incidents.

[77] Wilson, *op. cit.*, p. 119.

[78] Tomlinson, *op. cit.*

whites *must demand* that both the public and private sectors do everything possible to further black equality. As Carmichael and Hamilton have observed, "There is no black man in this country who can live 'simply as a man.' His blackness is an ever-present fact of this racist society, whether he recognizes it or not. It is unlikely that this or the next generation will witness the time when race will no longer be relevant in the conduct of public affairs and in public policy decision-making. To realize this and to attempt to deal with it . . . puts one in the forefront of a significant struggle. If there is no intense struggle today, there will be no meaningful results tomorrow."[79] Finally, blacks must begin to put their own house in order, so they are capable of collectively applying continuous pressure upon white institutions for change.[80]

[79] Carmichael and Hamilton, *Black Power*, p. 54. They define "racism" as the predication of decisions and policies on considerations of race for the purpose of subordinating a racial group and maintaining control over that group (p. 3).

[80] For a comprehensive discussion of a number of additional activities which probably should be undertaken see: *Report of the National Advisory Commission on Civil Disorders*, part III, pp. 283–483. Particularly important are the changes discussed in: "The Community Response," Chapter 10; "The Police and the Community," Chapter 11; and "Recommendations for National Action," Chapter 17.

25

Social Structure and the Negro Revolt: An Examination of Some Hypotheses*

JAMES A. GESCHWENDER**
UNIVERSITY OF WESTERN ONTARIO

T HE SUMMER OF 1963 HAS BEEN REFERRED TO AS "THE SUMMER OF THE Negro Revolt." Negroes have rebelled against their status in the United States from the earliest days of slavery to the present time,[1] but the rebellion reached its peak to date the summer of 1963, when it became a nationwide movement with protests and demonstrations in three-fourths of our states in all mainland regions of the country.[2]

It is true that this revolt did not simply emerge spontaneously and full-blown in one summer. Yet, we cannot validly view this present protest as a simple continuation of the protest begun during slavery. Intense and widespread support makes today's protest basically different. Lomax chooses to date today's revolt from December 1, 1955, when Mrs. Rosa Parks refused to give up her seat on a Montgomery, Alabama, bus.[3] Others might prefer other dates, but this seems as good as any. The major question is not the precise date of its inception but rather the reasons for its existence.

Journalists have speculated as to these reasons.[4] It is time for a sociologist to attempt a structural explanation. The present writer will attempt to do this by searching the literature for sociological hypotheses which purport to be able to explain such revolts, examining empirical evidence pertaining to the living conditions of the Negro in order to test and evaluate these hypotheses, and drawing some general conclusions.

PROPOSED EXPLANATORY HYPOTHESES

Five general types of hypotheses which attempt to explain this type of revolt have appeared in the sociological literature.

* Reprinted by permission of the University of North Carolina Press from *Social Forces*, 43 (December, 1964), pp. 248-256.

** I am indebted to Elwood Guernsey for compiling much of the data upon which Tables 1 and 3 are based and to the Institute for Social Research, Florida State University, for the use of graduate assistants and machines. I have benefited from the critical comments on earlier drafts generously given by William A. Rushing and Henry J. Watts.

[1] For information on the slave revolts see Herbert Aptheker, *American Negro Slave Revolts* (New York: Columbia University Press, 1945), and for a brief history of other Negro protest activity see Gunnar Myrdal, *An American Dilemma* (New York: Harper & Bros., 1944), pp. 736–937.

[2] See files of *The New York Times* throughout the period from May to August, 1963.

[3] Louis E. Lomax, *The Negro Revolt* (New York: The New American Library, 1963), p. 92.

[4] Lomax, *op. cit.*, and Dan Wakefield, *Revolt in the South* (New York: Grove Press, 1960), are just two examples among many.

The first of these might be called "The Vulgar Marxist Hypothesis." It could be so named because of the general belief that this is the manner in which Marx believed revolutions originate.[5] This hypothesis may be stated: *As a group experiences a worsening of its conditions of life, it will become increasingly dissatisfied until it eventually rebels.* It is questionable if this is the correct interpretation of Marx's analysis of the cause of the revolution.[6] Nevertheless, this hypothesis has received support from Sorokin in his analysis of revolution and qualifies as a candidate hypothesis.[7]

The second type of hypothesis might be called "The Rising Expectations Hypothesis." This hypothesis may be stated: *As a group experiences an improvement in its conditions of life it will also experience a rise in its level of desires. The latter will rise more rapidly than the former, leading to dissatisfaction and rebellion.* The classic statement of this hypothesis was presented by L. P. Edwards though others have presented similar formulations.[8]

The third kind of explanation might be called "The Sophisticated Marxist Hypothesis," after its author, or "The Relative Deprivation Hypothesis," after its nature. This hypothesis may be stated: *As a group experiences an improvement in its conditions of life and simultaneously observes a second group experiencing a more rapid rate of improvement, it will become dissatisfied with its rate of improvement and rebel.* Marx saw the chain of events—including the alienation of labor, the development of class consciousness, and the proletarian revolution—as having its inception with feelings of relative deprivation resulting from a set of changes in objective conditions.[9]

The fourth type of hypothesis might be called "The Rise and Drop Hypothesis." It may be worded: *As a group experiences an improvement in its conditions of life followed by a sharp reversal of this improvement, it will become dissatisfied and rebel.* James C. Davies formulated this hypothesis.[10]

The fifth type of hypothesis might be called "The Status Inconsistency Hypothesis," and may be worded: *A group which possesses a number of status attributes which are differently ranked on the various status hierarchies will be dissatisfied and prone toward rebellion.* This hypothesis is

[5] Cf. James C. Davis, "Toward a Theory of Revolution," *American Sociological Review*, 27 (February 1962), pp. 5–18, esp. p. 5.

[6] Cf. Reinhard Bendix and Seymour Martin Lipset, " 'Karl Marx' Theory on Social Classes," Reinhard Bendix and Seymour Martin Lipset (eds.), *Class, Status and Power* (Glencoe, Illinois: The Free Press, 1953), pp. 26–27, esp. pp. 32–33.

[7] Pitirim A. Sorokin, *The Sociology of Revolution* (Philadelphia: J. B. Lippincott Co., 1925), p. 367.

[8] Lyford P. Edwards, *The Natural History of Revolution* (Chicago: The University of Chicago Press, 1927). See also the passage quoted from A. de Tocqueville in Davies, *op. cit.*, p. 6, and Crane Brinton, *The Anatomy of Revolution* (New York: W. W. Norton Co., 1938), esp. pp. 74–78 and pp. 44–46.

[9] See citations in Davies, *op. cit.*, p. 5; Bendix and Lipset, *op. cit.*, pp. 32–33 .

[10] Davies, *op. cit.*, p. 6.

probably best known through Lenski's work in status crystallization but is similar to propositions of Broom, Hughes, and Sorokin.[11]

THE POSITION OF THE NEGRO IN THE UNITED STATES

Having listed the various hypotheses purporting to explain phenomena such as "The Negro Revolt," it is time to examine the data which permit an evaluation of these hypotheses. Let us examine the position of the Negro in the United States in terms of the categories: education, occupation, and income. These particular categories are chosen for analysis because of the belief that they are most crucial in determining one's life chances and one's style of life.[12]

Unfortunately, direct data on Negroes are not available in most areas one would wish to examine. One is forced to rely upon data for nonwhites and infer to Negroes. This will introduce some distortion into the data. This distortion, however, should not be overestimated. The number of non-Negro nonwhites has been less than ten percent of the nonwhites throughout the time period with which we will be concerned. Furthermore, data are available showing both nonwhite and Negro occupational distributions for 1940 and 1950, and in no occupational category for either year do the two frequencies differ by over seven-tenths of one percent.[13] This lends support to the belief that the position of the nonwhite may be taken as a reasonable approximation of that of the Negro.

Table 1 portrays the changes that have taken place in male level of education by race between 1940 and 1960. There are two approaches one could take to the analysis of comparative rates of educational improvements of whites and nonwhites. One could compare the proportional distributions of whites and nonwhites by educational categories or one could examine rates based upon nonwhite proportional representation within educational categories. Each technique has its merits and they can be used to supplement one another. The first six columns of Table 1 represent the former and the last three columns represent the latter.

In analyzing the ethnic distribution by educational categories, levels of education may profitably be broken into three broad categories: low— from none to six years of elementary school; middle—seventh grade through eleventh grade; and high—high school graduates through four or more years of college. A much larger percentage of nonwhites than whites (24.3 to 8.5 percent) are moving out of the lower educational category. The middle educational category shows an increase in the pro-

[11] Gerhard Lenski, "Status Crystallization: A Non-Vertical Dimension of Social Status," *American Sociological Review,* 19 (August 1954), p. 412; Leonard Broom, "Social Differentiation and Stratification," Robert K. Merton, Leonard Broom and Leonard S. Cottrell (eds.), *Sociology Today* (New York: Basic Books, Inc., 1959), pp. 429–441; Everett C. Hughes, "Social Change and Status Protest: An Essay on the Marginal Man," *Phylon,* 10 (First Quarter 1949), pp. 58–65; Pitirim A. Sorokin, *Society, Culture and Personality* (New York: Harper & Bros., 1947).

[12] The crucial role played by the status dimensions of ethnicity, education, occupation, and income is supported by Lenski, *op. cit.,* and Broom, *op. cit.,* p. 431.

[13] These data were compiled from census data and are available from the present writer upon request.

TABLE 1

Level of Education by Color, Males, 1940 and 1960*

Level of Education	White			Nonwhite			Nonwhite as Per Cent of Tota		
	1940	1960	% Change	1940	1960	% Change	1940	1960	Ratio*
No schooling	3.2	2.0	− 1.2	11.7	6.6	− 5.1	26.1	26.3	0.94
Elementary:									
1–4 yrs.	8.8	5.5	− 3.3	34.5	21.1	−13.4	27.7	28.9	0.97
5–6 yrs.	11.1	7.1	− 4.0	20.6	14.8	− 5.8	15.3	17.9	1.09
7 yrs.	7.0	6.6	− 0.4	7.5	8.5	+ 1.0	9.5	11.8	1.16
8 yrs.	30.5	18.4	−12.1	11.4	12.3	+ 0.9	3.5	6.6	1.77
High:									
1–3 yrs.	15.1	18.9	+ 3.8	7.4	17.1	+ 9.7	4.6	8.7	1.77
4 yrs.	13.0	22.1	+ 9.1	3.8	11.7	+ 7.9	2.8	5.3	1.77
College:									
1–3 yrs.	5.3	9.0	+ 3.7	1.7	4.4	+ 2.7	3.0	4.9	1.52
4 yrs.	5.9	10.3	+ 4.4	1.4	3.4	+ 2.0	2.3	3.4	1.38
Total Reporting	99.9	99.9		99.9	99.9	0.1	8.9	9.5	1.00
	33,59	5,150	−43,157,862	3,27	9,786	−4,547,539			

* Source: United States Bureau of the Census, *Characteristics of the Population, United State Summary, 1940, 1960*, Alaska and Hawaii excluded.

** Standardized by number reporting education.

portion of nonwhites (11.6 percent) and a decrease in the proportion of whites (8.7 percent). This suggests that nonwhites are moving in larger numbers than whites out of the lower educational categories; that they are moving into the middle educational categories which the whites are moving out of; and that the nonwhites are moving into the upper educational categories in smaller numbers than whites.

Changes in the proportional representation of nonwhites in each educational category are measured by ratios comparing 1960 proportions to 1940 proportions standardized by numbers reporting education. The standardized ratios give a precise way of measuring the rate of educational improvement of nonwhites relative to that of the society as a whole. A ratio of one represents proportional improvement; less than one, improvement at a slower rate; and more than one, improvement at a more rapid rate. There was a net gain in proportion of nonwhites in all educational levels above the fourth grade. The size of the gain at the two highest levels was less than that for the three middle levels. Thus, it would appear that nonwhites are improving their level of education at a more rapid rate than whites.

The use of census data for comparing changing educational levels over time has one major weakness. Age distributions are not controlled, so it is not possible to know how much of the result is a reflection of different age distributions. Table 2 presents median years of schooling completed by age, sex, and color for 1959 and sheds some light on this difficulty. A comparison of the ratios of the nonwhite median to the white median for each of the age categories reveals that, with the singular exception of the 55 to 64 age category, there is a steady progression toward greater equal-

TABLE 2

Median Years of Schooling Completed Age 25 Years and Over by Age, Sex, and Color, March 1959[*]

	Male			Female		
Age	Total	Nonwhite	Nonwhite as Percent of Total	Total	Nonwhite	Nonwhite as Percent of Total
25–29	12.4	10.9	88	12.3	11.0	89
30–34	12.2	9.5	78	12.2	10.0	82
35–44	12.1	8.1	67	12.1	8.8	73
45–54	10.2	6.7	66	10.8	7.7	71
55–64	8.7	6.7	77	8.9	6.6	74
65 and over	8.2	3.8	46	8.4	5.4	64

[*] Source: Data taken from Murray Gendell and Hand L. Zetterberg, *A Sociological Almanac for the United States* (New York: Bedminister Press, 1961), Table 68, p. 70.

ity in level of education between white and nonwhite as age decreases. This can only reflect a situation in which nonwhites are improving their educational accomplishments relative to whites.

Thus, it may be concluded that the nonwhite is improving his educational level relative to previous generations of nonwhites and also is improving his educational level relative to whites. The data are ambiguous as to proportional gains in the upper educational categories.

OCCUPATION

Table 3 presents the changes which have taken place in male occupations by race from 1940 to 1960. It presents the data in the same two ways that were used earlier in the analysis of data on education. The first three columns portray the changes in the distribution of persons into occupational categories by race. It may be noted that nonwhites have increased their representation in all non-farm occupational categories and that whites have increased their representation in all non-farm occupational categories except labor. This makes it difficult to determine whether the increase in numbers of nonwhite professionals and managers represents occupational upgrading. Nonwhites increased their representation in the highest status non-farm occupations (professional-technical) and (manager-official-proprietor) by 13.8 percent but decreased their representation in the highest status category of farm occupations (farmer and farm manager) by 16.3 percent.

The second three columns present the distribution of persons into occupational categories by race when non-farm occupations only are considered. We now note that there is a decrease in the proportion of nonwhites in the two lowest status occupational categories (service and labor); an increase in representation in the upper blue collar and lower white collar categories (operatives, craftsmen-foremen, clerical-sales); an increase in the professional-technical occupational category and a negligible decrease in the manager-official-proprietor category.

TABLE 3

Occupation by Color, United States Males, 1940 and 1960*

Occupation	Color	All Occupations			Non-Farm Only			Nonwhite as Percent of Total		All Occupations: Ratio**	Non-Farm Only: Ratio***
		1940	1960	Change	1940	1960	Change	1940	1960		
Professional Technical	White	6.0	11.4	+ 5.4	7.6	12.5	+ 4.9	3.0	3.3	1.16	0.82
	Nonwhite	1.9	4.1	+ 2.2	3.2	4.7	+ 1.5				
Farm-Farm Managers	White	14.2	5.9	− 8.3				13.1	7.3	0.59	
	Nonwhite	21.2	4.9	−16.3							
Managers-Prop Officials	White	10.7	12.0	+ 1.3	13.6	13.1	− 0.5	1.5	1.8	1.26	1.01
	Nonwhite	1.7	0.6	+ 0.6	2.9	2.6	− 0.3				
Clerical-Sales	White	14.1	15.2	+ 1.1	17.9	16.5	− 1.4	1.5	4.1	2.87	2.29
	Nonwhite	2.2	6.9	+ 4.7	3.7	7.9	+ 4.2				
Craftsmen-Foremen	White	15.8	21.4	+ 5.6	20.1	23.3	+ 3.2	2.7	4.5	1.76	1.40
	Nonwhite	4.4	10.7	+ 6.3	7.5	12.2	+ 4.7				
Operatives	White	19.1	20.4	+ 1.3	24.3	22.2	− 2.1	6.2	10.7	1.82	1.45
	Nonwhite	12.5	25.9	+13.4	21.3	29.6	+ 8.3				
Service	White	5.4	5.5	+ 0.1	6.9	6.0	− 0.9	22.2	21.5	1.02	0.82
	Nonwhite	15.3	16.0	+ .07	26.1	18.3	− 7.8				
Farm Labor	White	7.1	2.4	− 4.7				22.3	23.3	1.09	
	Nonwhite	20.1	7.8	−12.3							
Labor	White	7.6	5.9	− 1.7	9.7	6.4	− 3.3	21.5	25.6	1.25	1.00
	Nonwhite	20.7	21.4	+10.7	35.3	24.5	−10.8				
Total	White	30,480,640		37,846,354	24,000,434		34,620,227	9.1	8.6	1.00	1.00
	Nonwhite	3,072,006		3,558,946	1,801,092		3,107,859				

* Source: United States Bureau of the Census, *Characteristics of the Population, United States Summary, 1940, 1960,* Alaska and Hawaii excluded.

** Standardized by number reporting occupations.

*** Standardized by number reporting non-farm occupations.

These figures appear to demonstrate an occupational upgrading of non-whites. The data are unclear as to relative rates of upgrading. Nonwhites are shifting from farm to non-farm occupations in larger numbers than whites; shifting into the highest status occupations less rapidly than whites; shifting into the middle status occupations more rapidly than whites; and shifting out of the lowest status occupations more rapidly than whites, if we consider non-farm occupational data and, less rapidly than whites if we consider data on all occupations.

The seventh and eighth columns in Table 3 present the proportion of nonwhites in each occupational category for 1940 and 1960. The final two columns present ratios of the 1960 proportions to the 1940 proportions standardized by numbers reporting occupations for all occupations and non-farm occupations only. As in the case of education, a ratio of one represents changes at the same rate as the larger society; more than one, increase in proportional representation; less than one, decrease in proportional representation. The ratios computed on the basis of all occupations show a decrease in nonwhite representation in the farmer-farm manager occupational category and an increase in all other occupational categories (but a negligible increase in the service category). The ratios computed on the basis of non-farm occupations show a decrease in nonwhite representation in the occupational categories of professional-technical and service; relative stability in the occupational categories of labor and management-official-proprietor; and an increase in proportional representation in all other occupational categories.

When considered as a totality, the data on occupational changes indicate that nonwhites are leaving the farms more rapidly than whites, are being occupationally ugraded relative to previous generations of nonwhites; and are experiencing some occupational upgrading relative to whites but possibly not at the highest occupational status levels.

INCOME

It is difficult to examine income changes over extended periods of time because of the large number of different techniques of reporting income that are used, the difficulty in getting data from the same technique for many consecutive years, and the shifting value of the dollar in terms of purchasing power. We will consider the technique of measuring income which was reported over the longest time span, analyzed in both current and constant dollars. Constant dollars are computed by translating the purchasing power of current dollars into the average purchasing power of the dollar from 1947 to 1949.

Table 4 presents median income of males 14 and over having wage or salary income by color for those years in which such data were available from 1939 to 1961. Nonwhite income has shown a relatively steady increase in both current and constant dollars from 1939 to 1961. White income has shown a similar increase in both current and constant dollars. The difference between white and nonwhite median incomes in constant dollars increased from $1,276 in 1939 to $1,776 in 1961. Thus, nonwhite males have improved their income in both current and constant dollars,

TABLE 4

Median Income Males 14 and Over Having Wage or Salary Income in Current
and Constant Dollars in the United States for 1939 to 1961°

	White		Nonwhite		White Minus Nonwhite in Constant Dollars
Year	Current Dollars	Constant Dollars	Current Dollars	Constant Dollars	Constant Dollars
1939	1112	2176	460	900	1276
***	***	***	***	***	***
1947	2357	2468	1279	1339	1189
1948	2711	2637	1615	1571	1066
1949	2735	2686	1367	1342	1344
1950	2982	2901	1828	1779	1122
1951	3345	3014	2060	1856	1158
1952	3507	3090	2038	1795	1295
1953	3760	3286	2833	1826	1460
1954	3754	3270	2131	1856	1414
1955	3986	3480	2342	2045	1435
***	***	***	***	***	***
1961	5287	4134	3015	2358	1776

° Source: *Statistical Abstract of the United States*, Washington, D.C.: United States
Department of Commerce, Bureau of the Census, 1962, and earlier editions. 1961 income data from P.60 Series, *Current Population Reports*, 1962.

but have fallen further behind white males in so doing.[14] In other words,
nonwhites are raising their standard of living, but less rapidly than whites.

EVALUATION OF HYPOTHESES

Now that the changing position of the Negro (nonwhite) in the United
States has been examined, we are in a position to evaluate the hypotheses
presented earlier.

"The Vulgar Marxist Hypothesis," which predicted rebellion as a result
of a worsening of conditions of life, is clearly inconsistent with these data.
The position of the Negro is improving educationally, occupationally, and
income-wise.

"The Rising Expectations Hypothesis," which predicted rebellion as a
result of improvements in conditions of life, is consistent with the data examined. Negroes have improved their level of education; they have better
jobs, and they are earning more money with which they may purchase
more things. One might assume a more rapid rise in level of aspirations
but data are lacking to either substantiate or refute the assumption.

"The Sophisticated Marxist Hypothesis," which gave a relative deprivation basis for its prediction of rebellion, is also consistent with these data.
Negroes have improved their level of education and have done so more
rapidly than have whites. But education is not a direct measure of living
conditions either socially or economically. It is one source of status and,

[14] This same general pattern emerges regardless of the choice of income data. It
holds for median family income, female income, urban income, as well as the combined individual and family income.

as such, it carries with it certain satisfactions. Occupation may be viewed as a second source of status. The Negro has improved his occupational level, thus improving his status rewards as well as receiving other rewards in terms of better working conditions. The evidence is not clear as to the relative occupational gains or losses experienced by the Negro. He appears to be moving more rapidly than whites into the middle status occupations, but if urban occupations only are considered, he is moving more slowly into the higher status occupations. Whether this situation would produce feelings of relative loss or relative gain is a moot question which could only be settled through further empirical studies.

The area of income most directly affects conditions of life and presents the clearest picture. Negroes are improving their incomes in terms of both current and constant dollars. The gap between white and Negro incomes is also increasing in terms of both current and constant dollars. Thus, Negroes are improving their material conditions of life but are not doing so at the same rate as whites. This is the perfect situation to create feelings of relative deprivation leading to rebellion.

"The Rise and Drop Hypothesis," which predicted rebellion as a result of the reversal of past progress in conditions of life, is not consistent with the data examined. There appears to be relatively steady improvement in level of education, level of occupation, and income in both current and constant dollars. No reversal may be observed.

"The Status Inconsistency Hypothesis," which predicted rebellion as a result of an increase in the proportion of status inconsistents, is consistent with the data examined. There has been an increase in the proportion of status inconsistents among Negroes. This is true in both a trivial and a significant sense. Current research in status inconsistency emphasizes the dimensions of occupation, income, education, and ethnicity as the crucial ones for American society. Negroes have retained their low ethnic status, but they have improved their position on each of the other status dimensions. Thus, they have increased their status inconsistency in the trivial sense. They have increased the combination of low ethnic status with higher rankings on other dimensions.

Negroes have also increased their status inconsistency in a more significant sense. These data show that they are not only improving their level of education, but they are doing so at a more rapid rate than whites; while in the area of occupational gains there has not been as significant a gain relative to that of whites. Table 1 shows that nonwhites are increasing their proportional representation in the educational category of one-to-three-years-of-college 1.53 times as rapidly as is the total society, and they are increasing their representation in the four-or-more-years-of-college 1.38 times as rapidly. When the category of all those with any college is considered, nonwhites are increasing their representation 1.48 times as rapidly as is the general society. Yet Table 3, which covers the same time span, shows that nonwhites are increasing their representation in the occupational category of professional-technical workers only 1.16 times as rapidly as the general society, when all occupations are considered, or 0.82 times as rapidly when only non-farm occupations are considered. They are increasing their representation in the combined managerial and professional categories 1.19 times as rapidly as whites, when all occupations are considered, and 1.00 times as rapidly for non-farm occupations. This shows that nonwhites (and presumably Negroes) are improving their educational qualifications for professional and technical jobs more rapidly than they are receiving these jobs, thus causing an increased disparity between educational qualifications for jobs and level of occupational achievement.[15]

We may observe the same pattern if we consider proportional distributions of whites and nonwhites into educational and occupational categories. Nonwhites increased their representation in the category of some college or college graduate by 4.7 percent. These would presumably be the categories best qualifying them for upper white collar jobs. They increased their representation in the professional-technical occupational category by 2.2 percent (a gain which is 44.7 percent of the educational gain), and they increased their representation in the combined manager and professional-technical categories by 2.8 percent (59.6 percent of the educational gain). The corresponding figures for whites show an increase of 8.1 percent in the some college or college graduate category and an increase of 5.4 percent (66.7 percent of the educational gain) in the professional-technical categories and an increase in the combined professional-technical and manager categories of 6.7 percent (82.7 percent of the educational gain). These data show that whites are making gains in the occupational realm which are much more in proportion to their educational gains than are nonwhites. Data on non-farm occupations reveal the same pattern.[16] Nonwhites are increasing their discrepancy between education and occupation and becoming more status inconsistent.

It was shown in Table 4 that Negroes are not increasing their income level as rapidly as whites. Further evidence that improved educational achievements are not rewarded by increased incomes as rapidly for nonwhites as for whites may be derived from Table 5. Not only do nonwhites receive a lower median income than whites at each level of education, but the dollar gap between medians increases as level of education increases.

Even if we ignore their ethnicity, Negroes are becoming increasingly status inconsistent as a result of the fact that they are raising their level

[15] I say an increased discrepancy because Turner has already demonstrated the existence of the discrepancy in 1940. He showed that only 39 percent of the nonwhites' lower job status could be attributed to their lesser amount of education. See Ralph H. Turner, "Foci of Discrimination in the Employment of Non-Whites," *American Journal of Sociology*, 58 (November 1952), pp. 247–256.

[16] Nonwhites: Professional-technical—1.5 percent (31.9 percent of educational gains). Combined Manager and Professional-technical—1.2 percent (25.6 percent of educational gains).

Whites: Professional-technical—4.9 percent (60.5 percent of educational gains). Combined Manager and Professional-technical—4.4 percent (54.3 percent of educational gains).

TABLE 5

Median Income by Level of Education and Color—Males 14 and Over, 1961[*]

Level of Education	White	Nonwhite	Difference
Elementary:			
Less than 8 years	2303	1554	749
8 years	3617	2505	1112
High School:			
1–3 years	4090	2427	1663
4 years	5155	3381	1774
Some college	6379	4246	2133
Total	4432	2292	2140

[*] Source: *Current Population Reports*, P60 Series, United States Bureau of the Census, #39, p. 4.

of education but are being denied the occupational mobility or income level which would "normally" be associated with such progress.

DISCUSSION

Only two out of the five proposed hypotheses have been rejected. This leaves the task of either choosing among the remaining hypotheses or somehow reconciling them. It is a relatively simple task to reconcile the "Sophisticated Marxist Hypothesis" with "The Status Inconsistency Hypothesis," as the essence of each is the concept of the relative deprivation. The former is explicitly stated in these terms, while the latter's thesis is implied. It is the association between statuses which generally prevails in a society that determines what is status consistency. Deviations from this prevailing association are what constitute status inconsistency. It is the experiencing of these deviations to one's own detriment which causes the propensity to revolt among status inconsistents.[17]

It is also possible to reconcile "The Rising Expectations Hypothesis" with the "Status Inconsistency Hypothesis." Both Edwards and Brinton see blockages of social mobility as an essential basis for "The Rising Expectations Hypothesis."[18] People feel that they have legitimate aspirations which are blocked, thus interfering with the circulation of the elite, and creating a status inconsistent group. This is very similar to the interpretation that Broom gives to "The Status Inconsistency Hypothesis."[19]

It seems that "relative deprivation" is of the essence of all three hypotheses that are consistent with the observed data. It is only by observing the process of social mobility in society that one will develop aspirations for such mobility. Observation of the criteria used to select successful aspirants allows development of feelings that one's aspirations are legiti-

[17] Cf., George C. Homans, *Social Behavior: Its Elementary Forms* (New York: Harcourt Brace & World, 1961), pp. 232–264. Homans points out that anger leading to rebellion will result from the experiencing of this deviance to one's detriment, while guilt (which is a weaker emotion not calculated to lead to rebellion) will result from the experiencing of this deviance to one's benefit.

[18] Brinton, *op. cit.*, pp. 78–79; Edwards, *op. cit.*, p. 30.

mate. Possession of these characteristics without subsequent mobility creates status inconsistency. Without comparing one's own experiences with those of others in society and subsequently developing feelings of relative deprivation, no rebellion would take place.

CONCLUSIONS

Five hypotheses which purport to account for the current "Negro Revolt" were taken from the literature. Data were examined which resulted in the rejection of two of these. The three which remained were reconciled with each other in terms of their common basis in the concept of relative deprivation. This should not be misinterpreted as a claim that the psychological state of possessing feelings of relative deprivation will, regardless of objective conditions, produce rebellion. In contrast, the suggestion proposed herein is that certain types of objective conditions will produce feelings of relative deprivation, which will, in turn, produce rebellion.

The Negro in the United States has been exposed to just such a set of objective conditions. He is handicapped by blockages in the circulation of the elite, especially in the area of the professions. He is acquiring the education which is normally the key to occupational mobility and economic gain. He is not experiencing as rapid a rate of occupational mobility to which he feels he is entitled. He is not receiving the economic rewards which he feels he has earned. As a result, he is becoming increasingly status inconsistent and he sees himself falling further and further behind the white. He feels relatively deprived and unjustly so. Therefore, he revolts in order to correct the situation.

26

The Class and Status Bases of Negro Student Protest[1]

ANTHONY M. ORUM
EMORY UNIVERSITY
AMY W. ORUM
EMORY UNIVERSITY

MOST CONTEMPORARY ANALYSTS OF SOCIAL AND POLITICAL MOVEMENTS subscribe to the view that such movements originate from a number of different circumstances. Smelser, for instance, argues that social movements may emerge in response to conditions as diverse as economic depressions, wars, and actions of agencies like the police force.[2] Others assign the major impetus for social movements to economic and status-related deprivations.[3] Threats to the maintenance or improvement of a group's economic resources and status accoutrements, they argue, eventually can produce sufficient discontent to permit social movements to arise.

In the case of the present Negro protest movement in the United States, observers frequently trace its roots to barriers to Negroes' economic and status-related achievements.[4] With few exceptions, however, the connection between protest activity and economic or status-related deprivation among Negroes has been based on insufficient evidence.[5] By examining

---

[1] This article represents a revised portion of the senior author's doctoral dissertation, "Negro College Students and the Civil Rights Movement," (unpublished Ph.D. diss., University of Chicago, 1967). Norman Bradburn provided helpful suggestions on an earlier draft of this article.

[2] Neil Smelser, *A Theory of Collective Behavior* (New York: Free Press, 1963), Chs. 10 and 11.

[3] See especially the studies by Richard Hofstadter, "The Pseudo-Conservative Revolt," and "Pseudo-Conservatism Revisited: A Postscript," and by Seymour M. Lipset; "The Sources of the Radical Right," and "Three Decades of the Radical Right: Coughlinites, McCarthyites, and Birchers," in Daniel Bell, ed., *The Radical Right* (Garden City, N.Y.: Doubleday and Co., Inc., 1963), pp. 63–86, 259–377.

[4] See, for instance, William F. Soskin, "Riots, Ghettos, and the 'Negro Revolt,'" in Arthur M. Ross and Herbert Hill, eds., *Employment, Race and Poverty* (New York: Harcourt, Brace and World, Inc., 1967), p. 209.

[5] Studies of participation in the Negro protest movement mainly deal with the participation of students. These studies only briefly consider the relationship between economic and status-related factors and participation. See J. R. Fishman and F. Solomon, "Youth and Social Action: I. Perspective on the Student Sit-In Movement," *The American Journal of Orthopsychiatry*, 33 (Oct., 1963), pp. 872–882; Donald R. Matthews and James W. Prothro, *Negroes and the New Southern Politics* (New York: Harcourt, Brace & World, 1966); John M. Orbell, "Protest Participation Among Southern Negro College Students," *American Political Science Review*, 61 (June, 1967), pp. 446–456; Ruth Searles and J. Allen Williams, Jr., "Negro College Students' Participation in Sit-Ins," *Social Forces*, 40 (March, 1962), pp. 215–220; F. Solomon and J. R. Fishman, "Youth and Social Action: II. Action and Identity Formation in the First Student Sit-In Demonstration," *The Journal of Social Issues*, 20 (April, 1964), pp. 36–45; and Howard Zinn, *SNCC: The New Abolitionists* (Boston: Beacon Press, 1964). The only reported research on this topic among adults is in Gary T. Marx, *Protest and Prejudice: A Study of Belief in the Black Community* (New York: Harper and Row, 1967).

◆ First published in *Social Science Quarterly* 49, No. 3 (December, 1968).

data on Negro college students, the present study seeks to shed light on this matter. Specifically, we ask: To what extent is the participation of Negro college students in the Negro protest movement a response to economic or status-related deprivation?

PERSPECTIVES AND RESEARCH ON THE NEGRO PROTEST MOVEMENT

The literature about economic or status-related conditions and the Negro protest movement can best be viewed in terms of three explanations outlined by Geschwender.[6] In this section we shall examine the evidence for each explanation. The first interpretation, the "vulgar Marxist" orientation, claims that fundamental economic impoverishment may create the dissatisfaction required for a social movement to emerge.[7] Meier and other social scientists as well as Negro political leaders emphasize the importance of such basic economic motivations for the present Negro protest efforts.[8] For instance, in 1963, Whitney Young, Jr., a moderate Negro spokesman, dramatized the economic plight of Negroes by calling for a domestic "Marshall Plan" to help offset unemployment and poverty among Negroes.[9] Miller argues that "usually the long-term economically depressed are unlikely candidates for a dynamic political movement, but the race ethnic dimension, as well as the economic factor, is propelling the poor, whether Negro, Mexican-American, or Puerto Rican."[10] In addition, organizations engaged in the Negro protest movement, like the Student Nonviolent Coordinating Committee (SNCC), focus their campaigns on basic economic issues and problems. Such organizations often

[6] Geschwender provides a very interesting explication of five hypotheses about the relation between certain social and economic conditions and the rise of the Negro protest movement. James A. Geschwender, "Social Structure and the Negro Revolt: An Examination of Some Hypotheses," *Social Forces*, 43 (Dec., 1964), pp. 248–256.

[7] The type of evidence that supports this point of view can be found in: Leonard Broom and Norval Glenn, *Transformation of the Negro American* (New York: Harper and Row, 1965), Chs. 5 and 6; Rashi Fein, "An Economic and Social Profile of the Negro American," in Talcott Parsons and Kenneth B. Clark, eds., *The Negro American* (Boston: Houghton-Mifflin Co., 1966), pp. 102–133; Dale W. Hiestand, *Economic Growth and Employment Opportunities for Minorities* (New York: Columbia University Press, 1964); Herbert Hill, "Racial Inequality in Employment: The Patterns of Discrimination," in Arnold Rose, ed., *Annals of the American Academy of Political and Social Science*, Special Issue on The Negro Protest, 357 (Jan., 1965), pp. 30–47; Thomas Pettigrew, *A Profile of the Negro American* (Princeton, N.J.: D. Van Nostrand Co., Inc., 1964), esp. p. 189; and U.S. Department of Labor, "The Employment of Negroes: Some Demographic Considerations," in Raymond J. Murphy and Howard Elinson, eds., *Problems and Prospects of the Negro Movement* (Belmont, Calif.: Wadsworth Publishing Co., Inc., 1966), pp. 116–124.

[8] August Meier, "Civil Rights Strategies for Negro Employment," in Ross and Hill, eds., *Employment, Race and Poverty*, pp. 175–204.

[9] Whitney M. Young, Jr., "Domestic Marshall Plan," in *New York Times Magazine*, October 6, 1963, cited in Murphy and Elinson, eds., *Problems and Propsects*, pp. 45–49.

[10] S. M. Miller, "Poverty and Politics," in Irving Louis Horowitz, ed., *The New Sociology* (New York: Oxford University Press, 1964), p. 297, quoted in Michael Harrington, "The Economics of Protest," in Ross and Hill, eds., *Employment, Race and Poverty*, p. 236.

have demanded increased job opportunities for Negroes, sometimes in preference to voting rights or benefits in housing, frequently have employed economic boycotts to secure fair treatment for Negroes by white-owned or operated businesses, and, most recently, have urged the full-scale development of business enterprises in the ghettos.[11]

The second explanation, the "rising expectations" view, argues that if people of longstanding impoverishment are subject to heightened aspirations, due to partial fulfillment of certain goals, then they may become dissatisfied with gradual improvement of their situation and seek to channel their energies into a social movement. A number of writers accept this point of view as an interpretation of the present Negro protest efforts.[12] Kristol, for instance, remarks that "American Negroes . . . feel . . . that they have a special claim upon American society: they have had some centuries of resignation and now would like to see tangible benefits, quickly."[13] Evidence from public opinion polls conducted in the 1950's and 1960's indicates that Negroes had comparatively high expectations regarding their future. A 1954 nationwide study revealed that 64 per cent of the Negroes felt life would become better as compared with only 53 per cent of a matched group of whites who had this feeling.[14] Approximately 10 years later Brink and Harris found somewhat larger proportions of Negro respondents answering positively to similar questions.[15] However, such high aspirations of Negroes may quickly be transformed into anger and frustration when confronted with insurmountable barriers to their fulfillment. Along these lines, the discovery that the Negro-white income gap increases with additional education prompted Siegel to comment: "We might speak of the motivation provided the civil rights movement by the discovery on the part of thousands of young Negroes that their coveted education wasn't worth much on the open market."[16]

The third thesis, the "relative deprivation" perspective, states that discontent, and subsequently, social rebellion, may occur among people who evaluate their achievements by reference to the standards and accomplishments of some similarly situated persons who differ only in terms of having different or more numerous advantages. Karl Marx provided the essence of this notion by observing:

11 Broom and Glenn, *Transformation*, pp. 69–72; Jack L. Walker, "Protest and Negotiation: A Case Study of Negro Leadership in Atlanta," *Midwest Journal of Political Science*, 7 (May, 1963), pp. 99–124.

12 Broom and Glenn, *Transformation*, p. 59; Pettigrew, *A Profile*, pp. 170–191; and Everett Carll Ladd, Jr., *Negro Political Leadership in the South* (Ithaca, N.Y.: Cornell University Press, 1966), p. 24.

13 Irving Kristol, "It's Not a Bad Crisis To Live In," *New York Times Magazine*, January 22, 1967, p. 70.

14 Cited in Pettigrew, *A Profile*, pp. 184–185.

15 William Brink and Louis Harris, *The Negro Revolution in America* (New York: Simon and Schuster, 1964), p. 238.

16 Paul M. Siegel, "On the Cost of Being a Negro," *Sociological Inquiry*, 35 (Winter, 1965), p. 57. Siegel's results are also pertinent to the discussion on "relative deprivation."

A house may be large or small; as long as the surrounding houses are equally small it satisfies all social demands for a dwelling. But let a palace arise beside the little house, and it shrinks from a little house to a hut.[17]

In the case of the Negro protest activities, many observers claim that certain segments of the Negro community, especially for middle class, experience dissatisfaction as a result of comparing their achievements with those of their white counterparts.[18] The evidence for this argument certainly appears convincing. While Negro unemployment, for example, seems to have declined over the past 20 years, it has increased relative to that of whites.[19] In addition, the few studies of Negro participation in the Negro protest movement indicate that the more socially advantaged persons are over-represented in the protest activities. A recent study by G. Marx, for instance, demonstrates that Negroes who have more educational, occupational, and social privileges were more apt to be militant about the need for Negroes to gain equal rights.[20] After finding that middle-class Negro college students were over-represented among student participants, Searles and Williams suggest that many student participants adopted their white middle-class counterparts as a reference group.[21] Similar evidence on the background of Negro student protesters also is presented by Matthews and Prothro and Orbell.[22]

Each of the above interpretations attempts in a somewhat different manner to account for the current momentum of Negro protest efforts by virtue of economic or status-related deprivations among Negroes. In the analysis which follows, an attempt is made to determine whether the phenomenon of fundamental poverty, relative deprivation, or rising expectations is more characteristic of protest participants than of nonparticipants among Negro students.

DATA

The data upon which this study is based are part of a nationwide sample survey conducted in 1964 by the National Opinion Research Center (NORC). The purpose of the survey was to collect information on the graduate plans of seniors at colleges and universities throughout the na-

[17] Karl Marx, "Wage-Labor and Capital," in Karl Marx and Friederich Engels, *Selected Works* (Moscow, 1958), I, p. 93, quoted in Ladd, *Negro Political Leadership*, p. 24.

[18] This explanation is found in many discussions of the Negro protest movement. For illustrations: see Broom and Glenn, *Transformation*, p. 106; Joseph Gusfield, *Symbolic Crusade: Status Politics and the American Temperance Movement* (Urbana: University of Illinois Press, 1963), p. 22; Lewis M. Killian and Charles Grigg, *Racial Crisis in America: Leadership in Conflict* (Englewood Cliffs, N.J.; Prentice-Hall, Inc., 1964), pp. 133–134; Pettigrew, *A Profile*, pp. 178–179; and Daniel Thompson, "The Rise of the Negro Protest," in Rose, ed., *Annals of American Academy*, pp. 19–20.

[19] U.S. Department of Labor Report in Murphy and Elinson, eds., *Problems and Prospects*, p. 121.

[20] Gary T. Marx, *Protest and Prejudice*, pp. 55–70.

[21] Searles and Williams, "Negro College Students' Participation," p. 219.

[22] Matthews and Prothro, *Negroes and the New Southern Politics*, p. 419; and Orbell, "Protest Participation," p. 448. Orbell, incidentally, used the same data as Matthews and Prothro.

CLASS AND STATUS BASES OF NEGRO STUDENT PROTEST

tion. In April and May of 1964 a questionnaire was sent to a representative group of seniors at these institutions. In addition, a sample was chosen of seniors at predominantly Negro senior colleges and universities, designed to represent all students who received their bachelor's degrees in the spring of 1964.[23] Members of the NORC staff, together with personnel from the Department of Labor, identified 77 schools primarily attended by Negroes.[24] This list was comparable with one compiled independently and, for all practical purposes, exhausted the population of four-year predominantly Negro colleges and universities in the United States.[25] A two-stage probability design was employed in choosing the sample of students. Altogether, a total of 50 schools and roughly 7,000 students were included in the original sample.

Although respondents represent about one-third of all Negro college seniors who graduated in the spring of 1964, about 3,500 students, the response rate was only 49 per cent. In contrast, the response rate to the nationwide 1964 study was 74 per cent. No conclusive evidence was obtained to explain this low rate among Negroes, but one investigation suggests that a major factor was the greater length of the Negro college student questionnaire.[26] The low response rate probably accounts for certain biased characteristics of respondents. Those students who responded were more likely to be women, to have higher grade-point averages, and to have majors in areas such as the physical sciences and humanities. These biases, however, were similar in type and magnitude to those in the nationwide study. Hence, there appears to be no reason for anticipating that the biases affected the representativeness of this sample.

FINDINGS

The information on the participation of students in the protest activities comes from two separate questions. Students were asked, first of all, what major protest events had occurred on their campuses. As can be seen in Table 1, most students claimed that economic boycotts were the major activity at their school, an answer that confirms other evidence on the popularity of economic boycotts among Negro college students.[27] In addition, students were questioned about their own roles in these efforts. Approximately 70 per cent of the students reported participation and, of this group, 32 per cent claimed to be active participants or leaders. A comprehensive measure of participation probably should account for both the degree and type of involvement, but the ambiguity of the question on type of activity prevented our creating such a mseasure. Instead we chose to

[23] The results of this study of Negro seniors' career plans are reported in Joseph H. Fichter, "Neglected Talents: Background and Prospects of Negro College Graduates," National Opinion Research Center, Feb., 1966, multilithed.

[24] This group of schools does not include the fairly large number of predominantly Negro junior colleges in the United States.

[25] The other list was assembled by McGrath. See Earl J. McGrath, *The Predominantly Negro Colleges and Universities in Transition* (New York: Bureau of Publications, Teachers College, Columbia University, 1965).

[26] Fichter, "Neglected Talents," App. 1.

[27] Broom and Glenn, *Transformation*.

TABLE 1

Proportion of Students Reporting Major Types
of Protest Activities on Their Campus

	Per Cent	N
Holding rallies	36	1,244
Public addresses by civil rights leaders	40	1,378
Participation in "freedom rides"	19	655
Participation in boycott moves against		
segregated businesses	64	2,170
Sit-ins in segregated public places	61	2,098
Fund raising for civil rights movement	35	1,185
Voter registration campaigns	48	1,652
Marches on city hall	42	1,441
Participation in March on Washington	23	802
None of these	12	405
No answer	—	125
Total	380	13,165
Total N		3,423[a]

[a] Variations in total sample size from table to table are due to rounding off to
nearest whole number.

distinguish between students who said that they were nonparticipants and
those who reported taking an inactive, active, or leadership role.[28]

SOCIOECONOMIC STATUS AND PARTICIPATION. Most evidence concerning
the link between economic or status factors and involvement in the Negro
protest movement is based on the background characteristics of participants and nonparticipants. Without exception, such evidence indicates
that Negroes from middle-class, or in general, more privileged background were more apt to be protest participants. In Table 2 we have assembled information on fathers' education, family income, and protest
participation that allow us to re-examine these results. The education of
students' fathers shows no association with participation, whereas the income of students' families has a slight positive relationship with participation. Students from high SES backgrounds were slightly more apt to
participate in protest activities. The "relatively deprived" students, those
from families with high education but low income, were no more likely
to be protest participants than were their economic peers from families
with less education.

It will be recalled from our earlier discussion that one interpretation of
the Negro protest movement concerns the relative deprivation of Negroes
as compared with their white counterparts. Although the data do not per-

---

[28] Also examined were the correlates of activism by distinguishing between activists,
leaders or very active participants, and nonactivitists, inactive participants. The characteristics of the activists did not differ much from those who were inactive participants.
As a consequence, results were presented only on the dimension of participation.

mit systematic exploration of this hypothesis, we can examine the relative deprivation of Negro students in their college settings. Table 3 presents data on the SES composition of the school, the SES background of students, and protest participation.[29] If the relative-deprivation argument is correct, then we would anticipate more extensive participation among students whose SES background is lower than that of their fellow students. Specifically, students from homes of low SES should be more likely to participate in schools in which there is a medium or high proportion of students from

TABLE 2

Father's Education, Family Income, and Protest
Participation (per cent participating)

Father's Education	Family Income	
	Less than $5,000/yr.	$5,000 or more/yr.
Some high school or less	69	74
N =	(1,389)	(471)
High school grad- uate or more	69	74
N =	(456)	(617)
Total N		3,424[a]

[a] Variations in total sample size due to rounding.

TABLE 3

Socioeconomic Status Composition of Schools, Socioeconomic Status Background
of Students, and Protest Participation (per cent participating)

School SES (Proportion of students from high SES families)	Students' SES		Participating Total Per Cent
	Low	High	
Low	61	65	61
N =	(850)	(99)	(949)
Medium	76	73	75
N =	(677)	(175)	(852)
High	77	75	76
N=	(634)	(498)	(1,132)
Total N			3,423[a]

[a] Variations in total sample size due to rounding.

[29] An index of socioeconomic status was created by combining responses to questions on father's education, family income, and occupation of the chief wage earner. In terms of this index, a family of high socioeconomic status would be comprised of a man whose education included at least some college training, whose head—most often a man—held a professional, managerial, or clerical position, and whose annual income was at least $7,500. Of course such families appear to be more prevalent among the parents of the Negro student population than among the Negro population in general.

high SES backgrounds. An examination of data in Table 3, however, reveals virtually no difference in participation among students from low- and high-SES families in the different settings.[30]

STUDENT OCCUPATIONAL ASPIRATIONS AND PARTICIPATION. Some additional depth to our analysis of SES factors and participation in the protest activities is provided by examining students' choices of occupational careers. In order to make this analysis, we first examined the relationship between students' career preferences as freshmen and participation. Using freshman career preferences, the preference in 1960, rather than senior preferences, acts as a control for the possibility that protest participation from 1960 through 1964 might have had either beneficial or adverse consequences for students' aspirations.[31] Among both men and women we found that students with high career aspirations as freshmen were somewhat more apt to participate in the protest events.[32] Among 1,028 male students, 79 per cent of those with high aspirations were participants as compared to 76 per cent of those with low aspirations. Among 1,859 females, the percentages were 72 and 66, respectively. The relationship was stronger for women, but was not very strong in either case.

Let us suppose, however, that a shift in students' career aspirations from their freshman through senior year accompanied differential involvement in the protest movement. For example, some students may have shifted their aspirations from "high" to "low" during their college years because of their dissatisfaction with prospects for occupational success. And, as a con-

[30] The careful reader will note that the class composition of the school is related to the rate of participation. Specifically, the greater the proportion of students from high socioeconomic status (SES) homes, the greater is the rate of participation. This association can be explained by other variables that are related to the proportion of high SES students. For instance, schools of high quality generally have a greater proportion of students from high SES backgrounds and also have higher rates of student participation. See Matthews and Prothro, *Negroes and the New Southern Politics*, pp. 424–429; Orbell, "Protest Participation," pp. 448–450; and Anthony M. Orum, "Negro College Students and the Civil Rights Movement" (unpublished Ph.D. diss., University of Chicago, 1967), Ch. 6. The measures of school quality employed in these studies are based upon such indexes as the proportion of Ph.D.'s on the faculty, student-faculty ratio, ratio of library books per student, and number of books in the library.

[31] Pettigrew, for instance, claims that involvement in the protest might have advantageous effects for the self-respect and esteem of Negroes. He states that "the remedial powers of the movements themselves alter their followers in the process. . . . Negro Americans are learning how to be first-class citizens at the same time they are winning first-class citizenship." (Pettigrew, *A Profile*, p. 167).

[32] In order to measure the level of students' career aspirations, an index developed by James Davis was employed. It is based upon the number of years of postgraduate education required for a particular occupation. The careers tend to be ranked by skill level or loosely speaking, occupational status. See James A. Davis, *Great Aspirations* (Chicago: Aldine Press, 1964). Sex was used as a control variable in this and subsequent analyses. There were two reasons for this procedure. First, the anticipated associations between economic or status-related factors and participation might have been stronger for men, since occupational data often demonstrate that Negro males seem to face a greater inequality of opportunity than Negro females, particularly in the white-collar occupations. Second, Negro college men were more likely to participate in the protest than Negro women. This difference might have confounded other differences in the association between economic or status-related factors and participation.

sequence, they might have been more likely than other students to participate in the protest movement. Examination of the data in Table 4, however, indicates that such an argument is unwarranted.

PERCEPTION OF EMPLOYMENT OPPORTUNITIES AND PARTICIPATION. Both
the "rising expectations" and, to a lesser degree, the relative-deprivation
explanations suggest that protest activity may arise among Negroes who
confront unanticipated limits on their opportunities. Negro students tend,
as a group, to be one of the more upwardly mobile segments of the Negro
community. Yet their earnings are not commensurate with their educational attainment.[33] For that matter, their opportunities for employment
in the professions and in business also may not be commensurate with
their education.[34] Consequently, those Negro students who recognize the
existence of such barriers might turn to the Negro protest movement to
relieve their discontent.

Such arguments are examined here by looking at the association between students' perception of employment opportunities and protest participation. Students were asked the following question about job opportunities in the nation: "In your view, when will Negroes have equal job
opportunities as compared with whites of the same educational level?"
Students' responses to this question, together with the extent of their participation, are presented in Table 5. Among both male and female students, perception of opportunities for employment in the nation bore no
relationship to the extent of participation. A similar absence of association
is found between participation and the perception of employment opportunities in both the North and South.

TABLE 4

Sex, Freshman Career Preference, Senior Career Preference,
and Protest Participation (per cent participating)

Sex	Freshman Career Preference	Senior Career Preference	
		Low	High
Male	Low N=	74 (392)	78 (109)
	High N =	77 (167)	81 (340)
Female	Low N=	65 (1,123)	69 (127)
	High N =	72 (27)	72 (283)
Total N			3,423[a]

[a] Variations in total sample size due to rounding.

[33] Siegel, "On the Cost."
[34] For instance, see Hill, "Racial Inequality," pp. 30–47.

TABLE 5

Sex, Perception of Employment Opportunities in the Nation,
and Protest Participation (per cent participating)

Sex	Perception of Opportunities	
	Equal now/ten years	Equal twenty years or more
Male	77	77
N =	(510)	(501)
Female	66	67
N =	(1,032)	(780)
Total N		3,422[a]

[a] Variations in total sample size due to rounding.

TABLE 6

Gamma Coefficients for Association between Perception of
Employment Opportunities and Participation, Controlling
for Most Important Goal of Protest Movement and Sex

Type of Opportunity	Most Important Goal			
	Employment Opportunities		All Others	
	Male	Female	Male	Female
Employment opportunities in the nation[a]	+.06	−.01	−.02	−.04
Employment opportunities in the South	+.08	−.03	−.05	−.06
Employment opportunities in the North	+.05	−.06	+.01	−.03

[a] In each case, participation is counted as positive, (+), and nonparticipation as negative (−). Thus, a gamma coefficient with a plus sign, (+), means that students who thought equal employment opportunities for Negroes would be obtained in twenty years or more were more likely to be participants than students who thought such opportunities would be achieved more rapidly.

The analysis above assumes that many students thought that the expansion of employment opportunities for Negroes was an important goal of the Negro protest movement and, thus, joined the movement when confronted with limits on their own mobility. Undoubtedly, some dissatisfied students did not regard the protest movement as a vehicle for such purposes and therefore did not choose to participate in the protest. In order to take account of this possibility, let us examine the relationship between perception of employment opportunities and participation among students who did think that expanded opportunities were the most important goal. As the data in Table 6 indicate, even among the students who believed expanded job opportunities were the most significant aim of the

Negro protest movement, the perception of employment opportunities had neither a consistent nor a strong association with participation.

OCCUPATIONAL ASPIRATIONS, PERCEPTION OF OPPORTUNITIES AND PARTICIPATION. Although this investigation has provided less than convincing evidence for the connection between economic or status-related factors and protest participation, one additional hypothesis. It is plausible to argue that the occupational aspirations of students would, in Lazarsfeld's terms, specify the relationship between perception of opportunities and participation.[35] More precisely, we might anticipate that only among the Negro students with high aspirations will the perception of limited employment opportunities lead to protest participation. Table 7 presents data necessary to test this hypothesis. Although freshman career preference continues to be slightly related to participation, students' perception of employment opportunities has no association with participation, even among students with high aspirations.

DISCUSSION

There are three traditional explanations which have been used to account for the growth of the Negro protest movement in terms of economic and status-related deprivations. The "vulgar Marxist" explanation argues that fundamental economic impoverishment of Negroes produces the necessary conditions for the spread of Negro protest efforts. This argument

TABLE 7

Sex, Perception of Employment Opportunities in the Nation, Freshman Career Preference and Protest Participation (per cent participating)

| Sex | Opportunities | Freshman Career Preference | |
		Low	High
Male	Equal now/ten years	77	80
	N =	(250)	(208)
	Twenty years or more	78	82
	N =	(199)	(263)
Female	Equal now/ten years	66	73
	N =	(672)	(271)
	Twenty years or more	66	71
	N =	(474)	(235)
	Total N		3,424[a]

[a] Variations in total sample size due to rounding.

[35] Patricia L. Kendall and Paul L. Lazarsfeld, "Problems of Survey Analysis," in Robert K. Merton and Paul F. Lazarsfeld, eds., *Continuities in Social Research: Studies in the Scope and Method of "The American Soldier"* (New York: Free Press, 1950), pp. 154–165.

received no confirmation from our evidence on the participation of Negro college students. Students from poor families—lower socioeconomic status—were about equally likely to participate in protest activities as were students from wealthy backgrounds, higher SES.

The "rising expectations" thesis claims that many Negroes are unhappy with the pace of their recent achievements and, consequently, have channeled their frustrations into the protest activities. In order to test this argument, we looked at relationships among students' career aspirations, perception of employment opportunities, and protest participation. If this argument were correct, the perception of limited opportunities should have been associated with participation. However, this hypothesis received no support. We also found that there was no association between the perception of employment opportunities and participation even among students with high aspirations, who might be most dissatisfied with limited opportunities. Finally, we expected that many students who had lowered their career aims during college were unhappy with their occupational prospects and, therefore, would be most prone to participate. Instead, we discovered that students with high career aspirations throughout college were most likely to participate.

The third interpretation claims that the Negro protest movement arose largely as a means for expressing the discontent of many Negroes, especially middle-class Negroes, who feel "relatively deprived" compared with their Negro or white peers. In order to assess the effect of individual "deprivation" we examined the SES characteristics of student participants and nonparticipants, in general, and in different college settings. We found that students from relatively deprived backgrounds, homes in which the father's education was high and family income low, had no greater likelihood of participation than any other group. We also anticipated that students whose parents' SES was lower than that of the majority of their fellow students would feel relatively deprived and would be most likely to participate. There was no confirmation of this hypothesis. Of course, none of this evidence provides a basis for dismissing the importance of the relative deprivation that Negro students might feel toward their white counterparts.

By and large, all these results contradict those of previous research. Matthews and Protho as well as Orbell discovered that students from higher SES homes were more likely to be participants than were students from lower SES homes.[36] Searles and Williams also uncovered a similar finding.[37] The present study, however, differs in several respects from earlier research. First, it is based on a much larger and somewhat more representative sample of Negro students and therefore may furnish more reliable evidence of the link between economic and status-related factors and participation. In addition, it was conducted two years after the other studies and reveals about twice as much overall participation. During the intervening two years, it seems likely that many students of lower-class

---

[36] Matthews and Prothro, *Negroes and the New Southern Politics.*
[37] Searles and Williams, "Negro College Students' Participation."

origins became involved in the protest movement. Consequently, the earlier class differences between participants and nonparticipants would tend to disappear.

The different results also could be associated with the fact that the earlier studies used samples of students from all college classes, i.e., freshman through senior, whereas the present research dealt with seniors only. This analysis might indirectly confirm what Newcomb and other social scientists have observed about college students' political behavior: namely, that the impact of background factors such as parents' SES is gradually muted by salient dimensions of the college environment.[38] Along these lines, Matthews and Prothro's research demonstrates that characteristics of the college setting are much better predictors of students' participation in the protest movement than are economic or status-related background variables.[39]

In summary, we have found that several major interpretations of the growth of the Negro protest movement fail to explain student participation in these activities. The inadequacy of these interpretations might be due to the type of group analyzed in this study, or to their limited applicability as explanations of the Negro protest. In either case, the evidence from this research indicates that a re-evaluation should be made of these interpretations. Such a reassessment, moreover, should be conducted not only in light of the results from this study, which deals with Negro protest efforts of the past, but also with an eye to changes occurring in the character of the movement, especially in the strategies of protest organizations.

[38] Theodore M. Newcomb, *Personality and Social Change* (New York: The Dryden Press, 1943).

[39] Matthews and Prothro, *Negroes and the New Southern Politics*, esp. p. 429.

27

Religion: Opiate or Inspiration of Civil Rights Militancy Among Negroes?*

GARY T. MARX**

HARVARD UNIVERSITY

Let justice roll down like waters, and righteousness like a mighty stream.
—*Amos* 5:24

But God . . . is white. And if his love was so great, and if he loved all his children, why were we, the blacks, cast down so far?—*James Baldwin*

THE RELATIONSHIP BETWEEN RELIGION AND POLITICAL RADICALISM IS A confusing one. On the one hand, established religious institutions have generally had a stake in the status quo and hence have supported conservatism. Furthermore, with the masses having an otherworldly orientation, religious zeal, particularly as expressed in the more fundamentalist branches of Christianity, has been seen as an alternative to the development of political radicalism. On the other hand, as the source of universal humanistic values and the strength that can come from believing one is carrying out God's will in political matters, religion has occasionally played a strong positive role in movements for radical social change.

This dual role of religion is clearly indicated in the case of the American Negro and race protest. Slaves are said to have been first brought to this country on the "good ship Jesus Christ."[1] While there was occasional controversy over the effect that religion had on them it appears that most slave-owners eventually came to view supervised religion as an effective means of social control. Stampp, in commenting on the effect of religion notes:

. . . through religious instruction the bondsmen learned that slavery had divine sanction, that insolence was as much an offense against God as against the temporal master. They received the Biblical command that servants should obey their masters, and they heard of the punishments awaiting the disobedient slave in the hereafter. They heard, too, that eternal salvation would be their reward for faithful service . . .[2]

* Reprinted by permission of the American Sociological Association from the *American Sociological Review*, 32 (February, 1967), pp. 64-72.

** Revision of paper read at the annual meeting of the American Sociological Association, August, 1966. This paper may be identified as publication A-72 of the Survey Research Center, University of California, Berkeley. I am grateful to Gertrude J. Selznick and Stephen Steinberg for their work on the early phase of this project, and to the Anti-Defamation League for support.

1 Louis Lomax, *When the Word Is Given*, New York: New American Library, 1964, p. 34. It has often been noted that when the missionaries came to Africa they had the Bible and the people had the land. When the missionaries left, they had the land and the Africans had the Bible.

2 Kenneth Stampp, *The Peculiar Institution*, New York: Alfred A. Knopf, 1956, p. 158.

In discussing the period after the Civil War, Mydral states that ". . . under the pressure of political reaction, the Negro church in the South came to have much the same role as it did before the Civil War. Negro frustration was sublimated into emotionalism, and Negro hopes were fixed on the after world."[3] Many other analysts, in considering the consequences of Negro religion from the end of slavery until the early 1950's reached similar conclusions about the conservatizing effect of religion on race protest.[4]

However, the effect of religion on race protest throughout American history has by no means been exclusively in one direction. While many Negroes were no doubt seriously singing about chariots in the sky, Negro preachers such as Denmark Vesey and Nat Turner and the religiously inspired abolitionists were actively fighting slavery in their own way. All Negro churches first came into being as protest organizations and later some served as meeting places where protest strategy was planned, or as stations on the underground railroad. The richness of protest symbolism in Negro spirituals and sermons has often been noted. Beyond this symbolic role, as a totally Negro institution, the church brought together in privacy people with a shared problem. It was from the church experience that many leaders were exposed to a broad range of ideas legitimizing protest and obtained the savior faire, self-confidence, and organizational experience needed to challenge an oppressive system. A recent commentator states that the slave churches were "the nucleus of the Negro protest" and another that "in religion Negro leaders had begun to find sanction and support for their movements of protest more than 150 years ago."[5]

Differing perceptions of the varied consequences religion may have on protest have continued to the present time. While there has been very little in the way of empirical research on the effect of the Negro church

[3] Gunnar Myrdal *et al.*, *An American Dilemma*, New York: Harper, 1944, pp. 851–853. About the North he notes that the church remained far more independent "but on the whole even the Northern Negro church has remained a conservative institution with its interests directly upon other-worldly matters and has largely ignored the practical problems of the Negro's fate in this world."

[4] For example Dollard reports that "religion can be seen as a mechanism for the social control of Negroes" and that planters have always welcomed the building of a Negro church on the plantation but looked with less favor upon the building of a school. John Dollard, *Caste and Class in a Southern Town*, Garden City: Doubleday Anchor, 1957, p. 248. A few of the many others reaching similar conclusions are, Benjamin E. Mays and J. W. Nicholson, *The Negro's Church*, New York: Institute of Social and Religious Research, 1933; Hortense Powdermaker, *After Freedom*, New York: Viking Press, 1939, p. 285; Charles Johnson, *Growing Up in the Black Belt*, Washington, D.C.: American Council of Education, 1941, pp. 135–136; Horace Drake and St. Clair Cayton, *Black Metropolis*, New York: Harper and Row, 1962, pp. 424–429; George Simpson and Milton Yinger, *Racial and Cultural Minorities*, New York: Harper, rev. ed., 1958, pp. 582–587. In a more general context this social control consequence of religion has of course been noted throughout history from Plato to Montesquieu to Marx to Nietzsche to Freud to contemporary social theorists.

[5] Daniel Thompson, "The Rise of Negro Protest," *Annals of the American Academy of Political and Social Science*, 357 (January, 1965).

on protest,[6] the literature of race relations is rich with impressionistic statements which generally contradict each other about how the church either encourages and is the source of race protest or inhibits and retards its development. For example, two observers note, "as primitive evangelism gave way to a more sophisticated social consciousness, the church became the spearhead of Negro protest in the deep South,"[7] while another indicates "the Negro church is a sleeping giant. In civil rights participation its feet are hardly wet."[8] A civil rights activist, himself a clergyman, states: ". . . the church today is central to the movement . . . if there had been no Negro church, there would have been no civil rights movement today."[9] On the other hand, a sociologist, commenting on the more involved higher status ministers, notes: ". . . middle class Negro clergymen in the cities of the South generally advocated cautious gradualism in race activities until the mid-1950's when there was an upsurge of protest sentiment among urban Negroes . . . but most of them [ministers] did not embrace the more vigorous techniques of protest until other leaders took the initiative and gained widespread support."[10] Another sociologist states, "Whatever their previous conservative stance has been, the churches have now become 'spearheads of reform.' "[11] Still another indicates: ". . . the Negro church is particularly culpable for its general lack of concern for

[6] The empirical evidence is quite limited. The few studies that have been done have focused on the Negro minister. Thompson notes that in New Orleans Negro ministers constitute the largest segment of the Negro leadership class (a grouping which is not necessarily the same as "protest leaders") but that "The vast minority of ministers are primarily interested in their pastoral role . . . their sermons are essentially biblical, dealing only tangentially with social issues." Daniel Thompson, *The Negro Leadership Class*, Englewood Cliffs, New Jersey: Prentice-Hall, 1963, pp. 34–35. Studies of the Negro ministry in Detroit and Richmond, California also stress that only a small fraction of Negro clergymen show any active concern with the civil rights struggle. R. L. Johnstone, *Militant and Conservative Community Leadership Among Negro Clergymen*, Ph.D. dissertation, University of Michigan, Ann Arbor, 1963, and J. Bloom, *The Negro Church and the Movement for Equality*, M.A. thesis, University of California, Berkeley, Department of Sociology, 1966.

It is worthy of mention that, although the number of cases was small, the Negro ministers in our sample had the lowest percentage militant of any occupational group. With respect to the sons of clergymen, the situation seems somewhat different. While the myth of the preacher's son gone bad is almost a part of American folklore, one would think that a comparable myth might develop within the Negro community—that of the preacher's son gone radical. Malcolm X, James Baldwin, A. Philip Randolph, Martin Luther King, James Farmer, Adam Clayton Powell, Elijah Muhammad, and a number of others had clergymen as fathers. To be taken into consideration is that clergymen make up a relatively larger segment of the Negro middle class than of the white middle class.

[7] Jane Record and Wilson Record, "Ideological Forces and the Negro Protest," *Annals, op. cit.*, p. 92.

[8] G. Booker, *Black Man's America*, Englewood Cliffs, N.J.: Prentice-Hall, 1964, p. 111.

[9] Rev. W. T. Walker, as quoted in William Brink and Louis Harris, *The Negro Revolution in America*, New York: Simon and Schuster, 1964, p. 103.

[10] N. Glenn, "Negro Religion in the U.S." in L. Schneider, *Religion, Culture and Society*, New York: John Wiley, 1964.

[11] Joseph Fichter, "American Religion and the Negro," *Daedalus* (Fall, 1965), p. 1087.

the moral and social problems of the community . . . it has been accommodating. Fostering indulgence in religious sentimentality, and riveting the attention of the masses on the bounties of a hereafter, the Negro church remains a refuge, and escape from the cruel realities of the here and now."[12]

Thus one faces opposing views, or at best ambiguity, in contemplating the current effect of religion. The opiating consequences of religion are all too well known as is the fact that the segregated church is durable and offers some advantages to clergy and members that might be denied them in a more integrated society. On the other hand, the prominent role of the Negro church in supplying much of the ideology of the movement, many of its foremost leaders, and an institution around which struggle might be organized—particularly in the South—can hardly be denied. It would appear from the bombings of churches and the writings of Martin Luther King and other religiously inspired activists that for many, religion and protest are closely linked.

Part of this dilemma may lie in the distinction between the church as an institution in its totality and particular individual churches within it, and the further distinctions among different types of individual religious concern. This paper is concerned with the latter subject; it is an inquiry into the relationship between religiosity and response to the civil rights struggle. It first considers how religious denomination affects militancy, and then how various measures of religiosity, taken separately and together, are related to civil rights concern. The question is then asked of those classified as "very religious" and "quite religious," how an "otherworldly orientation"—as opposed to a "temporal" one—affects militancy.

In a nationwide study of Negroes living in metropolitan areas of the United States, a number of questions were asked about religious behavior and beliefs as well as about the civil rights struggle.[13] Seven of the questions dealing with civil rights protest have been combined into an index of conventional militancy.[14] Built into this index are a number of dimen-

---

[12] E. U. Essien-Udom, *Black Nationalism*, New York: Dell Publishing Co., 1962, p. 358.

Many other examples of contradictory statements could be offered, sometimes even in the same volume. For example, Carleton Lee stresses the importance of religion for protest while Rayford Logan sees the Negro pastor as an instrument of the white power structure (in a book published to commemorate 100 years of emancipation). Carleton Lee, "Religious Roots of Negro Protest," and Rayford Logan, "Educational Changes Affecting American Negroes," both in Arnold Rose, *Assuring Freedom to the Free*, Detroit: Wayne University Press, 1964.

[13] This survey was carried out in 1964 by the Survey Research Center, University of California, Berkeley, A non-Southern metropolitan area probability sample was drawn as well as special area samples of Negroes living in New York City, Chicago, Atlanta and Birmingham. Since the results reported here are essentially the same for each of these areas, they are treated together. More than 90% of the interviews were done with Negro interviewers. Additional methodological details may be found in Gary Marx, *Protest and Prejudice: A Study of Belief in the Black Community*, New York: Harper & Row [1967].

[14] Attention is directed to a conventional militancy rather than to that of the Black Nationalist variety because a very small percentage of the sample offered strong and consistent support for Black Nationalism. As in studying support for the KKK, the

sions of racial protest such as impatience over the speed of integration, opposition to discrimination in public facilities and the sale of property, perception of barriers to Negro advancement, support of civil rights demonstrations, and expressed willingness to take part in a demonstration. Those giving the militant response to five or more of the questions are considered militant, those giving such a response to three or four of the questions, moderate, and fewer than three, conservative.[15]

DENOMINATION

It has long been known that the more fundamentalist sects such as the Holiness groups and the Jehovah's Witnesses are relatively uninterested in movements for secular political change.[16] Such transvaluation movements with their otherworldly orientation and their promise that the last shall be first in the great beyond, are said to solace the individual for his lowly status in this world and to divert concern away from efforts at collective social change which might be brought about by man. While only a minority of Negroes actually belong to such groups, the proportion is higher than among whites. Negro literature is rich in descriptions of these churches and their position on race protest.

In Table 1 it can be seen that those belonging to sects are the least likely to be militant; they are followed by those in predominantly Negro denominations. Ironically those individuals in largely white denominations (Episcopalian, Presbyterian, United Church of Christ, and Roman

TABLE 1

Proportion Militant (%) by Denomination*

Denomination	% Militant
Episcopalian	46 (24)
United Church of Christ	42 (12)
Presbyterian	40 (25)
Catholic	40 (109)
Methodist	34 (142)
Baptist	32 (658)
Sects and Cults	20 (106)

* 25 respondents are not shown in this table because they did not specify a denomination, or belonged to a non-Christian religious group, or other small Christian group.

Birch Society or the Communist Party, a representative sample of normal size is inadequate.

[15] Each of the items in the index was positively related to every other and the index showed a high degree of internal validity. The index also received external validation from a number of additional questions. For example, the percentage belonging to a civil rights organization went from zero among those lowest in militancy to 38 percent for those who were highest, and the percentage thinking that civil rights demonstrations had helped a great deal increased from 23 percent to 58 percent. Those thinking that the police treated Negroes very well decreased from 35 percent to only 2 percent among those highest in militancy.

[16] Liston Pope, *Millhands and Preachers*, New Haven: Yale University Press, 1942, p. 137. J. Milton Yinger, *Religion, Society, and the Individual*, New York: The Macmillan Company, 1957, pp. 170–173.

Catholic) are those most likely to be militant, in spite of the perhaps greater civil rights activism of the Negro denominations. This pattern emerged even when social class was held constant.

In their comments members of the less conventional religious groups clearly expressed the classical attitude of their sects toward participation in the politics of the secular world. For example, an Evangelist in the Midwest said, "I don't believe in participating in politics. My church don't vote—they just depends on the plans of God." And an automobile serviceman in Philadelphia stated, "I, as a Jehovah's Witness, cannot express things involving the race issue." A housewife in the Far West ventured, "In my religion we do not approve of anything except living like it says in the Bible; demonstrations mean calling attention to you and it's sinful."

The finding that persons who belong to sects are less likely to be militant than the non-sect members is to be expected; clearly this type of religious involvement seems an alternative for most people to the development of radicalism. But what of the religious style of those in the more conventional churches which may put relatively less stress on the afterlife and encourage various forms of secular participation? Are the more religiously inclined within these groups also less likely to be militant?

RELIGIOSITY

The present study measured several dimensions of religious involvement. Those interviewed were asked how important religion was to them, several questions about orthodoxy of belief, and how frequently they attended worship service.[17] Even with the sects excluded, irrespective of the dimension of religiosity considered, the greater the religiosity the lower the percentage militant. (See Tables 2, 3 and 4.) For example, militancy increases consistently from a low of only 29 percent among those who said religion was "extremely important" to a high of 62 percent for those who indicated that religion was "not at all important" to

TABLE 2

Militancy by Subjective Importance Assigned to Religion*

Importance	% Militant	
Extremely important	29	(668)
Somewhat important	39	(195)
Fairly important	48	(96)
Not too important	56	(18)
Not at all important	62	(13)

* Sects are excluded here and in all subsequent tables.

17 These dimensions and several others are suggested by Charles Y. Glock in "On the Study of Religious Commitment," *Religious Education Research Supplement,* 57 (July–August, 1962), pp. 98–100. For another measure of religious involvement, the number of church organizations belonged to, the same inverse relationship was noted.

them. For those very high in orthodoxy (having no doubt about the existence of God or the devil) 27 percent were militant while for those totally
rejecting these ideas 54 percent indicated great concern over civil rights.
Militancy also varies inversely with frequency of attendance at worship
service.[18]

Each of these items was strongly related to every other; when taken
together they help us to better characterize religiosity. Accordingly they
have been combined into an overall measure of religiosity. Those scored
as "very religious" in terms of this index attended church as least once a
week, felt that religion was extremely important to them, and had no
doubts about the existence of God and the devil. For progressively lower
values of the index, frequency of church attendance, the importance of
religion, and acceptance of the belief items decline consistently until, for
those scored "not at all religious," church is rarely if ever attended, religion is not considered personally important and the belief items are
rejected.

TABLE 3

Militancy by Orthodoxy

Orthodoxy	% Militant
Very high	27 (414)
High	34 (333)
Medium	39 (144)
Low	47 (68)
Very low	54 (35)

TABLE 4

Militancy by Frequency of Attendance at Worship Services

Frequency	% Militant
More than once a week	27 (81)
Once a week	32 (311)
Once a month or more but less than once a week	34 (345)
Less than once a month	38 (240)

[18] There is a popular stereotype that Negroes are a "religious people." Social science
research has shown that they are "over-churched" relative to whites, i.e., the ratio of
Negro churches to the size of the Negro population is greater than the same ratio for
whites. Using data from a nation-wide survey of whites, by Gertrude Selznick and
Stephen Steinberg, some comparison of the religiosity of Negroes and whites was possible. When these various dimensions of religiosity were examined, with the effect of
education and region held constant, Negroes appeared as significantly more religious
only with respect to the subjective importance assigned to religion. In the North, whites
were more likely to attend church at least once a week than were Negroes; while in
the South rates of attendance were the same. About the same percentage of both groups
had no doubts about the existence of God. While Negroes were more likely to be sure
about the existence of a devil, whites, surprisingly, were more likely to be sure about a
life beyond death. Clearly, then, any assertions about the greater religiosity of Negroes
relative to whites are unwarranted unless one specifies the dimension of religiosity.

Using this measure for non-sect members, civil rights militancy increases from a low of 26 percent for those labeled "very religious" to 30 percent for the "somewhat religious" to 45 percent for those "not very religious" and up to a high of 70 percent for those "not at all religious."[19] (Table 5.)

Religiosity and militancy are also related to age, sex, education, religious denomination and region of the country. The older, the less educated, women, Southerners and those in Negro denominations are more likely to be religious and to have lower percentages as militant. Thus it is possible that the relationship observed is simply a consequence of the fact that both religiosity and militancy are related to some third factor. In Table 6 it can be seen, however, that even when these variables are controlled the relationship is maintained. That is, even among those in the North, the younger, male, more educated and those affiliated with predominantly white denominations, the greater the religiosity the less the militancy.

The incompatibility between piety and protest shown in these data becomes even more evident when considered in light of comments offered by the respondents. Many religious people hold beliefs which clearly inhibit race protest. For a few there was the notion that segregation and a lowly status for Negroes was somehow God's will and not for man to question. Thus a housewife in South Bend, Indiana, in saying that civil rights demonstrations had hurt Negroes, added: "God is the Creator of everything. We don't know why we all dark-skinned. We should try to put forth the effort to do what God wants and not question."[20]

A Negro spiritual contains the lines "I'm gonna wait upon the Lord till my change comes." For our respondents a more frequently stated belief

TABLE 5

Militancy by Religiosity

Religiosity	Very Religious	Somewhat Religious	Not Very Religious	Not at All Religious
% Militant	26	30	45	70
N	(230)	(523)	(195)	(36)

[19] When the sects are included in these tables the results are the same. The sects have been excluded because they offer almost no variation to be analyzed with respect to the independent variable. Since virtually all of the sect members scored as either "very religious" or "somewhat religious," it is hardly possible to measure the effect of their religious involvement on protest attitudes. In addition the import of the relationships shown in these tables is considerably strengthened when it is demonstrated that religious involvement inhibits militancy even when the most religious and least militant group, the sects, are excluded.

[20] Albert Cardinal Meyer notes that the Catholic Bishops of the U.S. said in their statement of 1958: "The heart of the race question is moral and religious." "Interracial Justice and Love," in M. Ahmann, ed., Race Challenge to Religion, Chicago: H. Regnery, 1963, p. 126. These data, viewed from the perspective of the activist seeking to motivate Negroes on behalf of the civil rights struggle, suggest that this statement has a meaning which Their Excellencies no doubt did not intend.

stressed that God as the absolute controller of the universe would bring about change in his own way and at his own time, rather than expressing segregation as God's will. In indicating her unwillingness to take part in a civil rights demonstration, a Detroit housewife said, "I don't go for demonstrations. I believe that God created all men equal and at His appointed time He will give every man his portion, no one can hinder it." And in response to a question about whether or not the government in Washington was pushing integration too slowly, a retired clerk in Atlanta said: "You can't hurry God. He has a certain time for this to take place. I don't know about Washington."

Others who desired integration more strongly and wanted immediate social change felt that (as Bob Dylan sings) God was on their side. Hence man need do nothing to help bring about change. Thus a worker in Cleveland, who was against having more civil rights demonstrations, said: "With God helping to fight our battle, I believe we can do with fewer demonstrations." And in response to a question about whether Negroes should spend more time praying and less time demonstrating, an Atlanta clergyman, who said "more time praying," added "praying is demonstrating."[21]

TABLE 6

Proportion Militant (%) by Religiosity, for Education,
Age, Region, Sex, and Denomination

	Very Religious	Somewhat Religious	Not Very Religious	Not at All Religious
Education				
Grammar school	17 (108)	22 (201)	31 (42)	50 (2)
High school	34 (96)	32 (270)	45 (119)	58 (19)
College	38 (26)	48 (61)	59 (34)	87 (15)
Age				
18–29	33 (30)	37 (126)	44 (62)	62 (13)
30–44	30 (53)	34 (180)	48 (83)	74 (19)
45–59	25 (71)	27 (131)	45 (33)	50 (2)
60+	22 (76)	18 (95)	33 (15)	100 (2)
Region				
Non-South	30 (123)	34 (331)	47 (159)	70 (33)
South	22 (107)	23 (202)	33 (36)	66 (3)
Sex				
Men	28 (83)	33 (220)	44 (123)	72 (29)
Women	26 (147)	28 (313)	46 (72)	57 (7)
Denomination				
Episcopalian, Presbyterian, United Church of Christ	20 (15)	27 (26)	33 (15)	60 (5)
Catholic	13 (15)	39 (56)	36 (25)	77 (13)
Methodist	46 (24)	22 (83)	50 (32)	100 (2)
Baptist	25 (172)	29 (354)	45 (117)	53 (15)

[21] A study of ministers in Richmond, California, notes that, although almost all questioned were opposed to discrimination, very few had taken concrete action, in part because of their belief that God would take care of them. One minister noted, "I

RELIGION AMONG THE MILITANTS

Although the net effect of religion is clearly to inhibit attitudes of protest it is interesting to consider this relationship in the opposite direction, i.e., observe religiosity among those characterized as militant, moderate, and conservative with respect to the civil rights struggle. As civil rights concern increases, religiosity decreases. (Table 7). Militants were twice

TABLE 7

Religiosity by Civil Rights Militancy

	Militants	Moderates	Conservatives
Very religious	18%	24%	28%
Somewhat religious	48	57	55
Not very religious	26	17	16
Not at all religious	8	2	1
Total	100	100	100
N	332	419	242

as likely to be scored "not very religious" or "not at all religious" as were conservatives. This table is also of interest because it shows that, even for the militants, a majority were scored either "very religious" or "somewhat religious." A study of Southern Negro CORE activists reports that less than one person in ten never attends church while almost six out of ten attended church weekly.[22] Clearly, for many, a religious orientation and a concern with racial protest are not mutually exclusive.

Given the active involvement of some churches, the singing of protest spirituals, and the ideology of the movement as it relates to Christian principles of love, equality, passive suffering,[23] and the appeal to a higher moral law, it would be surprising if there were only a few religious people among the militants.

A relevant question accordingly is: Among the religious, what are the intervening links which determine whether religion is related to an active concern with racial matters or has an opiating effect?[24] From the com-

---

believe that if we was as pure . . . as we ought to be, there would be no struggle. God will answer my prayer. If we just stay with God and have faith. *When Peter was up, did the people march to free him? No. He prayed, and God did something about it.* (Bloom, *op. cit.*, italics added.)

[22] Ingeborg B. Powell, *Ideology and Strategy of Direct Action: A Study of the Congress of Racial Equality* (Unpublished Ph.D. Dissertation, University of California, Berkeley, 1965), p. 207. In the North the same figure, four out of ten, report never attending as indicate that they go to church weekly.

[23] Non-violent resistance as it relates to Christianity's emphasis on suffering, sacrifice, and privation, is discussed by James W. Vander Zanden, "The Non-Violent Resistance Movement Against Segregation." *American Journal of Sociology*, 68 (March, 1963), pp. 544–550.

[24] Of course, a most relevant factor is the position of the particular church that an

ments reported above it seemed that, for some, belief in a highly deterministic God inhibited race protest. Unfortunately the study did not
measure beliefs about the role of God as against the role of men in the
structuring of human affairs. However, a related variable was measured
which would seem to have much relevance—the extent to which these
religious people were concerned with the here and now as opposed to the
after-life.

The classical indictment of religion from the Marxist perspective is that
by focusing concern on a glorious after-life the evils of this life are ignored. Of course there are important differences among religious institutions and among individuals with respect to the importance given to
other worldly concerns. Christianity, as with most ideologies, contains
within it, if not out-and-out contradictory themes, then certainly themes
which are likely to be in tension with one another. In this fact, no doubt,
lies part of the explanation of religion's varied consequences for protest.
One important strand of Christianity stresses acceptance of one's lot and
glorifies the after-life,[25] another is more concerned with the realization of
Judeo-Christian values in the current life. King and his followers clearly
represent this latter "social gospel" tradition.[26] Those with the type of
temporal concern that King represents would be expected to be higher in
militancy. A measure of temporal vs. otherworldly concern has been constructed. On the basis of two questions, those interviewed have been classified as having either an otherworldly or a temporal orientation.[27] The

---

individual is involved in. Unfortunately, it was difficult to obtain such information in a
nationwide survey.

[25] The Muslims have also made much of this theme within Christianity, and their
militancy is certainly tied to a rejection of other worldly religiosity. The Bible is referred
to as a "poison book" and the leader of the Muslims states, "No one after death has
ever gone any place but where they were carried. There is no heaven or hell other than
on earth for you and me, and Jesus was no exception. His body is still . . . in Palestine
and will remain there." (As quoted in C. Eric Lincoln, The Black Muslims in America,
Boston: Beacon Press, 1961, p. 123).

However, while they reject the otherworldly theme, they nevertheless rely heavily
on a deterministic Allah; according to E. U. Essien-Udom, this fact leads to political
inactivity. He notes, "The attainment of black power is relegated to the intervention
of "Almighty Allah" sometime in the future . . . Not unlike other religionists, the
Muslims too may wait for all eternity for the coming of the Messiah, the predicted
apocalypse in 1970 notwithstanding." E. U. Essien-Udom, Black Nationalism, op. cit.,
pp. 313–314.

[26] He states: "Any religion that professes to be concerned with the souls of men and
is not concerned with the slums that damn them, the economic conditions that strangle
them, and the social conditions that cripple them, is a dry-as-dust religion." He further
adds, perhaps in a concession, that "such a religion is the kind the Marxists like to see
—an opiate of the people." Martin Luther King, Stride Toward Freedom, New York:
Ballantine Books, 1958, pp. 28–29.

John Lewis, a former SNCC leader and once a Baptist Divinity student, is said to
have peered through the bars of a Southern jail and said, "Think not that I am come
to send peace on earth. I came not to send peace, but a sword." (Matthew 10:34.)

[27] The two items used in this index were: "How sure are you that there is a life
beyond death?"; and "Negroes should spend more time praying and less time demonstrating." The latter item may seem somewhat circular when observed in relation to
civil rights concern. However, this is precisely what militancy is all about. Still it

evidence is that religiosity and other worldly concern increase together. For example, almost 100 percent of the "not at all religious" group were considered to have a temporal orientation, but only 42 percent of the "very religious." (Table 8). Those in predominantly white denominations

TABLE 8

Proportion (%) with Temporal (as Against Otherworldly) Concern,
by Religiosity

Religiosity	% with Temporal Concern
Very religious	42 (225)
Somewhat religious	61 (531)
Not very religious	82 (193)
Not at all religious	98 (34)

were more likely to have a temporal orientation than those in all-black denominations.

Among the religious groups, if concern with the here and now is a relevant factor in overcoming the opiating effect of religion then it is to be anticipated that those considered to have a temporal religious orientation would be much higher in militancy than those scored as otherworldly. This is in fact the case. Among the otherworldly religious, only 16 percent were militant; this proportion increases to almost 40 percent among those considered "very religious" and "somewhat religious" who have a temporal religious outlook. (Table 9). Thus it would seem that an im-

TABLE 9

Proportion Militant (%) by Religiosity and Temporal
or Otherworldly Concern

Concern	Somewhat Religious	Very Religious
Temporal	39 (95)	38 (325)
Otherworldly	15 (130)	17 (206)

portant factor in determining the effect of religion on protest attitudes is the nature of an individual's religious commitment. It is quite possible, for those with a temporal religious orientation, that—rather than the effect of religion being somehow neutralized (as in the case of militancy among the "not religious" groups)—their religious concern serves to inspire and sustain race protest. This religious inspiration can, of course, be clearly noted among some active civil rights participants.

would have been better to measure otherwordly vs. temporal concern in a less direct fashion; unfortunately, no other items were available. Because of this the data shown here must be interpreted with caution. However it does seem almost self-evident that civil rights protest which is religiously inspired is related to a temporal religious outlook.

Conclusion

The effect of religiosity on race protest depends on the type of religiosity involved. Past literature is rich in suggestions that the religiosity of the fundamentalist sects is an alternative to the development of political radicalism. This seems true in the case of race protest as well. However, in an overall sense even for those who belong to the more conventional churches, the greater the religious involvement, whether measured in terms of ritual activity, orthodoxy of religious belief, subjective importance of religion, or the three taken together, the lower the degree of militancy.

Among sect members and religious people with an otherworldly orientation, religion and race protest appear to be, if not mutually exclusive, then certainly what one observer has referred to as "mutually corrosive kinds of commitments."[28] Until such time as religion loosens its hold over these people or comes to embody to a greater extent the belief that man as well as God can bring about secular change, and focuses more on the here and now, religious involvement may be seen as an important factor working against the widespread radicalization of the Negro public.

However, it has also been noted that many militant people are nevertheless religious. When a distinction is made among the religious between the "otherworldly" and the "temporal," for many of the latter group, religion seems to facilitate or at least not to inhibit protest. For these people religion and race protest may be mutually supportive.

Thirty years ago Donald Young wrote: "One function which a minority religion may serve is that of reconciliation with inferior status and its discriminatory consequences . . . on the other hand, religious institutions may also develop in such a way as to be an incitement and support of revolt against inferior status.[29] The current civil rights struggle and the data observed here certainly suggest that this is the case. These contradictory consequences of religion are somewhat reconciled when one distinguishes among different segments of the Negro church and types of religious concern among individuals.

[28] Rodney Stark, "Class, Radicalism, and Religious Involvement," *American Sociological Review*, 29 (October, 1964), p. 703.

[29] Donald Young, *American Minority Peoples*, New York: Harper, 1937, p. 204. These data are also consistent with Merton's statement that it is premature to conclude that "all religion everywhere has only the one consequence of making for mass apathy" and his insistence on recognizing the "multiple consequences" and "net balance of aggregate consequences" of a given institution such as religion. Robert Merton, *Social Theory and Social Structure*, Glencoe: Free Press, 1957, revised edition, p. 44.

28

Negro Political Strategy: Coalition or Independent Power Politics?

HARRY HOLLOWAY
UNIVERSITY OF OKLAHOMA

GROWING NEGRO POLITICAL POWER HAS BECOME AN INCREASINGLY IMPORtant fact of modern American politics. The Negro mayors elected in 1967 in Cleveland, Ohio, and Gary, Indiana, are among the recent, forceful reminders of this fact. According to a *Christian Science Monitor* story on November 4, 1967, about 600 Negroes then held elective office. The number had doubled in the previous four years and, the reporter noted, the number was expected to double again by 1970. The same story pointed out that in the South and border areas alone, 161 Negroes held elective office and the potential was "untapped." These figures are impressive, but the exact numbers at any given time are less important than the implications: the Negro is moving onto the American political scene on a scale far greater than ever before. And the process is likely to continue, for some time at least.[1]

This movement of Negroes into American politics presents problems as well as opportunities. One of the problems is strategy: how should Negroes direct their political strength so as to maximize the advantages to be gained from the exercise of political power? One can see this basic issue reflected today in the debate over the black power slogan. The meanings attributed to the phrase are varied and, at times, elusive. Nonetheless, throughout the discussion a recurring theme is that of the basic strategy Negroes ought to pursue. In the main there are three basic alternatives. One would be the formation of a liberal coalition to unite Negroes with "underdog" whites. A second would be the development of a conservative coalition to unite Negroes with "the better sort of white." A third would be a policy of independence and pragmatism in which ad hoc coalitions are accepted but continuing coalition ties are rejected.

THE FRAMEWORK AND METHODOLOGY

Before proceeding with analysis of these alternatives, some limitations and methodological questions need to be resolved. One, these alternatives oversimplify somewhat. They "stand for" a complex set of human relations that may continue for some time and involve many nuances of behavior.

[1] Contributions to the study of Negro politics by political scientists include the following: Everett Carll Ladd, *Negro Political Leadership in the South* (Ithaca, N.Y.: Cornell University Press, 1966); Donald R. Matthews and James W. Prothro, *Negroes and the New Southern Politics* (New York: Harcourt, Brace and World, 1966); Hugh D. Price, *The Negro and Southern Politics* (New York: New York University Press, 1957); James Q. Wilson, *Negro Politics* (Glencoe, Ill.: The Free Press, 1960). The classic by V. O. Key, Jr., *Southern Politics* (New York: Alfred A. Knopf, 1949), is now somewhat dated, but always deserves mention. In addition, see James Q. Wilson, "The Negro in Politics," *Daedalus*, 94 (Fall, 1965), pp. 949–973. This article has an overview of Negro problems of political strategy as of the mid-1960's.

♦ First published in *Social Science Quarterly* 49, No. 3 (December, 1968).

Furthermore, coalition ties may vary over a period of time from one type to another as local leaders experiment with alliances. Additionally, there may be dissidents who do not accept the leadership of the dominant group.

Nor are the three basic strategies cited above necessarily exhaustive. Another possible alternative would be separation and withdrawal politically, such as is advocated by some black nationalists.[2] Another would be a "back to Africa" movement entailing not only separation but a complete, physical withdrawal as well. A third, quite different, possibility would be the avoidance of ethnic or racial politics altogether and the advocacy, instead, of a neutral approach to politics uncolored by a sense of a distinct ethnic identity.[3] None of these last alternatives, however, seem likely to command large-scale followings in the foreseeable future. They will not, therefore, be dealt with here.

Another point that deserves mention in introducing this problem of strategy is its special relevance to the South, for in the North, Negroes have long been social and political participants. They have, therefore, formed organizational ties and loyalties that may operate as constraints. Chicago Negroes and the Democratic machine of Mayor Richard Daley are an obvious case in point. In the South, where Negro political power is a more recent development, such ties are apt to be less binding. In spite of the constraints that are bound to exist everywhere, Southern Negroes may have, paradoxically, more freedom to choose alternative courses than do their Northern brethern. Even so, the issue is a lively one. Chicago Negroes are active today in challenging the Daley machine, and ferment elsewhere in the North is apparent. Southern Negroes may have an advantage, then, but the issue is one of importance all over the United States.

The analysis and evaluation of the basic alternatives available will focus on three localities. Each of the places here dealt with is a large metropolitan center located in one of the states of the old Confederacy. In each, Negroes have for years been able to register to vote and have organized themselves politically. Houston serves as an example of the liberal coalition in operation. In Texas generally and in Houston specifically, the

---

[2] Survey data that is still relatively recent and which bears upon Negro attitudes toward black nationalism include the following: William Brink and Louis Harris, *Black and White* (New York: Simon and Schuster, 1966), pp. 260 ff.; Gary T. Marx, *Protest and Prejudice* (New York: Harper and Row, 1967), Ch. 5. In general these studies conclude that separation and withdrawal have markedly limited appeal.

A more recent, although localized, piece of evidence is that from a 1967 study of Bedford-Stuyvesant Negroes in the New York area. One finding was that "clearly, black separatism has no firm hold on this community" (*New York Times*, June 17, 1967, pp. 1, 22).

[3] This possibility may seem unreal and probably is on any scale today. One researcher, however, reports the reaction of a New Orleans Negro academician to the 1960 presidential election as one that fits this category. This academician confided to friends that he was voting Republican because "Nixon's fiscal policy is sounder than Kennedy's. In my opinion this is the basic issue in this campaign." During this same period, according to the researcher, a school desegregation crisis reached a climax so that "Negroes were victims of the bitterest villification by white supremacists and violence and threats of violence constituted a large proportion of the daily news." See Daniel C. Thompson, *The Negro Leadership Class* (Englewood Cliffs, N.J.: Prentice Hall, A Spectrum Book, 1963), p. 51.

liberal coalition has been more fully developed than anywhere else in the South. Atlanta serves as an example of the conservative coalition in operation. The city's image as a progressive Southern city has been related in no small part to the long-time operation of the conservative coalition. Independence and a pragmatic approach to politics are probably best illustrated by the Memphis pattern, an interesting one that has not received much attention.

The data from which the present analysis is drawn are part of a larger project on the politics of the Southern Negro. Basic hypotheses that shaped this study were that Southern Negroes may be viewed as an ethnic group emerging from a once traditional society.[4] Within this framework a variety of Southern localities were selected as illustrating, roughly, a continuum that varies in accord with the persistence of traditional attitudes toward the Negro.[5] These places, though selected on a somewhat impressionistic basis, do appear to illustrate significant variations in the overall pattern of the emergence of the Southern Negro. The big cities, such as those dealt with here, illustrate the full-blown emergence of the Negro with an organization, leadership, and mass of followers able to exert a continuing and significant influence upon local affairs. In such settings the questions of basic strategy that center on coalition versus independence become of great importance.

The field work for this study took the form of interviews with leaders in both the white and black communities in each of the localities studied. Those interviewed were selected chiefly on the basis of their reputation and/or official position on the local scene with respect to racial policies. Given the pressures and controversies that have surrounded race relations in the South, this procedure was probably as good as any available in the circumstances for singling out those worth interviewing. No claims are made here that the interviewees constituted a cross section of the local population or that all local leaders of possible relevance to this subject were interviewed. The interviews usually lasted less than an hour, but some lasted much longer. They were roughly structured to probe for broadly comparable results; flexibility in the conduct of the interviews was also necessary because of the great variation in personalities and situations from one place to another.

---

[4] Valuable sources in the study of ethnic politics include the following: Robert Dahl, *Who Governs?* (New Haven, Conn.: Yale University Press, 1961), Book I; Robert E. Lane, *Political Life* (New York: The Free Press of Glencoe, 1959), Ch. 17; Michael Parenti, "Ethnic Politics and the Persistence of Party Identification," *American Political Science Review*, 61 (Sept., 1967), pp. 717–726; Raymond E. Wolfinger, "The Development and Persistence of Ethnic Voting," *American Political Science Review*, 59 (Dec., 1965), pp. 896–908.

[5] There is precedent for viewing the South as a traditional or once traditional society. V. O. Key in his *Southern Politics* did not use the term as such, but he did explicitly compare the position of Black Belt whites in the past with the Dutch in the East Indies and the British in India. See, for instance, page 5 and the whole opening section, "Of the South."

A much more recent, although brief, example is in Donald R. Matthews and James W. Prothro, *Negroes and the New Southern Politics*, pp. 261–263.

The interviews were supplemented by examination of other sources, including census data, local registration and election records, campaign flyers, and the records and occasional brochures of political organizations. Also consulted were local newspapers and the surprisingly numerous reports and analyses available in national newspapers, magazines, and books. The *New York Times* proved to be a particularly helpful source.

There is much that is interesting, indeed fascinating, in the origin and consolidation of Negro political power in these cities, but that story must be told elsewhere.[6] Here the center of attention lies with the basic questions of strategy that Negro leaders face in deciding how to maximize black political power in their own communities. Therefore the analysis of each locality will focus on an assessment of the advantages and disadvantages, the profits and the losses that characterize each basic strategy.

One further troublesome methodological issue is that of chronology. In the present instance, field work was largely completed in 1964 and 1965; but what of more recent developments? Would events such as the sanitation employees' strike in Memphis or the assassination there of Martin Luther King, Jr., in the spring of 1968, have any effect on findings based upon an earlier period? Ultimately, only further field work can answer such questions. And at some point the field work must end and the writing begin. In the present instance, developments since 1965 must remain largely outside this analysis.

For that matter, the patterns here analyzed did not spring up overnight and did not dissolve in short order. They evolved over time and persisted, even if somewhat frayed, in spite of dissidence and considerable turbulence. In any case the final conclusions reached are not wholly dependent on particular cases. The conclusions draw upon the experience of specific localities, but they should be applicable beyond them in other times and places as long as political leaders are capable of exercising meaningful choices.

Houston and the Liberal Coalition

Briefly, the liberal coalition concept assumes that the "underdogs" in the community are potentially a majority and should be able to unite in pursuit of common economic interests. Those who are among the less well-off groups in the community should, it is thought, share a common interest in the enlargement of governmental activities to benefit the deprived. This interest in turn is presumed to override differences that might arise due to race, religion, creed, or culture. The component elements in the present study were the following: labor unions, with steelworkers being perhaps the most active; independent Anglo liberals drawn from the professional and business world; Negroes; and Latin Americans. In political campaigns they worked up an agreed ticket of candidates to support in a wide range of federal and state contests, but the coalition, as such, was not active in contests for local office, such as county, city council, or school board elections.

[6] A much more extended treatment will be the present writer's *The Politics of the Southern Negro* (New York: Random House, forthcoming).

How well, politically, did Houston's liberal coalition serve Negro inter-ests? Certainly the coalition offered some advantages. For one, Houston Negroes, comprising about 20 per cent of county population, did need allies, and Anglo liberals were generally the most sympathetic to Negro aspirations. Additionally, coalition ties gave Negroes some psychological support and a degree of respectability, and labor money provided much of the financial wherewithal for campaigns, including those of Negroes on the ticket. As for the liberal ideology, the concept of a coalition of underdogs has had perennial appeal.[7] In Texas the appeal was supple-mented by the presence of ideological divisions that date back to the late 1940's.[8] It seemed natural enough for Negroes, especially in the early days as they began to emerge as a significant force in city affairs, to align themselves with liberals.

But what of the disadvantages? Negro leaders by the mid-1960's were, themselves, willing to express some frustration and dissatisfaction. Few Negroes had gained office, either elective or appointive. Mrs. Charles E. White did win a place on the school board in 1958 and again in 1962, but her victories were not really coalition efforts.[9] A feeling arose that the effort expended through the coalition had not brought the results it should have.

A number of more specific complaints also appeared, many of which centered on labor's de facto domination of the coalition. Labor was in-terested in federal and state office; the leaders found it difficult to deliver labor votes in contests for local office, so the coalition, as such, did not function locally. But people in city, school board, and county office were the ones who could most directly influence the conditions of Houston Negroes. Local Negroes did interest themselves in local office but they had to do so largely on their own, with only the informal support of in-terested Anglo liberals.

Labor dominated the process of selecting tickets. Negro leaders felt that Negro candidates had to "over-qualify." As a result, until 1962 only one Negro, Miss Barbara Jordan, was included on the ticket, simply to provide "balance." But even her presence led to further complaints: she attracted the Negro vote to the ticket, but the Anglo vote for her, as the Negro on the ticket, was less than satisfactory. Even Anglo leaders admitted they

[7] Reference to this kind of a coalition effort occurred in interviews in various places across the South. One of the most prominent examples is that of the activists who or-ganized Mississippi's Freedom Democratic party in 1963 and 1964.

See also Bayard Rustin's well-known article, "From Protest to Politics: The Future of the Civil Rights Movement," *Commentary*, 39 (Jan., 1965), pp. 25–31.

[8] On ideological divisions in Texas, see James R. Soukup, Clifton McCleskey, and Harry Holloway, *Party and Factional Division in Texas* (Austin: The University of Texas Press, 1964).

[9] This victory meant more than non-Houstonians might realize. For years school board sessions were televised; local wags referred to them as the "Monday night fights." The ideological struggle between liberals and conservatives on the board was a major reason for the contention. The official coalition organization, the Harris County Demo-crats, did not endorse Mrs. White, although individual Anglo liberals did work in her campaign. As indicated above, the coalition simply did not take part in such contests for local office.

had not worked as hard for Miss Jordan, in 1962 and again in 1964, as for others. In any case, the blue-collar vote was hard to deliver for a Negro. As a large body of evidence from social science literature indicates, working-class whites are less sympathetic to Negro aspirations than are middle- and upper-class whites.[10] Miss Jordan, critics could charge, was being used to attract Negro votes to whites while whites failed to deliver to Negroes a comparable degree of support.

One other facet of labor domination was the existence of ample labor coffers and the tendency toward dependence upon labor money. A Negro candidacy without labor money looked problematic, at best. Yet Mrs. White raised "adequate" money for her campaigns without coalition support because she could appeal to sources of support in the Negro community who might well have been antagonized by official liberal coalition endorsement. Although Mrs. White's contests differed importantly from Miss Jordan's, it remains true that labor money added significantly to labor tendencies toward domination.

A further distinct liability of coalition politics was that liberals usually lost the elections. The conservatives usually won, whether called Republicans or conservative Democrats. The major exception in recent times was the election of Senator Ralph Yarborough. Otherwise, Negroes and their allies were on the outside looking in. In other words, labor domination might have been more palatable had the coalition won and been in a position to dispense benefits to component elements.

One last liability of the coalition was that participation in the coalition tended to draw Negroes into the factional feuding that periodically rends Texas liberals. The passions and the almost Byzantine intrigues that have engaged Texas liberals cannot here be detailed, but one small example may suffice. In 1961 and again in 1966 a number of Texas liberals openly supported conservative Republican John Tower! Whatever the rationale for such a maneuver, this factionalism did *not* help Houston Negroes to better their conditions in the city.

The main limitations on the effectiveness of the coalition, then, were a powerful tendency for labor to dominate and to use the coalition for its own purposes. Local office was neglected and the important Negro vote used to support the coalition ticket of state and federal candidates. In any case, Negroes tied their fortunes politically to that part of the white community, which is everywhere generally less sympathetic to the Negro.

---

[10] Sociologist Seymour M. Lipset refers to working-class intolerance generally as "working class authoritarianism." See his *Political Man* (Garden City, N.Y.: Doubleday, 1960), p. 98. On the South specifically and the correlates of tolerance, see Melvin Tumin, *Desegregation: Resistance and Readiness* (Princeton, N.J.: Princeton University Press, 1958), p. 198.

Also note Brink and Harris, *Black and White*, pp. 136 ff. Political scientist James Q. Wilson generalized this point to argue that "in the South the potential supporters of . . . current Negro objectives are the members of the commercial and industrial elite." See his "The Negro in Politics," *Daedalus*, 94 (1965), p. 968.

This conclusion is an important one and has its critics, but in the opinion of the present writer, these critics have yet to prove their point.

ATLANTA AND THE CONSERVATIVE COALITION

Atlanta's long-time mayor William B. Hartsfield provided much of the leadership for initiation and operation of the coalition there. Hartsfield identified closely with his beloved city. He also identified closely with Atlanta's power elite.[11] He had not much sympathy for the poor white and he was anxious to continue the policies of economic progress that had long been an Atlanta tradition. In these circumstances the possibilities inherent in a sizable bloc of Negro votes became apparent. Negroes, led by a bloc of 10 or 12 top men, could be one of the powerful electoral supports for a progressive economic elite.[12] In time it became a standard observation about Atlanta that the electorate consisted of three main groups: the Negroes, the "better sort of whites," and working-class whites. The last group was usually characterized as segregationist and fundamentalist; the first two formed the conservative coalition. Within the coalition Negroes organized themselves in a bipartisan group focused on local politics. They took their bipartisanship seriously. They deliberately sought to staff their organization with roughly equal numbers of Republicans and Democrats and to maintain the balance. At times an exception was made to their policy of concentration on local office when a vocally segregationist candidate ran for state office. Then, both Republicans and Democrats could agree on the importance of working in the Democratic primary to defeat such candidates. Otherwise, and unlike Houston, local office was the focus. With the eruption of direct-action protest in the early 1960's, the Negro bloc fragmented somewhat.[13] Yet the coalition, now under the leadership of Hartsfield's successor, Mayor Ivan Allen, continued to be a powerful force in city affairs.

What can be said for and against this type of coalition? Its merits are significant for it contributed much to the creation of a national image of Atlanta as a progressive city, in racial as well as in economic matters. The coalition enabled the city to continue the progressive economic policies that in turn enabled it to become the business center of the Southeastern region. Hartsfield's leadership helped mightily in the early 1950's in persuading the well-to-do suburbs to vote themselves into the city. Part of the package also included a reform of local government that won the attention and the praise of outsiders.

[11] Of Hartsfield, one writer stated that he was the "self-proclaimed 'viceroy'" of the business community. See Seymour Freedgood, "Life in Buckhead," *Fortune* (Sept., 1961), p. 184.

[12] The Negro vote was not simply important to the coalition; quite possibly it was crucial. For instance, when Ivan Allen won office in 1961 as mayor and leader of the coalition, there were some who doubted his claim that he carried more than half of the white vote. In other words, the coalition victory, then and perhaps on other occasions, may have rested on a *minority* of the white vote. See Reese Cleghorn, "Allen of Atlanta Collides with Black Power and White Racism," *New York Times Magazine,* Oct. 16, 1966, p. 138.

[13] On the split within the Negro community, see Jack L. Walter, "Protest and Negotiation: A Case Study of Negro Leadership in Atlanta, Georgia," *Midwest Journal of Political Science,* 7 (1963), pp. 120–122. Walker notes that the split among Negroes was so intense that contending factions in the Negro community seemed more hostile to one another than to the white segregationists.

Negroes benefited in a number of respects: the coalition created a climate of opinion at odds with the hostile temper that still pervaded many Southern cities, and this relatively benign racial temper (a quality whites would hardly notice) improved the quality of living for local Negroes. Then, by degrees, the desegregation of public facilities occurred. Federal courts, it is true, abetted this process; but without the coalition, resistance would have been greater and the transition more fraught with tension and conflict. In addition, city services improved in the Negro community. A Negro, Dr. Rufus Clement, won election in 1953 to the school board. In 1962 a Negro from Atlanta won a legislative office. Moderate whites, such as Charles Weltner, could on occasion also win. These more recent victories owed much to reapportionment, but the ground had been prepared by the coalition. Additionally, Negroes gained appointment to units of local government and to party office as their political strength made itself felt. All in all, Atlanta must be given credit, whatever its shortcomings, for leading the way in creating a new pattern in Southern race relations and political practices.

However great the benefits derived from such coalitions, there is another side. In Houston many of the faults centered on the domination of the liberal coalition by labor. In Atlanta many of the faults of the conservative coalition centered on the control exercised by an oligarchic elite.[14] This oligarchic control was not confined to the white community, for, essentially, the city was dominated through much of the post-World War II period by an oligarchy of both whites and Negroes. It is by no means certain that the white elite consistently commanded the support of a majority of the white electorate, but with the bulk of the Negro bloc vote on their side plus a share of the white vote, victory normally was theirs. When the vote focused on a racial issue and was fought out on a city-wide basis, however, a majority of whites were likely to side with segregation.[15] As for the Negro oligarchy with whom whites usually dealt, it was often reluctant to share power as new currents stirred in the Negro community. The result was a set of policies which furthered economic progress in a climate favorable to business and a gradual transition from a politics of race to a politics oriented to limited concessions to rising Negro demands. But the needs of the "little people" of Atlanta, both black and white, were still neglected.[16]

---

14 See Floyd Hunter's, *Community Power Structure* (Garden City, N.Y.: Doubleday Anchor Books, 1963). Since Hunter first published his study in 1953, it has been much discussed and criticized. It is not necessary here to add another version of "what Hunter really said," but insofar as Hunter's findings may be interpreted to mean that men like Hartsfield and Allen were mere puppets manipulated by powerful businessmen, the present writer disagrees. The research experience in Atlanta has left a strong impression that these men were powerful personalities who had an impact on events in Atlanta as influential persons in their own right.

15 One example is the re-election of the segregationist, Judge Durwood T. Pye, to local judicial office in the fall of 1964. In the presidential election of 1964, indications are that white Atlanta voted, on the whole, for Barry Goldwater.

16 See, for instance, Hunter, *Community Power*, Ch. 9. Hunter's study preceded much of the public discussion of ghetto conditions, a discussion that has since become

As regards the Negro specifically, the coalition disregarded the problems of the ghetto poor and their claims to speak out and to have their deprivations alleviated. New leaders, of whom Julian Bond was perhaps the most representative among the militants, arose to challenge the established leadership. To them, the coalition's accomplishments smacked of gradualism and tokenism. In other words, the coalition, in its heyday, was an improvement over the past, and very much so; but it did not really tackle the problems of the deprived in one of America's leading urban centers. Even worse, it tended to suppress expression of grievances, by both black and white, because of its oligarchic tendencies.

Is the conservative coalition, then, no better than the liberal coalition? Some among the militants in Atlanta, who seemed to dislike the established leadership almost as much as they disliked white segregationists, might agree. Furthermore, Atlanta Negroes amounted to roughly one-third of Fulton County population, but Negroes were only 20 per cent or so of Harris County population. Still and all, two basic facts stand out. For one, Atlanta Negroes were on the side of the winners, usually, in being part of the coalition that dominated the city. As such they won benefits that losers could not expect. Secondly, they focused on local office, not, as in Houston, on state and federal office. It is also true that in some respects the coalition was a product of chance rather than planning. It is difficult to see how local Negroes could have formed a tie with local white working-class elements. These constituted the base of segregationist sentiment in the city; some of them supported—or tolerated—the Klan. In this sense, the conservative coalition was not fortuitous, and its achievements, whatever its faults, were not negligible.

MEMPHIS AND INDEPENDENT POWER POLITICS

Negro politics in Memphis has taken a distinctive form due partly to the influence on Shelby County of its long-time political boss, Edward H. Crump. He was the virtually undisputed boss of Shelby County from the late 1920's until his death in 1954. During his reign, Crump used and manipulated the Negro vote; but this was not discrimination on Crump's part, for he manipulated the white vote as well.[17] In the years just before Crump's death, stirrings of independence emerged in the Negro community but were not notably successful. Crump's control was of a peculiarly personal nature, so that when he died his organization fell apart and a substantial power vacuum existed. Local liberals and Negroes organized what amounted to a liberal coalition although enthusiasm for the liberals began to wane among Negroes in succeeding years. As Negroes saw it, their allies were not pushing hard enough for desegregation. By 1959 Negro leaders had decided upon a frontal attack; they mounted this at-

---

prevalent; yet this chapter focuses on the "silence . . . found in the mass of the citizenry in Regional City" (p. 223).

[17] Memphis Negroes were able to participate in a wider range of elections than were most Negroes in the South, and, as V. O. Key pointed out, the manipulation was not wholly one-sided. They won a "fairer break than usual in public services." See his *Southern Politics*, p. 74.

tack with a ticket of Negro candidates headed by Russell Sugarmon seeking the office of public works commissioner. The Negro ticket lost but had a surprising effect, for Negro leaders felt they had won all but the election itself.[18] Henceforth whites would have to recognize their power and deal with them.

The following year, in 1960, they completed this evolution politically by making a deal with a well-known local segregationist who was influential in county affairs.[19] Liberals and urbanites were shocked but Negro leaders felt they had benefited in the outcome. A basic benefit was the proof of their independence. No one could now take them for granted. They would deal with anyone on a realistic down-to-earth basis without much heed to ideology. They would consider basically where they could make the best deal. Negro leaders called this a policy of "independent power politics." They admitted that their ideals at times might look questionable, but they defended their strategy as a legitimate means of maximizing their bargaining power. In the words of one leader, they "never doublecrossed anyone"; they always held up their end of any deal. Essentially, they wanted to let whites know that what they did was a matter of interests, not brotherly love. The cool, calculating temper of these words was far, far removed from the passion of Houston's ideologically oriented politics.

In assessing the Memphis strategy certain risks and limitations should first be pointed out. Whatever its merits, this policy of independent power politics is probably the most demanding and difficult of all to execute. One important risk is the danger of leadership isolation from followers. Whatever the risks of an ideologically oriented coalition, it does provide guidelines that help the ordinary voter in responding to the organization's leadership. On the other hand, an independent, pragmatic politics lacks such guidelines. To some extent the voter simply has to believe that leaders know what they are doing and that he should follow wherever they lead. In 1963 the leaders backed a man in the mayor's race whom they had earlier opposed. For this and other reasons as well, the followers failed to get the word and voted into office another man. The leadership regarded this as a major defeat and admitted to great discouragement after the election. At other times they were more successful. In 1962 they supported Frank Clement for governor; but in the 1964 Senate race they opposed Clement and switched to Ross Bass, who finally won. To execute these shifts was not easy. Among other things, it required good organization and a vigorous leadership able to maintain contact with grass-roots sentiment. By contrast, one cannot but wonder if established Atlanta leadership could apply such a strategy successfully.

Another risk related to the first is that of isolation from the white community and a tendency towards a go-it-alone confrontation. In 1959 Ne-

[18] William E. Wright, *Memphis Politics: A Study in Racial Bloc Voting* (New York: McGraw-Hill, Eagleton Institute Cases in Practical Politics, 1962), p. 31.

[19] Although a segregationist, this man was described by a reporter who knew him personally as one who was paternalistically benign in his relations with Negroes. He was not one to exploit and abuse them.

groes did just that, and whatever the favorable impact in some respects, they did lose the election. Certain conclusions were suggested by this experience. One was that this type of head-on confrontation aroused racial feelings that many among both whites and blacks saw as unhealthy. These racial feelings in turn led to an outpouring of strength in the white community. In the future Negroes felt they should use less dramatic publicity in trying to arouse their own people: otherwise, they added more to white strength than to their own. Another conclusion drawn from this 1959 experience was that Negroes were, after all, a minority; they could not win by themselves. They needed allies, so their antipathy to coalition should not mean opposition to ad hoc alliances with elements of the white community. On the contrary, they would ordinarily need at least some white votes to win and would have to go after them. Independence, then, meant that some alliances must be accepted and that tendencies toward go-it-alone policies and a confrontation must be checked.

Another major problem related to this policy of independence was that of raising money. In a coalition, Negro allies could provide money for the ticket and in Memphis some money was available on occasion from allies in the white community. But leaders admitted that raising money was a serious problem. Some money they could raise from their midde-class supporters, such as businessmen and ministers; and in Memphis middle-class Negroes appeared to be unusually active and supportive. Yet they were not a large group and most Negroes were poor. How could a large, vigorous political organization with thousands of workers and the hefty expenses of today's election campaigns support itself?

A major source of revenue was the candidates themselves: a candidate seeking support was given an estimate of campaign costs and asked to contribute. This practice raised uncomfortable questions. Above all, was a candidate supported on his merits or because of his "folding green"? Was Negro support still being bought much as it had been in earlier years in Memphis and elsewhere? The fact that the leaders frankly followed a pragmatic, realistic approach to politics added weight to this question. Yet the Shelby County Democratic Club leaders were widely regarded as honest, aggressive men who pressed hard to serve the interests of those they led.[20] They tried to cope with this sticky question by separating organizationally the functions of candidate screening and fund raising. But this solution was regarded as less than perfect. In the end it was hard to see how this large organization requiring many thousands of dollars for effective campaigns could avoid some reliance on candidate contributions, although to do so put the leaders and the organization itself "on the spot." Not all political leaders would be capable, to put it mildly, of sustaining good reputations in such circumstances.

Offsetting these hazards were advantages—and they are fundamental. As a policy, pragmatic independence means that the Negro builds his own power politically and directs it by coolly assessing where his own interests.

[20] Certainly some Memphis Negro leaders did not have such reputations. One reportedly had candidates bidding competitively for his support, threw his support to one whose "bid" included the promise of a truck, then lost the election!

lie. It is a form of black power largely stripped of slogans and a narrow, anti-white appeal. The Negro organizes the Negro or decides who is to do so. Negro leaders themselves decided upon their objectives, whether on a local or statewide level. They decide upon the candidates they are to support and for what reasons or objectives. They decide whether to run Negro candidates and under what conditions. They determine much of the strategy of the campaigns. They raise much of their own money, even in soliciting contributions from candidates. They manage their own campaigns, particularly among Negroes, and they can claim much of the reward of winning. Throughout it is a policy of the Negro doing mainly for himself and by himself. Win or lose, the responsibility falls upon Negroes themselves. And the pragmatic flexibility of being willing to deal with all manner of candidates enhances the bargaining power of the Negro bloc of votes. The Negro bargains with the white as one who has his own independent political influence to expend as he, the Negro, sees fit.

Further considerations reinforce these advantages. No other ethnic group in American history experienced slavery and the caste-subordination and isolation forced, until recently, upon Negroes in the South.[21] These are conditions, understandably enough, likely to produce a heightened ethnic sensitivity and a certain detachment from, or hostility toward, the dominant society. All in all, Negro experience in the United States might lead to the view that the Negro should look after himself and should view white proposals of support with some reservations. Such an outlook obviously fits in many ways with a pattern of independent power politics.[22]

Conclusions

A basic difficulty with any coalition strategy is a tendency for whites to dominate. After all, they have many advantages. They are the majority in most places.[23] They have great economic resources at their disposal, including the wealth and prestige of top businessmen. They have the skills

[21] On the legacy of the Negro and its effects, see the following: Lerone Bennett, Jr., *Confrontation: Black and White* (Baltimore: Penguin Books, 1966); Stanley Elkins, *Slavery* (Chicago: University of Chicago Press, 1959); Gunnar Myrdal, *An American Dilemma* (New York: Harper and Row, 1944); Abram Kardiner and Lionel Ovesey, *The Mark of Oppression* (New York: W. W. Norton, 1951); Charles E. Silberman, *Crisis in Black and White* (New York: Random House, 1964). Silberman's book deserves special mention as a well-written and perceptive account, especially Chapters 3 through 7.

[22] In Brink and Harris, *Black and White*, the authors stress the independence and selectivity of the Negro vote, pp. 74 ff. They note that Negro registration is heavily Democratic (p. 92), but also concluded, "Fundamentally, this is one vote for one issue: civil rights. . . . It is a vote no army of ward heelers can deliver. Yet it will deliver itself more massively than any machine ever attempted. It will be a vote that can shift independently for President, governor, Congress, or for mayor . . ." (p. 78).

[23] On Negro population movement and the percentage of Negro population in the nation's major cities, see the *Report of the National Advisory Commission on Civil Disorders* (New York: Bantam Books, 1968), Ch. 6 and pp. 289 ff. A projection of present trends leads the authors to conclude that 11 major cities will become over 50 per cent Negro by 1984 (p. 391). Even so, white majorities will prevail in much of urban America.

and established organization, and they dominate all the organs of government. Negroes, on the other hand, are relatively recent arrivals emerging from a past of repression and deprivation. For these two groups to join in a coalition can hardly result in anything but domination by whites.

Negroes, as relatively recent additions to the Southern political scene on any scale, admittedly need help. They badly need the various resources that white allies can bring them. Yet each coalition form has its own distinct disadvantages. In the liberal coalition Negroes ally themselves with that segment of the white population usually least receptive to racial change. Furthermore, liberals, and especially Texas liberals, tend to be ideologically oriented. This tendency in turn may accentuate factional disagreements, and it may lead to a concern with major federal and state contests and a neglect of the relatively nonideological local contests. As for the conservative coalition, it accentuates oligarchic tendencies which are likely to be present in all political organizations. Here Negroes are dealing with those at the top of the hierarchy in political, economic, and social matters, and such people may lack awareness of conditions in much of the Negro (and poor white) community.[24] Furthermore, those militant Negro leaders who feel they themselves have this awareness may be suspicious and resentful of the white power elite. The result may then be, as in Atlanta, a fragmentation of the Negro bloc and a rather frayed coalition.

As for independence and a pragmatic approach to bargaining, it is a strategy with at once the greatest peril and the greatest promise. The perils include the risk of leadership isolation from followers as the leaders shift from one alliance to another. The leaders must know their followers, have their trust and confidence, and be able to judge what they will and will not accept. As for their relations with whites, the Negro leaders must avoid the risk of isolation from all elements in the white community and a confrontation that pits white against black. In certain circumstances, it is true, such a confrontation may be desirable. In Memphis in 1959, it probably gained in the long haul more than was lost. But as a regular strategy it is unrealistic and likely to result in defeat, frustration, and increasing estrangement from whites. The situation in which Negroes have the majority is not necessarily an exception, for the leaders must still meet and bargain with white officials in other cities and at the state and federal level. In particular, federal aid could be endangered if black versus white confrontations occur repeatedly.[25]

[24] Among all Southern mayors, Ivan Allen of Atlanta least deserves criticism on this score. In 1966 a reporter described him as lecturing businessmen about wearing blinders and not wanting to do business with the poor. He also took nine of his city department heads on a tour of the slums. See Reese Cleghorn, "Allen of Atlanta," p. 137.

[25] In the spring of 1968 Carl Stokes, Negro mayor of Cleveland, was reported as saying of his city that its problems were "going to take a maximum effort by the federal government. And there's going to have to be support from the state . . . at the local level, there's going to have to be unprecedented private involvement. . . ." See *Christian Science Monitor,* April 26, 1968, Second Section.

These words would surely apply to virtually all American cities to mean that a controlling Negro majority can hardly afford a massive estrangement of whites on the local level.

This point relates to another weakness of independent power politics: the necessity for much self-support. If the purse of a coalition ally is unavailable, Negroes must somehow provide for themselves; large-scale political organizations do not run on "good will" alone. Whatever benefits improved fund-raising in the Negro community might provide, some reliance on contributions from candidates appears inevitable.

The other side of the strategy—the promise—is great. It means that the Negro largely does for himself and bargains with white allies, in ad hoc alliances, as an equal with his own power and influence to dispense. The bargaining power of the Negro bloc is maximized and the tendency of white allies to take the Negro vote for granted is minimized. It would appear to fit the legacy of a group that, more than any other, has known acute subordination, isolation, and deprivation. Perhaps at some time in the future when, and if, this legacy has been largely overcome and Negroes need no longer be motivated by a sharp ethnic sensitivity, then other forms of political relationships may become desirable. For the near future a good deal of independence and a hard-headed pragmatism in assessing Negro interests would seem to be in order. The Negro needs allies; black power cannot win alone or, rather, it can win only limited, local victories. But this fact should not be allowed to obscure the contribution that a hefty infusion of black power can make.

29

Civil Rights Protest and Riots:
A Disappearing Distinction

JAMES A. GESCHWENDER
THE UNIVERSITY OF WESTERN ONTARIO

The civil rights movement has dominated much of the American scene from 1954 to the present, with urban disorders pretty well taking over center stage since 1963. The liberal segment of white America has generally had a positive image of the civil rights movement but has viewed big city riots with a mixture of fear and disgust. A number of social scientists also view civil rights activities and riots as two different and contradictory types of phenomena. This paper will take the assumption of difference as a hypothesis rather than a postulate. In this discussion sociologists' conceptualizations of social movements and riots will be examined, characteristics of recent urban disorders will be evaluated, and conclusions will be drawn.

It must be emphasized that the problem to be examined is not one of mere labeling. This paper is concerned with the proper label for recent urban disorders, but only because the question has broader implications. First, there are important theoretical considerations. The nature of the concepts used, the theories invoked, and the hypotheses drawn all will be influenced by the correct classification of the disorders as riots or as parts of a developing social movement, for the problem cannot be understood accurately by using an invalid classificatory scheme. If predictions of the future are to be accurate, we must start with a valid base.

The second implication—the application of sociological principles—is closely related to the need for accurate prediction. Social scientists cannot make useful recommendations for action to politicians or segments of society unless they have a correct image of the current expressions of black unrest, a correct image of the depth and intensity of unrest, a perception of the extent to which this unrest has crystallized into a prerevolutionary movement, and some reasonably accurate predictions for the future. The types of societal changes that will ameliorate conditions producing hostile outbursts will not be sufficient to change the direction of a social movement which is developing along potentially revolutionary lines.

HOSTILE OUTBURSTS AND SOCIAL MOVEMENTS

Neil J. Smelser has developed a highly elaborate conceptual framework for the analysis of collective behavior.[1] He uses a value-added approach in which six determinants (necessary conditions) of collective behavior combine to specify the nature and characteristics of any particular collective episode. The six determinants are structural conduciveness, structural strain, growth and spread of a generalized belief, precipitating factors, mobilization of participants for action, and the operation of social con-

[1] Neil J. Smelser, *Theory of Collective Behavior* (New York: The Free Press of Glencoe, 1963).

trol.[2] Any particular form of collective behavior produced by these determinants may be analyzed in terms of four basic components of social action: values, norms, mobilization of motivation for organized action, and situational facilities.[3] Each component of social action is categorized into seven levels of specificity, but present purposes do not require a detailed exposition of the theory.

For Smelser, the crucial distinction between hostile outbursts (riots) and norm-oriented movements (that category of social movements which includes the civil rights movement) lies in the area of growth and spread of generalized beliefs. The value-added analysis of the development of hostile outbursts begins by examining ambiguity and anxiety. Anxiety is fused with the mobilization series to produce a generalized belief that some agent, or agents, is responsible for the anxiety-producing situation. This suspicion of agents is short-circuited to the selection of a particular kind of agent. A desire to punish, restrict, damage, or remove the agent then emerges, and wish-fulfillment beliefs of two types manifest themselves. They take the form of an exaggerated belief in the ability to punish agents of evil and to remove the evils ascribed to the agents. This belief is basically a generalized sense of omnipotence which is short-circuited to specifc results.[4]

The early stages of the development of a norm-oriented movement are identical to those in the development of a hostile outburst. The norm-oriented movement, too, begins with ambiguity, anxiety, the attachment of the anixety to some agent, and the exaggeration of the threatening nature of that agent. At this point, however, its development diverges. A belief develops that the normative control of the agent is inadequate and this belief becomes directed toward a particular set of laws or customs. Thus it comes to be accepted that the problem can be solved by changing the normative structure. This expectation becomes channeled into a decision about the particular type of normative change that would be expected to immobilize or destroy the agent, eliminating the source of the problem.[5]

The distinction between hostile outbursts and social movements focuses attention on the belief system. If the episode of collective behavior is seen as a direct attempt to attack or punish the agents of evil (in this case, police and white businessmen), then it is classed as an hostile outburst (a riot). However, if the episode of collective behavior is seen as a means of bringing about normative change to prevent the agents from working their evil, then it is termed a social movement. The presence or absence of scapegoating and/or violence does not determine the classification of a particular episode, because violence and scapegoating are elements of both hostile outbursts and norm-oriented movements. Smelser states that

> hostile outbursts are frequently adjuncts of larger-scale social movements. On certain occasions reform movements . . . may erupt into violence.

2 *Ibid.*, pp. 14–17.
3 *Ibid.*, pp. 23–28.
4 *Ibid.*, pp. 101–103.
5 *Ibid.*, pp. 111–112.

Revolutionary movements . . . are frequently accompanied by violence. The primary difference among terms such as "riot," "revolt," "rebellion," "insurrection," and "revolution" all of which involve hostile outbursts— stems from the scope of their associated social movements.[6]

The task, then, is to determine whether the recent urban disorders are isolated outbursts of pent-up hostility directed against perceived oppressors, such as police and white businessmen in the black ghetto, or part of a larger movement aimed at bringing about fundamental alterations in the normative order of American society. Probably a majority of white liberals and many social scientists have decided on the former alternative.[7]

CHARACTERISTICS OF THE DISORDERS

Research reports suggest that three aspects of the disorders contribute most to the labeling of the disorders as riots. First, the prime activity of most participants was looting.[8] Second, the disorders were spontaneous, relatively unorganized, and leaderless.[9] Third, the participants apparently did not attempt to seize permanent control of an area or specify political demands.[10] These objections will be examined one at a time.

LOOTING. First, the existence of looting, per se, should be investigated. Oberschall makes two points with regard to looting. He suggests that many petty thieves and small-time professional crooks came into the Watts area to engage in looting but left prior to the major waves of arrests. He indicates further that looting is a frequent occurrence in all disasters, natural or otherwise.[11] Both of these points may be well taken. Fires, floods, tornadoes, and riots all represent periods of upheaval. At such times, the burden upon police and other agents of social control is greatly increased. They are not in a position to enforce all aspects of the law and many persons take this opportunity to improve their lot temporarily by acquiring a ham, a television set, furniture, or liquor. Looting during a riot may be, as Lee Rainwater describes it, "a kind of primitive attempt at an income redistribution."[12] In other words, the "have-nots"

6 *Ibid.*, p. 227.

7 See, for example, Allen D. Grimshaw, "Civil Disturbance, Racial Revolt, Class Assault: Three Views of Urban Violence," paper presented before the American Association for the Advancement of Science, New York, December 28, 1967; and Anthony Oberschall, "The Los Angeles Riot," *Social Problems*, 15 (Winter, 1968), pp. 322–341. For examples of sociologists taking positions similar to the one presented herein, see Lewis M. Killian, *The Impossible Revolution* (New York: Random House, 1968); and Robert Blauner, "Whitewash over Watts," *Transaction*, 3 (March-April, 1966), p. 9.

8 See, for example, Tom Parmenter, "Breakdown of Law and Order," *Transaction*, 9 (Sept., 1967), pp. 13–21; Oberschall, "Los Angeles Riot," p. 327; and *Report of the National Advisory Commission on Civil Disorders* (New York: Bantam Books, 1968), p. 93.

9 See, for example, Oberschall, "Los Angeles Riot," p. 341; *Report on Civil Disorders*, pp. 201–202; and Arthur I. Waskow, *From Race Riot to Sit-In* (Garden City, N.Y.: Doubleday-Anchor, 1967), p. 260.

10 Oberschall, "Los Angeles Riot," p. 340.

11 *Ibid.*, pp. 335–338.

12 Lee Rainwater, "Open Letter on White Justice and the Riots," *Transaction*, 9 (Sept., 1967), p. 25.

temporarily increase their possessions without seriously attacking the distributive system.

This view must be balanced with an alternative one, for theft of any sort may be considered an act of rebellion. Hobsbawm has documented the fact that banditry in peasant societies has often been a form of social protest and represents an archaic form of social movement.[13] In such a case, the bandit who followed the Robin Hood model of stealing from the privileged and redistributing a portion of his gains to the underprivileged often had the support and affection of the peasantry. American history has its counterparts. Jesse James, Pretty Boy Floyd, and Babyface Nelson are only a few of the many American bandits who have been renowned in song and legend for their fights against the propertied and their generosity toward the needy. Theft, when directed against the right targets, may be seen as a direct attack upon the exploiter and upon the whole system of exploitation.

There is evidence that looting during the recent urban disorders was so directed. Rustin indicates that in the Watts riot the victims of looting and arson were whites rather than blacks.[14] He further points out that not all whites were victims; the white-owned businesses that had reputations for fair dealing and nondiscriminatory practices were spared. In Detroit some black-owned businesses were also targets.[15] These, however, were black merchants who had the same reputation for exploitation as did many whites.[16] There is, incidentally, some indication that in Detroit a group of individuals provided leadership in looting without participating in it themselves.[17]

A more basic criticism of the Oberschall interpretation of looting must be made, however. Dynes and Quarantelli state that looting rarely occurs in natural disasters and the little that does occur differs in many significant respects from that which occurs in urban disorders.[18] They cite one example of major looting in a natural disaster (the Chicago snowstorms of January and February, 1967) but suggest that the similarity in area of incidence may mean that this looting was a continuation of the looting during the disorder of 1966.[19]

If looting is characteristic of the current urban disorders but rarely occurs in natural disasters, it cannot be explained in the same terms in both cases. It is doubtful that the Dynes-Quarantelli interpretation in terms of property redefinition is adequate.[20] Looting appears to be more than simply a protest against the prevailing definition of property rights. The

[13] E. J. Hobsbawm, *Primitive Rebels* (New York: W. W. Norton, 1959), esp. Ch. 2.
[14] Bayard Rustin, "The Watts 'Manifesto' and the McCone Report," *Commentary*, 41 (March, 1966), pp. 29–35.
[15] *Report on Civil Disorders*, p. 88.
[16] Private interviews with observers of the disorder.
[17] Louis E. Lomax, "Seeds of Riot Planted Here by Salesmen," *Detroit News*, August 6, 1967, pp. 1–2.
[18] Russell Dynes and E. L. Quarantelli, "What Looting in Civil Disturbances Really Means," *Transaction*, 5 (May, 1968), pp. 9–14.
[19] *Ibid.*, p. 12.
[20] *Ibid.*, pp. 13–14.

selection of white and black exploiters as targets of looting and arson suggests that it is an attack upon the system of distribution of property and that it also provides an opportunity to acquire property. In short, looting constitutes an attack upon exploitation rather than upon exploiters—an act more characteristic of social movements than of hostile outbursts.

ORGANIZATION. Second, the fact that the disorders were spontaneous rather than the result of conspiracy is informative. The Kerner Commission saw no evidence of conspiracy, of deliberate incitement, or of organization in the disorders.[21] This is, however, no reason to conclude that they are not part of a social movement. To make such a statement is to misunderstand the nature of a social movement.

The treatment of social movements by Lang and Lang provides instructive insights.[22] They define a social movement as a "large-scale, widespread, and continuing, elementary collective action in pursuit of an objective that affects and shapes the social order in some fundamental aspect."[23] A social movement is seen as having organized associations at its core that provide general direction and focus; but it also includes large, unorganized segments pushing in the same direction but not integrated with the core associations. Lang and Lang specifically state that "unless we are able to distinguish between the core group and a larger mass of supporters not formally joined, we are not dealing with a social movement."[24]

Not all participants in every social movement need to have identical definitions of goals, strategy, and tactics; it is only necessary that they share the same general objectives. The degree of mutual cooperation and coordination of activities is, in fact, problematic in any given social movement. Lang and Lang state:

> One group working for a cause . . . may appear to be so involved in its quarrels with another group sharing its objective that members of both groups hardly seem to be participants in the same movement. Yet, however riddled by factional disputes a movement may be, the knowledge that other groups are working toward the same ends gives each unit a sense of participation in it. They compete to see which is the purest representative of the doctrine.[25]

Thus it would seem that any definition of the civil rights movement must be broad enough to include such disparate organizations as the Urban League, National Association for the Advancement of Colored People, Southern Christian Leadership Conference, Student Nonviolent Coordinating Committee, and the Congress on Racial Equality, provided they are all working for the same general objectives, such as the furthering of the position and rights of the black American. The definition must also be

---

21 *Report on Civil Disorders*, pp. 201–202.
22 Kurt Lang and Gladys Engel Lang, *Collective Dynamics* (New York: Crowell, 1961), pp. 489–544.
23 *Ibid.*, p. 490.
24 *Ibid.*, p. 497.
25 *Ibid.*, p. 496.

broad enough to include the unorganized participants of demonstrations, boycotts, and even urban disorders, provided, again, that the participants have the same general goals.[26] The lack of organization does not, *ipso facto*, exclude looters, snipers, and arsonists from the civil rights movement. Their motives must be examined, which will be done later in this paper.

TACTICS. Third, does the absence of stated political demands and/or any attempt to seize permanent control of a geographic area exclude urban disorders from the category of social movements? The answer to this question requires a comprehensive analysis of the nature and role of tactics in a social movement.

The reluctance to treat urban disorders as a segment of the civil rights movement very likely stems from the tendency to define the movement in terms of its organized core associations and to define its tactics in terms of the more respectable ones of court suits, nonviolent direct action, and voter registration drives. Killian and Grigg note, however, that each of the above tactics emerged when previous modes of behavior proved inadequate in bringing about sufficiently broad results as rapidly as desired.[27] It is plausible to assume that segments of the black community have become dissatisfied with the slow, token changes brought about by the respectable tactics and are developing more drastic ones to increase the speed and scope of change. Oberschall lends support to this interpretation when he states:

> The collective significance of these events, however, is that the civil rights gains made by the Negro movement in the last few years, which have benefitted the Southern Negro and middle-class Negroes, have not altered the situation of the lower-class urban Negroes outside of the South and have not removed the fundamental sources of grievances of a large proportion of the Negro population in the U.S.[28]

The historical role of urban mobs in controlling ruling elites and in attempting to bring about changes is well documented. Hobsbawm states:

> Provided the ruler did his duty, the populace was prepared to defend him with enthusiasm. But if he did not, it rioted until he did. . . . The treatment of perennial rioting kept rulers ready to control prices and to distribute work or largess, or indeed to listen to their faithful commons on other matters.[29]

> Nevertheless, such a symbiosis of the "mob" and the people against whom it rioted was not necessarily the fundamental factor about its politics. The "mob" rioted, but it also sometimes made revolutions. . . . It was poor;

---

[26] Although probably clear from the context, the term "civil rights movement" is not here used in the narrow sense of attempts to acquire legal rights and legal equality through normative means. It is used in the broader sense of all attempts to gain legal rights and legal equality as well as those attempts to translate legal rights into actual functioning rights and equality.

[27] Lewis Killian and Charles Grigg, *Racial Crisis in America* (Englewood Cliffs, N.J.: Prentice Hall, 1964), pp. 18–23.

[28] Oberschall, "Los Angeles Riot," p. 341.

[29] Hobsbawm, *Primitive Rebels*, p. 116.

"they" were rich; life was fundamentally unjust for the poor. These were the foundations of its attitude. . . . The implicit revolutionism of the "mob" was primitive; in its way it was the metropolitan equivalent of the stage of political consciousness represented by social banditry in the countryside.[30]

Thus, a plausible assumption is that the civil rights movement has undergone an evolution of tactics. As one tactic proves inadequate to the task it is replaced by another seen as more adequate. In the recent past, accommodation gave way to court suits. The orderly tactics gave way to the less orderly tactics of direct action, which Waskow analyzes under the concept of "creative disorder."[31] "Creative disorder" may now be giving way to "creative rioting."[32] Ghetto riots may be an attempt to use violent disorder creatively to bring about change. This does not mean that all individuals involved in the civil rights movement are now, or will be, participating in riots. There always has been a tactical division of labor: some civil rights adherents use court suits; others engage in nonviolent direct action; others, however, may have moved on to creative rioting.[33]

The stating of political demands and the attempts to permanently occupy and control a given territory are tactics which are likely to appear in a fully developed insurrection or revolution. The tactic of creative rioting represents a move in this direction developing from creative disorder. It is an intermediate tactic which does not go as far as revolution. That is, it may appear in prerevolutionary situations—situations which have the potential for developing into revolutions but which will not necessarily do so.

Oberschall may not be entirely accurate when he states that political demands are missing in the current urban disorders. The Kerner Commission report states:

In 21 of the 24 disturbances surveyed, discussion or negotiation occurred during the disturbances. These took the form of relatively formal meetings

[30] *Ibid.*, p. 118.

[31] Waskow, *From Race Riot to Sit-In*, pp. 225–290.

[32] "Creative rioting" as used herein refers to a particular tactical type of behavior aimed at bringing about societal change. It involves the conscious and deliberate use of violent attacks against property and/or persons. The violence against property may be either of a destructive or of a confiscatory (theft) nature. Violence against persons usually is not directed randomly against persons as individuals or members of a group; rather, it is frequently directed against persons as symbols of authority or oppression. It tends to be incidental to attacks upon property or the system of exploitation.

Thus, creative rioting differs from creative disorder in that the latter is nonviolent and, while disruptive of societal processes, is not destructive of property. Creative rioting also differs from revolution in that it tends to be too short-lived, less organized, and less coordinated than required for a full-scale, violent attempt to seize control of society.

[33] Similarly, there may be a division of labor within a rioting mob. Some participants may consciously use rioting as a tactic to promote change, while others simply attempt to improve their personal well-being by acquiring more possessions, and still others try to avenge real or alleged wrongs. The latter two groups are not, strictly speaking, using creative rioting, but by swelling the numbers of rioters—thereby increasing the duration and intensity of the disorders—they contribute to the overall effect of the creative rioters.

between government officials and Negroes during which grievances and issues were discussed and means were sought to restore order.[34]

These meetings usually were with "established leaders" but youths were involved in 13 discussions. The combination of discussion of grievances and the presence of the more militant youths indicates the presence of some sort of political demands even though no attempt to occupy territory permanently may have been made. Urban disorders, therefore, may be a new civil rights tactic which stops short of revolution.

The case for creative rioting—ghetto riots as an integral part of the civil rights movement—has not yet been fully demonstrated. The nature and pattern of looting lend more support to this interpretation than they do to the alternative interpretation of urban disorders as hostile outbursts. The lack of deliberate instigation or organization in the disorders is neutral, as it is equally consistent with either interpretation. The lack of an attempt to assume permanent control of a given territory does not prevent the current ghetto riots from being a step in the evolution of tactics within the civil rights movement just short of full-blown insurrection. Due to the inconclusive nature of the foregoing, one must analyze the characteristics of riot participants prior to drawing final conclusions. The prime source of data will be the recent surveys of riot participation conducted in Detroit and Newark.

Characteristics of Riot Participants

A number of characteristics of self-identified rioters or riot supporters correspond to those noted in the sociological literature as characterizing individuals who are prone to participate in social movements or revolutions. Both Lyford P. Edwards and Crane Brinton state that individuals who perceive their legitimate aspirations for mobility to be blocked are especially prone to engage in revolutionary behavior.[35] The Kerner Commission report notes that the self-identified rioters in Newark were significantly ($p<.05$) more likely than the self-reported noninvolved individuals to believe that their level of education entitled them to a job with more income and responsibility than the one they presently possessed.[36] The Newark rioters were also less likely than the noninvolved to perceive that there was an opportunity for them to acquire their desired job ($p<.06$) and significantly more likely ($p<.025$) to believe that discrimination was the factor preventing them from so doing.[37] No comparable data from Detroit are available. Taken jointly, these characteristics indicate the existence of the blocked-mobility syndrome that Edwards and Brinton find typical of potential revolutionaries.

Status inconsistency also has been interpreted as a characteristic that

---

[34] *Report on Civil Disorders*, pp. 126–127.

[35] Lyford P. Edwards, *The Natural History of Revolution* (Chicago: The University of Chicago Press, 1927), p. 30; and Crane Brinton, *The Anatomy of Revolution* (New York: W. W. Norton, 1938), p. 78.

[36] *Report on Civil Disorders*, p. 127, n. 130. Henceforth, self-reported rioters and self-reported noninvolved will be referred to, respectively, as rioters and noninvolved.

[37] *Ibid.*, p. 175, nn. 131 and 132.

predisposes individuals toward participation in social movements or revolutions.[38] Evidence suggests that rioters tend to be status-inconsistent. The Detroit rioters were significantly *better educated* than the noninvolved (p<.05) and the Newark rioters, too, tended to be better educated than the noninvolved (p<.06).[39] Both Newark and Detroit rioters tended to have *lower incomes* than the noninvolved, although neither difference is statistically significant.[40] The Newark rioters also tended to have lower job status than the noninvolved (p<.06).[41] No data on occupational status are available from Detroit. While there is no difference between rioters and the noninvolved in terms of current rate of unemployment, the Newark rioters were significantly more likely to have been unemployed for a month or longer within the past year (p<.05).[42] No comparable data are available from Detroit.

These data together indicate that rioters were considerably less likely to be able to bring their occupational status, income, or employment status up to a level comparable to their level of education. When this observation is combined with the fact that Negroes are more likely than whites to have their levels of occupation and income lag behind their educational level, then there can be no doubt that active rioters are status inconsistent —and inconsistent to a greater degree than the noninvolved.[43] More important, the rioters' "profiles" are inconsistent with high education–low income or high education-low occupation profiles, which are precisely the ones most likely to produce participation in extremist social movements of leftist inclinations.[44]

The fact that rioters exhibit status inconsistency and possess thwarted aspirations does not in itself demonstrate that riots are part of a social movement. One additional factor, however, lends credence to this interpretation. Ransford found that Watts Negroes who were socially isolated from whites were significantly more willing to use violence than were those with greater contact with whites.[45] This conclusion agrees with the suggestion by Marx that the isolation of an aggrieved category of persons into an interacting collectivity is likely to produce a conflict group with a high degree of group consciousness and an awareness of a common enemy.[46] The likelihood that racially isolated blacks may develop "black con-

[38] For a summary of such literature see James A. Geschwender, "Continuities in Theories of Status Inconsistency and Cognitive Dissonance," *Social Forces*, 46 (Dec., 1967), pp. 160–171.

[39] *Report on Civil Disorders*, p. 174, n. 126.

[40] *Ibid.*, p. 174, n. 124.

[41] *Ibid.*, p. 175, n. 129.

[42] *Ibid.*, p. 175, nn. 127 and 128.

[43] James A. Geschwender, "Negro Education: The False Faith," *Phylon* (forthcoming); and James A. Geschwender, "Social Structure and the Negro Revolt: An Examination of Some Hypotheses," *Social Forces*, 43 (Dec., 1964), pp. 248–256.

[44] Geschwender, "Continuities in Theories," pp. 169–171.

[45] H. Edward Ransford, "Isolation, Powerlessness, and Violence: A Study of Attitudes and Participation in the Watts Riot," *American Journal of Sociology*, 73 (March, 1968), p. 586.

[46] Reinhard Bendix and Seymour Martin Lipset, "Karl Marx' Theory of Social

sciousness" and a hostility toward whites which could manifest itself in rioting as revolutionary activity gains support from data on the Detroit and Newark rioters. Both Newark and Detroit rioters were significantly more likely than the noninvolved to believe that Negroes are more dependable than whites ($p<.05$ and $<.001$, respectively) and that Negroes are "nicer" than whites ($p<.025$ and $<.001$, respectively).[47] Newark rioters were significantly more likely than the noninvolved to describe themselves as "black" ($p<.025$) and were more prone to believe that all Negroes should study African history and languages ($p<.06$).[48] No comparable data are available from Detroit. Newark rioters were significantly more likely than the noninvolved to believe that presently integrated civil rights groups would be more effective without whites ($p<.005$) and to admit that sometimes they hated whites ($p<.001$).[49] While there are no data on the likelihood that Detroit rioters hated whites, they, also, were more likely than the noninvolved to say that integrated civil rights groups would be more effective without whites ($p<.10$).[50]

These data strongly suggest that rioters are individuals largely isolated from whites, that they interact with blacks who share common grievances, that they develop a high level of hostility toward whites, combined with a high level of black consciousness, and that they subsequently participate in riots as a means of attacking the "system." In short, they are participating in a social movement that may or may not reach revolutionary proportions.

The suggestion presented above—that urban riots may represent an evolution of tactics from the more respectable to the more violent—gains support from the following facts. Newark rioters were significantly more likely than the noninvolved to participate in discussions of Negro rights ($p<.025$), to participate in activities of civil rights groups ($p<.05$), to identify political figures ($p<.205$), to be politically knowledgeable ($p<.025$), and to not trust the Newark government to do what is right ($p<.10$).[51] While there are no directly comparable data from Detroit, the rioters there were significantly more likely than the noninvolved to feel that anger toward politicians ($p<.05$) and toward the police ($p<.05$) had much to do with causing the riots.[52]

Conclusion

The rioters discussed above are not the normally apathetic, noninvolved individuals who participate in hostile outbursts. They tend to be politically knowledgeable and active in civil rights activities. Many of them have apparently come to the conclusion that traditional political and civil rights

---

Classes," in Reinhard Bendix and Seymour Martin Lipset, eds., *Class, Status and Power* (New York: Free Press of Glencoe, 1953), pp. 26–35.

[47] *Report on Civil Disorders*, p. 175, n. 134.

[48] *Ibid.*, p. 175, n. 135.

[49] *Ibid.*, p. 175, n. 136.

[50] *Ibid.*

[51] *Ibid.*, pp. 177–178, nn. 140, 139, 141.

[52] *Ibid.*, p. 178, n. 142.

tactics cannot bring about desired results and thus they have shifted to newer tactics. This interpretation is supported by the desire of a large number of rioters to exclude whites from civil rights organizations. The theoretically relevant characteristics of thwarted aspirations and status inconsistency suggest, but do not demonstrate, this conclusion. The factor of racial isolation, though, pushes further in the direction indicated. Political knowledgeability, civil rights activities, black consciousness, hostility toward whites, and mistrust of government "put the icing on the cake" and make the conclusion emphatic.

The earlier discussion of looting strongly suggested that current urban disorders were a developing part of the civil rights movement. The discussions of degree of organization of riots and of tactics were consistent with the interpretation of urban disorders as either hostile outbursts or segments of a social movement. The discussion of the characteristics of rioters, however, removed remaining doubts. The present author no longer questions that the urban disorders are, in fact, creative rioting. Creative rioting falls clearly within the evolutionary pattern of the civil rights movement, a social movement which may or may not eventually become revolutionary.

This thesis should not be misconstrued; this paper does not contend that all urban disorders were creative rioting. The outbreaks of 1964 in Harlem, Rochester, Jersey City, and Philadelphia may have been simple hostile outbursts, although they did bring about a response on the community, state, and national levels. As subsequent riots continued to bring about real, if limited, results, individuals may have become aware of riots as a potentially successful tactic. This is not to say that the riots were deliberately instigated. Rather, a potential riot situation may have made some individuals aware of the utility of rioting, which in turn stimulated riot behavior. Once a riot was underway, other individuals were motivated to continue and direct it. Thus, rioting shifts from the category of a hostile outburst to that of a creative force in the civil rights movement.

30

Riot Ideology in Los Angeles: A Study of Negro Attitudes[1]

DAVID O. SEARS
UNIVERSITY OF CALIFORNIA, LOS ANGELES

T. M. TOMLINSON
OFFICE OF ECONOMIC OPPORTUNITY

Each summer from 1964 through 1967 saw urban Negroes in America involved in a series of violent riots. Among the most critical consequences of the riots were the decisions made by the white population about the social changes required to prevent further rioting. These decisions rested in part on the whites' assumptions about the nature and extent of the Negro community's involvement in the riots. Matters of simple fact such as how many people took part in the riots, whether the rest of the Negro community repudiated the rioters, and whether it viewed the riots as representing some form of collective protest against injustice and poverty, were initially quite unclear. Yet whites quickly made their own assumptions about such matters, and these strongly influenced their stance toward the riots and the entire racial problem.

There appear to be three widely held myths about the Negro community's response to riots. The first is that the riots are participated in and viewed favorably by only a tiny segment of the Negro community. The figure often cited by news media and political spokesmen (both black and white) is between 2 and 5 per cent of the Negro population. Since riot supporters are thought to be so few in number, a further assumption is that they come from such commonly condemned fringe groups as Communists, hoodlums, and Black Muslims.[2]

The second myth is that most Negroes see the riots as purposeless, meaningless, senseless outbursts of criminality. Many white public officials certainly professed to see nothing in the riots but blind hostility and malicious mischief, drunkenness, and material greed. Perhaps because they held this view so strongly themselves, they tended to assume that Negroes shared it as well.

The third myth is that Negroes generally believe that no benefit will result from the riots. Negroes are supposed to view them with horror, seeing the physical destruction wrought in black ghettos, as well as the

[1] This study was conducted under a contract between the Office of Economic Opportunity and the Institute for Government and Public Affairs at UCLA, while both authors were members of the Department of Psychology, UCLA. The Coordinator of the research was Nathan E. Cohen. We owe a profound debt of gratitude to the many persons who worked on the Los Angeles Riot Study, with special thanks to Diana Ten-Houten and John B. McConahay. We also wish to express our appreciation to Esther Spachner for editorial help and to Peter Orleans for his comments on an earlier draft of this paper.

[2] See the attributions of the Watts riot to "young hoodlums," "the criminal element," and black nationalists by the mayor and police chief of Los Angeles, in the *New York Times*, Aug. 13, 1965, p. 26; Aug. 14, 1965, p. 8; Sept. 14, 1965, p. 22.

destruction of the good will patiently accumulated during early days of campaigning for civil rights. According to this myth, Negroes foresee "white backlash" and cities laid waste, rather than betterment in their life situations, as the main effect of the riots.

The response of the Negro community to the riots is a crucial consideration in determining how the society as a whole should respond to them. If these three myths are correct, perhaps the customary mechanisms for dealing with individual criminal behavior are not only morally justified but also the most practicable means for handling riots. If these myths are incorrect, if Negroes support the riots, see them as expressing meaningful goals, and expect them to better the conditions of their lives, then the responses traditionally used for dealing with criminals would be inappropriate. They would be impractical, ineffective, and likely to exacerbate an already difficult situation. Instead it would be essential to devise policies which took into account the fact that the riot highlighted a problem pervading the whole Negro community, rather than one limited to a few deviant individuals.

It is apparent that many Americans, black and white alike, have already rejected these myths. Others, however, retain them—those in positions of authority as well as those in the broader white community. Moreover, systematic data on them have not been widely available. Since these myths have had and will continue to have great influence in determining the white population's response to urban problems, it is vital that their validity be subjected to close empirical test. The primary purpose of this article is to present some convincing evidence of their inaccuracy, at least in the important case of the Los Angeles Negro community's response to the Watts riots.

METHOD[3]

The data on which this article is based were obtained from interviews conducted with three samples of respondents in Los Angeles County in late 1965 and early 1966. The most important was a representative sample of Negroes living in the large area (46.5 square miles) of South-Central Los Angeles sealed off by a curfew imposed during the rioting. This sample, numbering 586 respondents, will be referred to below as the "Negro curfew zone" sample. The curfew zone contains about three-fourths of the more than 450,000 Negroes living in Los Angeles County, and is over 80 per cent Negro.[4] Hence it represents the major concentration of Negroes in the Los Angeles area. The sampling was done by randomly choosing

---

[3] For more complete accounts of the method, see T. M. Tomlinson and Diana L. Ten-Houten, "Method: Negro Reaction Survey," and Richard T. Morris and Vincent Jeffries, "The White Reaction Study," *Los Angeles Riot Study* (Los Angeles: Institute of Government and Public Affairs, University of California, 1967). See also R. T. Morris and V. Jeffries, "Violence Next Door," *Social Forces*, 46 (March, 1968), pp. 352–358.

[4] See U.S., Bureau of the Census, *U.S. Census of Population: 1960*, Vol. 1: *Characteristics of the Population*, Part 6: California (Washington, D.C.: U.S. Government Printing Office, 1963). Also David O. Sears and John B. McConahay, "Riot Participation," *Los Angeles Riot Study*.

names from the 1960 census lists, then over-sampling poverty-level census tracts by a cluster-sampling procedure to compensate for the underrepresentation of low-income respondents due to residential transience. Another 124 Negro respondents, all arrested in the riot, were contacted principally through lawyers providing free legal aid. This "arrestee" sample was not representative but provided a useful reference point. Both Negro samples were interviewed by black interviewers living in the curfew zone. Though the interviews were long (averaging about two hours), interest was high and the refusal rate low. Checks were run on the possible biases introduced by the interviewers' own views and these do not give unusual reason for concern. The same interview schedule was used for all Negro respondents; it was structured, and included both open-ended and closed-ended items.

The third sample included 586 white respondents from six communities in Los Angeles County, half of which were racially integrated and half nonintegrated, with high, medium, and low socioeconomic levels. This sample is thus not wholly representative of the county, overrepresenting high SES and racially integrated areas, thus probably underestimating racial hostilities. Some, but not all, of the items on the Negro interview schedule were also used with white respondents. The main emphasis in this article is upon Negro opinion, so the white sample is not referred to except when explicitly indicated.

THE THREE MYTHS

Data relevant to the first myth—that only a small fraction of the Negro community participated in the riot of August, 1965, and that nearly everyone else was antagonistic to it—show that it was clearly erroneous on both counts.

The authors' best estimate is that approximately 15 per cent of the Negroes in the area participated in the riot. This was the proportion of curfew zone respondents who stated that they had been "very" or "somewhat" active in the riot and that they had seen crowds of people, and stores being burned and looted. The self-report of active participation, whether wholly accurate or not, indicates, at least, that numerous Los Angeles Negroes (22 per cent of the sample) were willing to identify themselves with the riot.[5]

Furthermore, the Negro community as a whole was not overwhelmingly antagonistic to the riot. This point may be demonstrated in two ways. First, respondents were asked to estimate the proportion of "people in the area" (referring generally to the curfew zone) who had supported or opposed the riot. The mean estimate was that 34 per cent had "supported" the riot, and that 56 per cent had been "against it."

Second, each respondent was asked his own feeling about the riot in a series of open-ended questions. He was asked directly how he felt about

[5] For a detailed consideration of these data, see Sears and McConahay, *ibid.* Rates of participation in the Newark and Detroit riots of 1967 appear to have been similarly high, according to data published in *The Report of the National Advisory Commission on Civil Disorders* (New York: Bantam Books, 1968), p. 172.

the riot, how he felt about the events of the riot, and how he felt about the people who were involved. Answers to these questions yielded three measures of feeling or affect toward the riot.[6] A little under one-third of the Negro curfew zone sample expressed approval of the riot on each of these three measures, and about half disapproved of the riot, as shown in Table 1. This finding closely resembled the respondents' own estimates of public opinion in the area, as cited above.

Clearly, then, support for the riot was far more extensive than the public has been led to believe, numbering about a third of the area's adult residents, though a majority did disapprove of it. Even while disapproving, however, Negro respondents were markedly more lenient toward the riot's supporters than they were toward the destruction of life and property that occurred. Table 1 shows that 42 per cent disapproved of the participants, while 67 per cent disapproved of the events of the riot.

THE RIOT AS A PROTEST. The second myth—that the riot was a meaningless, haphazard expression of disregard for law and order—was not com-

TABLE 1

Evaluation of Riot and Rioters[a]

	Overall Feeling about Riot	Feeling about Events	Feeling about Participants
Negro curfew zone (N=586)			
Very or somewhat favorable	27%	29%	30%
Ambivalent or neutral	16	1	19
Strongly or moderately unfavorable	50	67	42
Don't know, no answer	7	3	8
Total	100%	100%	99%
Arrestee sample (N=124)			
Very or somewhat favorable	52%	50%	57%
Ambivalent or neutral	10	4	12
Strongly or moderately unfavorable	32	45	23
Don't know, no answer	6	1	7
Total	100%	100%	99%

[a] The specific questions were as follows:
For column 1, "Now that it is over, how do you feel about what happened?"
For column 2, "What did you like about what was going on?" and
      "What did you dislike about what was going on?"
For column 3, "What kinds of people supported it?" and "What kinds of people
      were against it?"
These questions were not asked of the white sample.

---

[6] For a detailed description of the coding procedure, see Tomlinson and TenHouten, "Method: Negro Reaction Survey." The coding reliabilities were all over .95.

monly held among Negroes in Los Angeles. Many viewed the riot in revolutionary or insurrectional terms; most thought it had a purpose and that the purpose was, in part at least, a Negro protest.

Official utterances and the mass media, almost without exception, had described the events as being a "riot." Each respondent was asked what term he would use to describe the events. Table 2 shows that, given this free choice, over a third of the Negro sample selected "revolt," "insurrection," "rebellion," "uprising," "revenge," or other revolutionary term, thus

TABLE 2

The Riot as Protest

	Whites	Negroes (Curfew Zone)	Arrestees
What word or term would you use in talking about it?			
Riot	58%	46%	44%
Revolt, revolution, insurrection	13	38	45
Other (disaster, tragedy, mess, disgrace, etc.)	27	8	10
Don't know, no answer	2	8	2
Total	100%	100%	101%
Why were targets attacked?[a]			
Deserved attack	—	64%	75%
Ambivalent, don't know	—	17	21
Did not deserve attack	—	14	0
No answer	—	5	4
Total		100%	100%
Did it have a purpose or goal?			
Yes	33%	56%	56%
Don't know, other	4	11	13
No	62	28	29
No answer	—	5	2
Total	99%	100%	100%
Was it a Negro protest?			
Yes	54%	62%	66%
Don't know, other	3	12	15
No	42	23	16
No answer	—	2	3
Total	99%	99%	100%

[a] This question was not asked of white respondents.

flying in the face of the conventional definition. Other items given in Table 2 posed the question of a meaningful protest more directly, and show that a majority of the Negro community did indeed see the riot in these terms. Substantial majorities felt that it did have a purpose, that it was a Negro protest, and that those outsiders attacked in the riot deserved what they got.

ANTICIPATING FAVORABLE EFFECTS. The third myth—that Negroes viewed the riot with alarm for the future—also was not subscribed to in Los Angeles. Most (58 per cent) foresaw predominantly beneficial effects, and only a minority (26 per cent) anticipated predominantly unfavorable effects. Similarly, more thought it would "help" the Negro cause than thought it would "hurt" it. These data are given in Table 3.

Thus, a large minority of the Negroes in the curfew zone, about one-third, were favorable to the rioting, and the others' disapproval focused more upon the events than upon the participants. Over half saw the riot as a purposeful protest, many even speaking of it in revolutionary terms. Favorable effects were much more widely anticipated than unfavorable effects. This evidence indicates that the three myths cited above were invalid for the Los Angeles Negro community. It did not wholeheartedly reject and condemn its 1965 riot.

PARTICIPANTS' ATTITUDES. Negroes clearly had more sympathy for the participants than for the events of the riot. In fact, the participants and the community as a whole had rather similar attitudes about the riot. The arrestees were considerably more favorable toward the riot than was the

TABLE 3

Expected Effects of the Riot

	Whites	Negroes (Curfew Zone)	Arrestees
What will the main effects be?[a]			
Very or somewhat favorable	—	58%	57%
Neutral, ambivalent, don't know	—	12	14
Very or somewhat unfavorable	—	26	27
No answer	—	3	2
Total		99%	100%
Do you think it helped or hurt the Negro's cause?			
Helped	19%	38%	54%
No difference, don't know	5	30	33
Hurt	75	24	9
No answers, other	1	8	4
Total	100%	100%	100%

[a] This question was not asked of white respondents.

community as a whole (see Table 1), but the community was equally optimistic about the effects of the riot, and as willing to interpret it as a purposeful protest (see Tables 2 and 3). Data presented elsewhere compare participants and nonparticipants within the Negro curfew zone sample, and yield almost exactly the same picture. Most participants tended to approve of the riot, while more nonparticipants disapproved than approved of it. However, in both groups a majority expressed optimism about the effects of the riot, and interpreted it as a meaningful protest. In fact participants and nonparticipants hardly differed at all in the latter two respects.[7] This similarity of feeling between the participants (whether arrested or not) and the Negro community as a whole suggests both that the participants were not particularly unusual or deviant in their thinking, and that members of the community were not wholly willing to condemn nor to symbolically ostracize the rioters.

WHITE ATTITUDES. The picture is quite different with respect to whites. As might now be expected, their attitudes toward the riot were considerably less favorable. Table 2 shows that whites thought it was nothing more meaningful than a "riot." Though most did feel it was a Negro protest, the consensus of opinion was that it was a purposeless, meaningless outburst. Table 3 shows that whites felt it definitely had "hurt" the Negro cause. Thus the cleavage in opinion that developed in Los Angeles after the riot was not so much between rioters and the law-abiding people of both races as between whites and blacks.

OTHER RIOTS, OTHER COMMUNITIES. This is not the place to attempt a complete review of Negro opinion in other communities, or about other riots, but a brief discussion will indicate that results obtained here were similar to those obtained elsewhere in this nation.

Items directly analogous to those here evaluating riots and rioters have not been widely used. A *Fortune Magazine* national survey in 1967 did find that only 14 per cent felt the "violence and rioting that has already occurred" was "essentially good," while 58 per cent felt it was "essentially bad."[8] Similarly, a 1967 Harris national survey found that 10 per cent felt "most Negroes support riots" and 75 per cent felt that "only a minority" supports them.[9] These results indicate disapproval of riots by a substantial majority of Negroes. Yet the same Harris poll reveals that 62 per cent felt looters should not be shot, and 27 per cent felt they should be (in contrast to the 62 per cent of whites who felt shooting was appropriate for looters).[10] Clearly there are substantial limits on the strength of Negro disapproval and condemnation of Negro rioters.

Optimism about the effects of riots has also been characteristic. In sev-

---

[7] See David O. Sears and John B. McConahay, "The Politics of Discontent: Blocked Mechanisms of Grievance Redress and the Psychology of the New Urban Black Man," *Los Angeles Riot Study.*

[8] Roger Beardwood, "The New Negro Mood," *Fortune,* 77 (Jan., 1968), p. 146.

[9] See Hazel Erskine, "The Polls: Demonstrations and Race Riots," *Public Opinion Quarterly,* 31 (Winter, 1967), pp. 655–677, for many of the results of these polls. This finding is given on p. 671.

[10] *Ibid.,* p. 674.

eral studies, Negroes have been asked whether riots "help" or "hurt" their cause, and the preferred answer has generally been that they "help." This was the result of a 1966 Harris national survey, a 1966 Harris survey of Negro leadership, and surveys of the Negro populations of Los Angeles (1966) and Oakland (1967).[11] The two exceptions have been a 1966 survey in Houston, a Southern city, where a slight plurality felt that riots "hurt," and the 1967 Harris survey (presumably national), which reported that only 12 per cent felt they would help—a result that is grossly out of line with all other surveys and thus difficult to interpret.

THE RIOT IDEOLOGY OF THE NEGRO COMMUNITY

Ambivalent evaluations of the riot, the feeling that it was meaningful, and optimism about its effects represent the simple elements around which a more complex belief system about the riot developed within the Negro community. This centered on a view of the riot as an instrument of Negro protest against real grievances. The substance of this view may be examined through the content of the protest and the grievances. First, let us consider in more detail the question of general community sympathy for the rioters.

RIOT EVENTS AND PARTICIPANTS: THE COMMUNITY'S SYMPATHETIC DEFENSE. Evaluations of the riot events and riot participants, shown in Table 1, gave the impression that the events of the riot were condemned more heartily than the rioters. Does the content of the respondents' attitudes support this impression?

The actual events of the riot were almost universally condemned. When asked "What did you like about what was going on?" 63 per cent of the Negroes sampled replied, "Nothing." The others gave widely dispersed responses. Crimes against property (such as burning and looting) and crimes against persons (such as killing and shooting) were cited about equally often as disliked aspects of the riot, as shown in Table 4. However, while the events of the riot were generally disliked and disapproved, they were not flatly repudiated. About 75 per cent couched their disapproval in terms suggesting sorrow and remorse (e.g., "regretful," "a sad thing," "a shame," "glad it's over") while only 25 per cent responded in a fashion suggesting repudiation of the riot (e.g., "disgusted," "disgrace," "unnecessary," "senseless"). Since disapproval of the riot did not necessarily include total disociation from and repudiation of it, it is perhaps not surprising that the rioters and riot supporters were less harshly criticized than the event they created.

Indeed, the Negro community's description of the riot supporters, on the one hand, and the authorities on the other, reveal considerably more sympathy for those fomenting the riot than for those who tried to stop it.

---

11 See W. Brink and Louis Harris, *Black and White* (New York: Simon and Schuster, 1966), pp. 264–265; *Federal Role in Urban Affairs*, Hearings before the Subcommittee on Executive Reorganization of the Committee on Government Operations, U.S. 89th Congress, 2nd Sesssion, Senate, Part 6, p. 1387; William McCord and John Howard, "Negro Opinions in Three Riot Cities," *American Behavioral Scientist*, 11 (March–April, 1968), p. 26.

The descriptions of who had supported the riot, shown in Table 5, indicate that such sympathetic and understanding descriptions as "people who suffer" or "people wanting freedom" outnumbered such unsympa-

TABLE 4

What Did You Dislike About the Riot?[a]

	Negroes (Curfew Zone)	Arrestees
Crimes against property (burning, destruction, looting)	47%	26%
Crimes against persons	43	70
Negro attacks on white	(1)	(0)
Police shooting, killing, brutality	(14)	(32)
Killing, bloodshed, violence, shooting in general	(28)	(38)
Practical inconveniences	9	5
Negroes breaking law	1	0
Total	100%	100%

[a]Not asked of white respondents.

TABLE 5

What Kinds of People Supported the Riot?"

	Negroes (Curfew Zone)	Arrestees
Sympathetic descriptions	45%	59%
Everyone	(10)	(15)
Good people (people wanting freedom, sympathetic people, etc.)	(5)	(8)
Deprived, mistreated (unemployed people who suffer, have-nots, poor people)	(30)	(36)
Unsympathetic descriptions	34	16
Anti-social (hoodlums, corrupt)	(12)	(10)
Political (Communists, Muslims)	(2)	(0)
Irresponsible (teenagers, fools, uneducated, thrill seekers)	(20)	(6)
Other	21	25
Estranged people (hopeless people, old people)	(5)	(9)
Middle class (business people)	(1)	(1)
Don't know, no answer	(15)	(15)
Total	100%	100%

[a] Not asked of white respondents.

thetic and repudiating responses as "hoodlums" or "Communists." The predominant conception of a riot supporter was not of a criminal, or of a dis-
reputable or despicable person, but evidently of a person not so very
dissimilar from the respondent himself, though perhaps somewhat down
on his luck.

In contrast, much antagonism was expressed toward the authorities'
role in the riot. Only 28 per cent thought the authorities had handled the
riot "well," and 65 per cent felt they had handled it "badly." The further
breakdown of these responses is shown in Table 6; Negroes who thought
the authorities had done badly were split between those who felt they
should have put an end to the riot earlier, and those who felt the authorities had exacerbated the situation. Many Negro respondents did not
like what had happened then, but their disposition was to defend and
justify the actions of Negro rioters, and to criticize the actions of the white
authorities.

Explanations of the causes of the riot also demonstrated a sympathetic
defense of the rioters, as shown in Table 7. The dominant tendency was
to blame the riot on legitimate grievances, such as discrimination, poverty,
or police mistreatment (38 per cent), or on long-standing hostility and
other pent-up emotions (26 per cent). Relatively few attributed the riot
mainly to the incident that precipitated it, the fracas with the Frye family,
or blamed any of the obvious candidates for a scapegoat, such as the Communists or gang members.

The contrast with opinions expressed by white residents of Los Angeles
was a vivid one. By attributing the riot to grievances and to years of frustration, the Negro respondents suggested that the people who supported
the riot had legitimate reasons for doing so. Whites, on the other hand,
praised the work of the authorities, or even criticized them for not being
more punitive with the rioters (Table 6). Whites were much more inclined to attribute the riot to agitators, Communists, criminals, the weath-
er, or simply to write it off as arising from the Frye incident (Table 7).

TABLE 6

Did the Authorities Handle It Well or Badly?

	Whites	Negroes (Curfew Zone)	Arrestees
Well	66%	28%	15%
Badly	32	65	77
Should have stopped it sooner	(26)	(27)	(14)
They made it worse, were intransigent	(6)	(33)	(56)
Other	(0)	(5)	(7)
Don't know, no answer, other	2	8	9
Total	100%	101%	101%

The Negro community as a whole was much closer to the explicit sympathy for the rioters expressed by the arrestees. Both gave relatively sympathetic descriptions of the rioters (Table 5), harshly criticized the authorities (Table 6), and attributed the riot to legitimate grievances rather than to chance or whimsical or illegal and un-American factors (Table 7).

This contrast between black sympathy for the rioters and white condemnation of them, as reflected in explanations for the riot, has also been obtained in several more recent surveys made in other areas. For example, in Harris's 1967 survey, Negroes were about twice as likely as whites to attribute recent riots to grievances over jobs, education, housing, police, and inequality. Whites were more likely than Negroes to blame outside agitation, lack of firmness by government authorities, the desire to loot, or a desire for violence.[12] Negroes thought the riots were spontaneous; a vast majority of the whites thought they had been organized.[13] Negroes thought the looted stores had been charging exorbitant prices; whites thought they had not.[14] Among whites, 62 per cent felt looters should be

TABLE 7

What Caused The Riot?

	Whites	Negroes (Curfew Zone)	Arrestees
Specific grievances	20%	38%	51%
Discrimination, mistreatment by whites	(5)	(7)	(4)
Poverty, economic deprivation, inadequate services	(11)	(10)	(5)
Police mistreatment	(4)	(21)	(42)
Pent-up hostility, desire for revenge, fed-up	14	26	34
Frye incident	18	11	8
Undesirable groups	29	9	2
Communists, Muslims, civil rights groups, organized groups, KKK, agitators	(16)	(3)	(0)
Criminals, looters	(8)	(2)	(0)
Foolish people, teenagers, Southerners	(5)	(4)	(2)
Spontaneous explosion, accident, weather	10	0	0
Don't know, no answer	10	17	6
Total	101%	101%	101%

[12] McCord and Howard, *ibid.*; Erskine, "The Polls," p. 662.
[13] Erskine, "The Polls," p. 666.
[14] *Ibid.*, p. 665.

shot; among Negroes, only 27 per cent felt that action was justifiable.[15] In other post-riot surveys, Negroes in Detroit and in Watts have generally explained the rioting in terms of a response to grievances about housing, jobs, the police, and poverty.[16] The most impressive difference of opinion about the rioters, then, is not between the law-abiders and the law-breakers in the Negro community, but between blacks and whites.

THE PURPOSE OF THE RIOT: TO CALL ATTENTION. Looking back on the riot, Los Angeles Negroes were largely agreed that it had been a purposeful, directed protest. But if Negroes saw the riot as a meaningful event, what was the meaning? What was the purpose of the riot; what was it supposed to accomplish? Negroes' perceptions on these matters may illuminate in what respects their hopes have subsequently been frustrated or fulfilled.

The dominant "purpose" of the riot, according to retrospective Negro perceptions, was to call the attention of whites to Negro problems. Fifty-six per cent of the Negro curfew zone sample had felt the riot had a purpose (see Table 2); of these, 41 per cent identified it as an attempt to call attention to Negro problems, and most of these saw the call directed specifically at white people. Smaller numbers saw it as an expression of accumulated hostility and resentment (33 per cent) or thought it was intended to implement some specific social or economic changes (26 per cent), e.g., to get more jobs, improve conditions, or get equal rights. The "message" from the Negro citizenry to the broader, predominantly white community is thus a two-edged one: a request for attention to their problems, and at the same time, an expression of accumulated angers and resentments from past grievances.

The specific problems being protested follow a line now familiar. The main targets of attack were seen as being merchants (38 per cent), white people in general (28 per cent), and the police (17 per cent). As already indicated (Table 2), most respondents felt these targets deserved the attacks they received. The predominant reasons given for the attacks had to do with justifiable grievances. Mistreatment of Negroes, in terms of discrimination or brutality, was the most common (31 per cent). Economic exploitation or disadvantage (e.g., overcharging, or unemployment) was next most frequent (19 per cent). These two categories accounted for the reasons given by half the Negro curfew zone respondents. "Chance" (10 per cent) and mere "criminal intent" (1 per cent) were relatively rare responses. However, 17 per cent explained the attacks in terms of the rioters' longstanding frustration, anger, and resentment.

So, Los Angeles Negroes tended to interpret the riot as a purposeful protest. In retrospect, they saw its aims as twofold: a call for attention to their problems, and an expression of hostility and resentment over

[15] *Ibid.*, p. 674.
[16] Detroit Urban League, "A Survey of Attitudes of Detroit Negroes after the Riot of 1967," Detroit, 1967. See also *Federal Role in Urban Affairs*, p. 1387. The vivid contrast between whites and Negroes also appears in a Brandeis University survey: Lemberg Center for the Study of Violence, "A Survey of Racial Attitudes in Six Northern Cities: Preliminary Findings," Waltham, Mass., 1967, pp. 15–16. (Mimeographed.)

genuine grievances. Much of this interpretation must represent a rationale constructed after the fact for a violent and confusing series of events that almost certainly had no single cause and was not deliberately planned.[17] Nevertheless, the riot was a widely based outburst of Negro hostility, fed upon reservoirs of resentment and hatred that had not been perceived earlier or understood well by white people. It had a clear focus on racial antagonisms: the objects of hos lity were not other Negroes, but white people, primarily merchants, and almost any symbol of constituted authority. Even if the "purposeful" quality of the riot was a rationalization, it described a moderately "rational" series of events.

EXPECTED OUTCOMES OF THE RIOT: HELP FOR THE GHETTO. In seeing the riot as a protest, a majority of the Negro population thought of it as a social-change action the principal aims of which were change in living conditions and aggression against the oppressor. Expectations about outcomes should thus serve as critical considerations in Negroes' thinking about the value of riots as instruments of social change. In the most general terms, these expectations were mostly optimistic, as seen earlier (Table 3). A further question is how Negroes expected the riot to affect the conditions of their lives, and, particularly, how they expected constituted authority and the broader white community to react.

By all odds the most salient expectation was that whites would begin to redress Negro grievances. The effect of the riot mentioned first by 43 per cent of the Negro respondents was help from outside the Negro community. An additional 13 per cent cited the effect of greater white awareness of Negro problems, and more comfortable relations between whites and Negroes. Thus, a majority thought first of favorable change among whites. These data are shown in Table 8. Similar thoughts were expressed by those who thought the riot would affect the Negro's cause, or affect the gap between the races. Table 9 shows that the most common reasons Negroes gave for why the riot might help or hurt the Negro's cause had to do with white reactions to it. Similarly, of those who thought it would increase or decrease the gap between the races, 54 per cent expected some change in whites, 28 per cent expected change in both races, and only 12 per cent expected change among Negroes themselves. Hence the clearest expectation among Negro respondents was that the riot would effect favorable change among white people.

While Negroes expected a favorable response from whites, they did not expect a massive one. Table 10 shows that greater white awareness of Negro problems was almost universally expected, and most Negroes expected more sympathetic treatment. However, opinion was much more

---

[17] Some surveys may elicit a grander ideological structure than actually exists by utilizing a carefully designed Socratic progression of questions. However the section of the present schedule dealing with the riot began with only the simplest open-ended items; i.e., those listed in Tables 1, 4, 5, 6, 7, the first two items of Table 2, and the first item of Table 3. Only later were more leading structured questions raised (e.g., the remaining items in Tables 2 and 3). Hence most of the discussion of "riot ideology" rests on spontaneously reported responses, not on interviews "leading" the respondent on.

TABLE 8

What Will the Main Effects of the Riot Be?

	Negroes (Curfew Zone)
Negroes will be helped or rewarded by others	43%
Negro-white relations will be changed for the better	13
Whites will be more aware of Negroes	(11)
Negroes and whites will get along together	(2)
Negro-white relations will change for the worse	13
Negroes will gain self-respect, get new leadership	2
Hope for something good	3
Nothing, no change	11
Don't know, no answer	14
Total	99%

TABLE 9

Why Will It Help or Hurt Negroes?[a]

	Negroes (Curfew Zone)
Change whites for the better	42%
Greater attention to Negroes	(29)
More positive toward Negroes	(13)
Change whites for the worse, more prejudice, etc.	8
Change Negroes	15
For worse (give bad name, make worse off)	(12)
For better (greater self-confidence, morale)	(3)
Economic effects (fewer jobs, stores)	30
Other	5
Total	100%

[a] Asked of the 62 per cent of the sample who said the riot would help or hurt the Negro cause.

divided with respect to changes in the social distance between the races.[18] About the same number of Negroes felt "more at ease" (10 per cent) than felt "less at ease" (8 per cent) in the contacts with white people after the riot, and no change was reported in the frequency of contact with whites.

[18] An additional coding of the "increased gap" responses indicated that few Negroes thought increased separation a good thing, despite the popularity of separatist ideology among many activists.

So most Negroes seem to have expected more sympathetic attention to their problems, but relatively few expected more commitment from whites at the level of personal relationships.

Two possibilities Negroes rarely mentioned, curiously enough, were "white backlash" and greater Negro solidarity. Anticipation of greater white hostility or greater racial prejudice was mentioned by only 13 per cent as the most likely effect of the riot (Table 8) and by 8 per cent as the main reason why the riot might help or hurt the Negro cause (Table 9). Effects upon Negroes aside from effects upon whites were also rarely mentioned. Two per cent saw new self-respect or leadership among Negroes as a main effect of the riot, and 15 per cent and 12 per cent, respectively, cited change among Negroes as the main reasons why the riot might help or hurt the Negro's cause and increase or decrease the gap between the races.

In retrospect this seems surprising because these two effects seem to have materialized to a far greater degree than the generally predicted white sympathetic attention. At the time, whites indeed felt more aware of Negro problems, but scarcely more sympathetic, as shown in Table 10. And whites predicted a considerable widening of the gap between the races. The rise in Negro solidarity is more difficult to determine di-

TABLE 10

Perceived Effects of Riot on Negro-White Relations

	Whites	Negroes (Curfew Zone)	Arrestees
Are whites more aware of Negro problems?			
More aware	79%	84%	80%
No change	18	13	17
Less aware	2	2	1
Other	1	2	2
Total	100%	101%	100%
Are whites more sympathetic to Negro problems?			
More sympathetic	32%	51%	49%
No change	27	31	38
Less sympathetic	37	12	9
Other	4	6	4
Total	100%	100%	100%
Did the riot increase or decrease the gap between the races?			
Increase	71%	23%	15%
No change	11	38	37
Decrease	13	24	22
Other	4	16	27
Total	99%	101%	100%

rectly from these data, but it seems evident that the riot drew more support from Negroes than anyone could have expected, and that in many respects the community as a whole rallied behind the rioters.

Thus the changes described by both races follow a well-worn path in American race relations. The white population is mainly willing to adjust when it is easy and convenient to do so. Both races expected the riot to increase the awereness of Negro problems among the dominant majority whites, and it seems to have done just that. However, a misjudgment occurred on the more difficult issue of white sympathy with Negro problems. Here Negroes hoped for change, while whites frankly expected a deterioration of race relations. More helpful, perhaps, are the social distance data. Here Negroes' expectations may have been more accurate than those of whites. The white population's racial nightmares have traditionally been filled with the horrors of intimate social contact with Negroes, rather than the more ritualized contacts of occupational or political interdependence. So more pessimism on the social distance dimension than on the awareness or sympathy dimensions could reasonably have been expected. But these data (and Negroes' expectations) do not reveal an actual widening of the gap between the races, contrary to whites' expectations.[19] The "backlash" may mean a slowdown rather than an actual deterioration in race relations.

Preferred Mechanisms of Grievance Redress

A riot ideology appears to have developed among Negroes in the curfew zone, in part justifying the Los Angeles riot as an instrument of protest. To what extent did rioting thus become thought of as a legitimate and effective mechanism of grievance redress for the future? Not widely, apparently. Answers to the open-ended question "What must Negroes do to get what they want?" reveal a preponderantly conventional approach to equal rights, as shown in Table 11. Over half of the Negro respondents see some form of conventional middle-class behavior as the road to success (e.g., more education and hard work). Another 19 per cent see more efficient and active political participation as the answer, while only 3 per cent contend that violence is necessary for equal rights. So the majority of Negroes in Los Angeles, even after a riot they perceived as likely to have beneficial effects, still opted for moderate grievance redress procedures and for traditional methods of personal advancement.

The question still remains how strong this preference for conventional mechanisms actually is, and whether or not the riot affected it. A sizable number of respondents expressed interest in demonstrations and nonviolent protest. Only a few (6 per cent) had participated in pre-riot civil rights activity, but 37 per cent said after the riot that they were willing to participate in demonstrations. Thirteen per cent said the riot had made them more willing to do so; so perhaps the riot made some Negroes more militant and unified.

It is hard to determine from the data whether it also increased their

19 See also Morris and Jeffries, "The White Reaction Study."

TABLE 11

What Must Negroes Do To Get What They Want?

	Negroes (Curfew Zone)	Arrestees
Conventional approaches	56%	51%
Get more education	(27)	(15)
Work hard, strive and succeed	(23)	(32)
Get jobs, acquire wealth	(2)	(2)
Change stereotyped qualities	(4)	(2)
Political action	19	15
Vote more, follow their leaders, etc.	(6)	(6)
Protest, make needs known	(13)	(9)
Violent action	3	10
Increase morale	7	12
Remove self-hatred	(1)	(0)
Increase racial solidarity	(6)	(12)
Change whites, change both races	1	0
Other	5	7
Don't know, no answer	9	5
Total	100%	100%

attraction to violence. However, when asked the most effective method to use in protest, given the alternatives of negotiation and nonviolent protest, 12 per cent selected violent protest (of the arrestees, 22 per cent did so). And 34 per cent thought there would be a recurrence of rioting in Los Angeles. Another 37 per cent felt they could not predict whether or not there would be another riot, thereby reflecting a lack of confidence in the durability of civic peace. While these data do not suggest that a majority of Negroes in Los Angeles advocate violence, the minority that does is rather sizable, and the expectation of further violence on the part of many others is an ominous sign; prophecies of that kind have a way of becoming self-fulfilling.[20]

[20] Particularly ominous, as might be expected, were the attitudes of the more militant respondents. Subdividing the curfew zone sample in terms of relative militance reveals considerably greater support for riots and higher endorsement of violence among the militants than among the more conservative respondents. For a detailed account of these data, see T. M. Tomlinson, "Ideological Foundations for Negro Action: A Comparative Analysis of Militant and Non-Militant Views of the Los Angeles Riot," *Los Angeles Riot Study*. See also T. M. Tomlinson, "The Development of a Riot Ideology Among Urban Negroes," *American Behavioral Scientist*, 11 (March–April, 1968), pp. 27–31.

Findings from other surveys on the level of endorsement of violence are not strictly comparable, because of different question wording. The range of estimates is substantial. In 1964, Kraft surveys in Harlem, Chicago, and Baltimore found 5 per cent saying violence was necessary, but one in Watts after the riot found that 14 per cent thought

CONCLUSIONS

This paper has been primarily concerned with the reaction of the Los Angeles Negro population to the Watts Riots of 1965. The principal findings follow:

1) It is not correct that all but a small minority strongly disapproved of the riots, felt they were a meaningless and random outburst of violence, and felt deeply pessimistic about the probable effects of the riots on the welfare of Negroes. Actually, a large minority (about one-third) approved of the rioting, most Negro residents of the riot area felt it had been a meaningful protest, and most were optimistic about its effects on their life situation.

2) A widespread "riot ideology" appears to have developed in the Negro community following the riot, with the following elements. The events of the riot were deplored, and the wish was expressed that the authorities had stopped it earlier. Yet the authorities tended to be criticized and the rioters defended. The causes of the riot were described in terms of genuine grievances with those who were attacked; e.g., a history of friction, discrimination, and economic exploitation with local merchants and police. The purpose of the riot was seen as being, on the one hand, to call the attention of whites to Negro problems, and on the other, to express resentment against malefactors. The riot was expected to bring help to the Negro population from whites, though major improvement in interracial personal relationships was not expected. This "riot ideology" seemed to justify and defend the riot, but violence was not often advocated for the future.[21]

3) The major cleavage that developed after the riot was between the white and black populations of Los Angeles, not between lawbreakers and lawabiders within the black population. Whites were much readier to condemn the riot, to see only purposeless violence in it, and to foresee a gloomy future for race relations. Whites were likely to ascribe the riot to agitators and criminal impulse, and less likely to attribute it to genuine grievances. These divisions of opinion along racial lines seem to be character-

---

it was. See *Federal Role in Urban Affairs*, p. 1399. A complex question used by Harris in national surveys in 1963 and 1966 found 22 per cent and 21 per cent, respectively, thinking violence was needed. See Brink and Harris, *Black and White*, p. 260. After the Detroit riot of 1967, an Urban League survey found 24 per cent feeling there was more to gain than lose with violence (see Detroit Urban League, "A Survey of Attitudes"). And the 1967 *Fortune* survey found 35 per cent saying that riots and violence are necessary (see Beardwood, "The New Negro Mood," p. 148). Whether these represent secular changes or merely differently worded questions is unclear.

[21] There is considerable justification for speaking of this pattern of beliefs in terms of an "ideology," based on the pattern of interrelationships between various of them. Approval of the riot, optimism about its effects, and perceiving the riot as a meaningful protest were all strongly correlated with one another.

istic of the ways in which the two racial groups have responded across the country to recent race riots.[22]

Perhaps the most important fact of all is that so many Negroes felt disposed to justify and ennoble the riot after it was all over. It was not viewed as an alien disruption of their peaceful lives, but as an expression of protest by the Negro community as a whole, against an oppressive majority. Here perhaps lies one of the tragedies of the riot. While it was, in the eyes of many Negroes, an outburst against an oppressive social system, the response of whites to the call for attention and help was hoped to be favorable. Perhaps this was an analogy taken from the white response to the Southern civil rights battles of the preceding decade. However, relatively little help has in fact been forthcoming, and it is not clear that whites expect to give very much. Awareness of the problem seems obviously to have increased, but the retaliatory aspect of the "message" of the riot seems as salient to whites as the plea for help.

[22] This observation of racial differences might seem to set a new record for banality in social science. The impressive finding here is not that whites and Negroes disagree, but that disagreement penetrates so deeply into each group, well beyond those that normally concern themselves with public affairs. It could be, for example, that relatively few people care very much about riots, and that most people of both races reject them as they reject criminal behavior in general. That is not the case, however.

31

Social and Political Characteristics of Riot Cities: A Comparative Study[1]

BRYAN T. DOWNES
MICHIGAN STATE UNIVERSITY

LIKE OTHER CONFLICTS WHICH OUR SOCIETY HAS EXPERIENCED, RACIAL CONflict has all too frequently given rise to incidents of violence. Beatings, shootings, lynchings, pogroms, riots, and even rebellions have been an integral part of the historical development of race relations and black protest, occurring with varying frequency and intensity since slavery was first introduced into this country in the 1600's.[2]

The majority of these outbursts of racial violence are examples of that which Smelser labels collective behavior: the mobilization of individuals to act on the basis of a belief which redefines social action.[3]

One type of collective behavior which has been occurring with greater frequency in urban areas are the hostile outbursts which have become an integral part of the current black protest movement. Smelser defines a hostile outburst as simply the mobilization of individuals for action under a hostile belief.[4] In the last four years a large number of urban blacks have been mobilized for action on the basis of such beliefs. According to Smelser, these individuals are bent upon attacking someone, such as police and white merchants, who they consider responsible for a "disturbing state of affairs."[5]

It is not surprising that in its current phase black protest is characterized by violence. Many blacks have become impatient with the pace of integration; this is nowhere more apparent than in the case of younger black inhabitants of our nation's urban ghettos. Their "dream" of integration, social justice, and equality has been deferred too long, and since 1964 it has "exploded" in the form of over 225 hostile outbursts—incidents which involve rock throwing, fighting, looting, burning, and killing.[6] Be-

---

[1] Portions of this article have been drawn from "The Black Protest Movement and and Urban Violence," a paper presented at the 1968 annual meeting of the American Political Science Association, Washington, D.C., September 2–7, 1968. The author gratefully acknowledges the support of the department of political science at Michigan State University and the assistance of Stephen W. Burks in the preparation and analysis of the data presented in this article. It should be stressed that this analysis represents a *preliminary examination* of the information we have collected. In the future we plan to undertake a more sophisticated statistical analysis of some of these data.

[2] For an examination of early racial violence, see Arthur I. Waskow, *From Race Riot to Sit-In, 1919 and the 1960's* (Garden City, N.Y., Doubleday, 1966).

[3] Neil J. Smelser, *Theory of Collective Behavior* (New York: The Free Press, 1962), p. 8.

[4] *Ibid.*, p. 226. See also Smelser's discussion of the determinants of hostile outbursts in Ch. 8.

[5] *Ibid.*, pp. 224–225.

[6] The changes which many blacks expected would occur after the 1954 Supreme Court school desegregation decision have simply not been forthcoming. This refers to

---

fore turning to the central concern of this article, which is to analyze some of the characteristics of cities experiencing racial violence since 1964, let us briefly examine the nature of current outbursts.

HOSTILE OUTBURSTS, 1964–1968

Today's hostile outbursts differ quite markedly from either outbreaks of collective racial violence. For example, in early pogroms, or "southern-style riots," whites attacked and killed Negroes they thought were responsible for "disturbing states of affairs," sometimes burning their homes, with blacks offering little or no resistance. On the other hand, in the race riots which occurred in many northern cities in 1919, 1935, and 1943, large numbers of both blacks and whites engaged in collective violence against each other. In these race riots, which occurred in cities such as Washington, D. C., New York, and Detroit, blacks actively defended themselves and even initiated violence against whites.

The hostile outbursts which we are witnessing today have taken still a different form.[7] In these incidents, blacks have been the primary participants, directing their hostility against police and merchants who they consider responsible for a great deal of racial injustice. Because police are representatives of the dominant white society in the ghetto (as are merchants to a lesser degree), they become symbols of a far greater source of dissatisfaction for many blacks. Although most of the hostile outbursts which we examined were spontaneous and therefore displayed only a primitive organization, some of the most recent incidents occurring this past summer began to take on a greater degree of organization. For example, the outburst which occurred in Cleveland was set off by a systematic ambush of white policemen by black militants.

Not all behavior of participants in these hostile outbursts, however, is instrumental in achieving specific objectives. Many participate simply because such involvement is intrinsically satisfying or satisfying because it allows them to give expression to a state of mind. Although recent hostile outbursts do not carry "the war" to the enemy's ("whitey's") territory, they are directed against rather specific enemies. Furthermore, although many outbursts are precipitated by specific incidents which involve police, these outbursts are also linked to a variety of grievances which exist in the minds of urban ghetto-dwellers.[8]

DATA ON HOSTILE OUTBURSTS. Our data on hostile outbursts has been drawn primarily from a *Congressional Quarterly* special report, entitled, *Urban Problems and Civil Disorder*, and from the *New York Times*.[9] An

the lines in a poem by Langston Hughes entitled, "Harlem," in *Selected Poem of Langston Hughes* (New York: Alfred A. Knopf, 1959), p. 268.

[7] See the materials in, Louis H. Masotti, ed., "Urban Violence and Disorder," *American Behavioral Scientist*, 11 (March–April, 1968).

[8] Some of these points are raised in: James Q. Wilson, "Why Are We Having A Wave of Violence," *The New York Magazine*, May 19, 1968, pp. 23–24, 116–120. However, Professor Wilson and I differ quite markedly in our interpretations of the behavior of participants in hostile outbursts.

[9] *Urban Problems and Civil Disorder* (Washington, D.C.: Congressional Quarterly Service, Special Report No. 36, Sept. 8, 1967).

initial examination of "civil disorders" listings in the *Congressional Quarterly* publication, compiled by the Legislative Reference Service of the Library of Congress, provided us with a brief description of 113 hostile outbursts which occurred from January 1, 1964 to January 1, 1968. In order to check on the accuracy of these listings, however, we consulted the *New York Times Index* for the same period and found 61 additional incidents. Further information on all incidents was then gathered directly from the *New York Times* as were data on outbursts which occurred during the first five months of 1968.

Reliance on journalistic accounts for our basic universe of incidents meant that the study was vulnerable to any selectivity in the hostile outbursts actually reported in the newspapers. For example, following the recent assassination of Martin Luther King, Jr., the *New York Times* published a report prepared by the United Press International giving the 110 cities which experienced varying degrees of violence during the week following Dr. King's death.[10] Of the 110 cities listed, we could find adequate information on only 60 of these in the *New York Times*. This may say something about the accuracy of the report as well as point up a critical problem which we faced. It also means that we have definitely under-reported smaller incidents simply because of a lack of available data.[11]

Another problem encountered was the amount and accuracy of the information reported; this varied considerably from incident to incident, with the greatest amount of accurate information being provided on more violent outbursts. Outside the *Congressional Quarterly* publication and the *New York Times*, however, we generally found a paucity of data except on the most violent incidents.[12] Our data, therefore, should be looked upon as *approximate* and subject to some change as more complete information becomes available.

THE NATURE OF HOSTILE OUTBURSTS. Everyone has read that large numbers of blacks were mobilized for action in the most recent outbreak of hostile outbursts. However, studies indicate that only a small percentage of the total Negro population in any given city actually become involved in these outbursts.[13] Although in the most violent incidents the percentage

[10] *New York Times*, April 10, 1968. The news media generally tend to over-report smaller. less violent, incidents.

[11] Although we culled all available sources, there simply were not very much data available on the hostile outbursts which had occurred since 1964. The Lemberg Center for the Study of Violence at Brandeis University has recently begun to coordinate systematically the efforts of various researchers in this area.

[12] For instance see, The National Advisory Commission on Civil Disorders, *Report of the National Advisory Commission on Civil Disorders* (Washington, D.C.: U.S. Government Printing Office, March 1, 1968); Governor's Select Commission on Civil Disorder State of New Jersey, *Report for Action* (Trenton: Governor's Office, Feb., 1968); Mayor's Development Team, *Report to Mayor Jerome P. Cavanagh* (Detroit, Mich.: Mayor's Office, Oct., 1967); and publications of the Los Angeles Riot Study undertaken by the Institute of Government and Public Affairs, University of California at Los Angeles.

[13] T. M. Tomlinson, "The Development of a Riot Ideology among Urban Negroes," *American Behavioral Scientist*, 11 (March–April, 1968), pp. 27–31. See also the recent supplement to the *Report of the National Advisory Commission on Civil Disorders*.

may go as high as 15 per cent, this still represents a relatively small proportion of the Negro population. Furthermore, studies have shown those individuals most likely to participate in hostile outbursts tend to be younger Negroes, roughly between the ages of 15 and 24 years, who were born in the North. These younger Negroes are, by and large, as well educated and are earning about as much money as nonparticipants, although there seems to be somewhat more unemployment (or underemployment) among their ranks.[14]

During the period of January 1, 1964, to May 31, 1968, 239 hostile outbursts occurred. Our data on the number of persons involved in these outbursts are not accurate because: (1) we could find no information on 112 (47 per cent) of the 239 outbursts, and (2) the data which we did find on the remaining 127 were not very useful. For example, many reports in the *New York Times* simply indicated that 100's, *etc.*, had participated. As we have already noted, social scientists, who studied cities in which hostile outbursts took place, indicate that in the most violent incidents—such as those which occurred in Watts, Newark, and Detroit—about 15 per cent of the Negro population in the outburst area became involved.

On the basis of the information we did have, we estimate that about 150,000 persons actively participated in the 239 outbursts, although this figure could probably go as high as 250,000. This still represents a small percentage of the 21.5 million Negroes in the United States in 1968 and only about 10 per cent of the 15 million who reside in our metropolitan areas. The news media, particularly television, have been largely responsible for creating the impression that greater numbers of Negroes participate in hostile outbursts, for they tend to devote most of their coverage to only the most violent outbursts. We did, however, find that the number of participants varies considerably from incident to incident, with the greatest number generally participating in more violent outbursts.

The individuals who were involved in the 239 outbursts wrought tremendous havoc upon certain areas in many of our largest cities. Not only have millions of dollars been lost due to arson and looting, and further millions expended by government to restore order, many individuals were killed and thousands seriously wounded. During the 523 days of hostilities which occurred over the 53 month period, for example, 49,607 persons were arrested, 7,942 were wounded, and 191 were killed. Although these latter figures appear quite high, they are considerably less than the number reported wounded or killed in many early pogroms and race riots or those maimed and killed by firearms in any given year in this country.[15]

While the averages are about the same for participants and nonparticipants, the distributions differ. Persons from both the very low and very high educational and income levels are under-represented among the participants.

[14] For example, see *A Survey of Attitudes of Detroit Negroes After the Riot of 1967* (Detroit: Detroit Urban League, 1967); and Kurt Lang and Gladys E. Lang, "Racial Disturbances as Collective Protest," *American Behavioral Scientist*, 11 (March-April, 1968), pp. 11–13.

[15] For example, a recent Associated Press survey reported that 149 persons had been killed by firearms in the United States during the week of June 16 to June 23, 1968. This included 80 homicides, 58 suicides, and 11 accidental shootings. In 1966, the

These figures are low because most outbursts never reached a point where blacks invaded white territory or systematically killed police who were attempting to control them.[16]

Instead, Negroes involved in these outbursts directed their attention primarily to the destruction of property and looting and were only marginally concerned with physically assaulting or killing whites. The amount of property damage and economic loss due to rock throwing, burning, and looting was very high; in 1965, 1966, and 1967, it was estimated that there were $210.6 million in property damages and $504.2 million in economic losses; and these appear to be very conservative estimates.[17]

The preceding information is broken down by yearly totals in Table 1. These data indicate there generally has been an increase in all totals since 1964, except in 1966 when the numbers arrested, wounded, and killed decreased. However, all totals went up quite markedly in 1967. Our information for 1968 is incomplete, and thus it is hard to draw any conclusions at this time. Nevertheless, the number of incidents occurring in July and August approached the number which took place in 1967; therefore, the upward trend in these figures will continue in 1968.[18] One interesting figure in Table 1 is the drastic upswing in the number of persons arrested in 1968. Police are reacting much more quickly and effectively in their attempts to control incidents of collective violence. A more effective policy adopted increasingly by police is to use maximum force in the initial stage of an outburst. This does give rise to a greater number of arrests but less overall violence and property damage. The police used this technique very effectively in Washington, D.C. early this summer when an outburst broke out following the conclusion of the Poor People's Campaign.

Almost all incidents occurring each year were of relatively short duration, lasting only one or two days. Also, most outbursts, on which we had data, involved less than 500 persons. Similarly, in 30 per cent of the 239 outbursts no arrests were reported and in an additional 46 per cent a maximum of 50 arrests were made by law enforcement personnel. In over 46 per cent of the incidents no individuals were reported wounded and in 77 per cent no deaths occurred. These percentages do not necessarily remain stable when one examines the number arrested, wounded, and killed each year. In addition, many of these figures have shown some increases since 1964.

If one views hostile outbursts as occurring in a series of stages, it ap-

---

Federal Bureau of Investigation indicated that an average of 125 Americans were killed *each week* during that year by firearms.

[16] In the last several months, blacks have precipitated a number of hostile outbursts by systematically ambushing and attempting to kill police. This is very different from the anomic pattern of most post-1964 incidents.

[17] These estimates were prepared by the Permanent Subcommittee on Investigations of the Committee on Governmental Operations of the U.S. Senate, the so-called McClellan Committee.

[18] Our initial tabulation indicates that some 45 hostile outbursts have occurred during June, July, and August. With the exception of incidents occurring in Cleveland, Ohio; Miami and St. Petersburg, Florida; Little Rock, Arkansas; and Grand Rapids, Michigan; most of these outbursts were quite minor.

TABLE 1

Yearly Breakdown of Information on Hostile Outbursts

| Data on | Totals for Period 1964–May 31, 1968 | | | | | |
Hostile Outbursts	1964	1965	1966	1967	1968	Total
Number of cities having outbursts	16	20	44	71	64	215[a]
Number of outbursts	16	23	53	82	65	239[b]
Total number of days of hostility	42	31	92	236	122	523
Total number arrested	2,000	10,245	2,216	16,471	18,675	49,607
Total number wounded	580	1,206	467	3,348	2,341	7,942
Total number killed	9	43	9	85	46	191

[a] Because many of the same cities have incidents each year, this figure is high.
[b] Smaller (less violent) incidents are under-reported.

pears that most incidents which have occurred since 1964 never move beyond the first or primarily symbolic looting stage, where destruction rather than plunder appears to be the intent of the participants.[19] Approximately 75 per cent of the outbursts never progressed beyond this initial stage of window breaking, car burning, and the occasional tossing of fire bombs.

An additional 20 per cent of the outbursts progress to a second stage where looting of goods as well as greater destruction of property (equipment and facilities) takes place. In this stage white and even black merchants dealing in consumer goods become the objects of attack. The racial dimension, while never absent, may become secondary to the economic factor in motivating the behavior of looters.

Finally, only about five per cent of the outbursts progress to a third stage in which there is a full redefinition of certain property rights.[20] At this point plundering becomes the normative, the socially supported thing to do. For example, as one social scientist has observed, "the carnival spirit particularly commented upon in the Newark and Detroit outbursts does not represent anarchy. It is, instead, an overt manifestation of widespread localized social support for the new definition of the situation."[21] At this stage, participation of blacks is at its height as is the level of violence. Property damage and economic loss among both whites and blacks is widespread and complete due to arson and looting. When an outburst reaches this stage, any attempt at control usually results in large numbers of blacks being arrested, wounded, and killed.

[19] See the discussion of these stages in E. L. Quarantelli and Russell R. Dynes, "Looting in Civil Disorders: An Index of Social Change," *American Behavioral Scientist*, 11 (March-April, 1968), pp. 8–9. These percentages are the same as those reported in the Kerner Report for the 164 "disorders" reported occurring during the first nine months of 1967.

[20] See the discussion in E. L. Quarantelli and Russell R. Dynes, "What Looting in Civil Disturbances Really Means," *Transaction*, 5 (May, 1968), pp. 9–14.

[21] Quarantelli and Dynes, *op. cit.*, p. 9.

TYPES OF CITIES EXPERIENCING HOSTILE OUTBURSTS

Now that we have briefly examined the nature of hostile outbursts which have occurred since 1964, we can turn to the central concern of this article. Is there anything distinctive about the environmental context in cities in which hostile outbursts have occurred during the last 53 months? What conditions in these cities are associated with the occurrence of incidents of racial violence?

Lieberson and Silverman, in their earlier analysis of conditions thought to underly 76 Negro-white "race riots" occurring in the United States from 1913 through 1963, found that population growth, proportion Negro-white unemployment rate, Negro income, and proportion of Negroes living on substantial housing were substantially the same in matched cities in which racial violence did occur as in cities where such violence did not occur.[22] Although some additional conditions were found to be associated with the occurrence of riots, they were only weakly associated.[23]

The Lieberson and Silverman study provides perhaps the first systematic attempt to assess selected conditions thought to underlie racial violence. But the results, although based on incomplete data, generally failed to provide empirical support for many commonly held beliefs regarding the occurrence of earlier riots.

Bloombaum, in his re-analysis of the Lieberson and Silverman data, also found that no single factor discriminated between riot and control cities.[24] However, he did find the job effect of the nine conditions examined did discriminate between riot cities and their controls much better than any one factor could do.

Our examination of the characteristics of cities experiencing racial violence begins where Lieberson and Silverman ended their study. Although we are using a very different method of analysis, as indicated below, we are concerned with investigating the contextual conditions found in cities which have and have not experienced hostile outbursts. Because of this difference in methodology, however, it is difficult to compare our findings with those of Lieberson and Silverman. Where they could make no inferences about differences between riot cities and all other American cities, and could only conclude that riot cities do not differ from nonriot cities of the same *size and region*, we can systematically undertake the former but not the latter type of comparison.[25]

[22] Stanley Lieberson and Arnold R. Silverman, "The Precipitants and Underlying Conditions of Race Riots," *American Sociological Review*, 30 (Dec., 1965), pp. 887–898. They define "riots" as involving an assault on persons and property simply because they are part of a given subgroup of the community. In terms of our conceptualization, riots are simply one type of hostile outburst.

[23] For a summary of these conditions, see Milton Bloombaum, "The Conditions Underlying Race Riots as Portrayed by Multidimensional Scalogram Analysis: A Reanalysis of Lieberson and Silverman's Data," *American Sociological Review*, 33 (Feb., 1968), p. 77.

[24] *Ibid.*, pp. 76–91.

[25] In their analysis, Lieberson and Silverman made use of *paired comparisons*; that is, each city experiencing a riot was compared with a city as similar as possible in *size* and *region* which had no riot in the ten years preceding or following the riot date.

METHOD. In order to begin in a preliminary manner to answer the questions posed initially in this section, data in the 1960 Census and the 1963 *Municipal Yearbook*[26] were used. (Professor Robert Alford of the University of Wisconsin collected information from these two sources and was kind enough to let us use his data in our analysis. However, he collected data only on cities of 25,000 or more persons at the time of the 1960 census.) In 1960, there were 676 cities which had 25,000 or more persons; of the 676, 129 (19 per cent) had experienced one or more hostile outbursts since 1964. Furthermore, in these 129 cities, 190 incidents of collective racial violence occurred, with an additional 49 incidents taking place in cities under 25,000 persons.

Our analysis began by dividing cities over 25,000 persons into two groups, those which had no hostile outbursts and those which had, and by running this dichotomous variable against the Alford census data. We next ranked each city according to the intensity of violence of its most hostile outburst and made a second series of computer runs. Since this *preliminary analysis* yielded so much information, we will present only those results which provide a balanced *descriptive characterization* of cities in which hostile outbursts took place and which allow us to examine some of the environmental conditions thought to underlie racial violence in the United States.

THE ANALYSIS. Most outbursts of collective racial violence are sparked by a very specific incident which channels generalized hostile beliefs into specific hopes, fears, and antagonisms. The data in Table 2 give some indication of the type of precipitants of hostile outbursts which have occurred since 1913. Noting the very different precipitant(s) which have touched off recent outbursts, one finds in the case of many current incidents, it seems the killing, arrest, interference, assault, or search of Negro men and women by police has either confirmed or justified existing generalized fears and hatreds about police in the ghetto and/or signalized a "failure" on the part of the police which demanded explanation and assignment of responsibility. The data also indicate how easily recent outbursts were precipitated; over 30 per cent of these incidents were either spontaneous or set off by the death of Martin Luther King, Jr. What are the conditions in a community which increase the probability that a precipitating incident will lead to an outburst? What are the conditions which give rise to strain and encourage the spread of hostile beliefs which ultimately results in generalized aggression?

POPULATION CHARACTERISTICS. Our data support the argument that hostile outbursts are more likely to occur in densely populated areas where people are forced to live in very close proximity to each other. Hostile outbursts are more likely to occur, also, in larger municipalities which have lost population or gained very little since 1950. In addition, these same

---

One of the real problems which plagues such studies is the problem of selecting "appropriate" control cities.

[26] *The Municipal Yearbook, 1963* (Chicago: International City Manager's Association, 1963).

TABLE 2

Immediate Precipitants of Hostile Outbursts,
1913–1963 and 1964–1968

Immediate Precipitants	1913–1963[a] (N=76) Per Cent	1964–May 31, 1968[b] (N=239) Per Cent
Rape, murder, attack, or hold-up of white women by Negro men	13	0
Killings, arrest, interference, assault, or search of Negro men (and women) by police	20	27
Other inter-racial murder or shooting	15	4
Inter-racial rock throwing or fight, no mention of lethal weapons	21	10
Civil liberties, public facilities, segregation, political events, housing	18	10
Negro strikebreakers, upgrading, or other job based conflicts	7	1
Burning of an American flag by Negroes	1	0
Inflammatory speeches by civil rights or black power leaders	0	2
Spontaneous (no immediate apparent precipitant)	0	10
Other (death of civil rights leader, building blown up, vandals, ambulance failure to respond quickly to Negro heart attack victim, Halloween prank)	0	26
No information available	5	10

[a] Source, 1913–1963 data: Stanley Lieberson and Arnold R. Silverman, "The Precipitants and Underlying Conditions of Race Riots," *American Sociological Review*, 30 (Dec., 1965), p. 889.

[b] Source, 1964–1968 data: *New York Times*.

densely populated, large cities have higher percentages of deaths per 1,000 persons. On the other hand, cities which have not experienced such outbursts tend to be somewhat smaller, less densely populated, faster growing communities with somewhat lower death rates. The gamma coefficients in Table 6 give some indication of the strength of the relationship between intensity of violence in a hostile outburst and the above population data.

Lieberson and Silverman found very little difference in their study between the proportion of blacks in riot and control cities. They also found no sizable differences between riot and control cities in their percentage gains in Negro population during the period 1913–1963.[27] On the other hand, we found that cities which experienced hostile outbursts since 1964

[27] Lieberson and Silverman, "The Precipitants," pp. 893–894.

had, on the whole, a much higher proportion of nonwhites (primarily Negroes) in their populations than cities which experienced no incidents of racial violence. The nonwhite populations in these cities have also increased, some quite drastically, since 1950. Thus it would appear that the rapid influx of nonwhites may be an important condition underlying hostile outbursts, primarily because such an influx may disrupt the on-going social order and create or accentuate existing problems in the black community.

EDUCATION, INCOME, AND EMPLOYMENT. As one might expect, there tends to be an inverse relationship between the occurrence of hostile out-

TABLE 3

Population Characteristics of Cities
Experiencing Hostile Outbursts

Population Characteristics of Cities of 25,000 or More Persons, 1960	No Hostile Outburst[a] (N=547) Per Cent	Hostile Outburst[a] (N=129) Per Cent	Total[a] (N=676) Per Cent
1960 population:			
25,000– 99,999	89	45	81
100,000– 199,999	7	22	10
200,000– 499,999	3	19	6
500,000–1,000,000 or more	1	14	3
Population growth or decline, 1950–1960:			
Declined (0–29%)	14	37	19
Increased (0–44%)	50	46	50
Increased (45% or more)	29	16	26
Not ascertainable	7	0	5
Population per square mile:			
3,999 or less	45	29	42
4,000–4,999	18	12	17
5,000–7,000 or more	37	59	41
Deaths per 1,000, 1959:			
7 or less	30	10	26
8–9	23	27	24
10 or more	40	63	44
Not ascertainable	7	0	6
Per cent nonwhite:			
4.9% or less	61	12	52
5.0–14.9%	21	33	24
15% or more	18	55	24
Change in per cent nonwhite, 1950–1960:			
Decreased by 1.0% or more	34	22	32
Increased 0.0–0.9%	35	3	29
Increased 1.0% or more	27	75	36
Not ascertainable	4	0	3

[a] If some columns do not add up to 100% it is due to rounding error or missing data.

bursts in a city and the level of education of its inhabitants. Incidents of collective violence are much more likely to take place in cities in which the educational attainment of its citizenry is quite low, with the most violent incidents occurring in those municipalities whose populations have the lowest level of educational attainment (see Table 4).

Also not unexpectedly, we found that in cities which had hostile outbursts, the median income of families tends to be somewhat lower than in cities which experienced no outbursts, with the most hostile incidents occurring in cities which had the lowest median family incomes. Thus, hostile outbursts also appear to be a consequence of generally low educational and income levels in a city (which, in turn, may be a function of the per cent nonwhite).

Unemployment was also much higher in cities which had hostile outbursts, with the most violent incidents occurring in communities with the highest unemployment rates. We know that unemployment tends to be almost twice as high among the black inhabitants in urban ghettos; therefore, this finding generally supports the expectation hostile outbursts are more likely to occur in a city when either Negroes or whites have relatively high unemployment rates.

The Lieberson and Silverman study failed to find any tendency whatsoever for housing to be of lower quality in cities which had experienced riots when they were compared with cities of the same size and region.[28] Our analysis indicates housing units tend to be less sound in cities which had outbursts, with more intensely violent incidents taking place in cities with the lowest percentages of sound housing units. Thus racial violence may also be attributable to poor housing conditions, particularly among blacks, in a city.

Furthermore, in cities in which hostile outbursts did take place, the percentage of housing units which were owner occupied was quite low, particularly when compared to cities which had no outbursts. In almost half of these cities, 50 per cent or less of the housing units were owner occupied. As one might expect, cities which had more violent outbursts also tended to have the least number of dwelling units which were owner occupied.

METROPOLITAN STATUS AND ECONOMIC BASE. Of those cities which experienced hostile outbursts, 57 per cent were classified as central employing (see Table 4). As the intensity of violence increased in these cities, so did the number of cities falling into that category—including some 90 per cent of the 10 cities having the highest level of violence. On the other hand, only 15 per cent of the cities which experienced no outbursts fell into the central employing category. Communities which had no incidents were likely to be classified as suburban dormitory (23 per cent), independent employing (14 per cent), or independent balanced (13 per cent). Thus, it would appear that most incidents of racial violence, particularly those which are most destructive, are taking place within the largest central cities.

[28] Ibid., p. 895.

TABLE 4

Population, Housing, and Economic Characteristics
of Cities Experiencing Hostile Outbursts

Population, Housing, and Economic Characteristics of Cities of 25,000 or More Persons, 1960	No Hostile Outburst[a] (N=547) Per Cent	Hostile Outburst[a] (N=129) Per Cent	Total[a] (N=676) Per Cent
Per cent persons 25 years and over who have completed 4 years of high school or more:			
43% or less	44	65	48
44–51%	25	21	24
52–99%	31	14	28
Median family income:			
$0000–5399	22	31	24
$5400–6749	51	58	52
$6750 and over	27	12	24
Per cent of labor force unemployed:			
0–3%	32	17	30
4%	24	18	22
5% or more	44	65	48
Per cent housing units sound with plumbing facilities:			
74.9% or less	20	33	22
75.0–87.9%	49	57	51
88.0% or more	31	10	27
Per cent occupied housing units owner occupied:			
49.9% or less	16	40	21
50.0–66.9%	51	52	51
67.0% or more	33	8	28
Metropolitan status:			
Central employing	15	57	23
Suburban dormitory	23	3	19
Independent balanced	13	4	11
Independent employing	14	9	13
Other	35	27	34
Economic base:			
Manufacturing	34	33	34
Diversified manufacturing	14	29	17
Diversified retail	21	24	21
Retail trade	19	8	17
Other	12	6	11
Per cent employed in white collar occupations:			
0–44%	47	59	50
45–99%	53	41	50

[a] If some columns do not add up to 100% it is due to rounding error or missing data.

In terms of their economic bases, cities in which hostile outbursts took place were likely to have manufacturing or diversified manufacturing economies; however, more violent outbursts occurred in diversified manufacturing communities. Cities which experienced no outbursts were just as likely to be manufacturing centers, but less likely to have diversified manufacturing economies. Persons in cities which had outbursts were, therefore, somewhat less likely to be employed in white-collar occupations; this was particularly true in municipalities having more violent outbursts. Although we are unable to substantiate the following observation, we might expect greater antagonism on the part of Negroes toward whites in cities where Negroes are relatively restricted in occupational opportunities—that is, where most blacks are restricted to traditional pursuits because of lack of requisite skills or job opportunities.

GOVERNMENTAL STRUCTURE. Lieberson and Silverman argue the more direct the relationship between the voter and government, the less likely hostile outbursts will occur.[29] "A more responsive government makes riots less likely because it provides regular institutional channels for expressing grievances."[30] On the basis of this sort of reasoning, we would expect hostile outbursts to occur in cities with the council-manager form of government, in which councilmen are elected to small councils (at large) on a nonpartisan basis. The assumption underlying this observation is that councilmen elected at large to small councils on a nonpartisan ballot will be less responsive to special interests and groups within the population.

Our findings offer very little support for this particular interpretation of municipal political structure. A closer examination of the actual functioning of many of these local governments, however, probably would indicate that they are relatively unresponsive or unable to respond to the demands of black Americans. Cities in which hostile outbursts took place tend to be just as likely to have either the mayor-council or council-manager forms of government, while communities which had no incidents were somewhat more likely to have the council-manager plan. The most violent outbursts, however, occurred in cities which had the mayor-council form.

In addition, cities which experienced incidents of violent collective behavior were somewhat less likely to have nonpartisan elections for municipal offices, but were more likely to have larger councils in which councilmen served for longer terms. These relationships were simply more pronounced in cities which had more violent outbursts. On the other hand, communities which had no hostile outbursts were somewhat more likely to have nonpartisan elections, smaller councils, and councilmen whose terms of office were shorter.

[29] *Ibid.*, p. 896.

[30] "County Official's Guide to the Kerner Report," *American County Government*, 33 (June, 1968), p. 16. As our data indicate, then, cities experiencing hostile outbursts tend to exhibit many overt signs of social and economic decay. For a more detailed discussion of these factors, see Kenneth B. Clark, *Dark Ghetto, Dilemmas of Social Power* (New York: Harper, 1965). Professor Clark also discusses some of the psychological implications of environmental decay.

With regard to voting behavior among people in communities which had hostile outbursts, we found that in 1960, individuals in these cities were less likely to register to vote. Those who did register, however, were more likely to turn out at the polls and to vote overwhelmingly for the Democratic party's presidential candidate. In cities which experienced no outbursts, inhabitants were more likely to register, but less likely to vote;

TABLE 5

Political Structure and Expenditure Characteristics
of Cities Experiencing Hostile Outbursts

Political Structure and Expenditure Characteristics of Cities of 25,000 or More Persons, 1963	No Hostile Outburst[a] (N=547) Per Cent	Hostile Outburst[a] (N=129) Per Cent	Total[a] (N=676) Per Cent
Form of government:			
Mayor-council	37	45	38
Commission	11	12	11
City manager	52	42	50
Type of election:			
Nonpartisan	73	62	71
Partisan	26	36	28
Term of office:			
Less than four years	45	36	43
Four years or more	55	64	57
Number of councilmen:			
Less than 5	51	28	38
5–9	42	45	43
10 or more	17	27	19
Per capita general expenditure:			
$00–48	25	12	23
$49–66	22	15	20
$67–98	20	28	22
$99	32	46	34
Per capita sanitation expenditure:			
$00–08	50	34	47
$09–13	23	32	25
$14–99	24	33	26
Not ascertainable	3	0	2
Per capita debt outstanding end of year, in $10 units:			
$00–12	49	37	47
$13–20	23	25	24
$21–99	25	38	27
Not ascertainable	3	0	2

[a] If some columns do not add up to 100% it is due to rounding error or missing data.

although they did cast their ballots for the Democratic presidential candidate. These same relationships were simply accentuated when voter registration, per cent voting, and party receiving the greatest plurality in the presidential election were examined in communities in which more intensely violent outbursts took place.

CITY EXPENDITURES. In cities which experienced hostile outbursts, local government expenditures were generally quite high. For example, in such cities both per capita general expenditure and per capita expenditure for sanitation were higher than in cities in which no outbursts occurred (see Table 5). These expenditures were also highest in cities in which more violent incidents took place. The outstanding debt of local government was also higher in communities in which outbursts occurred. Again, this was particularly true of cities experiencing more violent outbursts.

Demands placed upon city services by the type of population living in cities which have experienced hostile outbursts are very high. These are the cities, however, which can least afford to pay for the expansion of basic services—let alone the establishment of new ones—because of their steadily deteriorating tax base. Such municipalities are in a particularly difficult position and are being forced to rely on new sources of revenue, such as the city income tax, and to look to other levels of government for financial assistance.

CONCLUSION

The information presented on cities in the United States with 25,000 or more persons clearly indicates that the environmental context one finds in cities in which hostile outbursts took place tends to be quite different from that found in communities in which no incidents occurred. Cities experiencing hostile outbursts have a very distinctive set of social, economic, and even political structural characteristics. Hostile outbursts are not randomly distributed among our universe of municipalities; this in itself is a significant finding, given the number of cities in which one or more outbursts have taken place. In addition, the data show that contextual differences tend to be further accentuated in those cities in which more violent outbursts occurred (see Table 6). By solving the major problems confronting our largest cities, the data indicate we would also be taking a giant step toward solving many of the problems of the black people who live in them, thus removing some of the environmental conditions underlying hostile outbursts. For as the Kerner Commission has observed:[31]

> Social and economic conditions in the riot cities constituted a clear pattern of severe disadvantage for Negroes compared with whites, whether the Negroes lived in the area where the riot took place or outside it. Negroes had completed fewer years of education and fewer had attended high school. Negroes were twice as likely to be unemployed and three times as likely to be in unskilled and service jobs. Negroes averaged 70 per cent of the income earned by whites and were more than twice as likely to be living in poverty. Although housing cost Negroes relatively more, they had

[31] Tomlinson, "A Development of a Riot Ideology," p. 29.

worse housing—three times as likely to be overcrowded and substandard. When compared to white suburbs, the relative disadvantage is even more pronounced.

Thus many of the general characteristics of the population in cities experiencing hostile outbursts are simply accentuated among blacks living in the urban ghettos or the largest, least rapidly growing, most densely populated central cities.

We are well aware that none of the conditions examined individually cause a hostile outburst to occur. These factors are highly intercorrelated and are probably largely a function of the size and age of a community. Taken together, however, such a set of conditions may provide the basis for an outbreak of racial violence in any given city. Indeed, one might

TABLE 6

Conditions Found to be Associated with the Intensity of Hostile Outbursts[a]

Social, Economic, and Political Characteristics of Cities with 25,000 or more Persons	Intensity of Violence of Hostile Outburst (gamma coefficients)
Population, 1960	.75
Population change, 1950–1960	—.39
Population per sq. mile, 1960	.43
Deaths per 1,000, 1959	.36
Per cent nonwhite, 1960	.70
Change in per cent nonwhite, 1950–1960	.65
Median age, 1960	.31
Per cent persons 25 years old and over who have completed four years of high school or more, 1960	—.41
Median family income, 1960	—.14
Per cent of labor force unemployed, 1960	.30
Per cent housing units sound with plumbing facilities, 1960	—.26
Per cent occupied housing units owner occupied, 1960	—.47
Employment residence ratio, 1960	.37
Manufacturing ratio, 1960	.12
Per cent employed in white collar occupations, 1960	—.15
Form of government, 1963	—.21
Type of election, 1963	.21
Number of individuals on council, 1963	.32
Term of office, 1963	.17
Per capita general government expenditure, 1963	.41
Per capita expenditure on sanitation, 1963	.29
Per capita debt outstanding end of year in $10 units, 1963	.31

[a] In measuring the intensity of violence of a hostile outburst, we made use of the following ordinal scale:
1. Low intensity (rock and bottle throwing, window breaking, fighting)
2. Medium intensity (the above plus some looting and arson)
3. High intensity (the above plus much looting and arson, reports of sniping)
4. Very high intensity (the above plus widespread looting and arson, sniping)

hypothesize that collective racial violence is likely to occur in a municipality when a certain *threshold* in some of these conditions is reached—that is, when environmental conditions within a particular city reach a particularly "explosive" point. This implies that hostile outbursts occur largely because a set of contextual conditions become such that strains arise which further the spread of hostile beliefs among individuals in the black community. When these generalized hostile beliefs are channeled into specific fears, antagonisms, and hopes by a precipitating factor, blacks are ready to be mobilized for participation in a hostile outburst.

Some will continue to argue that in this analysis we have simply confirmed the obvious; however, because social scientists have not had adequate data on (1) the number and character of current hostile outbursts, and (2) the number and types of cities in which such outbursts have been occurring, a number of erroneous conclusions about these outbursts have been drawn. For instance, some have argued that causes of hostile outbursts are not related to social, economic, or political differences between cities; our analysis, while only preliminary, raises doubts about the validity of such a statement. Furthermore, as Tomlinson has observed:[32]

> What produces riots is the shared agreement by most Negro Americans that their lot in life is unacceptable, coupled with the view by a significant minority that riots are a legitimate and productive mode of protest. What is unacceptable about Negro life does not vary much from city to city, and the differences in Negro life from city to city are *irrelevant*. The unifying feature is the consensus that Negroes have been misused by whites and this perception exists in every city in America. . . . urban riots in the North will continue until the well of available cities runs dry. They will continue because the mood of many Negroes in the urban North demands them, because there is a quasi-political ideology which jusitfies them and because there is *no presently effective deterrent or antidote*. (Emphasis added.

Some of these comments are probably quite correct. What Tomlinson does not emphasize is that many of the conditions (which give rise to the psychological state of mind he discusses and which may affect, quite dramatically, the course of any given hostile outburst) are rooted in the context of cities in which Negroes live. For example, conditions such as overcrowding, inadequate housing, unemployment, low income, lack of education, poor schools, high death rates, and unresponsive political institutions are not only responsible for maintaining the self-perpetuating cycle of poverty within which many Negroes find themselves, but also for the development of the attitudes Tomlinson discusses. Perhaps the ultimate determinants of hostile outbursts are psychological in nature; however, this is an empirical question. But we should also be concerned with asking why blacks hold such attitudes; we should be asking why they are acting on the basis of these hostile beliefs. This is particularly important when developing deterrents and antidotes, for the attitudes and behavior of Negroes are shaped to a considerable degree by conditions in the environment within which they live, work, and play.

[32] *Ibid.*, p. 30.

What 'Black Power' Means to Negroes in Mississippi*

JOYCE LADNER
SOUTHERN ILLINOIS UNIVERSITY

FOR THREE MONTHS DURING THE SUMMER OF LAST YEAR, I CONDUCTED A study aimed at finding out how Mississippi Negroes who endorsed "black power" interpreted this new concept. I learned that even those civil-rights activists who welcomed the concept attached curiously different meanings to it. My research also helped me understand why the black-power slogan proved so welcome to these activists—and why its acceptance was accompanied by the expulsion of whites from positions of leadership. Finally, my investigation provided some hints on the usefulness of the black-power slogan in helping Mississippi Negroes achieve their goals.

The black-power concept that emerged during the past year created fierce controversy, not only among white liberals but among Negro activists and conservatives. Most of the nation's top civil-rights leaders denounced the slogan—or vigorously embraced it. Instead of "black power," Martin Luther King Jr. advocated the acquisition of "power for all people." The N.A.A.C.P.'s Roy Wilkins, in condemning the slogan, used such terms as "anti-white power . . . a reverse Hitler . . . a reverse Ku Klux Klan and . . . can only mean black death." On the other hand, Stokely Carmichael, former head of SNCC, was the chief advocate of the slogan, which he defined as "the ability of black people to politically get together and organize themselves so that they can speak from a position of strength rather than a position of weakness." CORE's Floyd McKissick agreed.

But though Negro civil-rights leaders were divided about black power, the slogan was welcomed by many disenchanted Negroes living in Northern ghettos. These Negroes tended to view black power as a tangible goal that, when acquired, would lift them from their inferior positions in the social structure. Still, despite the positive identification that Negroes in the Northern ghettos had with the rhetoric of black power, SNCC and CORE made no massive attempts to involve these Negroes in black-power programs.

But what about the South? How did Negroes in Mississippi, and civil-rights organizations in Mississippi, interpret the new slogan? This was what I wanted to find out.

I used two methods of study. The first was *participant-observation*—in informal, small meetings of civil-rights activists; in civil-rights rallies; and in protest demonstrations, including the historic Meredith march. The second was the *focused interview*. I chose to interview 30 Negroes who, I had found, were in favor of black power. All were friends or acquaint-

* Reprinted by permission from *Trans-Action*, 5 (November, 1967), pp. 7-15. Copyright © 1967 by *Trans-Action* magazine, St. Louis, Missouri.

ances of mine, and all had had long experience in Southern civil-rights work. They represented about two-thirds of the black-power leaders in the state. (My personal involvement with the civil-rights movement helped provide the rapport needed to acquire the observational data, as well as the interview data.)

Among other things, I learned that many Negro activists in Mississippi had immediately embraced the black-power slogan—because of the already widely-held belief that power *was* an effective tool for obtaining demands from the ruling elite in Mississippi. Since 1960, civil-rights organizations have been playing a major role in involving Mississippi Negroes in the fight for equality. As a result, these Negroes became more and more dissatisfied with their impoverished, powerless positions in the social structure. The 1960 census reports that the median family income for Mississippi Negroes (who constitute 42.3 percent of Mississippi's population) was $1168, as opposed to $3565 for whites. Until fewer than five years ago, only 6 percent of the eligible Negroes were registered to vote. Today, the traditional all-white primary still exists—in almost the same form as it did 25 years ago. Since many of the efforts Mississippi Negroes made to change the social structure—through integration—were futile, they began to reconceptualize their fight for equality from a different perspective, one designed to acquire long-sought goals through building bases of power.

The black-power concept was, then, successfully communicated to Mississippi Negroes because of the failure of integration. But it was also communicated to them by the shooting of James Meredith on his march through Mississippi. This act of violence made Negro activists feel justified in calling for "audacious black power." For only with black power, they contended, would black people be able to prevent events like the shooting.

Locals and Cosmopolitans

But there were varying degrees of acceptance of the slogan among Mississippi Negroes. Some, of course, did not accept the slogan at all—those who were never part of the civil-rights movement. Despite the fact that Mississippi has been one of the centers of civil-rights activity in the United States for the past six or seven years, no more than half the Negro population (I would surmise) has ever been actively involved in the movement. In such areas as Sunflower County, a very high percentage of Negroes have participated; but in many other areas, like Laurel, only a small percentage of the Negroes have taken part.

As for those Negroes active in the movement, they can be broadly classified into two groups. The first: the traditional, moderate, N.A.A.C.P.-style activists, who boast of having been "freedom fighters" before the "new movement" came into existence. They include ministers; small-businessmen; professionals; a sizable following of middle-class people; and a small number of the rank and file. Frequently the white ruling elite calls these activists the "responsible" leaders. The primary activities of this group include selling N.A.A.C.P. memberships; initiating legal action against segregation and discriminatory practices; negotiating with the ruling elite; and conducting limited boycotts and voter-registration campaigns.

The second group of activists are the less economically advantaged. Although a small number were once members of the N.A.A.C.P., most of them joined the movement only since 1960. They are readily identified with such organizations as the Freedom Democratic Party, CORE, SNCC, the Delta Ministry, and the Southern Christian Leadership Conference. Members of this group include plantation workers, students, the average lower-class Negro, and a small number of ministers, professionals, and businessmen. More militant than the first group, these activists conduct mass marches, large-scale boycotts, sit-ins, dramatic voter-registration campaigns, and so forth.

Members of the traditional organizations, in sum, are still committed to working for integration. It is the militants who are oriented toward a black-power ideology, who consider integration irrelevant to what they see as the major task at hand—uniting black people to build black institutions. I suspect that a larger number of activists identify with traditional organizations like the N.A.A.C.P. than with the more militant ones.

The 30 black-power advocates I interviewed were, of course, the militant activists. Even so, I found that even these 30 could be further classified—into categories that Robert K. Merton has called *local* and *cosmopolitan*:

The localite largely confines his interest to this [town of Rovere] community. Devoting little thought or energy to the Great Society he is preoccupied with local problems, to the virtual exclusion of the national and international scene. He is, strictly speaking, parochial.

Contrariwise with the cosmopolitan type. He has some interest in Rovere and must of course maintain a minimum of relations within the community since he, too, exerts influence there. But he is also oriented significantly to the world outside Rovere and regards himself as an integral part of the world. . . . The cosmopolitan is ecumenical.

In this paper, I shall use "local" to refer to those long-term residents of Mississippi—usually uneducated, unskilled adults—whose strong commitment to civil-rights activity stemmed primarily from their desire to produce massive changes in the "home-front," the area they call home.

I shall use "cosmopolitan" to refer to the urbane, educated, highly skilled young civil-rights activists who are usually newcomers to Mississippi. Because they went to the state to work in the civil-rights movement only temporarily, their identification with the area tends to be weak.

THE MOVEMENT'S PHILOSOPHERS

One-third of my respondents, I found, hold the cosmopolitan view. The majority are Negro men, but there are a small group of Negro women and a very small group of white sympathizers. The mean age is about 23 or 24. About half are from the North; the remainder are from Mississippi and other Southern states. Most of the cosmopolitans are formally educated and many have come from middle-class Northern families and gone to the better universities. They are widely read and widely traveled. They are also artistic: Writers, painters, photographers, musicians, and the like are often found in the cosmopolitan group. Their general orientation toward life is an intellectual one. They are associated with SNCC, the Freedom Democratic Party, and CORE. Although a few are actively engaged in organizing black people in the various counties, much of their work in the state is centered on philosophical discussions, writing, and so forth. All of the cosmopolitans have had wide associations with white people. Some grew up and attended school with whites; others had contact with whites in the civil-rights movement. The cosmopolitans maintain that black people in American society must redefine the term "black" and all that it symbolizes, and that black pride and dignity must be implanted in all Negro Americans. The cosmopolitan position embraces the belief that the plight of Negro Americans is comparable to neocolonialized "colored peoples" of the world.

The cosmopolitans' participation in the Southern civil-rights scene, by and large, dates back to 1960 and the beginning of the student movement in the South. Their present ideology has to be viewed in the framework of the history of their involvement in the movement, with special emphasis on the negative experiences they encountered.

Some six years ago, black Americans began to seek their long-desired civil rights with a new sense of urgency. The N.A.A.C.P.'s painstaking effort to obtain legal, theoretical rights for Negroes was challenged. Groups of Negro college students in the South decided to fight the gradualism that had become traditional and to substitute radical action aimed at bringing about rapid social change. These students began their drive for equal rights with lunch-counter demonstrations. After much immediate success, they spread their drive to the political arena. Their only hope for the future, they felt, lay in the ballot. Much to their disappointment, acquiring political power was not so easy as integrating lunch counters. The students met their strongest resistance from whites in full possession of the sought-after political power. To deal with this resistance, the Federal Government passed two civil-rights laws: public accommodation and voting rights. But the Government did little to implement these laws. Still, in the early 1960s, student civil-rights workers had an almost unrelenting faith in the Federal Government and believed that changes in the laws would rapidly pave the way for sweeping changes in the social structure. This was the era when students were much involved in hard-core organizing. They paid little attention to abstract philosophizing. Instead they occupied themselves with such pressing problems as the mass arrests of Negroes in Greenwood, Miss.

As time went on, the cosmopolitans became more and more discouraged about their organizing efforts. They began to seriously question the feasibility of their strategies and tactics. By the end of 1964, after the historic Mississippi Summer Project, the cosmopolitans began to feel that their organizational methods were just not effective. For roughly a year and a half, they groped and searched for more effective strategies. Frequently they felt frustrated; sometimes they despaired. A number of them returned to the North and got well-paying jobs or went to graduate and professional schools. Others were alienated from some of the basic values of American society. Some students developed a strong interest in Africa and began to look to various African states as possible havens. Still others, after deciding that they had accomplished all that was possible through organizations such as SNCC, associated themselves with radical leftist groups.

It was during the tail end of this six-year period that two position papers were written by the cosmopolitans. One was by a group that insisted that Negroes expel whites from leadership roles in civil-rights organizations, and that Negroes develop "black consciousness" and "black nationalism." "Black consciousness" refers to a set of ideas and behavior patterns affirming the beauty of blackness and dispelling any negative images that black people may have incorporated about blackness. "Black nationalism" is a kind of patriotic devotion to the development of the Negro's own political, economic, and social institutions. Black nationalism is *not* a racist ideology with separatist overtones, however, but simply a move toward independence from the dominant group, the whites. This paper states:

If we are to proceed toward true liberation, we must cut ourselves off from white people. We must form our own institutions, credit unions, co-ops, political parties, write our own histories. . . . SNCC, by allowing whites to remain in the organization, can have its efforts subverted. . . . Indigenous leadership cannot be built with whites in the positions they now hold. They [whites] can participate on a voluntary basis . . . but in no way can they participate on a policy-making level.

In response, one white civil-rights worker—Pat McGauley—wrote a paper acceding to the demands of the black-consciousness group:

The time has indeed come for blacks and whites in the movement to separate; however, it must always be kept in mind that the final goal of the revolution we are all working for is a multi-racial society.

The cosmopolitans I interviewed conceived of black power in highly philosophical terms—as an ideology that would unite black people as never before. To most of them, black power was intricately bound up with black consciousness. To a long-time SNCC worker, black consciousness was:

. . . an awareness of oneself as a removed nation of black people who are capable of running and developing their own governments and who have pride in their blackness to the extent that they won't sell out. . . . To the extent that he can say, "I'm no longer ashamed of my blackness." The individual redefines the society's rules in terms of his own being. There is a new kind of awakening of the individual, a new kind of realization of self, a type of security, and a type of self-confidence.

Another cosmopolitan equated black consciousness with community loyalty:

Black consciousness is not the question but rather [the question is] from which community one comes from. If you know that, you can identify with black people anywhere in the world then. That is all that is necessary.

These young people firmly believe that even the term "black" has to be redefined. To one of them, "Black has never had any favorable expression in the English language." To another, "American society has characterized black as the symbol for strength, evil, potency and malignancy. . . . People are afraid of the night, of blackness."

Most cosmopolitans feel that black people must acquire black consciousness before they can successfully develop the tools and techniques for acquiring black power. As one of them put it:

Black consciousness is the developmental stage of black power. Black power will be incomplete without black consciousness. Black consciousness is basically the search for identity; or working out one's own identity. . . . There must be a long process of learning and unlearning in between and a period of self-questing.

In short, by developing black consciousness, a Negro can appreciate his blackness and thus develop a kind of community loyalty to other colored peoples of the world.

Most of the cosmopolitans feel that the redefinition of blackness must take place in the black community *on the black man's terms*. When such a redefinition has taken place, black men who feel psychologically castrated because of their blackness will be able to compete with whites as psychological equals. ("Psychologically castrated" is a popular term among cosmopolitans, and refers to Negroes whose beliefs and behavior have become so warped by the values of white American society that they have come to regard themselves as inferior.)

HEROES OF THE BLACK REVOLUTION

Cosmopolitans are familiar with the works of Marcus Garvey, Malcolm X, Franz Fanon, Kwame Nkrumah, and other revolutionary nationalists. Some can quote passages from their works. To the cosmopolitans, Marcus Garvey (1887–1940), who tried to instill racial pride in Negroes, was a pioneer of black nationalism and black consciousness in America. The greatest impact on the cosmopolitans, however, comes from the contemporary Malcolm X, whose philosophy—toward the latter period of his life —reflected a revolutionary spirit and a total dissatisfaction with the plight of Negroes in this country. One of the cosmopolitans had this to say about Malcolm X:

Malcolm was very much together. . . . He was a man who knew what he was doing and would have eventually showed everyone what he was capable of doing. . . . Malcolm had history behind him and was with the cat on the block.

To another:

Malcolm X . . . was able to relate to people and to the press. The press is your right arm. . . . In order to be a real militant, you have to use the man [press] and that is what Malcolm did. They [the press] didn't create Malcolm. . . . The press was attuned to Malcolm. . . . Malcolm was not attuned to the press.

Some cosmopolitans call themselves students of Malcolm X and express the hope that another such leader will soon emerge.

Another symbolic leader is the late Algerian revolutionary, Franz Fanon, whose *The Wretched of the Earth* has become a veritable Bible to the cosmopolitans. Fanon tried to justify the use of violence by the oppressed against the oppressor, and to relate the neocolonization of the black man in Algeria to the plight of colored peoples everywhere. Similarly, the cosmopolitans have great admiration for Stokely Carmichael, one of their associates, whose philsophy is highlighted in this passage:

> The colonies of the United States—and this includes the black ghettos within its borders, north and south—must be liberated. For a century this nation has been like an octopus of exploitation, its tentacles stretching from Mississippi and Harlem to South America, the Middle East, southern Africa, and Vietnam; the form of exploitation varies from area to area but the essential result has been the same—a powerful few have been maintained and enriched at the expense of the poor and voiceless colored masses. This pattern must be broken. As its grip loosens here and there around the world, the hopes of black Americans become more realistic. For racism to die, a totally different America must be born.

Embodied within the philosophy of the cosmopolitans is an essential proposition that American society is inherently racist, that the majority of white Americans harbor prejudice against black people. Few make any distinction between whites—for example, the white Southerner as opposed to the Northern liberal. Whites are considered symbolic of the black man's oppression, and therefore one should not differentiate between sympathetic whites and unsympathetic whites. The conclusion of the cosmopolitans is that any sweeping structural changes in American society can come about only through the black man's taking an aggressive role in organizing his political, economic, and social institutions. The black man must control his destiny.

THE PRACTICAL ORIENTATION

I have categorized the remaining two-thirds of my 30 respondents as locals. (Of what significance these ratios are, by the way, I am not sure.) The locals are almost as committed to solving the pressing problems of inadequate income, education, housing, and second-class citizenship *practically* as the cosmopolitans are committed to solving them *philosophically*. Most of the locals are life-long residents of their communities or other Mississippi communities. Most of them, like the cosmopolitans, have been drawn into the movement only since 1960. Unlike the generally youthful cosmopolitans, the age range of the locals is from young adult to elderly. Many locals are indigenous leaders in their communities and in state-wide organizations. Whereas cosmopolitans tend to be middle-class, locals are members of the lower-class black communities and they range from plantation workers to a few who have acquired modest homes and a somewhat comfortable style of life. Many are leaders in the Mississippi Freedom Democratic Party, which in 1964 challenged the legality of the all-white

Mississippi delegation to the national Democratic convention and in 1965 challenged the constitutionality of the elected white Representatives to serve in the U.S. House of Representatives. (Both challenges were based upon the fact that Negroes did not participate in the election of the delegates and Representatives.)

Although most of the locals are native Mississippians who have always been victimized by segregation and discrimination, I have also placed a number of middle-class students in this category—because of their very practical orientation to black power. The backgrounds of these students are somewhat similar to those of the cosmopolitans, except that the majority come from the South and are perhaps from lower-status families than the cosmopolitans are. These students are deeply involved in attempts to organize black-power programs.

Because of segregation and discrimination, the locals are largely uneducated; they subsist on a totally inadequate income; and they are denied the privileges of first-class citizenship. They have had a lot of experience with the usual forms of harrassment and intimidation from local whites. Their entire existence can be perceived in terms of their constant groping for a better way of life. Because of many factors—like their low level of income and education and their Southern, rural, small-town mentality (which to some extent prevents one from acquiring an intellectualized world view)—the definition they have given to black power is a very practical one.

The black-power locals can be considered militants to much the same degree as the cosmopolitans, but on a different level. In essence, the nature and kind of activities in which they are willing to participate (voter registration, running for political office, boycotts, etc.) are indeed militant and are not surpassed by the nature and kind to which the cosmopolitans orient themselves. Indeed, in some cases the locals are deeply involved in realizing black-power programs: In certain counties, women have organized leathercraft and dress-making cooperatives. And in Senator Eastland's home county of Sunflower, an unsuccessful effort was even made to elect an all-black slate of public officials.

The great difference between cosmopolitans and locals is that the locals are committed to concrete economic and political programs, while the cosmopolitans—to varying degrees—endorse such programs but actually have made little effort to realize them.

Most locals perceived black power as a more effective, alternate method of organizing and acquiring those rights they had been seeking. In the past they had been committed to integration. Power had not originally been considered important in and of itself, for it was hoped that America would voluntary give Negroes civil rights. Therefore the locals sought coalition politics—they aligned themselves with Northern labor groups, liberals, national church groups, and so forth. During their several years of involvement, they—like the cosmopolitans—suffered many defeats. For example, many were involved with the Mississippi Summer Project, which brought hundreds of Northerners into the state in 1964. At that time the locals were convinced that such a program would bring about the wide structural changes they desired. But, to their disappointment, once the volunteers returned to the North the old patterns of segregation and discrimination returned. Some of the locals had gone to the Democratic Convention in Atlantic City, N.J., in 1964 hoping to unseat the all-white slate of delegates from Mississippi. When this failed, they invested further moral and physical resources into challenging the legality of the all-white slate of Mississippi Representatives in the U.S. House. Another set-back came when a large contingent pitched their tents on the White House lawn in a last-ditch effort to obtain poverty funds to aid in building adequate housing. All were sharecroppers, evicted because their participation in voter-registration programs was contrary to the desires of their plantation landlords. These evicted sharecroppers later set up residence in the buildings of the inactive Air Force base in Greenville, Miss. They were deeply depressed when officials of the Air Force ordered military police to remove them. One of the leaders of this group remarked, "If the United States Government cares so little about its citizens that it will not allow them to live in its abandoned buildings rather than in unheated tents [this occurred during winter], then that government can't be for real."

I submit that the events outlined above, among many others, caused a large number of the locals—like the cosmopolitans—to pause and question the effectiveness of their traditional organizational tactics and goals. Indeed, many even came to seriously question the Federal Government's sincerity about alleviating the problems of the Negro. A number of the participants in these events stopped being active in the movement. Others began to express strong anti-white sentiments.

The Attractions of Black Power

Black power was embraced by many of the locals from the very beginning, and they began to reconceptualize their activities within the new framework. To the locals, black power was defined in various ways, some of which follow:

Voter registration is black power. Power is invested in the ballot and that's why the white man worked like hell to keep you away from it. . . . We were even taught that it was not right to register [to vote]. The civil-rights movement in this state started around the issue of voting—we shouldn't forget that.

Black power is political power held by Negroes. It means political control in places where they comprise a majority. . . . Black power is legitimate because any time people are in a majority, they should be able to decide what will and what will not happen to them.

Black power was further viewed as a means of combining Negroes into a bond of solidarity. It was seen as a rallying cry, a symbol of identification, and a very concrete tool for action. Many said that former slogans and concepts such as "Freedom Now" were ambiguous. One could easily ask, "Freedom for what and from what?" One local said:

First we wanted Freedom Now. I ran around for six years trying to get my freedom. I really didn't know what it was.

Black power, they felt, was more concrete, for it had as its central thesis the acquisition of power. (Actually, the locals have also defined black power in various ways, and to some the slogan is as ambiguous as "Freedom Now.") The locals felt that Negroes would be able to acquire certain rights only through the control of their economic and political institutions, which—in some cases—also involves the eventual control of the black community. One black power advocate put it succinctly when he said:

Black power means controlling the Negro community. It means that if the Negro community doesn't want white cops coming in, they can't come in. It means political, economic, and social control.

Asked how this control could be obtained, he replied:

We will have to start putting our money together to organize cooperatives, and other kinds of businesses. We can get political power by putting Negroes into public offices. . . . We will have to tell them to vote only for Negro candidates.

To others, control over the black community was not the goal, but rather a *share* in the existing power:

All we're saying to the white man is we want some power. Black power is just plain power. . . . It just means that Negroes are tired of being without power and want to share in it.

Thus, we can observe that there are several variations of the concept, all revolving around a central theme: the acquisition of power by Negroes for their own use, both offensively and defensively.

Despite the obvious practical orientation of the locals, there can also be found traces of black consciousness and black nationalism in their thought patterns. Most have never read Garvy, Fanon, Malcolm X, and other nationalists, but they tend to readily identify with the content of speeches made by Stokely Carmichael bearing the message of black nationalism. They are prone to agree with the cosmopolitans who speak to them about ridding themselves of their "oppressors." When the chairman of the Mississippi Freedom Democratic Party speaks of overthrowing neocolonialism in Mississippi, shouts of "Amen—" can be heard from the audience. There is also a tendency in this group to oppose the current war in Vietnam on the grounds that America should first concentrate on liberating Negroes within the United States' borders. The locals also believe that the war is indeed an unjust one. Perhaps the following statement is typical:

Black men have been stripped of everything. If it takes black power to do something about this, let us have it. Black power has got the country moving and white people don't like it. We marched into Dominica, we marched into Vietnam. Now if we [black people] can conquer this country, we will conquer the world.

There is a growing feeling among both locals and cosmopolitans of kinship with the colored peoples of the world, including the Vietnamese. To engage in warfare against other colored people is regarded as a contradiction of this bond of solidarity.

For both the Mississippi cosmopolitans and locals, then, it was mainly frustration that drew them to the concept of black power.

Why Whites Were Expelled

The black-power slogan should be viewed in the perspective of the overall civil-rights movement, one of the most popular social movements in the history of this country. Now, there are some scholars who maintain that, by viewing a particular social movement over a period of time, one can discern a typical sequence: the movement's crystallization of social unrest; its phase of active agitation and proselytism; its organized phase; and the achievement of its objectives. The civil-rights movement, with much success, achieved each of these phases—except the final one, the achievement of objectives. Despite the great amount of effort and resources expended by black people and their allies to obtain civil rights, there was a disproportionate lack of gains. Indeed, in much of Mississippi and the South, conditions have barely changed from 10 or even 20 years ago. Many black people are still earning their livelihood from sharecropping and tenant farming; many household heads are still unable to earn more than $500 a year; many black children are still deprived of adequate education because of the lack of facilities and adequately trained teachers. To date, only 42.1 percent of Negroes of voting age are registered as opposed to 78.9 percent of whites. We still hear of lynchings and other forms of violence of which Negroes are the victims.

The black-power thrust is thus an inevitable outgrowth of the disillusionment that black people have experienced in their intense efforts to become integrated into the mainstream of American society. Thwarted by traditional formulas and organizational restrictions, some Mississippi Negroes have responded to the black-power concept in a sometimes semirational, emotionally charged manner—because it seemed the only available resource with which they could confront white American society.

How was the black-power concept related to the expulsion of whites from leadership positions in the movement? The fact is that the alienation and disaffection found throughout the entire black-power group also resulted from strained interpersonal relations with white civil-rights workers. During the past two years, there has been a growing belief among black people in Mississippi that white civil-rights workers should go into the *white* communities of that state to work. Only then, they contended, could the "inherent racism" in American society, with particular reference to the "Southern racist," begin to be dealt with. Even the seriousness of white civil-rights workers was questioned. Many Negroes felt that a sizable number of them had come South mainly to resolve their very personal emotional difficulties, and not to help impoverished black Mississippians. Rather, they were considered rebellious youth who wanted only to act out their rebellion in the most unconventional ways. Stokely Carmichael stated:

Too many young, middle-class Americans, like some sort of Pepsi generation, have wanted to come alive through the black community; they've wanted to be where the action was—and the action has been in the black community. . . .

It's important to note that those white people who feel alienated from white society and run into the black society are incapable of confronting the white society with its racism where it really does exist.

Much strain also resulted from the inability of many black civil-rights activists—skilled organizers but lacking the formal education and other technical skills white workers possessed—to deal with the increased bureaucratization of the civil-rights movement (writing proposals for foundation grants, for example). Black activists, in addition, constantly complained about the focus of the mass media on white "all-American" volunteers who had come South to work in the movement. The media never paid attention to the thousands of black people who frequently took far greater risks. These factors played a major role in destroying the bond of solidarity that had once existed between whites and blacks in the movement. Before the emergence of the black-power concept, it is true, many young black civil-rights workers had cast white civil-rights workers in the same category as all other white people. The new slogan was, to some extent, a form of justification for their own prejudice against whites.

In terms of practical considerations, however, urging the white volunteers to leave the black communities has had negative effects. SNCC and CORE, which at one time directed most of the grass-roots organizing, have always depended upon the economic and volunteer resources of liberal white individuals and groups. These resources are scarce nowadays.

On another level, there have been positive results from removing whites from black communities. Black activists—all cosmopolitans and some locals—contend that, now that the whites have gone, they feel more self-confident and capable of running their own programs. They tend to view the earlier period of the movement, when whites played active roles in executing the programs, as having been a necessary phase; but they maintain that the time has arrived when black people must launch and execute their own programs.

Cosmopolitans vs. Locals

Clearly, the long-range aims of the locals and cosmopolitans are basically the same. Unlike Negroes in such traditional organizations as the N.A.A.C.P., locals and cosmopolitans have turned away from integration. Both groups want to unite black people and build political, economic, and social institutions that will render a certain amount of control to the black community. For some time, however, the two groups have been operating on different levels. The cosmopolitans focus on developing black consciousness among black people, which they consider a necessary step to developing black power; the locals concentrate on solving the immediate problems resulting from segregation and discrimination.

While it may seem that the locals are more prudent and realistic than the cosmopolitans, it should be said that there are many positive features to black nationalism and black consciousness. It *is* important to establish a positive black identity in a great many sectors of the black communities, both North and South, rural and urban, lower and middle class. Indeed, it is both important and legitimate to teach black people (or any other ethnic minority) about their history, placing emphasis upon the positive contributions of other black people. Thus black consciousness has the potential to create unity and solidarity among black people and to give them hope and self-confidence. Perhaps it fulfills certain needs in black people that society, on the whole, cannot. Martin Luther King has made the following statement about black consciousness:

One must not overlook the positive value in calling the Negro to a new sense of manhood, to a deep feeling of racial pride and to an audacious appreciation of his heritage. The Negro must be grasped by a new realization of his dignity and worth. He must stand up amid a system that still oppresses him and develop an unassailable and majestic sense of his own value. *He must no longer be ashamed of being black.* (Emphasis mine.)

Moreover, the task of getting blacks to act *as blacks, by* themselves and *for* themselves, is necessary for developing black conciousness, or psychological equality. Thus one is led to the conclusion that black consciousness does *necessarily* call for the expulsion of whites from leadership roles in the black communities.

The locals, on the other hand, have adopted concrete strategies that, in reality, involve the same kind of techniques that existed in the integration era. Specifically, when they refer to developing black-power programs, they speak of registering to vote, running for political office, and building independent political parties. As for the economic situation, they have begun to concentrate on building cooperatives and small businesses, and on almost-exclusively patronizing black merchants in an effort to "keep the money in the black community." If we turn back two years, however, we find that the same strategies, though somewhat modified, were being used then. In the past, the locals concentrated on registering large numbers of black people to vote, in an effort to be able to have a voice in the decision-making apparatus. The emphasis is now on registering to vote so that the Negro can have control over his community and eventual control over his political destiny. Cooperatives were organized at least a year before the black-power concept emerged, but—ever since emphasis was put on economic control—there has been an expansion and intensification in certain sectors of this area. At present, cooperatives are still operating on a small-scale, though, considering the masses of people whose lives could be immensely improved by cooperatives.

The differences in the emphasis on priorities of achieving black power between locals and cosmopolitans can be viewed as complementary rather than oppositional, because each level of emphasis is vital for the achievement of their goals. This is becoming increasingly true since, within the last year, black-power advocates have taken a far more aggressive and militant stance toward the realization of such aims. Locals who a year ago might have questioned the importance and feasibility of "Black Liberation" schools, which teach black history and culture, are less likely to do so now. This is an indication that there is a trend toward unity between the groups. Because of the strong emphasis among some sectors of the black-power movement with that of the inhabitants of the Third World, locals are quite likely to become more cosmopolitan through time.

Through the development of such unity, there is a great possibility that black-power advocates in Mississippi will again turn to creative, large-scale organizing that would incorporate the major emphases of each group: black consciousness and immediate gains.

THE FUTURE OF BLACK POWER

The key question, of course, is, what are the prospects for Mississippi Negroes' developing black-power institutions in the near future? Clearly, this will depend to a great extent upon the number of organizers in the field, on adequate economic resources, and on commitments from major civil-rights organizations to the Mississippi scene. Certainly the presence of a local charismatic leader also would aid in the development of pervasive black-power institutions. Indeed, a black-power "prophet" whose task was to keep the message before all the advocates would give them immeasurable support and strength for their undertakings.

Where black-power institutions have a good chance of developing at present are in the small number of Mississippi counties where there are strong black-power organizations with large Negro voting populations. Since the cosmopolitans are reentering the field and beginning to organize (and some of the most skilled organizers are in this group), the prospects—here at least—seem favorable. On the other hand, it seems highly doubtful at this point that the needed resources can be obtained from the traditional sources (Northern students, white liberals, church and labor organizations). So these resources (inadequate as they may be) may have to be obtained from the black community. CORE and SNCC have already begun to establish financial bases in the black communities throughout the country. Should this tactic fail, perhaps there will be a revaluation of the strategies employed in the acquisition of black power.

33

The Prejudice-Interaction Hypothesis from the Point of View of the Negro Minority Group[*]

ERNEST WORKS[1]
CALIFORNIA STATE COLLEGE AT FULLERTON

RECENT STUDIES REVEAL THAT WHITE TENANTS IN INTEGRATED HOUSING ARE more likely than are their counterparts in segregated housing to experience intimate interracial contacts of persons equal in status.[2] These studies also reveal that the integrated tenants, when compared with the segregated, exhibit less prejudice against the Negro minority. This may be said to validate a prejudice-interaction hypothesis: that outgroup prejudice is reduced when contacts are intimate and of those of equal status. The present study was designed to test this hypothesis among the Negro minority.[3] We assume that the hypothesis is merely a specific demonstration of a hypothesis with general applicability. If so, it should hold in all instances of ingroup-outgroup relations, for members of the minority and the dominant group.

HYPOTHESES

The independent variable in the hypothesis is intergroup contact, and the dependent variable is intergroup prejudice. Intergroup contact is seen as reducing outgroup prejudice. The earlier studies reveal that such contacts are more probable in integrated than in segregated housing. (We assume this but will demonstrate its validity below.) Therefore, Negro tenants in integrated housing are expected to be less prejudiced toward whites than are their counterparts in segregated housing, and this should hold for husbands as well as for wives (hypothesis 1). The earlier studies failed to test the hypothesis among husbands.

Integrated housewives have more opportunities for interracial contacts than do their husbands. Greater opportunity should result in greater con-

[*] Reprinted from *American Journal of Sociology*, 67 (1961), by permission of the University of Chicago Press. Copyright © 1961 by the University of Chicago Press.

[1] This study was supported by grants from the Society for the Psychological Study of Social Issues and from the National Institutes of Health. The author also wishes to acknowledge the advice and assistance of Professors Daniel Glaser and Bernard Farber of the University of Illinois and Richard Dewey of the University of New Hampshire and of Paul D. Strait and the staff of the Youngstown Metropolitan Housing Authority for making their facilities available.

[2] For a summary of these studies see Daniel M. Wilner, Rosabelle P. Walkley, and Stuart W. Cook, *Human Relations in Interracial Housing* (Minneapolis: University of Minnesota Press, 1955).

[3] For studies on Negro prejudice against whites see Tilman C. Cothran, "Negro Conceptions of White People," *American Journal of Sociology*, LVI (March, 1951), 458–467. Also see Robert Johnson, "Negro Reactions to Minority Status," pp. 192–214, in Milton L. Barron (ed.), *American Minorities* (New York: Alfred A. Knopf, Inc., 1957).

tact (hypothesis 2; to be tested below). Assuming no sexual difference in outgroup prejudice, integrated housewives are expected to be less prejudiced toward whites than are their Negro husbands.

The opportunities for interracial contacts of segregated wives are about equal to those of their husbands (to be tested below). We therefore expect to find no significant difference in antiwhite prejudice between housewives and husbands in all-Negro housing (hypothesis 3).

The initial plan was to conduct the interviews among tenants residing in an integrated project and among tenants residing in an all-Negro project, both located in the same city and having similar occupants. The interviewing was actually conducted in a single housing project which was partly integrated and partly segregated. This project, located in a middle-sized midwestern metropolis, was laid out along both sides of an east-west thoroughfare with two-thirds of the units on the north side. Of the units on the north side, 54 per cent were occupied by Negroes and 46 per cent by whites. This was accepted as satisfying the requirement of an integrated pattern of occupancy. Of the south side units, Negroes occupied 94 per cent and whites only 6 per cent. Because of the negligible percentage of white tenants on this side of the project, it was accepted as a pattern of all-Negro occupancy.[4]

In order to control relevant variables, we decided to restrict the sample to families satisfying the following requirements: (1) both spouses living together, (2) both between the ages of twenty and forty-five, (3) employed husband, and (4) at least six months residence in the project. At the time the interviewing began there were forty-eight integrated and forty-nine segregated families meeting the first requirement. Twenty-nine interviews with integrated tenants were lost, and sixteen with segregated tenants were lost.[5] Twenty-one of the losses among integrated tenants were due to "move-outs" and changes in status, five to refusals by husbands, and two to refusals by wives. Of the losses among segregated tenants, fourteen were due to "move-outs" and changes in status, two to refusals by husbands, and the remaining one to unavailability of one wife.

---

[4] The housing authority in charge of the project had an open-occupancy policy, in view of which it seemed strange that one side of the project could remain predominantly uniracial. An interview was conducted with the assistant manager in charge of placement on the subject of the placement of tenants; she contended that no selective factor operated in assignment of tenants to units. A casual chat with the assistant manager's assistant confirmed this assertion.

[5] The interviewing took place between October, 1957, and February, 1958, by a Negro male and female in their late twenties. The female interviewed the wives, while the husbands were interviewed by the male. Each interviewer was familiar with the instrument, have pretested it on tenants in a similar project. Contact with the tenants was arranged through a brief one-page letter which introduced the researcher, explained the purpose of the research, requested an interview, indicated the role of the interviewer in the interview, and specified the date and time the interviewer would call. Each Monday morning ten letters were placed in the mail boxes of the families scheduled for that week. In no case were husband and wife interviewed at the same time in the same room.

In addition, there were six segregated husbands whose ages fell beyond the upper limit. These men were excluded from the study, but their wives were retained to prevent too-drastic reduction in size of sample.

Three sets of interview items were used to collect the data reported in this paper. One focused upon socioeconomic characteristics thought relevant to the dependent variable; the second upon levels of neighborly Negro-white contacts; and the third upon antiwhite prejudice. The latter was defined as a categorical way of thinking, feeling, or acting about those of the outgroup. Accordingly, it was approached in three ways, thereby increasing the number of hypotheses to nine.[6] First, the tenants were requested to indicate agreement, disagreement, or uncertainty with a check list of attitudes to the white families. Second, they were requested to respond to the broad question: "How do you feel toward the white tenants?" Third, they were directed to respond to a hypothetical situation in which they were being evicted from the present quarters and could elect to move into either a "separate but equal" project, a "separate but unequal" project in favor of the Negroes, or an integrated project with joint use of facilities.[7]

TESTS OF ASSUMPTIONS

A number of studies have revealed relationships between certain socioeconomic characteristics and intergroup prejudice. The data summarized in Table 1 checked the similarity of the groups as to these characteristics.

Table 1 reveals substantial differences in earlier residence in the South, years of residence in the project, education, preproject interracial contacts, and awareness that whites were in the project before moving in. The differences in the first and latter three attributes favor the integrated tenants, the group predicted to have less of the dependent variable. These attributes were, therefore, cross-tabulated with the measures of the dependent variable to determine their possible influence upon it. The analysis revealed that none of the differences between marginals was large enough to suggest a relationship. However, it appears plausible that education and earlier residence in the South may serve as predisposing factors to change or remain stable.

Table 2 summarizes the data which checked the assumptions underlying the hypotheses.[8] The table indicates that all three assumptions are

---

[6] Separate treatment seemed warranted since research reveals imperfect correlation of these three components (see Isidor Chein, "Notes on a Framework for the Measurement of Discrimination and Prejudice," in Marie Jahoda, Morton Deutsch, and Stuart W. Cook (eds.), *Research Methods in Social Relations*, I [New York: Dryden Press, 1951], 381–390; also see Bernard Kramer, "Dimensions of Prejudice," *Journal of Psychology*, XXXVI [1949], 389–451).

[7] Correlation between these three measures was far from perfect; *r* between attitude and feeling was .24; between attitude and action, .26; and between feeling and action, .002. Such low values for *r*, of course, may reflect crudeness in our indexes.

[8] These items covered contacts inside other tenants' apartments, stopping and hold-in a conversation outside the apartments on the grounds, knowing other tenants by name, speaking, and no contacts at all. They met the criteria of an unidimensional scale, with a coefficient of reproducibility of .95.

TABLE 1

Summary of Socioeconomic Characteristics

Characteristic	Segregated	Integrated
Mean income	$2,740	$2,518
Mean monthly rent	43	40
Median number of children	2	2
Mean age		
Housewives	29.7	25.3
Husbands	30.9	29.2
Percentage with prior residence in South		
Housewives	29.2	33.3
Husbands	36.1	24.2
Mean years lived in project	3.6	1.9
Education (percentage):		
Housewives		
Completed high school	36.6	45.7
Grades 9–11	51.2	45.7
Through grade 8	12.2	8.6
Husbands		
Completed high school	38.9	70.9
Grades 9–11	50.0	19.4
Through grade 8	11.1	9.7
Preproject interracial contacts (percentage)		
Housewives	37	39
Husbands	42	58
Preproject interracial job contacts (percentage)		
Housewives	73	81
Husbands	81	88
Knowledge that whites were in project before moving in (percentage)		
Housewives	71	83
Husbands	81	79

TABLE 2

Pattern of Occupancy and Interracial Contacts* (Percent)

	Husbands		Housewives	
No. of Types of Contact	Integrated ($n=32$)	Segregated ($n=36$)	Integrated ($n=35$)	Segregated ($n=41$)
4	19	0	49	15
3	31	19	28	27
2	22	6	11	9
1	19	22	9	22
0	9	53	3	27

* x^2 between husbands and between wives significant at .01 level; between integrated spouses significant at .05 level; between segregated spouses significant at .15 level.

valid. The assumption about segregated spouses, however, is not as strongly supported as are the other two.

In analyzing the data on patterns of occupancy and intergroup prejudice, we shall examine the hypotheses on each measure of intergroup prejudice separately. Analysis of one hypothesis on all three measures, before going on the second hypothesis, would necessitate repetition of the tables or excessive reference to tables presented earlier.

ATTITUDES TOWARD WHITES

Tabulation of responses to the check list of attitudes yielded five items with a coefficient of reproducibility equal to .88. In their scale order the items were: "The white people in this project judge Negroes by the worse types of Negroes"; ". . . do not care to be among Negroes"; ". . . do not like for children to play with colored children"; ". . . are just as clean as the white;" ". . . never let you forget they are white and you are colored." As a test of the first hypothesis, the cases were ranked by percentage of "unprejudiced" response and significance of difference was tested by the Mann-Whitney U Test. As summarized in Table 3 these data support hypothesis 1 only for the wives. While in the expected direction, the difference between husbands lacks significance.

Hypothesis 2 was tested by establishing matched pairs between the score received by each integrated wife and that received by her spouse. Of thirty matched pairs, there was no difference in five, in fourteen the wife received a higher score, and in the remaining eleven the husband's score exceeded the wife's. These data, analyzed by means of the Wilcoxon Matched-Pairs Signed-Ranks Test, failed to substantiate hypothesis 2. A possible explanation for the failure of this hypothesis is that an assumption used in deriving it—that the conceptions of whites held by husbands would be independent of those held by their wives—was not valid. We began to doubt this assumption when a number of integrated husbands,

TABLE 3

Pattern of Occupancy and Indorsement of Unprejudiced Response
on Five Antiwhite Items* (Percent)

	Husbands		Housewives	
No. of Un- prejudiced Responses	Integrated ($n=32$)	Segregated ($n=36$)	Integrated ($n=35$)	Segregated ($n=41$
5	13	11	17	7
4	22	11	29	7
3	19	14	11	22
2	25	28	14	17
1	9	19	23	20
0	12	17	6	27

* z between husbands significant at .09 level; between wives significant at .01 level; between husbands and wives not significant.

who themselves reported no neighborly intergroup contacts, began talking about such contacts as experienced by their wives. For example, one husband described the white families thus: "They're nice. Can tell by the way they come over and talk with my wife." This was not an isolated remark. It suggests that the integrated husbands' conceptions of whites were not independent of the conceptions of whites held by their wives, thus causing the hypothesis to fail. An alternative explanation is that the greater education of the integrated husbands caused them to have already or be more readily disposed to hold less stereotyped conceptions.

Hypothesis 3, on no significant difference in antiwhite prejudice between spouses in segregated housing, was tested by the procedure employed for hypothesis 2. Of thirty-four matched pairs, eight revealed no difference, while thirteen disclosed more unprejudiced responses by the wife, and thirteen by the husband, thus supporting hypothesis 3.

Studies adopting the ex post facto from cause to effect design make only one comparison between the experimental and the control groups, this coming after the experimental group has been exposed to the independent variable.[9] The most serious shortcoming of these studies is their failure to establish group comparability prior to the assumed introduction of the causative variable. It is possible that the conceptions of whites held by integrated tenants were more positive than were those of segregated tenants prior to moving into the project. To check this, the following question was asked each tenant subsequent to completing the check list on attitudes: "Now if you had been asked to describe the white tenants prior to moving into the project, do you think you would have said the same thing, or do you think you would have said something different?" The following is the percentage distribution of those who responded, "something different": integrated wives, 37 percent; integrated husbands, 44 percent; segregated wives, 10 percent; and segregated husbands, 17 percent.

This reflects a greater tendency of the integrated tenants to give the response, "something different." Unfortunately, our instrument did not include a question on the direction of "something different," that is, whether it meant a less positive or a more positive response. However, a number of tenants made statements which suggest it meant an initially less positive response. For example, one husband stated, "when I first came in I did not know what they were going to be like. I thought they were going to be like some other people I have had dealings with. They have not been like that at all." Another remarked, "I thought they were going to be a lot worse than they are."

FEELINGS TOWARD WHITES

The question on feelings elicited responses which fell into the three categories: positive, neutral, and negative. Illustrative of the positive responses are: "I like them, they seem to be very nice"; "They treat me nice; okay toward them"; "They are nice; treat me nice." Examples of neutral responses are: "I feel neutral toward them"; "No feeling toward them"; "I

[9] Ernest Greenwood, *Experimental Sociology* (New York: King's Crown Press, 1945).

feel toward them just like I feel toward anyone else." Examples of negative responses are: "You can't tell what the whites are thinking. I don't visit or have anything to do with them"; "Whites prefer to live in their own section; they don't care for Negroes"; "Fine! Because they're not around me and don't bother me." The neutral and negative responses were combined, and the hypotheses were tested as to feelings by comparing the percentage of positive responses among the respective groups.[10]

Table 4 indicates support of all three hypotheses. The finding on integrated housewives and husbands is enigmatic in that earlier comparisons revealed no significant difference. An attempt to amplify it is made in a later section.

Quite interesting is the way in which respondents phrased their responses to the question on feelings toward the white tenants. Many made some reference to intergroup contacts; this percentage distribution is: integrated wives, 71 percent; integrated husbands, 41 percent; segregated wives, 39 percent; and segregated husbands, 8 percent.

Both cross-project and husband-wife comparisons are significant at the 1 percent level. The difference between segregated spouses was unexpected in that no significant difference was observed between these groups on intergroup feelings, Perhaps the greater tendency for segregated wives to experience neighborly contacts played some role in this unanticipated finding.

ORIENTATION TO ACTION

The hypotheses were tested on orientation to action by comparing the percentage of the respective groups indorsing the integrated housing arrangement (Table 5).

Table 5 supports hypothesis 1 as to orientations to action only for husbands. While in the expected direction, the difference between house-

TABLE 4

Pattern of Occupancy and Responses to Questions on How Negro Tenants Felt about White Tenants*

(Percent)

	Husbands		Housewives	
Response	Integrated ($n=32$)	Segregated ($n=36$)	Integrated ($n=35$)	Segregated ($n=41$)
Positive	59	39	31	44
Neutral and negative	41	61	9	56

* Critical ratio between husbands significant at .05 levels; between wives and between integrated spouses significant at .01 level; between segregated spouses not significant.

[10] Intercoder agreement when the two categories, "positive" and "neutral-negative," were employed was perfect.

TABLE 5

Pattern on Occupancy and Desirability of Living in an Integrated
or Segregated Project*
(Percent)

	Husbands		Housewives	
Project Indorsed	Integrated ($n=32$)	Segregated ($n=36$)	Integrated ($n=35$)	Segregated ($n=41$)
Integrated	91	69	86	76
Segregated	9	31	14	24

* Critical ratio between husbands significant at .02 level; between wives and between spouses not significant.

TABLE 6

Significance Levels for Contact and Prejudice

Comparison	Percent
Wives	
Attitudes	.05
Feelings	.05
Action	.10
Husbands	
Attitudes	.05
Feelings	.05
Action	.10

wives fails to achieve significance. The husband-wife comparisons refute hypothesis 2 but support hypothesis 3. A slight contradiction is indicated in the case of hypothesis 2; however, the difference is small and well within the range of chance.

CONTACT AND PREJUDICE

So far we have approached the prejudice-interaction hypothesis indirectly, by relating pattern of occupancy to intergroup contact, then relating the former to intergroup prejudice. Because of a number of tenants on the segregated side of the project experienced some interracial contact, contrary to expectations, it is possible to examine directly the relationship between it and intergroup prejudice. This can be done by combining the response of both integrated and segregated tenants and cross-tabulating contact with each measure of the dependent variable (Table 6). The differences on contact and attitudes and contact and feelings are significant at the .05 level. Cross-tabulations of contact and disposition to action, while in the expected direction, failed to reach significance. In retrospect, the question arises whether, perhaps, the technique employed in sampling orientations to action was not the strongest. We erroneously expected an appreciable number of segregated tenants to indorse the segregated housing arrangement. Apparently, this was unrealistic. Indorsement of the segregated housing pattern would be tantamount to rejection of first-class citizenship and many of the privileges which go with it. A stronger test might have sampled areas of action where making a choice would not deny rights and privileges to the individual.

While not all specific hypotheses were substantiated, the data as a whole appear to support the general hypothesis.

Of the hypotheses which failed to receive confirmation, those between integrated spouses are the most disturbing. We speculated that the reason these hypotheses failed to receive confirmation was that the wives discussed their neighborly contacts with their husbands, thus causing some of their own benefit to "rub off" on to the latter. This does not explain, however, a significant difference between integrated spouses on feelings. Perhaps it is less difficult to influence attitudes and dispositions to act than it is to influence feelings: studies suggest that children acquire outgroup stereotypes long before they acquire the feelings appropriate to them. In addition, many southern schools have been desegregated without prior or simultaneous modification of intergroup feelings. An alternative explanation is that the integrated husbands, because of their greater education, were more readily inclined to less stereotyped and more positive orientations to action.

If the former explanation is valid, it suggests that outgroup prejudice is reduced not only through intimate intergroup contacts of those of equal status, but also through contact with members of the ingroup who themselves experienced such contacts. This is similar to the way outgroup prejudice is acquired. Moreover, it is consistent with observations that individuals belonging to the same social group tend to have similar opinions despite differences in their first-hand observations or knowledge of the facts.

34

The Functions of Racial Conflict*

JOSEPH S. HIMES**

NORTH CAROLINA COLLEGE

W HEN ONE CONTEMPLATES THE CONTEMPORARY AMERICAN SCENE, HE MAY be appalled by the picture of internal conflict portrayed in the daily news. The nation is pictured as torn by dissension over Vietnam policy. The people are reported being split by racial strife that periodically erupts into open violence. Organized labor and management are locked in a perennial struggle that occasionally threatens the well-being of the society. The reapportionment issue has forced the ancient rural-urban conflict into public view. Religious denominations and faiths strive against ancient conflicts of theology and doctrine toward unification and ecumenism. Big government is joined in a continuing struggle against big industry, big business, big finance, and big labor on behalf of the "public interest."

The image created by such reports is that of a society "rocked," "split" or "torn" by its internal conflicts. The repetition of such phrases and the spotlighting of conflict suggest that the integration, if not the very existence of the society is threatened. It is thus implied, and indeed often stated that the elimination of internal conflict is the central problem for policy and action in the society.

These preliminary remarks tend to indicate that there is widespread popular disapproval of social conflict. In some quarters the absence of conflict is thought to signify the existence of social harmony and stability. According to the human relations theme, conflict, aggression, hostility, antagonism and such devisive motives and behaviors are regarded as social heresies and therefore to be avoided. Often the word conflict is associated with images of violence and destruction.

At the same time, in contemporary sociology the problem of social conflict has been largely neglected. As Coser, Dahrendorf and others have pointed out, this tendency issues from preoccupation with models of social structure and theories of equilibrium.[1] Conflicts are treated as strains, tensions or stresses of social structures and regarded as pathological. Little attention is devoted to the investigation of conflict as a functional social process.

* Reprinted by permission of the University of North Carolina Press from *Social Forces*, 45 (September, 1966), pp. 1-10.

** Presidential address delivered at the annual meeting of the Southern Sociological Society, New Orleans, April 8, 1966. I am indebted to Professors Ernest Borinski, Lewis A. Coser, Hylan G. Lewis, and Robin M. Williams, Jr., for their critical reading of this manuscript.

[1] Lewis A. Coser, *The Functions of Social Conflict* (Glencoe, Illinois: The Free Press, 1956), p. 20; Ralf Dahrendorf, *Class and Class Conflict in Industrial Society* (Stanford: Stanford University Press, 1959), chap. 5.

However, some of the earlier sociologists employed social conflict as one central element of their conceptual systems. Theory and analysis were cast in terms of a process model. Conflict was viewed as natural and as functioning as an integrative force in society.

To Ludwig Gumplowicz and Gustav Ratzenhofer conflict was the basic social process, while for Lester F. Ward and Albion W. Small it was one of the basic processes. Sumner, Ross, and Cooley envisaged conflict as one of the major forces operating to lace human society together.[2] Park and Burgess employed social conflict as one of the processual pillars of their sociological system.[3]

At bottom, however, the two analytic models of social organization are really not inconsistent. Dahrendorf argues that consensus-structure and conflict-process are "the two faces of society."[4] That is, social integration results simultaneously from both consensus of values and coercion to compliance. Indeed, in the present study it is observed that the two sources of social integration are complementary and mutually supporting.

Coser has led the revival of sociological attention to the study of social conflict. In this task he has injected the very considerable contributions of the German sociologist Georg Simmel into the stream of American sociological thought. Ralf Dahrendorf, among others, has made further substantial contributions to the sociology of social conflict. One latent consequence of this development has been to sensitize some sociologists to conflict as a perspective from which to investigate race relations. Thus race relations have been called "power relations" and it has been proposed that research should be cast in terms of a "conflict model."[5] This approach is consistent with Blumer's thesis that race prejudice is "a sense of group position" and that empirical study involves "a concern with the relationship of racial groups."[6]

In the present discussion the term racial conflict is used in a restricted and specific sense.[7] By racial conflict is meant rational organized overt

[2] William Graham Sumner, *Folkways* (Boston: Ginn, 1906); Edward Alsworth Ross, *The Principles of Sociology* (New York: Century, 1920); Charles Horton Cooley, *Social Progress* (New York: Charles Scribner's Sons, 1918), and *Social Organization* (New York: Charles Scribner's Sons, 1909).

[3] Robert E. Park and Ernest W. Burgess, *Introduction to the Science of Sociology* (Chicago: University of Chicago Press, 1924).

[4] Dahrendorf, *op. cit.*, pp. 157–165. Arthur I. Wastow makes the same point in his concepts of "church," state," and "government" as models of social integration. See *From Race Riot to Sit-In, 1919 and the 1960s: A Study in the Connections Between Conflict and Violence* (New York: Doubleday & Co., 1966).

[5] Lewis M. Killian and Charles M. Grigg, *Racial Crisis in America* (Englewood Cliffs, New Jersey: Prentice-Hall, 1964), p. 18 ff.; H. M. Blalock, Jr., "A Power Analysis of Racial Discrimination," *Social Forces*, 39 (October 1960), pp. 53–59; Ernst Borinski, "The Sociology of Coexistence—Conflict in Social and Political Power Systems," unpublished, pp. 6–7; Wilson Record, *Race and Radicalism* (Ithaca: Cornell University Press, 1964); Ernst Borinski, "The Litigation Curve and the Litigation Filibuster in Civil Rights Cases," *Social Forces*, 37 (December 1958), pp. 142–147.

[6] Herbert Blumer, "Race Prejudices as a Sense of Group Position," in J. Masuka and Preston Valien (eds.), *Race Relations* (Chapel Hill: The University of North Carolina Press, 1961), p. 217.

[7] In much authoritative literature the concept conflict in racial relations is used in

action by Negroes, initiating demands for specific social goals, and utilizing collective sanctions to enforce these demands. By definition, the following alternative forms of conflict behavior are excluded from the field of analysis.

1. The aggressive or exploitative actions of dominant groups and individuals toward minority groups or individuals.

2. Covert individual antagonisms or affective compensatory or reflexive aggressions, and

3. Spontaneous outbursts or nonrationalized violent behavior.

As here treated, racial conflict involves some rational assessment of both means and ends, and therefore is an instance of what Lewis Coser has called "realistic conflict."[8] Because of the calculating of means and ends, racial conflict is initiating action. It is a deliberate collective enterprise to achieve predetermined social goals. Of necessity, conflict includes a conscious attack upon an overtly defined social abuse.

Merton has pointed out that groups sometimes resort to culturally tabooed means to achieve culturally prescribed ends.[9] Under such circumstances one might assume that if legitimate means were available, they would be employed. But, Vander Zanden has observed, "Non-violent resistance is a tactic well suited to struggles in which a minority lacks access to major sources of power within a society and to the instruments of violent coercion."[10] He goes on to add that, "within the larger American society the Negro's tactic of non-violent resistance has gained a considerable degree of legitimacy."[11] Three principal manifestations of Negro behavior fit this definition of racial conflict.

1. Legal redress, or the calculated use of court action to achieve and sanction specific group goals. Legal redress has been used most often and successfully in the achievement of voting rights, educational opportunities and public accommodations.

2. Political action, or the use of voting, bloc voting and lobby techniques to achieve legislative and administrative changes and law enforcement.

3. Non-violent mass action, or organized collective participation in overt activity involving pressure and public relations techniques to enforce specific demands.

This paper examines some of the social functions of conflict as here defined. It is asked: Does realistic conflict by Negroes have any system-maintaining and system-enhancing consequences for the larger American society? To this question at least four affirmative answers can be given.

---

various other ways. See for example, George Simpson and J. Milton Yinger, *Racial and Cultural Minorities* (New York: Harper & Row, 1965), chap. 4; Killian and Grigg, *op. cit.*; Leonard Broom and Norval D. Glenn, *Transformation of the Negro American* New York: Harper & Row, 1965), esp. chaps. 3 and 4.

[8] Coser, *op. cit.*, pp. 48–55.

[9] Robert K. Merton, *Social Theory and Social Structure* (Glencoe, Illinois: The Free Press, 1957), pp. 123–149.

[10] James W. Vander Zanden, "The Non-Violent Resistance Movement Against Segregation," *American Journal of Sociology*, 68 (March 1963), p. 544.

[11] *Ibid.*, p. 544.

Realistic racial conflict (1) alters the social structure, (2) enhances social communication, (3) extends social solidarity and (4) facilitates personal identity. Because of space and time limitations, considerations of societal dysfunctions and goal achievements are omitted.

STRUCTURAL FUNCTIONS

H. M. Blalock has noted that within the American social structure race relations are power relations.[12] Thus, realistic social conflict is an enterprise in the calculated mobilization and application of social power to sanction collective demands for specific structural changes. Yet, because of minority status, Negroes have only limited access to the sources of social power. Robert Bierstedt has identified numbers, resources and organization as leading sources of power.[13] Of these categories, resources which Bierstedt specifies as including money, prestige, property and natural and supernatural phenomena, are least accessible to Negroes.

Perforce then, realistic racial conflict specializes in the mobilization of numbers and organization as accessible sources of power. Thus a boycott mobilizes and organizes numbers of individuals to withhold purchasing power. A demonstration organizes and mobilizes numbers of individuals to tap residual moral sentiments and to generate public opinion. Voter registration and bloc voting mobilize and organize numbers of citizens to influence legislative and administrative processes. Legal redress and lobby techniques mobilize organization to activate legal sanctions or the legislative process.

The application of mobilized social power in realistic racial conflict tends to reduce the power differential between actors, to restrict existing status differences, and to alter the directionality of social interaction. First, in conflict situations, race relations are defined unequivocally in power terms. Sentimentality and circumlocution are brushed aside. The power dimension is brought into central position in the structure of interaction. The differential between conflict partners along this dimension is thus reduced. The power advantage of the dominant group is significantly limited. In this connection and perhaps only in this connection, it may be correct to liken embattled Negroes and resisting whites to "armed camps."

Second, alteration of the power dimension of interracial structure tends to modify status arrangements. In the traditional racial structure, discrimination and segregation cast whites and Negroes in rigid and separate orders of superiority and inferiority. The limited and stylized intergroup contacts are confined to a rigid and sterile etiquette. However, in realistic conflict initiating actors assume, for they must, a status coordinate with that of the opposition.[14]

Status coordination is one evident consequence of power equalization.

---

12 Blalock, *op. cit.*, pp. 53–59.

13 Robert Bierstedt, "An Analysis of Social Power," *American Sociological Review*, 15 (December 1950), pp. 730–738. Bierstedt argues that numbers and organization as sources of social power are ineffectual without access to resources.

14 Thomas F. Pettigrew, *A Profile of the Negro American* (Princeton: D. Van Nostrand Co., 1964), p. 167.

Moreover, it is patently impossible to make demands and to sanction them while acting from the position of a suppliant. That is, the very process of realistic conflict functions to define adversaries in terms of self-conception as status equals. Martin Luther King perceives this function of realistic conflict in the following comment on the use of non-violent action and deliberately induced tension.[15]

Non-violent direct action seeks to create such a crisis and foster such a tension that a community which has constantly refused to negotiate is forced to confront the issue. It seeks so to dramatize the issue that it can no longer be ignored.

That is, social power is used to bring interactors into status relations where issues can be discussed, examined and compromised. There are no suppliants or petitioners and no condescending controllers in a negotiation relationship. By the very nature of the case, interactors occupy equal or approximately equal positions of both status and strength.

Third, power equalization and status coordination affect the interactional dimension of social structure. The up and down flow of interaction between super- and subordinates tends to level out in relations between positional equals. That is, rational demands enforced by calculated sanctions cannot be forced into the molds of supplication and condescension.

The leveling out of social interaction is inherent in such realistic conflict mechanisms as sit-ins, freedom rides, bloc voting, voter registration campaigns and boycotts. Thus, for example, the interruption of social interaction in a boycott implies an assumption of status equality and the leveling of interaction. The relationship that is interrupted is the up and down pattern inherent in the status structure of inequality. No relationship is revealed as preferable to the pattern of supplication and condescension. Whether such structural functions of realistic conflict become institutionalized in the larger social system will depend on the extent of goal achievement of the total Negro revolution. That is, structural consequences of conflict may be institutionalized through the desegregation and nondiscrimination of education, employment, housing, recreation and the like. Changes in these directions will provide system-relevant roles under terms of relatively coordinate status and power not only for the conflict participants, but also for many other individuals. Developments in these directions will also be influenced by many factors and trends apart from the process of realistic racial conflict.

We may now summarize the argument regarding the structural functions of realistic racial conflict in a series of propositions. Realistic conflict postulates race relations as power relations and undertakes to mobilize and apply the social power that is accessible to Negroes as a minority group.

In conflict, the traditional interracial structure is modified along three dimensions. The power differential between interactors is reduced; status differentials are restricted; and social interaction tends to level out in di-

15 Martin Luther King, *Why We Can't Wait* (New York: Harper & Row, 1963), p. 81.

rectionality. Whether these structural consequences of realistic conflict become institutionalized in the general social system will depend on the extent and duration of goal achievement in the larger social structure.

COMMUNICATIONAL FUNCTIONS

It is widely claimed that Negro aggression interrupts or reduces interracial communication. Whites and Negroes are thought to withdraw in suspicion and hostility from established practices of communication. The so-called "normal" agencies and bridges of intergroup contact and communication are believed to become inoperative. Such a view of conflict envisages Negroes and whites as hostile camps eyeing each other across a "no man's land" of antagonism and separation.

It is true that racial conflict tends to interrupt and reduce traditional communication between whites and Negroes. But traditional interracial communication assumes that communicators occupy fixed positions of superiority and inferiority, precludes the consideration of certain significant issues, and confines permitted interchanges to a rigid and sterile etiquette. "The Negro," write Killian and Grigg, "has always been able to stay in communication with the white man and gain many favors from him, so long as he approached him as a suppliant and as an inferior, and not as a conflict partner."[16]

It will be evident that intergroup communication under such structural conditions is both restricted in content and asymmetrical in form. However, our analysis indicates that realistic conflict functions to correct these distortions of content and form and to extend the communication process at the secondary mass media level.

First, realistic racial conflict heightens the individual level and extends the social range of attention to racial matters. Individuals who have by long custom learned to see Negroes only incidentally as part of the standard social landscape, are brought up sharply and forced to look at them in a new light. Persons who have been oblivious to Negroes are abruptly and insistently confronted by people and issues which they can neither avoid nor brush aside. Many individuals for the first time perceive Negroes as having problems, characteristics and aspirations that were never before recognized, nor at least so clearly recognized. Racial conflict thus rudely destroys what Gunnar Myrdal aptly called the "convenience of ignorance."[17]

In *Freedom Summer*, Sally Belfrage gives a graphic personal illustration of the attention-arresting function of realistic racial conflict.[18] In the most crowded and hottest part of an afternoon the daughter of one of Greenwood's (Mississippi) leading families walked into the civil rights headquarters. In a lilting southern voice she asked to everybody in general: "I jus' wanted to know what y'all are up to over here."

At the same time the "race problem" is brought into the focus of col-

[16] Killian and Grigg, *op. cit.*, p. 7.
[17] Gunnar Myrdal, *An American Dilemma* (New York: Harper & Bros., 1944), pp. 40–42.
[18] Sally Belfrage, *Freedom Summer* (New York: The Viking Press, 1965), p. 48.

lective attention by realistic conflict. Negroes as well as their problems and claims insist upon having both intensive and extensive consideration. To support this contention one has only to consider the volume of scientific, quasi-scientific and popular literature, the heavy racial loading of the mass media, and the vast number of organizations and meetings that are devoted to the racial issue.

Further, realistic racial conflict tends to modify both the cognitive and effective content of interracial communication. Under terms of conflict whites and Negroes can no longer engage in the exchange of standardized social amenities regarding safe topics within the protection of the status structure and the social etiquette. Communication is made to flow around substantive issues and the calculated demands of Negroes. Communication is about something that has real meaning for the communicators. It makes a difference that they communicate. In fact, under terms of realistic conflict it is no longer possible to avoid communicating. Thus Martin Luther King argued that non-violent mass action is employed to create such crisis and tension that a community which has refused to negotiate is forced to confront the issue.[19]

In conflict the effective character of communication becomes realistic. The communicators infuse their exchanges of recognition meanings with the feelings that, within the traditional structure, were required to be suppressed and avoided. That Negroes are permitted, indeed often expected to reveal the hurt and humiliation and anger that they formerly were required to bottle up inside. Many white people thus were shocked to discover that the "happy" Negroes whom they "knew" so well were in fact discontented and angry people.

Thus the cognitive-affective distortion of traditional interracial communication is in some measure at least corrected. The flow of understanding and affection that was permitted and encouraged is balanced by normal loading of dissension and hostility. The relationship thus reveals a more symmetrical character of content and form.

Finally, attrition of primary contacts between unequals within the traditional structure and etiquette is succeeded, in part at least, by an inclusive dialogue at the secondary communication level. The drama of conflict and the challenges of leaders tend to elevate the racial issue in the public opinion arena. The mass media respond by reporting and commenting on racial events in great detail. Thus millions of otherwise uninformed or indifferent individuals are drawn into the public opinion process which Ralph H. Turner and Lewis M. Killian have analyzed as defining and redefining the issue and specifying and solving the problem.[20]

Much obvious evidence reveals the secondary communication dialogue. Since 1954 a voluminous scientific, quasi-scientific and popular literature on the race issue has appeared. Further evidence is found in the heavy racial loading of newspapers, magazines, television and radio broadcast-

[19] King, op. cit., p. 81.
[20] Ralph H. Turner and Lewis M. Killian, Collective Behavior (Englewood Cliffs, New Jersey: Prentice-Hall 1957), chaps. 11 and 12.

ing and the motion pictures. The race problem has been the theme of numerous organizations and meetings at all levels of power and status. From such evidence it would seem reasonable to conclude that few if any Americans have escaped some degree of involvement in the dialogue over the race issue.

We may now summarize the argument briefly. Realistic racial conflict tends to reduce customary interracial communication between status unequals regarding trivial matters within the established communication etiquette. On the other hand, conflict tends to extend communication regarding significant issues with genuine feelings and with noncustomary structures and situations. At the secondary level both the volume of communication and the number of communicators are greatly increased by realistic conflict. These observations would seem to warrant the conclusion that communication within the general social system is extended by realistic racial conflict.

SOLIDARITY FUNCTIONS

A corollary of the claim that racial conflict interrupts communication is the assertion that conflict also is seriously, perhaps even radically disunifying. Struggles between Negroes and whites are thought to split the society and destroy social solidarity. It is at once evident that such a claim implies the prior existence of a unified or relatively unified biracial system. Notwithstanding difference of status and condition, the racial sectors are envisaged as joined in the consensus and structure of the society.

A judicious examination of the facts suggests that the claim that racial conflict is seriously, perhaps even radically disunifying is not altogether correct. On the one hand, the image of biracial solidarity tends to be exaggerated. On the other, realistic racial conflict serves some important unifying functions within the social system.

As Logan Wilson and William Kolb have observed, the consensus of the society is organized around a core of "ultimate values."[21] "In our own society," they assert, "we have developed such ultimate values as the dignity of the individual, equality of opportunity, the right of life, liberty, and the pursuit of happiness, and the growth of the free personality."

Far from rejecting or challenging these ultimate values, the ideological thrust of realistic racial conflict affirms them.[22] That is, the ultimate values of the society constitute starting points of ideology and action in racial conflict. As Wilson Record and others have observed, Negro protest and improvement movements are thoroughly American in assumption and objectives.[23]

This fact creates an interesting strategic dilemma for the White Citizens Councils, the resurgent Ku Klux Klan and similar manifestations of the so-called "white backlash." The ideology of racial conflict has preempted the traditional high ground of the core values and ultimate moral-

---

[21] Logan Wilson and William L. Kolb, *Sociological Analysis* (New York: Harcourt, Brace & Co., 1949), p. 513.

[22] Pettigrew, *op. cit.*, p. 193.

[23] Record, *op. cit.*; Pettigrew, *op. cit.*; Broom and Glenn, *op. cit.*

ity. The reactionary groups are thus left no defensible position within the national ethos from which to mount their attacks.

One consequence of realistic racial conflict, then, is to bring the core values of the society into sharp focus and national attention. People are exhorted, even forced to think about the basic societal tenets and to consider their meaning and applications. A dynamic force is thus joined to latent dedication in support of the unifying values of the society. Thus, as Coser has observed, far from being altogether disunifying, realistic conflict functions to reaffirm the core and unifying values of the society.[24] In other words the "two faces of society" are seen to be complementary and mutually supporting.

The primacy of core values in realistic racial conflict is revealed in many ways. Martin Luther King places the ultimate values of the society at the center of his theoretic system of non-violent mass action.[25] In his "Letter from Birmingham Jail" he refers to "justice," "freedom," "understanding," "brotherhood," "constitutional rights," "promise of democracy" and "truth." See how he identifies the goal of racial freedom with the basic societal value of freedom. "We will reach the goal of freedom in Birmingham and all over the nation, because the goal of America is freedom."[26]

One impact of realistic racial conflict is upon interpretation of core values and the means of their achievement. Thus, the issue is not whether or not men shall be free and equal, but whether these values are reserved to white men or are applicable to Negroes as well. Or again, the phrases "gradualism" and "direct action" depict an important point of disagreement over means to universally affirmed ends. But, it may be observed that when men agree on the ends of life, their quarrels are not in themselves disunifying.

Further, the very process of realistic racial conflict is intrinsically functional. Participants in the conflict are united by the process of struggle itself. The controversy is a unique and shared social possession. It fills an interactional vacuum maintained in the traditional structure by limited social contacts and alienation.

At the same time, as Coser has argued, a relationship established by conflict may lead in time to other forms of interaction.[27] It is conceivable that Negroes and whites who today struggle over freedom and justice and equality may tomorrow be joined in cooperation in the quest of these values.

Conflict is also unifying because the object of struggle is some social value that both parties to the conflict wish to possess or enjoy. The struggle tends to enhance the value and to reveal its importance to both actors. A new area of consensus is thus defined or a prior area of agreement is enlarged. For example, that Negroes and whites struggle through realistic

[24] Coser, op. cit., pp. 127–128.
[25] King, op. cit., pp. 77–100.
[26] Ibid., p. 97.
[27] Coser, op. cit., pp. 121–122.

conflict for justice or freedom or equality tends to clarify these values for both and join them in the consensus regarding their importance.

"Simultaneously," as Vander Zander observes, "within the larger American society the Negro's tactic of non-violent resistance has gained a considerable degree of legitimacy."[28] That is, conflict itself has been defined as coming within the arena of morally justifiable social action. The means as well as the ends, then, are enveloped within the national ethos and serve to enhance societal solidarity. In this respect realistic racial conflict, like labor-management conflict, tends to enter the "American way of life" and constitutes another point of social integration.

Many years ago Edward Alsworth Ross pointed out that nonradical conflicts may function to "sew" the society together.[29]

Every species of conflicts interferes with every other species in society . . . save only when lines of cleavage coincide; in which case they reinforce one another. . . . A society, therefore, which is ridden by a dozen oppositions along lines running in every direction may actually be in less danger of being torn with violence or falling to pieces than one split just along one line. For each new cleavage contributes to narrow the cross-clefts, so that one might say that society is sewn together by its inner conflicts.

In this sewing function, realistic racial conflict is interwoven with political, religious, regional, rural-urban, labor-management, class and the other persistent threads of struggle that characterize the American social fabric. What is decisive is the fact that variously struggling factions are united in the consensus of the ultimate societal values. The conflicts are therefore nonradical, crisscrossing and tend to mitigate each other.

The proposition on the solidarity function of realistic racial conflict can now be formulated briefly. The claims that racial conflict is disruptive of social solidarity, though partially true, tends to obscure other important consequences. Conflict not only projects the combatants into the social consensus; it also acts to reaffirm the ultimate values around which the consensus is organized. Moreover, conflict joins opposing actors in meaning interaction for ends, whose importance is a matter of further agreement. From this perspective and within a context of multifarious crisscrossing threads of opposition, realistic racial conflict is revealed as helping to "sew" the society together around its underlying societal consensus. We now turn to a consideration of certain social-psychological consequences of realistic racial conflict.

[28] Vander Zanden, *op. cit.*, p. 544.
[29] Ross, *op. cit.*, pp. 164–165. Dahrendorf, *op. cit.*, pp. 213–215, argues that conflicts tend to become "superimposed," thus threatening intensification. "Empirical evidence shows," he writes, "that different conflicts may be, and often are, superimposed in given historical societies, so that the multitude of possible conflict fronts is reduced to a few dominant conflicts . . . If this is the case, (class) conflicts of different associations appear superimposed; i.e., the opponents of one association meet again—with different titles, perhaps, but in identical relations—in another association." (Pp. 213–214.) Such an argument, however, fails to recognize that conflicts may superimpose along religious, regional, ethnic or other fronts and thus mitigate the strength of the class superimposition.

IDENTITY FUNCTIONS

The fact is often overlooked that realistic racial conflict permits many Negroes to achieve a substantial measure of identity within the American social system. This function of racial conflict is implied in the foregoing analyses of communication and solidarity. However, the analysis of the identity function of racial conflict begins with a consideration of the alienation of the American Negro people. Huddled into urban and rural slums and concentrated in menial and marginal positions in the work force, Negroes are relegated to inferior and collateral statuses in the social structure. Within this structural situation discrimination prevents their sharing in the valued possessions of the society. Legal and customary norms of segregation exclude them from many meaningful contacts and interactions with members of the dominant group.

Isolated and inferior, Negro people searched for the keys to identity and belonging. The social forces that exclude them from significant participation in the general society also keep them disorganized. Thus identity, the feeling of belonging and the sense of social purpose, could be found neither in membership in the larger society nor in participation in a cohesive racial group. Generation after generation of Negroes live out their lives in fruitless detachment and personal emptiness. In another place the alienation of Negro teenagers has been described as follows.[30]

The quality of Negro teenage culture is conditioned by four decisive factors: race, inferiority, deprivation and youthfulness. Virtually every experience of the Negro teenager is filtered through this complex qualifying medium; every act is a response to a distorted perception of the world. His world is a kind of nightmare, the creation of a carnival reflection chamber. The Negro teenager's culture, his customary modes of behavior, constitute his response to the distorted, frightening, and cruel world that he perceives with the guileless realism of youth.

Yet the search for identity goes on. It takes many forms. In the Negro press and voluntary organizations it is reflected in campaigns for race pride and race loyalty. One sector of the Negro intelligentsia invented the "Negro history movement" as a device to create a significant past for a "historyless" people. For the unlettered and unwashed masses the church is the prime agent of group cohesion and identity. The National Association for the Advancement of Colored People and other militant organizations provide an ego-enhancing rallying point for the emancipated and the aggressive. The cult of Negro business, escapist movements like Father Divine's Heaven, and nationalist movements like Marcus Garvey's Universal Negro Improvement Association, and the Black Muslims provide still other arenas for the Negro's search for identity.

Despite this variegated panorama of effort and search, the overriding experience of Negroes remains isolation, inferiority and the ineluctable sense of alienation. Whether involved in the search or not, or perhaps just

[30] Joseph S. Himes, "Negro Teen Age Culture," *Annals*, 338 (November 1961), pp. 92–93.

because of such involvement, individuals see themselves as existing outside the basic American social system. Vander Zanden puts it this way: "By virtue of his membership in the Negro group, the Negro suffers considerably in terms of self-esteem and has every incentive for self-hatred."[31] Thus self-conception reflects and in turn supports social experience in a repetition of the familiar self-fulfilling prophecy.

In this situation, collective conflict had an almost magical although unanticipated effect upon group cohesion and sense of identity among Negroes. Group struggle, as Coser and others have pointed out, functions to enhance group solidarity and to clarify group boundaries.[32] The separations among collective units are sharpened and the identity of groups within a social system is established. In the course of conflict collective aims are specified, defined and communicated. Cadres of leaders emerge in a division of labor that grows clearer and more definite. Individuals tend to find niches and become polarized around the collective enterprise. All participants are drawn closer together, both for prosecution of the struggle and for common defense.

As the racial conflict groups become more cohesive and organized, the boundaries with other groups within the American social system become clearer. The distinction between member and nonmember is sharpened. Individuals who stood indecisively between groups or outside the fray are induced or forced to take sides. The zones of intergroup ambiguity diminish. Internally, the conflict groups become more tightly unified and the positions of members are clarified and defined more precisely.

Further, conflict facilitates linkage between the individual and his local reference group as the agent of conflict. The individual thus achieves both a "commitment"[33] and a "role" as a quasi-official group representative in the collective struggle. Pettigrew writes:[34]

Consider the Student Non-Violent Coordinating Committee (SNICK), . . . The group is cohesive, highly regarded by Negro youth, and dedicated entirely to achieving both personal and societal racial change. Recruits willingly and eagerly devote themselves to the group's goals. And they find themselves systematically rewarded by SNICK for violating the 'Negro' role in every particular. They are expected to evince strong racial pride, to assert their full rights as citizens, to face jail and police brutality unhesitatingly for the cause. . . . Note, . . . that these expected and rewarded actions all publicly commit the member to the group and its aims.

In the general racial conflict system individuals may act as leaders, organizers and specialists. Some others function as sit-inners, picketers, boycotters, demonstrators, voter registration solicitors, etc. Many others, re-

---

[31] Vander Zanden, *op. cit.*, p. 546.

[32] Coser, *op. cit.*, p. 34.

[33] Amitai Etzioni employs the concept "commitment" to designate one dimension of cohesiveness and operational effectiveness in complex organizations. See his *Complex Organizations: A Sociological Reader* (New York: Henry Holt Co., 1961), p. 187; and *A Comparative Study of Complex Organization* (Glencoe, Illinois: The Free Press, 1961), pp. 8-22.

[34] Pettigrew, *op. cit.*, pp. 165–166.

moved from the areas of overt conflict, participate secondarily or vicariously as financial contributors, audience members, mass media respondents, verbal applauders, etc.

In the interactive process of organized group conflict self-involvement is the opposite side of the coin of overt action. Actors become absorbed by ego and emotion into the group and the group is projected through their actions. This linkage of individual and group in ego and action is the substance of identity.

Paradoxically, the personal rewards of participation in conflict groups tend to support and facilitate the larger conflict organization and process. Edward Shils and Morris Janowitz have noted this fact in the functions of primary groups in the German Army in World War II.[35] That is, for the individual actor the sense of identity is grounded and sustained by gratification of important personal needs.

In the case of realistic racial conflict, group-based identity functions to facilitate sociopsychic linkage between the individual and the inclusive social system. It was shown above that racial conflict is socially unifying in at least two ways. First, the conflict ideology identifies parties to the conflict with the core values of the social heritage. Thus sit-inners, and demonstrators and boycotters and all the others in the drama of racial conflict conceive themselves as the latter-day warriors for the freedom, justice and equality and the other moral values that are historically and essentially American. For many Negroes the sense of alienation is dispelled by a new sense of significance and purpose. The self-image of these embattled Negroes is consequently significantly enhanced.

Second, the conflict process draws organized Negroes into significant social interaction within the inclusive social system. Some of the crucial issues and part of the principal business of the society engage Negroes of all localities and stations in life. Though often only vicariously and by projection, life acquires a new meaning and quality for even the poorest ghetto dweller and meanest sharecropper. The sense of alienation is diminished and the feeling of membership in the inclusive society is enhanced.

We may now formulate the argument as follows. Intense alienation kept alive the Negro's quest for identity and meaning. Miraculously almost, realistic racial conflict with its ideological apparatus and action system functions to alleviate alienation and to facilitate identity. Conflict enhances group solidarity, clarifies group boundaries and strengthens the individual-group linkage through ego-emotion commitment and overt action. In-group identity is extended to the larger social system through the extension of communication, the enlargement of the network of social interactions and ideological devotion to national core values. It may be said, then, that through realistic racial conflict America gains some new Americans.

---

[35] Edward A. Shils and Morris Janowitz, "Cohesion and Disintegration in the Wehrmacht in World War II," *Public Opinion Quarterly*, 12 (Summer 1948), p. 281.

A Selected Bibliography on
Black Responses to White Reactions

Barbour, Floyd B. (editor), *The Black Power Revolt* (Boston: Porter Sargent, 1968).

Bell, Inge P., *CORE and the Strategy of Nonviolence* (New York: Random House, 1968).

Bennett, Lerone, Jr., *Confrontation: Black and White* (Baltimore: Penguin Books, 1966).

Berkowitz, Leonard, "The Study of Urban Violence: Some Implications of Laboratory Studies of Frustration and Aggression," in Louis H. Masotti and Don R. Bowen (editors), *Riots and Rebellion* (Beverly Hills: Sage Publications, 1968).

Bloombaum, Milton, "The Conditions Underlying Race Riots as Portrayed by Multidimensional Scalogram Analysis: A Reanalysis of Lieberson and Silverman's Data," *American Sociological Review*, 33 (February, 1968), pp. 76–91.

Brink, William, and Louis Harris, *Black and White: A Study of U.S. Racial Attitudes Today* (New York: Simon and Schuster, 1967).

Brink, William, and Louis Harris, *The Negro Revolution in America* (New York: Simon and Schuster, 1964).

Broom, Leonard, and Norval D. Glenn, *Transformation of the Negro American* (New York: Harper, 1965).

Carmichael, Stokely, and Charles V. Hamilton, *Black Power: The Politics of Liberation in America* (New York: Random House, 1967).

Clark, Kenneth B., *Dark Ghetto* (New York: Harper, 1965).

Clark, Kenneth B., "The Civil Rights Movement: Momentum and Organization," *Daedalus*, 95 (Winter, 1966), pp. 239–267.

Clark, Kenneth B., and Mamie P. Clark, "Racial Identification and Preference in Negro Children," in Theodore M. Newcomb and E. L. Hartley (editors), *Readings in Social Psychology* (New York: Holt, 1947).

Cloward, Richard A., and Frances Fox Piven, "The Urban Crisis and the Consolidation of National Power," in *Urban Riots: Violence and Social Change* (New York: Academy of Political Science, 1968).

Coleman, A. Lee, "Race Relations and Developmental Change," *Social Forces*, 47 (Sept., 1967), pp. 1–8.

Cothran, Tilman C., "The Negro Protest against Segregation in the South," *Annals of the American Academy of Political and Social Science*, 357 (1965), pp. 65–73.

Cox, Oliver C., *Caste, Class and Race* (Garden City: Doubleday, 1948).

Cruse, Harold, *The Crisis of the Negro Intellectual* (New York: Morrow, 1967).

David, Stephen M., "Leadership of the Poor in Poverty Programs," in *Urban Riots: Violence and Social Change* (New York: Academy of Political Science, 1968).

Detroit Urban League, *A Survey of Attitudes of Detroit Negroes after the Riot of 1967* (Detroit, 1967).

Dollard, John, *Caste and Class in a Southern Town,* third edition (Garden City: Doubleday, 1957).

Drake, St. Clair, "Urban Violence and American Social Movements," in *Urban Riots: Violence and Social Change* (New York: Academy of Political Science, 1968).

Drake, St. Clair, and Horace R. Cayton, *Black Metropolis,* revised edition (New York: Harper, 1962).

Dynes, Russell and E. L. Quarentelli, "What Looting in Civil Disturbances Really Means," *Trans-action,* 5 (May, 1968), pp. 9–14.

Edwards, G. Franklin, "Community and Class Realities: The Ordeal of Change," *Daedalus,* 95 (Winter, 1966), pp. 1–23.

Essien-Udom, E. U., *Black Nationalism: A Search for Identity in America* (Chicago: University of Chicago Press, 1962).

Evans, E. S., "Ghetto Riots and City Politics," in Louis H. Masotti and Don R. Bowen (editors), *Riots and Rebellion* (Beverly Hills: Sage Publications, 1968).

Feagin, Joe R., "Social Sources of Support for Violence and Nonviolence in a Negro Ghetto," *Social Problems,* 15 (Spring, 1968), pp. 432–441.

Feagin, Joe R., and Paul B. Sheatsley, "Ghetto Resident Appraisals of a Riot," *Public Opinion Quarterly,* 32 (Fall, 1968), pp. 352–362.

Fichter, Joseph H., "American Religion and the Negro," *Daedalus,* 94 (Fall, 1965), pp. 1085–1106.

Fleming, Walter L., *Documentary History of Reconstruction* (New York: Peter Smith, 1950).

Franklin, John Hope, *From Slavery to Freedom: A History of American Negroes,* revised edition (New York: Knopf, 1956).

Franklin, John Hope, "The Two Worlds of Race: A Historical View," *Daedalus,* 94 (Fall, 1965), pp. 899–920.

Frazier, E. Franklin, *Black Bourgeoisie* (New York: Free Press, 1957).

Frazier, E. Franklin, *The Negro in the United States* (New York: Macmillan, 1949).

Frazier, E. Franklin, "The Negro Middle Class and Desegregation," *Social Problems,* 4 (April, 1957), pp. 291–301.

Gans, Herbert J., "The Ghetto Rebellions and Urban Class Conflict," in *Urban Riots: Violence and Social Change* (New York: Academy of Political Science, 1968).

Garfinkel, Herbert, *When Negroes March* (New York: Free Press, 1959).

Geschwender, James A., "Desegregation, the Educated Negro, and the Future of Social Protest in the South," *Sociological Inquiry,* 35 (1965), pp. 58–69.

Geschwender, James A., "Social Structure and the Negro Revolt: An Examination of Some Hypotheses," *Social Forces,* 43 (Dec., 1964), pp. 248–256.

Geschwender, James A., "Status Inconsistency, Social Isolation, and Individual Unrest," *Social Forces,* 46 (June, 1968), pp. 477–483.

Glenn, Norval D., "Negro Religion and Negro Status in the United States," in Louis Schneider (editor), *Religion, Culture and Society* (New York: Wiley, 1964).

Gossett, Thomas F., *Race: The History of an Idea in America* (Dallas: Southern Methodist University Press, 1963).

Griffin, John Howard, *Black Like Me* (New York: Signet Books, 1962).

Grimshaw, Allen D., "Lawlessness and Violence in the United States and Their Special Manifestations in Changing Negro-White Relationships," *Journal of Negro History*, 44 (1959), pp. 52–72.

Grimshaw, Allen D., "Three Views of Urban Violence: Civil Disturbance, Racial Revolt, Class Assault," in Louis H. Masotti and Don R. Bowen (editors), *Riots and Rebellion* (Beverly Hills: Sage Publications, 1968).

Grimshaw, Allen D., "Urban Racial Violence in the United States: Changing Ecological Considerations," *American Journal of Sociology*, 66 (Sept., 1960), pp. 109–119.

Grindstaff, Carl F., "The Negro, Urbanization, and Relative Deprivation in the Deep South," *Social Problems*, 15 (Winter, 1968), pp. 342–352.

Gunterman, Stanley E., "A Bibliography on Violence and Social Change," in *Urban Riots: Violence and Social Change* (New York: Academy of Political Science, 1968).

Howard, David H., "An Exploratory Study of Attitudes of Negro Professionals toward Competition with Whites," *Social Forces*, 45 (Sept., 1966), pp. 20–27.

Howard, John R., "The Making of a Black Muslim," *Trans-action*, 4 (Dec., 1966), pp. 15–21.

Hughes, Everett C., "Race Relations and the Sociological Imagination," *American Sociological Review*, 28 (Dec., 1963), pp. 879–890.

Isaacs, Harold R., *The New World of Negro Americans* (New York: John Day, 1963).

Johnson, David W., "Racial Attitudes of Negro Freedom School Participants and Negro and White Civil Rights Participants," *Social Forces*, 45 (Dec., 1966), pp. 266–273.

Johnson, Robert B., "Negro Reactions to Minority Group Status," in Milton L. Barron (editor), *American Minorities* (New York: Knopf, 1957).

Kardiner, Abram, and Lionel Ovesey, *The Mark of Oppression: Explorations in the Personality of the American Negro* (New York: Norton, 1951).

Karon, Bertram P., *The Negro Personality: A Rigorous Investigation of the Effects of Culture* (New York: Springer, 1958).

Katz, Irwin, "Review of Evidence Relating to Effects of Desegregation on the Intellectual Performance of Negroes," *American Psychologist*, 19 (1964), pp. 381–399.

Katz, Irwin, James M. Robinson, Edgar G. Epps, and Patricia Waly, "The Influence of Race of the Experimenter and Instructions upon the Expression of Hostility by Negro Boys," *Journal of Social Issues*, 20 (1964), pp. 54–60.

Katz, Shlomo (editor), *Negro and Jew* (New York: Macmillan, 1967).

Keech, William R., *The Impact of Negro Voting: The Role of the Vote in the Quest for Equality* (Chicago: Rand McNally, 1968).

Killian, Lewis M., *The Impossible Revolution? Black Power and the American Dream* (New York: Random House, 1968).

Killian, Lewis M., and Charles Grigg, *Racial Crisis in America: Leadership in Conflict* (Englewood Cliffs: Prentice-Hall, 1964), pp. 18–23.

Killian, Lewis M., and Charles Grigg, "Negro Perceptions of Organizational Effectiveness," *Social Problems*, 11 (Spring, 1964), pp. 380–388.

Killian, Lewis M., and Charles U. Smith, "Negro Protest Leaders in a Southern Community," *Social Forces*, 38 (March, 1960), pp. 253–257.

King, Martin Luther, Jr., *Stride toward Freedom* (New York: Harper, 1958).

King, Martin Luther, Jr., *Why We Can't Wait* (New York: Signet, 1963).

Lamanna, Richard A., "The Negro Teacher and Desegregation: A Study of Strategic Decision-Makers and Their Vested Interests in Different Community Contexts," *Sociological Inquiry*, 35 (1965), pp. 26–41.

Lang, Kurt, and Gladys E. Lang, "Racial Disturbances as Collective Protest," *American Behavioral Scientist*, 11 (March–April, 1968), pp. 11–13.

Laue, James H., "The Changing Character of Negro Protest," *Annals of the American Academy of Political and Social Science*, 357 (1965), pp. 119–126.

Laue, James H., "A Contemporary Revitalization Movement in American Race Relations: The 'Black Muslims'," *Social Forces*, 42 (March, 1964), pp. 315–323.

Lieberson, Stanley, and Arnold R. Silverman, "The Precipitants and Underlying Conditions of Race Riots," *American Sociological Review*, 30 (Dec., 1965), pp. 887–898.

Lincoln, C. Eric, *The Black Muslims in America* (Boston: Beacon, 1961).

Lincoln, C. Eric, *My Face is Black* (Boston: Beacon, 1964).

Logan, Rayford W., *The Negro in the United States: A Brief History* (Princeton: Van Nostrand, 1957).

McCord, William, and John Howard, "Negro Opinions in Three Riot Cities," in Louis H. Masotti and Don R. Bowen (editors), *Riots and Rebellion* (Beverly Hills: Sage Publications, 1968).

McNamara, Robert J., "The Ethics of Violent Dissent," in *Urban Riots: Violence and Protest* (New York: Academy of Political Science, 1968).

Marden, Charles F., and Gladys Meyer, *Minorities in American Society*, third edition (New York: American Book, 1968).

Marx, Gary T., *Protest and Prejudice: A Study of Belief in the Black Community* (New York: Harper, 1967).

Masotti, Louis H., and Don R. Bowen (editors), *Riots and Rebellion: Civil Violence in an Urban Community* (Beverly Hills: Sage Publications, 1968). Selected articles from this work are listed separately.

Matthews, Donald R., and James W. Prothro, *Negroes and New Southern Politics* (New York: Harcourt, 1966).

Meier, August, "Civil Rights Strategies for Negro Employment," in Arthur M. Ross and Herbert Hill (editors), *Employment, Race and Poverty* (New York: Harcourt, 1967).

Meier, August, "Negro Class Structure and Ideology in the Age of Booker T. Washington," *Phylon*, 23 (Fall, 1962), pp. 258–266.

Meier, August, *Negro Thought in America, 1880–1915: Racial Ideologies in the Age of Booker T. Washington* (Ann Arbor: University of Michigan Press, 1964).

Middleton, Russell, "The Civil Rights Issue and Presidential Voting among Negroes and Whites," *Social Forces*, 40 (March, 1962), pp. 209–215.

Moore, Barrington, Jr., "Thoughts on Violence and Democracy," in *Urban Riots: Violence and Social Change* (New York: Academy of Political Science, 1968).

Myrdal, Gunnar, *An American Dilemma* (New York: Harper, 1944).

Murphy, Raymond J., and Howard Elinson (editors), *Problems and Prospects of the Negro Movement* (Belmont, California: Wadsworth, 1966).

Noel, Donald L., and Alphonso Pinkney, "Correlates of Prejudice: Some Racial Differences and Similarities," *American Journal of Sociology*, 69 (May, 1964), pp. 609–622.

Oberschall, Anthony, "The Los Angeles Riot of August 1965," *Social Problems*, 15 (Winter, 1968), pp. 322–341.

Olsen, Marvin E., "Perceived Legitimacy of Social Protest Actions," *Social Problems*, 15 (Winter, 1968), pp. 297–310.

Orbell, John M., "Protest Participation among Southern Negro College Students," *American Political Science Review*, 61 (June, 1967), pp. 446–456.

Parker, James H., "The Interaction of Negroes in an Integrated Church Setting," *Social Forces*, 46 (March, 1968), pp. 359–366.

Pettigrew, Thomas F., "Complexity and Change in American Racial Patterns: A Social Psychological View," *Daedalus*, 94 (Fall, 1965), pp. 974–1008.

Pettigrew, Thomas F., *A Profile of the Negro American* (Princeton: Van Nostrand, 1964).

Proudfoot, Merrill, *Diary of a Sit-in* (Chapel Hill: University of North Carolina Press, 1962).

Quarantelli, E. L., and Russell Dynes, "Looting in Civil Disorders: An Index of Social Change," in Louis H. Masotti and Don R. Bowen (editors), *Riots and Rebellion* (Beverly Hills: Sage Publications, 1968).

Rainwater, Lee, "Open Letter on White Justice and the Riots," *Trans-action*, 9 (Sept., 1967).

Ransford, H. Edward, "Isolation, Powerlessness, and Violence: A Study of

Attitudes and Participation in the Watts Riot," *American Journal of Sociology*, 73 (March, 1968), pp. 581–591.

Record, Wilson, *The Negro and the Communist Party* (Chapel Hill: University of North Carolina Press, 1951).

Record, Wilson, *Race and Radicalism: The NAACP and the Communist Party in Conflict* (Ithaca: Cornell University Press, 1964).

Report of the National Advisory Commission on Civil Disorders (New York: Bantam Books, 1968).

Reynolds, Harry W., Jr., "Black Power, Community Power, and Jobs," in Louis H. Masotti and Don R. Bowen (editors), *Riots and Rebellion* (Beverly Hills: Sage Publications, 1968).

Rose, Peter I., *They and We: Racial and Ethnic Relations in the United States* (New York: Random House, 1964).

Rossi, Peter H., and Robert A. Dentler, *The Politics of Urban Renewal: The Chicago Findings* (New York: Free Press, 1961).

Rustin, Bayard, "From Protest to Politics: The Future of the Civil Rights Movement," *Commentary*, 39 (Feb., 1965), pp. 25–31.

Schulman, Jay, "Ghetto-Area Residence, Political Alienation, and Riot Orientation," in Louis H. Masotti and Don R. Bowen (editors), *Riots and Rebellion* (Beverly Hills: Sage Publications, 1968).

Schwartz, Mildred A., *Trends in White Attitudes toward Negroes* (Chicago: National Opinion Research Center, 1967).

Scoble, Harry, "Effects of Riots on Negro Leadership," Louis H. Masotti and Don R. Bowen (editors), *Riots and Rebellion* (Beverly Hills: Sage Publications, 1968).

Searles, Ruth, and J. Allen Williams, Jr., "Negro College Students' Participation in Sit-ins," *Social Forces*, 40 (March, 1962), pp. 215–220.

Sears, David O., and John B. McConahay, "The Politics of Discontent: Blocked Mechanisms of Grievance Redress and the Psychology of the New Urban Black Man," *Los Angeles Riot Study* (Los Angeles: Institute of Government and Public Affairs, University of California, 1967).

Sears, David O., and John B. McConahay, "Riot Participation," *Los Angeles Riot Study* (Los Angeles: Institute of Government and Public Affairs, University of California, 1967).

Silberman, Charles E., *Crisis in Black and White* (New York: Random House, 1964).

Simpson, George E., and J. Milton Yinger, *Racial and Cultural Minorities: An Analysis of Prejudice and Discrimination*, third edition (New York: Harper, 1965).

Smith, Bruce L. R., "'The Politics of Protest: How Effective is Violence?'" in *Urban Violence and Social Change* (New York: Academy of Political Science, 1968).

Soskin, William W., "Riots, Ghettos, and the 'Negro Revolt'," in Arthur M. Ross and Herbert Hill (editors), *Employment, Race and Poverty* (New York: Harcourt, 1967).

Spergel, Irving A., "Youth Gangs and Urban Riots," in Louis H. Masotti and Don R. Bowen (editors), *Riots and Rebellion* (Beverly Hills: Sage Publications, 1968).

Street, David, and John C. Leggett, "Economic Deprivation and Extremism: A Study of Unemployed Negroes," *American Journal of Sociology*, 67 (July, 1961), pp. 53–57.

Surace, Samuel J., and Melvin Seeman, "Some Correlates of Civil Rights Activism," *Social Forces*, 46 (Dec., 1967), pp. 197–207.

Thompson, Daniel C., "The Rise of Negro Protest," *Annals of the American Academy of Political and Social Science*, 357 (1965), pp. 18–29.

Tomlinson, T. M., "The Development of a Riot Ideology among Urban Negroes," *American Behavorial Scientist*, 11 (March–April, 1968), pp. 27–31.

Vander Zanden, James W., *American Minority Relations*, second edition (New York: Ronald, 1966).

Vander Zanden, James W., "The Non-Violent Resistance Movement against Segregation," *American Journal of Sociology*, 68 (March, 1963), pp. 544–550.

Vander Zanden, James W., *Race Relations in Transition: The Segregation Crisis within the South* (New York: Random House, 1965).

Walker, Jack L., "Protest and Negotiation: A Case Study of Negro Leadership in Atlanta," *Midwest Journal of Political Science*, 7 (May, 1963), pp. 99–124.

Wanderer, Jules J., "1967 Riots: A Test of the Congruity of Events," *Social Problems*, 16 (Fall, 1968), pp. 191–198.

Waskow, Arthur I., *From Race Riot to Sit-In, 1919 and the 1960's* (Garden City: Doubleday, 1966).

Westie, Frank R., "Racial and Ethnic Relations," in Robert E. L. Faris (editor) *Handbook of Modern Sociology* (Chicago: Rand McNally, 1964).

Westie, Frank R., and David H. Howard, "Social Status Differentials and the Race Attitudes of Negroes," *American Sociological Review*, 19 (Oct., 1954), pp. 584–591.

Williams, Robin M., Jr., with the collaboration of John P. Dean and Edward A. Suchman, *Strangers Next Door: Ethnic Relations in American Communities* (Englewood Cliffs: Prentice-Hall, 1964).

Works, Ernest, "Residence in Integrated and Segregated Housing and Improvements in Self Concepts of Negroes," *Sociology and Social Research*, 46 (April, 1962), pp. 294–301.

Fogelson, Robert M., "Violence as Protest," in *Urban Riots: Violence and Social Change* (New York: Academy of Political Science, 1968).

Part IV

PUBLIC POLICY AND BLACKS
IN THE UNITED STATES

Contributions 35 through 42 in this section are the summary of the *Report of the National Advisory Commission on Civil Disorders* (commonly known as the *Kerner Report*) and a symposium on the *Report*. The background of the *Report* and the membership of the Commission on Civil Disorders are detailed in contribution 36, an introduction to the symposium, by Norval D. Glenn, a sociologist. The other contributors to the symposium are Elliott Rudwick, Raymond W. Mack, G. Franklin Edwards, and Clifton R. Jones, sociologists; August Meier, a historian; Eli Ginzberg, an economist; and Jewel Prestage and Carl Akins, political scientists. These scholars are concerned with explaining the contents of the *Report*, evaluating its explanations of racial violence, and predicting the consequences of the *Report* on public policy and on race relations. The *Report* is of special interest to social scientists because its contents are perhaps based more on social scientific findings than any previous report by a government commission appointed to investigate a problem of wide public concern.

Recommendations such as those made by the Kerner Commission may have little effect on public policy, and in fact the appointment of a study commission may often be a substitute for policy changes to deal with a problem condition, rather than the basis of such changes. However, in recent years there have been policy changes of major importance concerning black Americans, at the federal, state, and local levels. Perhaps the most important changes at the federal level were the enactments of the Civil Rights Act of 1964, the Civil Rights Act of 1965 (concerning voting rights), and the Open Housing Act of 1968.

The Civil Rights Act of 1964

. . . prohibits discrimination or refusal of service on account of race in hotels, motels, restaurants, gasoline stations, and places of amusement if their operations affect interstate commerce or if their discrimination "is supported by state action"; requires that Negroes have equal access to, and treatment in, publicly owned or operated facilities such as parks, stadiums, and swimming pools; empowers the Attorney General of the United States to bring school desegregation suits; and authorizes the use of federal technical and financial aid to assist school districts in desegregation.

The act further provides that no person shall be subjected to racial discrimination in any program receiving federal aid, and directs federal agencies to take steps against discrimination, including—as a last resort, and after hearings—withholding of federal funds from state or local agencies that discriminate. It bans discrimination by employers or unions with 100 or more employees or members the first year the act is effective, reducing over four years from 100 or more to 25 or more. And the statute permits the Attorney General of the United States to intervene in suits filed by private persons complaining that they have been denied rights guaranteed to them by the Fourteenth Amendment.[1]

The act also contains a voting right section, which applies to federal elections only. It provides

. . . that the same standards must be used in registering all voters; minor errors in applications cannot be used to disqualify registrants; a sixth-grade education is proof of literacy for voting purposes unless election officials can prove otherwise in court; literacy tests must be given in writing, with copies available to applicants; and a three-judge federal court must be impaneled to hear any case in which the Attorney General of the United States charges voting discrimination, with right of direct appeal to the U.S. Supreme Court.[2]

The Civil Rights Act of 1965 extends most of these provisions to cover state and local elections.

The 1964 legislation resulted in the opening of many public accommodations to Negroes within weeks after it was enacted, and the two acts are undoubtedly in large measure responsible for the substantial recent increase in Negro voter registration and voter turnout in the South.[3] It is impossible to tell to what extent the 1964 act is responsible for recent Negro occupational and economic gains,[4] but it may have had a substantial effect, especially on Negro representation in the skilled trades,

[1] James W. Vander Zanden, *American Minority Relations*, 2nd edition (New York: Ronald Press, 1966), pp. 469–470.

[2] *Ibid.*, p. 469.

[3] See Jewel Prestage, "Black Politics and the Kerner Report: Concerns and Directions," contribution 41 of this anthology.

[4] See contribution 3 of this anthology.

from which Negroes have often been excluded by discriminating labor unions.

The Open Housing Act of 1968 prohibits discrimination in the sale of housing, if the sale is handled by a real-estate agent, and it prohibits discrimination in rentals, except by owners of one or a few rental units. The provisions of the act go into effect in stages and are not yet all effective; therefore, it is too early to assess the impact of the act on the segregated pattern of housing that now exists in all cities of the United States.

The last three contributions in this anthology deal with some changes in public policy, the reasons for them, and their impact on blacks. The change in the armed forces from a fully segregated to a technically fully integrated institution occurred in a relatively short time and provides many lessons in directed social change. In "Racial Integration in the Armed Forces," Charles C. Moskos, Jr., outlines some of these lessons, deals with the effects of desegregation, and draws on the military experience for clues as to what one might expect in a fully integrated America.

The reasons for a historical policy decision concerning black Americans are treated in "Why Lincoln Said 'No': Congressional Attitudes toward Slavery Expansion, 1860–1961," by Charles Desmond Hart, whereas "Constituency Characteristics and Roll-Call Voting on Negro Rights in the 88th Congress," by Jack R. van der Slik deals with recent policy decisions. Although the periods of time covered by the studies are separated by more than a century, both reveal that public policies concerning blacks were shaped largely by an interplay of regionally based interests and values. However, van der Slik shows that Southern unity is not monolithic, that several Southern Democrats from culturally homogeneous districts have given moderate support for Negro rights.

35

Summary of the Report of the National Advisory Commission on Civil Disorders*

INTRODUCTION

The summer of 1967 again brought racial disorders to American cities, and with them shock, fear, and bewilderment to the Nation.

The worst came during a 2-week period in July, first in Newark and then in Detroit. Each set off a chain reaction in neighboring communities.

On July 28, 1967, the President of the United States established this Commission and directed us to answer three basic questions:

What happened?
Why did it happen?
What can be done to prevent it from happening again?

To respond to these questions, we have undertaken a broad range of studies and investigations. We have visited the riot cities; we have heard many witnesses; we have sought the counsel of experts across the country.

This is our basic conclusion: Our Nation is moving toward two societies, one black, one white—separate and unequal.

Reaction to last summer's disorders has quickened the movement and deepened the division. Discrimination and segregation have long permeated much of American life; they now threaten the future of every American.

This deepening racial division is not inevitable. The movement apart can be reversed. Choice is still possible. Our principal task is to define that choice and to press for a national resolution.

To pursue our present course will involve the continuing polarization of the American community and, ultimately, the destruction of basic democratic values.

The alternative is not blind repression or capitulation to lawlessness. It is the realization of common opportunities for all within a single society.

This alternative will require a commitment to national action—compassionate, massive, and sustained, backed by the resources of the most powerful and richest nation on this earth. From every American it will require new attitudes, new understanding, and, above all, new will.

The vital needs of the Nation must be met; hard choices must be made, and, if necessary, new taxes enacted.

Violence cannot build a better society. Disruption and disorder nourish repression, not justice. They strike at the freedom of every citizen. The community cannot—it will not—tolerate coercion and mob rule.

Violence and destruction must be ended—in the streets of the ghetto and in lives of people.

* Reprinted from *Report of the National Advisory Commission on Civil Disorders* (Washington, D.C.: United States Government Printing Office, 1968), pp. 1–13.

Segregation and poverty have created in the racial ghetto a destructive environment totally unknown to most white Americans.

What white Americans have never fully understood—but what the Negro can never forget—is that white society is deeply implicated in the ghetto. White institutions created it, white institutions maintain it, and white society condones it.

It is time now to turn with all the purpose at our command to the major unfinished business of this Nation. It is time to adopt strategies for action that will produce quick and visible progress. It is time to make good the promises of American democracy to all citizens—urban and rural, white and black, Spanish-surname, American Indian, and every minority group.

Our recommendations embrace three basic principles:

- To mount programs on a scale equal to the dimension of the problems;
- To aim these programs for high impact in the immediate future in order to close the gap between promise and performance;
- To undertake new initiatives and experiments that can change the system of failure and frustration that now dominates the ghetto and weakens our society.

These programs will require unprecedented levels of funding and performance, but they neither probe deeper nor demand more than the problems which called them forth. There can be no higher priority for national action and no higher claim on the Nation's conscience.

We issue this report now, 5 months before the date called for by the President. Much remains that can be learned. Continued study is essential.

As Commissioners we have worked together with a sense of the greatest urgency and have sought to compose whatever differences existed among us. Some differences remain. But the gravity of the problem and the pressing need for action are too clear to allow further delay in the issuance of this report.

I. WHAT HAPPENED?

Chapter 1.—Profiles of Disorder

The report contains profiles of a selection of the disorders that took place during the summer of 1967. These profiles are designed to indicate how the disorders happened, who participated in them, and how local officials, police forces, and the National Guard responded. Illustrative excerpts follow:

NEWARK

* * * It was decided to attempt to channel the energies of the people into a nonviolent protest. While Lofton promised the crowd that a full investigation would be made of the Smith incident, the other Negro leaders began urging those on the scene to form a line of march toward the city hall.

Some persons joined the line of march. Others milled about in the narrow street. From the dark grounds of the housing project came a barrage of rocks. Some of them fell among the crowd. Others hit persons in the line of march. Many smashed the windows of the police station. The rock throwing, it was believed, was the work of youngsters; approximately 2,500 children lived in the housing project.

Almost at the same time, an old car was set afire in a parking lot. The line of march began to disintegrate. The police, their heads protected by World War I-type helmets, sallied forth to disperse the crowd. A fire engine, arriving on the scene, was pelted with rocks. As police drove people away from the station, they scattered in all directions.

A few minutes later a nearby liquor store was broken into. Some persons, seeing a caravan of cabs appear at city hall to protest Smith's arrest, interpreted this as evidence that the disturbance had been organized, and generated rumors to that effect.

However, only a few stores were looted. Within a short period of time, the disorder appeared to have run its course.

        °   °   °   °   °   °

* * * On Saturday, July 15, [Director of Police Dominick] Spina received a report of snipers in a housing project. When he arrived he saw approximately 100 National Guardsmen and police officers crouching behind vehicles, hiding in corners, and lying on the ground around the edge of the courtyard.

Since everything appeared quiet and it was broad daylight, Spina walked directly down the middle of the street. Nothing happened. As he came to the last building of the complex, he heard a shot. All around him the troopers jumped, believing themselves to be under sniper fire. A moment later a young Guardsman ran from behind a building.

The director of police went over and asked him if he had fired the shot. The soldier said, "Yes," he had fired to scare a man away from a window; that his orders were to keep everyone away from windows.

Spina said he told the soldier: "Do you know what you just did? You have now created a state of hysteria. Every Guardsman up and down this street and every state policeman and every city policeman that is present thinks that somebody just fired a shot and that it is probably a sniper."

A short time later more "gunshots" were heard. Investigating, Spina came upon a Puerto Rican sitting on a wall. In reply to a question as to whether he knew "where the firing is coming from?" the man said:

"That's no firing. That's fireworks. If you look up to the fourth floor, you will see the people who are throwing down these cherry bombs."

By this time four truckloads of National Guardsmen had arrived and troopers and policemen were again crouched everywhere looking for a sniper. The director of police remained at the scene for 3 hours, and the only shot fired was the one by the Guardsman.

Nevertheless, at 6 o'clock that evening two columns of National Guardsmen and State troopers were directing mass fire at the Hayes housing project in response to what they believed were snipers. * * *

DETROIT

* * * A spirit of carefree nihilism was taking hold. To riot and destroy appeared more and more to become ends in themselves. Late Sunday afternoon it appeared to one observer that the young people were "dancing amidst the flames."

A Negro plainclothes officer was standing at an intersection when a man threw a Molotov cocktail into a business establishment at the corner. In the heat of the afternoon, fanned by the 20 to 25 miles per hour winds of both Sunday and Monday, the fire reached the home next door within minutes. As residents uselessly sprayed the flames with garden hoses, the fire jumped from roof to roof of adjacent two- and three-story buildings. Within the hour the entire block was in flames. The ninth house in the burning row belonged to the arsonist who had thrown the Molotov cocktail. ° ° °

   °   °   °   °   °   °

° ° ° Employed as a private guard, 55-year-old Julius L. Dorsey, a Negro, was standing in front of a market when accosted by two Negro men and a woman. They demanded he permit them to loot the market. He ignored their demands. They began to berate him. He asked a neighbor to call the police. As the argument grew more heated, Dorsey fired three shots from his pistol into the air.

The police radio reported: "Looters—they have rifles." A patrol car driven by a police officer and carrying three National Guardsmen arrived. As the looters fled, the law-enforcement personnel opened fire. When the firing ceased, one person lay dead.

He was Julius L. Dorsey. ° ° °

   °   °   °   °   °   °

° ° ° As the riot alternately waxed and waned, one area of the ghetto remained insulated. On the northeast side the residents of some 150 square blocks inhabited by 21,000 persons had, in 1966, banded together in the Positive Neighborhood Action Committee (PNAC). With professional help from the Institute of Urban Dynamics, they had organized block clubs and made plans for the improvement of the neighborhood. ° ° °

When the riot broke out, the residents, through the block clubs, were able to organize quickly. Youngsters, agreeing to stay in the neighborhood, participated in detouring traffic. While many persons reportedly sympathized with the idea of a rebellion against the "system" only two small fires were set—one in an empty building.

   °   °   °   °   °   °

° ° ° According to Lieutenant General Throckmorton and Colonel Bolling, the city, this time, was saturated with fear. The National Guardsmen were afraid, the citizens were afraid, and the police were afraid. Numerous persons, the majority of them Negroes, were being injured by gunshots of undetermined origin. The general and his staff felt that the major task of the troops was to reduce the fear and restore an air of normalcy.

In order to accomplish this, every effort was made to establish contact and rapport between the troops and the residents. The soldiers—20 percent of whom were Negro—began helping to clean up the streets, collect garbage, and trace persons who had disappeared in the confusion. Residents in the neighborhoods responded with soup and sandwiches for the troops. In areas where the National Guard tried to establish rapport with the citizens, there was a similar response.

NEW BRUNSWICK

° ° ° A short time later, elements of the crowd—an older and rougher one than the night before—appeared in front of the police station. The participants wanted to see the mayor.

Mayor [Patricia] Sheehan went out onto the steps of the station. Using a bull horn, she talked to the people and asked that she be given an opportunity to correct conditions. The crowd was boisterous. Some persons challenged the mayor. But, finally, the opinion, "She's new— Give her a chance!" prevailed.

A demand was issued by people in the crowd that all persons arrested the previous night be released. Told that this already had been done, the people were suspicious. They asked to be allowed to inspect the jail cells.

It was agreed to permit representatives of the people to look in the cells to satisfy themselves that everyone had been released.

The crowd dispersed. The New Brunswick riot had failed to materialize.

CHAPTER 2.—PATTERNS OF DISORDER

The "typical" riot did not take place. The disorders of 1967 were unusual, irregular, complex, and unpredictable social processes. Like most human events, they did not unfold in an orderly sequence. However, an analysis of our survey information leads to some conclusions about the riot process.

In general:

- The civil disorders of 1967 involved Negroes acting against local symbols of white American society, authority, and property in Negro neighborhoods—rather than against white persons.
- Of 164 disorders reported during the first nine months of 1967, eight (5 percent) were major in terms of violence and damage; 33 (20 percent) were serious but not major; 123 (75 percent) were minor and undoubtedly would not have received national attention as riots had the Nation not been sensitized by the more serious outbreaks.
- In the 75 disorders studied by a Senate subcommittee, 83 deaths were reported. Eighty-two percent of the deaths and more than half the injuries occurred in Newark and Detroit. About 10 percent of the dead and 36 percent of the injured were public employees, primarily law officers and firemen. The overwhelming majority of the persons killed or injured in all the disorders were Negro civilians.
- Initial damage estimates were greatly exaggerated. In Detroit, newspaper damage estimates at first ranged from $200 to $500 million; the highest recent estimate is $45 million. In Newark, early estimates ranged from $15 to $25 million. A month later damage was estimated at $10.2 million, 80 percent in inventory losses.

In the 24 disorders in 23 cities which we surveyed:

- The final incident before the outbreak of disorder, and the initial violence itself, generally took place in the evening or at night at a place in which it was normal for many people to be on the streets.
- Violence usually occurred almost immediately following the occurrence of the final precipitating incident, and then escalated rapidly. With but few exceptions, violence subsided during the day, and flared rapidly again at night. The night-day cycles continued through the early period of the major disorders.
- Disorder generally began with rock and bottle throwing and window breaking. Once store windows were broken, looting usually followed.
- Disorders did not erupt as a result of a single "triggering" or "precipitating" incident. Instead, it was generated out of an increasingly disturbed social atmosphere, in which typically a series of tension-heightening incidents over a period of weeks or months became linked in the minds of many in the Negro community with a reservoir of underlying grievances. At some point in the mounting tension, a further incident—in itself often routine or trivial—became the breaking point and the tension spilled over into violence.
- "Prior" incidents, which increased tensions and ultimately led to violence, were police actions in almost half the cases; police actions were "final" incidents before the outbreak of violence in 12 of the 24 surveyed disorders.

■ No particular control tactic was successful in every situation. The varied effectiveness of control techniques emphasizes the need for advance training, planning, adequate intelligence systems, and knowledge of the ghetto community.

■ Negotiations between Negroes—including young militants as well as older Negro leaders—and white officials concerning "terms of peace" occurred during virtually all the disorders surveyed. In many cases, these negotiations involved discussion of underlying grievances as well as the handling of the disorder by control authorities.

■ The typical rioter was a teenager or young adult, a lifelong resident of the city in which he rioted, a high school dropout; he was, nevertheless, somewhat better educated than his nonrioting Negro neighbor, and was usually underemployed or employed in a menial job. He was proud of his race, extremely hostile to both whites and middle-class Negroes and, although informed about politics, highly distrustful of the political system.

A Detroit survey revealed that approximately 11 percent of the total residents of two riot areas admitted participation in the rioting, 20 to 25 percent identified themselves as "bystanders," over 16 percent identified themselves as "counterrioters" who urged rioters to "cool it," and the remaining 48 to 53 percent said they were at home or elsewhere and did not participate. In a survey of Negro males between the ages of 15 and 35 residing in the disturbance area in Newark, about 45 percent identified themselves as rioters, and about 55 percent as "noninvolved."

■ Most rioters were young Negro males. Nearly 53 percent of arrestees were between 15 and 24 years of age; nearly 81 percent between 15 and 35.

■ In Detroit and Newark about 74 percent of the rioters were brought up in the North. In contrast, of the noninvolved, 36 percent in Detroit and 52 percent in Newark were brought up in the North.

■ What the rioters appeared to be seeking was fuller participation in the social order and the material benefits enjoyed by the majority of American citizens. Rather than rejecting the American system, they were anxious to obtain a place for themselves in it.

■ Numerous Negro counterrioters walked the streets urging rioters to "cool it." The typical counterrioter was better educated and had higher income than either the rioter or the noninvolved.

■ The proportion of Negroes in local government was substantially smaller than the Negro proportion of population. Only three of the 20 cities studied had more than one Negro legislator; none had ever had a Negro mayor or city manager. In only four cities did Negroes hold other important policy-making positions or serve as heads of municipal departments.

■ Although almost all cities had some sort of formal grievance mechanism for handling citizen complaints, this typically was regarded by Negroes as ineffective and was generally ignored.

■ Although specific grievances varied from city to city, at least 12 deeply held grievances can be identified and ranked into three levels of relative intensity:

First level of intensity:

1. Police practices.
2. Unemployment and underemployment.
3. Inadequate housing.

Second level of intensity:

4. Inadequate education.
5. Poor recreation facilities and programs.
6. Ineffectiveness of the political structure and grievance mechanisms.

Third level of intensity:

7. Disrespectful white attitudes.
8. Discriminatory administration of justice.
9. Inadequacy of Federal programs.
10. Inadequacy of municipal services.
11. Discriminatory consumer and credit practices.
12. Inadequate welfare programs.

▪ The results of a three-city survey of various Federal programs—manpower, education, housing, welfare and community action—indicate that, despite substantial expenditures, the number of persons assisted constitute only a fraction of those in need.

The background of disorder is often as complex and difficult to analyze as the disorder itself. But we find that certain general conclusions can be drawn:

▪ Social and economic conditions in the riot cities constituted a clear pattern of severe disadvantage for Negroes compared with whites, whether the Negroes lived in the areas where the riot took place or outside it. Negroes had completed fewer years of education and fewer had attended high school. Negroes were twice as likely to be unemployed and three times as likely to be in unskilled and service jobs. Negroes averaged 70 percent of the income earned by whites and were more than twice as likely to be living in poverty. Although housing cost Negroes relatively more, they had worse housing—three times as likely to be overcrowded and substandard. When compared to white suburbs, the relative disadvantage was even more pronounced.

A study of the aftermath of disorder leads to disturbing conclusions. We find that, despite the institution of some postriot programs:

▪ Little basic change in the conditions underlying the outbreak of disorder has taken place. Actions to ameliorate Negro grievances have been limited and sporadic; with but few exceptions, they have not significantly reduced tensions.
▪ In several cities, the principal official response has been to train and equip the police with more sophisticated weapons.
▪ In several cities, increasing polarization is evident, with continuing breakdown of interracial communication, and growth of white segregationist or black separatist groups.

Chapter 3.—Organized Activity

The President directed the Commission to investigate "to what extent, if any, there has been planning or organization in any of the riots."

To carry out this part of the President's charge, the Commission established a special investigative staff supplementing the field teams that made the general examination of the riots in 23 cities. The unit examined data collected by Federal agencies and congressional committees, including thousands of documents supplied by the Federal Bureau of Investigation, gathered and evaluated information from local and state law enforcement agencies and officials, and conducted its own field investigation in selected cities.

On the basis of all the information collected, the Commission concludes that:

The urban disorders of the summer of 1967 were not caused by, nor were they the consequence of, any organized plan or "conspiracy."

Specifically, the Commission has found no evidence that all or any of the disorders or the incidents that led to them were planned or directed by any organization or group, international, national, or local.

Militant organizations, local and national, and individual agitators, who repeatedly forecast and called for violence, were active in the spring and summer of 1967. We believe that they sought to encourage violence, and that they helped to create an atmosphere that contributed to the outbreak of disorder.

We recognize that the continuation of disorders and the polarization of the races would provide fertile ground for organized exploitation in the future.

Investigations of organized activity are continuing at all levels of government, including committees of Congress. These investigations relate not only to the disorders of 1967 but also to the actions of groups and individuals, particularly in schools and colleges, during this last fall and winter. The Commission has cooperated in these investigations. They should continue.

II. WHY DID IT HAPPEN?

CHAPTER 4.—THE BASIC CAUSES

In addressing the question "Why did it happen?" we shift our focus from the local to the national scene, from the particular events of the summer of 1967 to the factors within the society at large that created a mood of violence among many urban Negroes.

These factors are complex and interacting; they vary significantly in their effect from city to city and from year to year; and the consequences of one disorder, generating new grievances and new demands, become the causes of the next. Thus was created the "thicket of tension, conflicting evidence, and extreme opinions" cited by the President.

Despite the complexities, certain fundamental matters are clear. Of these, the most fundamental is the racial attitude and behavior of white Americans toward black Americans.

Race prejudice has shaped our history decisively; it now threatens to affect our future.

White racism is essentially responsible for the explosive mixture which has been accumulating in our cities since the end of World War II. Among the ingredients of this mixture are:

■ *Pervasive discrimination and segregation* in employment, education, and housing, which have resulted in the continuing exclusion of great numbers of Negroes from the benefits of economic progress.

■ *Black in-migration and white exodus,* which have produced the massive and growing concentrations of impoverished Negroes in our major cities, creating a growing crisis of deteriorating facilities and services and unmet human needs.
■ *The black ghettos,* where segregation and poverty converge on the young to destroy opportunity and enforce failure. Crime, drug addiction, dependency on welfare, and bitterness and resentment against society in general and white society in particular are the result.

At the same time, most whites and some Negroes outside the ghetto have prospered to a degree unparalleled in the history of civilization. Through television and other media, this affluence has been flaunted before the eyes of the Negro poor and the jobless ghetto youth.

Yet these facts alone cannot be said to have caused the disorders. Recently, other powerful ingredients have begun to catalyze the mixture:

■ *Frustrated hopes* are the residue of the unfulfilled expectations aroused by the great judicial and legislative victories of the civil rights movement and the dramatic struggle for equal rights in the South.
■ *A climate that tends toward approval and encouragement of violence* as a form of protest has been created by white terrorism directed against nonviolent protest; by the open defiance of law and Federal authority by state and local officials resisting desegregation; and by some protest groups engaging in civil disobedience who turn their back on nonviolence, go beyond the constitutionally protected rights of petition and free assembly, and resort to violence to attempt to compel alteration of laws and policies with which they disagree.
■ *The frustrations of powerlessness* have led some Negroes to the conviction that there is no effective alternative to violence as a means of achieving redress of grievances, and of "moving the system." These frustrations are reflected in alienation and hostility toward the institutions of law and government and the white society which controls them, and in the reach toward racial consciousness and solidarity reflected in the slogan "Black Power."
■ *A new mood* has sprung up among Negroes, particularly among the young, in which self-esteem and enhanced racial pride are replacing apathy and submission to "the system."
■ *The police are not merely a "spark" factor.* To some Negroes police have come to symbolize white power, white racism, and white repression. And the fact is that many police do reflect and express these white attitudes. The atmosphere of hostility and cynicism is reinforced by a widespread belief among Negroes in the existence of police brutality and in a "double standard" of justice and protection —one for Negroes and one for whites.

❖   ❖   ❖   ❖   ❖   ❖

To this point, we have attempted only to identify the prime components of the "explosive mixture." In the chapters that follow we seek to analyze them in the perspective of history. Their meaning, however, is clear:

In the summer of 1967, we have seen in our cities a chain reaction of racial violence. If we are heedless, none of us shall escape the consequences.

CHAPTER 5.—REJECTION AND PROTEST: AN HISTORICAL SKETCH

The causes of recent racial disorders are embedded in a tangle of issues and circumstances—social, economic, political, and psychological—which arise out of the historic pattern of Negro-white relations in America.

In this chapter we trace the pattern, identify the recurrent themes of

Negro protest and, most importantly, provide a perspective on the protest activities of the present era.

We describe the Negro's experience in America and the development of slavery as an institution. We show his persistent striving for equality in the face of rigidly maintained social, economic, and educational barriers, and repeated mob violence. We portray the ebb and flow of the doctrinal tides—accommodation, separatism, and self-help—and their relationship to the current theme of Black Power. We conclude:

The Black Power advocates of today consciously feel that they are the most militant group in the Negro protest movement. Yet they have retreated from a direct confrontation with American society on the issue of integration and, by preaching separatism, unconsciously function as an accommodation to white racism. Much of their economic program, as well as their interest in Negro history, self-help racial solidarity and separation, is reminiscent of Booker T. Washington. The rhetoric is different, but the ideas are remarkably similar.

CHAPTER 6.—THE FORMATION OF THE RACIAL GHETTOS[1]

Throughout the 20th century the Negro population of the United States has been moving steadily from rural areas to urban and from South to North and West. In 1910, 91 percent of the Nation's 9.8 million Negroes lived in the South and only 27 percent of American Negroes lived in cities of 2,500 persons or more. Between 1910 and 1966 the total Negro population more than doubled, reaching 21.5 million, and the number living in metropolitan areas rose more than fivefold (from 2.6 million to 14.8 million). The number outside the South rose elevenfold (from 885,000 to 9.7 million.)

Negro migration from the South has resulted from the expectation of thousands of new and highly paid jobs for unskilled workers in the North and the shift to mechanized farming in the South. However, the Negro migration is small when compared to earlier waves of European immigrants. Even between 1960 and 1966, there were 1.8 million immigrants from abroad compared to the 613,000 Negroes who arrived in the North and west from the South.

As a result of the growing numbers of Negroes in urban areas, natural increase has replaced migration as the primary source of Negro population increase in the cities. Nevertheless, Negro migration from the South will continue unless economic conditions there change dramatically.

Basic data concerning Negro urbanization trends indicate that:

▪ Almost all Negro population growth (98 percent from 1950 to 1966) is occurring within metropolitan areas, primarily within central cities.[2]

▪ The vast majority of white population growth (78 percent from 1960 to 1966) is occurring in suburban portions of metropolitan areas. Since 1960, white central-city population has declined by 1.3 million.

[1] The term "ghetto" as used in this Report refers to an area within a city characterized by poverty and acute social disorganization and inhabited by members of a racial or ethnic group under conditions of involuntary segregation.

[2] A "central city" is the largest city of a standard metropolitan statistical area, that is, a metropolitan area containing at least one city of 50,000 or more inhabitants.

■ As a result, central cities are becoming more heavily Negro while the suburban fringes around them remain almost entirely white.
■ The 12 largest central cities now contain over two-thirds of the Negro population outside the South, and almost one-third of the Negro total in the United States.

Within the cities, Negroes have been excluded from white residential areas through discriminatory practices. Just as significant is the withdrawal of white families from, or their refusal to enter, neighborhoods where Negroes are moving or already residing. About 20 percent of the urban population of the United States changes residence every year. The refusal of whites to move into "changing" areas when vacancies occur means that most vacancies eventually are occupied by Negroes.

The result, according to a recent study, is that in 1960 the average segregation index for 207 of the largest U.S. cities was 86.2. In other words, to create an unsegregated population distribution, an average of over 86 percent of all Negroes would have to change their place of residence within the city.

Chapter 7.—Unemployment, Family Structure, and Social
Disorganization

Although there have been gains in Negro income nationally, and a decline in the number of Negroes below the "poverty level," the condition Negroes in the central city remains in a state of crisis. Between 2 and 2.5 million Negroes—16 to 20 percent of the total Negro population of all central cities—live in squalor and deprivation in ghetto neighborhoods.

Employment is a key problem. It not only controls the present for the Negro American but, in a most profound way, it is creating the future as well. Yet, despite continuing economic growth and declining national unemployment rates, the unemployment rate for Negroes in 1967 was more than double that for whites.

Equally important is the undesirable nature of many jobs open to Negroes and other minorities. Negro men are more than three times as likely as white men to be in low-paying, unskilled, or service jobs. This concentration of male Negro employment at the lowest end of the occupational scale is the single most important cause of poverty among Negroes.

In one study of low-income neighborhoods, the "sub-employment rate," including both unemployment and underemployment, was about 33 percent, or 8.8 times greater than the overall unemployment rate for all U.S. workers.

Employment problems, aggravated by the constant arrival of new unemployed migrants, many of them from depressed rural areas, create persistent poverty in the ghetto. In 1966, about 11.9 percent of the Nation's whites and 40.6 percent of its nonwhites were below the poverty level defined by the Social Security Administration (in 1966, $3,335 per year for an urban family of four). Over 40 percent of the nonwhites below the poverty level live in the central cities.

Employment problems have drastic social impact in the ghetto. Men who are chronically unemployed or employed in the lowest status jobs are often unable or unwilling to remain with their families. The handicap imposed on children growing up without fathers in an atmosphere of deprivation is increased as mothers are forced to work to provide support.

The culture of poverty that results from unemployment and family breakup generates a system of ruthless, exploitative relationships within the ghetto. Prostitution, dope addiction, and crime create an environmental "jungle" characterized by personal insecurity and tension. Children growing up under such conditions are likely participants in civil disorder.

CHAPTER 8.—CONDITIONS OF LIFE IN THE RACIAL GHETTO

A striking difference in environment from that of white, middle-class Americans profoundly influences the lives of residents of the ghetto.

Crime rates, consistently higher than in other areas, create a pronounced sense of insecurity. For example, in one city one low-income Negro district had 35 times as many serious crimes against persons as a high-income white district. Unless drastic steps are taken, the crime problems in poverty areas are likely to continue to multiply as the growing youth and rapid urbanization of the population outstrip resources.

Poor health and sanitation conditions in the ghetto result in higher mortality rates, a higher incidence of major diseases, and lower availability and utilization of medical services. The infant mortality rate for nonwhite babies under the age of 1 month is 58 percent higher than for whites; for 1 to 12 months it is almost three times as high. The level of sanitation in the ghetto is far below that in high-income areas. Garbage collection is often inadequate. Of an estimated 14,000 cases of rat bite in the United States in 1965, most were in ghetto neighborhoods.

Ghetto residents believe they are exploited by local merchants; and evidence substantiates some of these beliefs. A study conducted in one city by the Federal Trade Commission showed that higher prices were charged for goods sold in ghetto stores than in other areas.

Lack of knowledge regarding credit purchasing creates special pitfalls for the disadvantaged. In many states, garnishment practices compound these difficulties by allowing creditors to deprive individuals of their wages without hearing or trial.

CHAPTER 9.—COMPARING THE IMMIGRANT AND NEGRO EXPERIENCE

In this chapter, we address ourselves to a fundamental question that many white Americans are asking: Why have so many Negroes, unlike the European immigrant, been unable to escape from the ghetto and from poverty?

We believe the following factors play a part:

■ *The maturing economy.*—When the European immigrants arrived, they gained an economic foothold by providing the unskilled labor needed by industry. Unlike the immigrant, the Negro migrant found little opportunity in the city. The economy, by then matured, had little use for the unskilled labor he had to offer.

■ *The disability of race.*—The structure of discrimination has stringently narrowed opportunities for the Negro and restricted his prospects. European immigrants suffered from discrimination, but never so pervasively.

■ *Entry into the political system.*—The immigrants usually settled in rapidly growing cities with powerful and expanding political machines, which traded economic advantages for political support. Ward-level grievance machinery, as well as personal representation, enabled the immigrant to make his voice heard and his power felt.

By the time the Negro arrived, these political machines were no longer so powerful or so well equipped to provide jobs or other favors, and in many cases were unwilling to share their remaining influence with Negroes.

■ *Cultural factors.*—Coming from societies with a low standard of living and at a time when job aspirations were low, the immigrants sensed little deprivation in being forced to take the less desirable and poorer paying jobs. Their large and cohesive families contributed to total income. Their vision of the future—one that led to a life outside of the ghetto—provided the incentive necessary to endure the present.

Although Negro men worked as hard as the immigrants, they were unable to support their families. The entrepreneurial opportunities had vanished. As a result of slavery and long periods of unemployment, the Negro family structure had become matriarchal; the males played a secondary and marginal family role —one which offered little compensation for their hard and unrewarding labor. Above all, segregation denied Negroes access to good jobs and the opportunity to leave the ghetto. For them, the future seemed to lead only to a dead end.

Today, whites tend to exaggerate how well and quickly they escaped from poverty. The fact is that immigrants who came from rural backgrounds, as many Negroes do, are only now, after three generations, finally beginning to move into the middle class.

By contrast, Negroes began concentrating in the city less than two generations ago, and under much less favorable conditions. Although some Negroes have escaped poverty, few have been able to escape the urban ghetto.

III. WHAT CAN BE DONE?

CHAPTER 10.—THE COMMUNITY RESPONSE

Our investigation of the 1967 riot cities establishes that virtually every major episode of violence was foreshadowed by an accumulation of unresolved grievances and by widespread dissatisfaction among Negroes with the unwillingness or inability of local government to respond.

Overcoming these conditions is essential for community support of law enforcement and civil order. City governments need new and more vital channels of communication to the residents of the ghetto; they need to improve their capacity to respond effectively to community needs before they become community grievances; and they need to provide opportunity for meaningful involvement of ghetto residents in shaping policies and programs which affect the community.

The Commission recommends that local governments:

■ Develop Neighborhood Action Task Forces as joint community-government efforts through which more effective communication can be achieved, and the delivery of city services to ghetto residents improved.

■ Establish comprehensive grievance-response mechanisms in order to bring all public agencies under public scrutiny.
■ Bring the institutions of local government closer to the people they serve by establishing neighborhood outlets for local, state, and Federal administrative and public service agencies.
■ Expand opportunities for ghetto residents to participate in the formulation of public policy and the implementation of programs affecting them through improved political representation, creation of institutional channels for community action, expansion of legal services, and legislative hearings on ghetto problems.

In this effort, city governments will require State and Federal support. The Commission recommends:

■ State and Federal financial assistance for mayors and city councils to support the research, consultants, staff, and other resources needed to respond effectively to Federal program initiatives.
■ State cooperation in providing municipalities with the jurisdictional tools needed to deal with their problems; a fuller measure of financial aid to urban areas; and the focusing of the interests of suburban communities on the physical, social, and cultural environment of the central city.

CHAPTER 11.—POLICE AND THE COMMUNITY

The abrasive relationship between the police and minority communities has been a major—and explosive—source of grievance, tension, and disorder. The blame must be shared by the total society.

The police are faced with demands for increased protection and service in the ghetto. Yet the aggressive patrol practices thought necessary to meet these demands themselves create tension and hostility. The resulting grievances have been further aggravated by the lack of effective mechanisms for handling complaints against the police. Special programs for bettering police-community relations have been instituted, but these alone are not enough. Police administrators, with the guidance of public officials, and the support of the entire community, must take vigorous action to improve law enforcement and to decrease the potential for disorder.

The Commission recommends that city government and police authorities:

■ Review police operations in the ghetto to ensure proper conduct by police officers, and eliminate abrasive practices.
■ Provide more adequate police protection to ghetto residents to eliminate their high sense of insecurity and the belief in the existence of a dual standard of law enforcement.
■ Establish fair and effective mechanisms for the redress of grievances against the police and other municipal employees.
■ Develop and adopt policy guidelines to assist officers in making critical decisions in areas where police conduct can create tension.
■ Develop and use innovative programs to insure widespread community support for law enforcement.
■ Recruit more Negroes into the police force, and review promotion policies to insure fair promotion for Negro officers.
■ Establish a "Community Service Officer" program to attract ghetto youths between the ages of 17 and 21 to police work. These junior officers would perform

duties in ghetto neighborhoods, but would not have full police authority. The Federal Government should provide support equal to 90 percent of the costs of employing CSO's on the basis of one for every 10 regular officers.

CHAPTER 12.—CONTROL OF DISORDER

Preserving civil peace is the first responsibility of government. Unless the rule of law prevails, our society will lack not only order but also the environment essential to social and economic progress.

The maintenance of civil order cannot be left to the police alone. The police need guidance, as well as support, from mayors and other public officials. It is the responsibility of public officials to determine proper police policies, support adequate police standards for personnel and performance, and participate in planning for the control of disorders.

To maintain control of incidents which could lead to disorders, the Commission recommends that local officials:

- Assign seasoned, well-trained policemen and supervisory officers to patrol ghetto areas, and to respond to disturbances.
- Develop plans which will quickly muster maximum police manpower and highly qualified senior commanders at the outbreak of disorders.
- Provide special training in the prevention of disorders, and prepare police for riot control and for operation in units, with adequate command and control and field communication for proper discipline and effectiveness.
- Develop guidelines governing the use of control equipment and provide alternatives to the use of lethal weapons. Federal support for research in this area is needed.
- Establish an intelligence system to provide police and other public officials with reliable information that may help to prevent the outbreak of a disorder and to institute effective control measures in the event a riot erupts.
- Develop continuing contacts with ghetto residents to make use of the forces for order which exist within the community.
- Establish machinery for neutralizing rumors, and enabling Negro leaders and residents to obtain the facts. Create special rumor details to collect, evaluate, and dispel rumors that may lead to a civil disorder.

The Commission believes there is a grave danger that some communities may resort to the indiscriminate and excessive use of force. The harmful effects of overreaction are incalculable. The Commission condemns moves to equip police departments with mass destruction weapons, such as automatic rifles, machine guns, and tanks. Weapons which are designed to destroy, not to control, have no place in densely populated urban communities.

The Commission recommends that the Federal Government share in the financing of programs for improvement of police forces, both in their normal law enforcement activities as well as in their response to civil disorders.

To assist government authorities in planning their response to civil disorder, this report contains a Supplement on Control of Disorder. It deals with specific problems encountered during riot control operations, and includes:

■ Assessment of the present capabilities of police, National Guard and Army forces to control major riots, and recommendations for improvement.

■ Recommended means by which the control operations of those forces may be coordinated with the response of other agencies, such as fire departments, and with the community at large.

■ Recommendations for review and revision of Federal, state and local laws needed to provide the framework for control efforts and for the callup and inter-related action of public safety forces.

Chapter 13.—The Administration of Justice Under Emergency Conditions

In many of the cities which experienced disorders last summer, there were recurring breakdowns in the mechanisms for processing, prosecuting, and protecting arrested persons. These resulted mainly from long-standing structural deficiencies in criminal court systems, and from the failure of communities to anticipate and plan for the emergency demands of civil disorders.

In part, because of this, there were few successful prosecutions for serious crimes committed during the riots. In those cities where mass arrests occurred, many arrestees were deprived of basic legal rights.

The Commission recommends that the cities and states:

■ Undertake reform of the lower courts so as to improve the quality of justice rendered under normal conditions.

■ Plan comprehensive measures by which the criminal justice system may be supplemented during civil disorders so that its deliberative functions are protected, and the quality of justice is maintained.

Such emergency plans require broad community participation and dedicated leadership by the bench and bar. They should include:

■ Laws sufficient to deter and punish riot conduct.

■ Additional judges, bail and probation officers, and clerical staff.

■ Arrangements for volunteer lawyers to help prosecutors and to represent riot defendants at every stage of proceedings.

■ Policies to insure proper and individual bail, arraignment, pretrial, trial, and sentencing proceedings.

■ Adequate emergency processing and detention facilities.

Chapter 14.—Damages: Repair and Compensation

The Commission recommends that the Federal Government:

■ Amend the Federal Disaster Act—which now applies only to natural disasters —to permit Federal emergency food and medical assistance to cities during major civil disorders, and provide long-term economic assistance afterwards.

■ With the cooperation of the states, create incentives for the private insurance industry to provide more adequate property insurance coverage in inner-city areas.

The Commission endorses the report of the National Advisory Panel on Insurance in Riot-Affected Areas: "Meeting the Insurance Crisis of our Cities."

CHAPTER 15.—THE NEWS MEDIA AND THE DISORDERS

In his charge to the Commission, the President asked: "What effect do the mass media have on the riots?"

The Commission determined that the answer to the President's question did not lie solely in the performance of the press and broadcasters in reporting the riots. Our analysis had to consider also the overall treatment by the media of the Negro ghettos, community relations, racial attitudes, and poverty—day by day and month by month, year in and year out.

A wide range of interviews with Government officials, law enforcement authorities, media personnel and other citizens, including ghetto residents, as well as quantitative analysis of riot coverage and a special conference with industry representatives, leads us to conclude that:

▪ Despite instances of sensationalism, inaccuracy and distortion, newspapers, radio and television tried on the whole to give a balanced, factual account of the 1967 disorders.
▪ Elements of the news media failed to portray accurately the scale and character of the violence that occurred last summer. The overall effect was, we believe, an exaggeration of both mood and event.
▪ Important segments of the media failed to report adequately on the causes and consequences of civil disorders and on the underlying problems of race relations. They have not communicated to the majority of their audience—which is white—a sense of the degradation, misery, and hopelessness of life in the ghetto.

These failings must be corrected, and the improvement must come from within the industry. Freedom of the press is not the issue. Any effort to impose governmental restrictions would be inconsistent with fundamental constitutional precepts.

We have seen evidence that the news media are becoming aware of and concerned about their performance in this field. As that concern grows, coverage will improve. But much more must be done, and it must be done soon.

The Commission recommends that the media:

▪ Expand coverage of the Negro community and of race problems through permanent assignment of reporters familiar with urban and racial affairs, and through establishment of more and better links with the Negro community.
▪ Integrate Negroes and Negro activities into all aspects of coverage and content, including newspaper articles and television programming. The news media must publish newspapers and produce programs that recognize the existence and activities of Negroes as a group within the community and as a part of the larger community.
▪ Recruit more Negroes into journalism and broadcasting and promote those who are qualified to positions of significant responsibility. Recruitment should begin in high schools and continue through college; where necessary, aid for training should be provided.
▪ Improve coordination with police in reporting riot news through advance planning, and cooperate with the police in the designation of police information officers, establishment of information centers, and development of mutually acceptable guidelines for riot reporting and the conduct of media personnel.
▪ Accelerate efforts to insure accurate and responsible reporting of riot and

racial news, through adoption by all news-gathering organizations of stringent internal staff guidelines.

■ Cooperate in the establishment of a privately organized and funded Institute of Urban Communications to train and educate journalists in urban affairs, recruit and train more Negro journalists, develop methods for improving police-press relations, review coverage of riots and racial issues, and support continuing research in the urban field.

CHAPTER 16.—THE FUTURE OF THE CITIES

By 1985, the Negro population in central cities is expected to increase by 68 percent to approximately 20.3 million. Coupled with the continued exodus of white families to the suburbs, this growth will produce majority Negro populations in many of the Nation's largest cities.

The future of these cities, and of their burgeoning Negro populations, is grim. Most new employment opportunities are being created in suburbs and outlying areas. This trend will continue unless important changes in public policy are made.

In prospect, therefore, is further deterioration of already inadequate municipal tax bases in the face of increasing demands for public services, and continuing unemployment and poverty among the urban Negro population:

Three choices are open to the Nation:

■ We can maintain present policies, continuing both the proportion of the Nation's resources now allocated to programs for the unemployed and the disadvantaged, and the inadequate and failing effort to achieve an integrated society.

■ We can adopt a policy of "enrichment" aimed at improving dramatically the quality of ghetto life while abandoning integration as a goal.

■ We can pursue integration by combining ghetto "enrichment" with policies which will encourage Negro movement out of central city areas.

The first choice, continuance of present policies, has ominous consequences for our society. The share of the Nation's resources now allocated to programs for the disadvantaged is insufficient to arrest the deterioration of life in central-city ghettos. Under such conditions, a rising proportion of Negroes may come to see in the deprivation and segregation they experience, a justification for violent protests, or for extending support to now isolated extremists who advocate civil disruption. Large-scale and continuing violence could result, followed by white retaliation, and ultimately, the separation of the two communities in a garrison state.

Even if violence does not occur, the consequences are unacceptable. Development of a racially integrated society, extraordinarily difficult today, will be virtually impossible when the present black central-city population of 12.1 million has grown to almost 21 million.

To continue present policies is to make permanent the division of our country into two societies: one, largely Negro and poor, located in the central cities; the other, predominantly white and affluent, located in the suburbs and in outlying areas.

The second choice, ghetto enrichment coupled with abandonment of integration, is also unacceptable. It is another way of choosing a permanently divided country. Moreover, equality cannot be achieved under conditions of nearly complete separation. In a country where the economy, and particularly the resources of employment, are predominantly white, a policy of separation can only relegate Negroes to a permanently inferior economic status.

We believe that the only possible choice for America is the third—a policy which combines ghetto enrichment with programs designed to encourage integration of substantial numbers of Negroes into the society outside the ghetto.

Enrichment must be an important adjunct to integration, for no matter how ambitious or energetic the program, few Negroes now living in central cities can be quickly integrated. In the meantime, large-scale improvement in the quality of ghetto life is essential.

But this can be no more than an interim strategy. Programs must be developed which will permit substantial Negro movement out of the ghettos. The primary goal must be a single society, in which every citizen will be free to live and work according to his capabilities and desires, not his color.

CHAPTER 17.—RECOMMENDATIONS FOR NATIONAL ACTION

INTRODUCTION. No American—white or black—can escape the consequences of the continuing social and economic decay of our major cities.

Only a commitment to national action on an unprecedented scale can shape a future compatible with the historic ideals of American society.

The great productivity of our economy, and a Federal revenue system which is highly responsive to economic growth, can provide the resources.

The major need is to generate new will—the will to tax ourselves to the extent necessary to meet the vital needs of the Nation.

We have set forth goals and proposed strategies to reach those goals. We discuss and recommend programs not to commit each of us to specific parts of such programs, but to illustrate the type and dimension of action needed.

The major goal is the creation of a true union—a single society and a single American identity. Toward that goal we propose the following objectives for national action:

▪ Opening up opportunities to those who are restricted by racial segregation and discrimination, and eliminating all barriers to their choice of jobs, education, and housing.
▪ Removing the frustration of powerlessness among the disadvantaged by providing the means for them to deal with the problems that affect their own lives and by increasing the capacity of our public and private institutions to respond to these problems.
▪ Increasing communication across racial lines to destroy stereotypes, halt polarization, end distrust and hostility, and create common ground for efforts toward public order and social justice.

We propose these aims to fulfill our pledge of equality and to meet the fundamental needs of a democratic and civilized society—domestic peace and social justice.

EMPLOYMENT. Pervasive unemployment and underemployment are the most persistent and serious grievances in minority areas. They are inextricably linked to the problem of civil disorder.

Despite growing Federal expenditures for manpower development and training programs, and sustained general economic prosperity and increasing demands for skilled workers, about 2 million—white and nonwhite—are permanently unemployed. About 10 million are underemployed, of whom 6.5 million work full time for wages below the poverty line.

The 500,000 "hard-core" unemployed in the central cities who lack a basic education and are unable to hold a steady job are made up in large part of Negro males between the ages of 18 and 25. In the riot cities which we surveyed, Negroes were three times as likely as whites to hold unskilled jobs, which are often part time, seasonal, low paying and "dead end."

Negro males between the ages of 15 and 25 predominated among the rioters. More than 20 percent of the rioters were unemployed, and many who were employed held intermittent, low status, unskilled jobs which they regarded as below their education and ability.

The Commission recommends that the Federal Government:

■ Undertake joint efforts with cities and states to consolidate existing manpower programs to avoid fragmentation and duplication.
■ Take immediate action to create 2 million new jobs over the next 3 years—1 million in the public sector and 1 million in the private sector—to absorb the hard-core unemployed and materially reduce the level of underemployment for all workers, black and white. We propose 250,000 public sector and 300,000 private sector jobs in the first year.
■ Provide on-the-job training by both public and private employers with reimbursement to private employers for the extra costs of training the hard-core unemployed, by contract or by tax credits.
■ Provide tax and other incentives to investment in rural as well as urban poverty areas in order to offer to the rural poor an alternative to migration to urban centers.
■ Take new and vigorous action to remove artificial barriers to employment and promotion, including not only racial discrimination but, in certain cases, arrest records or lack of a high school diploma. Strengthen those agencies such as the Equal Employment Opportunity Commission, charged with eliminating discriminatory practices, and provide full support for Title VI of the 1964 Civil Rights Act allowing Federal grant-in-aid funds to be withheld from activities which discriminate on grounds of color or race.

The Commission commends the recent public commitment of the National Council of the Building and Construction Trade Unions, AFL-CIO, to encourage and recruit Negro membership in apprenticeship programs. This commitment should be intensified and implemented.

EDUCATION. Education in a democratic society must equip children to develop their potential and to participate fully in American life. For the community at large, the schools have discharged this responsibility well. But for many minorities, and particularly for the children of the ghetto, the schools have failed to provide the educational experience which could overcome the effects of discrimination and deprivation.

This failure is one of the persistent sources of grievance and resentment within the Negro community. The hostility of Negro parents and students toward the school system is generating increased conflict and causing disruption within many city school districts. But the most dramatic evidence of the relationship between educational practices and civil disorders lies in the high incidence of riot participation by ghetto youth who have not completed high school.

The bleak record of public education for ghetto children is growing worse. In the critical skills—verbal and reading ability—Negro students are falling further behind whites with each year of school completed. The high unemployment and underemployment rate for Negro youth is evidence, in part, of the growing educational crisis.

We support integration as the priority education strategy; it is essential to the future of American society. In last summer's disorders we have seen the consequences of racial isolation at all levels, and of attitudes toward race, on both sides, produced by three centuries of myth, ignorance, and bias. It is indispensable that opportunities for integration between the races be expanded.

We recognize that the growing dominance of pupils from disadvantaged minorities in city school populations will not soon be reversed. No matter how great the effort toward desegregation, many children of the ghetto will not, within their school careers, attend integrated schools.

If existing disadvantages are not to be perpetuated, we must drastically improve the quality of ghetto education. Equality of results with all-white schools must be the goal.

To implement these strategies, the Commission recommends:

■ Sharply increased efforts to eliminate de facto segregation in our schools through substantial federal aid to school systems seeking to desegregate either within the system or in cooperation with neighboring school systems.
■ Elimination of racial discrimination in Northern as well as Southern schools by vigorous application of Title VI of the Civil Rights Act of 1964.
■ Extension of quality early childhood education to every disadvantaged child in the country.
■ Efforts to improve dramatically schools serving disadvantaged children through substantial federal funding of year-round quality compensatory education programs, improved teaching, and expanded experimentation and research.
■ Elimination of illiteracy through greater Federal support for adult basic education.
■ Enlarged opportunities for parent and community participation in the public schools.
■ Reoriented vocational education emphasizing work-experience training and the involvement of business and industry.
■ Expanded opportunities for higher education through increased federal assistance to disadvantaged students.
■ Revision of state aid formulas to assure more per student aid to districts having a high proportion of disadvantaged school age children.

THE WELFARE SYSTEM. Our present system of public welfare is designed to save money instead of people, and tragically ends up doing neither. This system has two critical deficiencies:

First, it excludes large numbers of persons who are in great need, and who, if provided a decent level of support, might be able to become more productive and self-sufficient. No Federal funds are available for millions of unemployed and underemployed men and women who are needy but neither aged, handicapped nor the parents of minor children.

Second, for those included, the system provides assistance well below the minimum necessary for a decent level of existence, and imposes restrictions that encourage continued dependency on welfare and undermine self-respect.

A welter of statutory requirements and administrative practices and regulations operate to remind recipients that they are considered untrustworthy, promiscuous, and lazy. Residence requirements prevent assistance to people in need who are newly arrived in the state. Searches of recipients' homes violate privacy. Inadequate social services compound the problems.

The Commission recommends that the Federal Government, acting with state and local governments where necessary, reform the existing welfare system to:

■ Establish, for recipients in existing welfare categories, uniform national standards of assistance at least as high as the annual "poverty level" of income, now set by the Social Security Administration at $3,335 per year for an urban family of four.
■ Require that all states receiving Federal welfare contributions participate in the Aid to Families with Dependent Children-Unemployed Parents Program (AFDC-UP) that permits assistance to families with both father and mother in the home, thus aiding the family while it is still intact.
■ Bear a substantially greater portion of all welfare costs—at least 90 percent of total payments.
■ Increase incentives for seeking employment and job training, but remove restrictions recently enacted by the Congress that would compel mothers of young children to work.
■ Provide more adequate social services through neighborhood centers and family-planning program.
■ Remove the freeze placed by the 1967 welfare amendments on the percentage of children in a State that can be covered by Federal assistance.
■ Eliminate residence requirements.

As a long-range goal, the Commission recommends that the Federal Government seek to develop a national system of income supplementation based strictly on need with two broad and basic purposes:

■ To provide, for those who can work or who do work, any necessary supplements in such a way as to develop incentives for fuller employment.
■ To provide, for those who cannot work and for mothers who decide to remain with their children, a minimum standard of decent living, and to aid in saving children from the prison of poverty that has held their parents.

A broad system of supplementation would involve substantially greater Federal expenditures than anything now contemplated. The cost will range widely depending on the standard of need accepted as the "basic allowance" to individuals and families, and on the rate at which additional income above this level is taxed. Yet if the deepening cycle of poverty and dependence on welfare can be broken, if the children of the poor can be given the opportunity to scale the wall that now separates them from the rest of society, the return on this investment will be great indeed.

HOUSING. After more than three decades of fragmented and grossly underfunded Federal housing programs, nearly 6 million substandard housing units remain occupied in the United States.

The housing problem is particularly acute in the minority ghettos. Nearly two-thirds of all nonwhite families living in the central cities today live in neighborhoods marked by substandard housing and general urban blight. Two major 'factors are responsible:

First: Many ghetto residents simply cannot pay the rent necessary to support decent housing. In Detroit, for example, over 40 percent of the nonwhite-occupied units in 1960 required rent of over 35 percent of the tenants' income.

Second: Discrimination prevents access to many nonslum areas, particularly the suburbs, where good housing exists. In addition, by creating a "back pressure" in the racial ghettos, it makes it possible for landlords to break up apartments for denser occupancy, and keeps prices and rents of deteriorated ghetto housing higher than they would be in a truly free market.

To date, Federal programs have been able to do comparatively little to provide housing for the disadvantaged. In the 31-year history of subsidized Federal housing, only about 800,000 units have been constructed, with recent production averaging about 50,000 units a year. By comparison, over a period only 3 years longer, FHA insurance guarantees have made possible the construction of over 10 million middle and upper income units.

Two points are fundamental to the Commission's recommendations:

First: Federal housing programs must be given a new thrust aimed at overcoming the prevailing patterns of racial segregation. If this is not done, those programs will continue to concentrate the most impoverished and dependent segments of the population into the central-city ghettos where there is already a critical gap between the needs of the population and the public resources to deal with them.

Second: The private sector must be brought into the production and financing of low and moderate-rental housing to supply the capabilities and capital necessary to meet the housing needs of the Nation.

The Commission recommends that the Federal Government:

■ Enact a comprehensive and enforceable Federal open-housing law to cover the sale or rental of all housing, including single-family homes.
■ Reorient Federal housing programs to place more low- and moderate-income housing outside of ghetto areas.

■ Bring within the reach of low- and moderate-income families within the next 5 years 6 million new and existing units of decent housing, beginning with 600,000 units in the next year.

To reach this goal we recommend:

■ Expansion and modification of the rent supplement program to permit use of supplements for existing housing, thus greatly increasing the reach of the program.
■ Expansion and modification of the below-market interest rate program to enlarge the interest subsidy to all sponsors, provide interest-free loans to non-profit sponsors to cover preconstruction costs, and permit sale of projects to nonprofit corporations, co-operatives, or condominiums.
■ Creation of an ownership supplement program similar to present rent supplements to make home ownership possible for low-income families.
■ Federal writedown of interest rates on loans to private builders constructing moderate-rent housing.
■ Expansion of the public housing program, with emphasis on small units on scattered sites, and leasing and "turnkey" programs.
■ Expansion of the Model Cities program.
■ Expansion and reorientation of the urban renewal program to give priority to projects directly assisting low-income households to obtain adequate housing.

CONCLUSION. One of the first witnesses to be invited to appear before this Commission was Dr. Kenneth B. Clark, a distinguished and perceptive scholar. Referring to the reports of earlier riot commissions, he said:

I read that report ° ° ° of the 1919 riot in Chicago, and it is as if I were reading the report of the investigating committee on the Harlem riot of '35, the report of the investigating committee on the Harlem riot of '43, the report of the McCone Commission on the Watts riot.

I must again in candor say to you members of this Commission—it is a kind of Alice in Wonderland—with the same moving picture reshown over and over again, the same analysis, the same recommendations, and the same inaction.

These words come to our minds as we conclude this report.

We have provided an honest beginning. We have learned much. But we have uncovered no startling truths, no unique insights, no simple solutions. The destruction and the bitterness of racial disorder, the harsh polemics of black revolt and white repression have been seen and heard before in this country.

It is time now to end the destruction and the violence, not only in the streets of the ghetto but in the lives of people.

36

The Kerner Report, Social Scientists, and the American Public: Introduction to a Symposium

NORVAL D. GLENN

THE UNIVERSITY OF TEXAS AT AUSTIN

IN THE EARLY SUMMER OF 1967 RIOTING BROKE OUT IN BLACK NEIGHBOR-hoods in Newark, Detroit, and several other cities in the United States.[1] In Newark and Detroit alone, 68 persons were killed, hundreds were injured, and property damage was as high as $55 million (initially estimated to be much higher). The losses in life and property from racial disturbances in the summer of 1967 exceeded those of 1965, when the riot in the Watts area of Los Angeles left 34 dead, and greatly exceeded the losses of any recent year other than 1965. Violent outbreaks in black ghettoes have not increased steadily from year to year, but the overall trend during the 1960's has clearly been toward greater violence.

Although most white Americans were not directly affected by the violence in Newark, Detroit, and other cities (fewer than 10 whites were killed in the major outbreaks), it led to what was perhaps unprecedented national concern about the "urban problem," or, less euphemistically, the "Negro problem."[2] In part in response to this concern, on July 27, 1967, President Lyndon Johnson appointed the National Advisory Commission on Civil Disorders and directed it to determine what happened and why, and to make recommendations for action to prevent a recurrence. After an intensive investigation, the Commission issued its *Report* February, 1968, four months prior to the deadline set by the President.

Tom Wicker, in his introduction to the preliminary edition of the *Report*, wrote the Commission consisted of representatives of the "moderate Establishment."[3] The chairman was Otto Kerner, then Governor of Illinois (hence, the *Report* is often called the "Kerner Report"). Other members were New York City Mayor John Lindsay; U.S. Senator Fred Harris, Oklahoma (Democrat); U.S. Representative James Corman, California (Democrat); U.S. Representative William McCulloch, Ohio (Republican); Herbert Jenkins, Atlanta Chief of Police; Katherine Peden, former Kentucky Commissioner of Commerce; I. W. Abel, president, United Steelworkers of America; and Charles Thornton, chairman, board of Litton Industries. The two black members of the Commission, U.S. Senator Edward Brooke, Massachusetts, and Roy Wilkins, executive director of the NAACP, are moderates; and in the minds of many young militant blacks, they are "Uncle Toms."

---

[1] Some observers insist that these outbreaks were insurrections rather than riots. I apply the more usual label to them without denying the validity of the claims that they were more nearly insurrections.

[2] However, as I point out below, this concern among the white public still was not extremely great, in an absolute sense.

[3] *Report of the National Advisory Commission on Civil Disorders* (New York: Bantam Books, 1968), p. v.

In view of the composition of the Commission, many observers predicted a whitewash, or a seeking of "political truth" rather than objective
truth, *a la* the highly criticized McCone Commission, which was appointed
by the California governor to investigate the Watts disorder.[4] Perhaps the
predictions that the Riot Commission *Report* would not grapple with the
real issues or place any major responsibility on moderate northern whites
were self-defeating;[5] perhaps the Riot Commission was determined to
avoid the kind of criticism the McCone Commission received. At any rate,
the Kerner Report is not as it was predicted to be. It places the blame for
violence in the ghettoes squarely on whites, including (at least by implication) the moderate majority. "White racism" receives the ultimate blame
throughout the *Report*. Shortcomings of Negroes are not overlooked; but
these shortcomings are always attributed to one or more of the many
manifestations of racism. "What white Americans have never fully understood—but what the Negro can never forget—is that white society is
deeply implicated in the ghetto. White institutions created it, white institutions maintain it, and white society condones it."[6]

"White racism" is a pejorative term too vague to have much explanatory
utility, but the Kerner Report spells out in considerable detail the specific
white attitudes and behavior it blames for the trouble. For instance, the
Report contains pages of evidence, always convincing if not absolutely
conclusive, of continued widespread discrimination in employment, administration of justice, police treatment, housing, and consumer and credit
practices. The *Report* does not attribute recent ghetto violence only to
discrimination and prejudice, however, but rather states that white racism
is "essentially responsible" for the "explosive mixture" that includes such
ingredients as a new mood of racial pride among Negroes, the growing
concentration of Negroes in the central cities, and the unfulfilled expectations aroused by the judicial and legislative victories of the Civil Rights
Movement.[7]

The recommendations of the Kerner Report go well beyond those of
earlier commissions that investigated racial disorders, and in the eyes of
many whites, some approach being radical. For instance, the report recommends a national system of income supplementation based strictly on
need (a negative income tax) to provide a minimum standard of decent
living for all citizens. And it recommends that the federal government
provide at least 90 per cent of all welfare costs, make available six million
new and existing housing units to low-income families within five years,
and provide funds for year-around compensatory education programs in

---

[4] For discussion of the concept of political truth, see Carl Akins, "The Riot Commission and Political Science," in this symposium.

[5] Just as prophesies sometimes lead to their fulfillment, they sometimes prevent their
fulfillment, and many are intended to do so. For some reason, the self-defeating
prophesy has received less attention from social scientists than the self-fulfilling prophesy, although the former may be the more frequent phenomenon.

[6] *Report of the National Advisory Commission on Civil Disorders*, p. 2.

[7] However, August Meier and Elliott Rudwick, in their contribution to this symposium, correctly point out that the *Report* does not make sufficiently clear the role of
the recent *decline* in racism in producing violence.

disadvantaged neighborhoods. In short, implementation of the *Report's* recommendations would entail considerable costs to white taxpayers, the majority of whom are not yet vitally concerned about ghetto violence.

To social scientists, there is nothing new and original in the *Report*, and certainly the conclusion that whites are ultimately responsible for the problems and pathologies of black America is not new. Most of us have espoused this view for many years. In fact, some of us have written, spoken, heard, and read it so often that a restatement of this "obvious truth" seems almost trite. However, when one realizes that this "trite" conclusion sharply contradicts the majority opinion of American whites, and that it was arrived at by a President's commission (more than half of whose members were public officials elected by largely white electorates), it then loses its triteness.

A Gallup poll conducted in May, 1968, just weeks after the conclusions of the Kerner Commission were made public, reveals how far the *Report* diverges from the majority views of white America.[8] Gallup asked of a national area probability sample (N=approximately 1,500): "Who do you think is MORE to blame for the present conditions in which Negroes find themselves—white people or Negroes themselves?" Only 23 per cent of the white respondents replied "white people," 58 per cent said "Negroes themselves," and 19 per cent reported no opinion. The whites most likely to blame their own race for the plight of Negroes were those with a college education, but only a third of these did so. Furthermore, most whites denied there was discrimination against Negroes in their home communities. Only 17 per cent said labor unions discriminate, only 18 per cent said most businesses discriminate in their hiring practices, and only 17 per cent said Negroes are not treated as well as whites. In view of these data, it is not surprising that most whites expressed little sympathy for Negro participants in ghetto violence, and especially little sympathy for looters. Fifty-eight per cent said police should shoot looters on sight—a position one is not likely to take if he feels that he, or a majority of whites, are to any great extent responsible for the behavior of the looters.

The general agreement of social scientists, in contrast to the white lay public, with the major conclusion of the Kerner Report is illustrated by the six other contributions to this symposium. None of the contributors disagree with the notion that whites are responsible for the plight and the unrest of black people in the United States. Although the contributions by Meier and Rudwick and by Mack stress that racism itself is not a sufficient explanation for the recent violence, they agree that it is a necessary condition. Meier and Rudwick and Edwards and Jones note criticisms that can be made of the *Report* when it is viewed as a scholarly document, but all these authors clearly believe the *Report* will tend to enlighten the white lay public, to the extent that it has any influence on those people. Furthermore, Edwards and Jones believe the *Report* signifies greater acceptance of social scientific findings by laymen and a "value drift" favorable to massive corrective action to aid Negroes.

Prestage has only minor criticisms of the conclusions of the *Report*; her

[8] The data reported here are from the *Gallup Opinion Index* (July, 1968), pp. 17–22.

contribution goes beyond the *Report* and grapples with crucial and relevant topics concerning black politics with which the Riot Commission did not directly deal. However, both she and Ginzberg express reservations about the Commission's recommendations. Prestage says the Commission may have placed too much emphasis on the material aspects of the black man's problems, and Ginzberg, modifying if not reversing an opinion he gave in testimony to the Commission, expresses doubts about the efficacy of federal money as a solution to those problems. In addition, Prestage considers the *Report* futile if it does not lead to radical corrective action.

Akins is not so concerned with evaluating the validity of the *Report*'s conclusions and the wisdom of its recommendations as with explaining its contents. He concludes that even though the *Report* is not the whitewash some observers predicted, it still may be viewed as a statement of "political truth."

I cannot refrain from adding my own evaluation of the *Report* to those of other contributors to this symposium. I am somewhat less sanguine about the *Report*'s value, and about the social trends its signifies, than are most of the other authors. Social scientists may be gratified that the *Report*, although occasionally prone to vagueness and oversimplification, generally reflects the social scientific and "liberal" points of view. This, however, may be more of a victory for social science than for black America; as of this writing, it seems highly unlikely that most of the recommendations of the Commission will soon be implemented. Whereas the Kerner Report, unlike the McCone Report, passes the test of acceptability to social scientists and liberals, it may well fail the test of political efficacy.[9] It tells what should be done but not how it can be done, in the face of overwhelming public opposition to such action.[10] Whereas the *Report* correctly identifies white racism as essentially responsible for the trouble, it proposes no realistic program to overcome racism.

Furthermore, the *Report* fails to deal realistically with another factor that may be as important an obstacle as racism to implementation of its recommendations. This factor is the apathy, the lack of concern, the lack of feelings of responsibility for black problems that characterize some of the less racist segments of the white population.

Many whites who verbally espouse egalitarian values and are not highly prejudiced feel little or no personal guilt about the plight of their black countrymen.[11] They will readily admit the guilt of their forefathers, and if they live in the North or West, of southern "rednecks." They con-

[9] After I wrote the first draft of this paper, I read a very similar conclusion in a paper by Amitai Etzioni ("Making Riots Mandatory," *Psychiatry and Social Science Review* [May, 1968], as excerpted in *Current* [Sept., 1968], pp. 23–26). In my final draft, my conclusion is even more similar to Etzioni's than it was in the first draft, and I acknowledge Etzioni's influence.

[10] Etzioni, *op. cit.*, correctly points out that the commitment of resources in Viet Nam is also a major obstacle to implementation of the Commission's recommendations. I doubt, however, that chances of early implementation would be very great even if there were no commitment in Viet Nam.

[11] I base this conclusion mainly on recent national poll data, including those reported above. I recognize the deficiencies of this evidence but have a strong "gut feeling" that

veniently ignore that they have inherited from their discriminating forefathers a legacy of occupational, economic, and social advantages over
Negroes; even though they may not now discriminate, they very likely
continue to benefit from past discrimination.[12] If they were consistent,
they would also accept from their forefathers a legacy of guilt and obligation to compensate for the centuries of wrongs blacks have experienced at
the hands of whites. But it is not the nature of human thought to be consistent when self-interest is not served by consistency. Therefore, the
typical liberal and relatively unprejudiced white American opposes "reverse discrimination" with at least as much fervor as he opposes discrimination against Negroes. The feeling that whites owe Negroes a social debt
for past wrongs appears to be very rare, even among the more liberal
segments of the white lay public.

Realistically, the guilt feelings, conscience, and altruism of whites cannot be relied on to bring about the programs and changes needed to satisfy the rising aspirations of blacks. As I have argued elsewhere, white
action that has significantly aided Negro advancement has been motivated
primarily by considerations of self-interest, or at least has not been contrary to perceived self-interest.[13] The corrective action necessary to prevent racial disturbances is not likely to be taken until a large number of
whites with enough power to effect the action feel definitely threatened.[14]
Unfortunately, that time does not seem close at hand. According to a Gallup poll conducted in June, 1968, only 19 per cent of the whites said they
expected serious racial trouble in their communities during the following
six months.[15] And undoubtedly many of those who expect trouble are not
fearful enough to pay the necessary costs—in higher taxes, increased competition from Negroes, and the like—to eliminate the threat of violence.
Some of the others probably are fearful enough that they would pay the
costs if they thought they must, but they believe repression can remove
the threat.

If this view is correct, the Kerner Report is largely irrelevant to the
course of race relations in the United States, or it may even tend to increase violence. It may intensify the feelings of blacks that their demands
are legitimate, and thus increase their frustrations and restiveness as it
becomes apparent that the federal administration and the white public
are going to take little action on the basis of the *Report*'s recommendations.

more adequate evidence still would not reveal widespread feelings of personal guilt,
even among liberals.

[12] See my "White Gains from Negro Subordination," *Social Problems*, 14 (Fall,
1966), pp. 159–178.

[13] "The Role of White Resistance and Facilitation in the Negro Struggle for Equality," *Phylon*, 26 (Summer, 1965), pp. 105–116.

[14] I must stress that the necessary corrective action might not be taken even under
those conditions. The powerful whites who feel threatened must perceive that corrective action rather than repression is the more effective means of dealing with the threat.
Some corrective and repressive measures are not mutually exclusive and I suspect that
if more whites were to feel threatened by racial violence, both corrective action and
certain kinds of repressive measures would be more likely.

[15] *Gallup Opinion Index* (July, 1968), p. 16.

37

Negro Protest and Urban Unrest

AUGUST MEIER
KENT STATE UNIVERSITY

ELLIOTT RUDWICK
KENT STATE UNIVERSITY

As a call to action, the Report of the National Advisory Commission on Civil Disorders is a superb document. Just because its main function is to marshal white public opinion to change the appalling conditions in the black ghettos, it inevitably leaves something to be desired as a work of scholarship.

Our function, of course, is to examine the *Report* from the point of view of historical and sociological scholarship. There are many things in the *Report* that deserve comment and detailed discussion, but space restricts us to an examination and amplification of two major points: the treatment of the causes of the riots of the 1960's and the historical sketch of the Negro protest movement.

The *Report* states,

> ". . . certain fundamental matters are clear. Of these, the most fundamental is the racial attitude and behavior of white Americans toward black Americans. Race prejudice has shaped our history decisively. . . . White racism is essentially responsible for the explosive mixture which has been accumulating in our cities. . . ."[1]

Historically it is absolutely true that the roots of the current racial crisis lie in the doctrine of white supremacy and the subordination of Negroes in the American social order. Yet, this view is an oversimplification, if not a distortion, of what has happened in the 1960's. It neglects to take into account that American institutions changed. The policies of the media of mass communication, of the federal and of many state and local governments indicated that for most of the articulate sectors of American public opinion, doctrines of white superiority and white racism were discredited. The fact is that while racism still exists among many white people, there is less of it today than there has ever been in American history. Indeed, it is just because of the lessening of American racism and the growing guilt of whites about their past—and present—treatment of Negroes, that the riots have occurred. The Commission mentions "the expectations aroused by the great judicial and legislative victories of the civil rights movement," and the resultant "frustration, hostility and cynicism in the face of the persistent gap between promise and fulfillment," as one of the ingredients in the explosive mixture that has produced the riots of the 1960's. But what the *Report* does not make clear is the tragic irony that without the retreat from racism which the judicial and legislative victories symbolize, the riots would not have occurred.

[1] *Report of the National Advisory Commission on Civil Disorders* (New York: Bantam Books, 1968), p. 203.

♦ First published in *Social Science Quarterly* 49, No. 3 (December, 1968).

The *Report's* handling of the data about distribution of the 1967 riots reflects the way in which the Commission has obscured this very important fact. One would expect, if white racism is the basic present-day cause of the riots, that these urban disorders would be most likely to occur where racist repression is most severe and the area where the majority of the nation's Negroes still reside. By the *Report's* own figures over half of the nation's black people still live in the South, the region still most repressive in its policies toward Negroes. Yet of the eight riots of 1967 which the *Report* lists as "major,"[2] only one—that in Tampa—was in the South. Of the 33 riots in 1967 which the *Report* lists as "serious," seven occurred in southern states Atlanta, Georgia; Birmingham, Alabama; Cambridge, Maryland; Houston, Texas; Jackson, Mississippi; Nashville, Tennessee; and Riviera Beach, Florida. It will be noted, however, that most of these southern riots took place in the more progressive areas of the South—that is, in Atlanta, and in what Matthews and Prothro have referred to as the "Peripheral South," both of which are more liberal than the Deep South in racial attitudes. In fact, the *Report*, on page 114, confuses matters by bracketing the southern and border states together as a region comparable to the West, the Midwest, and the Northeast, to support its conclusion that "violence was not limited to any one section of the country." Outside of Birmingham and Jackson, the Deep South had no major or serious rioting in 1967. And there, more than in any other section of the country, are found the variables associated with white racism which the Commission regards as so fundamental—that is, pervasive discrimination and segregation, white terrorism, defiance of federal authority by state and local officials, black ghettos, police brutality, unemployment and underemployment, and political powerlessness.

Thus, the basic factor responsible for the rioting of the 1960's is something more complex than white racism as such. Rather, it is due to the thwarting of rapidly rising expectations, to the failure to achieve quickly full equality and racial justice. And the expectation that racial justice could be rapidly attained occurred because white racism had perceptibly declined.

As the *Report* points out, the civil rights movement itself—from the founding of the National Association for the Advancement of Colored People (NAACP) in 1909 through the turbulent events of the 1950's and early 1960's—played a crucial role in bringing about the changes that in turn produced the revolution in expectations we have described. Yet, on the other hand, the *Report* fails to analyze the reasons for the increasing fragmentation, disunity, and ineffectiveness of the civil rights movement in the middle 1960's—a condition which was a major factor in producing the alienation and cynicism of the black power militants.

The process of growing fragmentation and ineffectiveness of the Negro protest movement was due basically to the disillusionment that came from the frustration of radically heightened expectation. Yet the process also

2 We are not in complete agreement with the way in which the *Report* classifies certain cities as having had "major" and "serious" riots. However, for the purposes of this discusssion, we are accepting the *Report's* classification.

was hastened by certain policies of the Johnson administration, which inadvertently and unintentionally interacted in a circular fashion with this mood of disillusionment to exacerbate the feelings of anger, cynicism, and pessimism among the most militant. The policies of the Johnson administration to which we refer were: the compromise effected as a result of the challenge of the Mississippi Freedom Democratic party (MFDP) at the 1964 Democratic party convention; the country's involvement in the Viet Nam War; and the War on Poverty. The *Report* basically failed to take these politically sensitive matters into account and, consequently, obscured the fact that one of the things producing the racial crisis of 1967 was what was happening in the civil rights movement itself.

The 1964 Democratic party convention, in the eyes of the militants, thoroughly discredited both the Democratic party establishment and the white liberal elements in the interracial coalition backing the national civil rights legislative program. The black militants believed that the party's compromise offer of two delegates-at-large was mere tokenism which proved the insincerity and untrustworthiness of the Johnson administration. Moreover, the radicals' growing distrust of white liberals like Walter Reuther—people who had originally supported the challenge but in the end advocated accepting the compromise—became complete. The liberals saw the compromise as significant progress, while Student Nonviolent Coordinating Committee (SNCC) and Congress of Racial Equality (CORE) regarded it as a bitter defeat. Finally the Negroes were deeply divided, with SNCC and CORE refusing to accept the compromise, while NAACP elements in the Freedom Democratic party and men like Bayard Rustin and Martin Luther King urged its acceptance.

In any case, even without the upshot of the Freedom Democratic party challenge, the various segments of the Negro protest movement became increasingly divided on how to tackle the problems of the ghettos. The growing cleavages were exacerbated by the war in Viet Nam. Opinion both within the movement and among its supporters was sharply split on this issue. Some believed that the Viet Nam War diverted attention and funds away from solving the country's leading domestic problem and that no serious steps would be taken toward alleviating conditions of the black masses until the war was ended. Others went even further and regarded the Viet Nam War as cut of the same cloth as internal racism within the United States, charging that both involved the attempt of the American "white power structure" to keep a colored race in a colonial status. At the opposite extreme were those who held that the Viet Nam issue was irrelevant as far as the Negro protest was concerned, and that to mix the two issues was tactically dangerous since it would lose support for the Negroes' cause among some friends who supported the Johnson administration's policy in Viet Nam.

The conflict over this issue weakened the Negro protest movement. A number of people, heretofore devoting their full time and energy to fighting racial discrimination, were diverted to working against the war in Viet Nam. Moreover, the debate intensified the cleavage in the coalition of Negro protest and other organizations that had supported the March on

Washington in 1963 and lobbied for the civil rights bills of 1964 and 1965. The Urban League and NAACP refused to identify themselves with the Viet Nam issue, while Martin Luther King, previously a key figure in the coalition strategy, openly attacked United States policy in Viet Nam (as did SNCC and CORE). The white supporters of the coalition were similarly split, with organized labor particularly endorsing the Johnson administration's war program.

By 1965, white funding of the direct-action organizations was drying up. All along the NAACP had been financed primarily by Negroes, and the Urban League continued to receive money from white business. Various factors appear to have accounted for the financial problems of CORE, SCLC, and SNCC—those groups which primarily used direct action tactics. Certainly the riots of 1964 and the following summer alienated some sympathetic whites. Many white financial supporters, impressed with the recognition which the Mississippi Freedom Democratic party had succeeded in obtaining at the Democratic convention were annoyed by the refusal of SNCC, MFDP, and CORE to accept the compromise. Finally the direct-action organizations lost white financial support because of their position on the Viet Nam War; even King, who had urged MFDP to accept the compromise at the 1964 Democratic convention, found that his opposition to the Viet Nam policy produced a sharp drop in SCLC's income.

The financial situation exacerbated distrust for the white liberals, and accelerated the decline in the activities of CORE and SNCC. Many individual workers in these organizations turned to peace activities. Others, including many among the most effective local leaders in the protest movement, were siphoned off into administrative positions—often well-paid—with the anti-poverty programs.

The anti-poverty program had several effects on the protest movement. For one thing, it accelerated the shift, already evident by 1964, from an emphasis on a national legislative program to local community action. The Office of Economic Opportunity (OEO) encouraged the development and widespread popularity of the idea of the importance of creating local community organizations as a prerequisite to the solution of the problems facing the masses of Negroes. The program, also, by virtue of its emphasis upon involving the poor in the decision-making process, accelerated tendencies already evident—and encouraged by CORE and SNCC in their southern work from 1963 on—in the direction of developing grass-roots indigenous leadership among the poor in their local communities.

The OEO programs played a key role both in the diminution of the traditional civil rights activities of certain of the major national civil rights organizations and in the process of fragmentation of the Negro protest movement. As we have already noted, one of the first results of the initial anti-poverty programs was to siphon off much of the ablest leadership—particularly in the more militant organizations.

This prominence of militant types from CORE and SNCC in the anti-poverty programs was undoubtedly one of the reasons for the development of a struggle within the black community over the administration of the CAP programs. On the one side were the more moderate middle-class leaders, often NAACP and Urban League types who traditionally had been the recognized leaders of the Negro community and the people with whom the white political and business establishment had been dealing for years. On the other side were the newer, more radical types, some of whom had emerged out of the nonviolent direct-action phase of the movement (these being chiefly middle-class types who found the NAACP program too gradualist), and others who were emerging from the ranks of the poor themselves. The struggle between these two groups accentuated and polarized cleavages along class lines that already existed within the Negro community and thus was a prime factor in the dissolution of the earlier trends toward unity of strategy, if not of personalities.

Finally, the OEO programs unintentionally served to increase the frustration and discontent among the black poor. The aims and rhetoric of the anti-poverty program further escalated the expectations of the Negro masses; yet, OEO failed to deliver anything substantial, at best did little to improve the conditions of the people whom it aimed to help. And at worst the OEO projects were obviously make-work ones designed to "cool it" for a summer. Poor people involved in these projects came to view them as just another "hustle," and attention was often centered on fighting over which groups or cliques within the minority community would share in the limited available resources. Moreover, even the best programs suffered as funds were cut back and projects discontinued. The result was increased cynicism about the "system" and the "power structure." Ironically, it is even likely that the failure of OEO to achieve anything near what it had seemed to promise, may have been a significant factor in augmenting the climate of angry discontent that produced the widespread rioting of 1967.

On the other hand, if, as the saying goes, some were "turned off" by the anti-poverty programs, others were "turned on" by the vision of community organization, self-help, and the idea of the poor administering the spending of resources supplied by the federal government for their advancement. Indeed, one legacy of the War on Poverty appears to be a widespread feeling that the government should allocate resources to the ghetto, to be spent for programs initiated and administered by the ghetto-dwellers. Thus, paradoxically, the OEO programs, while not solving the problems of the poor, led to a heightened militance among them.

It should be pointed out that the *Report of the National Advisory Commission on Civil Disorders* shows an awareness of the limitations of the federal programs intended to help the slumdwellers; however, while criticizing these efforts for being nowhere nearly large enough to solve the problems they were supposed to ameliorate, the *Report* fails to analyze the role of the War on Poverty in changing the nature of the Negro protest movement, or its ironic contribution to the heightened urban unrest.

We have chosen to focus on what we consider to be major weaknesses in the *Report*. Yet, despite its oversimplification of certain important matters, the *Report* is, nevertheless, useful. In fact, it handles some subjects with considerable expertise and sophistication—particularly the description of the "typical rioter," the contrast between the immigrant experience and the Negro experience in northern cities, and the discussion of the results of the riots.

The *Report* has made an enormous contribution to the popular discussion of race relations in America. Thus, in the final analysis, to judge it by the yardstick of scholarship may well be irrelevant.

38

Of White Racism and Black Mobilization

RAYMOND W. MACK
NORTHWESTERN UNIVERSITY

Neither peaceful protests nor large-scale riots result simply from the existence of an oppressed class. It is true that we have in America both an oppressed class and a pattern of violence and protest. But the pattern of violence we have seen over the past three or four years and the pattern of protest which has developed over a period of nearly twenty years are both relatively new phenomena. The pattern of oppression, on the other hand, is older than the nation itself.

The protest and the violence involve a large, discriminated-against lower class, socially defined on the basis of race. When this class is analyzed statistically as a social category, its median members are poor, over-crowded, poorly educated, discriminated against, and under-privileged in their access to political power, to economic opportunity, and to human dignity. But the protest and the violence are relatively new, whereas black Americans have been under-privileged and discriminated against for over three centuries. It is indeed poor social science analysis then simply to say that the position of black Americans in the stratification structure is the cause of civil disorder.

This is not to say that oppression is not a causative factor. But throughout most of our history, oppression has not resulted in militant protest or in widespread violence. We must ask as social scientists what other factors America has added to the pattern of oppression we have always practiced against our black citizens. American Negroes have been poor and discriminated against for over three centuries. What have we added to the equation in the past two decades that leads us to a National Advisory Commission on Civil Disorders?

Social scientists can identify four variables which differentiate black Americans today from their parents, grandparents, and enslaved ancestors: (1) marked upward mobility in that most critical of stratification factors, education, leading to (2) markedly higher expectations for equality of opportunity, for human dignity, for access to political power, and for economic payoff in the society's reward structure, leading to (3) social organization to protest the discrimination which serves as a road block in gaining access to these expectations, with all three of these occurring at the same time that black Americans have suffered (4) the dislocation of the mass migration which has removed them from their traditional rural southern homes to the concentration of northern urban ghettos.

Educational mobility. Only a little over a century ago, it was illegal in many states with large Negro populations to teach Negroes to read and write; at the beginning of this century, most black Americans were still illiterate. In 1940 the median years of school completed by white males 25–29 years old was more than ten; for black males it was only a little over six. The gap has narrowed rapidly; by 1960 the median years completed by males 25–29 years old was just over twelve for whites and just over ten for blacks. By 1966 that two-year gap had narrowed to one of only half a year: twelve and one-half years for white males, twelve years for black males. Only ten years ago two-thirds of young Negroes dropped out before completing high school; today more than half are finishing.

INCREASED EXPECTATIONS. In American society, education is viewed as perfume for the "sweet smell of success." But as Blau and Duncan point out:

> A Negro's chances of occupational success in the United States are far inferior to those of a Caucasian. Whereas this hardly comes as a surprise to anyone familiar with the American scene, it is noteworthy that Negroes are handicapped at every step in their attempts to achieve economic success, and these cumulative disadvantages are what produces the great inequalities of opportunities under which the Negro American suffers. Disproportionate numbers of Negroes live in the South, where occupational opportunities are not so good as in the North. Within each region, moreover, Negroes are seriously disadvantaged. They have lower social origins than whites, and they receive less education. Even when Negroes and whites with the same amount of education are compared, Negroes enter the job market on lower levels. Furthermore, if all these differences are statistically controlled and we ask how Negroes would fare if they had the same origins, education, and career beginnings as whites, the chances of occupational achievement of Negroes are still considerably inferior to those of whites. Within the same occupation, finally, the income of Negroes is lower than that of whites. The multiple handicaps associated with being an American Negro are cumulative in their deleterious consequences for a man's career.[1]

In this sense, it is whites who have initiated conflict in American society. Conflict arises when, in competition, one of the competitors refuses to abide by the rules—when a runner in a race trips his competitor. The rules of the American stratification competition teach Americans that if they achieve in the educational race they will be rewarded in the spheres of occupation, income, and social respect. White Americans have used institutionalized race discrimination as a means of avoiding this open competition.

It is one thing to live in a caste society where one is taught to expect to stay in his place, but black Americans have been taught—by schools, by churches, by patriotic pronouncements, and by the mass media—to expect the rewards available in an open competitive society and have been frustrated by the denial of these rewards.

ORGANIZATION. Sociologists know that revolutions, whether peaceful or violent, are made not by the most down-trodden and oppressed participants in a social order, but by those whose status has been improving and who then find that access to further improvement is blocked. This society became a nation when a revolution was organized by the thirteen best-governed colonies in the world. A few years later a revolution was made

[1] Peter M. Blau and Otis Dudley Duncan, *The American Occupational Structure* (New York: John Wiley and Sons, 1967).

in France—not by the serfs, but by the bourgeoisie. The civil rights protest movement of the 1950's and 1960's was led not by sharecroppers or by unemployed, unskilled laborers, but by clergymen, lawyers, and college students.

We, as social scientists, should not be thrown off the trail by the skillful press relations of a Bob Moses when he appears on television in his tattered sweater and overalls to talk about grass roots leadership. Moses is a leader all right; he is also the holder of an M.A. in philosophy from Harvard. It is not accidental that the early effective organization and vigorous protest occurred in the Deep South where the discrepancy was most marked between the achievement of middle class characteristics, such as a college education, and the access to middle class perquisites, such as respectful service in a restaurant.

MIGRATION AND DISLOCATION. In 1940, 77 per cent of black Americans still lived in the South. By now, nearly half live outside the South and nearly three-fourths of those outside the South live in the central cities of metropolitan areas. This upheaval from a rural and, for many, essentially feudal mode of living means that a generation of northern urban Negroes is being reared in northern ghettos by parents ill equipped to help them learn to live in this alien environment.

What the Commission has addressed is the violence which has erupted particularly among the young, ill-socialized males in these northern central cities. Many readers of the *Report* were startled to learn that the rioters were not essentially an uneducated underclass of criminals and recent migrants. Rather than migrants, they were products of the costs of migration. The typical rioter in the summer of 1967 was an unmarried black male between the ages of 15 and 24, somewhat better educated than the average inner-city Negro, but working in a menial or low-status job as an unskilled laborer in a position where his income was frequently interrupted by periods of unemployment. "He feels strongly that he deserves a better job, and that he is barred from achieving it, not because of lack of training, ability, or ambition, but because of discrimination by employers."[2]

Certainly one caution is in order. Social scientists should not join the general public in overestimating and exaggerating the extent of the civil disorders. Of the 164 disorders analyzed in the *Report of the National Advisory Commission of Civil Disorders,*

> One hundred and twenty-three disorders, 75 percent of the total, were minor. These would not have been classified as 'riots' or received wide press attention without national conditioning to a 'riot climate.' They were characterized generally by: (1) a few fires and broken windows; (2) violence lasting generally less than one day; (3) participation by only small numbers of people; and (4) use, in most cases, only of local police or police from a neighboring community.[3]

[2] *Report of the National Advisory Commission on Civil Disorders* (New York: Bantam Books, 1968), p. 203.
[3] *Ibid.*, p. 113.

It is poignant that with all the pious talk of white racism as the root cause of the rioting, most of the programs that have been proposed by industry, by government, and by voluntary agencies are programs calculated to do something to, with, or about black citizens. As the Commission says in its introduction to the *Report*, "What white Americans have never fully understood—but what the Negro can never forget—is that white society is deeply implicated in the ghetto. White institutions created it, white institutions maintain it, and white society condones it."[4] This is not to argue that many of the *Report*'s recommendations for national action in unemployment, education, welfare, and housing are not sorely needed, but we should bear in mind that these programs are unlikely to point us toward a solution to the problem of two societies, one black, one white—separate and unequal—unless they are accompanied by programs to alter the structure of the society which brought us to the need for a National Advisory Commission on Civil Disorders.

Of course we need six million low- and middle-income housing units, but we also need to have them sprinkled through previously all-white residential areas rather than packed into the central city ghettos which brought us to our present tragic confrontation.

Social scientists have helped American society to comprehend the dilemma by their careful research on the ten per cent of our population which is black. Perhaps the time is past due for us to exert equal energy on careful research into the 90 per cent which is white, and which defines what it means to be black in America.

[4] *Ibid.*, p. 2.

39

The Commission's Report: Some Sociological and Policy Considerations

G. FRANKLIN EDWARDS
HOWARD UNIVERSITY

CLIFTON R. JONES
HOWARD UNIVERSITY

T HE *Report of the National Advisory Commission on Civil Disorders* IS A significant document which brings together much of what social scientists have learned of the underlying causes of racial disturbances in general and the factors involved in the civil disorders of the summer of 1967 in particular, along with a list of recommendations designed to prevent the recurrence of such disorders. In many respects the document resembles the reports of other commissions on the subject of racial disturbances and civil disorders, but in other respects the present *Report* can be distinguished from the earlier ones.[1]

Unlike others, the present *Report* is forthright in placing the major blame for the civil disorders of 1967 upon "white racism" and finds the causes of disruptions in the control of ghetto institutions by whites. Analyzing available data on many aspects of institutional life—economic, political, educational and social—the Commission concludes that a systematic pattern of discrimination and prejudice exists on the part of whites. It is this exclusionary pattern to which Negroes have reacted. Although this general finding has been included in other reports on the subject of race riots in this country, the present *Report* makes it indubitably clear and a central, organizing theme upon which its recommendations are based.

While all previous reports have underscored the role of the migration of Negroes to cities and the disadvantages under which they have lived in the large urban communities to which they have moved as factors contributing to the development of racial tensions, none of the earlier documents have had to consider these factors in conjunction with the recent and rapid rise in the level of Negro expectations. What is of crucial significance is that the rising expectations occur at a time when many avenues to goal achievement are blocked. What Negroes are demanding is not only a more equitable share of the housing, employment, and educational resources of the nation, but also, as one student has pointed out,[2] admission on an equal basis to membership in the community.

[1] Reference is made specifically to the following reports: Chicago Commission on Race Relations, *The Negro in Chicago* (Chicago: The University of Chicago Press, 1922); New York (City) Mayor's Commission to Inquire into Conditions in Harlem during the March, 1935, Riots in Harlem; and A Report by the Governor's Commission on the Los Angeles Riots, *Violence in the City—An End or a Beginning?*, Los Angeles, California, December 2, 1965.

[2] Harold Pfautz, "The American Dilemma: Prospects and Proposals," paper delivered at the Conference on "Short Term and Emergency Measures to Avert Urban Violence," Center for Policy Study, University of Chicago, November, 1967.

◆ First published in *Social Science Quarterly* 49, No. 3 (December, 1968).

The *Report*, therefore, was developed under a different set of conditions and reaches the conclusion that a mere reduction of tensions will not suffice to prevent future disturbances. What is required are broad-based programs which will move the Negro closer to the goals of equality, both in the sharing of opportunities and as members of the community. There also is a sense of urgency about the actions recommended which is notably absent in other reports. The explosiveness of our central cities is not episodic, as witnessed by the 150 communities which experienced racial disturbances in the summer of 1967.[3] What is recognized is that, given the disabilities under which Negroes live at present and the boundaries which circumscribe their movement toward a more legitimate place in the society, violent disruptions are endemic to contemporary urban life in the United States. The problem, moreover, is not alone one of resolving the position of the Negro, but, by so doing, of relieving the intractable conditions of the American city in which Negroes are disproportionately represented in the central cities and whites concentrated in the suburbs. The economic and political viability of the city is seriously impaired by the separation of racial groups, but, even more, such physical patterning helps generate and sustain the "racism" which, in the Commission's judgment, is responsible for the disorders investigated.

The Commission's analysis, in focusing upon the inter-related problems of race, poverty, and civil disorders, benefits from advances in social science knowledge over the past two decades. While poverty has been a subject of social investigation for almost a century, during much of that period it was approached in moral and religious terms (the Marxian analysis represents an important exception). Only in recent years has the influence of poverty upon aspirations and achievement begun to be documented and understood. The retarding effects of disadvantaged home conditions upon a child's cognitive development and the meaning of such experience for later learning are now better understood. This, in turn, has led to more serious study of the school system, and the slum school in particular, with regard to its capacity to meet the needs of a large segment of the student population. The *Report* notes that both inadequate preschool preparation and the inferior quality of education available in ghetto schools contribute to school dropouts and to teen-age and young adult unemployment which have contributed to the disorders.

Further reliance of the *Report* upon social science research may be gained from its acceptance of findings from the Coleman report on *Equality of Educational Opportunity*, the Civil Rights Commission's report on *Racial Isolation in the Public Schools*, the Taeubers' *Negroes in American Cities*, and other recent studies.[4] It accepts, for example, the Coleman finding that segregated education is damaging to Negro children from

[3] *Report of the National Advisory Commission on Civil Disorders* (New York: Bantam Books Edition, 1968), p. 32.

[4] James S. Coleman *et al.*, *Equality of Educational Opportunity* (Washington: U.S. Government Printing Office, 1966); *Racial Isolation in the Public Schools*, a Report of the United States Civil Rights Commission, 1967; and Karl Taeuber and Alma Taeuber, *Negroes in American Cities* (Chicago: Aldine Publishing Co., 1965).

disadvantaged homes; such children perform better academically when they attend school with other children having superior educational advantages. In like manner "destiny control"—the belief of the Negro child in his ability to shape the future—is related to the proportion of whites in the school. This latter factor was found to have a more important relationship to the Negro child's achievement than all other factors together.[5]

In indicating the linkage between the *Report* and social science research, it should be indicated that the use of the survey technique in three separate studies by researchers at the University of Michigan, the Johns Hopkins University, the Massachusetts Institute of Technology and Columbia University has provided more systematic information on racial attitudes, the operation of ghetto institutions and the characteristics of rioters than was available to other studies of racial disturbances.[6]

To indicate that the *Report* makes use of social science research findings and that its conclusions have been shaped in large part by such findings is not to suggest that all social scientists agree with the *Report*'s analysis or all of its conclusions. Some students assert that it contains important omissions and distortions. One student, for example, notes that racism is too abstract to explain the dynamic relationships between Negroes and whites. The concept is used in such a blanket fashion that no one in fact is condemned. It is further observed that the *Report* fails to recognize the positive aspects of civil disorder and violence; analytically, it does not establish a relationship between the civil disorders and the Viet Nam War, and it demonstrates a sociological naiveté in lumping all civil disturbances together and in failing to recognize that the disorders represent an emergent process rather than a number of discrete events.[7]

However well-founded these criticisms, it should be remembered that the document is not a piece of scientific research. Its failure to make greater use of social science analysis doubtless results from staff and time limitations. But it is clear that the work done by social scientists in studying the problems of the disadvantaged and the processes which operate in their community life, initiated within the past two decades and now developing on a substantial scale, has made a significant impact upon the *Report*.

A primary value of the *Report* is that it calls attention to the *national* significance of the problem of civil disorders and their underlying causes. Whereas earlier reports dealt with disruptions in Chicago, Detroit, East St. Louis, New York, and other local communities, the broadened scope of this form of behavior, along with its intensity and seriousness, calls for national action.

If, indeed, these disorders are symptoms of the failure of the existing structure to satisfy fundamental needs, it can be expected that changes at

[5] *Report of the National Advisory Commission on Civil Disorders,* p. 427.

[6] *Supplemental Studies for the National Advisory Commission on Civil Disorders* (Washington: U.S. Government Printing Office, July, 1968).

[7] Gary T. Marx, "Two Cheers for the Riot Commission Report," *The Harvard Review,* 4 (Summer, 1968), pp. 3–14.

many levels will occur. One such change doubtless will be an increased interest of social scientists in problems of the ghetto and the larger community and the direction of their skill to a further understanding of existing conditions. Whether this results from conscious effort to make social science more relevant or simply to understand the dynamic forces at work, the outcome will be salutary. In this connection, one may point to the increase in studies dealing with police systems and police-community relations, citizen participation, model cities and educational programs, and to the decentralization of community services and control, areas in which the *Report* calls for action.

On the action side, the *Report* makes an impressive list of recommendations in the areas of employment, education, housing, welfare, and in the administration of justice. None of these are particularly new; most, in fact, have been recommended previously by liberal congressmen, the Johnson administration, and civil rights groups. The significance of these recommendations lies in the scale and scope of the action suggested and, by implication, the manner in which programs in various areas must be inter-related to provide a concerted attack on the underlying causes of disorders. A reading of these recommendations leads to the conclusion that they constitute a most enlightened summary of programs to relieve the immediate causes of deprivations and unrest.

Students of contemporary community life and of the problems of the disadvantaged applaud these recommendations, but remain skeptical regarding the possibility of their being implemented in the immediate future. Bayard Rustin, for example, regards the *Report*'s major deficiencies, on the action side, as "its lack of cost-analysis, the slowness with which it urges implementation of programs, and its failure to call for the destruction of ghettos and the construction of new towns."[8] Regarding full employment, he notes that ". . . the *Report* failed to declare unequivocally that the government must be the employer of first and last resort for the hard-core poor."[9]

Certainly the costs of the programs recommended are important considerations, and the position of the skeptics is thus well taken, given past performances by Congress and the national preoccupation with the Viet Nam War. But the significance of the recommendations may be viewed in another way. They add to the emerging consensus that only drastic reform in our community and institutional life will eliminate the costly failure of the society to provide opportunities for all of its members and thus forestall disorders. There is a "value drift" which permits action programs to develop on a scale far broader than was possible in previous periods.

Even in a year which experiences a large budget deficit and a continuation of war costs to escalate, Congress has passed a housing bill which goes beyond previous housing legislation in scope and costs.

The Housing Act of 1968 does build upon previous legislation in the

[8] Bayard Rustin, "The Report of the National Advisory Commission on Civil Disorders: An Analysis," (New York: A. Philip Randolph Institute, n.d.), p. 2.
[9] *Ibid.*

housing field, such as its proposal to expand the number of dwelling units built for low-income and middle-income families, and by expanding the urban renewal and rent-supplement programs. But it also introduces some new and challenging concepts by which government would assist low- and middle-income families to become homeowners by making it possible for such families to commit only one per cent of their income to interest payments and only twenty per cent of family income to total monthly payments.

The observation that changes such as the above are occurring is small compensation in view of what needs to be done. The fact is that the pace of change can be accelerated, given a national will to do so. There must, however, be a readiness for such acceleration to occur. The civil disorders and the Advisory Commission's *Report*, by inviting attention to the need for more rapid and more broadly-gauged action, doubtless will contribute to the preparation of such readiness.

It is enough to conclude these comments with the observations that in terms of its content, the type of report discussed could not have been produced twenty years ago. Nor could it be expected that such recommendations as the *Report* advances would have been made as recently as fifteen years ago. The *Report*, therefore, is not only a commentary on the ills of our society, but is as well a document which informs us of the tortuous nature of the change process.

40

The Economist Who Changed His Mind

ELI GINZBERG
COLUMBIA UNIVERSITY

W HEN I TESTIFIED BEFORE THE NATIONAL ADVISORY COMMISSION ON CIVIL Disorders I stressed two points—one historical, the other economic. Drawing on our 1964 study, *The Troublesome Presence: American Democracy and the Negro,* I tried to convince the Commission that white America has been racist in conviction and action, and that there will be no prospect of domestic tranquility until white America is willing to recognize the Negro as a full-fledged citizen and to grant him the rights and privileges of citizenship. Nothing has happened in the intervening nine months —not even the howling of the liberals who feel that the Commission made an error in analysis and tactics in stressing the racist character of the United States—to change this historical view.

My second approach was to stress the need for expanded government programs aimed at improving the preparation of Negro children and youth for work and life, and the concomitant need for an expanded and strengthened manpower policy that would provide jobs for many Negroes who are currently out of the labor force, unemployed or underemployed. I underscore the need for Congress to expand its support for ghetto-impacted schools and to implement the Employment Act of 1946 by launching a large-scale job creation program.

I have changed my opinions with respect to this part of my testimony. Why? Can there be any question that since only 60 per cent of the age group graduate from high school in New York City and many of these have earned a diploma that attests more to their deportment than to their knowledge, something is awry with the education of Negro and Puerto Rican youth in New York? And let us look at testimony from the South: rates of rejection for military service based on an eighth grade equivalency examination runs above 50 per cent for Negro youth in South Carolina. How can anybody question the need for more federal financing for public education?

The employment situation is correspondingly bleak. In general, Negro unemployment rates run at twice that of whites; but the rate for teenage Negro girls fluctuates above the 30 per cent level—more than three times the comparable white rate. Moreover, we know from the special surveys conducted by the U.S. Department of Labor that the subemployment rate in the heart of the ghettos among Negroes—those not in the labor force, unemployed, underemployed or earning under $60 a week (poverty level for head of household with two dependents)—totals 35 per cent or more. Who can doubt that a strong government job creation program is required?

Ever since Keynes, most economists have been impressed with the potency of governmental spending as a way to absorb unused resources. And ever since the New Deal, most social scientists have agreed with the prop-

osition that when localities and states are unable to provide a minimum
level of services—educational, health, welfare—it is both right and proper that the federal government step in and make sizable funds available.

Given these preconceptions—these scholarly convictions that have
gained increasing approval from the voting public—why was my initial
advice to the Commission stressing more money for ghetto schools and
more jobs for the Negro unemployed and underemployed wrong? Can
anyone doubt that the money and the jobs are needed, and that if they
become available the position of the Negro would be significantly improved? I have now joined the doubters because of the criterion of "significant improvement."

We have seen experiments underwritten with both foundation and governmental funds that have raised per pupil expenditures by as much as
50 per cent over a reasonable base figure. While all the evidence is not
yet in, enough is at hand to warn against the blithe assumption that Negro
youngsters who today show three years retardation in basic skills at the
ninth grade level will be at their appropriate age level or close to it if
only more money were spent on their education.

To oversimplify a complex matter, it is probably true that no matter
how much money is spent, children will not learn if those who teach them
do not believe that they are capable of learning and if the principal objective of the educational system continues to be the avoidance of trouble.
More money is essential if this national scandal of the incapacity of the
public school to educate the Negro child is to be terminated. But the
money will be productive only in a new environment and with a new
source of teaching manpower. We sorely need a year's service from college juniors, or seniors or graduate students who, out of commitment and
conviction, can prove that Negro students can learn. We need such an
input, not for three or five years, or even ten years, but for a generation.

Education is a subtle process, not easily responsive to reform. But
what about the challenge of jobs for those who need them? What possible
objection can there be to a large-scale job creation program by the federal
government? One of the most revealing findings reported in city after
city torn by riots was that most of the participants who were arrested
were job-holders—a great many were earning $100 or more weekly.
Young unemployed Negroes also were picked up by the police, but most
of those who were booked were employed. Here is one reason to go
slowly in seeing a panacea in more jobs.

But there are further reasons. A regular job is no longer a prerequisite
for the receipt of income. About a million persons in New York City are
on relief and included in this group are many women and children. Many
men can get a bed, a meal and even a little spending money from their
mothers or girl friends. And they can pick up a little more by doing odd
jobs now and again. Subsistence agriculture has long served as the farmers' social security; the equivalent for the urban poor is relief.

Among the dimensions of ghetto life about which we are ignorant is
the quasi-legal and illegal employment which yield relatively high incomes to the participants. Why should a young Negro man wash dishes

for 40 hours a week for $60 when he can earn as much in four hours push-ing drugs?

Since there are not sufficient good jobs—that is, jobs that pay reason-ably well and that lead somewhere—many young Negroes, especially those who are not only alienated from but who reject outright the culture and values of white middle-class America, avoid regular employment. Employment at a poor job, especially one where the boss is white, is proof to the Negro of his powerlessness.

Since there is little prospect that Congress will be able to fashion a job creation program that would provide a large number of "good jobs" for Negroes, faith should not be pinned to a federal manpower program to remedy the malaise that afflicts so many American Negroes, as they stand outside the society with little prospect of making the grade even if white attitudes and behavior improve spectacularly and quickly.

Another drawback to large-scale government job expansion programs is the way in which such an effort would act as a magnet and draw into the already overcrowded slum areas of our large cities many hundreds of thousands of poor whites and poor Negroes who today are unable to earn a living wage. As the recent report by the President's Commission on Rural Poverty indicated, there are 13 million rural people who have been left behind—10 million of them white. A truly effective governmental pro-gram directed to improving the lot of the urban Negro can succeed only if a parallel large-scale program devoted to the sources of rural poverty is instituted to slow down and, it is hoped, stop the flooding of the city with poor migrants.

This cautionary view about the ability of federal financing to make a *significant* dent in the short-run on either the quality of the education or the employment of disadvantaged Negroes would not command assent from many of my fellow economists. A minority might be opposed to large-scale programs not on the ground that they would fail the Negro but simply because they would entail too high a cost in inflation and taxes on white Americans. The majority might agree with the Commission's finding that a vastly expanded federal effort for education and employ-ment as well as for housing and welfare holds the best prospects for rapid progress on the racial front. But the success of a market economy depends on the effective functioning of a vast array of social institutions including the family, the school, the corporation, the trade union, and government.

Three hundred and fifty years of aggressive discrimination has taken a terrible toll by crippling the ability of each of these institutions to per-form their basic functions effectively for the Negro minority. One of the reasons that I argue against the assumption that money, even lots of money, will prove effective is that these basic institutions must be radical-ly transformed before they can function effectively where Negroes are concerned. And money alone cannot transform them.

As long as white teachers remain prejudiced and Negro teachers con-tinue to be poorly prepared, Negro children will not be properly educat-ed. As long as white homeowners in the suburbs and white apartment dwellers in the city are determined to prevent Negroes from moving into their communities, many Negroes will be kept from getting jobs that they could handle and many others will not even make the effort to work and improve themselves.

Negroes have made more progress objectively measured in terms of employment, income, and living standards since 1940 than any other minority group in the history of this country in a comparable period of time. But so little improvement in the lot of the Negroes occurred between 1619 and 1940 that the recent gains have not sufficed to contain more than three centuries of mounting frustration and hostility.

More and more Negroes—those who are the spokesmen for black power and the millions who support it—are demanding that racism be exorcised from American life. This is their first and overriding demand. And unless and until it is exorcised, white America must recognize that all other efforts will at best be palliatives. If, and only if, there is a national commitment to this goal will the many necessary and essential programs of specific assistance to the Negro community have some prospect of succeeding. American Negroes need help, but they need acceptance and respect even more. The quicker white America understands that it has no option but to grant the Negro what is his right of humanity and citizenship, the shorter will be the period of its travail. If white America balks, it is inviting disaster. No metropolitan society can long survive if even a small number of its members will risk death rather than continue to suffer the indignities of rejection and exclusion.

41

Black Politics and the Kerner Report
Concerns and Direction

JEWEL L. PRESTAGE
SOUTHERN UNIVERSITY

Reactions to the report of the *National Advisory Commission on Civil Disorders*[1] have been widespread and varied, both in terms of their sources and their content. This discussion is essentially an effort to relate the *Report* to some of the theories and research findings in three areas of political science; namely, political socialization, democratic theory, and black political strategy. Any value accruing from this effort will probably be the results of the questions raised rather than directions or answers given.

POLITICAL SOCIALIZATION

One of the comparatively new and rapidly developing fields of inquiry for political scientists is political socialization.[2] Greenstein defines political socialization as ". . . all political learning formal and informal, deliberate and unplanned, at every stage of the life cycle, including not only explicitly political learning but also nominally nonpolitical learning which affects political behavior. . . ."[3]

[1] National Advisory Committee on Civil Disorders, *Report of the National Advisory Commission on Civil Disorders* (New York: Bantam Books, 1968) (hereafter referred to as the *Report*).

[2] Major studies include Herbert Hyman, *Political Socialization* (Glencoe, Ill.: The Free Press, 1959); Fred Greenstein, *Children and Politics* (New Haven: Yale University Press, 1965); Gabriel Almond and Sidney Verba, *The Civic Culture* (Boston: Little, Brown and Company, 1965); Lewis Froman, "Personality and Political Socialization," *Journal of Politics*, 23 (May, 1961), pp. 341–352; David Easton and Robert D. Hess, "Youth and the Political System" in Seymour M. Lipset and Leo Lowenthal, eds., *Culture and Social Character* (New York: The Free Press of Glencoe, 1961), pp. 226–251; David Easton and Robert D. Hess, "The Child's Political World," *Midwest Journal of Political Science*, 6 (Aug., 1962), pp. 229–246; Roberta Sigel, "Political Socialization: Some Reactions on Current Approaches and Conceptualizations," paper read at the 62nd annual meeting of the American Political Science Association, New York City, September, 1966; John J. Patrick, "Political Socialization of American Youth: A Review of Research with Implications for Secondary School Social Studies," High School Curriculum Center in Government, Indiana University, Bloomington, Indiana, March, 1967, mimeographed paper; Jack Dennis, "Major Problems of Political Socialization Research," *Midwest Journal of Political Science*, 12 (Feb., 1968), pp. 85–114.

[3] Fred Greenstein, "Political Socialization," in *International Encyclopedia of the Social Sciences* (New York: Crowell-Collier Macmillan Publishing Company, 1968); Roberta Sigel defines political socialization as "the gradual learning of the norms, attitudes, and behavior accepted and practiced by the ongoing political system." See Roberta Sigel, "Assumptions About the Learning of Political Values," *Annals of the American Academy of Political and Social Science*, 361 (Sept., 1965), pp. 1–9; of political socialization, Gabriel Almond writes, "What do we mean by the function of political socialization? We mean that all political systems tend to perpetuate their cultures and structures through time, and that they do this mainly by means of the socializing influences of the primary and secondary structures through which the young of the society pass in the process of maturation." See Gabriel Almond and James Cole-

Because political socialization has been interpreted as involving "all political learning at every stage of the life cycle" the dimensions of research possibilities are indeterminable.[4] It has been suggested that a full-blown characterization of political socialization would include classifications of: (1) who learns, (2) what is learned, (3) the agents of political socialization, (4) the circumstances of political socialization, and (5) the effects of political learning.[5]

An understanding of the political socialization function is essential to the understanding and analysis of any political system, and the stability and continued existence of a political system depend, in no small measure, on the extent to which the citizenry internalizes political norms and attitudes supportive of the system.[6] Political socialization, then, is induction into the political culture,[7] the means by which an individual "comes to terms" with his political system. The *Report* would seem to suggest that "coming to terms" is an especially traumatic experience for black people in America.

Examined in the context of current findings of political socialization research, the *Report* gives rise to several crucial concerns. The nature of these concerns is implicit in the observations which follow.

First, the political world of American blacks is so radically different from the political world of American whites that it might well constitute a "subculture" within a dominant or major culture. Even though there has been a great volume of writing and research on political socialization, very little has been directed to political socialization of American blacks.[8] The studies suggest that black people tend to relate rather differently to the political system and have a far greater sense of personal aliena-

man, eds., *The Politics of Developing Areas* (Princeton, N.J.: Princeton University Press, 1960), p. 27.

[4] The varied nature of such studies may be discerned from the foci of the following studies: Philip E. Converse and George Dupeux, "Politicization of the Electorate in France and the United States," *Public Opinion Quarterly*, 26 (Spring, 1962), pp. 1–23; Fred Greenstein, "Sex-Related Political Differences in Childhood," *Journal of Politics*, 23 (May, 1961), pp. 353–371; M. Kent Jennings and Richard Niemi, "Family Structure and the Transmission of Political Values," *American Political Science Review*, 62 (March, 1968), pp. 169–184; Heinz Eulau, William Buchanan, Leroy G. Ferguson, and John C. Wahlke, "The Political Socialization of American State Legislators" in John Wahlke and Heinz Eulau, eds., *Legislative Behavior: A Reader in Theory and Research* (Glencoe: The Free Press, 1959); Edgar Litt, "Civic Education, Community Norms and Political Indoctrination," *American Sociological Review*, 28 (Feb., 1963), pp. 69–75.

[5] Fred I. Greenstein, *Children and Politics* (New Haven: Yale University Press, 1965), p. 12.

[6] Almond and Coleman, *Politics of Developing Areas*, p. 31.

[7] Almond and Verba state, "When we speak of the political culture of a society, we refer to the political system as internalized in the cognitions, feelings and evaluations of its population." Almond and Verba, *The Civic Culture*, p. 13.

[8] See Dwaine Marvick, "The Political Socialization of the American Negro," *Annals of the American Academy of Political and Social Science*, 361 (Sept., 1965), pp. 112–127; and Bradbury Seasholes, "Political Socialization of Negroes: Image Development of Self and Polity" in William C. Kvaraceus, ed., *Negro Self-Concept: Implications for School and Citizenship* (New York: McGraw-Hill Book Company, 1965), pp. 52–90.

tion and political futility than do similarly located whites.[9] Ghetto residents, like other citizens, tend to formulate their attitudes toward the political system largely on the basis of their contact with the system. For example, ghetto blacks believe that police brutality and harrassment occur in their neighborhoods to a much greater extent than whites believe that violations occur in white areas. In Detroit, for example, 91 per cent of the rioters believed anger at police had something to do with causing the riots.[10] It is not surprising that the policeman, primarily a symbol of law and order in white neighborhoods, is for ghetto people a symbol of injustice, inhumanity and of a society from which they are alien as well as alienated. Studies of white policemen assigned to ghetto areas indicate that black fears and reservations about the police may not be entirely imaginary.[11] Bobby Richardson, writing about police brutality in New Orleans, states ". . . brutality, man is a state of mine, not just a whipping with a billy, although plenty of the brothers get beat up on. They know that brutality is the way you are treated and the way a policemen will arrest one man and not another. And the way he will talk to you and treat you. Brutality is just an extension of prejudice, and it is easier to brutalize one man than it is another."[12]

Similarly, blacks tend to be less trusting of their political systems (local and national) than do their white counterparts.[13] Surveys done in Newark reveal that both "rioters" and "non-involved" blacks have a high distrust

---

[9] See Dwaine Marvick, *ibid.* When Negro respondents were matched with whites (counterpart groups) having similar socioeconomic characteristics, Negroes expressed considerably less confidence that they would receive "equal treatment" from governmental officials or from the police.

In a study of Gary, Indiana, James T. Jones found that more Caucasian children than Negro children agreed that "A person owes his first duty to the community and the nation and next to himself." James T. Jones, *Political Socialization in a Midwestern Industrial Community* (Ph.D. diss., Department of Political Science, University of Illinois, 1965), p. 228.

Roberta Sigel found that Negro children were considerably more upset and worried than white children over the assassination of President Kennedy. These differences maintained themselves even when partisanship and socioeconomic status were taken into account. Roberta Sigel, "An Exploration into Some Aspects of Political Socialization: School Childrens' Reaction to the Death of a President" in Martha Wolfenstein and Gilbert Kilman, eds., *Children and the Death of a President* (Garden City: Doubleday and Company, 1965), pp. 34–69.

[10] The *Report*, p. 178.

[11] See the *Report*, p. 306. From a study by Albert Reiss, director of the Center for Research on Social Organization, University of Michigan, "In predominantely Negro precincts, over three-fourths of the white policemen expressed prejudice or highly prejudiced attitudes toward Negroes. Only one per cent of the officers expressed attitudes which could be described as sympathetic towards Negroes. Indeed, close to the one-half of all the police officers in predominantly Negro high crime rate areas showed extreme prejudice against Negroes. What do I mean by extreme racial prejudice? I mean that they describe Negroes in terms that are not people terms. They describe them in terms of the animal kingdom."

[12] Robert Richardson, "Every Black Man is My Brother," *New Orleans Magazine*, 2 (June, 1968), pp. 30–31; and see also Eldridge Cleaver, "Black People and Police Routine," *Black Politics: A Journal of Liberation*, 1 (April–May, 1968), pp. 33–36.

[13] Marvick, "Political Socialization of the American Negro," *loc. cit.*

of local government with 44.2 per cent and 33.9 per cent, respectively, reporting they could "almost never" trust the Newark government to do what is right. In Detroit, 75 per cent of the rioters and 58.7 per cent of the non-involved felt that "anger with politicians" had a "great deal" or "something" to do with causing riots.[14]

Especially crucial for students of political socialization is the proportion of blacks, rioters and non-involved, who indicated that the country was not worth fighting for in a major world war. In Detroit the percentages were 39.4 for rioters and 15.5 for the non-involved, while the Newark survey revealed these sentiments on the part of 52.8 per cent of the rioters and 27.8 per cent of the non-involved.[15] These figures are striking, especially those related to the non-involved blacks, and would seem to indicate substantial disaffection among blacks. Similar results were ascertained in a recent study of black youth in Atlanta where 49 per cent took a negative stance on the proposition, "Black Americans should be proud to be fighting in Viet Nam."[16]

Given the above data, it is interesting to note the Commission's contrasting finding that rioters were not seeking to change the American system, but merely to gain full participation in it. However, the deep disaffection from the system by blacks and the continued reluctance of the system to accept blacks as full participants might lead one to question the Commission's conclusion. Could it be that black rioters were attempting to change the system and to gain full participation simultaneously? Or, more directly, would not full participation by blacks in itself represent a fundamental change in the system? Such reservations regarding the goals of rioters receive some support from the recent report of Mayor Richard Daley's committee to study Chicago's riots of April, 1968. This committee reported a growing feeling among blacks that "the existing system must be toppled by violent means." This feeling was said to have its strongest expression among black teenagers, where there is "an alarming hatred for whites." Such feelings were found to be based on the attitude that "the entire-existing political-economic-educational structure is anti-black."[17]

Assuming the blacks of the ghetto have internalized the American dream of freedom, equality and justice, there is small wonder that "coming to terms" with the system has produced deep alienation, frustration and despair. Throughout the history of this country, blacks have, for the most part, been excluded from full benefits of this society. The fact that the rest of the country has experienced progressive affluence (flagrantly paraded before blacks through mass media) while blacks became poorer is a story much too familiar to belabor here. In the face of "the American dream" of equal opportunity and abundance, blacks have been forced to live "the American nightmare" of poverty, discrimination and deprivation.

[14] The *Report*, p. 178.
[15] *Ibid.*
[16] James E. Conyers and William Farmer, *Black Youth in a Southern Metropolis* (Atlanta: Southern Regional Council, 1968), p. 13.
[17] "Survey of Chicago Riots Reveals 'Black Racism,'" *Baton Rouge Morning Advocate*, August 8, 1968, p. 12-D.

Despite some progress, American blacks continue to live in this "credability gap" and part of the results are distrust, estrangement and violence.[18]

Data from the Detroit survey indicate that all blacks included in the survey were not equally alienated and distrusting. Least alienated were the "counter-rioters," a major portion of whom (86.9 per cent) regarded the country as worth fighting for.[19] Of this group, 88.9 per cent felt that getting what you want out of life is a matter of "ability" rather than "being in the right place" as compared to 76.9 per cent of the rioters and 76.1 per cent of the non-involved.[20] The typical counter-rioter was described as an active supporter of existing social institutions and considerably better educated and more affluent than either the rioter or the non-involved. This would lead one to speculate that black attitudes or perceptions may be changed when "reality" changes.

Finally, the *Report* attributes responsibility for the present civil disorders to "white racism" in America, "the racial attitude and behavior of white Americans toward black Americans." The fact that a political system theoretically committed to democratic values finds itself embroiled in a major crisis resulting from undemocratic practices raises some fundamental questions regarding the real operative values of the system. How do white Americans reconcile theory and reality? What are the special problems which this situation suggests relative to political socialization of white Americans? Is resocialization of American whites a prerequisite for the fundamental policy changes recommended by the Commission? A number of scholars and writers, some black and some white, have long maintained that the race problem in America is essentially a white problem, created and perpetuated by whites.[21] If the problem is to be solved it must be solved by whites. As Myrdal stated many years ago, "all our attempts to reach scientific explanations of why the Negroes are what they are and why they live as they do have regularly led to determinants on the white side of the race line."

Coming to grips with the fundamental cause of the riots, white racism, is more a task for American whites than for blacks. The process will no doubt necessitate an admission on the part of white Americans that the American dream remains a dream, that full democracy in America is yet to be realized. In short, it will entail alteration of the American political culture, a re-examination of basic values and possibly a rewriting of American history to revise the image of blacks in the minds of whites and blacks. More fundamentally, it will possibly require a restructuring of the socialization process for blacks and whites if our commitments to democratic

---

18 "Characteristically, violence has been employed by those groups in the political system which feel that they have least to lose from chaotic upheaval, and which face an enormous gap between possessions and expectations." See Gabriel Almond and Bingham Powell, *Comparative Politics: A Developmental Approach* (Boston: Little, Brown and Company, 1966), p. 82.

19 The *Report*, p. 178.

20 *Ibid.*, p. 176.

21 See James Baldwin, *The Fire Next Time* (New York: The Dial Press, 1963); Gunnar Myrdal, *An American Dilemma* (New York: Harper and Row, 1944); and *Ebony Magazine* (special issue) "The White Problem in America," 20, August, 1965.

values are to be translated into actual practices. The question for which the *Report* provides no answer is "how can this be done?" It is in the delineation of the broad outlines of such a process that political science and other social science research can possibly make its most significant contribution.

DEMOCRATIC THEORY

"Democracy is . . . characterized by the fact that power over significant authoritative decisions in a society is distributed among the population. The ordinary man is expected to take an active part in governmental affairs, to be aware of how decisions are made and to make his views known."[22]

Any attempt to view the *Report* in the context of democratic theory would seem to raise an array of tantalizing questions,[23] one of which is the relationship between *political obligation* and *consent*.

In a democracy the basis of political obligation is consent.[24] Such consent implies a high level of citizen participation in the political process or at least the unrestricted right of the interested citizen to participate. Consequently, democratic political systems have traditionally institutionalized certain structures and practices that allow for the orderly and periodic involvement of citizens in decision-making. A brief examination of the record tends to substantiate the Commission's contention that throughout the course of American history, black men have been essentially "subjects" rather than "participants" in the political process.[25]

Black men arrived in America in 1619 and began what was to become a 244-year legacy of chattel slavery. Slaves were, by definition, nonparticipants in the political process. The lot of free Negroes was not markedly different from that of slaves. The end of the Civil War, the Emancipation Proclamation, and ratification of the Fourteenth and Fifteenth Amendments heralded the period of Reconstruction and relatively widespread participation in politics by black people. A return to white control and patterns of excluding Negroes from southern politics followed the Compromise of 1877 and withdrawal of federal troops from the South. South-

---

[22] Almond and Verba, *The Civic Culture*, p. 19.

[23] For critical commentary on this general subject see Lane Davis, "The Cost of Realism: Contemporary Restatements of Democracy," *Western Political Science Quarterly*, 17 (1964), pp. 37–46; Jack Walker, "A Critique of the Elitist Theory of Democracy," *American Political Science Review*, 60 (June, 1966), pp. 285–295; Robert Dahl, "Further Reflections on the Elitist Theory of Democracy," *American Political Science Review*, 60 (June, 1966), pp. 296–305. See also Joseph Tussman, *Obligation and the Body Politic* (New York: Oxford University Press, 1960).

[24] For an extensive treatment of the principle of consent in the American political experience see David W. Minar, *Ideas and Politics: The American Experience* (Homewood. Ill.: The Dorsey Press, 1964), Ch. 4.

[25] "Subjects" are those individuals who are oriented to the political system and the impact which its outputs, such as welfare benefits, laws, etc., may have upon their lives, but who are not oriented to participation in the input structures. "Participants" are those individuals who are oriented to the input structures and processes, and engage in, or view themselves as potentially engaging in, the articulation of demands and the making of decisions. See Almond and Powell, *Comparative Politics*, p. 53.

ern states revised their constitutions to deny the franchise to Negroes and as the Negro entered the twentieth century, his political future looked dismal and bleak.[26] Since 1900, blacks have staged an uphill battle in quest of full participation in the body politic. Most significant among legal victories for blacks have been the outlawing of white primaries in 1944, the passage of Civil Rights acts in 1957, 1960, and 1964, the Anti-Poll Tax Amendment in 1963 and finally the Federal Voting Rights Act of 1965.[27]

Perhaps the most reliable source of information on current black registration and voting in the South is the Voter Education Project of the Southern Regional Council. According to its director, Vernon Jordan, the 1965 Voting Rights Act has had a marked impact on voter registration among southern Negroes. He states that significant gains have come in Alabama, Louisiana, Georgia, South Carolina, Virginia, and Mississippi. In Mississippi, Negro registration jumped from 8 per cent to nearly 60 per cent in just two and a half years.[28]

The most recent figures on voter registration supplied by the Voter Education Project are presented in Table 1.

Also noteworthy is the election of over 200 blacks to public office in the South since the Voting Rights Act was passed.[29] There are presently 50

TABLE 1

Voter Registration in the South,
Winter–Spring, 1968

	White Registered	Per Cent White VAP[a] Registered	Negro Registered	Per Cent Negro VAP[a] Registered
Alabama	1,119,000	82.7	271,000	56.3
Arkansas	616,000	72.4	121,000	62.8
Florida	2,194,000	83.8	293,000	62.3
Georgia	1,450,000	80.6	334,000	54.5
Louisiana	1,122,000	87.0	301,000	58.5
Mississippi	655,000	88.9	264,000	62.5
North Carolina	1,555,000	77.5	293,000	53.2
South Carolina	567,000	63.6	183,000	49.3
Tennessee	1,434,000	80.6	225,000	71.7
Texas	3,532,000	72.3	540,000	83.1
Virginia	1,200,000	63.9	247,000	56.6
Totals	15,454,000	76.9	3,072,000	61.2

Source: Voter Education Project, *News*, 2 (June, 1968).
[a] VAP=Voter Age Population

[26] For a detailed account of this period, see John Hope Franklin, *From Slavery to Freedom* (New York: Alfred A. Knopf, 1967).

[27] See *Revolution in Civil Rights*, 3rd ed., (Washington, D.C.: Congressional Quarterly Service, 1967).

[28] Vernon E. Jordan, "New Forces of Urban Political Power," *The New South*, 23 (Spring, 1968), p. 47.

[29] United States Commission on Civil Rights, *Political Participation* (Washington D.C.: U.S. Government Printing Office, 1968), p. 15.

blacks holding local, parish, and state offices in Louisiana, all elected since 1965.[30]

These accelerated advances in black registration and election are indeed impressive, but they do not eradicate the voting problem. With the exception of Texas, black registration percentages are still below white percentages in all the states included in the Voter Education Project survey, and in many areas blacks still experience substantial difficulties in gaining the franchise. Also, the number of blacks holding statewide positions in government and political parties is in no way proportionate to the number of blacks in the population.

Wilson observes, "that the political participation of the Negro in the North is significantly higher than in the South but even so is lower than than that of most other Northern population groups."[31] It ought to be pointed out that low participation in the North cannot be attributed to the type of legal restrictions historically operative in the South. Social science surveys have indicated that persons with low socioeconomic status tend to vote less than persons of higher socioeconomic status.[32] In addition, Negroes in the urban North are more geographically mobile than whites and are less likely to be able to satisfy residence requirements for voting. Nonpartisan elections, candidates running at-large and weak party organization also contribute to low turnout among low income voters. And it could well be that "the extent to which an individual feels effective as part of the institutionalized process may well determine the degree to which he participates in those processes. In sum, the individual's perception of his personal effectiveness should be supportive to the values he places on participation."[33] Thus, while there are no legal deterrents to Negro voting in the North, the cultural deterrents (income, education, occupation) are attributable to the system. That is, the prevailing social, economic and educational arrangements operate in a manner which relegates Negroes to this status, and as long as Negroes face these artificial barriers it is reasonable to assume that their level of political participation will not change.[34]

[30] These include 8 constables, 9 justices of the peace, 11 party executive committee members, 5 school board members, 6 city and town councilmen, 10 police jurors and only one statewide officer. a member of the state House of Representatives. Source: List of Negro Elected Officials of Louisiana prepared for Workshop for Louisiana Negro Elected Officials held at Southern University, Baton Rouge, Louisiana, July 13, 1968.

[31] James Q. Wilson, "The Negro in American Politics: The Present" in John P. Davis, ed., *The American Negro Reference Book* (Englewood Cliffs, N.J.: Prentice-Hall, Inc., 1966), p. 431.

[32] See Angus Campbell *et al.*, *The American Voter* (New York: John Wiley and Sons, Inc., 1964).

[33] James T. Jones, *Political Socialization in a Midwestern Industrial Community*, pp. 218–219.

[34] This point is developed in Philip Meranto, "Negro Majorities and Political Power: The Defeat of an All-Negro Ticket in East St. Louis" prepared for Herbert Hill, ed., *The Revolt of the Powerless: Negroes in the Cities* (New York: Random House, forthcoming); in earlier studies similar projections had been made regarding Negro registration and voting in the South. Donald R. Matthews and James W. Prothro, "Social and Economic Factors and Negro Voter Registration in the South," *American Political*

The extent of constraints on black participation, North and South, would seem to suggest an absence of consent by blacks and thus possible relief from obligations traditionally incumbent upon citizens in a democracy. Of interest in this connection is a recent re-examination of the principles of obligation and consent and related problems rendered by Pitkin.[35]

Pitkin, in a highly provocative treatise, holds that obligation depends not on any actual act of consenting, past or present, but on the character of the government. If it is just government, doing what a government should, then you must obey it. If it is unjust, then you have no such obligation. Or, your obligation depends not on whether you have consented but on whether the government is such that you ought to consent to it. Are its actions consistent with the type of government men in a hypothetical state of nature would have consented to establish and obey? Pitkin's study would suggest that any assessment of the riots and the rioters would of necessity involve grappling with these kinds of concerns.

The propensity among blacks to disobey certain basic canons of the political system has produced strains in the system which threaten to destroy its very foundation. Could this propensity derive fundamentally from the unwillingness of the system to incorporate blacks as full partners in the political process? Cook has projected that "on the empirical level, a tradition of exclusion from participation in the political system breeds disrespect for, and disloyalty to, that system."[36] "Men rarely question the legitimacy of an established order when all is going well; the problem of political obligation is urgent when the state is sick. . . ."[37]

Does exclusion from participation, coupled with exclusion from benefits of "the good life" of the system, not only remove the obligation to obey, but also give rise to the obligation to disobey or revolt? These queries are relevant, but they are also difficult in as much as they solicit precise guidance in specific and varied kinds of situations. Pitkin underscores the inadequacy of classical democratic theory as well as her own theory on consent by noting that both provide insufficient cues for determining what authority to resist and under what conditions. In the same way, both provide only imperfect guidelines for assessing and evaluating the consistency between civil disorder of the magnitude of riots and the obliga-

---

Science Review, 57 (March, 1963), pp. 24–44. On the national scene, there are one black U.S. Senator and five black Representatives (Adam Powell excluded). About 80 blacks were among over 2,600 delegates and alternates at the 1968 Republican Convention and some 301 were among 5,611 delegates and alternates at the Democratic Convention. "Has the GOP Written off Black Votes," in *Pittsburgh Courier*, nat'l ed., August 17, 1968, p. 1; and "Negro Delegates to Confab Shows Gain, Chairman Says" in *Baton Rouge, Morning Advocate*, August 15, 1968, p. 18-A.

35 Hanna Pitkin, "Obligation and Consent—I," and "Obligation and Consent—II," *American Political Science Review*, 59 and 60 (Dec., 1965 and March, 1966), pp. 990–999; pp. 39–52.

36 Samuel D. Cook, "The Negro and the American Political System: Obligation and Resistance," (unpublished paper presented at the Conference on Political Obligation and Resistance to Authority, Gatlingburg, Tennessee, April 18–20, 1968), p. 1.

37 S. I. Benn and R. S. Peters, *Social Principles and the Democratic State* (London: George Allen and Urwin, 1959), pp. 299–300.

tion of citizens to obey the authority of society invested with the duty of enforcing the law.

BLACK POLITICAL STRATEGY

Scoble suggests that Negro leadership and politics represent a quest for effective political power. Negro politics can be best understood if viewed as pursuit of power and influence over authoritative policy decisions.[38] On the other hand, Wilson, in a recent article on the subject, writes, "Because of the structure of American politics as well as the nature of the Negro community, Negro politics will accomplish only limited objectives. This does not mean that Negroes will be content with those accomplishments or resigned to that political style. If Negroes do not make radical gains, radical sentiments may grow."[39] The crucial problem of the black man in the American political arena seems to revolve around the magnitude of the needs of the black people, (as set forth in the *Report* and elsewhere) in relationship to the limited potential of politics as a vehicle for ministering to those needs.[40] More succinctly put, it now seems incumbent upon black men to decide if politics, in the traditional sense, is now more of an irrelevancy rather than an imperative in the search for solutions to their problems. If politics is relevant, then what types of strategies will best serve the needs of the black community, North and South? If irrelevant, what are the alternatives?

Questions of strategy are significant and there are those who feel that this aspect of the black protest movement has not received sufficient attention from leaders in that movement. In fact, the alleged absence of a programmatic element in radical politics in America today, especially the black protest movement, provoked Lasch to state, "the very gravity of the crisis makes it all the more imperative that radicals try to formulate at least a provisional theory which will serve them as a guide to tactics in the immediate future as well as to long range questions of strategy."[41] Along the same general lines, Crozier points out that America is now committed to the omnipotence of reason and the black protest movements are out of step with that development. Very pointedly, he reflects that "it is no longer possible to make good through mere numbers, through the vote

[38] Harry Scoble, *Negro Politics in Los Angeles: The Quest for Power* (Los Angeles: Institute of Government and Public Affairs, University of California, 1967), p. 2.

[39] See James Q. Wilson, "The Negro in Politics" in Kenneth B. Clark and Talcott Parsons, eds., *The Negro American* (Boston: Houghton Mifflin Company, 1966), p. 444. He notes that "American political institutions provide no way for the organized political pressure of a particular disadvantaged group to reshape in any fundamental sense social and economic conditions. . . . That politics seems irrelevant to their daily pre-occupation is not necessarily an expression of neurotic withdrawal . . . but may well be the rational conclusion of a reasonably well-informed citizen." Also, see Carey McWilliams, "Protest, Power and the Future of Politics," *Nation*, 206 (Jan. 15, 1968), pp. 71–77.

[40] On the changing nature of the black protest, see Bayard Rustin, "From Protest to Politics: The Future of the Civil Rights Movement," *Commentary* (Feb., 1965), pp. 25–31.

[41] Christopher Lasch, "The Trouble with Black Power," *The New York Review of Books*, 10, February 29, 1968, p. 14.

or through manual labor, but only through the ability to play the game of modern calculation. And in that area the Negro is still fundamentally disadvantaged. The more rational the society becomes, the more he loses his foothold."[42] Could it be that traditional politics characterize the black subculture while a more rational-calculating variety of politics has long been the pattern in the dominant political culture?[43]

The literature of the discipline and popular periodicals are replete with suggestions of appropriate strategies and/or programs for solving the race problem. Some of the more popularly suggested and researched strategies include black-liberal white coalitions, black-conservative white coalitions, fluctuating or *ad hoc* coalitions, separate black political parties, Black Power, ghetto power.[44] No examination of this proliferation of literature can be made in this limited commentary. Nor will any full-blown theory or strategy be offered. However, it does seem reasonable to submit that any strategy designed to redefine the status of black people in America must of necessity be devised with certain considerations.

First, political strategy for blacks must take into account the difficulties inherent in being a numerical minority. Minority strategy must be highly flexibly based, to a large degree, on the fluctuating attitudes and actions of the white majority in any given setting. It must also be directed toward overcoming traditional constraints on the exertion of effective power by Negroes endemic to the black community itself. Second, any therapeutic strategy must acknowledge the reality that blacks in the ghetto already constitute a "separate society,"[45] and must address itself seriously to black charges of control by "alien, outside" agents. Indigenous control of the ghetto and similar demands cannot be summarily dismissed as, for example, "old wine in new bottles."[46] Third, given the general apathy and insensitivity of whites toward problems of blacks, it seems reasonable to

[42] Michel Crozier, "America Revisited: The Lonely Frontier of Reason," *Nation*, 206 (May 27, 1968), p. 693. See also Harold Cruse, *The Crisis of the Negro Intellectual* (New York: William Morrow and Company, Inc., 1967).

[43] This writer's personal ambivalence on this question leads to the belief that some effort to apply developmental theory to the study of black politics in America would seem to provide interesting and meaningful research possibilities.

[44] On the white conservative-black coalition in Atlanta, see Edward C. Banfield, *Big City Politics* (New York: Random House, 1955), pp. 18–36. The coalition of blacks with liberal whites in Houston, Texas, is reported by Harry Holloway, "Negro Political Strategy: Coalition or Independent Power Politics," a paper in this issue of the *Quarterly*. See also Ronald Moskowitz, "Education and Politics in Boomtown," *Saturday Review*, February 17, 1968, pp. 52–54, 66–67. James W. Wilson suggests that blacks form coalitions on an issue-to-issue basis. See "The Negro in Politics" in Parsons and Clark, *The Negro American*, pp. 434–435. Also see Bayard Rustin, "Black Power and Coalition Politics," *Commentary*, 42, (Sept., 1966), pp. 35–40; Stokley Carmichael and Charles V. Hamilton, *Black Power: The Politics of Liberation in America* (New York: Random House, 1967); Floyd McKissick, "Programs for Black Power" in Floyd B. Barbour, ed., *The Black Power Revolt* (Boston: Porter Sargent Publisher, 1968), pp. 179–181; Hubert M. Blalock, Jr., *Toward a Theory of Minority Group Relations* (New York: John Wiley and Sons, Inc., 1967).

[45] Kenneth B. Clark, *Dark Ghetto* (New York: Harper & Row, 1965).

[46] See W. H. Ferry, "Blacktown and Whitetown: The Case for a New Federalism," *Saturday Review*, June 15, 1968, pp. 14–17.

suggest that any meaningful gains for blacks will come as a result of *demands*, supported by evidence of black willingness to cause great inconvenience to the community at large if these legitimate demands are ignored. Fourth, it might be that the Commission placed too much emphasis on the material aspects of the black man's problem (and the material aspects are indeed important) and did not devote enough attention to such psychological needs as dignity, self-respect and identity and to the relationship between the latter and any corrective actions, political or otherwise. Taking these psychological dimensions into account will probably necessitate innovations in and restatements of traditional concepts and theories regarding democracy, civil disobedience, protest, and other forms of political activity. New tactics, new rhetoric and new sources of leadership will most probably emerge and must be accommodated by the system.[47] Fifth, and in a similar view, it would seem that black strategy and black strategists ought not be constrained to political alternatives if these alternatives prove to be mostly dysfunctional for blacks, and there is a growing body of opinion which holds that they may well be. Finally, the magnitude of the problems faced by blacks is such that the correctives must be radical. If radical programs are not adopted, the Kerner Report may be more a prelude to, rather than a summation of, the worst race riots in the history of this nation, for there seems to be little reason to believe that black rioters will be satisfied with anything less than radical corrective action.

[47] In the last decade, black sit-ins, mass marches and general obstruction of operations of various governmental and educational enterprises have become commonplace. These tactics have found widespread acceptance by nonblack groups such as students against university administrations and protesters against the draft. It would seem reasonable to suggest that similar creativity with regard to tactics will characterize the black struggle in the future.

42

The Riot Commission Report and the Notion of "Political Truth"

CARL AKINS

UNIVERSITY OF HOUSTON

THE *Report of the National Advisory Commission on Civil Disorders* IS OF interest to political scientists in several ways for it raises both theoretical and policy questions of importance. Not only is the document itself important; its preparation and its reception are also of great importance.

Final evaluation of the preparation of the *Report* must await the publication of the supplemental studies which have been promised, the transcripts of the closed hearings, and the other data on which the Commission based its report. Until these materials are available, it is difficult to tell if the *Report* is fully substantiated by the evidence collected. From what is presented in the *Report* itself, it appears that there is ample evidence for the Commission's findings and conclusions. Though there have been a few comments disputing some points of the *Report* and probably will be more, thus far most of these have been minor or have been directed against the recommendations rather than the findings.

On this point the contrast between the Riot Commission and the Mc-Cone Commission which investigated the Watts disorder of 1965 is worth noting. Several evaluations of the work of the McCone Commission have shown that its report was not substantiated by the evidence which it collected.[1] Indeed, the Riot Commission *Report* appears as if it were deliberately designed to avoid the criticisms which were made of the Mc-Cone report. Certainly the specific charge that the McCone Commission ignored racism in spite of evidence that showed "manifestations of problems of race even more than class"[2] is one that cannot be made of the Riot *Report*.

One evaluation of the McCone Commission report is largely based on the notion of "political truth"—a notion which was also used to speculate on the probable report of the Riot Commission before it appeared.[3] This notion of "political truth" is a simple one—that the "truth" found is based on political acceptability rather than objectivity. A thesis often advanced to explain the work of a particular commission is that it was seeking some sort of political truth instead of a more accurate explanation or description of what actually happened. Thus Edward Jay Epstein, in what is probably the most widely known use of the notion, explained the work of the Warren Commission as a search for political truth.[4]

[1] Robert M. Fogelson, "White on Black: A Critique of the McCone Commission Report on the Los Angeles Riots," *Political Science Quarterly*, 82 (Sept., 1967), pp. 337–367.

[2] *Ibid.*, p. 347.

[3] *Ibid.*, p. 341; T. M. Tomlinson, "The Development of a Riot Ideology among Urban Negroes," *American Behavioral Scientist*, 11 (March-April, 1968), pp. 29–30 and footnote 5, p. 31.

[4] Edward Jay Epstein, *Inquest* (New York: The Viking Press, 1966), esp. pp. 31–42.

Writing some months before the Riot Commission delivered its *Report* (although his paper did not appear until after release of the *Report*), T. M. Tomlinson used the notion to explain in advance why the *Report* could not be expected to deal with the actual issues.[5] In terms of political truth, the Riot Commission *Report* should have been a very different document: more subdued in tone and less sweeping in its condemnations, emphasizing different items, and finding fault with different groups. The Commission itself was certainly not a radical one in any way; the members were all persons from the broad center of American politics and were persons with considerable political experience and/or knowledge. Both in terms of findings and recommendations, the Commission could be expected to be both "reasonable" and "realistic."

The staff of the Commission, especially at its upper levels, included a disproportionate numbers of lawyers, a common feature of such staffs given the legalistic style of much of American politics. Social scientists were on the staff in large numbers, and many more served as consultants. If the Commisssion sought political truth, there would be no reasons to expect it to use social science data any differently from the McCone Commission which had issued its report in the face of conflicting evidence provided by social scientists. Dismissal of many of the social scientists on the staff several months before release of the *Report* as well as stories of dissension among the Commission's members also pointed toward political truth. Since the Commission did not arrive at the predicted conclusion, it is tempting to assume that it did not seek political truth or that the notion itself is not a very useful one.

Examination of the *Report* itself shows, however, that the Commission did both seek and find political truth, although the truth discovered was different from the one expected. The major finding of the Commission was that, in the words of the summary chapter, "Our nation is moving toward two societies, one black, one white—separate and unequal."[6] In addition, the Commission found no evidence of any conspiracy, found that the "typical" rioter was not "riff-raff" of the sort described by the McCone Commission, and found that the situation of Negroes today was vastly different from that of the earlier disadvantaged immigrant groups.[7] In its recommendations, the Commission refused to assign specific price tags but called for massive specific actions by the federal government as well as local communities, private business, and the press. In evaluating what current programs are accomplishing, the Commission used as the basis for comparison what needs to be done rather than what has been done in the past.

These findings and the need for the recommendations are generally backed in the *Report* itself by impressive evidence, but whether accepted as "telling it like it is," they constitute a sort of political truth. The political truth is basically the Commission's findings of pervasive racism—a

[5] Tomlinson, "Development of a Riot Ideology."
[6] *Report of the National Advisory Commission on Civil Disorders* (New York: Bantam Books, 1968), p. 1.
[7] *Ibid.*, pp. 7, 9, 15–16, 128–135, 201–202, 278–282.

finding which largely ignores all the poverty which the Commission also described. Though both poverty and racism are documented by the *Report*, the former is at least as pervasive as the latter, if not more so. Certainly the Commission does not ignore poverty in its findings or its recommendations; the latter deal with poverty even more than they do with racism. But by emphasizing racism, the Commission found a political truth.

Racism is a simple answer to the question of why the riots occurred, and it is comforting to both the supporters and opponents of the Commission's recommendations. The supporters approve for they find justification for continuation of the "War on Poverty" and/or the existing welfare programs; the opponents approve because the problem has now become one of the "hearts of men" which they all know cannot be changed by law. Racism is as nebulous as the notion of collective guilt—meaningful yet vaguely disturbing. Both upset a little but not too much, and neither is specific enough to require meaningful action. Thus the finding of racism is politically acceptable.

The conclusion of divisive racism is a political truth in another way also; it focused public attention on a new problem and gave the press a new topic on which to write. The news media generally rose to the occasion and emphasized racism while ignoring poverty. Poverty had become "old hat"; it was and is dull and unpleasant for the public. A report emphasizing poverty was bound to have little impact; one emphasizing racism might have a significant impact on the policy process. If the concept of political truth is broadened to include this interpretation of the *Report*, the notion once again becomes useful in explaining the *Report*. This use of the notion does not require attributing conscious- of even unconscious-motivation to the Commission, only that the results of its actions can be interpreted as "political truth."

Whether the above interpretation is accepted, the reception of the *Report* remains of importance to political science and social science in general. Thus far the reception appears to be another instance in which social data and/or findings and recommendations based on such data are accepted by some political leaders but not be enough to effect a major change in policy. Though such receptions have occurred with some frequency, political scientists have done little to study them. The usual approach has been a case study approach; thus, even the best studies have had limitations. The most notable recent study of such an instance has been on the Moynihan Report;[8] and it is to be hoped that a similar study will be done on the Riot *Report*. In addition to a well done case study, a more generalized study of the uses of such reports in the policy-making process is needed. Not only do the receptions of such reports need to be studied in a systematic way; the uses of social science data and the findings and recommendations based on such data should also be an important area of study.

[8] Lee Rainwater and William L. Yancey, *The Moynihan Report and the Politics of Controversy* (Cambridge: The M.I.T. Press, 1967), pp. 1–313.

The notion of political truth is useful in explaining instances in which reports are "white-washes" or fail to change policy. If a broad view of the notion is taken, it is also useful in cases in which policies are changed. For example, the above interpretation of the Riot Commission *Report* as one which found a different sort of political truth from that expected could also be used, if the bold action of the Commission had been successful in changing public policy. Even if an interpretation based on political truth is not accepted, the phenomenon of a group of "moderates" (after careful study) advocating a set of "radical" conclusions and policy recommendations is not a new one in American policy-making. Such boldness is frequently used, often with success.

The boldness of the Riot *Report* appears at this time (June, 1968) to have largely been a failure, at least at the national level. Although some of the policy recommendations for local units have been adopted in some of the country's cities, other cities have adopted policies almost exactly opposite of those recommended. The reception of the *Report* by President Johnson has been especially cool. This coolness is underscored by the fact that there is no official letter of transmittal in the *Report*, as is the usual practice. Some of the recommendations for national action have been vaguely endorsed, most notably in the area of riot control, but the basic finding has been largely rejected and the recommendations which involve large costs ignored.

Why has the reception of the *Report* by most political leaders been one of rejection? Certainly the process of preparation is not a major reason for the rejection. The document itself does not provide a very clear reason for rejection either, though two major criticisms—failure to give credit for what has been done and failure to consider costs—have been levied against it. *Ad hoc* reasons can be advanced for the *Report*'s rejection, and they are helpful in answering questions concerning the direction of policy. The more general questions on the policy process are left unanswered, however, as are those concerning public reception and political use of social science data. Thus the *Report* provides a challenge for political science and the social sciences in general.

Recent events emphasize the importance of this challenge. That such special Presidential investigating commissions and reports are an increasingly important feature of our political life is shown once again by President Johnson's recent appointment of a commission on violence. The use this new commission makes of social science data will most certainly be interesting, as will the reception of its report. But similar reactions to this new commission by the *New York Times* and Mrs. Martin Luther King, Jr., illustrate the distressingly limited nature of our knowledge of policy-making by such commissions. Both made the point that action on the recommendations of the Riot Commission was needed rather than another commission,[9] and thus raised the question of why have these recommendations been so widely ignored or rejected.

At present the answer to this question of "why" must be that political

---

[9] *New York Times*, June 7, 1968, p. 36; *Washington Post*, June 13, 1968, p. B1.

science does not know. The notion of political truth, like racism or collective guilt or "sick society," is of limited value. As a concept to be used by political scientists it lacks much; more is needed. The problem is being considered; the American Political Science Association will have a panel specifically on the Riot Commission and its *Report* at its 1968 meeting. Hopefully, there will be answers to such questions as what impact do independent investigating commissions have on policy outcomes. If such a commission wishes to have maximum impact, what is its best strategy? And how do such independent commissions fit into the general behavioral and institutional patterns of American politics?

To answer these questions, political science offers several alternatives. As is common with most questions of political science, none of the answers are entirely satisfactory, but most do offer some useful insights. For example, such commissions can be viewed in terms of group theory either as institutions which aggregate the interests of several groups or as institutions which express interests. Alternatively, such commissions may be compared to the independent regulatory commissions in their operations and functions. Or such commissions can simply be compared with one another (including, for example, the Wickersham Commission and the Hoover Commission) in order to develop answers to the questions.

These possible ways of answering the questions are certainly not the only ones; nor are the questions the only ones for which we do not have answers—they are only suggestive of the work to be done. In doing this work, political scientists (and other social scientists as well) must continually answer for themselves one other question: Are their efforts contributing to political truth, or are they "telling it like it is"?

43

Racial Integration in the Armed Forces*

CHARLES C. MOSKOS, JR.[1]
NORTHWESTERN UNIVERSITY

On July 28, 1948, President Truman issued an executive order abol-ishing racial segregation in the armed forces of the United States. By the middle 1950's this policy was an accomplished fact. The lessons of the racial integration of the military are many. Within a remarkably short period the makeup of a major American institution underwent a far-reaching transformation. At the same time, the desegregation of the military can be used to trace some of the mutual permeations between the internal organization of the military establishment and the racial and social cleavages found in the larger setting of American society. Further, because of the favorable contrast in the military performance of integrated Negro servicemen with that of all-Negro units, the integration of the armed services is a demonstration of how changes in social organization can bring about a marked and rapid improvement in individual and group achievement. The desegregated military, moreover, offers itself as a graphic example of the abilities of both whites and Negroes to adjust to egalitarian racial relations with surprisingly little strain. Also, an examination of the racial situation in the contemporary military establishment can serve as a partial guideline as to what one might expect in a racially integrated America. It is to these and related issues that this paper is addressed.[2]

* Reprinted from *American Journal of Sociology*, 72 (1966), by permission of the University of Chicago Press. Copyright © 1966 by the University of Chicago Press.

[1] Many persons have given the writer invaluable assistance during his collection and analysis of the materials for this paper. I would especially like to thank Lieutenant Colonel Roger W. Little, U.S. Military Academy, John B. Spore, editor of *Army* magazine, Philip M. Timpane, staff assistant for civil rights, Department of Defense, and Morris Janowitz, University of Chicago. Also, the writer's access to military personnel at all levels was made possible by the more than perfunctory co-operation of numerous military information officers, men who perform a difficult task with both efficiency and good humor. Financial support was given by the Inter-University Seminar on Armed Forces and Society sponsored by the Russell Sage Foundation. Additional funds for travel were made available by the University of Michigan, and the Council for Inter-societal Studies of Northwestern University. It must be stressed, however, that the usual caveat that the author alone accepts responsibility for the interpretations and conclusions is especially relevant here.

[2] The information on which the observations presented in this paper are based is of a varied sort. A primary source are Department of Defense statistics and those United States government reports dealing with racial relations in the armed forces: President's Committee on Equality of Treatment and Opportunity in the Armed Forces ("Fahy Committee"), *Freedom To Serve: Equality of Treatment and Opportunity in the Armed Forces* (Washington, D.C.: Government Printing Office, 1950); U.S. Commission on Civil Rights, "The Negro in the Armed Forces," *Civil Rights '63* (Washington, D.C.: Government Printing Office, 1963), pp. 169–224; President's Committee on

Desegregating the Military[3]

Negroes have taken part in all of this country's wars. An estimated 5,000 Negroes, some scattered as individuals and others in segregated units, fought on the American side of the War of Independence. Several thou-

---

Equal Opportunity in the Armed Forces ("Gesell Committee"), "Initial Report: Equality of Treatment and Opportunity for Negro Personnel Stationed within the United States" (mimeographed; June, 1963), and "Final Report: Military Personnel Stationed Overseas and Membership and Participation in the National Guard" (mimeographed; November, 1964). Also, participant observations were made by the writer while on active duty in the Army and during field trips to military installations in Germany, Viet Nam, and Korea in the summer of 1965 and in the Dominican Republic in the spring of 1966. Additionally, sixty-seven formal interviews were conducted with soldiers who made up nearly all of the total Negro enlisted personnel in two Army companies. Another source of data is found in Operations Research Office ("ORO"), *Project Clear: The Utilization of Negro Manpower in the Army* (Chevy Chase, Md.: Operations Research Office, Johns Hopkins University, April, 1955). The ORO surveys queried several thousand servicemen during the Korean War on a variety of items relating to attitudes toward racial integration in the Army. The findings of Project Clear, heretofore classified, have now been made available for professional scrutiny. Some comparable data were obtained from the section dealing with Negro soldiers in Samuel A. Stouffer *et al., The American Soldier: Adjustment during Army Life*, Vol. I (Princeton, N.J.: Princeton University Press, 1949), pp. 486–599.

[3] This background of the Negro's role in the American military is derived, in addition to the sources cited above, from Seymour J. Schoenfeld, *The Negro in the Armed Forces* (Washington, D.C.: Associated Publishers, 1945); Paul C. Davis, "The Negro in the Armed Services," *Virginia Quarterly*, XXIV (Autumn, 1948), 449–520; Herbert Aptheker, *Essays in the History of the American Negro* (New York: International Publishers, 1945); Arnold M. Rose, "Army Policies toward Negro Soldiers," *Annals of the American Academy of Political and Social Science*, CCXLIV (March, 1946), 90–94; Eli Ginzburg, "The Negro Soldier," in his *The Negro Potential* (New York: Columbia University Press, 1956), pp. 61–91; David G. Mandelbaum, *Soldiers Groups and Negro Soldiers* (Berkeley: University of California Press, 1952); and Benjamin Quarles, *The Negro in the Making of America* (New York: Collier Books, 1964), *passim.* A good account of the early days of military desegregation is Lee Nichols, *Breakthrough on the Color Front* (New York: Random House, 1954).

Though the last several years have seen little social science research on racial relations in the armed forces, there has recently been a spate of novels dealing with this theme. See, e.g., John Oliver Killens, *And Then We Heard the Thunder* (New York: Alfred A. Knopf, Inc., 1963); James Drought, *Mover* (New York: Avon Books, 1963); Webb Beech, *Article 92* (Greenwich, Conn.: Gold Medal Books, 1964); Gene L. Coon, *The Short End* (New York: Dell Publishing Co., 1964); Hari Rhodes, *A Chosen Few* (New York: Bantam Books, 1965); and Jack Pearl, *Stockade* (New York: Pocket Books, 1965).

It should be noted that Negroes have not been the only ethnic or racial group to occupy a unique position in the American military. Indians served in separate battalions in the Civil War and were used as scouts in the frontier wars. Filipinos have long been a major source of recruitment for stewards in the Navy. The much decorated 442nd ("Go For Broke") Infantry Regiment of World War II was composed entirely of Japanese-Americans. Also in World War II, a separate battalion of Norwegian-Americans was drawn up for intended service in Scandinavia. The participation of Puerto Ricans in the American military deserves special attention. A recent case of large-scale use of non-American soldiers are the Korean fillers or "Katusas" (from Korean Augmentation to the U.S. Army) who make up roughly one-sixth of the current personnel in the Eighth Army.

sand Negroes saw service in the War of 1812. During the Civil War 180,000 Negroes were recruited into the Union army and served in segregated regiments.[4] Following the Civil War four Negro regiments were established and were active in the Indian wars on the Western frontier and later fought with distinction in Cuba during the Spanish-American War. In the early twentieth century, however, owing to a general rise in American racial tensions and specific outbreaks of violence between Negro troops and whites, opinion began to turn against the use of Negro soldiers. Evaluation of Negro soldiers was further lowered by events in World War I. The combat performance of the all-Negro 92nd Infantry, one of its regiments having fled in the German offensive at Meuse-Argonne, came under heavy criticism. Yet it was also observed that Negro units operating under French command, in a more racially tolerant situation, performed well.

In the interval between the two world wars, the Army not only remained segregated but also adopted a policy of a Negro quota that was to keep the number of Negroes in the Army proportionate to the total population. Never in the pre-World War II period, however, did the number of Negroes approach this quota. On the eve of Pearl Harbor, Negroes constituted 5.9 percent of the Army; and there were only five Negro officers, three of whom were chaplains. During World War II Negroes entered the Army in larger numbers, but at no time did they exceed 10 percent of total personnel. Negro soldiers remained in segregated units, and approximately three-quarters served in the quartermaster, engineer, and transportation corps. To make matters worse from the viewpoint of "the right to fight," a slogan loudly echoed by Negro organizations in the United States, even Negro combat units were frequently used for heavy-duty labor. This was highlighted when the 2nd Cavalry was broken up into service units owing to command apprehension over the combat qualities, even though untested, of this all-Negro division. The record of those Negro units that did see combat in World War II was mixed. The performance of the 92nd Infantry Division again came under heavy criticism, this time for alleged unreliability in the Italian campaign.

An important exception to the general pattern of utilization of Negro troops in World War II occurred in the winter months of 1944–1945 in the Ardennes battle. Desperate shortages of combat personnel resulted in the Army asking for Negro volunteers. The plan was to have platoons (approximately 40 men) of Negroes serve in companies (approximately 200 men) previously all-white. Some 2,500 Negroes volunteered for this assignment. Both in terms of Negro combat performance and white soldiers' reactions, the Ardennes experiment was an unqualified success. This incident would later be used to support arguments for integration.

After World War II, pressure from Negro and liberal groups coupled with an acknowledgment that Negro soldiers were being poorly utilized

---

[4] A particularly insightful contemporary report on Negro soldiers in the Civil War is Thomas Wentworth Higgins[on], *Army Life in a Black Regiment* (New York: Collier Books, 1962).

led the Army to reexamine its racial policies. A report by an Army board in 1945, while holding racial integration to be a desirable goal and while making recommendations to improve Negro opportunity in the Army, concluded that practical considerations required a maintenance of segregation and the quota system. In light of World War II experiences, the report further recommended that Negro personnel be exclusively assigned to support rather than combat units. Another Army board report came out in 1950 with essentially the same conclusions.[5] Both reports placed heavy stress on the supervisory and disciplinary problems resulting from the disproportionate number of Negroes, as established by Army examinations, found in the lower mental and aptitude classification levels. In 1950, for example, 60 percent of the Negro personnel fell into the Army's lowest categories compared with 29 percent of the white soldiers. From the standpoint of the performance requirements of the military, such facts could not be lightly dismissed.

After the Truman desegregation order of 1948, however, the die was cast. The President followed his edict by setting up a committee, chaired by Charles Fahy, to pursue the implementation of equal treatment and opportunity for armed forces personnel. Under the impetus of the Fahy committee, the Army abolished the quota system in 1950, and was beginning to integrate some training camps when the conflict in Korea broke out. The Korean War was the coup de grâce for segregation in the Army. Manpower requirements in the field for combat soldiers resulted in many instances of *ad hoc* integration. As was true in the Ardennes experience, Negro soldiers in previously all-white units performed well in combat. As integration in Korea became more standard, observers consistently noted that the fighting abilities of Negroes differed little from those of whites.[6] This contrasted with the blemished record of the all-Negro 24th Infantry Regiment.[7] Its performance in the Korean War was judged to be so poor that its divisional commander recommended the unit be dissolved as quickly as possible. Concurrent with events in Korea, integration was introduced in the United States. By 1956, three years after the end of the Korean War, the remnants of Army Jim Crow disappeared at home and in overseas installations. At the time of the Truman order, Negroes constituted 8.8 percent of Army personnel. In 1964 the figure was 12.3 percent.

In each of the other services, the history of desegregation varied from the Army pattern. The Army Air Force, like its parent body, generally assigned Negroes to segregated support units. (However, a unique military

[5] The 1945 and 1950 Army board reports are commonly referred to by the names of the officers who headed these boards: respectively, Lieutenant General Alvan C. Gillem, Jr., and Lieutenant General S. J. Chamberlin.

[6] These evaluations are summarized in ORO, *op. cit.*, pp. 16–19, 47–105, and 582–83.

[7] The notoriety of the 24th Infantry Regiment was aggravated by a song—"The Bug-Out Boogie"—attributed to it: "When them Chinese mortars begin to thud / The old Deuce-Four begin to bug / When they started falling 'round the CP [command post] tent/ Everybody wonder where the high brass went / They were buggin' out / Just movin' on."

venture taken during the war was the formation of three all-Negro, including officers, air combat units.) At the end of World War II the proportion of Negroes in the Army Air Force was only 4 percent, less than half what it was in the Army. Upon its establishment as an independent service in 1947, the Air Force began to take steps toward integration even before the Truman order. By the time of the Fahy committee report in 1950, the Air Force was already largely integrated. Since integration there has been a substantial increase in the proportion of Negroes serving in the Air Force, from less than 5 percent in 1949 to 8.6 percent in 1964.

Although large numbers of Negroes had served in the Navy during the Civil War and for some period afterward, restrictive policies were introduced in the early 1900's, and by the end of World War I only about 1 per cent of Navy personnel were Negroes. In 1920 the Navy adopted a policy of total racial exclusion and barred all Negro enlistments. This policy was changed in 1932 when Negroes, along with Filipinos, were again allowed to join the Navy but only as stewards in the messman's branch. Further modifications were made in Navy policy in 1942 when some openings in general service for Negroes were created. Negro sailors in these positions, however, were limited to segregated harbor and shore assignments.[8] In 1944, in the first effort toward desegregation in any of the armed services, a small number of Negro sailors in general service were integrated on ocean-going vessels. After the end of World War II the Navy, again ahead of the other services, began to take major steps toward elimination of racial barriers. Even in the integrated Navy of today, however, approximately a quarter of Negro personnel still serve as stewards. Also, despite the early steps toward integration taken by the Navy, the proportion of Negro sailors has remained fairly constant over the past two decades, averaging around 5 percent.

The Marine Corps has gone from a policy of exclusion to segregation to integration. Before World War II there were no Negro marines. In 1942 Negroes were accepted into the Marine Corps but assigned to segregated units where they were heavy-duty laborers, ammunition handlers, and anti-aircraft gunners. After the war small-scale integration of Negro marines into white units was begun. In 1949 and 1950 Marine Corps training units were integrated, and by 1954 the color line was largely erased throughout the Corps. Since integration began, the proportion of Negroes has increased markedly. In 1949 less than 2 percent of all marines were Negroes compared with 8.2 percent in 1964.

Although the various military services are all similar in being integrated today, they differ in their proportion of Negroes. As shown in Table 1, the Negro distribution in the total armed forces in 1962 and 1964, respectively, was 8.2 percent and 9.0 percent, lower than the 11–12 percent constituting the Negro proportion in the total population. It is virtually certain, however, that among those *eligible*, a higher proportion of Ne-

[8] A lesson in the rewriting of history is gained from the movie *PT-109*, a dramatization of John Kennedy's war exploits. In this film, released in the early 1960's, the Navy is portrayed as racially integrated in World War II.

TABLE 1

Negroes in the Armed Forces and Each Service as a Percentage
of Total Personnel, 1962 and 1964

Service	1962	1964
Army	11.1	12.3
Air Force	7.8	8.6
Navy	4.7	5.1
Marine Corps	7.0	8.2
Total armed forces	8.2	9.0

Source: U.S. Commission on Civil Rights, *op. cit.*, p. 218; Department of Defense statistics.

TABLE 2

Negroes in Each of the Armed Services as a Percentage
of Initial Enlistments, 1961, 1963, and 1965

Year	Army	Air Force	Navy	Marine Corps
1961	8.2	9.5	2.9	5.9
1963	11.2	10.5	4.3	5.5
1965	14.1	13.1	5.8	8.4

Source: Department of Defense statistics.

groes than whites enter the armed forces. That is, a much larger number of Negroes do not meet the entrance standards required by the military services. In 1962, for example, 56.1 percent of Negroes did not pass the preinduction mental examinations given to draftees, almost four times the 15.4 percent of whites who failed these same tests.[9] Because of the relatively low number of Negroes obtaining student or occupational deferments, however, it is the Army drawing upon the draft that is the only military service where the percentage of Negroes approximates the national proportion. Thus, despite the high number of Negroes who fail to meet induction standards, Army statistics for 1960–1965 show Negroes constituted about 15 percent of those drafted.

Even if one takes account of the Army's reliance on the selective service for much of its personnel, the most recent figures still show important differences in the number of Negroes in those services meeting their manpower requirements solely through voluntary enlistments; the 5.1 percent Negro in the Navy is lower than the 8.2 percent for the Marine Corps or the 8.6 percent for the Air Force. Moreover, the Army, besides its drawing upon the draft, also has the highest Negro initial enlistment rate of any of the services. As reported in Table 2, we find in 1965 that the Army drew 14.1 percent of its volunteer incoming personnel from Negroes as

[9] Department of Labor ("Moynihan Report"), *The Negro Family: The Case for National Action* (Washington, D.C.: Government Printing Office, 1965), p. 75.

compared with 13.1 percent for the Air Force, 8.4 percent for the Marine Corps, and 5.8 percent for the Navy. As also shown in Table 2, there has been a very sizable increase in Negro enlistments from 1961 to 1965 in all four of the armed services.

There are also diverse patterns between the individual services as to the rank or grade distribution of Negroes. Looking at Table 3, we find the ratio of Negro to white officers is roughly 1 to 30 in the Army, 1 to 70 in the Air Force, 1 to 250 in the Marine Corps, and 1 to 300 in the Navy. Among enlisted men, Negroes are underrepresented in the top three enlisted ranks in the Army and the top four ranks in the other three services. We also find a disproportionate concentration of Negroes in the lower noncommissioned officer ranks in all of the armed forces, but especially so in the Army. An assessment of these data reveals that the Army, followed by the Air Force, has not only the largest proportion of Negroes in its total personnel, but also the most equitable distribution of Negroes throughout its ranks. Although the Navy was the first service to integrate and the Army the last, in a kind of tortoise and hare fashion, it is the Army that has become the most representative service for Negroes.

TABLE 3

Negroes as a Percentage of Total Personnel in Each
Grade for Each Service, 1964

Grade	Army	Air Force	Navy	Marine Corps
Officers:				
Generals/admirals	–	0.2	–	–
Colonels/captains	0.2	0.2	–	–
Lt. cols./commanders	1.1	0.5	0.6	–
Majors/lt. commanders	3.6	0.8	0.3	0.3
Captains/lieutenants	5.4	2.0	0.5	0.4
1st lieutenants/lts. (j.g.)	3.8	1.8	0.2	0.4
2d lieutenants/ensigns	2.7	2.5	0.7	0.3
Total officers	3.4	1.5	0.3	0.4
Enlisted:*				
E–9 (sgt. major)	3.5	1.2	1.5	0.8
E–8 (master sgt.)	6.1	2.2	1.9	1.2
E–7 (sgt. 1st class)	8.5	3.2	2.9	2.3
E–6 (staff sgt.)	13.9	5.3	4.7	5.0
E–5 (sgt.)	17.4	10.8	6.6	11.2
E–4 (corp.)	14.2	12.7	5.9	10.4
E–3 (pvt. 1st class)	13.6	9.7	6.6	7.8
E–2 (private)	13.1	11.7	5.7	9.5
E–1 (recruit)	6.8	14.4	7.1	9.1
Total enlisted men	13.4	10.0	5.8	8.7

* Army and Marine Corps enlisted titles indicated in parentheses have equivalent grades in Navy and Air Force.

Source: Department of Defense statistics.

CHANGING MILITARY REQUIREMENTS AND NEGRO OPPORTUNITIES

A pervasive trend within the military establishment singled out by students of this institution is the long-term direction toward greater technical complexity and narrowing of civilian-military occupational skills.[10] An indicator, albeit a crude one, of this trend toward "professionalization" of military roles is the changing proportion of men assigned to combat arms. Given in Table 4, along with concomitant white-Negro distributions, are figures comparing the percentage of Army enlisted personnel in combat arms (e.g., infantry, armor, artillery) for the years 1945 and 1962. We find that the proportion of men in combat arms—that is, traditional military specialties—dropped from 44.5 percent in 1945 to 26.0 percent in 1962. Also, the percentage of white personnel in traditional military specialties approximates the total proportional decrease in the combat arms over the seventeen-year period.

For Negro soldiers, however, a different picture emerges. While the percentage of Negro enlisted men in the Army increased only slightly between 1945 and 1962, the likelihood of a Negro serving in a combat arm is almost three times greater in 1962 than it was at the end of World War II. Further, when comparisons are made between military specialties within the combat arms, the Negro proportion is noticeably higher in line rather than staff assignments. This is especially the case in airborne and marine units. Put in another way, the direction in assignment of Negro soldiers in the desegregated military is testimony to the continuing consequences of differential Negro opportunity originating in the larger society. That is, even though integration of the military has led to great improvement in the performance of Negro servicemen, the social and particularly educational deprivations suffered by the Negro in American society can be mitigated but not entirely eliminated by the racial egalitarianism existing within the armed forces.[11] These findings need not be interpreted as a de-

TABLE 4

Total Negro Army Enlisted Personnel and White and Negro
Enlisted Personnel in Combat Arms, 1945 and 1962

Category	1945*	1962
Negroes as percentage of total personnel	10.5	12.2
Percentage of total personnel in combat arms	44.5	26.0
Percentage of total white personnel in combat arms	48.2	24.9
Percentage of total Negro personnel in combat arms	12.1	33.4

* Excludes Army Air Force.
Source: ORO, *op. cit.*, pp. 563–64; U.S. Civil Rights Commission, *op. cit.*, pp. 219–222.

[10] Morris Janowitz with Roger Little, *Sociology and the Military Establishment* (New York: Russell Sage Foundation, 1965), pp. 17–49; and Kurt Lang, "Technology and Career Management in the Military Establishment," in Morris Janowitz (ed.), *The New Military: Changing Patterns of Organization* (New York: Russell Sage Foundation, 1964), pp. 39–81.
[11] World War II evidence shows much of the incidence of psychoneurotic break-

cline in the "status" of the Negro in the integrated military. Actually there is evidence that higher prestige—but not envy—is accorded combat personnel by those in non-combat activities within the military.[12] And taken within the historical context of the "right to fight," the Negro's overrepresentation in the combat arms is a kind of ironic step forward.[13]

Moreover, the military at the enlisted ranks has become a major avenue of career mobility for many Negro men.[14] As shown earlier in Table 3, in all four services, and especially in the Army, there is some overrepresentation of Negroes at the junior NCO levels (pay grades E-4–E-6). The disproportionate concentration of Negroes at these levels implies a higher than average reenlistment as these grades are not normally attained until after a second enlistment. This assumption is supported by the data given in Table 5. We find that in 1965 for all four services the Negro reenlistment rate is approximately twice that of white servicemen. Indeed, about half of all first-term Negro servicemen chose to remain in the armed forces for at least a second term. The greater likelihood of Negroes to select a service career suggests that the military establishment is undergoing a significant change in its NCO core. Such an outcome would reflect not only the "pull" of the appeals offered by a racially egalitarian institution, but also the "push" generated by the plight of the Negro in the American economy.[15] At the minimum, it is very probable that as the present cohort of Negro junior NCO's attains seniority there will be a greater representation of Negroes in the advanced NCO grades. The expansion of the armed forces arising from the war in Viet Nam and the resulting opening up of "rank" will accelerate this development.

ATTITUDES OF SOLDIERS

So far the discussion has sought to document the degree of penetration and the kind of distribution characterizing Negro servicemen in the inte-

---

down among Negro soldiers, compared to whites, was associated with psychological handicaps originating before entrance into military service (Arnold M. Rose, "Psychoneurotic Breakdown among Negro Soldiers," *Phylon*, XVII, No. 1 [1956], pp. 61–73).

[12] Stouffer *et al.*, *op. cit.*, II, 242–89; Raymond W. Mack, "The Prestige System of an Air Base: Squadron Rankings and Morale," *American Sociological Review*, XIX (June, 1954), 281–87; Morris Janowitz, *The Professional Soldier* (Glencoe, Ill.: Free Press, 1960), pp. 31–36.

[13] There are, as should be expected, differences among Negro soldiers as to their desire to see combat. From data not shown here, interviews with Negro soldiers stationed in Germany revealed reluctance to go to Viet Nam was greatest among those with high-school or better education, and northern home residence. This is in direct contrast with the findings reported in *The American Soldier*. In the segregated Army of World War II, northern and more highly educated Negro soldiers were most likely to want to get into combat, an outcome of the onus of inferiority felt to accompany service in support units (Stouffer, *op. cit.*, I, 523–24).

[14] The emphasis on academic education for officer careers effectively limits most Negro opportunity to the enlisted levels (Lang, *op. cit.*, p. 62).

[15] Documentation shows the gap between Negro and white job opportunities has not diminished appreciably, if at all, in the past twenty years (Department of Labor, *op. cit.*, pp. 19–21; Thomas F. Pettigrew, *A Profile of the Negro American* [Princeton, N.J.: D. Van Nostrand Co., 1964], pp. 168–74).

grated military establishment. We now introduce certain survey and interview data dealing more directly with the question of soldiers' attitudes toward military desegregation. Commenting on the difficulties of social analysis, the authors of *The American Soldier* wrote that few problems are "more formidable than that of obtaining dependable records of attitudes toward racial separation in the Army."[16] Without underestimating the continuing difficulty of this problem, an opportunity exists to compare attitudes toward racial integration held by American soldiers in two different periods. This is done by contrasting responses to equivalent items given in World War II as reported in *The American Soldier* with those reported in Project Clear a study sponsored by the Defense Department during the Korean War.[17]

In both *The American Soldier* and Project Clear (the surveys under consideration were conducted in 1943 and 1951, respectively) large samples of Army personnel in segregated military settings were categorized as to whether they were favorable, indifferent, or opposed to racial integration in Army units. We find, as presented in Table 6, massive shifts in soldiers' attitudes over the eight-year period, shifts showing a much more positive disposition toward racial integration among both whites and Negroes in the later year. A look at the distribution of attitudes held by white soldiers reveals opposition to integration goes from 84 percent in 1943 to less than half in 1951. That such a change could occur in less than a decade counters viewpoints that see basic social attitudes in large populations being prone to glacial-like changes. Yet, an even more remarkable change is found among the Negro soldiers. Where in 1945, favorable, indifferent, or opposing attitudes were roughly equally distributed among the Negro soldiers, by 1951 opposition or indifference to racial integration had become negligible. Such a finding is strongly indicative of a ref-

TABLE 5

First-Term Re-enlistment Rates in the Armed Forces and
Each Service by Race, 1965
(Percent)

Race	Total Armed Forces	Army	Air Force		Marine Corps
White	21.6	18.5	27.4	21.6	12.9
Negro	46.6	49.3	50.3	41.3	50.3

Source: Department of Defense statistics.

[16] Stouffer *et al.*, *op. cit.*, p. 566.

[17] What methodological bias exists is that the Korean War question was a stronger description of racial integration than the item used in World War II. Compare "What is your feeling about serving in a platoon containing both whites and colored soldiers, all working and training together, sleeping in the same barracks and eating in the same mess hall?" with "Do you think white and Negro soldiers should be in separate outfits or should they be together in the same outfits?" (respectively, ORO, *op. cit.*, p. 453, and Stouffer *et al.*, *op. cit.*, p. 568).

TABLE 6

Attitudes of White and Negro Soldiers toward Racial Integration
in the Segregated Army, 1943 and 1951

Attitude toward Integration	White Soldiers Percent		Negro Soldiers Percent	
	1943	1951	1943	1951
Favorable	12	25	37	90
Indifferent	4	31	27	6
Oppose	84	44	36	4
Total	100	100	100	100
(No. of cases)	(4,800)	(1,983)	(3,000)	(1,384)

Source: Stouffer *et al., op cit.*, p. 568; ORO, *op. cit.*, pp. 322, 433.

TABLE 7

Attitudes of Negro Soldiers in 1965 Comparing Racial Equality in
Military and Civilian Life, Total and by Home Region

Where More Racial Equality	Total	Percent Home Region	
		North	South
Military life	84	75	93
Civilian life	3	6	0
No difference	13	19	7
Total	100	100	100
(No. of cases)	(67)	(36)	(31)

ormation in Negro public opinion from traditional acquiescence to Jim Crow to the ground swell that laid the basis for the subsequent civil rights movement.

While the data on Negro attitudes toward integration given in Table 6 were elicited during the segregated military of 1943 and 1951, we also have evidence on how Negro soldiers react to military integration in the contemporary setting. As reported in Table 7, the Army is overwhelmingly thought to be more racially egalitarian than civilian life. Only 16 percent of sixty-seven Negro soldiers interviewed in 1965 said civilian life was more racially equal or no different than the Army. By region, as might be expected, we find southern Negroes more likely than northern Negroes to take a benign view of racial relations in the Army when these are compared to civilian life. The data in Table 7 support the proposition that, despite existing deviations from military policy at the level of informal discrimination, the military establishment stands in sharp and favorable contrast to the racial relations prevalent in the larger American society.

One of the most celebrated findings of *The American Soldier* was the discovery that the more contact white soldiers had with Negro troops, the more favorable was their reaction toward racial integration.[18] This conclusion is consistently supported in the surveys conducted by Project Clear. Again and again, comparisons of white soldiers in integrated units with those in segregated units show the former to be more supportive of desegregation. Illustrative of this pattern are the data shown in Table 8. Among combat infantrymen in Korea, 51 percent in all-white units say outfits are better segregated as compared to 31 percent in integrated units. For enlisted personnel stationed in the United States, strong objection to integration characterizes 44 percent serving in segregated units while less than one-fifth of the men in integrated units feel the same way. Seventy-nine percent of officers on segregated posts rate Negroes worse than white soldiers as compared with 28 percent holding similar beliefs on integrated posts.

OFFICIAL POLICY AND ACTUAL PRACTICE

For the man newly entering the armed forces, it is hard to conceive that the military was one of America's most segregated institutions less than two decades ago. For today color barriers at the formal level are absent throughout the military establishment. Equal treatment regardless of race is official policy in such non-duty facilities as swimming pools, chapels, barbershops, post exchanges, movie theaters, snack bars, and dependents' housing as well as in the more strictly military endeavors involved in the assignment, promotion, and living conditions of members of the armed services.[19] Moreover, white personnel are often commanded by Negro superiors, a situation rarely obtaining in civilian life. Recently the military has sought to implement its policy of equal opportunity by exerting pressure on local communities where segregated patterns affect military personnel. This policy deserves careful examination owing to its ramifications on the traditional separation of civilian and military spheres

TABLE 8

Racial Attitudes of White Soldiers in Segregated and Integrated Settings, 1951

Racial Attitudes	All-White Units		Integrated Units	
	Percent	No.	Percent	No.
Combat infantrymen in Korea saying segregated outfits better	51	(195)	31	(1,024)
Enlisted personnel in the U.S. strongly objecting to racial integration	44	(1,983)	17	(1,683)
Officers rating Negroes worse than white soldiers	79	(233)	28	(385)

Source: ORO, *op. cit.*, pp. 141, 322, 333, 356.

[18] *Ibid.*, p. 594.

[19] The comprehensive scope of military integration is found in the official guidelines set forth under "Equal Opportunity and Treatment of Military Personnel," in *Army Regulation 600-21, Air Force Regulation 35-78*, and *Secretary of the Navy Instruction 5350.6*.

in American society. A measure of the extent and thoroughness of military desegregation is found in comparing the 1950 President's committee report dealing with racial integration and the 1963 and 1964 reports of a second President's committee. Where the earlier report dealt entirely with internal military organizations, the recent reports address themselves primarily to the National Guard and off-base discrimination.[20] Along this same line, Congressman Adam Clayton Powell has said that up to the middle 1950's he used to receive 5,000 letters a year from Negro servicemen complaining of discrimination in the military. In recent years, he receives less than 1,500 such letters annually and these largely pertain to off-base problems.[21] In brief, military life is characterized by an interracial equalitarianism of a quantity and of a kind that is seldom found in the other major institutions of American society.

In their performance of military duties, whites and Negroes work together with little display of racial tension. This is not to say racial animosity is absent in the military. Racial incidents do occur, but these are reduced by the severe sanctions imposed by the military for such acts. Such confrontations are almost always off-duty, if not off-base. In no sense, however, is the military sitting on top of a racial volcano, a state of affairs differing from the frequent clashes between the races that were a feature of the military in the segregated era. Additionally, it must be stressed that conflict situations stemming from non-racial causes characterize most sources of friction in the military establishment, for example, enlisted men versus officers, lower-ranking enlisted men versus non-commissioned officers, soldiers of middle-class background versus those of the working-class, conscriptees versus volunteers, line units versus staff units, rear echelon versus front echelon, combat units versus non-combat units, newly arrived units versus earlier stationed units, etc.

Yet the fact remains that the general pattern of day-to-day relationships *off the job* is usually one of mutual racial exclusivism. As one Negro soldier put it, "A man can be my best buddy in the Army, but he won't ask me to go to town with him." Closest friendships normally develop within races between individuals of similar educational background. Beyond one's hard core of friends there exists a level of friendly acquaintances. Here the pattern seems to be one of educational similarities overriding racial differences. On the whole, racial integration at informal as well as formal levels works best on-duty vis-à-vis off-duty, on-base vis-à-vis off-base, basic training and maneuvers vis-à-vis garrison, sea vis-à-vis shore duty, and combat vis-à-vis non-combat. In other words, the behavior of servicemen resembles the racial (and class) separatism of the larger

[20] Cf. the Fahy committee report (1950), with the Gesell committee reports (1963 and 1964). The Moynihan Report comments, "Service in the United States Armed Forces is the only experience open to the Negro American in which he is truly treated as an equal . . . If this is a statement of the ideal rather than reality, it is an ideal that is close to realization" (Department of Labor, *op. cit.*, p. 42).

[21] In an interview with the *Overseas Weekly*, a newspaper published in Germany with a large readership among American servicemen. Personal communication with staff members.

American society, the more they are removed from the military environment.

For nearly all white soldiers the military is a first experience with close and equal contact with a large group of Negroes. There has developed what has become practically a military custom: the look over the shoulder, upon the telling of a racial joke, to see if there are any Negroes in hearing distance. Some racial animosity is reflected in accusations that Negro soldiers use the defense of racial discrimination to avoid disciplinary action. Many white soldiers claim they like Negroes as individuals but "can't stand them in bunches." In a few extreme cases, white married personnel may even live off the military base and pay higher rents rather than live in integrated military housing. On the whole, however, the segregationist-inclined white soldier regards racial integration as something to be accepted pragmatically, if not enthusiastically, as are so many situations in military life.

The most overt source of racial unrest in the military community centers in dancing situations. A commentary on American mores is a finding reported in Project Clear: three-quarters of a large sample of white soldiers said they would not mind Negro couples on the same dance floor, but approximately the same number disapproved of Negro soldiers dancing with white girls.[22] In many non-commissioned officer (NCO) clubs, the likelihood of interracial dancing partners is a constant producer of tension. In fact, the only major exception to integration within the military community is on a number of large posts where there are two or more NCO clubs. In such situations one of the clubs usually becomes tacitly designated as the Negro club.

Although there is almost universal support for racial integration by Negro soldiers, some strains are also evident among Negro personnel in the military. There seems to be a tendency among lower-ranking Negro enlisted men, especially conscriptees, to view Negro NCO's as "Uncle Toms" or "handkerchief heads." Negro NCO's are alleged to pick on Negroes when it comes time to assign men unpleasant duties. Negro officers are sometimes seen as being too strict or "chicken" when it comes to enforcing military discipline on Negro soldiers. As one Negro serviceman said, "I'm proud when I see a Negro officer, but not in my company."

One Negro writer, who served in the segregated Army and now has two sons in the integrated military, has proposed that what was thought by soldiers in all-Negro units to be racial discrimination was sometimes nothing more than harassment of lower-ranking enlisted personnel.[23] In fact, the analogy between enlisted men vis-à-vis officers in the military and Negroes vis-à-vis whites in the larger society has often been noted.[24]

---

[22] ORO, *op. cit.*, p. 388.

[23] James Anderson, "Fathers and Sons: An Evaluation of Military Racial Relations in Two Generations" (term paper, University of Michigan, December, 1965).

[24] Stouffer and his associates, for example, report enlisted men as compared to officers, as Negro soldiers to white soldiers, were more prone to have "low spirits," to be less desirous of entering combat, and to be more dissatisfied than perceived by others (Stouffer *et al.*, *op. cit.*, II, 345, and I, 392–94, 506, 521, and 538).

It has been less frequently observed, however, that enlisted men's behavior is often similar to many of the stereotypes associated with Negroes, for example, laziness, boisterousness, emphasis on sexual prowess, consciously acting stupid, obsequiousness in front of superiors combined with ridicule of absent superiors, etc. Placement of white adult males in a subordinate position within a rigidly stratified system, that is, appears to produce behavior not all that different from the so-called personality traits commonly held to be an outcome of cultural or psychological patterns unique to Negro life. Indeed, it might be argued that relatively little adjustment on the part of the command structure was required when the infusion of Negroes into the enlisted ranks occurred as the military establishment was desegregated. It is suggested, in other words, one factor contributing to the generally smooth racial integration of the military might be due to the standard treatment—"like Negroes" in a sense—accorded to all lower-ranking enlisted personnel.

Looking at changes in Negro behavior in the integrated military we find other indications of the immediate effects of social organization on individual behavior. Even though I am fully cognizant of the almost insurmountable difficulties involved in comparing crime statistics, the fact remains that students of the problem agree Negro crime is far higher than white crime.[25] There is no consensus, however, on what amount of the difference is due, on the one hand, to Negro cultural or psychological conditions or, on the other, to structural and class variables. Presented here, in a very preliminary fashion, is some evidence bearing on the consequences arising from changes in social organization on Negro crime. Reported by Project Clear are Negro-white crime differentials for three segregated posts in 1950. Proportionately, Negro soldiers committed four times more crime than white soldiers.[26] In 1964, in the integrated military, statistics of a major Army Command in Europe show Negroes accounting for 21 per cent of the crime while constituting 16 per cent of the total personnel. In a large combat unit in Viet Nam, for a three-month period in the summer of 1965, Negroes received 19 per cent of the disciplinary reports but made up 22 per cent of the troop assignment. These are the only Negro-white crime ratios in the integrated military that the writer has seen.[27] Although these findings, of course, are incomplete, they do point to a marked drop in Negro crime as compared with both the earlier segregated military as well as contemporary civilian life.[28]

[25] Marvin E. Wolfgang, *Crime and Race* (New York: Institute of Human Relations Press, 1964); and Department of Labor, *op. cit.*, pp. 38–40.

[26] ORO, *op. cit.*, p. 354.

[27] The data reported here are from offices of the Military Police, private communication.

[28] A caution to be introduced in assessing these findings is that the Army discharged many personnel of limited potential as determined by aptitude tests in 1957–58. Negroes were disproportionately represented in the released personnel (U.S. Commission on Civil Rights, *op. cit.*, pp. 176–77). Although Negroes are still overrepresented in the lower classification levels, there are probably proportionately fewer in these categories today than in 1950, and this most likely has some effect on the drop in Negro crime in the Army.

THE NEGRO SOLDIER OVERSEAS

Some special remarks are needed concerning Negro servicemen over-seas. Suffice it to say for prefatory purposes, the American soldier, be he either white or Negro, is usually in a place where he does not understand the language, is received with mixed feelings by the local population, spends the greater part of his time in a transplanted American environ-ment, sometimes plays the role of tourist, is relatively affluent in relation to the local economy, takes advantage and is at the mercy of a *comprador* class, and in comparison with his counterpart at home is more heavily in-volved in military duties.

In general, the pattern of racial relations observed in the United States —integration in the military setting and racial exclusivism off-duty—pre-vails in overseas assignments as well. This norm is reflected in one of the most characteristic features of American military life overseas, a bifur-cation of the vice structure into groups that pander almost exclusively (or assert they do) to only one of the races. A frequent claim of local bar owners is that they discourage racially mixed trade because of the de-mands of their G.I. clientele. And, indeed, many of the establishments catering to American personnel that ring most military installations are segregated in practice. To a similar degree this is true of shore towns where Navy personnel take liberty. Violation of these implicit taboos can lead to physical threat if not violence.

The pattern of off-duty racial separatism is most pronounced in Japan and Germany, and less so in Korea. A major exception to this norm is found in the Dominican Republic. There all troops are restricted and leaving the military compound necessitates soldiers collaborating if they are not to be detected; such ventures are often as not interracial. In cer-tain off-duty areas on Okinawa, on the other hand, racial separatism is complicated by interservice rivalries and a fourfold ecological pattern shows up: white-Army, Negro-Army, white-Marine Corps, and Negro-Marine Corps. Combat conditions in Viet Nam make the issue of off-duty racial relations academic for those troops in the field. In the cities, how-ever, racial separatism off-duty is already apparent. It is said that the riverfront district in Saigon, Kanh Hoi, frequented by American Negro soldiers was formerly patronized by Senegalese troops during the French occupation.

In Germany one impact on that country's economic boom has been to depress the relative position of the American soldier vis-à-vis the German working man. In the Germany of ten or fifteen years ago (or the Korea of today) all American military personnel were affluent by local standards with all that implied. This was (and is in Korea) an especially novel ex-perience for the Negro soldier. The status drop of American soldiers sta-tioned in Germany has particularly affected the Negro serviceman, who has the additional handicap of being black in a country where there are no Negro girls. The old "good duty" days for Negro soldiers in Germany are now coming to an end as he finds his previous access to girls other than prostitutes severely reduced. The German economic boom has affected Negro soldiers in another way. In recent years there has been some friction between foreign laborers (mostly Mediterranean) and Negro soldiers. Both groups of men apparently are competing for the same girls. At the same time, the foreign workers have little contact with white soldiers who move in a different segment of the vice structure.

Nonetheless, overseas duty for the Negro serviceman, in Germany as well as the Far East, gives him an opportunity, even if peripheral, to witness societies where racial discrimination is less practiced than it is in his home country. Although the level of Negro acceptance in societies other than America is usually exaggerated, the Negro soldier is hard put not to make invidious comparisons with the American scene.[29] In interviews conducted with Negro servicemen in Germany, 64 percent said there was more racial equality in Germany than America, 30 percent saw little difference between the two countries, and only 6 per cent believed Negroes were treated better in the United States.

Observers of overseas American personnel have told the writer that Negro soldiers are more likely than whites to learn local languages (though for both groups of servicemen this is a very small number). Evidence for this supposition is given in Table 9. Three German-national barbers, who were permanently hired to cut the hair of all the men in one battalion, were asked by the writer to evaluate the German language proficiency of the individual personnel in that battalion.[30] When these evaluations were correlated with race, it was found that Negro soldiers were five times more likely to know "conversational" German, and three times more likely to know "some" German than were white soldiers.[31] Actually, the

TABLE 9

Command of German Language by White and Negro Soldiers
in a German-Based U.S. Army Battalion, 1965

Command of German*	Percent	
	White Soldiers	Negro Soldiers
Conversational	1.4	7.4
Some	3.0	7.4
Little or none	95.6	85.2
Total	100.0	100.0
No. of cases)	(629)	(98)

* Based on evaluations of German-national battalion employees.

[29] A social-distance study conducted among Korean college students found the following placement, from near to far: Chinese, Europeans and white Americans, Filipinos, Indians (from India), and Negroes (Man Gap Lee, Seoul National University, personal communication).

[30] These barbers were focal points of much of the battalion's gossip and between themselves saw every man in the battalion on the average of at least twice a month.

[31] The same data, in tables not shown here, reveal that there is an *inverse* correlation between formal education (as ascertained from battalion personnel records) and like-

likelihood of Negro soldiers compared to whites in learning the language of the country in which they are stationed may be even greater than indicated in Table 9. Several of the German-speaking white soldiers were of German ethnic background and acquired some knowledge of the language in their home environments back in the United States. These data testify, then, that the Negro soldiers overseas, perhaps because of the more favorable racial climate, are more willing to take advantage of participation at informal levels with local populations.[32]

CIVIL RIGHTS AT HOME AND WAR ABROAD

It is important to remember that the military establishment was desegregated before the current civil rights drive gained momentum. In the segregated military, embroilments between Negro units and whites were an ever present problem. In the light of subsequent developments in the domestic racial picture, it is likely that severe disciplinary problems would have occurred had military integration not come about when it did. The timing of desegregation in the military defused an ingredient—all-Negro military units—that would have been potentially explosive in this nation's current racial strife.[33]

It is also probable, however, that military experience contributes to an activist posture on the part of Negro servicemen returning to civilian life. The Negro ex-serviceman, that is, may be less willing to accommodate himself to second-class citizenship after participation in the racially egalitarian military establishment. Further, especially in situations where Negroes are intimidated by physical threat or force, techniques of violence and organizational skill acquired in military service may be a new factor in the Negro's quest for equality. Robert F. Williams, the leading advocate of armed self-defense for Negroes, explicitly states that his Marine Corps experience led to his beliefs.[34] It also seems more than coincidence that the ten founders of the Deacons for Defense and Justice, a paramilitary group organized in 1964 to counter Ku Klux Klan terrorism, were all veterans of Korea or World War II.[35]

One must also take into account the possible consequences of the civil rights movement on Negro military behavior. Much attention has been given to a convergence of an important segment of the civil rights movement with the movement against the war in Viet Nam. The Student Non-

---

lihood of learning German! This reflects the greater likelihood of Negro soldiers, compared to whites, to learn German while averaging fewer years of formal education.

[32] In 1965 a widely seen German television commercial portrayed two American soldiers, one white and the other Negro. Only the Negro soldier spoke German.

[33] Although non-violence is the hallmark of the main thrust of the modern civil rights movement, there is, nevertheless, the leitmotiv of a Negro insurrection in the thinking of such Negro figures as James Baldwin, Malcolm X, William Epton, Warren Miller, and LeRoi Jones. Congruent with the idea of armed conflict between the races are the gothic endings—whites and Negro soldiers engaging in a bloodbath—in recent Negro-authored novels (see Killens, *op cit.*, and Rhodes, *op. cit.*).

[34] Robert F. Williams, *Negroes with Guns* (New York: Marzani & Munsell, 1962).

[35] *The Militant*, November 22, 1965, p. 1.

violent Coordinating Committee has formally denounced American action in Viet Nam as aggression. Civil rights organizers claim they find
Negroes who do not want to fight "whitey's war." A Negro is barred from
taking his seat in the Georgia legislature because he condones violations
of the draft law. Rumors are heard of isolated incidents of Negro insub-
ordination in the armed services. Despite this chain of events, however,
the main stream of the civil rights drive has remained largely removed
from those groups highly critical of this country's recent military policies.
Indeed, the antiwar movement will likely aggravate an already existing
cleavage between moderate and radical leaders—between those who accept versus those who reject the legitimacy of the American political system—in the civil rights movement itself. The more pertinent question at
this time appears to be not what are the implications of the civil rights
movement for the military establishment, but what will be the effects of
the Viet Nam war on the civil rights movement itself. Although it would
be premature to offer a definitive statement on any future interpenetra-
tions between the civil rights and antiwar movements, a major turning
away of Negroes per se from military commitment is viewed as highly
doubtful. Most likely, and somewhat paradoxically, we will witness more
vocal antiwar sentiment within certain civil rights organizations at the
same time that the military is becoming an avenue of career opportunity
for many Negro men.

Nevertheless, there has usually been and is today a presumption on the
part of America's military opponents that Negroes should be less committed soldiers than whites. Whether for tactical or ideological reasons,
the Negro serviceman has been frequently defined as a special target for
propaganda by forces opposing America in military conflicts. In World
War II the Japanese directed radio appeals specifically to Negro servicemen in the Pacific theater. The Chinese in the Korean War used racial
arguments on Negro prisoners of war. Yet a careful study of American
POW behavior in Korea made no mention of differences in Negro and
white behavior except to note that the segregation of Negro POW's by
the Chinese had a boomerang effect on Communist indoctrination methods.[36]

The current military involvement of the United States on the international scene raises again the question of the motivation and performance
of Negro soldiers in combat. A spokesman for the National Liberation
Front of South Viet Nam has recently asserted that "liberation forces
have a special attitude toward American soldiers who happen to be Negroes."[37] Up to now at least, however, efforts to test the loyalty of Negro
soldiers have not met with success. This writer, as well as others, detected
no differences in white or Negro combat performance in Viet Nam.[38] In
the Dominican Republic, where the proportion of Negroes in line units

[36] Albert D. Biderman, *March to Calumny* (New York: Macmillan Co., 1964), p. 60.

[37] *The Minority of One*, October, 1965, p. 9.

[38] "Only One Color," *Newsweek*, December 6, 1965, pp. 42–43; Robin Moore, *The
Green Berets* (New York: Avon Books, 1965), *passim*; and Herbert Mitgang, "Looking
for a War," *New York Times Magazine*, May 22, 1966, pp. 114–15.

runs as high as 40 percent, a pamphlet was distributed to Negro soldiers exhorting them to "turn your guns on your white oppressors and join your Dominican brothers."[39] Again, personal observation buttressed by comments from Dominicans revealed no significant differences between white and Negro military performance.[40]

The writer's appraisal is that among officers and NCO's there is no discernible difference between the races concerning military commitment in either the Dominican Republic or Viet Nam. Among Negro soldiers in the lower enlisted ranks, however, there is somewhat greater disenchantment compared to whites as to the merits of America's current military ventures. Such unease, however, has little effect on military performance, most especially in the actual combat situation. The evidence strongly suggests that the racial integration of the armed forces, coming about when it did, effectively precluded any potential success on the part of America's military opponents to differentiate Negro from white soldiers.

CONCLUSION

Although the military was until recent times one of America's most segregated institutions, it has leaped into the forefront of racial equality in the past decade. What features of the military establishment can account for this about-face? There is a combination of mutually supporting factors that operate in the successful racial integration of the armed forces. For one thing, the military—an institution revolving around techniques of violence—is to an important degree discontinuous from other areas of social life. And this apartness served to allow, once the course had been decided, a rapid and complete racial integration. The path of desegregation was further made easier by characteristics peculiar or at least more pronounced in the military compared to other institutions. With its hierarchical power structure, predicated on stable and patterned relationships, decisions need take relatively little account of the personal desires of service personnel. Additionally, because roles and activities are more defined and specific in the military than in most other social arenas, conflicts that might have ensued within a more diffuse and ambiguous setting were largely absent. Likewise, desegregation was facilitated by the pervasiveness in the military of a bureaucratic ethos, with its concomitant formality and high social distance, that mitigated tensions arising from individual or personal feelings.

At the same time it must also be remembered that the military estab-

[39] A copy of the entire pamphlet is reproduced in the Dominican news magazine *Ahora* (No. 108, September 18, 1965). Although many whites were unaware of the pamphlet's existence, virtually every Negro soldier the writer talked to in Santo Domingo said he had seen the pamphlet. The effectiveness of the pamphlet on Negro soldiers was minimal, among other reasons, because it claimed Negro equality existed in the Dominican Republic, a statement belied by brief observation of the Dominican social scene.

[40] Similarly in an interview with a Negro reporter, the commandant of "constitutionalist rebel" forces in Santo Domingo stated that to his dismay Negro American soldiers fought no differently than whites (Laurence Harvey, "Report from the Dominican Republic," *Realist*, June, 1965, p. 18).

lishment has means of coercion not readily available in most civilian pursuits. Violations of norms are both more visible and subject to quicker sanctions. The military is premised, moreover, on the accountability of its members for effective performance. Owing to the aptly termed "chain of command," failures in policy implementation can be pinpointed. This in turn means that satisfactory carrying of stated policy advances one's own position. In other words, it is to each individual's personal interest, if he anticipates receiving the rewards of a military career, to insure that decisions going through him are executed with minimum difficulty. Or put it another way, whatever the internal policy decided upon, racial integration being a paramount but only one example, the military establishment is uniquely suited to realize its implementation.

What implications does the military integration experience have for civilian society? Although it is certainly true that the means by which desegregation was accomplished in the military establishment are not easily translated to the civilian community, the end result of integration in the contemporary armed forces can suggest some qualities of what—if it came about—an integrated American society would be *within the context of the prevailing structural and value system*. Equality of treatment would be the rule in formal and task-specific relationships. Racial animosity would diminish but not disappear. We would expect a sharp improvement in Negro mobility and performance in the occupational sphere even taking into consideration on-going social and educational handicaps arising from existing inequities. Yet, because of these inequities, Negroes would still be overconcentrated in less skilled positions. We would also expect primary group ties and informal associations to remain largely within one's own racial group. But even at primary group levels, the integrated society would exhibit a much higher interracial intimacy than exists in the non-integrated society.

Such a description of the racially integrated society is, of course, what one finds in today's military establishment. Although the advent of the integrated society in this country is yet to occur, the desegregation of the armed forces has served to bring that day closer.

44

Why Lincoln Said "No": Congressional Attitudes on Slavery Expansion, 1860-1861

CHARLES DESMOND HART
YORK UNIVERSITY, TORONTO

E VEN BEFORE THE SOUTH CAROLINA CONVENTION PASSED THE ORDINANCE OF secession on December 20, 1860, which severed the ties of the Palmetto State with the Union, discussions of another sectional compromise in the tradition of 1820, 1833, and 1850 had already commenced in Congress. On December 18, Senator John J. Crittenden (Whig, Kentucky) introduced the last of the great antebellum plans of compromise, and for the remainder of the winter, as six more slaveholding states joined South Carolina as members of the Confederacy, the Crittenden Compromise dominated discussions of the slavery question, both in Congress and in the country at large. Building on the Missouri Compromise of 1820, Crittenden proposed, in his most important resolution, that in all territory then held or "hereafter acquired," slavery would be prohibited above the line of 36°30′ north latitude; below the line, slavery would be recognized and protected.[1] Although in its waning hours Congress approved a Constitutional amendment which would have prohibited for all time federal interference with slavery in the states, President-elect Abraham Lincoln and the Republicans in Congress used their influence to prevent the passage of the Crittenden Compromise. Within six weeks of the adjournment of Congress, Fort Sumter was fired upon and the American Civil War had begun.

Lincoln's refusal to support a territorial compromise during the winter of 1860–1861 probably has been the subject of more criticism than any other decision in his political life. Some historians have maintained that had the Crittenden Compromise been submitted to the people of the North in 1861 it would have been accepted; thus when Lincoln "moved to defeat compromise, he did not move as the champion of democracy, but as a partisan leader."[2] Had Lincoln supported the Crittenden Compromise, a historian favorable to the President-elect has written, "he probably could have carried enough Republicans with him" to have brought about its

---

[1] Most secondary accounts of Senator Crittenden's territorial proposal are vague or inaccurate. Too often it is forgotten that Crittenden's suggestion differed from the Missouri Compromise of 1820 in three important ways: all lands *"hereafter acquired"* were involved; slavery would have been *recognized and protected* below the 36° 30′ line; and Crittenden's proposal was offered in the form of *irrepealable* amendments to the Constitution. U.S., Congress, Senate, *Congressional Globe*, 36th Cong., 2d sess., 1860, pp. 112–114.

[2] David M. Potter, *Lincoln and his Party in the Secession Crisis*, 2d ed. (New Haven and London: Yale University Press, 1962), pp. 195–200. For a different view of Northern opinion see Kenneth M. Stampp, *And the War Came: The North and the Secession Crisis, 1860–1861*, 2d ed. (Chicago and London: The University of Chicago Press, 1964), pp. 141–147.

adoption.[3] Underlying the whole discussion is the important historiographical controversy on "the natural limits of slavery expansion," which is fundamental to most interpretations of the coming of the Civil War.[4] Even renowned Lincoln scholars have defended his refusal to endorse the Crittenden resolutions by attempting to demonstrate that slavery was a variable institution which might have been adapted to the cultivation of wheat on the western prairies, or to the orchards, mines, and factories of the United States today.[5] Yet in no less than five of the eight letters which Lincoln wrote on slavery in the territories during the winter of 1860–1861 he made it clear that he opposed the Crittenden Compromise because it made possible slavery expansion to Southern territory which might be acquired in the future. The Crittenden resolutions would only lead to "filibustering for all South of us, and making slave states of it;"[6] a year would not pass "till we should have to take Cuba as a condition upon which [the South] will stay in the Union."[7] On other aspects of the slavery question—fugitive slaves, slavery in the District of Columbia, the domestic slave trade—he cared "but little," as long as what was done "be comely and not altogether outrageous." Indeed, Lincoln did not even "care much" about New Mexico Territory, the storm center of the territorial controversy for much of the time since 1846, "if further expansion was hedged against."[8]

In brief, as Lincoln waited in Springfield to take over the government from James Buchanan, he kept an open mind on most aspects of the slavery question; he was firmly opposed, however, to any settlement of the territorial issue which would have permitted future slavery expansion to lands hereafter acquired to the south of the United States, and for this reason he could not support the Crittenden Compromise. With historians in disagreement about contemporary opinion on the possible territorial compromise, the time is opportune for systematic and comprehensive studies of certain important sources of that opinion in an attempt to discover whether the attitudes expressed by Lincoln were more widely held among Northerners. Since any territorial compromise would have had to receive the approval of Congress, an obvious starting point for such investigations is the congressional debate on slavery in the territories during the winter of 1860–1861. This debate commenced almost as soon as the reading of President Buchanan's last Annual Message was completed on December 3, 1860, and by the end of the session in March no less than 144, or ap-

[3] Richard N. Current, *The Lincoln Nobody Knows*, 2d ed. (New York: Hill and Wang, 1963), p. 94.

[4] There is a brief discussion of this controversy in C. R. Desmond Hart, "Congressmen and the Expansion of Slavery into the Territories: A Study in Attitudes, 1846–1861," (Ph.D. diss., University of Washington, Seattle, 1965), pp. iv–xi.

[5] Current, *The Lincoln Nobody Knows*, Ch. 4, esp. pp. 94–100; T. Harry Williams, "Lincoln and the Causes of the Civil War," in O. Fritiof Ander, ed., *Lincoln Images* (Rock Island, Ill.: Augusta Library Publications, No. 29, 1960) pp. 33–35.

[6] Lincoln, *Collected Works*, ed. Roy P. Basler (New Brunswick: Rutgers University Press, 1953–1955), pp. 154–155.

[7] *Ibid.*, p. 172.

[8] *Ibid.*, p. 183.

proximately 46 per cent of the 311 congressmen—66 senators, 240 representatives, 5 territorial delegates—who were eligible to serve in the second session of the Thirty-sixth Congress had spoken on slavery in the territories. An analysis of these speeches throws new light on Lincoln's territorial policy, on the historiographical controversy over the limits of slavery expansion, and on the compromise debacle of the secession winter.

Forty-three of the 144 senators and representatives specifically discussed the limits of slavery expansion in floor speeches delivered between December, 1860, and March, 1861. One group of 18 congressmen, which included such well-known political leaders as Crittenden, Stephen A. Douglas, and William H. Seward, expressed the opinion that slavery could not be taken beyond the states of the Old South where it was then established. Like his illustrious predecessor from Kentucky, Henry Clay in 1850, Crittenden in 1860 based his territorial plan on the understanding that slavery could never be established in any of the territories which would be affected. He said:

> By these resolutions, in all the territory north of the line designated, slavery is prohibited; all south of it, which in reference to our present territory, is nothing more than the Territory of New Mexico, the most sterile and worthless of its extent upon this whole continent, is reserved for the South.[9]

> What are the worth and value of that Territory [New Mexico] to white or black? It is the most sterile region of country belonging to the United States, the least happy. . . . as I believe, it can never be made a slave State. It is not a country where slaves can be profitably employed; and the great law of profit and loss governs with invariable power and invariable efficacy.[10]

Crittenden also believed that the line of 36°30′ north latitude had been adopted as the boundary between freedom and slavery because wise men had wanted to avoid further controversy by striking a line north of which slave labor never could be useful. As several antislavery congressmen pointed out, Crittenden's own argument was proof that his so-called "compromise" would provide nothing for the North which was not already secure.

Douglas (Democrat, Illinois) and Seward (Republican, New York), the other two senators most actively involved in the compromise negotiations, agreed with Crittenden that slavery would not become one of the permanent institutions in the territories remaining for settlement.[11] Douglas, who had frequently said over the years that slavery depended more upon "the necessities of climate, health, and productions than upon con-

---

[9] *Congressional Globe*, p. 864.

[10] *Ibid.*, p. 1376.

[11] Although most discussions of slavery in the territories were concerned with New Mexico Territory (which then included Arizona), when Congress met in early December, 1860, any territorial settlement would have had to take into account Kansas (which soon received statehood), Colorado, Nevada, and the Dakotas (which were organized as territories that winter), as well as Nebraska, Washington, and Utah Territories, along with the unorganized Indian country of the Southwest.

gressional and territorial enactments," contended that the events of the last dozen years had shown that one might as well attempt by act of Congress "to compel cotton to grow upon the tops of the Rocky Mountains and rice upon the summits of the Sierra Nevada" as to compel slavery to exist in such a region, where the climate was adverse and the inhabitants opposed the institution.[12] Speaking in the Senate on January 31, 1861, the day after Kansas was admitted to the Union, Seward admitted that everything "vital and important" had been secured the previous afternoon. Although in March, 1850, he had demanded the passage of the Wilmot Proviso to preserve the Mexican Territories for freedom, Seward was now convinced that his fears had been groundless. In phrases which were frequently quoted by other congressmen, Seward explained that he had no fear of slavery where only one slave had been planted in every twenty-four thousand miles of territory during a dozen years when the courts, the legislature, and the administration had "maintained, protected, defended, and guaranteed" the institution.[13]

Four other senators expressed similar sentiments on slavery expansion. The dilemma faced by a number of Republicans was brought out in the remarks of Senator Edward D. Baker of Oregon, a close friend of Abraham Lincoln (who would be killed in the early months of the Civil War). Baker believed that God Almighty had "registered a decree in Heaven" which protected the territory north of the 36°30′ line from slavery, while south of the line there was only barren New Mexico Territory. Yet Baker, like Lincoln, found it impossible to support a territorial compromise which applied to lands "hereafter acquired."[14] The other three senators, all of them Democrats, supported the Crittenden plan of compromise. According to Milton S. Latham of California, even if New Mexico entered the Union as a slaveholding state, five years would not pass before this condition would be changed.[15] Lazarus W. Powell of Kentucky, who had prevailed upon Crittenden to include the controversial "hereafter acquired" clause in his resolution on the territories, argued that there was no territory south of the United States out of which more than one or two slave states could be formed, nor was it possible that such territory could be acquired in the future without the approval of the non-slaveholding states.[16] Thomas L. Clingman of North Carolina agreed with Powell that it was "idle" for Northern Congressmen to attempt to convince anyone that they were afraid of future territorial "acquisitions against their wishes," especially since the new states coming into the Union from the Northwest would soon swell Northern majorities even more.[17]

Eleven members of the House of Representatives agreed that slavery could never be established in the remaining territories, some of them supporting the Crittenden Compromise and others opposing it. John Sherman

---

[12] *Congressional Globe*, pp. 661, 1391; App. p. 36.
[13] *Ibid.*, p. 658.
[14] *Ibid.*, pp. 1315, 1385.
[15] *Ibid.*, p. 403.
[16] *Ibid.*, App., p. 93.
[17] *Ibid.*, p. 727.

(Republican, Ohio) was certain that no matter what Congress or the Supreme Court decided, Northern public opinion, if nothing else, guaranteed that slavery could never be established in any of the lands above the 36°30′ line. Although Sherman was not so definite when he turned to New Mexico Territory, he did refer to the region as "a narrow, thinly populated country," a territory of "but little value."[18] John W. Killinger and William Stewart of Pennsylvania and Albert G. Porter of Indiana, all Republicans, admitted that slavery already existed in New Mexico.[19] They pointed out, however, that the future of the institution was bleak in a region of high mountain ranges, where the rivers ran dry in the summer and where irrigation was necessary to cultivate the valleys. Two other Republicans, James Humphrey of New York and William Kellogg of Illinois, together with William J. Morris (Whig, Pennsylvania), also stated that the climate, soil, and products of New Mexico Territory would prevent any large number of slaves being taken to that region.[20]

John A. Logan of Illinois and three Southerners discussed the limits of slavery expansion on the Democratic side of the House of Representatives. According to Logan, who was ready to support any of the various compromise proposals, the God of Nature had so arranged the soil and climate of the remaining territory that slavery could never enter.[21] Andrew J. Hamilton of Texas, one of the few men in Congress who knew firsthand the territory in question, expressed sentiments similar to those of John R. Barret of Missouri and William N. H. Smith of North Carolina:[22]

> I have heard New Mexico will ultimately be a non-slaveholding State; and that, although we may admit it as a slave State, it will not, in the opinion of some, remain a slave State. I admit the correctness of that opinion. It is my own opinion. . . . If I know anything about that country, I know that it cannot remain a slave State. No man who has ever traveled through it, no man who has ever been on the contiguous soil in my own State can, for a moment, delude himself with any such idea.[23]

While 18 congressmen expressed the opinion that the expansive capacities of slavery were limited, a second and larger group of 25 senators and representatives emphasized in their speeches that slavery was an institution which was capable of further expansion, either to the remaining territories of the West or to the lands south of the United States which might be acquired in the future.

Three of the 25 expansionists, all Republicans in the House of Representatives, contended that New Mexico would become a slaveholding state. For who could tell, queried Alfred Wells of New York, the result if New Mexico and Arizona, vast enough to produce 24 states the size of Massachusetts, were forever in contact with the fertile cotton fields of Texas and the other lands capable of maintaining 60 million slaves? Who

18 *Ibid.*, p. 455.
19 *Ibid.*, pp. 695, 1042; App., p. 257.
20 *Ibid.*, App., pp. 159, 194, 218.
21 *Ibid.*, App., p. 180.
22 *Ibid.*, App., pp. 248, 206.
23 *Ibid.*, App., pp. 176–177.

could tell what new arts, what new appliances, what unimagined discoveries might convert the desert into a garden? Might not the same industry and skill which had made rocky New England sustain a dense population and which had reclaimed the plains of Holland from the waters yet give fertility to the plains and mountains of New Mexico and Arizona?[24] Daniel W. Gooch of Massachusetts warned that when slavery was guaranteed and protected in New Mexico the number of slaves would rapidly increase, for no longer would slaveholders have to fear that when the territory entered the Union it would enter as a non-slaveholding state. Since the experience in Kansas had settled forever the question of slavery in lands north of the 36°30′ line, the Crittenden Compromise seemed to Gooch a dishonest and worthless proposal, an attempt to deceive the people of the North.[25] Daniel E. Somes of Maine maintained that unless Southerners believed that New Mexico would be as profitable for slave-breeding as Virginia and Maryland, they would not be as anxious to secure the region.[26]

Twenty-two of the 25 expansionists agreed with Abraham Lincoln that slavery might well be expanded southward to lands which would be acquired in the future. This group, which included such men as Henry Wilson and Charles Sumner, the Republican senators from Massachusetts, contained some of the most outspoken opponents of slavery expansion in general and of the Crittenden Compromise in particular. To Wilson the Crittenden proposals were "a cheat, a delusion, a snare. . . . an unqualified concession, a complete surrender of all the practical issues concerning slavery in the Territories to the demands of slave propagandism." The proslavery leaders were practical statesmen who saw clearly that "the mighty currents of advancing civilization were bearing them away from the Territories of the Northwest." They knew that no legal protection could permanently stamp their peculiar institution on the territory north of the 36°30′ line: Dakota, Colorado, Utah, Nevada, and Washington. The Southerners realized, as had the Republicans, that the great struggle between slavery and freedom in Kansas was a contest not only for Kansas, but for the territory north and west of its southern boundary. Thus they had not been fighting for a mere abstraction when, the previous spring, they had demanded that the Democratic party recognize the right to take slave property into the territories and to have it protected there by positive federal laws; indeed, they had contested the election of 1860 for the Indian country, New Mexico, Arizona, Cuba, and portions of Mexico and Central America. Senators Crittenden and Douglas now proposed to prohibit slavery in all the territory which had been won for freedom by the victory in Kansas and to recognize and protect slavery in all the territory involved in the great contest of the previous autumn. Such a settlement Wilson would never sanction.[27]

To Sumner, who considered freedom in the territories a matter of principle—"the Fort Sumter of the North"—the Crittenden Compromise

24 *Ibid.*, App., p. 191.
25 *Ibid.*, App., pp. 262–263.
26 *Ibid.*, p. 968.
27 *Ibid.*, p. 1092.

was worse than the Breckenridge platform which had been condemned at the recent election.[28] To make these proposals even more offensive and unacceptable to the North, they applied to all territories hereafter acquired; thus the flag of the Republic would always be the flag of slavery, and every future acquisition in a southwardly direction would be Africanized.[29] Two other Republican senators, Lot M. Morrill of Maine and John C. Ten Eyck of New Jersey, were willing to abide by the Compromise of 1850, even though New Mexico might enter the Union as a slave state; but they were concerned by what the latter described as "a well-established purpose and design, in certain quarters, as shown by past events, to extend the power of this Government over Mexico, Central America, Cuba, and the islands of the sea."[30] A third Republican senator, Henry B. Anthony of Rhode Island, warned that the provision which made Crittenden's territorial proposal applicable to all territory hereafter acquired would be regarded all over the North "as an invitation to filibusterism and a provocation to war with Mexico." Instead of anticipating difficulties which might never come, it would be better to admit New Mexico into the Union with whatever constitution her people adopted and give public opinion time to cool.[31]

Seventeen members of the House of Representatives expressed views similar to those of President-elect Lincoln on the question of slavery expansion. Roscoe Conkling of New York was one of several Republicans willing to carry out the Compromise of 1850, but no matter in what guise or from what quarter it originated, he could never support the Crittenden Compromise. It would amount, he claimed, to "a perpetual covenant of war against every people, tribe, and State owning a foot of land between here and Tierra del Fuego," making the federal government the armed missionary of slavery, and launching the United States upon "a shoreless and starless sea of war and filibustering."[32] Since nobody was credulous enough to suppose that the Union was to be sundered because slavery could not obtain a constitutional license to enter the arid and parched wilderness of New Mexico, Samuel S. Blair of Pennsylvania was convinced that Crittenden's offer to prohibit slavery in the major part of the remaining territories was only "a cloak to cover the nakedness of the attempt" to introduce slavery into Mexico or the portions of her dominions which might be acquired by treaty or acts of lawless aggression.[33] Francis W. Kellogg of Michigan agreed that since the residents of the Northern territories were opposed to slavery, the Crittenden proposals gave "a shadow for a substance; an imaginary title to the mountains in the moon for the promised possession of the provinces of Mexico." Their adoption would

---

[28] Numerous antislavery congressmen compared the platform on which John C. Breckenridge contested the presidential election in 1860 with the territorial proposal suggested by Senator Crittenden. See *Congressional Globe, ibid.*, App. p. 224.

[29] *Ibid.*, pp. 862–863.

[30] *Ibid.*, pp. 682, 1392.

[31] *Ibid.*, pp. 408–409.

[32] *Ibid.*, p. 651.

[33] *Ibid.*, App., pp. 252–253.

prepare the way for the agitation which would presently result in the conquest of Mexico and Central America.[34]

Included in this group of Republican representatives were some of the most outspoken opponents of compromise of the territorial issue. Several agreed with Justin M. Morrill of Vermont, who remarked that it was useless to trifle about the admission of New Mexico, even as a slaveholding state, when it left open what the South held to be "the paramount question—the disposal of *territory hereafter to be acquired*."[35] Only the transfer of the territorial controversy to foreign lands, which the United States did not own and had no right to assume that she ever would own, could satisfy the secessionists, declared Alfred Ely of New York.[36] Charles H. Van Wyck, also of New York, preferred to perish "on the threshold of the Capitol, defending the stars and stripes which float over it," rather than vote for any settlement which would satisfy Southern "dreams of Cuba, Mexico, the Central and South American States."[37] Carey A. Trimble of Ohio objected to the Crittenden Compromise because it would be held out as a bribe to marauders and filibusterers who would involve the United States in wars of conquest against all the weak neighboring states whose lands might be adapted to slavery.[38] James Wilson of Indiana objected because it would result in the dismemberment of Mexico, Cuba, and Central America and the creation of "an empire of slavery such as the world has never before witnessed."[39] John B. Haskin (Democrat, New York) capsulized the sentiments of this predominantly Republican group:

> The Crittenden proposals ask too much. It asks more for the extension of slavery than even the Breckinridge men demanded at Charleston, Baltimore, or Richmond. It provides for recognizing slavery in territory hereafter acquired, and offers a premium to the filibustering spirit which I supposed had been destroyed when the marauder General William Walker was executed in Central America. It invites the stealing of Mexico, the robbing of Central America, and the piratical acquisition of Cuba.[40]

All told, 43 senators and representatives discussed the limits of slavery expansion on the floor of Congress betweeen December, 1860, and March, 1861. Of these 43 Congressmen, 25 expressed the opinion that slavery was capable of expansion beyond the states of the Old South. All but one of

[34] *Ibid.*, App., p. 271.

[35] *Ibid.*, p. 1007. Cadwallader C. Washburn of Wisconsin (pp. 514–515) and Charles B. Sedgwick of New York (p. 796) spoke in a similar vein. Washburn was also the fourth member of the House of Representatives who believed that New Mexico could become a slaveholding state.

[36] *Ibid.*, App., p. 244.

[37] *Ibid.*, pp. 629–632.

[38] *Ibid.*, App., p. 162.

[39] *Ibid.*, App., p. 132.

[40] *Ibid.*, App., p. 268. The other representatives in this group were Charles Francis Adams of Massachusetts (App., pp. 125–126); Harrison G. O. Blake of Ohio (App., pp. 223–225); Alfred A. Burnham of Connecticut (App., pp. 969–973); James H. Campbell of Pennsylvania (pp. 911–912); Henry Winter Davis of Maryland (App., p. 183); and John U. Pettit of Indiana (App., p. 286). All were Republicans except Pettit, who was a Democrat, and Campbell, who was a Whig.

these men (Henry Winter Davis) represented non-slaveholding states (22 Republicans, 2 Democrats, 1 Whig). In contrast, 18 of the 43 expressed the opinion that slavery could not expand beyond the states where it was then established. Twelve of these men (8 Republicans, 3 Democrats, 1 Whig) represented non-slaveholding states, and 6 (5 Democrats and 1 Whig) represented slaveholding states. Since many Southern congressmen took little or no part in the proceedings of the second session of the Thirty-sixth Congress, the division between two groups of Northern congressmen, which had been evident since the beginning of the territorial debate in August, 1846, was brought into sharp focus. This division among congressmen from the non-slaveholding states was responsible for much of the bitterness on the territorial issue in the later 1850's, and was an important factor in the failure of Congress to consider seriously a compromise during the secession winter. Many Northerners were convinced that they had been betrayed on New Mexico and Kansas. In each instance men such as Stephen A. Douglas had declared that slaves were barred from the territories by a law of nature; yet in each instance Negro slaves had made an appearance and a slave code had been adopted. As long as some of their free-state colleagues dismissed the possibility of further slavery expansion, an important group of Northern congressmen refused to consider any territorial settlement which might allow the slaveholding interest (still in control of the federal government) to take advantage of a divided North once again and extend the territory open to slavery.[41]

In addition, a majority of the congressmen who discussed the limits of slavery expansion agreed with Abraham Lincoln that the real danger of future extension was to those Southern lands which might become part of the United States. This was an argument which had seldom appeared in the previous 15 years of the great debate on slavery in the territories; indeed, the reasoning of the antislavery congressmen followed much different lines in 1860–1861 than in either 1850 or 1854.[42] Since only 4 of 43 congressmen expressed a belief that slavery could become one of the permanent institutions in the territories than part of the United States, it should not be surprising that Congress organized Colorado, Dakota, and the Nevada Territories that same winter without any restrictions on slavery. Yet historians such as James G. Randall have made much of this action in an attempt to show that Lincoln and the Republicans had not been serious a few months before when they campaigned on a platform promising freedom from slavery in the remaining territories.[43] Too often it has been forgotten that the 1860 Republican platform called for federal legislation prohibiting slavery in the territories only when it was considered

[41] *Ibid.*, 31st Cong., 1st sess., App., p. 515; 33rd Cong., 2d sess., App., p. 249; 36th Cong., 2d sess., pp. 514–515, p. 682; App., p. 271.

[42] See Charles Desmond Hart, "Slavery Expansion to the Territories, 1850: A Forgotten Speech by Truman Smith," *New Mexico Historical Review,* 41 (Oct., 1966), pp. 269–287; " 'The Natural Limits of Slavery Expansion': Kansas-Nebraska, 1854," *Kansas Historical Quarterly,* 34 (Spring, 1968), pp. 32–50.

[43] "The Civil War Restudied," *Journal of Southern History,* 6 (Nov., 1940), pp. 439–457, esp. pp. 447–448.

"necessary" to keep a territory free; that in 1861 both Lincoln and his colleagues in Congress were concerned about the expansion of slavery to the south, not to the west. As Arthur Bestor and Kenneth M. Stampp have pointed out, there were ample reasons for this concern.[44]

Since only 43 of the 144 congressmen who discussed slavery in the territories during the last of the antebellum sessions of Congress specifically discussed the limits of slavery expansion, and since an analysis of the speeches of all 144 leaves little doubt that the territorial issue was now a matter of principle to most of them,[45] one might argue that by 1860 the question of the limits of slavery expansion was no longer an important consideration. Yet assumptions by historians on this question continue to be fundamental to most interpretations of the Civil War. Moreover, the question of the limits of slavery expansion determined the framework within which the whole discussion of slavery in the territories was conducted during the crucial winter of 1860–1861. Events of the later 1850's had convinced observers from both the North and South that the remaining territories of the West would never support slavery, that expansion of the institution must be confined to future acquisitions of territory to the south. Thus Southerners demanded a territorial settlement which would provide for slavery in any lands later acquired below the line of 36°30′, while even compromise-minded Northerners were determined to resist any settlement which opened the door for slavery expansion to the one region where they thought it could prosper. Although Lincoln and a majority of Republicans might well have compromised on the remaining territories of the United States, for good and practical reasons they uttered an emphatic "no" when presented with the Crittenden Compromise, for under such a settlement slavery might have been extended to the very region of greatest concern in 1861—Central and South America.

[44] Stampp, *And The War Came*, pp. 166–170; Arthur Bestor, "The American Civil War as a Constitutional Crisis," *American Historical Review*, 79 (Jan., 1964), pp. 334, 336.

[45] Hart, "Congressmen and the Expansion of Slavery into the Territories," Ch. 6, esp. pp. 138–139.

Constituency Characteristics and Roll Call Voting on Negro Rights in the 88th Congress[1]

JACK R. VAN DER SLIK

SOUTHERN ILLINOIS UNIVERSITY

A COMPELLING ISSUE IN CONTEMPORARY AMERICAN LIFE CONCERNS THE INtegration of black Americans into all structures and activities of society. The issue arises and the implications are being contested in many aspects of social life, but a major arena for resolving the political questions involved is the United States Congress. The purpose of this study is to measure and, if possible, explain recent roll call voting on questions of Negro rights in the House of Representatives. The inquiry will focus specifically upon the term of the 88th Congress, serving in 1963 and 1964.

Congressional roll call votes are consequential primarily because of their authoritative character for public policy. But they are also important in that they can be interpreted as indicators of popular demands; this is particularly true for the issue of Negro rights. Miller and Stokes' study of the attitudes and perceptions of representatives and constituents indicates that of the three policy areas they studied (social welfare, foreign involvement, and civil rights for Negroes) the latter is the one in which the correlation between constituents' attitudes and representatives' perceptions of constituent attitudes is highest.[2] They also stress that in this policy area representatives' roll call voting is highly correlated with representatives' perceptions of constituency attitudes. As a result there is a substantial correspondence between representatives' roll call votes and constituency attitudes on Negro rights. As Miller and Stokes explain, "the charged and polarized nature" of the Negro rights issue accounts for the relatively high degree of relationship between roll call voting on it and constituency attitudes. Because the salience of the Negro rights issue has heightened since their research in 1958, it is reasonable to assume these relationships would be even stronger for the period studied here.

METHODS OF ANALYSIS

The essential measure for this study is a cumulative (Guttman) scale of Negro rights voting which is based upon several roll call votes.[3] What

[1] I wish to thank Charles Press, Chairman of the Political Science Department at Michigan State University for his help and encouragement in undertaking this research. I completed this study with support from the Public Affairs Research Bureau and the Department of Government at Southern Illinois University. The findings and conclusions are my own and not the responsibility of the agencies with which I have been affiliated.

[2] Warren E. Miller and Donald E. Stokes, "Constituency Influence in Congress," *American Political Science Review*, 57 (March, 1963), pp. 45–56.

[3] Duncan MacRae, Jr., has done the most extensive analyses of roll call voting with cumulative scaling. See his *Dimensions of Congressional Voting: A Statistical Study of the House of Representatives in the Eighty-first Congress* (Berkeley and Los Angeles:

recommends the roll call vote for attention is its "hard" empirical nature,[4] and the fact that it puts each representative "on the record," making him an open target for political rivals.[5] For this inquiry all the roll call votes in the House during the 88th Congress were examined to establish an a priori set of roll calls which manifestly concerned Negro rights. The roll calls selected were decisions directly affecting public policy which would change the scope of rights, services, and protection afforded to Negroes. Only six roll calls seemed to fit this description. One roll call was eliminated from the original set of six, yielding a five-item Negro rights scale with remarkably high internal consistency.[6] There were 17 nonscale responses among 1,921 recorded positions.[7]

University of California Press, 1958), pp. 203–390; with Hugh D. Price, "Scale Positions and 'Power' in the Senate," *Behavioral Science*, 4 (July, 1959), pp. 212–218; and "A Method for Identifying Issues and Factions from Legislative Votes," *American Political Science Review*, 59 (Dec., 1965), pp. 909–926.

[4] See David B. Truman, *The Congressional Party: A Case Study* (New York: John Wiley and Sons, Inc., 1959), pp. 11–13.

[5] As Gross indicates, many activities consume more time and effort for the representative—committee activity, bill preparations, speeches, etc. Nevertheless the floor vote has a more tangible and conspicuous quality. See Bertram M. Gross, *The Legislative Struggle* (New York: McGraw-Hill Book Company, 1953), p. 30.

[6] *Congressional Quarterly* numbers and briefly identifies the roll calls. The reflected items, those roll calls whose numbers are accompanied by an R, indicate that *Nay* is the liberal position. The roll calls are as follows:

1. 1963–96R; HR 9124. Revise the junior and senior Reserve Officers Training Corps programs of the Army, Air Force, and Navy. Hebert (D, La. 1) motion to pass the bill under suspension of the rules (two-thirds majority vote required). Rejected 177–154.
2. 1964–9; HR 7152. Civil Rights Act of 1964. Passage of the bill to enforce the right to vote; prevent discrimination in access to public accommodations and public facilities; expedite public school desegregation; extend the life of the Civil Rights Commission for four years and broaden its powers; prevent discrimination in administration of federally assisted programs; prevent discrimination based on race, color, religion, sex, or national origin; establish a Community Relations Service to mediate racial disputes; and permit the Attorney General to instigate or intervene in certain civil rights cases. Passed 290–130.
3. 1964–63; HR 7152. Civil Rights Act of 1964. Adoption of a resolution (H Res 789) providing for House approval of the bill as amended by the Senate, thus clearing it for the President to sign into law. Resolution adopted 289–126.
4. 1963–72; HR 3369. Private bill for the relief of Mrs. Elizabeth G. Mason to which an amendment extending the life of the Civil Rights Commission for one year had been added by the Senate. Considered under suspension of the rules (two-thirds affirmative vote required). Passed 265–80.
5. 1963–33R; Roosevelt (D, Calif. 26)—Williams (D, Miss. 3) motion to adjourn the House. The purpose of the motion was to stop Reps. Lindsay (R, N.Y. 17), MacGregor (R, Minn. 3), and other Republicans from discussing civil rights legislation under previously approved special orders for House speeches. Rejected 53–276.

The roll call eliminated from the a priori set is 1964–64; H. Res. 795. Authorization for a special House committee to sit during the adjournment of the 88th Congress to investigate and report on campaign expenditures of candidates for nomination or election to the House. Adopted 264–92.

[7] Live pairs and declared positions to the *Congressional Quarterly* poll are considered

This Negro rights scale constitutes an ordinal measure of support for liberalizing political, social, and economic opportunities for Negroes.[8] In the scale the roll calls are recorded according to the proportion of representatives favoring improved Negro rights as implied in the content of the roll call in question. The scale scores correspond to the pattern of response made by each representative on the roll calls in the scale. Scores range from 0 (opposition to the proposal endorsed by the largest proportion of the representatives) to 5 (support for the proposal endorsed by the smallest proportion of the representatives). High scores indicate an orientation favoring the liberalization of Negro rights and low scores imply a conservative orientation on Negro rights.

Constituency characteristics examined in this study come from the 1960 Census and are reported in *The Congressional District Data Book (88th Congress)*. From the large number of variables available there, 21 were selected which seemed conceptually useful and were available conveniently as a percentage or median. These are listed as a part of Table 2 below.

FINDINGS

The distribution of scale scores on the Negro rights dimension indicates the polarization of attitudes in the Congress during the 88th Congress. In Table 1 the "all representatives" distribution reveals concentrations of representatives at both ends of the scale, but not many in the middle. The discrimination afforded by the scale is sufficiently substantial to relate roll call voting scores to other variables.

The findings by Miller and Stokes relating roll call voting to constituency attitudes via the perceptions that representatives have of constituency attitudes suggests the possible utility in examining the characteristics of constituencies associated with the scale scores.[9] If there is substantial covariation between roll call voting and constituency attitudes this may be partly explained by the constituency attributes of social, economic, and demographic character. Froman has argued that particular population variables may be taken as indicators of political values, life styles, and policy preferences because shared attitudes arise as people participate in

---

as votes. Roll call data are taken from appropriate *Congressional Quarterly Weekly Reports* for 1963 and 1964. CR=992 and CS, Menzel's coefficient of scalability,=.970. Menzel's suggested minimum value is .65; see Herbert Menzel, "A New Coefficient for Scalagram Analysis," *Public Opinion Quarterly*, 17 (1953), pp. 268–280.

[8] The Civil Rights Act of 1964, which occasioned two of the votes in the scale, has been described by one political scientist as "perhaps, the most crucial piece of action taken by the government recently in the direction of changing the status of Negroes favorably in American society." See Harry A. Bailey, Jr., ed., *Negro Politics in America* (Columbus, Ohio: Charles E. Merrill Books, Inc., 1967), p. 378.

[9] Miller and Stokes, "Constituency Influence"; see also the extension of their analysis by Charles F. Cnudde and Donald J. McCrone, "The Linkage Between Consistency Attitudes and Congressional Voting Behavior: A Causal Model," *American Political Science Review*, 60 (March, 1966), pp. 66–72.

TABLE 1

Distributions of Negro Rights Scale Scores for the 88th Congress

Scale scores	0	0.5[a]	1	1.5	2	2.5	3	3.5	4	4.5	5	Totals
All representatives	46	23	25	8	26	1	4	0	94	36	162	425[b]
Southern[c] representatives												
Democrats	44	20	13	0	6	0	1	0	4	0	0	88
Republicans	1	0	6	1	0	0	0	0	0	0	0	8
Non-Southern representatives												
Democrats	1	3	3	2	4	1	1	0	30	15	104	164
Republicans	0	0	3	5	16	0	2	0	60	21	58	165

[a] An advantage in scale analysis is that it can be used to deal with occasions when the representatives do not vote or declare a position. Often the non-response does not disturb an existing voting pattern. However, if the non-response intervenes between votes of support and opposition, it is reasonable to split the difference and assign a "half" score. Similarly, non-response on an extreme item of the scale raises ambiguity. Representative Howard Smith (D, Va. 8) opposed Negro rights in all the roll calls of the scale except the one in which Negro rights were endorsed by the largest proportion of representatives. Had he opposed Negro rights here his score would be 0. Support for Negro rights on this roll call would have resulted in a score of 1. Because he did not vote or declare a position, his score is 0.5.

[b] Representatives who participated in fewer than three of the five roll calls were not scored.

[c] Southern here refers to Alabama, Arkansas, Florida, Georgia, Louisiana, Mississippi, North Carolina, South Carolina, Texas, and Virginia.

and confront similar environments and problems.[10] Similarly organized groups, which press group demands upon representatives, are based upon shared characteristics and attitudes, and "the size and strength of these groups will roughly correspond with gross sociological differences in the general population (e.g., race, ethnicity, religion, occupation)."[11] Additionally, representatives, who are expected to "know their districts," probably are acquainted with the socioeconomic and demographic profiles of their constituencies to the extent that they can respond to home-owner interests, ethnic blocs, income groups, newcomers, etc. If representatives' perceptions are reasonably accurate, the prominent aspects of their constituencies which they take into account in their behavior may be discoverable in the population data available for the constituencies.

Table 2 presents Spearman rank-order correlation coefficients showing the relationship between voting scale scores and 21 constituency variables for all districts, Republican districts, and Democratic districts.

Given the tenuous linkage of constituency variables to roll call voting, several of the All Districts correlations are substantial.[12] Conventional wisdom suggests that level of education and urbanism would be strong correlates of Negro rights scale scores.[13] Urbanism, as measured by percentage urban and percentage farmers, and percentage foreign stock (a strong correlate of urbanism) are among the variables most highly related to Negro rights scale scores. Level of education is only modestly related to Negro rights, as evidenced by the correlations with low education, high school, college, and median years of schooling. However, all the indicators of economic well being—median income, percentage of sound homes, median home value, and median rent—are strong correlates of support for Negro rights. So too are median age and percentage of children in private elementary schools. It is also noteworthy that there is a substantial negative correlation between percentages of Negroes and Negro rights support.

The negative direction of the relationship between percentage Negroes and support for Negro rights indicates the explanation for the strength of the correlations. Most of the opposition to Negro rights is from Southern representatives with substantial proportions of Negroes in their constituencies. Likewise Southern constituencies evidence low educational achievement, low economic achievement, small proportions of foreign

[10] Lewis A. Froman, Jr., "Inter-Party Constituency Differences and Congressional Voting Behavior," *American Political Science Review*, 57 (March, 1963), pp. 57–61.

[11] *Ibid.*, p. 57.

[12] Thomas A. Flinn suggested a useful rule of thumb for interpreting correlations between roll call voting and consistency variables by saying, "As a matter of fact [correlation] coefficients above .4 are remarkably good in a system as complex as the legislative system." See his "Party Responsibility in the States: Some Causal Factors," *American Political Science Review*, 58 (March, 1964), pp. 60–71.

[13] A slender volume which is especially enlightening is Alan P. Grimes, *Equality in America: Religion, Race, and the Urban Majority* (New York: Oxford University Press, 1964). In particular, see pp. v–x, and 83–85.

TABLE 2

Spearman Rho Correlations between 21 Constituency Variables and Negro Rights Scale Scores for All Representatives, Democrats, and Republicans[a]

Constituency Variables	All Representatives	Democrats	Republicans
1. Per cent population change[b]	.028	−.041	.081
2. Per cent urban[b]	.434	.548	.183
3. Per cent Negro[b]	−.360	−.508	.040
4. Per cent foreign stock[b]	.643	.767	.230
5. Median age[b]	.430	.478	.276
6. Per cent elem. in private schools[b]	.586	.676	.326
7. Per cent low education[b]	−.388	−.567	−.050
8. Per cent high school[b]	.297	.347	.114
9. Per cent college[b]	.132	.079	.173
10. Median education[b]	.330	.413	.134
11. Median income[b]	.546	.669	.310
12. Per cent unemployed[c]	.071	.233	−.164
13. Per cent owner-occupancy[b]	.091	−.027	.146
14. Per cent sound homes, all plumbing[b]	.492	.592	.241
15. Median rooms per unit[b]	.228	.109	.319
16. Median persons per unit[b]	−.156	−.267	.112
17. Median home value[b]	.469	.555	.243
18. Median rent[b]	.478	.609	.188
19. Per cent white collar[c]	.346	.408	.198
20. Per cent blue collar[c]	.063	.125	−.003
21. Per cent farmer[c]	−.468	−.561	−.234

[a] Correlations are possible for only the 425 representatives assigned scale scores.

[b] Source: U.S. Bureau of the Census, *Congressional District Data Book (Districts of the 88th Congress)*—A Statistical Abstract Supplement. U. S. Government Printing Office, Washington, D.C., 1963. Source notes, definitions and explanations of the items are on pp. xv–xxvii.

[c] Source: *CQ Census Analysis: Congressional Districts of the United States* (Washington, D.C.: Congressional Quarterly Service, 1964), pp. 1818–1828.

stock, little private school education, and low urbanization. The variables on which the South is not generally different from the rest of the country have low correlations with Negro rights scale scores. These include percentage population increase, college education, home ownership, median rooms per unit, and blue-collar workers.

This interpretation receives support by doing the analysis for each party separately. Those variables which produced substantial correlations using all districts reveal stronger relationships using only Democratic representatives and the constituencies they represent. However, the correlations for Republican voting and constituency variables for Republican districts are much lower. The main effect of producing correlations with Republican districts alone is to remove the constituency variation present in the South. Only eight of the 178 Republican districts are in Southern states. Variation in Republican constituencies is not systematically related to variation in degree of support for Negro rights by Republican representatives.

The importance of regional variation in Negro rights voting is obvious in Table 1, which reports scale scores by region and party. Half the Southern Democrats have the lowest possible scale score and only a few have scale positions of two or higher. Southern Republicans have scores nearly as low. But what is more striking is the degree of unity manifest in the scale scores of non-Southern representatives, particularly the 164 non-Southern Democrats. The definition for the South is purposely narrow in this analysis; included among the non-Southern Democrats are all the "border state" representatives of Tennessee, Maryland, West Virginia, and Oklahoma. Among all these constituencies there is great variation on social, economic, and ethnic characteristics. Also the extent of electoral competition is variable. Nevertheless, the scale scores of these Democrats are heavily concentrated at the high end of the scale, with nearly two-thirds supporting Negro rights in every roll call opportunity. Republican voting is not as united with 24 non-Southern members registering scale scores below two and less than one-third taking the most liberal position.

An interesting subset revealed in the regional breakdown of scale scores is the 11 Southern Democrats with scale scores of two or higher. They are noteworthy because they have taken public positions in favor of at least two Negro rights proposals. They may be forerunners to the crumbling of segregationist unity in the South. All supported the extension of the Civil Rights Commission, five favored the Civil Rights Act as amended in the Senate, and four supported its passage when it first emerged from the House on February 10, 1964. Their support was obviously public on an issue presumed to be the most salient one in Southern politics.[14] There was no ambiguity about the implications of the bills. Accompanying each roll call in question was the mobilization of pro- and anti-Negro rights voting blocs. Probably the single most conspicuous vote was that by Representative Weltner (D, Ga. 5). After opposing the Civil Rights Act on the February 10 roll call, on July 2, 1964, he voted for the resolution to accept Senate amendments on the Civil Rights Act of 1964. Weltner is the only "Deep South"[15] member in this group of 11 moderates, and, of course, the

14 An interesting manifestation of this salience is the high participation on these roll calls by Southerners. The only Southern constituency that lacks a scaled representative in this analysis is Texas 10. Once Lyndon Johnson's constituency, it was represented by Homer Thornberry until his resignation December 20, 1963, to take an appointment by Johnson to a federal judgeship. Jake J. Pickle completed the term. Were their votes to be combined for scale purposes, however, the result would be a 4, putting them among the Southern moderates. Pickle voted in favor of the Civil Rights Act on both occasions. Thornberry took a conservative position concerning the Reserve Officers Training Corps programs.

15 For Matthews and Prothro, Alabama, Georgia, Louisiana, Mississippi and South Carolina are the "Deep South." See Donald R. Matthews and James W. Prothro,

only Deep South representative favoring the Civil Rights Act on a record vote. It is significant too that these moderate Southerners took their positions despite the fact that their votes were not needed for passage. In each instance more than two-thirds of the participating representatives favored the extension of Negro rights and passage was certain at roll call time. Each might have given covert support to the legislation while going on record against the Negro rights position, or simply taken a walk, avoiding public positions for or against the bills.

Because of the substantial linkage between roll call voting and constituency attitudes which Miller and Stokes found in relation to Negro rights voting, it is interesting to examine these Southern constituencies in a bit more detail. The question of interest is whether the districts represented by Southern Democrats, who are moderates on Negro rights, are in any way different from those whose representatives seek to preserve the conventional Southern way of life. However, to discover explanatory differences, one other subset of the Southern districts is included, namely, the Southern Republican districts, whose representatives were almost uniformly conservative on Negro rights. Table 3 indicates that differences between the constituencies of moderate and conservative Southern Democrats are numerous and often substantial. But the meaning of the differences cannot be assumed without looking at the characteristics of the Republican districts, all of whose representatives voted conservatively on Negro rights. For example, the average net increase in population is much higher in Southern moderates' districts than those of Southern conservatives. But in Republican districts, growth rates are still higher. Parallel findings occur with the economic indicators (median income, sound homes, home value, median rent), median age, and others. Similarly, proportions of Negroes and farmers are lower in moderates' districts than in those of conservatives; but are even lower in Republican districts. Nevertheless, certain suggestive differences are present. The moderates' districts are higher on per cent urban, foreign stock, private school enrollment, and unemployed. In sum, if the districts of the Southern Democratic moderates have a distinctive character, it is that they are more culturally diverse than those of the conservative Southern Democrats or the Southern Republicans. Foreign stock is perhaps the key variable, but the private school enrollment is probably an indication of religious diversity. The private school enrollment variable particularly varies with strong minority religious groups such as Roman Catholic and Lutheran, and these percentages are low in the districts of conservative Southern Democrats. The heterogeneity implicit in percentage urban receives accent from the unemployment levels in moderate Democrats' districts. Most of the remaining constituency variables used here shed little light on the analysis, and appear here only as evidence that they do *not* explain this representational behavior.[16] It is noteworthy, for example, that the level of educa-

---

Negroes and the New Southern Politics (New York: Harcourt, Brace and World, Inc., 1966), p. 169.

16 Although the data are not included here, a cursory analysis of primary and elec-

TABLE 3

Mean Values for 21 Constituency Variables in the Districts of All Representatives,[a] All Southern Representatives,[b] Conservative Southern Democrats,[c] Moderate Southern Democrats,[d] and Southern Republicans[e]

Constituency Variables	All Representatives	All Southern Representatives	Conservative Southern Dems. (scale scores<2)	Moderate Southern Dems. (scale scores ≥2)	Southern Republicans
1. Per cent population change	23.10	22.38	15.41	40.31	66.10
2. Per cent urban	67.67	54.75	49.26	78.97	72.46
3. Per cent Negro	10.60	23.51	26.28	12.91	12.49
4. Per cent foreign stock	18.81	5.41	3.36	15.76	10.06
5. Median age	29.60	26.95	26.65	27.18	29.46
6. Per cent elem. in private schools	14.82	4.82	4.17	7.90	6.68
7. Low education	8.79	15.88	16.57	15.76	9.29
8. Per cent high school	40.19	34.09	32.45	37.23	45.01
9. Per cent college	7.35	6.68	6.26	6.91	9.93
10. Median education	10.42	9.44	9.22	9.88	10.91
11. Median income	5503.60	4187.06	3976.10	4753.55	5442.75

12.	Per cent unemployed	5.31	4.92	4.94	5.46	4.14
13.	Per cent owner-occupancy	62.36	61.66	60.83	64.43	65.58
14.	Per cent sound homes, all plumbing	71.72	59.60	56.47	69.21	75.93
15.	Median rooms per unit	4.87	4.65	4.66	4.51	4.81
16.	Median persons per unit	2.96	3.09	3.10	3.08	3.03
17.	Median home value	115.78	87.81	83.97	95.00	114.88
18.	Median rent	68.49	54.33	51.74	60.82	70.00
19.	Per cent white collar	42.50	37.71	35.85	43.25	46.79
20.	Per cent blue collar	49.54	50.25	50.65	50.17	47.76
21.	Per cent farmers	7.88	11.73	13.19	6.58	4.58

a All 435 districts, using state figures for At Large seats.

b All districts for Alabama, Arkansas, Florida, Georgia, Louisiana, Mississippi, North Carolina, South Carolina, Texas, and Virginia.

c Includes eight Alabama representatives who were elected At Large in 1962. Alabama state figures are used eight times.

d Pepper (Fla. 3), Fascell (Fla. 4), Gibbons (Fla. 10), Weltner (Ga. 5), Brooks (Tex. 2), Thomas (Tex. 8), Wright (Tex. 12), Young (Tex. 14), Kilgore (Tex. 15), Gonzales (Tex. 20), and Jennings (Va. 9).

e Gurney (Fla. 11), Cramer (Fla. 12), Jonas (N.C. 8), Broyhill (N.C. 9), Alger (Tex. 5), Foreman (Tex. 16), Poff (Va. 6), and Broyhill (Va. 10).

tional achievement in the constituencies is unrelated to support for Negro rights.[17] That economic development, population increase, and higher proportions of white-collar workers do not of themselves explain Negro rights support is indicated by the data for the districts of Southern Republicans.

CONCLUSIONS

The social scientists' byword when presenting interpretations and conclusions is always *caution*. Nevertheless the following summary statements appear to be warranted:

1. Although there are substantial correlations between Negro rights scale scores and constituency characteristics for all congressional districts, the covariation producing these correlations is mostly regional in nature. Conservatism on Negro rights is concentrated in the South, which is marked by lower urbanization, economic, and educational achievement.

2. The correlations between constituency characteristics and Negro rights scale scores among Republicans are not substantial. Considering Republicans and their districts separately has the effect of removing the South from the analysis. The resulting findings are that variations in the constituency variables considered do not explain variations in Negro rights voting in the 88th Congress.

3. Non-Southern Democrats demonstrated highly unified support for Negro rights proposals despite substantial variation in districts on constituency variables and electoral competition.

4. Southern opposition to Negro rights legislation remained substantial, but 11 Southern Democrats manifested "moderate" voting records.

5. The constituencies of the moderate Southern Democrats are not sharply different from those of both Southern Democratic conservatives and Southern Republicans. The data suggest that moderate voting patterns and hopefully, moderate attitudes among constituents, emerge in culturally heterogeneous districts; where urbanization, growth, and economic development are ac-

---

toral competitiveness in the Southern constituencies does not yield persuasive evidence that such competition constitutes either necessary or sufficient conditions for moderation on Negro rights. It is noteworthy that in the 1964 elections the moderates did not meet more vigorous competition stemming from their Negro rights voting than they had met in 1962, and none were defeated, although Kilgore (Texas 15) did retire.

[17] This is not to deny Matthews and Prothro's findings; "The proportion of whites who are strict segregationists decreases with every increase in formal education." Instead, it is consistent with what they cautiously go on to say: "But a careful examination of the findings [relating amount of schooling to racial attitudes] suggests that they provide no basis for expecting large-scale change in southern attitudes within the near future. The combined number of moderates and integrationists does not exceed the number of strict segregationists within any educational level below completion of college—and only 8 per cent of the southern whites have a college degree." Matthews and Prothro, *Negroes*, p. 343.

companied by culturally different foreign backgrounds, industrial interdependence is indicated by unemployment levels typical in the larger society, and religious differentiation seems apparent.

Census data on the constituencies only provide suggestions about the political attitudes of large aggregates of people. To better project future patterns in this and other policy issues, political scientists will have to get closer to the interaction of constituents among themselves and with those who represent them. This is particularly true because these data portray only conditions at a particular point in time. Attitudes of both constituents and representatives change in response to events and trends not apparent in these sources. If moderation in Negro rights attitudes is associated only with the factors noted here, future change toward moderation in the South will be slow and spotty indeed. However, policy progress legitimated by congressional enactment may gradually obtain broad assent in the South if Southern political leaders are willing to endorse the legitimacy of this kind of policy change. In that connection the electoral success of the moderates in 1964 should be noted. Perhaps the integration of Negro rights moderates among the conservatives in the Southern contingent to the House is a harbinger of more meaningful racial integration.

A Selected Bibliography on
Public Policy and Blacks in the United States

Blauner, Robert, "Whitewash over Watts," *Trans-action*, 3 (March–April, 1966), p. 9.

Dwyer, Robert J., "The Negro in the U.S. Army," *Sociology and Social Research*, 38 (Nov., 1953), pp. 103–112.

Fogelson, Robert M., "White on Black: A Critique of the McCone Commission Report on the Los Angeles Riots," *Political Science Quarterly*, 82 (Sept., 1967), pp. 337–367.

Frazier, E. Franklin, *The Negro in the United States* (New York: Macmillan, 1949).

The Governor's Commission on the Los Angeles Riots, *Violence in the City—An End or a Beginning?* (Los Angeles: Dec., 1965).

Greenberg, Jack, *Race Relations and American Law* (New York: Columbia University Press, 1959).

Grimshaw, Allen D., "Actions of Police and the Military in American Race Riots," *Phylon*, 24 (Fall, 1963), pp. 271–289.

Krause, Elliot A., "Functions of a Bureaucratic Ideology: Citizen Participation," *Social Problems*, 16 (Fall, 1968), pp. 129–143.

Mendelson, Wallace, *Discrimination* (Englewood Cliffs: Prentice-Hall, 1962).

Moynihan, Daniel Patrick, *The Negro Family: The Case for National Action* (Washington, D.C.: Department of Labor, 1965).

Rainwater, Lee, and William L. Yancey, "Black Families and the White House," *Trans-action*, 5 (July–August, 1966), pp. 6–11.

Rainwater, Lee, and William Yancey, *The Moynihan Report and the Politics of Controversy* (Boston: MIT Press, 1967).

Report of the National Advisory Commission on Civil Disorders (New York: Bantam Books, 1968).

Rustin, Bayard, "The Watts 'Manifesto' and the McCone Report," *Commentary*, 41 (March, 1966), pp. 29–35.

Silver, Allan, "Official Interpretations of Racial Riots," in *Urban Riots: Violence and Protest* (New York: Academy of Political Science, 1968).

Walker, David B., "Intergovernmental Response to Urban Riots," in *Urban Riots: Violence and Social Change* (New York: Academy of Political Science, 1968).

Index